MW01625901

OTTO FREUNDLICH
COSMIC COMMUNISM

OTTO FREUNDLICH
COSMIC COMMUNISM

Edited by Julia Friedrich

Museum Ludwig, Cologne
Kunstmuseum Basel

PRESTEL
Munich · London · New York

Otto Freundlich

Confessions of a Revolutionary Painter[1]

Part I. We shall be understood by those for whom we fight.[2] We must fight with them, side by side, we must fight on the side of the revolutionary proletariat. All that we have thought and created is of no value in the present struggle. Yet, it is not worthless. But it lacks the supportive power of the people, the comrades. Why shouldn't they be willing to grasp something difficult once they know that it was intended and created for them. But first they must know that we do not wish to shirk the strict obligations of revolutionary solidarity and want to fulfill them with joy. Perhaps that will rob us of the time to continue our work on what we consider to be true, which today is useless, though, for the cause itself. That is likely. But we must be prepared for that as well. We must be willing to regard this artistic development, to which we have dedicated ourselves exclusively our whole life long, and which brought us boycott and poverty, as finished.

Because now the *ideal* humanity, for which more serious artists always created their works, has become the *real* humanity. It is here, it has taken the great ethical task in its hands. Fulfilling this task is both a necessity for it and its purpose in life. But that has altered time and space. The artist, who saw before him the lofty idea of human solidarity as a new start to the universe in a broad temporal and spatial form, somewhere *and* some time on Earth, but as something certain, something that has to come, now sees it as a demand from the masses in the present *and* in his immediate surroundings. The great inspirational power, which the best and most gifted of artists had as their great distant goal, and which is most magnificently expressed in Beethoven's IX Symphony, this inspirational force is now expected from close by. But for this, the bridge is still missing. And we must not pretend to ourselves that it is *not* missing. And even if we are at a loss as to how it should be built, it nevertheless remains for us to leap *in one go* across the trenches and stand suddenly amidst those without whom the practical work of living will never be a reality, who themselves realize the new society of humanity one stage after another at jeopardy to their own lives.

These stalwart fighters and modest heroes are not representative, their pathos is the "Internationale," illegal work, abuse, jail, and often certain death. Their sacrifice is their pathos, they sacrifice themselves and will continue to sacrifice themselves until the duty, which they perform for all humanity, is vindicated and has attained its goal. They cannot abstract themselves from their very selves, history does not permit that; because history has placed them in a predicament in which they must die or from which they must free themselves. How much worse it would be for them if they did not have their great teachers. But they do have their great teachers, and these great teachers have also learned an infinite amount from them. For if the great teachers had not learnt such a great deal from the working people, whom they wanted to enlighten about their miserable conditions, they may well have remained misunderstood.

We artists likewise wish to learn from the working people. But how? We have rent much that was cruel from our hearts: petty bourgeois sentiments, in opposition to the petty bourgeois. Bourgeois sentiments, in opposition to the bourgeoisie, and much based on many other oppositions. Because we hail from the petty bourgeoisie, from the bourgeoisie; certainly many of the most famous artists also come from the proletariat. But before they could be anything they first had to become middle-class citizens, attend middle-class art schools, and assimilate the high intellectual culture of the bourgeoisie. Many were drunk from their successes, i.e. from material successes and recognition in the press. They had acquired a steady fame, and the doors of the rich and powerful were wide open to them. Even the artist who savagely criticized bourgeois society in his drawings and paintings received great admiration from precisely this section of society, and the museums could not afford not to have his works. But he scarcely existed for the proletariat, they did not know him, even though this art was inspired by their suffering.

How did this come about?—because other artists, whose astute minds had realized that, however they looked at it, every form that they depicted was inevitably conventional, i.e. obeyed the demands of the society which they thanked for their training, remained in that respect artists who summoned every element of the great art of the past, from every country in the world, yet saw that in the best case they would remain skillful monkeys if they continued in that way, because it would never lead them to liberation from the yoke of convention. With that the entire world of forms was damned and besmirched for them, and everything turned in a circle. The leap had to be ventured away from all the myths down the ages, as well as from the realm of nature, which the philistines, the moneyed large and small, always invoked; nature had become their categorical imperative, the one in fact that they imposed on the artist; nature the α and ω of their aesthetic, by which they saw whether the artist kept to the straight and narrow or not. Nature knew no criticism, and all who copied it were also without criticism, and criticism was not wished for from the artists.

The eye of the artist is, however, an incorruptible critic. It sees through the masks, even if they are made of iron. And even if every bush, every flower, every brook, every cliff were hidden by a mask, the artist would see it and say: you're lying. And he stood there one day, looked around, and saw himself surrounded by a nature that wore masks, and by people who all wore masks, and he said: you're lying, off with those masks. But they were stuck tight and had turned to skin. That was a terrible discovery. And that's where we are today. Turn whichever way you will: we're still there. We tried to divine the truth from things and produce a true art that affirms the entire world of things. We have failed. Failed through the passive resistance of the things themselves. Because things were passive behind the masks and they wore their masks passively. Unredeemed by any romanticism. We saw just one thing: the technique of the painter, which is the flesh, blood, and bone by which he constructs, it yielded nothing but the *effect* chewed over a thousand times; nor was it meant to be anything but the thousand-times-chewed-over effect. And worst of all this tendency to present this effect was rooted in the artist himself, from even the most vacuous kitsch painter to the richest and most noble talent, yes, even the genius.

There were geniuses who had fought death struggles over it: Cézanne and Van Gogh. We need not wonder that their work remained a fragment, but simply admire all the more how they forged so far ahead with their work and try to make it clear to ourselves what an enormous achievement in terms of character strength and bold invention has been stored in their works. As we were young, we had to take up this bequest. Which meant we had to continue it. Many of us simply repeated what the masters said, and arrived in that way at fame and glory. We, however, had to proceed further. Which is something different. Going further is not repeating. In all this it must be emphasized that the old costumes in which we alone recognize and acknowledge the world of appearances as such is the sole existing, sole possible image of nature. Is it the only possible one? And do we need another? For the majority, even these questions seem to be blasphemy.

We have nevertheless proceeded a long way along this road and every work we created is the answer: no, this nature is not the only possible one, and we need another. May those who have the courage to develop from individualism to collectivism also have the courage to make the world of things disappear for once. Otherwise they will remain with grandpa, who hangs there in a papier maché frame above the sofa, and with the Biedermeier style. Let them tell themselves: the things you are looking at are visual memories, rendered as a physiological function by heredity, but they came about through the one and the same educational principle that came to be repeated over many generations. This educational principle had the aim of isolating things, because this principle of isolation corresponded with the character of human society, in which there were only individual egos.

But who was it that characterized society as the summation of millions of individual egos? Well, that was private ownership, which always spawned, more or less, high capitalism. Only what is individual can be left be; and whoever is to be left be must be isolated. From this, one can see that our world of things, which we call nature, is already very old. And that the reason why we have smashed this convention has very deep social causes. That collectivism, which is to say Communism, which has got rid of the individual as an end in itself, is unable to escape the consequences that emerge from a mind freed of property and being possessed. One day we shall be understood. The epoch of discovering nature anew for art will first be able to arrive once art has gone through an epoch free of nature.

The consequences that emerge from a mind freed of property and being possessed reveal themselves in painting insofar as it dispenses with the illusion of feigning three-dimensionality. Not that it in any way dispenses with space and form. What it dispenses with initially is the division (dualism) between foreground and background. Dispensing with this dualism means foregoing the world of things, i.e. its depiction. Its depiction is only possible by means of a painting technique that aspires to feign three-dimensionality and requires the foreground, middle ground, and background.[3]

So what remains? When nature has been eliminated as a motif of painting that has become unable to imitate an object what then is the positive, the distinguishing property that such painting depends on?

At the beginning of the steam engine was the kettle. When George Stevenson observed that the boiling water in his kettle not only sent steam issuing from the spout but also created an exit for itself by rhythmically lifting the lid, his attention was diverted from the immediate purpose of the boiling water, which served to make a cup of tea; Stevenson had observed this and had the great revelation that steam is a *force* capable of lifting a weight. This was the discovery of a natural law that was also proved to be of the greatest importance for physics and astronomy. Just what resistance people placed in the way of the inventor of the steam engine, what struggles it took before the first railway could forge a connection between two towns, is written down in the history of the origins of the railway. I want to compare the invention of the railway and its history with what I have to say about that development of painting/sculpture that did not imitate the objects of nature.

The purpose of representational painting and sculpture is comparable to the purpose of water for tea. Both arts were an excellent means for the historical portrayal of the religious and political powers, of the views and deeds in their eras. And yet there is a driving force in these artworks that does not completely equate with the purposes they served, and this is precisely the temporal connection which—unlike with languages—instantly permits us to establish a living relationship with the artworks of every epoch purely by looking. This driving force is comparable with the physical forces of nature—not that I wish to say that it is a physical force. But just as the power of steam was revealed to Stevenson while boiling water for tea, a force that is one of the mightiest in the universe, it became evident to a number of painters and sculptors in our era that while fashioning landscapes and people, this fashioning proceeds according to the laws of forces that go beyond the specific purpose of the given motifs and that can only then reveal the greatness, the enormity of their universal validity when they are released from any representational motif. Through this realization the artist was placed at a crossroads.

Here we wish to hand the word over to two different artists, each of whom will give his views on this insight in his own way: The first artist says: What's it to me that the power that enables me to depict landscapes and human figures has some deeper reason and purpose than to depict these landscapes and figures? It is enough for me that I can paint a landscape or a portrait the way I want to paint them. It is enough for me when I have an idea for a picture with human figures on it, with streets, factories, and trees, that I do studies and then execute it all in the technique I learned and further perfected in accordance with my needs. The finished painting is always that, at least, which I can achieve in precisely this period of my life. There is no end to an artist's progress, as I know, and every further accomplished work still leaves much that I must struggle to attain, and that keeps my spirits alert.

The second artist says:[4] As I began to paint and to sculpt, I had an ideal of art. I studied the art of the Greeks and old masters, the masters of Impressionism, and also went to various art schools, where I did life drawing and painting. I created pictures according to my own ideas and modeled portraits and human figures in clay. But since I was dissatisfied with working as an epigone using the techniques of the Impressionists or Rodin, I strived to find a means of expression whose form and content was personally experienced. What had bothered me most of all was that there was a trick for depicting people, landscapes, and objects, which doubtless existed quite unconsciously as one of the artists' conventions, but that bowed to the demands of the *beholder* to receive a certain illusion from the painting. This illusion that the beholder demanded was three-dimensionality.

I investigated the means, how in fact the three-dimensionality of bodies and space was achieved and what was the psychological reason why the beholder found such satisfaction in front of the painting when he felt it could be grasped, i.e. is plastic. As for the painting or drawing technique for this plastic effect, I discovered a trick there which tied even the revolutionaries of Impressionist painting to the ground of a convention that contradicted their revolutionary initiative. As for the beholder of such pictures, who demands a three-dimensional illusion for the objects on them, I discovered that the hand that always wants something graspable, also wants to grab, i.e. catch, hold, and possess. So it was the old, deep-rooted urge to possess that demanded this illusion of three-dimensionality from the painter.

My viewpoint was not so clear when it came to sculpture. Or rather, sculpture kept me fixed on the depiction of the person. Even if the relationships in a head were perceived according to plastic measurements, the highlights fell on the more prominent curves, the shadows in more sharply defined depths, heads remained heads with forehead, eyes, nose, mouth, and chin. In painting I had been quick to abandon the naturalistic technique and dispense with the threefold gradation of colors, which alone were always sufficient to create the illusion of plasticity in both painting and drawing. I sought to overcome this suggestion forever rendered by the same means by looking carefully.

In a vaulted cellar in an old edifice that served as a tavern, the walls had been painted with pilasters. What is it, I asked myself, that makes these painted pilasters seem to me to be plastic bas-reliefs. For I know they have not been tooled in stone, but simply painted on the wall in watercolors. With great application I began to study the individual color nuances painted next to one another and attempted to determine their juxtapositions in every detail, just as the hand of the painter had actually painted them. That was terribly hard: I managed to distinguish the deeper gray from medium gray, but my analysis failed when it came to light gray, and I felt solely the plastic suggestion of the pilaster. But I did not flag and finally I succeeded in training my eye so that it remained keen and alert in its discrimination, even with this third brightest nuance of the three grays, the dangerous spot where looking misted over and became plastic illusion. It now became increasingly easy for me to see the colors next to one another, the way they were painted, and even there, where the transitions had been done, I looked long and attentively and, satisfied by the feeling of plasticity, did not turn away. I now even looked attentively at street signs with plastically painted letters. There the plastic suggestion was produced with the most diverse technical means, ranging from academic painting technique to modern poster technique.[5]

While I also dispensed pretty early on in my artistic development with a technique of the kind used for the painted pilaster and painted purely flat surfaces, each placed tightly and without transition next to the other, and built up the entire picture in that way, the primal element of this planar art was nevertheless a bowed curved surface, i.e. a plastic element. But the one thing regarding the origin and meaning of these efforts was achieved: the elements of the mural had been realized. And I had the opportunity to make a large mosaic in which everything was composed according to the law of the pure surface.[6] But when I made a window with colored panes and my design was to be produced in a small studio for stained glass painting, the master glazer taught me that a planar curve cannot be cut out of the glass in one piece.[7] So the curved surface had to be cut out in numerous pieces, which were then separated from one another by the lead but, viewed against the light, still retained their unity.

But not all of the surfaces from this first design were curved. Instinctively, and wiser from my studies of ancient stained glass from the XII + XIII century, I had also painted trapezoidal surfaces in my design, and these could easily be cut from the glass with a diamond. This experience was of great importance to me when I designed a second window, but it was to be of even greater importance for my further artistic development, although at that time I did not yet realize as much. But when I painted my second design for a stained glass window measuring 1 meter wide and 2 meters high,[8] I did not paint in the lead glass with narrow black surfaces, but instead placed the colored trapezoidal shapes directly next to each other. While painting these colored trapezoidal surfaces directly next to one another I was beset by an excitement as if by a new kind of life in painting.

Not until many years later was I taken thither to where this new life was fully revealed to me. The intimate connection between all the surfaces on one picture, in which like a cell in an organism each passes the energy on to the next cell until there is but an unbroken circulation of these energies throughout the entire organism, this could first be realized by the accumulation of all colors in one picture. And this was the one goal that I strived to attain, because it tallied with my social convictions: with Socialism. For this reason I had to proceed step by step to an ever greater de-individualization. I had to eliminate the egocentric aspect that is closely connected with the depiction of people, plants, and things, I had to arrive at a kind of dialectical language of the colors themselves. I combined complexes of kindred colors with one another, which for their part joined up with complexes of other color units, and so on, until the entire picture was covered. Every color complex could contain its own ultimate chromatic dynamism, which bordered seamlessly on all sides on the neighboring color complexes, and made the contrasts of the others, and with that its difference to them, clearly recognizable; but since every color complex obeyed the same law, an organism could form in which there was no more individualism, in which the entire richness of the color scale could be brought to fruition, without one color unit living at the cost of or repressing the others. Every color complex, whether it was formed solely of strong reds or solely of grays, asserted itself alongside the others, maintaining its self all the more strongly the more it set off the self of the other. The coexistence of all these color complexes, each of which represents a color individuality, results in the perfect collective of all the colors on a picture surface.

The picture that I was able to paint in this manner was like a fine line for me, dividing the past from the future. Everything resembling a motif was overcome. The contrast and amalgamation of the color surfaces constituted the dialectical language of the picture. But even on this path there is a development. Because after the technique of glass cutting forced me to break up the curve-shaped, finely tapered surface into sub-sections consisting of trapezoidal surfaces, and also because being rectangular, they could be cut from the glass pane with a diamond, this curve-like, finely tapered surface no longer seemed sufficient to me to enable the whole rich instrument of planar painting to be brought to its full effect. The planar curve was itself like a body, which lay however nicely and without gap beside the other planar curves, but which did not grant the richness of the dynamism that was attained through the juxtaposition of trapezoidal, rectangular forms.

Thus it was as if the tips of these planar curves had been snapped off, and remained, seemingly like something curved in my picture, as a bent rectangle with one convex and one parallel curve, one convex and one concave. This bent rectangle, which was, for instance, blue throughout, now consisted of lots of rectangular blue surfaces in various shades of blue, with their tones alluding to the adjoining color complexes in other colors.

The concept behind the picture, which freed itself after great efforts of self-mastery from the motif of nature and which had drawn on the realm of pure energies, now underwent a transformation. The energies themselves proved to be of differing quality. One part belonged to the province of pure energies, another to the realm of forms. But while previously the energies that engendered form were the superior in painting, if not almost the only ones, they were now assigned to the pure energies and with that lost their exclusiveness, i.e. their manifestations, which shaped the world of perception. But even if we no longer include the manifestations of our perceived world in our concept of the picture, we nevertheless find ourselves on the fundament of experience, of a new manifestation that results from the ongoing development of the [...][9] law governing images and the energies expressed therein and thereby. So if the depiction of these pure energies is not an aim in itself, but contains rather the tendency to delve into this world of forms and to assimilate to them, we have described the two elements which, by eliminating the insulating layer that divides them, join up in the picture to form a new unity. This unity is a dialectical whole, i.e. a whole in which the erstwhile antitheses of pure forces with a [...][10] of the experiential world exist as values. The possibility of transposing the entire world of appearances into a unity of tensions must be regarded as the prerequisite for a new kind of experience.

The stages in this new manifestation are still few. Nor can it be any other way. All the longer is the path that lies before us. But why not joyfully avow this distant vision. Why not rise up here into a stratosphere and over and beyond that. Why bemoan that the sylvan idyll and the intimacy of the hearth are not to be found in the regions of this greater purview. Nobody is forced to leave the firm enduring Earth. But the results of an experience must be checked on the fundament on which they were established. And one cannot reach this fundament by good intentions alone, but also by work. Because much that is important in other fields is replaced here by another discipline. [...][11] A highly interesting fact has been brought to light by planar art, which artists have struggled over for a good thirty years: the forms of the world of appearances are not their final nor their sole expression, rather that after abandoning this manifestation a newly formed unity can be created, with the pure i.e. formless energies that become the content of a new experience. This self-sacrifice cannot be forced but only voluntary. We shall try to explain this from the artist's experience.

Part II.[12] The yearning for heaven, which prompted the Christian people to stretch up their arms longingly to the sky, did not bridge the abyss. With that, the wish had to become deed. With that, the power that separated people, unattainably outside and over the world, had to be drawn into the world. With that, passion had to become action. With that, the kind of dualism had to be abandoned that presented a sharply delineated body vis-à-vis an unattainable counterpart. With that, the air space disappeared as emptiness. That is how the silhouette of the body filled up with an anatomy of planar functions, which likewise filled all that surrounded the body with densely packed lines of action. With that, the inside and the outside were established on the same universal law. The vehicle of this law was, however, purely the individuality of the artist. His universal ideal stood in contrast to a reality in which only particularism, only private bourgeois life prevailed.

The artist thus created his universal artworks despite reality and counter to it. Which meant he had constantly to break down resistances, external resistances that were also internal ones. So he created his universal artworks not only in defiance of reality and counter to it, but also in defiance of his own personal reality and against *himself*. Which means the artistic act of creation was aided by violence. It is this that many are unable to excuse in the works of this epoch and reproach as a shortcoming. Doubtless their violence is their shortcoming, and yet the reproach is unjustified. Because how could one ever take a step forward, which has always to be wrested from the resistance of the surrounding world, if one didn't take things in hand, didn't go against the stream, didn't *force* the recalcitrant material into the new form. Those who are allotted this task are fighters, and their decisions are made in the heat and energy of battle, and what they manage to present contains the victory and the vanquished opponent. That adheres to them, to these presentations, battle born, and that which within ourselves is still a foe, a vanquished foe, feels affected.

But gradually even the opponent becomes a fellow fighter and with that there is no more enmity and instead of enmity there is the doubled power of creative collaboration that is open to the entire world. The violence has disappeared.

Being a fellow worker, fellow fighter, that is the answer to the riddle by which dualism disappears from the artwork and from the world. Off into a future without boundaries. That is our rosy dawn in which a socially united humanity experiences its first day of creation. More than with the discovery of America, with the discovery of the future comes the spirit of modern civilization, the establishment of universal solidarity among the whole of humanity. Every social utopia is directed to a better future, and the scientific socialism of Marx and Engels has raised the solidarity of all humanity to certainty. The avowal of the Internationale is the positive law, the constructive work in the midst of the revolutionary struggles. So demand no more from the revolutionary artist than he can achieve. The law that guides him is the impending law of the Internationale; what it must smash are empty conventions, what it puts in their place are the facts of total interconnectedness. What is attached to it, the struggle against egocentric self-assertion, already contains in real artworks the victory over egocentric self-assertion and the affirmative powers of the great, universal solidarity. And this, which lives and is alight in thousands upon thousands of revolutionaries, will be recognized in all that people have produced in its spirit and will produce in the entire future.

But there are two questions which each must ponder. The first question is that of the *old* individualism: "Does this face show the marks that a personality has been constructed?" The second question is that of the *new* individualism: "Does this face show the marks that a world has been constructed?" The portraiture that we are familiar with is that of the *old* individualism. A portraiture of the *new* individualism does not yet exist, because the marks, the building blocks of a new world, of the *collectives* of all energies must be visible therein. But how are we to render this visible with the old technique of individualistic *and* egocentric portraiture? How could one convey in that way a moral that denies the individual as an end in itself?

Because the technique of the old portraiture has evolved from morals: that the individual and every single thing is an end in itself, which is why they were depicted as isolated manifestations. And why on the works painted in this technique we find a sum of isolated things. Thus the morality of the collectives, which denies the individual thing as an end in itself and is there to realize the collectives as the principle overriding the individual, requires a different technique that accords with its morals. Now that we have distinguished the two different ethical, i.e. socio-ethical drives that determine the two different kinds of painting, we can look at the two techniques that produce these two different genres of painting.

The purely individualist technique of painting comes from Italian Renaissance portraiture. It was the Renaissance that founded the haughtiness of the individual. Instead of the static self-containment of the primitives, which still prevailed in Giotto, the Renaissance began to liberate the individual from this self-containment and thus liberate his movements. The liberation of the human body from its static, i.e. architectonic constraints could only be convincingly achieved however by mastering anatomy, and in order to depict the anatomically constructed body, geometrical perspective was required.

When viewed foreshortened, an arm, leg, or body had to be drawn or painted as it appears from a certain angle to an eye skilled in perspective. That requires immense studies with models and thus heralded painting from models. So perspective, the anatomy of the human body, liberation of the individual from the laws of architecture, all came together to give expression to one sole tendency in painting, to wit: that of depicting the human body in its perspectival-anatomical, i.e. plastic, three-dimensional manifestation. While even the three-dimensional spatial depth of a street or a room could now be depicted purely by lines, this was only possible for the corporeal with the help of gradations of light and shade and the colors. One can of course interpret a body cubistically, as the Cubists have done in our epoch. But what can be done effortlessly with a row of buildings, being as they are geometrically constructed, does not succeed that simply with rounded bodily forms. And while Cubism continues to deserve our admiration as a bold and necessary feat, it was only by an act of violence that it was able to force the individuals and objects freed from their architectonic restrictions into an architectonic unity. That was its tragedy, our tragedy, even if we attempted to convey architectonic unity not by a Cubist break-up of the picture surface but by building up painted surfaces.

The ever-progressive release of the individual manifestation since the Renaissance from architectonic, i.e. collective constraints had taken such root as a centuries-old habit of idolizing the self that all life was understood, perceived, experienced, and painted as simply a loose connection between mutually incomplete, isolated individualities. This unproblematic view of life was the prerequisite for the invention of photography.

Certainly the photographic exposure demonstrates the same gradations of light and shade with which the painters of the Renaissance attained the illusion of spatiality and plasticity, because this illusion is perfectly achieved by three color values painted side by side, changing from the darker shade to the medium and the lightest. By these means one can simulate the plasticity of a sphere or cone.[13] But it will be shown that the technique of Renaissance painting will pass on completely into photography as soon as color photographs or color movie film are widely manufactured, because this painting technique from the Renaissance, invented so as to depict the individual manifestation as an autonomous whole and to release it from its surroundings, has elevated as an end-in-itself in painting something that was only of secondary importance in the times of architectonic, i.e. collective constraints. This is why we see the glass painters of the XII *and* XIII centuries[14] build up and organize their large colored windows by the means of the surface. The corporeal aspect of the forms is alluded to discretely, but it fully aligns itself with and obeys the planar law that determines the power, beauty, and consistency of these windows. Thus the validity of the relief-like effect in painting and drawing is by no means as universal as it seems to us as heirs to the Renaissance and photography.

As little as we can cling to the ideal of man who stands today against the collective development of humanity in the form of a condottiere in Italy and his monkeys in Germany, and demonstrates the epigonal barrenness of authoritarian arrogance, we can just as little use a painterly technique that was created for the aggrandizement of authoritarian and arrogant individualism, even if this individual is simply a bottle or an apple.

But people continue to feel that they are Lorenzo di Medici; and still the revolutionary comrades believe that photography and photographic film are the last word in modernism, or indeed the first and only word of the collective, socialist world art. They regard us, who have already abjured the Renaissance ideal for thirty years now, with distrust and incomprehension and, in the light of the great results of a lengthy past, dispense with the knowledge and critique of the means by which they were achieved. For which reason they denied the artists who had departed from the basis on which Renaissance art was built, denied them their moral co-operation, and with that the process of developing a universal art has further been hampered: hampered by the resistance of the individuals, which is transposed from there to things and the whole of the visible world.

Thus the artist, who has been assigned the task of releasing and liberating the energies that are *bound* to the physical by the old individualism, finds himself before closed doors. And yet he has the hope or indeed the certainty that one day they will swing wide open. Because once the comrades have realized that the old myths are dead, that the myth itself, which only half a millennium ago seemed to embody humanity's longing for a community spanning the world, has shown that it does not match up to this ideal, and for that reason was forsaken by the old creative energies of art. Because a myth is dead as soon as the creative energies of art are no longer able to sustain themselves from it and thus abandon it. Which is to say the arts themselves die and are dead as soon as the power of truth in which they once believed, and which always renewed and rejuvenated its powers of innovation, as soon as this power of truth is extinguished and merely continues to be practiced as an old habit.

But the *vital aspect* of art, which saved it from being a dead teaching, had to turn to life itself, centralized life not spent by any myths. Thus art tore itself from the hierarchy of the church and, above all during the times that saw the blossoming of not only the dictatorship of the church but also the dictatorship of the imperialisms and of capital, freed itself from all these dictatorships. The process by which this struggle for liberty took place cannot be described here, it deserves to be treated by art history as a special field of study. Just this much though: the church's power dogma was: control over the human soul in this life brings an afterlife. The power dogma of imperialism was: control over all mineral resources on Earth. The power dogma of capitalism was: control over and exploitation of manpower. All three dogmas have this in common: conquest and subjugation, property. This thousand-year dictatorship of property has been totally instilled into human nature, yes, it has even rendered the complexion of our ideas of nature completely in its own likeness. And not even the naturalist and Impressionist artists were able to free themselves from this likeness of the dictatorship of property. Because even property is a myth. Just like the church, a finely branching ideology has developed and established on this its method for raising people in the family and the state.[15]

But how is it possible that even nature can be impregnated by the dictatorship of property. Do the trees, the hills, the landscapes and the rivers, the apples and the bottles all look like an industrial magnate? The answer to this depends on the values we hold. The value that things, that the world have for a person is introduced to it by him, is seen in it by him, that is how he depicts them. A new value generates a new depiction, which does not compare itself with the old, contemporary or foregoing values, but recognizes its difference from them and is now able to activate new creative energies which for their part shape matter itself; a new value of this kind is weak and will only be short-lived. But if it does not flinch from shining into all that lives in the present and that lived in the past, nor flinch even from shining into the heart of *those who establish values*, into all of his atavisms, slowly an unused, unspoiled material appears that is strong enough to summon up a new world of appearances.

But for this we need fact-based ideology and morals as our guide, which can be no other than a social ideology and morality and one alone that surmounts and eliminates the principle of property: only scientific socialism can achieve this. It alone is the arbiter between an old and a new form of being. It alone can give time, space, and form a new meaning, a new face. It alone can wean people from the illusion of property and power. And thus once individual being has completely identified with collective being, the individual manifestation will have also become identical with the human collective. But, people will ask, will we ever be able to see this collective humanity? And hasn't the individual manifestation been perfectly captured in the photographs of crowds and in film footage of crowds? Of course. Every single person in this crowd belongs to a family, has himself a family, has a small amount of property and works fully dedicated on building up the socialist collective. This however is a view of the collective as seen by the individual; only a very small fraction of the collective becomes visible in this way. But the larger the exposures of crowds taken with a camera, the smaller the number of recognizable individuals, the more they lose their collective character. But we need the means of representation in order to give the *collective* its *universal* character, because by this means alone is its permanency given. Only through such means of representation does the intrinsic nature, the materiality, the concrete distribution of the energies in the collective become visible. The collective, as an organizational principle of energies, permits these energies to appear under a law of configuration. And in order that this law and its application appear, i.e. can be made visible, the clarity and unity of the collective structure must be *capable of being portrayed*. But these can only be portrayed if the portrayal of the individual is relinquished: the portrayal of human individuality as well of animal and objective individuality. Only in this way will the collective be elevated to the visible fact that dualism has been overcome by it.

So we have no other choice at the moment for depicting the surmounting of dualism through the collective than by foregoing the portrayal of people, animals, things, and the entire objective world. [We] require [the] introduction of units which together permit an unbroken synthesis. That every individual, every discrete thing must actually be seen as egocentric and thus adverse to the collective is obvious to every painter who has attempted to break through the individualistic structure in order to join up with a universal one.

As the universal could still be expressed by mythology, it was enough to let the individual perform a mythological function. Everything remained here in the gesture, all that was required was the wish, the longing to bridge the abyss in dualism. But the universal has stepped out of the framework of the myth, has become an active, practical potential, it is the meaning behind the human community, has become its collective law, it is recognizable and workable, it is active. Passion has no creative place in it, such as was the case in dualistic mythologies; suffering is no longer a self-centered suffering but a collective suffering which does *not* resign itself.

Here are two powerful minds that have shaken the proletariat from its resignation: Marx and Engels. Dualism disappears from history and with that the individual as bearer of dualism. The collective becomes universal and produces individualities who are bearers of the collective. The painters, sculptors, and architects who hurry ahead and accompany the development and never make compromises with impunity must dig ever deeper into the laws of collectivity and universalism. And their honest decisions, which are precipitated in paintings, will one day be recognized for their true importance alongside the paintings from the dualist world era. In them the revolutionary world proletariat, united in the socialist world collective, will again recognize the strong discipline and self-denial that brought it to victory.

Finished in Paris November 1935.

1 Complete version of a text from Otto Freundlich's estate—a forty-two page manuscript written in sütterlin script, transcribed by Eric Wychlacz—previously published only in excerpts, here with the kind permission of Association Les Amis de Jeanne et Otto Freundlich. Cf. Otto Freundlich, "Bekenntnisse eines revolutionären Malers," in Uli Bohnen, ed., *Otto Freundlich: Schriften. Ein Wegbereiter der gegenstandslosen Kunst* (Cologne, 1982), pp. 197–202.

2 Freundlich originally wrote here: "who we love. We must fight for love."

3 The following passage was deleted here by Freundlich: "The sculpture is body and remains body. Working in stone and clay means working bodily; because the clay is by nature body and so is the clay. So here the attempt to try to fake physical, i.e. three-dimensional things, does not even arise. The sculpture is thus what remains by its nature isolated and can be possessed. Certainly, the painting is isolated inasmuch as it has four edges, however large it may be, i.e. as a mural or stained glass. What is needed is a third factor that resolves this isolation of the painted surface or the plastic art form, and this third term is architecture."

4 Here Freundlich deleted: "I am an autodidact."

5 Freundlich deleted the following at this juncture: "The plastic effect can be achieved in black and white graphics and in painting by placing 3 gradations next to one another. In black and white graphics it is enough to go from black to dark gray, from dark gray to paler gray and to place them within the contours of a drawing. In painting the same plastic effect can be obtained from the transition from a dark color to the middle tone and from that to the paler tone. This principle must be obeyed, regardless of which colors may be used in the painting or watercolor, this triple gradation of the light color from darker to lighter can thus be viewed as the underlying principle for depicting a plastic effect in drawing or painting. I think that this trinity in the gradation of the colors can be referred to, without doing any violence to it, as a dialectical principle. Only once the workings of this 'dialectic' have been introduced into aesthetic understanding will it be possible for me to advance from the dialectical schema of dark, middle, light to a non-schematic dialectic of color and black-and-white graphics, and to describe it."

6 *The Birth of Man,* 1919, HvW 8, p. 131.

7 Freundlich executed his first window in 1922, in an unidentified workshop in Naumberg an der Saale.

8 HvW 11, p. 140.

9 One word illegible.

10 One word illegible.

11 One illegible sentence.

12 Freundlich deleted the following paragraph here: "The second artist who has been allowed to speak in this report is me. I have not availed myself of mythological terms in order to depict my course of development as an artist. But philosophical, ethical, and religious ideas dominated my youth and my first artistic and intellectual awakenings. Already I experienced social injustice very early on, the way it led to poverty and unemployment, and tried in my own personal way to actively help by denying myself even what was absolutely necessary for me, until my energies were drained. Throughout my artistic development I was never a Naturalist or Impressionist, because they lacked for me the universalism which medieval art had through Christianity. Nor, however, have I imitated Christian art, because I knew that only a universalism personally acquired and applied by modern man could make up for the shortcoming. The pure surface, which I already employed very early on as the primal element in my paintings, was the means for me to convey this universalism in an image. Which meant that once I had decided on the pure surface, I employed none of the technical means of expression from Naturalism and Impressionism and thus also felt essentially alien to their way of looking at nature. But I saw my pictures as a conception of universal nature, which were one with the technical construction of the image. This technical construction was, as I said, the pure flatness of every color, which lay sharply delineated side by side as curve-like surfaces tapering to a point."

13 Freundlich deleted here: "There is no need of a light-and-shade effect in order to simulate the three-dimensionality of a cube or a pyramid on a surface, this can be done by lines alone."

14 Freundlich originally inserted here: "during which the Catholic Church represented the collective universal element in all its cathedrals."

15 An early draft of the text contained the words: "Already today a great many know what it means to be boycotted by property. This fate was not so widely known in our youth."

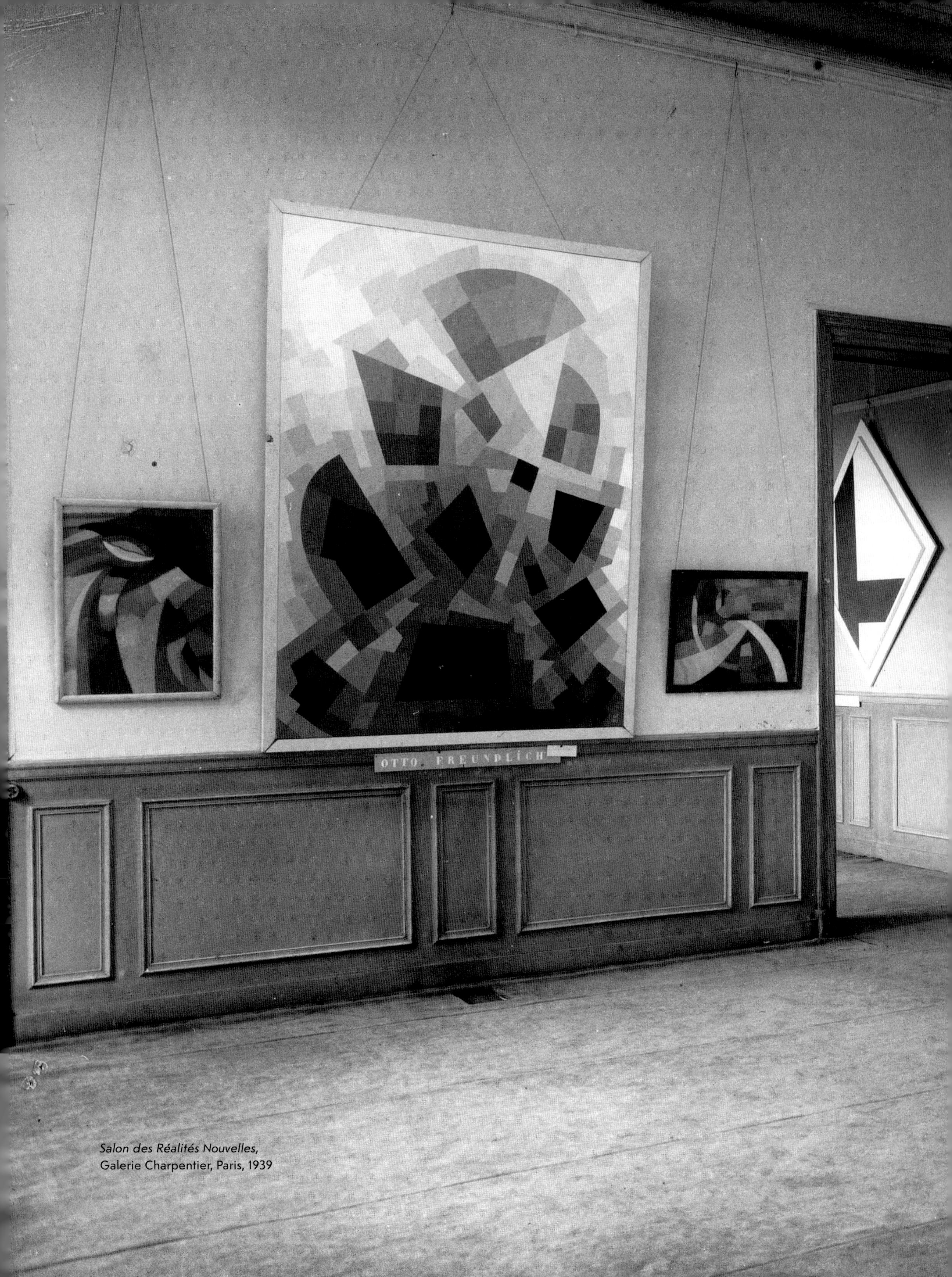

Salon des Réalités Nouvelles,
Galerie Charpentier, Paris, 1939

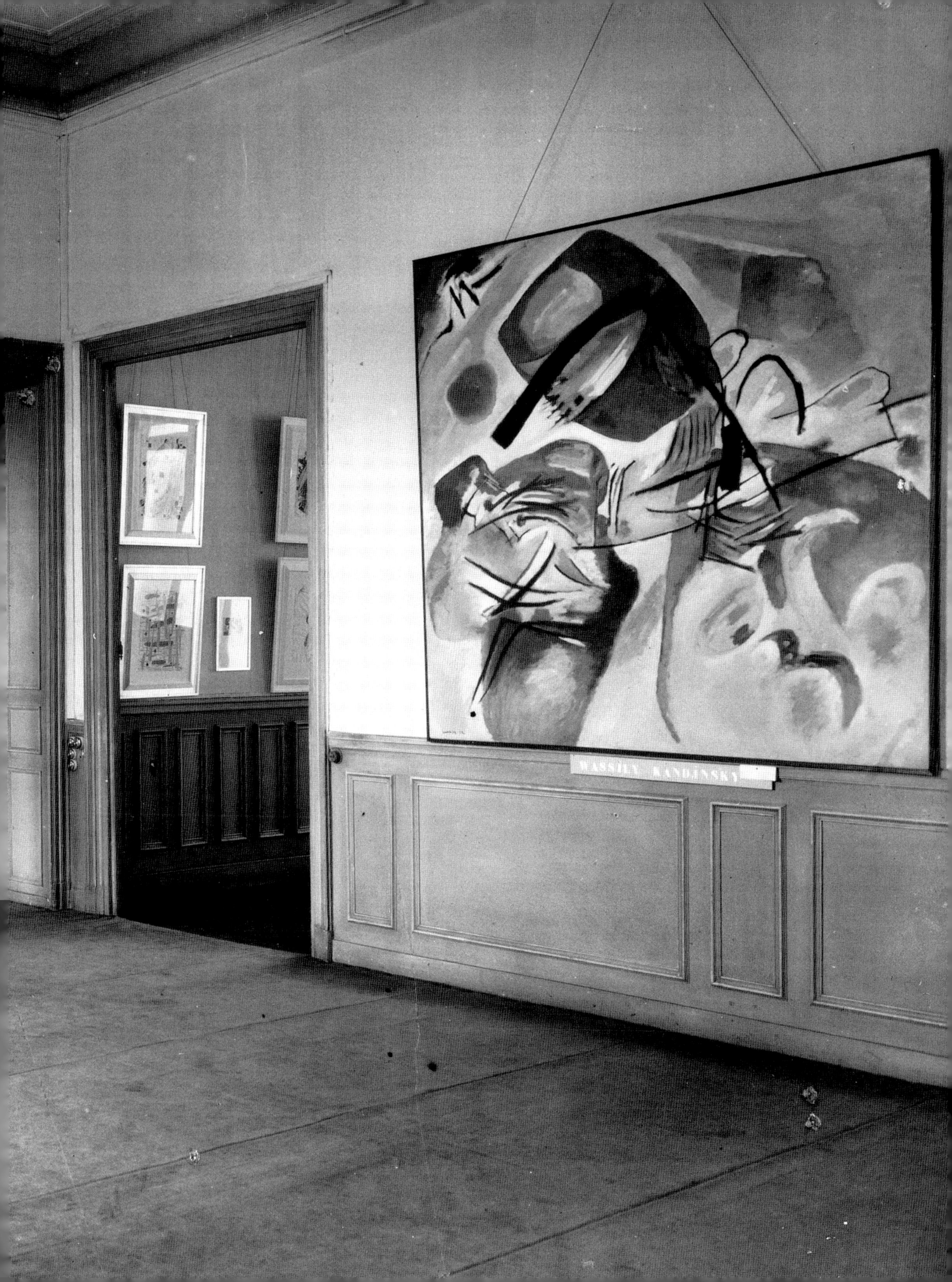
WASSILY KANDINSKY

Contents

A Word of Welcome

It was an unprecedented gesture of solidarity and appreciation: in 1938, a large number of distinguished modernist artists—including Jean Arp, Georges Braque, Alfred Döblin, André Derain, Robert and Sonia Delaunay, Max Ernst, Walter Gropius, Wassily Kandinsky, Oskar Kokoschka, Fernand Léger, Pablo Picasso, and Sophie Taeuber-Arp—signed an appeal to the French government on behalf of Otto Freundlich, a pioneer of abstract art. They drew attention to the precarious financial situation of the artist, who had been denounced as "degenerate" by the Nazis, and called for donations toward the purchase of one of his major works for the Musée du Jeu de Paume as a means of supporting him. This initiative and the famous names associated with it are sufficient to underscore the outstanding importance of an artist to whom the Nazis paid "unconscious tribute" in seeking to use him for their own ends (to quote the words of the appeal). Because his monumental 1912 sculpture *Large Head* appeared on the cover of the catalogue for the infamous Munich exhibition *Degenerate Art* in 1937, Otto Freundlich still stands today as an emblem for the vilification of the artistic avant-garde in the Nazi period. The artwork went missing as the defamatory exhibition traveled to various cities and is now regarded as lost. The Jewish Museum in Berlin exhibits a "Black Mark" in its place as a symbol of the loss and destruction of artworks under National Socialism.

Unfortunately, the reputation enjoyed by Otto Freundlich in the art world of his day, the reception of his work in the work of other artists, and his role as a pioneer of modernism are almost completely forgotten today, as are his theory of abstraction and his dream of a "new man in a kind of cosmic communism." As art historian Joachim Heusinger von Waldegg has observed, Otto Freundlich pursued "the ideal of a socially engaged, ethically committed art." For him, the development of a new art and a new society were intimately linked. In this, he was a forerunner of the conception of art that was expanded after 1960 by Fluxus and action artists such as Joseph Beuys. He himself never had the chance to resume his once so promising artistic career after World War II. In 1943, he was denounced as a Jew in the South of France, arrested, deported to an extermination camp, and murdered there.

For far too long, his extraordinary work was denied the public attention it deserves, in part because critical portions of his oeuvre were lost or destroyed as a result of his persecution, including thirteen of the fourteen works confiscated from German museums and collections for the exhibition *Degenerate Art*. This makes the exhibition *Otto Freundlich: Cosmic Communism*, which was developed by the Museum Ludwig in Cologne and the Kunstmuseum Basel in close collaboration with the Musée Tavet-Delacour in Pontoise, all the more important, indeed overdue.

In Germany, it represents the first major retrospective of the artist's work since the exhibitions at the Wallraf-Richartz-Museum in Cologne in 1960 and the Rheinisches Landesmuseum Bonn in 1978–79. It provides the first comprehensive overview of Otto Freundlich's activity and influence and makes it possible to trace the development of his artistic and theoretical approaches.

It is with gratitude and pleasure that I have agreed to become the patron of this very special exhibition. It not only constitutes a worthy monument to one of the most distinguished artists of the avant-garde; it also recalls the terrible suffering and injustice inflicted on artists—especially those with Jewish roots—under the Nazi reign of terror. It is our historical and moral obligation to keep these memories alive. Not least in this spirit, I wish the exhibition great success and many interested visitors.

Prof. Monika Grütters MdB
Minister of State to the Federal Chancellor

Foreword

It is a pleasure and an honor for us to be able to mount the first retrospective of Otto Freundlich's work in almost forty years at our museums. There is much about our cities that connects them with this artist. He left traces behind in both of them, which this exhibition reveals. They were also home to figures who very early on admired and supported Freundlich and his art.

In Cologne, the most important of these was the tobacconist and art patron Josef Feinhals, who not only rented a studio for the artist but also commissioned his mosaic *The Birth of Man* (1919, HvW 8, pp. 131–132), which still survives today. It was in Cologne in 1931 that Freundlich had his only solo exhibition in Germany during his lifetime. It was organized by the gallerist Andreas Becker in his spaces in Wallraf-Platz. Also based in Cologne were artists Franz Wilhelm Seiwert, Heinrich Hoerle, Gerd Arntz, Walter Stern, and August Sander, the so-called Cologne Progressives, with whom Freundlich was closely tied. This intimate connection to the Rhineland is almost certainly the reason why the Wallraf-Richartz-Museum was the first public institution to devote a solo exhibition to the artist in 1960. Curator Günter Aust was still able to speak with some of Freundlich's fellow artists and gain information from them firsthand, which made his exhibition a milestone. It represented the inexcusably belated recognition of an artist who had not only been persecuted as "degenerate" but was murdered because of his Jewish origins and political convictions. Aust's monograph, published by Dumont Verlag, remains a standard-bearer on the artist even today.

Because of the Nazi madness and its aftermath, Freundlich's rehabilitation did not take place in Germany until 1960, but it occurred in Switzerland decades earlier thanks to clear-sighted connoisseurs. In 1939, as director of the Kunstmuseum Basel, Georg Schmidt began to acquire the art that had been seized from German museums as "degenerate." Freundlich's works, however, were not among those that reached Switzerland as "internationally exploitable." In 1936, while he was still the librarian of Basel's Kunstgewerbemuseum, Schmidt visited Freundlich in Paris, and in 1937 he invited the artist to participate in the exhibition *Constructivists*, which he organized for Kunsthalle Basel together with curator Richard Lichtenhan. In addition to Wassily Kandinsky, Piet Mondrian, and Kazimir Malevich, he included a number of works by Otto Freundlich in the show. Schmidt owned a painting by Freundlich as part of his private collection and also sought to acquire his works as director of the Kunstmuseum Basel. Thus, the large painting *Composition* from 1932 (HvW 165, p. 233) was added to the collection as early as 1947 with the help of Richard Doetsch-Benziger. It was later followed by a small but very fine painting on wood (HvW 166, p. 265) and a pastel (HvW 252, p. 174), both of which formed part of the donation of Marguerite Arp-Hagenbach. Freundlich enjoyed a lifelong friendship with Jean and Sophie Taeuber-Arp, which was also expressed in an artistic kinship among them.

In many ways, however, Freundlich's most important supporter was the Basel-based elementary school teacher Hedwig Muschg. She met the artist in 1929, probably through her brother, Hans—a sculptor who moved to Paris—and supported him selflessly, sparing whatever she could from her meager salary. Freundlich thanked her with artworks, which grew into a sizeable collection over the years. The painting from Museum Ludwig's collection (HvW 199, p. 249) as well as the one from Kunstmuseum Basel (HvW 165, p. 233) are both dedicated to her. We are grateful to her half-brother, Adolf Muschg, for contributing his reminiscences of this great friend and supporter of the artist to our catalogue.

But the circle of Freundlich's supporters and fellow artists was not restricted to Cologne and Basel. Museum directors in other towns and cities also rendered outstanding services to his work. One of these was Max Sauerlandt of the Museum für Kunst und Gewerbe in Hamburg, who acquired Freundlich's works for his collection as early as the late 1920s, including *Large Head* (1912; HvW 63, p. 77), which would eventually come to a baleful end on the cover of the visitors' guide to the defamatory exhibition *Degenerate Art*. Another of Freundlich's early admirers was Wilhelm Wartmann, director of Kunsthaus Zürich. He exhibited the large sculpture *Ascension* (1912; HvW 76, pp. 186–187) not long after its production together with works by Jean Arp, Constantin Brâncuşi, Robert Delaunay, and many others at the large exhibition *Abstract and Surrealist Painting and Sculpture*, held in October–November 1929.

Freundlich also had a circle of fellow artists in France, where he relocated permanently in 1924. From 1930 on, he lived with the artist Jeanne Kosnick-Kloss. She followed Freundlich to the Pyrenees when he was forced to hide from the Nazis and their French collaborators and managed his estate until her death in 1968. The couple's legacy went to the Musées de Pontoise outside Paris at the initiative of their then director, Edda Maillet. Maillet, assisted by Hedwig Muschg, spent decades painstakingly reviewing and organizing the artist's estate and making it accessible to scholars and art historians, for which she is owed a heartfelt debt of gratitude. Also deserving of thanks is her successor in the position, Christophe Duvivier, who published a monograph on Freundlich in 2009 and did everything he could to support our project with loan works and information. Professor Emeritus Joachim Heusinger von Waldegg organized a retrospective of Freundlich's work for the Rheinisches Landesmuseum in Bonn in 1978, at which time he also compiled the catalogue raisonné. We wish to thank him most sincerely for sharing his research and vast knowledge with us and for supporting this project from beginning to end.

We have also received valuable support from the highly commendable Association des Amis de Jeanne et Otto Freundlich, all of whose members we would like to thank in the person of its chairman, Jérôme Serri. There is one of them, however, whom we wish to single out for special mention. Had it not been for the energetic involvement of Swiss patron Gerson Waechter, this exhibition might never have taken place, at least not at this time or in this form. In 2014, his passionate interest in Freundlich set a ball rolling which was passed by Rita Kersting—who at that time was still at the Israel Museum—to Museum Ludwig and from there back to Switzerland and the Kunstmuseum Basel. We cannot thank him enough for the initial impulse as well as for financially supporting the exhibition.

We have been moved and excited by the tremendous amount of support we have received since we began preparing this exhibition. In agreeing to become its patron, the German Minister for Culture and the Media, Prof. Monika Grütters, sent a clear signal of support. The Kulturstiftung der Länder with its Secretary General Isabel Pfeiffer-Poensgen, Switzerland's Art Mentor Foundation Lucerne, the Landschaftsverband Rheinland, and the KPMG AG made substantial funding available, which gave us the security to move forward with our plans and ensured our creative freedom. If we have been able to assemble an exhibition consistent with our vision and in the spirit of the artist, it is thanks to the domestic and foreign institutions and private lenders whose pledges also sent a signal of solidarity with Freundlich. We wish to thank above all the Berlinische Galerie, one of the exhibition's principal lenders, for its active and scholarly support.

A highlight of our exhibition is the presentation of Freundlich's mosaic *The Birth of Man*. Freundlich always regarded this 1919 mosaic as one of his major works, and he was heartbroken to know that it was shut up in a box and languishing in a shed. In the end, it was that box that enabled the work to survive the war, so that in 1954 it could be installed at the Cologne Opera. Thanks to the support of director Birgit Meyer, her technical director Patrik Wasserbauer, municipal conservator Dr. Thomas Werner, his colleague Dr. Marion Grams-Thieme, and restorer Gereon Lindlar, the work is now in a position to demonstrate its pioneering character for Freundlich's oeuvre. In this connection, we wish to convey our special thanks to Deputy for Art and Culture Susanne Laugwitz-Aulbach and to Mayor Henriette Reker for their energetic support. Thanks also to the Friends of the Wallraf-Richartz-Museum and Museum Ludwig for supporting the not exactly routine undertaking of transporting the mosaic from the opera house to the museum.

Both exhibition and catalogue also have scholarly ambitions. It was important to us that we incorporate into this project the research carried out at universities and museums, in order to make it accessible to a broader audience. We are grateful in this connection to the catalogue's contributors as well as to the libraries and archives that originally made this research possible, especially the IMEC Archive in Caen and in particular Nathalie Léger, Dr. André Derval, and Dr. Yves Chevrefils Desbiolles, who supported our research unreservedly.

We have also embarked on a research project of our own, which seeks to take an in-depth look at Freundlich's painting technique. Under the direction of restorer Verena Franken, works by Freundlich have been studied systematically for the first time; initial findings are published in this volume. We wish to extend our heartfelt thanks to the Rathgen Research Laboratory of the National Museums in Berlin with Prof. Ina Reiche and her team; the Laboratoire d'Archéologie Moléculaire et Structurale, Paris, with Dr. Philippe Walter and Dr. Katharina Müller; and the Technische Hochschule of Cologne, in particular Prof. Gunnar Heydenreich, Prof. Doris Oltrogge, and Prof. Hans Portsteffen; as well as to all the museums and private collectors who made their works available for this interdisciplinary project. We are indebted to the Wallraf-Richartz and Bröhan Museums for their ever straightforward and uncomplicated administrative assistance.

We wish to thank our colleagues and collaborators who worked on this exhibition and the accompanying catalogue. Above all, however, we are deeply grateful to the exhibition's curator, Dr. Julia Friedrich, who began working on this project in 2014 and is principally responsible for the fact that exhibition and catalogue are now able to shed new light on this important artist.

We are firmly convinced that this exhibition makes clear the significance of Otto Freundlich's work and shows that his name belongs beside those of his fellow artists, from Pablo Picasso to Robert Delaunay and Wassily Kandinsky.

Yilmaz Dziewior
Director, Museum Ludwig, Cologne

Josef Helfenstein
Director, Kunstmuseum Basel

Julia Friedrich

Abstraction as Opening Up
An Introduction to Otto Freundlich's Aesthetics

Abstraction is not a formal property. It is a relationship. Everything abstract relates, whether positively or negatively, to something concrete. This is rarely clearer than in the pioneering work by Otto Freundlich, who was one of the first to produce abstract art. Abstraction for him was not a self-reflection on the medium. It mirrored complex processes in nature and society. The manner in which this was done should have raised Freundlich to the ranks of the most compelling and interesting artists of his century—but the Nazis thought otherwise.

Indeed, when it comes to this artist the Nazis seem to have been the victors. Even today, a long shadow has been cast over his life and work because he was doomed to play a leading role in the vilifying *Degenerate Art* exhibition, which opened in 1937 in Munich before touring the country and giving the philistines a lesson in horror. His *Large Head* (HvW 63, p. 77) was depicted on the cover of the exhibition guide and titled in the text "The New Man" so as to suggest that what Freundlich, the Communist Jew, was up to was the very thing the Nazis had reserved for themselves: fabricating people. And that was not the only one of their manipulations, whose entire scope has been charted out by Mandy Wignanek in the present volume.

Worse than any manipulation, though, were the acts of destruction, because afterwards no amount of investigation can help. Of the fourteen works that the Nazis seized from German museums, only one has re-emerged (HvW 109, p. 84). Freundlich had to part with a great deal during his life. The Nazis severed the connection between him, as he lived in France, and his early work, which was stored in his old studio in Berlin at Kaiserplatz (now Bundesplatz) 17. The building survived the war, but all that he left there is now deemed lost.

In the desperate knowledge of no longer being able to access a part of his oeuvre, Freundlich drew up a list around 1941, while fleeing the Nazis and their French collaborators, containing all the titles of the works he could remember from 1923 on (pp. 282–301). He added small sketches to it, and even painted three of the works again from memory (HvW 101, p. 111; HvW 105, p. 90; and HvW 111, p. 91). All these attempts at reconstructing his work are a help, as are old photos, but they cannot undo what was done. Especially painful is the loss of the sculptures. They were built to be viewed from any angle, so not even a photograph can serve as more than a reference. The gap that the Nazis ripped out must be filled as best it can by research, but it must also remain recognizable for what it is.

In 1978 the research received a valuable boost in the form of the catalogue raisonné compiled by Joachim Heusinger von Waldegg.[1] A further piece of fortune is that the artist's singular texts have been preserved in Freundlich's estate, for they must be seen as part of this highly philosophical person's art, which would lose a lot without them. Günter Aust, who in 1960 mounted the first major exhibition of Freundlich's works, already edited a volume of Freundlich's writings to follow on from his monograph.[2] Heusinger von Waldegg similarly appended a reader to his catalogue raisonné containing important texts and letters, and finally Uli Bohnen presented the essential volume of his writings, the *Schriften.*[3]

One of Freundlich's most mature and considered texts, his "Bekenntnisse eines revolutionären Malers" ("Confessions of a Revolutionary Painter"), written in 1935 in Paris, had only previously been available in abbreviated form. It has been freshly transcribed for the present volume from the original manuscript. In these "Confessions" Freundlich explains his artistic program, which over the following pages will be located in the context of his work and times. The latest findings on the various groups of related works, his techniques, and the periods in his artistic development can be found in the essays, which have been written for this volume by some of the leading Freundlich researchers.

Old and New Nature Freundlich commences his "Confessions" on a hopeful note: "We shall be understood by those for whom we fight."[4] The most telling aspect of this sentence is the use of the future passive. Freundlich will be understood by the revolutionary proletariat for whom he is fighting. Which means that up until the time of writing, 1935, he had yet to be understood by it, let alone by the middle classes, although they were of no importance to him.

There is no need to put it as polemically as John Heartfield did when he wrote that not even Freundlich's "most logical thoughts on color" would be able to mobilize "as many as a dozen workers,"[5] but there is no escaping the question of how the revolutionary proletariat was supposed to grasp from his painting and sculptures that Freundlich was on its side. With very few exceptions—which include the central mosaic *The Birth of Man* (HvW, p. 131) and the painting *My Sky is Red* (HvW 168, p. 272)[6]—Freundlich never conveyed unequivocal signals in his works, except perhaps in the titles. In this he differed fundamentally from the Cologne Progressives, whose political goals he shared and with whom he was also closely connected.

Although the Progressives kept coming very close to artistic abstraction, it remained a boundary line which the artists dared not cross out of consideration towards the "worker-beholder." Franz Wilhelm Seiwert stated for instance that he knew that "the imagery of abstraction is still very poorly understood today."[7] The workers were able to identify their lives and struggles in the Progressives' works. Typical of Freundlich's advanced pieces are, by contrast, the colorful, prismatic surfaces he developed from stained glass painting and mosaics.

The artist gave his reasons for choosing the path to abstraction in his "Confessions." He underscored in them his renunciation of objective nature. It is not, he notes, the only possible one—"we need another."[8] He illustrated the discovery of this new, other nature with the (unfounded) anecdote that George Stephenson arrived at the principle behind the steam engine on observing how the steam in a kettle forced up the lid. According to Freundlich, in this way Stephenson discovered the action of a hitherto unharnessed force. A "driving force" of this kind also resides in representational painting and sculpture, he writes, and "is *comparable* with the physical forces of nature," even if that is not to say "it *is* a physical force." And yet it goes "beyond the specific purpose of the given motifs" and can "only then reveal the greatness, the enormity of its universal validity when it is released from any representational motif."[9]

So the driving force Freundlich refers to was already present in art up until that time, but like water contained by a dam, it had been penned in by motifs, blocked, held fast. It would only be able to produce its full effect once it was liberated from that. Not simply a mental energy, it is on a par with the very forces of nature.

The force that Freundlich outlines, which only develops once freed from the material, motivic aspects, is highly reminiscent of the views held by the natural sciences at that time. Science had likewise encountered processes which, although demonstrable and in certain ways also "physical," could no longer be pictured, and as such were both real and, at the same time, abstract. Everything that had previously been regarded as tangible mass and substance suddenly seemed to have dissipated. Freundlich kept informed about the latest developments in, among other things, physics through his cousin Erwin Finlay-Freundlich, who was an associate of Albert Einstein.[10]

The world of modern physics consists of quanta, energies, charges, tensions, processes, and fields which, in the majority of cases, can only be observed indirectly and in some cases only gleaned theoretically. There are now no substances, masses, or forms; physical understanding has departed from Euclidean space. Rita Wildegans, who is the first to study the influence of scientific thought on Freundlich, has analyzed how his surface was conceived of as an "extra-Euclidean space," and his curve appears to be in keeping with the "curved space-time manifold" in the Theory of Relativity.[11] But these can only be taken as "comparisons," as Freundlich himself emphasized. Painting and sculpture are not collections of formulae.

Even if Freundlich's art was based, like the new physics, on processes rather than static substances, like all art (even Conceptual Art) it remained bound to a substantial basis—in his case paint, canvas, bronze, which can be directly seen, touched, and experienced. The artist did not wish to deprive anyone of a naive, sensual encounter with his works and the attending joys. But he pointed emphatically to an intellectual, abstract motion, to an energy lying behind the sensual. This is of a complexity not yet conceived of by the old art, an as yet untapped force whose "universal validity," says Freundlich, is only first revealed when freed of motif, of figuration and representation.

At this point Freundlich extends his argument to include society. The driving forces in the nature and art of yore are bound to objects. But this can be seen as a property relationship: the ego as subject puffs itself up to become the owner of the objects. And since the subject as proprietor confronts the object as property in a dualistic modus, everything gets trapped in a fateful inertia. Freundlich felt that all thing-based perceptions of the world are permeated by this property-mindset.

The "hand that always wants something graspable" wants to possess, for which reason the eye likewise demands the "illusion of three-dimensionality"[12] as an illusion of ownership. Ultimately even nature appears to be "imbued with the dictatorship of property."[13]

Freundlich was not alone in his rejection of a dualistic world picture. Walter Gropius wrote in 1919 that "the old, dualistic world-concept which envisaged the ego in opposition to the universe is losing ground. In its place is rising the idea of a universal unity in which all opposing forces exist in a state of absolute balance."[14] But Freundlich went much farther than Gropius, he located the ego in the realm of property, which in his view was doomed to extinction. With that the driving force that overturns the ingrained property structure, and also the reified world of bodies and motifs, becomes a revolutionary force. Because "the object as antithesis to the individual will disappear, as will a person's existence as an object for another."[15] No longer will proprietors and their property, subjects and objects rule over society; their place is to be taken by an active, anonymous proletariat, not as a monolithic block but as complex motion. The proletariat will be grasped as a collective of equals in motion. It is this collective that will first make the "concrete distribution of the forces" visible, it is this collective that for the first time will be the "organizational principle for forces."[16]

A complexity of this kind is not to be found in the works of other Communist artists, who, in the service of propaganda, resorted to a simplified, at times crudely simple depiction of reality. Freundlich, on the contrary, could have appealed to Marx, who in his preface to *Das Kapital* wrote: "In the analysis of economic forms, moreover, neither microscopes nor chemical reagents are of use. The power of abstraction must replace both."[17] The outcome of an individual's work can still be observed, but not that of an entire industry; a single commodity can be touched and looked at, but not commodity exchange; a single person can attend an eviction or demonstration, but not class struggle.

Freundlich considered that art should be abreast of the times, or indeed ahead of them, that it should offer the whole wealth of not only perception but also thought. "Today, being political means changing the forms,"[18] he wrote. For which reason he could have seconded Max Raphael's complaint: "No one today shows you as clearly as socialist artists what art is not."[19] That, along with the political aspect, was a reason why Freundlich left the Novembergruppe in 1919. It was his desire that "artists would become creative and a model not only in outward form, but truly, emphatically in their inner form."[20] But if, on the other hand, art were to restrict itself to purely aesthetic relationships, he would have rejected that with equal vehemence. That is why he left the Abstraction-Création group in 1934, of which he had been an early member, just as he had been in the previous group, Cercle et Carré (Kandinsky, Mondrian, Vantongerloo, et al.).[21]

Unlike other abstract artists of his day, Freundlich's artistic abstraction was not restricted to the artwork's internal relationships. It stood for a "comparison" with natural and social processes which can no longer be observed as such with the naked eye. But his abstraction wanted more than simply to describe these processes, these "driving forces," it wanted to be *driven* by them: Freundlich wanted to be a "fellow worker, fellow fighter,"[22] even if he could only first be understood by the workers and fighters of the future. If not the purposes of today, he nevertheless served those of tomorrow.

Guild and Future Even if Freundlich was more daring with his abstraction than the Cologne Progressives, like them he loved the medieval artisans' guilds.[23] These guilds were already a part of the anonymous collective he was working towards. They pursued an art tailored to practical ends, which at that time was still innocent about property and the bourgeoisie, and thus of the dualism between subject and object, owner and possessions, and often had a broad cosmological horizon. Freundlich did not look back to the Middle Ages in nostalgia: they appeared to him to anticipate a time when privilege and private property will have been surmounted.

Undoubtedly Freundlich's most intense encounter with artisanal art was in 1914 when he lived for five months in the north tower of Chartres cathedral. His passion for stained glass and mosaics came from that time. His high esteem for craftsmanship arose, however, at an earlier date. He not only opposed the rejection it so frequently met with, he countered it: "Applied art differs in principle ... in no way from high art," as he wrote to Max Sauerlandt, "but the two differ today inasmuch as applied art draws on *evolving* life and high art recognizes a historical, social and visually complete world picture as the sole and definitive one."[24]

By applied art he was on no account referring to an art that worked with traditional methods along traditional lines, but to one that invoked the guiding ideas of the medieval guilds. Only then is the meaning of "*evolving* life" comprehensible, because he saw the future as governed by the action of the collective. The "historical, social and visually complete world picture" is however the one defined by property-mindedness and thingness, against which he pitted the "driving forces" of social change.

Applied art was thus not a safe and tranquil niche for him but the realm for realizing the future. In this spirit of the future, Freundlich produced designs in 1911 for Adya van Rees, who later wove them into carpets. While one of the first (HvW 3, fig. 1) was still largely figurative and resembles in its composition and form of depiction Freundlich's painting *Composition with Figure* (HvW 108, fig. 2), another (HvW 5, fig. 3), dated 1912–13 in the Herbstsalon catalogue, is perfectly abstract and resembles his *Composition* from 1911 (HvW 107, fig. 4), which in the artist's own words was his first abstract painting.[25] He had yet to arrive at his typical spatial compartmentalization, at the energetic charge in the fields that distinguish his mature work, but already Freundlich's first abstraction is pure movement and as such presents the dissolution of materiality and boundaries. "Abstraction here is the abolition of objective and formal limitation in favor of an illimitable perceptual dynamism,"[26] as Erich Franz noted. Although the work with its long-drawn-out strips still evinces Jugendstil influences, the colors have already been placed side by side without delimiting lines.

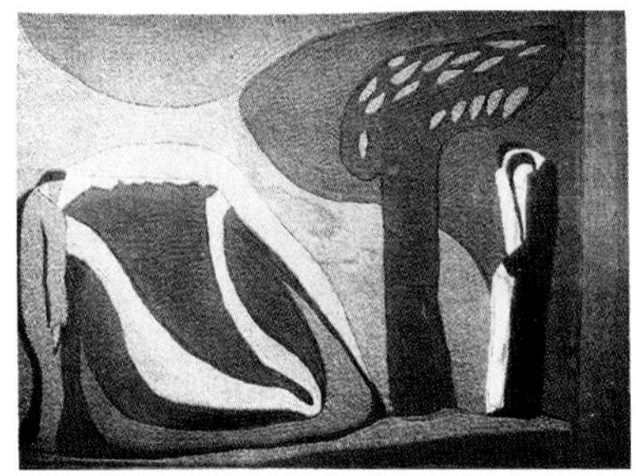

Fig. 1 Adya van Rees, after a design by Otto Freundlich
Composition, 1912
HvW 3
Tapestry in wool
Lost

Fig. 2 Otto Freundlich
Composition with Figure, 1911
HvW 108
Oil on canvas
54 x 65 cm
Donation Freundlich – Musées de Pontoise

As in a *Head* Freundlich did later in 1923 (HvW 131, p. 133), he presented here strips of paint set next to one another. The altered chromaticity and the geometrical surfaces show the influence of mosaic work. After World War I and through his acquaintanceship with Gottfried Heinersdorff, he developed his special glass and mosaic technique. Once again, his orientation to the guild idea in general and the influence of Chartres in particular was decisive for this work. Freundlich wanted to return with all force to the period prior to the Renaissance cult of the ego, into the communally minded Middle Ages. He drew intellectual and formal inspiration from this period, without wanting personally to become a late-Gothicist. Time and again he pointed out that the ego of the Renaissance had been accompanied by the introduction of illusionism in art. And even in Cubism, illusionism had persisted in the form of bodies—or in Freundlich's reading: possessions. This set him apart from the Cubists, with whom he had already established contact in 1908 and even lived with for a time. In fact, he shared a lifelong friendship with Picasso.

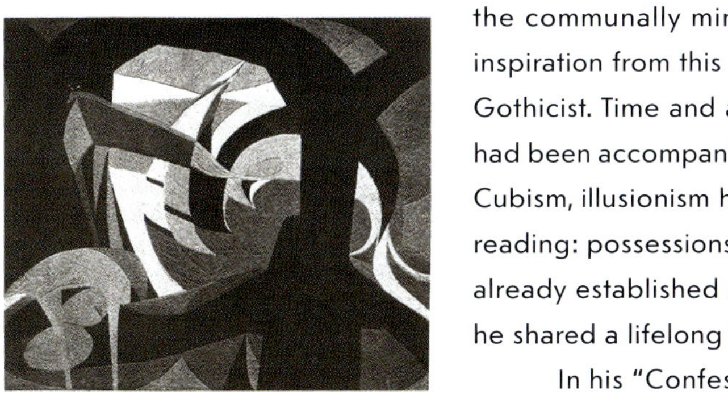

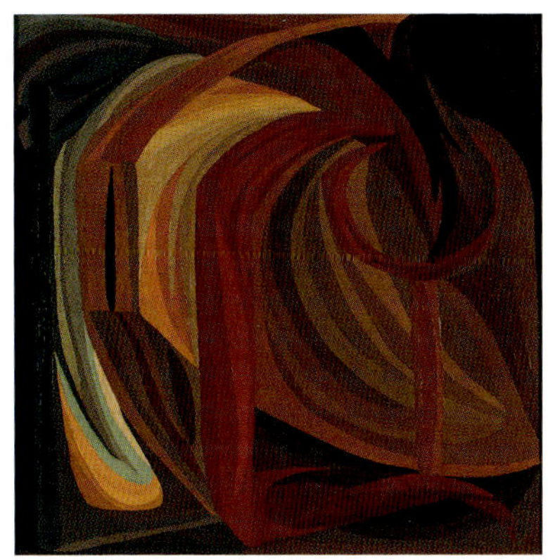

Fig. 3 Adya van Rees, after a design by Otto Freundlich
Composition, 1912–13
HvW 5
Tapestry in wool
Lost

Fig. 4 Otto Freundlich
Composition, 1911
HvW 107
Oil on canvas
200 x 200 cm
Musée d'Art moderne de la Ville de Paris

In his "Confessions" Freundlich gives a vivid description of how he liberated himself from the "illusion of plasticity"[27] and put a more intelligent, "dialectic" art in its place. This was an art of surfaces, albeit interrelated surfaces. And even there he took his bearings from the Middle Ages: "The old murals done in mosaics, the stained glass windows in the old cathedrals up until the thirteenth century, are all composed in a planar manner."[28]

Similarly what had always been the most striking element in his painting gained further importance after Chartres: color. Unlike most other German painters of his day, his feeling for color sensitized him to the "life-affirming, optimistic chromatic euphoria of Orphism";[29] he was friends with the Delaunays as well.

After World War I, color actually became more important to him than form, because it is the colors themselves that create the space, the force fields and contacts,[30] and dissolve all that is firm and material. For this they have to enter into a mutual tension, an exchange with one another. "In keeping with the energetic conception of the picture structure, Freundlich understood the interaction between the colors as a force with a concrete effect that was capable of crushing the stubborn resistance of things," as Heusinger von Waldegg observes.[31] Thus color is neither an end in itself nor material, but is also always thought of in a functional and emblematic way in the picture. Color ideally remains what it is in the pane of a cathedral window flooded by sunlight: the expression of a sense of motion.[32] Since Freundlich avoided illusionist effects, he never attempted to produce this, but he certainly saw it as his task to stimulate motion by means of objective color relations.

Contour and Cosmos The model of the glass window, which was to determine Freundlich's art from 1914 onward, shifted the previously cited requirements for abstraction to a larger if not cosmic context. Since the term "abstraction" is often used in a vague manner, it is worth recapitulating what Freundlich meant by it.

Strictly speaking, representational art is already abstract because quite simply a painted tree is not a tree. As Freundlich pointed out, "even the best painting that depicts natural things is simply an abstraction of nature and can only be abstract nature. Despite this, a landscape by Corot is felt to be like a living thing. So there is a difference between our feeling and judgment of life when faced with a painting and our feeling and judgment of life when faced with nature. . . . We always feel we are *in front of* a painting, but always feel ourselves *in* nature."[33]

This also means that the dualism which Freundlich aimed to surmount carries on in the viewing situation. The viewer continues to stand as a subject in front of the painting as object. But just as a person beholding a Corot succeeds in placing himself in the artist's landscape, which consists of old nature, so a viewer of Freundlich's works should be able to think his way into a landscape that is comprised of new nature. Paraphrasing the title of one of Freundlich's essays,[34] we can say: When the viewer goes under art begins. Just as the viewer in front of the art should neutralize himself, as it were, and become part of the collective and a "new nature," or indeed the cosmos, he should also neutralize what is necessarily left in the artwork in terms of adherence to matter and its remnants of objecthood. Freundlich's aesthetic not only articulates itself then on an abstract plane, it also promotes the capacity for abstraction.

The abstraction that Freundlich performs may be characterized as one that shifts away from an old, representational, and rigid nature into a new, non-representational, motile nature. But a relationship to nature remains. His painterly and sculptural abstraction stands for natural and social processes that are not as such directly perceptible, and which shake up the entrenched order based on things and property. For which reason abstraction should overcome the old subject-object dualism and the attending illusion of space and bodies. Abstraction replaces substances and forms with fields and relationships between fields. Abstraction assimilates itself into the art of the anonymous collective forces of a new era and simultaneously joins up with those of the guilds. In a word, Freundlich's abstraction is an opening up.

This opening up must be directed to a totality of society and nature, which Freundlich calls "cosmos." The Greek word (κόσμος) refers to the universe under the aspect of "order," but it goes almost without saying that Freundlich was not aiming at some divine order. And yet his cosmos is certainly not a kind of chaos but rather an open-ended space in which certain laws of nature hold sway, although the viewer should not envisage them too simply. In Freundlich's day the cosmos had become one of the great topics of modern physics with Einstein's Theory of Relativity. At the same time an intelligentsia that had lost its bearings was inclined toward spiritualist ideas—which makes it all the more important to know where Freundlich actually stood.

Despite some passing similarities,[35] there was a lot that separated him from Paul Klee, for instance, who wrote in his diary in summer 1916: "What my art lacks is / a passionate humanity. . . . The Earth idea gives way to the Universal idea. My love is . . . religious. . . . I am a cosmic point of reference, not / a species. . . . Art is ideal creation."[36] Although we also find in Freundlich that the "Earth idea gives way to the Universal idea," this is very much propelled by "passionate humanity." When Freundlich picked up on the cosmic notions of the Middle Ages and rediscovered a "cosmic law" in the "structure of old glass windows and mosaics," an "intellectual principle from life back then rendered as form,"[37] he was not referring to some divine or religious principle. That can be seen by comparing a window from Chartres with his own designs.

A distinction must be made however in the stained glass at Chartres between the geometrical structure, which tells of harmony and unity, or in other words divine perfection, and the narrative structure, which is not only independent of the geometrical aspect but also does not simply begin and end in biblical tales. The stories told on the windows frequently go back to contemporary literature,[38] and are often worldly rather than other-worldly.

Neither of these characteristics squares with Freundlich's art. He employed open rather than closed systems and, with the exception of a few graphic works, was never narrative. These in fact are the marks of his art. So the structural analogy with Chartres lies not in the closed and narrative elements, but in the shared "aspiration to the universal"[39] and in the ornamental means for reaching this goal. In this context the stained glass itself becomes noticeable, because it appears as a membrane between inside and out, between viewer and cosmos.[40] In keeping with Freundlich, one must say it enables the individual to extrapolate himself out into the universe. Although the "cosmic communism"[41] he called for in 1919 found its beginnings during a political revolution, it did not stay there. The aim was that people should at long last open themselves to the world that had so long been alien to them. They should think of it as a whole and be released as free and equal beings into that whole.

It is impressive with just what intellectual stringency the artist worked out this program of openness in even the design details, as for instance in his compositional technique. As he understood it, the "free color surfaces" in his paintings form an "open community" which can appear both as curves or ornaments. At the same time it is important to note that a surface enclosed by a curved or circular line must be regarded as an "object at rest." Likewise closed in his view were all things framed with some kind of border (one is involuntarily reminded of his earliest abstracts). A surface with four angles is by contrast an open ornament because it can link up. If one side of a triangle is concave, the other convex, we have a spatial curve before us (as for instance in HvW 176, p. 257). Circles were for him "half open" ornaments.

Having said this, it is not difficult to guess the macrostructure he aspired to—the "openness of all the surfaces on the picture to one another." The premise for this is that the "movements, as circle or curve . . . must be borne by various complexes of surfaces that are completely open to one another."[42] Like the circle, the curve generates movement, in this way making substance fluid,[43] and already appears in this function in Van Gogh, who Freundlich hailed as a precursor as late as 1930: "Curves and chromatic functions in the surfaces, which penetrate the motifs with concerted energy and rouse them from static to dynamic life," are in his view Van Gogh's "achievement." His aim was to transpose "shackled nature" into the "realm of freedom."[44]

This dynamization of the surfaces results conversely in the need to open up all the contours—to the environment and the cosmos. This opening up is demonstrated by a pair of sketches he did for his large mosaic *Homage to the Peoples of Color* (HvW 36, p. 245), a major work from the year 1938. The scheme for the contours set down by the artist in roughly 1935–36 (HvW 359 and HvW 360, fig. 5/6, p. 37) shows, on the one hand, the closed contour of a humanlike form as a traced silhouette: old nature. In the open contour, however, the place of the lines is taken by convex and concave sections of curves that can link up on all sides: new nature.

Even in these details he remained true to his principles from at latest the end of World War I. The contour had to be dissolved in accordance with the latest insights in physics,[45] which in place of delineated bodies now only recognized energy flows and particles which merely join together in forms before our sluggish eyes. The contour had to be dissolved, just as the armored ego and every form of delineation had to be broken down for political reasons. "The sight of sharply delineated bodies or surfaces corresponds with the officialdom and bureaucracy of the state."[46] And it must be dissolved in order that humanity can "extend out into the 'cosmic,'"[47] an example of which, according to Anita Beloubek-Hammer, is his sculpture *Head with its Externalizations* from 1916 (HvW 66, fig. 11, p. 50).

Freundlich was aware that the "act of transfixing the contours"[48] remains a symbolic, representative "simile" for the viewer, who has to rely on his limited senses and is forced to perceive the world as forms. Our natural perceptions are based on contours and figures. But he was not solely concerned with the factual products of art, but rather with their relationship to the whole, to the sphere of possibilities they open up. Against this he rejected everything that slipped back into the old substantialist schema, saying for instance that for him photography was nothing but "contour art."[49]

As such, his aesthetic is completely free of esotericism, even when the dissolution of the individual into the collective may be reminiscent of the self-renunciation taught by mystics such as Meister Eckhart, whom Freundlich studied.[50]

Individual and Opening Up Nothing distinguishes Freundlich's philosophy so much from our own times as his much invoked "supra-personal principle,"[51] his attempt to "overcome private, individualistic values" and "egocentric feelings and attitudes."[52] In our society, in which as a result of the economic system one can scarcely envisage anything but individualism, it is hard to grasp how noble Freundlich's intention was; this means a vital dimension of his visual thinking threatens to be lost to us.

Although he came from a middle-class family, he developed his distaste for bourgeois individualism at an extremely early age and with exceptional intensity. He wrote to Wilhelm Niemeyer in 1912 that "ignoring the individual is doubtless a heroic deed: reshaping the individual as a creative spiritual being is however higher, more difficult & more powerful."[53] There were many in fact who agreed with him during the interwar period. Jean Arp recalled his own firm conviction that artists should work in communities, as in the Middle Ages. In this, he added, he was in full agreement with his wife Sophie Taeuber-Arp, the artists Otto and Adya van Rees, and with Otto Freundlich.[54]

The individual aspect was viewed by these artists not as liberating but rather as restricting. Yet the concern was not with repressing personal impulses, but rather with refashioning, expanding, and opening them. Just how this process of restructuring was to take place is intimated to us in a number of passages in Freundlich's "Confessions."

Presented with a portrait, the old individualism asks: "Does this face show the marks of the construction of a personality?" The new question, by contrast, is: "Does this face show the marks of the construction of a world?"[55] Which is to say Freundlich's art, as already evinced in his *Large Head* from 1912, is not *impersonal* but rather *supra-personal*. He aims neither at the individual person, nor at the person as type (whether typical of a culture or a class), but rather at the world in which humanity first realizes itself. He seeks in people the world, the whole in the single case, by which the human aspect does not disappear but simply loses its narrowness and inflexibility.

An aesthetic like this was already at odds with the current trends. Although today's globalized liberal individualism had by no means established itself in the 1920s and 1930s, Freundlich sensed that things were none too favorable for his cause: "For a long time we believed in the transformation of the visible world by people, in the new man, in the new meaning of the world of appearances on the basis of a deep turnabout in the individual himself. But slowly we learnt to recognize just how distant man had become from the creative forces, how the sense of being at home in the universe had extinguished, how the paths to it soon returned to the point of departure. We ourselves were all burdened by the mistakes, the prejudices, the egoism, the self-worship of our contemporaries," as he noted a few months before his murder.[56]

The tone is exceptionally bitter for him. But his estimate of the situation is anything but false. Although art set out after the war on paths that superficially were not far removed from his—the Nouvelle École de Paris, for instance, also contained students of his in the form of Maurice Estève, Serge Poliakoff, and Raoul Ubac[57]—his collectivist approach received little attention in the age of individualism.

Without his thoughts his art loses depth and coherency. Otto Freundlich's art demonstrates in its euphoric, gaily colored way that the rejection of an opinionated individualism does not have to end up with marching in rank and file, but is rewarded by openness. And that is how cosmic communism should be grasped: as an attempt at opening up.

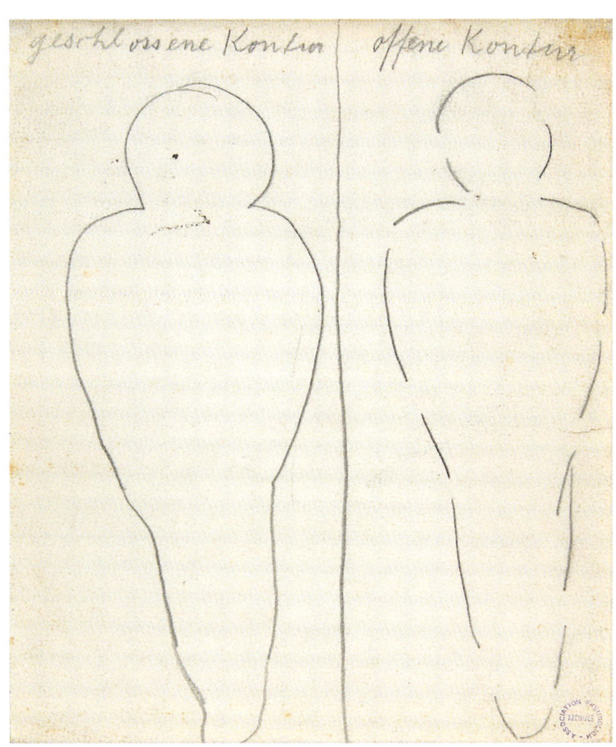

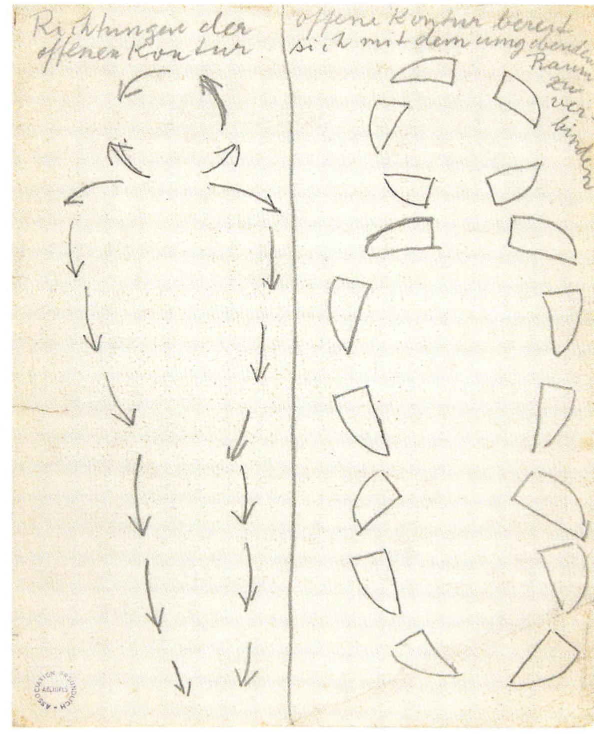

Fig. 5/6 Otto Freundlich
Contour Scheme, ca. 1935–36
HvW 359, 360
Pencil on paper (recto and verso of the same sheet)
29 × 22 cm
Association Les Amis de Jeanne et Otto Freundlich, Musées de Pontoise

1 *Otto Freundlich: Monographie mit Dokumentation und Werkverzeichnis*, ed. Joachim Heusinger von Waldegg, exh. cat. Rheinisches Landesmuseum Bonn at al. (Cologne, 1978).

2 Günter Aust, *Otto Freundlich: 1878–1943* (Cologne, 1960); Otto Freundlich, *Aus Briefen und Aufsätzen*, ed. Günter Aust (Cologne, undated [1966]).

3 Uli Bohnen, ed., *Otto Freundlich: Schriften. Ein Wegbereiter der gegenstandslosen Kunst* (Cologne, 1982).

4 Otto Freundlich, "Bekenntnisse eines revolutionären Malers" [1935]; Eng. trans. "Confessions of a Revolutionary Painter," in the current volume, pp. 4–16, here p. 4.

5 John Heartfield, "Grün oder—Rot," *Die Weltbühne* 22 (1926), p. 434, reprinted in John Heartfield, *Der Schnitt entlang der Zeit* (Dresden, 1981), p. 143.

6 Joachim Heusinger von Waldegg, "Otto Freundlich, 'Mon ciel est rouge' (1933): Zum Realitätsgehalt ungegenständlicher Malerei," *Pantheon* 46 (1988), pp. 131–141.

7 Franz Wilhelm Seiwert, "Unser Maibild," *Sozialistische Republik* 103 (1929), cited from Lynette Roth, "Malerei als 'Waffe,'" in *köln progressiv: seiwert–hoerle–arntz 1920–33*, exh. cat. Museum Ludwig (Cologne, 2008), pp. 15–132, here p. 83.

8 Freundlich, "Confessions," op. cit. (note 4), p. 6.

9 Ibid., p. 7.

10 See in this context Uli Bohnen, "Otto Freundlich—Entwürfe zum kosmischen Kommunismus," in Bohnen, *Otto Freundlich: Schriften*, op. cit. (note 3), p. 27, as well as Rita Wildegans-Krollpfeiffer, "Otto Freundlichs Werk im Kontext naturwissenschaftlicher und gesellschaftlicher Erkenntnisse," PhD diss., Universität Hamburg (Hamburg, 1989), pp. 9–10.

11 Wildegans-Krollpfeiffer, "Otto Freundlichs Werk im Kontext," op. cit. (note 10), pp. 32 and 42.

12 Freundlich, "Confessions," op. cit. (note 4), p. 8.

13 Ibid., p. 14.

14 Walter Gropius, "Programm des staatlichen Bauhauses in Weimar, April 1919," translated as "The Theory and Organization of the Bauhaus," in *Art in Theory, 1900–2000*, ed. Charles Harrison & Paul Wood (Oxford, 2003), p. 309, translation (slightly modified) by Herbert Bayer, originally in Bayer, Walter Gropius, and Ilse Gropius, eds., *Bauhaus 1919–1928* (New York, 1938), pp. 22–31. Cf. Aust, *Freundlich*, op. cit. (note 2), p. 21.

15 Otto Freundlich, "Die Verwandlung der sichtbaren Welt" [1921], in Bohnen, *Otto Freundlich: Schriften*, op. cit. (note 3), pp. 118–119, here p. 118.

16 Freundlich, "Confessions," op. cit. (note 4), p. 15.

17 Karl Marx, *Das Kapital: Kritik der politischen Ökonomie*, preface to the first German edition (Berlin, 1867); published in English as *Capital: A Critique of Political Economy*, trans. Samuel Moore and Edward Aveling (1887).

18 Otto Freundlich, "Die Politik ist die Religion der Zukunft" [ca. 1921], archive Association Les Amis de Jeanne et Otto Freundlich (AAJOF), IMEC, FRN 20.5.

19 Max Raphael, *Lebens-Erinnerungen: Briefe. Tagebücher. Skizzen. Essays*, ed. Hans-Jürgen Heinrichs (Frankfurt am Main and New York, 1985), p. 178.

20 Otto Freundlich, "An die Novembergruppe" [February 11, 1919], in Bohnen, *Otto Freundlich: Schriften*, op. cit. (note 3), pp. 108–109, here p. 109. For other reasons behind the distance he took to the Novembergruppe, cf. Helga Kliemann, *Die Novembergruppe* (Berlin, 1969), p. 63, and also Anita Beloubek-Hammer, "Wider die 'Stand- und Spielbein'-Skulptur: Die Bildhauer der Novembergruppe," in *Novembergruppe*, exh. cat. Galerie Bodo Niemann (Berlin, 1993), pp. 29–48, here p. 32.

21 Otto Freundlich, "Brief an 'abstraction—création,' Paris" [November 22, 1934], in Bohnen, *Otto Freundlich: Schriften*, op. cit. (note 3), p. 195.

22 Freundlich, "Confessions," op. cit. (note 4), p. 11.

23 Roth, "Malerei," op. cit. (note 7), pp. 53–57.

24 Letter from Freundlich to Sauerlandt, December 26, 1925, Archiv Museum für Kunst und Gewerbe (MKG), Hamburg.

25 Otto Freundlich, "Biographische Notiz des Malers und Bildhauers Otto Freundlich, von ihm selbst verfaßt" [1941], in Bohnen, *Otto Freundlich: Schriften*, op. cit. (note 3), pp. 252–253, here p. 252.

26 Erich Franz, "Otto Freundlich—Dynamischer Raum," in *Freiheit der Linie: Von Obrist und dem Jugendstil zu Marc, Klee und Kirchner*, ed. Erich Franz, exh. cat. Landesmuseum für Kunst und Kulturgeschichte, Westfälisches Landesmuseum Münster (Bönen, 2007), pp. 242–244, here p. 243.

27 Freundlich, "Confessions," op. cit. (note 4), p. 8.

28 Otto Freundlich, "Ideen und Bilder: Aufzeichnungen eines Malers (Auszug)" [1940–42], in Bohnen, *Otto Freundlich: Schriften*, op. cit. (note 3), pp. 221–249, here p. 228.

29 Thomas W. Gaehtgens, "Delaunay in Berlin," in *Delaunay und Deutschland*, ed. Peter-Klaus Schuster, exh. cat. Staatsgalerie moderner Kunst im Haus der Kunst, Munich (Cologne, 1985), pp. 264–284, here p. 283.

30 Cf. Franz, "Dynamischer Raum," op. cit. (note 26), p. 244.

31 Heusinger, "Mon ciel," op. cit. (note 6), p. 132.

32 Cf. Maria-Katharina Schulz, *Glasmalerei der klassischen Moderne in Deutschland* (Frankfurt am Main et al., 1987), p. 172.

33 Otto Freundlich, advertisement for Le Mur art school, archive AAJOF, IMEC, FRN 22.3.

34 Otto Freundlich, "Wenn der Künstler untergeht, fängt der Mensch an; Wenn der Mensch untergeht, fängt der Künstler an" [When the artist goes under the person begins; When the person goes under, the artist begins], *Der Strom* 4 (1919), pp. 8–11.

35 Lorenz Dittmann, "Otto Freundlich und die Farbe," *Otto Freundlich: Ein Wegbereiter der abstrakten Kunst*, ed. Gerhard Leistner and Thorsten Rodiek, exh. cat. Ostdeutsche Galerie Regensburg et al. (Regensburg, 1994), pp. 40–46, here p. 41.

36 Paul Klee, *The Diaries of Paul Klee, 1898–1918*, ed. Ernst Klee (California, 1992), p. 348. Translation slightly amended.

37 Freundlich, "Ideen und Bilder," op. cit. (note 28), p. 230.

38 Brigitte Kurmann-Schwarz, "Récits, programme, commanditaires, concepteurs, donateurs: Publications récentes sur l'iconographie des vitraux de la cathédrale de Chartres," *Bulletin Monumental* 2 (1996), pp. 55–71, here pp. 56 and 58.

39 Otto Freundlich, "Brief an Gottfried Heinersdorff, Berlin" [August 24, 1924], in Bohnen, *Otto Freundlich: Schriften*, op. cit. (note 3), pp. 134–136, here p. 135.

40 Joël Mettay, Edda Maillet, *Otto Freundlich et la France: Un amour trahi* (Perpignan, 2004), p. 39.

41 Otto Freundlich, "An die Novembergruppe," op. cit. (note 20), p. 108.

42 Otto Freundlich, "Die Wege der abstrakten Kunst" [1934], in Bohnen, *Otto Freundlich: Schriften*, op. cit. (note 3), pp. 188–194.

43 Otto Freundlich, "Der Raum," *Die weissen Blätter* 2 (1919), p. 83, cited in Joachim Heusinger von Waldegg, "Otto Freundlich—Leben und Werk," in Heusinger, *Otto Freundlich: Werkverzeichnis*, op. cit. (note 1), pp. 11–43, here p. 32.

44 Otto Freundlich, "Zu van Gogh's 40. Todestag" [1930], excerpted in Bohnen, *Otto Freundlich: Schriften*, op. cit. (note 3), pp. 165–166, here p. 165.

45 Wildegans-Krollpfeiffer, *Otto Freundlichs Werk im Kontext*, op. cit. (note 10), p. 50.

46 Otto Freundlich, "Welt-Urwelt" (1918), in Bohnen, *Otto Freundlich: Schriften*, op. cit. (note 3), pp. 103–105, here p. 105.

47 Anita Beloubek-Hammer, *Die schönen Gestalten der besseren Zukunft: Die Bildhauerkunst des Expressionismus und ihr geistiges Umfeld*, 2 vols. (Cologne, 2007), vol. 1, p. 252.

48 Freundlich, "Ideen und Bilder," op. cit. (note 28), p. 242.

49 Bohnen, "Entwürfe," op. cit. (note 10), p. 42.

50 Heusinger, "Leben und Werk," op. cit. (note 42), p. 26. Freundlich's distance to mystic teachings is also demonstrated in Denise Vernerey-Laplace, *Regards de l'est sur l'abstraction, Otto Freundlich, Etienne Béothy, Jean Leppien* (Villeneuve d'Ascq, undated), p. 377.

51 Otto Freundlich, "Picasso, zu seinem 50. Geburtstag" [1931], in Bohnen, *Otto Freundlich: Schriften,* op. cit. (note 3), pp. 178–180, here p. 179.

52 Otto Freundlich, "Gino Severini" [1930], in ibid., pp. 163–165, here p. 164.

53 Cited in Joachim Heusinger von Waldegg, *Otto Freundlich und die rheinische Kunstszene mit Briefen an Herwarth Walden und Wilhelm Niemeyer*, ed. Verein August Macke Haus, exh. cat. August Macke Haus (Bonn, 2006), p. 142.

54 Cf. Bibiana K. Obler, *Intimate Collaborations: Kandinsky & Münter, Arp & Taeuber* (New Haven and London, 2014), p. 140.

55 Freundlich, "Confessions," op. cit. (note 4), p. 12.

56 Freundlich, "Ideen und Bilder," op. cit. (note 28), p. 222.

57 "Pupil" in a literal and metaphorical sense; Bohnen presumes that Ubac took part in Freundlich's art school, Le Mur. Cf. Bohnen, "Entwürfe," op. cit. (note 10), p. 39. The influence Freundlich exerted on Estève und Poliakoff is analyzed in Karena Lütge, "Otto Freundlich und die Rezeption seiner Kunst nach 1945," in Leistner, Rodiek, *Wegbereiter*, op. cit. (note 35), pp. 71–75.

Lena Schrage

"Nothing is there simply for its own sake" Paintings, Drawings, and Watercolors in Otto Freundlich's Early Period

"When I began my career as an artist fifteen years ago I created according to my inner conviction, which demanded that I depart from the traditions,"[1] observed Otto Freundlich in retrospect. Driven by this "inner conviction," he soon developed his own abstract geometrical grammar of forms which prevailed in his paintings and drawings up until 1914.[2] Only a handful of the works from these years have survived in private collections and international museums. But various bundles of letters, handwritten notes on his works, and his own texts help us to reconstruct his early works, the majority of which are considered lost.

Freundlich grew up in a wealthy Jewish merchant family that was acculturated to its largely Protestant surroundings.[3] He relinquished his family ties when he decided that rather than train as a merchant, he would study literature, philosophy, and art history.[4] From April 1903 he lived in Berlin and was in contact with artists and writers of the Berlin bohemia, in particular the composer and later Sturm gallerist Herwarth Walden. Freundlich, who found in him a like-minded mentor, took lessons from Walden in music theory[5] until his departure from Berlin in summer 1904.[6]

Beginning in autumn 1904 Freundlich enrolled at the philosophical faculty in Munich[7] and continued his theoretical studies. He eagerly read Hermann von Helmholtz's *On the Sensations of Tone as a Physiological Basis for the Theory of Music*,[8] in which the physical occurrences in the auditory canal and their effects were examined as a new sensory-aesthetic sensation. This holistic viewpoint played a major part in Freundlich's turn to a non-representational language of forms. Indeed, his music theory studies were the actual origin of his break with the object from 1910 onward.

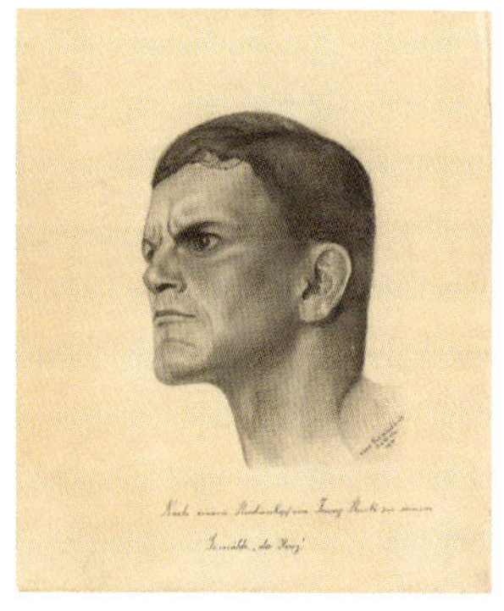

Fig. 7 Otto Freundlich
Copy after Franz von Stuck, 1901
HvW 259
Charcoal on paper
42 x 36 cm
Private collection, Cologne

In the first two drawings we know from Freundlich, dating from 1901 (HvW 259, fig. 7) and 1905, the break is not yet recognizable, but already in *Opera Scene* from 1905 (HvW 260, p. 99) we see a planar emphasis and a departure from the dictates of perspective. Governed by a pair of lovers locked in an embrace, who bear a distant resemblance to Gustav Klimt's symbolistic depictions of couples, Freundlich presents a view of a stage, the orchestra pit, and a slender segment of the auditorium in which the white silhouette of a spectator can be surmised. Another is located in a box to the right, above the stage. The deliberate abandonment of perspective, as well as the play with the white of the paper to create a strong contrast to the dark surfaces hatched in various shades of gray, dominate the drawing and already point to Freundlich's understanding of space as a compositional element in its own right.

This was an understanding that he further developed, above all from 1908 onward in the circles around the artists' haunt Le Bateau-Lavoir in Paris. He took a studio there for the months of June and July 1908 and once again from May to

June 1909.[9] But unlike many of the artists who lived at the Bateau-Lavoir, he did not join the "bande à Picasso,"[10] even if the art critic Maurice Raynal recalled that "Freundlich, the new man at the 'Bateau Lavoir,' was at once accepted into the artists' group."[11] Freundlich was in fact somewhat dismissive of the artists, who "nourished themselves from him [Picasso] and for half a decade partook of scarcely any other intellectual sustenance."[12] It may be assumed that he had already conveyed his reservations during his sojourns in Paris in 1908 and 1909, because he reported to Walden: "I'm doing fine—on the loftiest Montmartre . . . acquainted with the fine artists and literati of the martyr's mount, even if not *much* loved by them."[13] Although Freundlich knew Montmartre artists such as Max Jacob, Georges Braque, Juan Gris, André Derain, and Guillaume Apollinaire, and had exchanged ideas with them "on art, society, and the future of mankind,"[14] as he later recalled, ultimately he chose to adopt an outsider stance. "Although friends with the artists from the various movements, I was unable to impose art forms on my nature which for them seemed to be the one and only. [This] compromise was not permitted me."[15]

At the same time Freundlich's study of the Cubist approach to space was formative to his own understanding of the importance of space. Because as he showed so vividly in his later works, especially *Composition* from 1911 (HvW 107, p.113), his rejection of Cubism led to a language of forms in which he elevated the exploration of form and space to its own aesthetic principle. Thus he emphasized: "Space is sacred, space is generative, more generative than all the forms within it, it is the father of the planets and all beings thereon."[16]

In the second half of June 1909 Freundlich returned to Germany, lived variously in Berlin and Munich, and then returned once and for all to Paris in 1910. This time he moved not to Montmartre but to Montparnasse, the new arts center in the metropolis.[17] Even prior to his return to Paris he had embarked on a group of works featuring symbolistic figures. The results were the works *Robed Figure with Bowed Head* (HvW 263, p.87), *Three Parallel Figures* (HvW 102, lost), and *Four Parallel Figures* (HvW 103, p.87), as well as *Cosmic Composition* (HvW 264, p.89), followed in 1911 in Paris by *Group* (HvW 265, p.107). The depictions of the parallel figures highlight Freundlich's idea of a symbolist connection between movement and inner calm, which in his first art theory text "Eine Umrahmung für manche Bilder" ("A Framework for Certain Pictures")[18] from 1912 he described as "behold, keep silence, wait,"[19] "the three ways that bring people to themselves." In this text he also wrote: "Man's relationship to all temporal distances and all spatial distances is artificial, not natural. Entertaining relationships with the temporally distant, the past, is the accomplishment of the intermediary creature man."[20]

The paintings *Composition with Figure* (HvW 108, p.88) and *Composition with Three Figures* (HvW 111, p.91)[21] should be viewed in this light. One or three figures have been placed in a seemingly random arrangement of variously shaped patches of color, which fit together to form a flat background. In *Composition with Figure*, the figure already begins to join this planar composition, so that here the "intermediary creature man" enters an intimate relationship with the surrounding cosmos.

In Freundlich's aforementioned painting *Composition* (HvW 107, p. 113), this process of inclusion has already been completed. Color and form dominate, figurative traits have completely disappeared. Here for the first time Freundlich broke completely with representation and gave full expression to his constructive grammar of forms, which already begins to be discernible in the two works just named. The large format square work was presumably done in the second half of 1911 in Paris.[22] It is composed from a single, long drawn-out color surface climbing upwards, at times in parallel. Large and smaller elements done in uniform colors join together to make larger configurations of forms, with reddish and ochre-hued strips of color dominating. Swirling about them are arrangements of forms in matt greens, which are further embedded in darker colored elements at the outermost edges. Movement and the interplay of the individual color elements are at the center of this work. With the colored strips, which are in part shown soaring upwards and tracing curve-like paths, Freundlich also creates the impression that the surfaces are struggling to free themselves of their bounds, to overcome the actual space. But unlike the works in the 1930s they do not yet overcome them, the darker strips of color along the lower left-hand margin suggest there is still a restriction.

As Freundlich recalled: "While I also dispensed pretty early on in my artistic development with a technique of the kind used for the painted pilaster and painted purely flat surfaces, each placed tightly and without transition next to the other, and built up the entire picture in that way, the primal element of this planar art was nevertheless a bowed curved surface, i.e. a plastic element."[23] This curved surface—which already begins to announce itself in the drawing *Cosmic Composition* from 1910 (HvW 264, p. 89), is taken further in the painting *Composition with Figure*, and reaches its zenith in *Composition* from 1911—is key to the development of Freundlich's own abstract grammar of forms. Individual element and overall composition interact here in a balanced correlation of forces, a compositional idea that was founded by Freundlich's intensive studies of music theory. Thus he had already emphasized in 1905 the importance of the note as an individual element which, while existing in its own right, only first rises to become a "single organism in which nothing is there solely for its own sake" by interacting with the overall composition.[24]

Before he felt obliged to leave France on the outbreak of World War I, Freundlich went to Chartres, probably on the advice of the Portuguese artist Amadeo de Souza-Cardoso, with whom he had already become acquainted in 1911 in Paris. In all likelihood he took a studio in the north tower of the cathedral. Here for the first time he formulated his idea of abstraction: "I feel it is important in this context to study the tendency in composition and the tendency of life itself and its beauty. A life of energy comes from the power of decomposition, which means: spiritualizing so that life becomes an eternal flow that streams towards its dissolution [*négation*], but this dissolution must be wished for and cheerful. Congratulate me on this discovery, which is as follows: Decomposition is far more mysterious than composition."[25] Freundlich not only names the connections he considered important between society, man, nature, cosmos, and art as form lending expression, he also emphasizes a holistic way of viewing which he had already developed in his music studies under Walden as his underlying idea of art, a holism that can first emerge by splitting into individual elements. With that, Freundlich's claim to holism with regard to composition and the individual element and his turn to non-representation became characteristic marks of his art.

Although Freundlich's early work can only partly be reconstructed today, the existing works, notes and recollections, the correspondence we have, and finally the reconstruction of his circles in Paris give the picture of a self-confident artist who early on began working according to an "inner conviction,"[26] without submitting to ruling traditions or contemporary styles. As he stressed: "I am not afraid of being smashed to pieces because I am forever smashing myself to pieces."[27]

1 Otto Freundlich, "Bekenntnisse eines Intellektuellen" [1924], in Uli Bohnen, ed., *Otto Freundlich: Schriften. Ein Wegbereiter der gegenstandslosen Kunst* (Cologne, 1982), pp. 132–134, here p. 132.

2 See Lena Schrage, *Otto Freundlich (1878–1943): Individualist im Netzwerk der Pariser Avantgarde. Das Frühwerk*, PhD diss., Dresden (Frankfurt am Main, 2017).

3 Cf. ibid., p. 37. In addition Geneviève Debien's "Otto Freundlich, Künstler and Universalist im Kampf gegen die 'Nationalisierung des Geistes,'" in *Irreparabel: Lebenswege jüdischer Künstlerinnen, Künstler and Kunstkenner auf der Flucht aus dem "Dritten Reich" in Frankreich* [Veröffentlichungen der Koordinierungsstelle Magdeburg, vol. 9], 2013, pp. 202–227, here p. 203.

4 Study certificate for the Königlichen Friedrich-Wilhelms-Universität zu Berlin listing the seminars and lectures he attended, Bestand AZ 1459, Archiv der Humboldt-Universität zu Berlin.

5 Ibid.

6 Letter from Freundlich to Walden, May 25, 1904, in Joachim Heusinger von Waldegg, *Otto Freundlich and die rheinische Kunstszene mit Briefen an Herwarth Walden and Wilhelm Niemeyer*, ed. Verein August Macke Haus, exh. cat. August Macke Haus (Bonn, 2006), p. 78.

7 Official staff list of teachers, civil servants, and students at the Königlich Bayerische Ludwig-Maximilians-Universität zu München; Winter Semester 1904–1905; list of students, p. 60; accessible at https://epub.ub.uni-muenchen.de/9657/1/pvz_lmu_1904_05_wise.pdf (accessed March 2016).

8 Hermann von Helmholtz, *Die Lehre von den Tonempfindungen als physiologische Grundlage für die Theorie der Musik* (Braunschweig, 1863). The English edition was first published in 1875.

9 Otto Freundlich, "Handschriftliches Werkverzeichnis, Bl. 2," in *Otto Freundlich: Monographie mit Dokumentation and Werkverzeichnis*, ed. Joachim Heusinger von Waldegg, exh. cat. Rheinisches Landesmuseum Bonn et. al. (Cologne, 1978), p. 67.

10 David Raynal, ed., *Maurice Raynal: La bande à Picasso* (Rennes, 2008).

11 Maurice Raynal, "Le souvenir d'Otto Freundlich," in *Deux sculptures monumentales de Otto Freundlich*, ed. Galerie Claude Bernard, exh. cat. Galerie Claude Bernard (Paris, 1992), unpag.

12 Otto Freundlich, "Was wollt ihr von Picasso?" [1922], in Bohnen, *Otto Freundlich: Schriften*, op. cit. (note 1), pp. 128–129, here p. 128.

13 Letter from Freundlich to Walden, March 5, 1908/July 5, 1908, in Heusinger, *Rheinische Kunstszene*, op. cit. (note 6), p. 116. For the dating of this letter see Schrage, *Otto Freundlich*, op. cit. (note 2).

14 Otto Freundlich, "Ein deutscher Maler in Paris (Erinnerungen an das Künstlerleben in Paris vor dem Kriege 1914)" [1930], in Bohnen, *Otto Freundlich: Schriften*, op. cit. (note 1), pp. 166–172, here p. 169.

15 Otto Freundlich, "Bekenntnisse eines Intellektuellen," in Bohnen, *Otto Freundlich: Schriften*, op. cit. (note 1), p. 132.

16 Otto Freundlich, "Der Raum" [1919], in Bohnen, *Otto Freundlich: Schriften*, op. cit. (note 1), pp. 106–107, here p. 107.

17 Nicholas Hewitt, "Montmartre: Artistic Revolution," in *Paris: Capital of the Arts 1900–1968*, ed. Sarah Wilson, exh. cat. Royal Academy of Arts, London/Guggenheim Museum, Bilbao (London, 2002), pp. 28–39, here p. 38.

18 Otto Freundlich, "Eine Umrahmung für manche Bilder" [1912] in Heusinger, *Rheinische Kunstszene*, op. cit. (note 6), pp. 249–251.

19 Ibid., p. 251.

20 Ibid., p. 249.

21 *Composition with Three Figures* from 1911 no longer exists. In 1941, however, Freundlich did a gouache with the same motif either from memory or from a still extant sketch.

22 Otto Freundlich, "Ein deutscher Maler in Paris," op. cit. (note 14), p. 170.

23 Otto Freundlich, "Bekenntnisse eines revolutionären Malers" [1935]; Eng. trans. "Confessions of a Revolutionary Painter," in the present volume, pp. 4–16, here pp. 8–9.

24 Otto Freundlich, "Herwarth Waldens Tonlyrik," *Kampf: Zeitschrift für gesunden Menschenverstand* 18 (1905), pp. 529–530.

25 Postcard from Freundlich to de Souza-Cardoso, July 6, 1914, in Coleção Amadeo de Souza-Cardoso, I ASC 13/29; ASC 13/30; ASC 13/31 I FCG-BA, Biblioteca de Arte, Fundação Calouste Gulbenkian, Lisbon.

26 Otto Freundlich, "Bekenntnisse eines Intellektuellen," op. cit. (note 1), p. 132.

27 Ibid.

Christiane Wanken

Otto Freundlich's Early Sculptures as an Expression of his Image of Humankind

Otto Freundlich's *Large Head* (HvW 63, fig. 9) from 1912 is programmatic for his sculptures from the period prior to World War I. With its block-like construction and upward-directed gaze, even in photographs the sculpture has an enormous presence and seems like an icon. It is not surprising, then, that the Nazis placed it on the cover of the guide to their exhibition *Degenerate Art* (fig. 56, p. 208). The artist was a Jew and a Communist, his artwork rejected classicist aesthetics and subscribed rather to an abstractive grammar of forms with references to non-European art, and with that proclaimed a utopia of boundless liberty in a new society.

Striking here is the construction of the sculpture using elementary masses that shape the head and give it a voluminous, block-like appearance from the front, but a cubic and broken up look from the side. The block-like aspect demonstrates a great kinship with *moai* (fig. 8), the monumental stone figures on Easter Island.[1] Non-European art was held in early-twentieth-century discourse to be pristine, as having a primal creative power and as hailing from an everyday reality far removed from European civilization and its perceived decadence. Borrowing from the formal language of the *moai* denoted a turn from the handed-down forms of art, such as was taught at the academies and blessed by the Kaiser.

Three years after Freundlich's *Large Head* was made, Carl Einstein published his book *Negerplastik* (*Negro Sculpture*). The book was eagerly read by artists, for as Einstein notes: "What previously had been seen as meaningless has taken on significance in the recent efforts of young sculptors, because it has been intuited that no one else has dealt with the precise problems of space and the formulation of the means of artistic production with such purity as the Africans."[2] Einstein's exploration of African sculpture also directed attention to the Cubist theory of space, and as such his book was actually a polemic for the Cubist view of art.[3] European sculpture had, in his view, lost its own specific sculptural vitality and was "strongly imbricated with painterly surrogates,"[4] whereas in African sculpture the cubic concept of space and with that the underlying premise of sculptural work was met in exemplary fashion.[5] For Einstein the "three dimensional," which is to say space and the sculpture, are to be an independent, concentrated form and not a naturalistic or imitative depiction that can only ever remain relative. Form must always be built up without reference to anything alien to it.[6] According to his theory, sculptures should always create space and not, as in European art, have any spatial references of either a representational or draftsmanly kind.[7]

Like Einstein as well as his French artist colleagues, Freundlich saw the renunciation of naturalist, mimetic depiction and the autonomy of sculpture and space as essential to art, both European as well as non-European. Freundlich had gone to Paris in 1908 and moved in the circles of Pablo Picasso and the Fauves, through whom he also came in contact with African art.

African or non-European art was cited by European artists and intellectuals as legitimization for their own art, because it was seen to have freed itself from form and content. It was taken to have a pure, abstract character. The art historian Wilhelm Niemeyer wrote at the time: "In one point Rodin's creation resembles the work in African art: it is a thing in itself, living in non-visual space, enclosed in its own circle of being."[8] Niemeyer, who had constantly backed Freundlich and conducted an intensive correspondence with him, opined that the new yardstick and more profound concept that African sculpture had given European artists allowed a new kind of sculpture in Europe and a new understanding. Freundlich expressed himself in 1912 in much the same terms in a letter to Niemeyer: "Dear friend, I set to work on my sculpture today, an enormous head, and in addition a painting whose name and form came to me in a flash: The Oath. I've purchased a Negro sculpture very cheaply, a full-length figure in wood, black with a little red paint: it's standing under the photograph of my bronze mask. The comparison shows me how much the specific intellectual cast of the last two centuries is based on a fundamental change in form in the inner person, as is becoming increasingly apparent."[9]

So Freundlich is looking aside here from any concrete formal kinship. He is more concerned with a spiritual similarity and with the assumed similarity in the creative force, in the alleged purity and the concept of abstraction. Nevertheless, formal similarities can be observed to works from Africa and Oceania. For instance, in his *Male Mask* (HvW 64, p. 101) from 1915, the additive approach to form in the mouth, nose, and eyebrows, which have been affixed to the head as almost geometrical elements, is comparable to the formal principles behind many African masks, in which the facial features are dealt with in similar summary fashion: the closed mouth, the nose which is attached in the shape of a rectangle, and the closed eyes, which are overshadowed by a bulge forming the forehead.

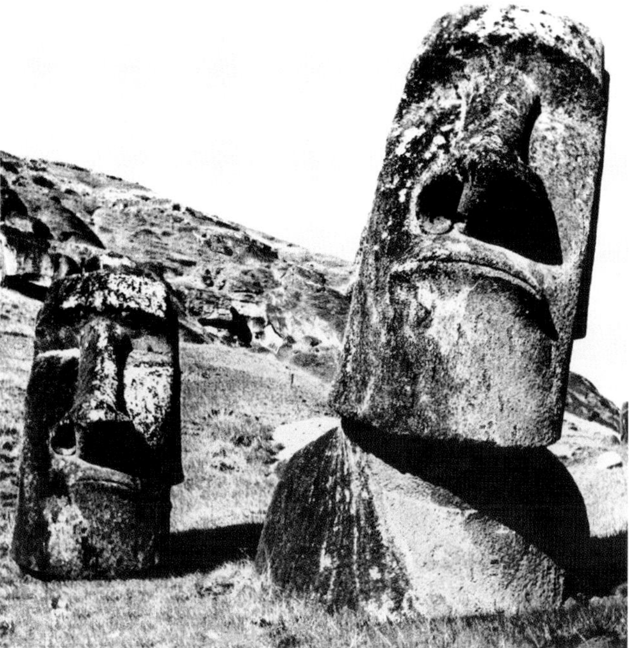

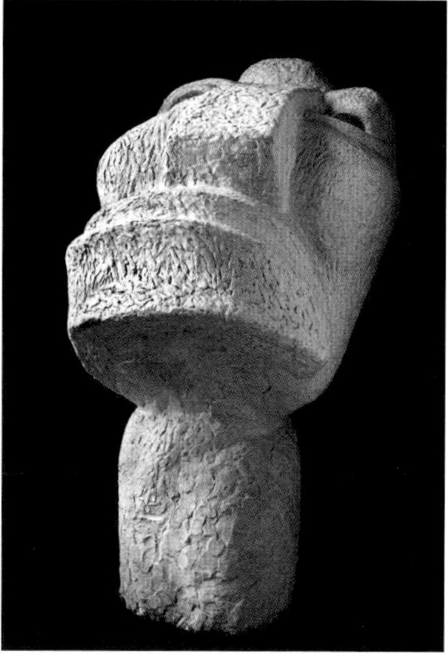

Fig. 8 Moai, Easter Island
Stone
H. 400 cm

Fig. 9 Otto Freundlich
Large Head, 1912
HvW 63
Plaster
H. 139 cm
Lost

The Mask as Abstraction and the Renunciation of the Bourgeois Stance A further aspect of so-called primitive art may be seen in the motif of the mask in Freundlich's oeuvre. Only a *Self-Portrait* from 1908 (HvW 51, fig. 10) allows us to distinguish personal features in its face. All his other sculpted heads are supraindividual, having a masklike look through the absence of individuality and facial expression, and often titled "Mask"—as with the *Mask* from 1909 hanging beside the place where Freundlich put his "Negro Sculpture."

The mask was regarded at the beginning of the twentieth century as the quintessence of non-European art and appeared to be the focus of the spiritual in those cultures. For Eckart von Sydow, an expert on both the Expressionists and non-European art, and moreover a close companion of Karl Schmidt-Rottluff, whom Freundlich greatly admired,[10] the spiritual was manifest in the masks. With that he saw them not simply as artworks, but as "true power centers," as an intensive heightening of the emotions and of life.[11] Gustav Friedrich Hartlaub, the founding director of the Kunsthalle in Mannheim, where he collected the Expressionists, recognized that "South Sea and Negro masks, as an object of art today from Picasso to Pechstein," possess something quite symbolic: "The mask conceals the visible, mutable, and mortal to reveal the immutable, immortal countenance."[12]

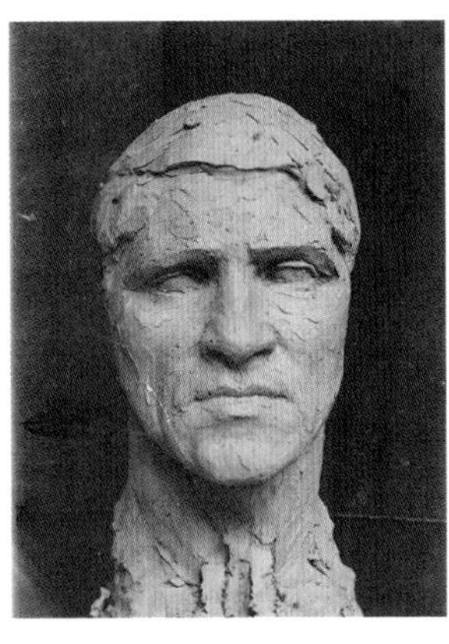

Fig. 10 Otto Freundlich
Head (Self-Portrait), 1908
HvW 51
Clay
Lost

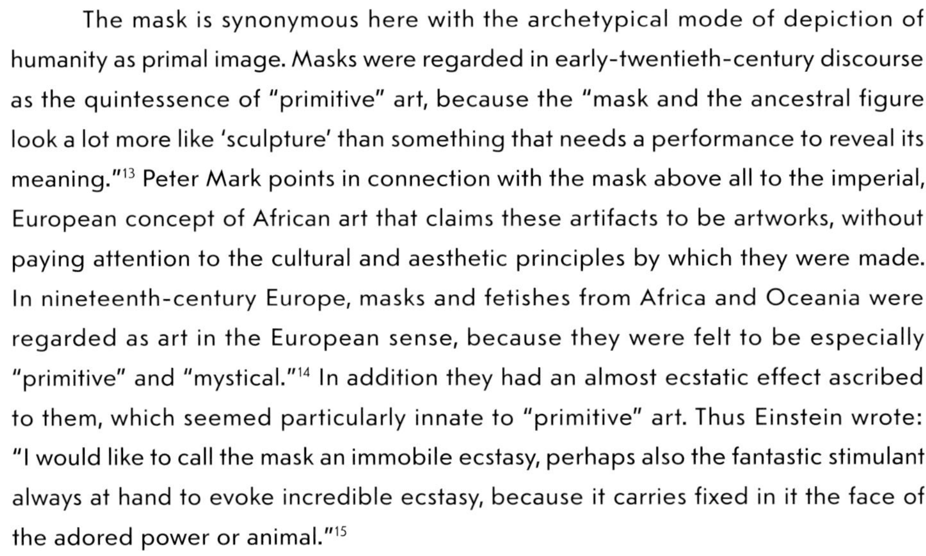

The mask is synonymous here with the archetypical mode of depiction of humanity as primal image. Masks were regarded in early-twentieth-century discourse as the quintessence of "primitive" art, because the "mask and the ancestral figure look a lot more like 'sculpture' than something that needs a performance to reveal its meaning."[13] Peter Mark points in connection with the mask above all to the imperial, European concept of African art that claims these artifacts to be artworks, without paying attention to the cultural and aesthetic principles by which they were made. In nineteenth-century Europe, masks and fetishes from Africa and Oceania were regarded as art in the European sense, because they were felt to be especially "primitive" and "mystical."[14] In addition they had an almost ecstatic effect ascribed to them, which seemed particularly innate to "primitive" art. Thus Einstein wrote: "I would like to call the mask an immobile ecstasy, perhaps also the fantastic stimulant always at hand to evoke incredible ecstasy, because it carries fixed in it the face of the adored power or animal."[15]

Einstein saw in the mask, as esthetic experience, "the force of a three-dimensional vision that lets the surfaces collide."[16] It is precisely this aestheticization of the cubic and of abstraction that is at the root of their suprapersonal quality, in keeping with Freundlich's various mask types. Likewise the spirituality located in the mask is to be found in Freundlich's masklike heads. The head, as Schmidt-Rottluff put it, is the "focal point of the whole psyche, of all expression."[17]

At the same time the European context of the mask, which arose from the Greek theater tradition,[18] should not be ignored when studying Freundlich's works. An interesting aspect here is that our term "person" (L. *persona*) comes from the word for "mask," while the Romans for their part distinguished between face (*facies*) and countenance (*vultus*). This etymology shows the interaction performed by the mask: on the one hand, the face as part of the body, whose appearance and facial expressions make a human being a person, and on the other hand, the face as an element of cultic practices and also of artificial crafting and design.[19] The interplay between showing and concealing manifests in the mask, it becomes a "social person" who, unlike the "I" or "ego," assumes a fixed type and communicates through that role with society.[20]

However, in an article from 1935 Freundlich also saw the mask as a means of obscuring the truth and of forcing a person into his or her role: "The eye of the artist is ... an incorruptible critic.... And he stood there one day, looked around, and saw himself surrounded by a nature that wore masks, and by people who all wore masks, and he said: you're lying, off with those masks. But they were stuck tight and had turned to skin. That was a terrible discovery."[21]

In his cultural history of the face, *Faces*, Hans Belting shows how closely connected the idea of the mask is with that of the portrait, and that ultimately the European portrait arose as an alternative to the mask.[22] The portrait became the mirror of society: the tighter a society was organized, the more binding were the role faces that belonged to it, so that a person's respective role would be shown. The portrait arose as an artifact with a lifeless surface that allowed the face to become the symbolic surface.[23]

The turn of the twentieth century brought the swan song of the portrait. Liberation from the portrait was seen by artists as a liberation from a bourgeois convention.[24] Freundlich also distanced himself clearly from the art of the portrait, which had been handed down since the Renaissance, and regarded it as a hyper-individualized bourgeois convention: "But there are two questions which each must ponder. The first question is that of the *old* individualism: 'Does this face show the marks that a personality has been constructed?' The second question is that of the *new* individualism: 'Does this face show the marks that a world has been constructed?' The portraiture that we are familiar with is that of the *old* individualism. A portraiture of the *new* individualism does not yet exist, because the marks, the building blocks of a new world, of the *collectives* of all energies must be visible therein. But how are we to render this visible with the old technique of individualistic *and* egocentric portraiture? How could one convey in that way a moral that denies the individual as an end in itself? ... It was the Renaissance that founded the haughtiness of the individual."[25]

The mask appears here as a tool for abandoning the portrait by artistic means, but also as a possibility for trying out a new role. While the face was supposed to grant insight into people—not least thanks to physiognomy, a popular middle-class practice in the nineteenth and early twentieth century—the refusal of personal and facial expression posed by the mask is a denial of bourgeois conventions. That is evident for instance in the yellow *Bust of a Woman* (HvW 56, p. 106). The bust, which enjoyed great popularity during the nineteenth century, seems to be a deeply bourgeois device, from which Freundlich wished to distance himself. The yellow *Bust of a Woman* resembles on first sight a traditional bust, but on closer inspection one sees her masklike features and vacant gaze staring into the distance. The intense yellow, which can be grasped as an autonomous design element in the sculpture, completes the sculpture's defamiliarization. Here Freundlich is not showing the portrait of a particular woman, but rather a form for surmounting the personal. He presents a woman who corresponds to his search for an image of twentieth-century humanity.

Abstraction as Liberation

Although Freundlich's heads always remain recognizable as such, they nevertheless evince an ongoing process of abstraction. This is made clear by the reference to non-European art, by the notion of this kind of art as being representative of a collective and of the supraindividual, as well as by the use of the mask to gain distance from the traditional portrait. Similarly the strategy of monumentalizing the heads is part of a progressive abstraction. The outsize heads, such as the *Large Head* (HvW 63, p. 77), the *Standing Mask* (HvW 55, p. 86), and *Head* (HvW 65, p. 80) from 1916, are from their size alone supraindividual and less naturalistic than the real model. Their monumentality is intended rather to visualize their intellectuality and their supraindividual power.[26] Likewise the additive and block-like approach to form in the heads, as for instance in *Head* from 1925 (HvW 75, p. 95), shows the artist's urge to abstract. His aim was not to depict nature, because nature was "looked at today profanely. The means can at last be acquired again for an intellectual view."[27] In fact the turn from the individual was also intended to bring the artist to the path of abstraction. Here he saw Picasso as a pioneer: "Ignoring the individual is already doubtless a heroic deed (Pikasso) [*sic*]: but restructuring the individual as a creative spirit is higher, harder & stronger."[28] Thus he also saw Picasso as the artist who in *Guitar Player* (1910) "turned the picture surface into a symbol of a supraindividual principle . . . and thus overcame the depiction of the individual as an end in itself."[29] In *Head with its Externalizations* (HvW 66, fig. 11) from 1916, Freundlich was quite evidently looking at Picasso's creative principles. The head involves similarly disintegrating elements to those used by Picasso in his bronze *Woman's Head (Fernande)* from 1909 (fig. 12). The sculpture breaks up the woman's head, the volumes of the individual forms of the face become facets undergoing perspectival shifts, so that the convex and concave elements in the elevations differ between side and front. Freundlich goes even further in disintegrating the woman's head. By dismantling the form into circular segments, he arrives at an almost complete release from the head motif, to a pure perception of form. The outline of the head and the emphasis on a vertical and a horizontal shape at the middle of the sculpture nevertheless allow the head motif to still emerge. Only on viewing the work *en face* (fig. 13, left) does the abstraction of this sculpture really hit the viewer. All that one perceives here is a pile of semicircular segments that seem to completely dissolve the form. In one *Head* (ca. 1919, HvW 68, fig. 13, right), which follows the same principle of disintegration, we still distinguish parts of the face, the hair, eyebrows, nose and mouth, and yet they merge into different volumes and remain abstract.[30]

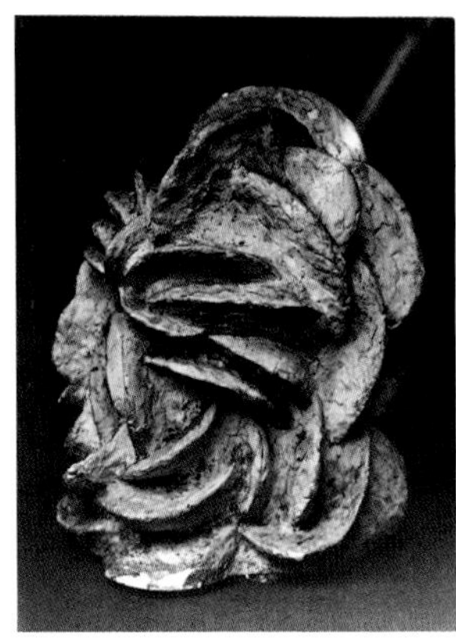

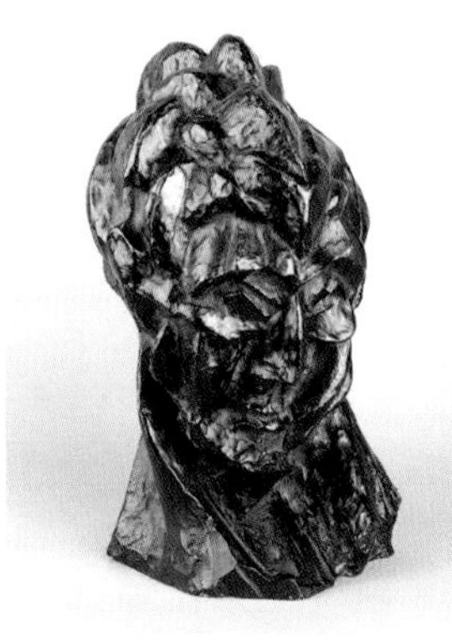

Fig. 11 Otto Freundlich
Head with its Externalizations/ Abstract Sculpture (Head Signs), 1916
HvW 66
Plaster
Lost

Fig. 12 Pablo Picasso
Woman's Head (Fernande), 1909
Bronze
41.3 × 24.4 × 26.6 cm
Museo Nacional Centro de Arte Reina Sofía, Madrid

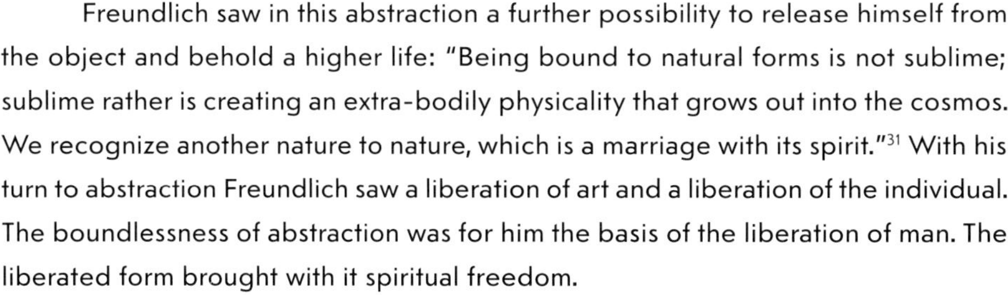

Freundlich saw in this abstraction a further possibility to release himself from the object and behold a higher life: "Being bound to natural forms is not sublime; sublime rather is creating an extra-bodily physicality that grows out into the cosmos. We recognize another nature to nature, which is a marriage with its spirit."[31] With his turn to abstraction Freundlich saw a liberation of art and a liberation of the individual. The boundlessness of abstraction was for him the basis of the liberation of man. The liberated form brought with it spiritual freedom.

1 Regarding the moai statues on Easter Island, see Terry L. Hunt, Carl P. Lipo, *The Statues That Walked: Unraveling the Mystery of Easter Island* (New York, 2011).

2 Carl Einstein, *Negerplastik* (Berlin, 1915), accessible at https://archive.org/details/negerplastik00einsuoft (accessed September 2016); bilingual e-edition *Negro Sculpture*, trans. Patrick Healy (Amsterdam, 2014), Kindle Book, position 176.

3 See also Dirk Heißerer, "Das 'Problem der Form,' der *Blaue Reiter* und die *Negerplastik*: Zu den Voraussetzungen der Kunstkritik Carl Einsteins," in Klaus H. Kiefer, ed., *Die visuelle Wende der Moderne: Carl Einsteins Kunst des 20. Jahrhunderts* (Munich, 2003), pp. 21–38.

4 Einstein, *Negro Sculpture,* op. cit. (note 2), pos. 222.

5 See Uwe Fleckner, *Carl Einstein und sein Jahrhundert: Fragmente einer intellektuellen Biographie* (Berlin, 2006), p. 77.

6 Einstein, *Negro Sculpture*, op. cit. (note 2), pos. 353–365ff.

7 See Fleckner, *Einstein*, op. cit. (note 5), p. 77.

8 Wilhelm Niemeyer, "Von Wesen und Wandlung der Plastik," *Genius* 1 (1919), pp. 77–89, here p. 88.

9 Letter from Freundlich to Niemeyer, August 15, 1912, cited in Joachim Heusinger von Waldegg, *Otto Freundlich und die rheinische Kunstszene mit Briefen an Herwarth Walden und Wilhelm Niemeyer*, ed. Verein August Macke Haus, exh. cat. August Macke Haus (Bonn, 2006), p. 145. By "enormous head" Freundlich might be referring to the *Large Head* (HvW 63) from 1912 and by "bronze mask" to *Mask* (HvW 54, p. 102) from 1909.

10 Letter from Freundlich to Niemeyer, August 3, 1913, cited in Heusinger, *Rheinische Kunstszene,* op. cit. (note 9), p. 159.

11 Eckart von Sydow, *Die Kunst der Naturvölker und der Vorzeit* (Berlin, 1927), p. 34.

12 Gustav Friedrich Hartlaub, *Kunst und Religion: Ein Versuch über die Möglichkeit neuer religiöser Kunst* (Leipzig, 1919), p. 90.

13 Shelly Errington, "What Became Authentic Primitive Art?" *Cultural Anthropology* 2 (1994), pp. 201–226, here p. 207.

14 According to Mark, the reception by European artists completely changed the perception of African art: its significance, context, use, etc. were put completely aside, all that was of interest was the form. Through this reception African art became part of art history, according to the yardsticks that defined Western art history. It became art, not of itself but because it was taken in as a source of inspiration for European artists. In connection with this reception, African art was always regarded as "primitive." Mark is vocal in demanding that artifacts of African

Fig. 13 Excerpt from *Reclams Universum* 45, Aug. 7, 1919 with, left, *Head with its Externalizations / Abstract Sculpture (Head Signs)*, 1916 HvW 66 and, right, *Head*, ca. 1919 HvW 68 Both plaster, both lost

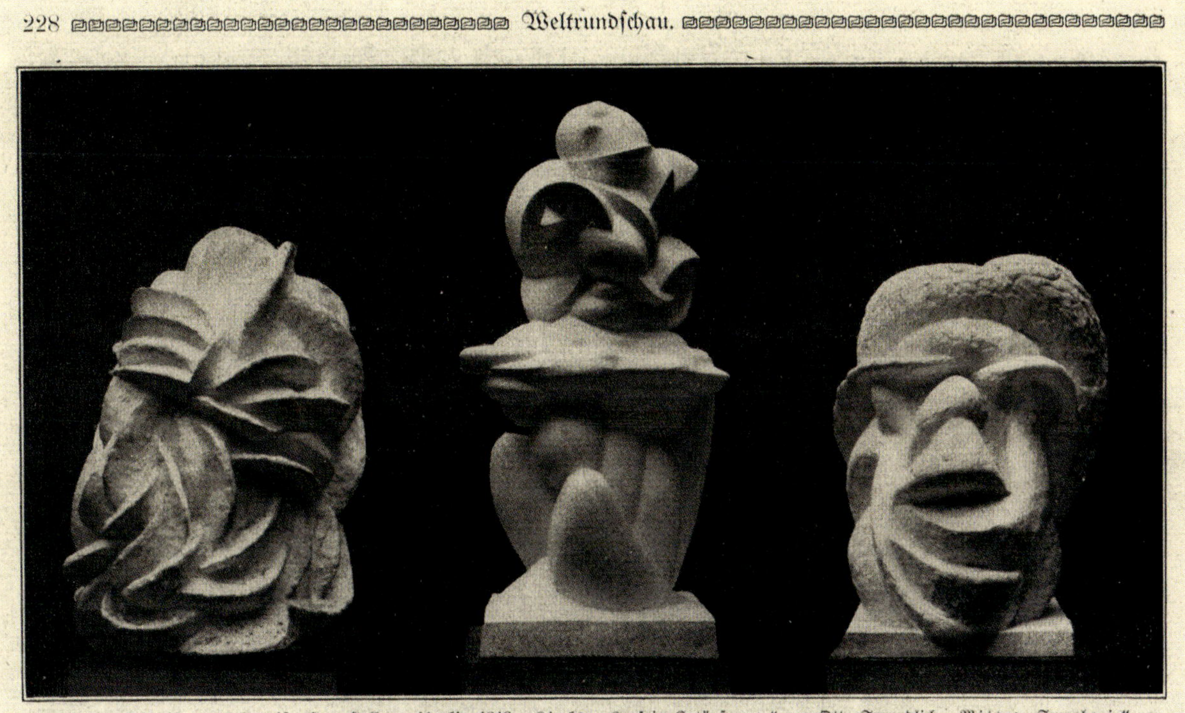

228 Weltrundschau.

Eigenartige Plastiken auf der Kunstausstellung Berlin 1919. Links: „Kopf in Entäußerung" von Otto Freundlich. Mitte: „Symphonie" von Oswald Herzog. Rechts: „Kopf" von Otto Freundlich. Phot. R. Sennecke.

material culture should not be placed side by side without comment, because just like European artifacts, these have undergone enormous changes through trading contacts, wars, or migration. Which means works from the sixteenth century differ greatly from those of the nineteenth. "To be Yoruba meant one thing in the sixteenth century and quite another in the early twentieth century." Peter Mark, "Is there Such a Thing as African Art?" *Record of the Art Museum: Princeton University* 1–2 (1999), pp. 7–15.

15 Einstein, *Negro Sculpture,* op. cit. (note 2), position 473. Translation modified.

16 Ibid., position 493. Translation modified.

17 Cited in Gerhard Wietek, *Karl Schmidt-Rottluff: Plastik und Kunsthandwerk. Werkverzeichnis* (Munich, 2001), p. 173.

18 See Richard Weihe, *Die Paradoxie der Maske: Geschichte einer Form* (Munich, 2004).

19 See Sigrid Weigel, "Das Gesicht als Artefakt: Zu einer Kulturgeschichte des menschlichen Bildes," in Weigel, ed., *Gesichter: Kulturgeschichtliche Szenen aus der Arbeit am Bildnis des Menschen* (Paderborn, 2013), pp. 7–29, here p. 9.

20 Hans Belting, *Faces: Eine Geschichte des Gesichts* (Munich, 2013), p. 13.

21 Otto Freundlich, "Bekenntnisse eines revolutionären Malers" [1935]; Eng. trans. "Confessions of a Revolutionary Painter," in the present volume, pp. 4–16, here p. 5.

22 Belting, *Faces*, op. cit. (note 20), pp. 118–136.

23 Ibid., p. 120.

24 See ibid., pp. 118–119. Belting does not regard the portrait as a bourgeois invention.

25 Freundlich, "Bekenntnisse," op. cit. (note 21), p. 12.

26 Joachim Heusinger von Waldegg, "Über Otto Freundlichs plastisches Werk," in *Bruckmanns Pantheon* 39 (1981), pp. 347–351, here pp. 347–348.

27 Letter from Freundlich to Niemeyer, June 6, 1913, cited in Heusinger, *Rheinische Kunstszene*, op. cit. (note 9), p. 161.

28 Letter from Freundlich to Niemeyer, prior to June/July 1912, cited in ibid., p. 142.

29 Otto Freundlich, "Picasso, zu seinem 50. Geburtstag. 25.10.1931," cited in *Otto Freundlich. Monographie mit Dokumentation und Werkverzeichnis,* ed. Joachim Heusinger von Waldegg, exh. cat. Rheinisches Landesmuseum Bonn et al. (Cologne, 1978), pp. 257–259, here p. 259.

30 I would like to thank Anita Beloubek-Hammer for bringing the illustration in *Reclams Universum* to my attention.

31 Otto Freundlich, "Der Raum," *Die weissen Blätter* 2 (1919), pp. 82–87, cited in Heusinger, *Otto Freundlich: Werkverzeichnis*, op. cit. (note 29), pp. 254–256, here p. 256.

Joachim Heusinger von Waldegg

Eccentric Sensoriality

Situation in Cologne 1915–1918 In January 1915 Otto Freundlich, a war volunteer, returned to Cologne after being prematurely discharged from military service on account of a hearing disability. He felt nicely situated in this city with its proximity to Paris and its heritage of medieval sacred architecture. Here, where patrons, collectors, museum curators, and art historians had backed him following the 1912 Sonderbund exhibition, he hoped to be able to build up a network on his return to civilian life.[1]

Freundlich made friends in the anti-war movement and published articles in René Schickele's *Weisse Blätter* and Franz Pfemfert's pacifist magazine *Die Aktion* (1917–1922), a melting pot for committed Expressionist art. Freundlich enjoyed a reputation as a pioneer of a new spiritual art in the "fourth dimension" among the younger staff members on the magazine—including the later Dadaists Johannes Theodor Baargeld (Alfred F. Gruenwald), Hans Richter, Raoul Hausmann, and the Cologne Progressives Heinrich Hoerle and Franz Wilhelm Seiwert.[2]

Freundlich's efforts to find his feet again in both his artistic and his private life—he married in 1916—were severely limited by wartime conditions and his alternative service as a paramedic. Consequently his graphic works for *Die Aktion* with their "black-and-white principle" (Erwin Piscator)—mainly woodcuts, linocuts, and drawings—demand all the more of our attention. They form a clearly delineated complex of works.

Works for *Die Aktion* The works during the artist's Cologne period were done under the banner of decomposition. Central ideas of Expressionism, such as brotherhood, suffering, redemption, and the birth of the New Man, were interpreted from the angle of spiritual regeneration and the disbandment of all boundaries, including those of the self. Individual motifs from his prewar oeuvre were deconstructed. It should be

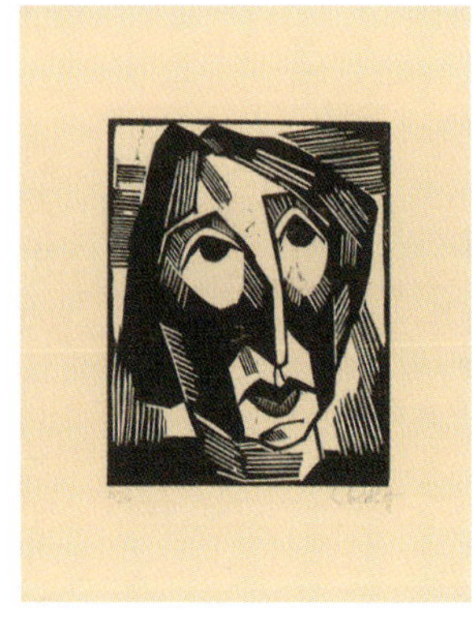

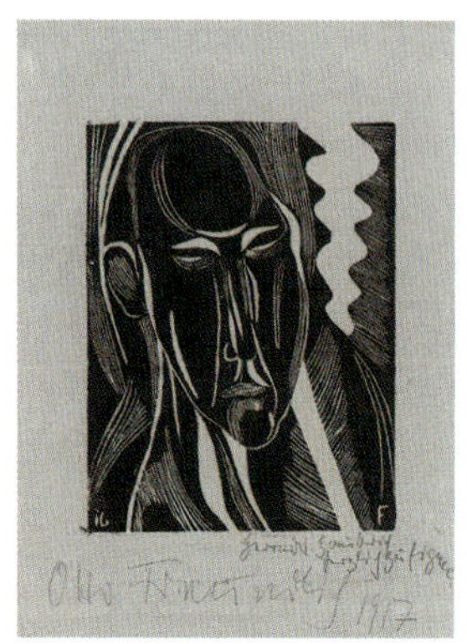

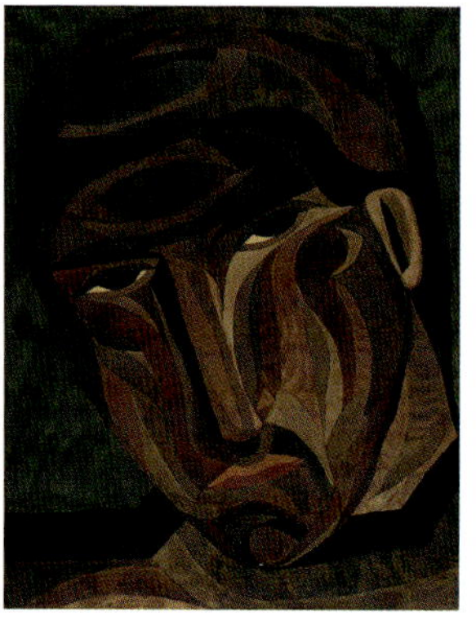

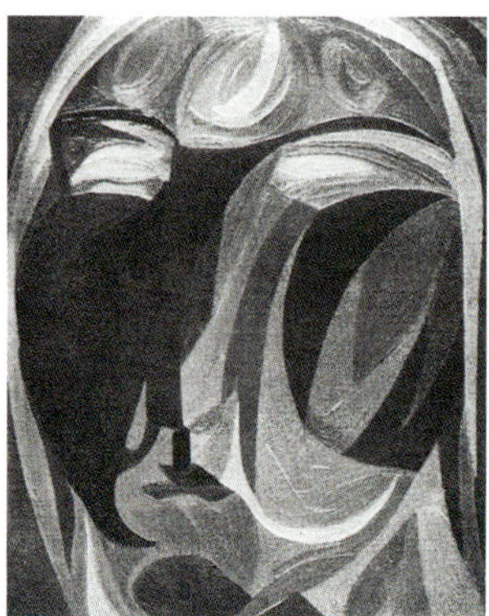

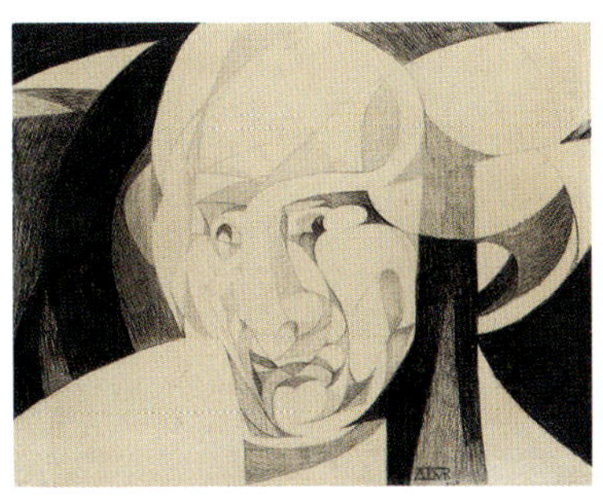

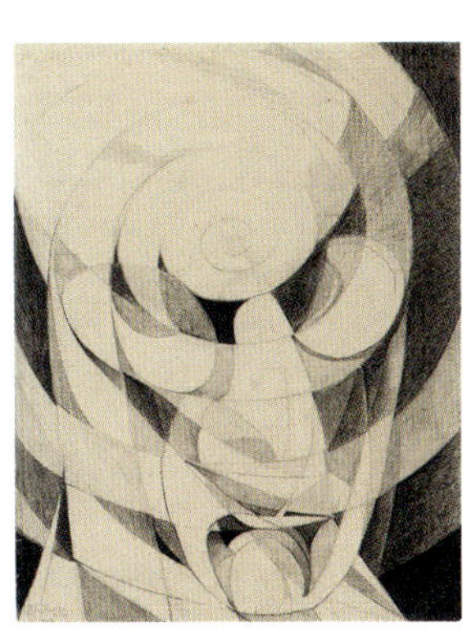

Fig. 18 Adya van Rees
Portrait of the Poet Ludwig Rubiner, 1913
Conté crayon on paper
32.6 x 41.5 cm
Gemeentemuseum, The Hague

Fig. 19 Adya van Rees
The Free Spirit, 1913
Conté crayon on paper
41.5 x 32.7 cm
Gemeentemuseum, The Hague

observed that Freundlich's path to abstraction was not a linear reductive development, in the manner of Piet Mondrian, but was spasmodic and with lapses, much like his notion of the "transformation of the visible world."[3] He was not concerned with formal experiments, but with gaining opportunities for transcendental experiences and dissolving the figure in light (HvW 442, p. 109). Already on a postcard from Chartres to Amadeo de Souza-Cardoso on July 6, 1914, Freundlich described decomposition as "more mysterious" (*plus mystérieuse*) than composition.

Anyone who compares Freundlich's heads with the kindred motifs in the work of his friend Karl Schmidt-Rottluff, a member of the art group Die Brücke, will notice marked differences. In one work, for example, in place of the typically angular Brücke style with its powerful contrasts (fig. 14), the concrete forms in Freundlich's face recede into the delicate lines that play about it and the surrounding space lit up as by a lightning bolt (HvW 441, fig. 15). The aim was to visualize hidden "tensions of a spiritual kind."[4]

A temporal bridge can be found in the spiritual portraits of literary contemporaries that Dutch artist Adya van Rees (Adriana van Rees-Dutilh) did in the prewar years. These include one of the writer and political activist Ludwig Rubiner, who put Freundlich in connection with *Die Aktion* (1913, fig. 18). The portraits by van Rees, who Freundlich had regularly worked with in the summers since 1911 at an artists' colony near Paris, reveal their topical relevance against the backdrop of the war. In keeping with van Rees, Freundlich contrasted the outer reality of war with the inner world of the spirit and thus, comparable to Paul Klee, produced a spiritual counter-reality. At the same time the portraits by both van Rees and Freundlich evince flowing transitions between mimesis and abstraction. Thus the individual shapes in the physiognomies, such as the eyes, mouth, and nose in van Rees's large-scale drawing *The Free Spirit* (1913, fig. 19), have a distinct similarity to Otto Freundlich's flat broad facial forms. Superimposed on these are motile spiraling shapes that have their starting point in the forehead. In Freundlich's portraits, precisely these parts of the face, which he equated with the seat of the spirit, are often emphasized (HvW 109, fig. 16,and HvW 115, fig. 17).

His written contributions and graphic works for *Die Aktion* have not only an illustrative function but also convey a particular content by the means of reflection and abstraction. The difference between conventional works like *Landscape*, *Nude*, or *Head* and the decompositional method directs the interest to the movements of the viewer's gaze, with the aim of stimulating him or her to witness the dissolution of all that is firm and creates borders. Pieced together from fragmentary parts, the connections in the motifs first emerge from the sequence when looked at in the right rhythmic direction: seeing as a creative act. Only occasionally does a figural cipher or the signature "F" give the direction for a reading (HvW 445, fig. 22, p. 56). Accoutred in a Christian narrative and staged instructively as the contrast between above and below, the miracle of global linguistic communication is equated on the *Leaflet on the Communist Manifesto* (HvW 446, p. 108) with the Pentecost. The experience of unity is visualized by licking flames that descend on the community of the enlightened (Acts 2:2–4). Also in this issue from June 1, 1918, Freundlich attacked

Fig. 14 Karl Schmidt-Rottluff
Portrait of Rosa Schapire, 1915
Woodcut
36 x 29 cm
Staatliche Graphische Sammlung, Munich

Fig. 15 Otto Freundlich
Head, 1916
HvW 441
Woodcut
29 x 23 cm
Museum Ludwig, Cologne

Fig. 16 Otto Freundlich
Head, 1911
HvW 109
Watercolor and ink on paper
63 x 48.5 cm
Private collection, Paris

Fig. 17 Otto Freundlich
Head, 1911
HvW 115
Oil on canvas
Lost

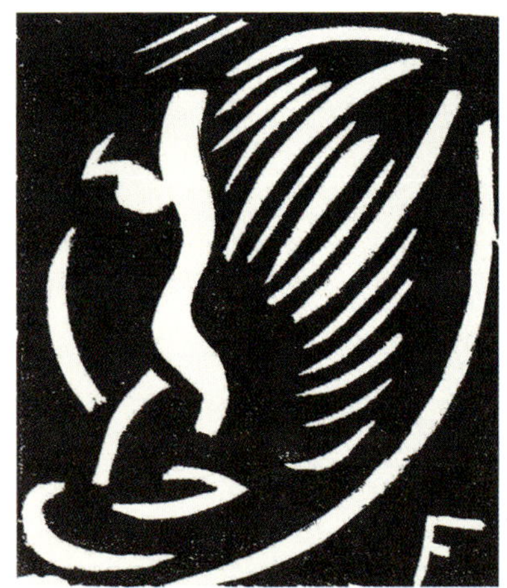

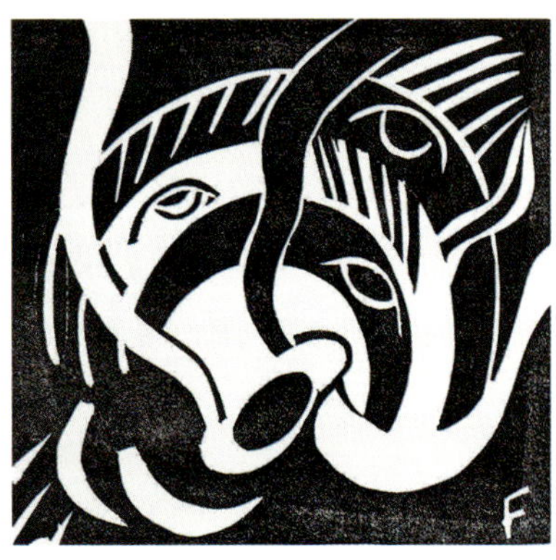

in his text "Der Turm zu Babel" the political terminology of the day, which wrongly identified "liberation" with the exercise of "power." By contrast he presented his vision of a "cosmic communism."

A similarly confessional character is to be found in *Self-Portrait* as the frontispiece for the special Otto Freundlich issue of *Die Aktion* on September 21, 1918 (HvW 449, p. 61), and the pen and ink drawing *Head* from the same year (HvW 295, fig. 28, p. 60). While his choice of this self-portrait underlines the importance of self-instantiation in his work, the ray-shaped aura indicates a visionary sense of mission—the artist as "spiritual leader." Against this, an intimate self-depiction done shortly after the political uprisings in November 1918 hints at skepticism and uncertainty in the questioning gaze and subjective framing of the image (HvW 296, p. 114). Its creation at the end of a year that began programmatically with the design of the mosaic *The Birth of Man* (HvW 127, p. 130) testifies to the artist's critical self-image, independent of any party doctrine. This draft of a logically consistent, personal, social utopian concept for social change can be traced all the way through to Joseph Beuys's self-presentation in *La rivoluzione siamo Noi* (1968).

A title like *Ecstacy* (HvW 443, fig. 20) or a woodcut like *Cello Player* (HvW 453, p. 69) point to out-of-body experiences or "eccentric sensoriality" (Ernst Marcus), especially in the faculty of vision, which envisages an activation of our powers of perception and their extension into cosmic dimensions. Against this, *Vision* (HvW 447, fig. 21) reaches out into speculative regions on the suprasensory fringe. The forms of the face dissolve into a sequence of radially arranged segments. On the cover of *Die Aktion* from July 18, 1914, is Adya van Rees's drawing *Fantômas,* which pictures a masked phantom with similar means (fig. 24). Freundlich adopted this ghostly scenario from the dime novel with mold-breaking dramatics in *The Dagger* (HvW 448, fig. 23) as point of departure for his pre-Dada critique of the middle-class understanding of art. Distortion, intermingling styles, and defamiliarization point to his search for new means of expression. Subsequently Baargeld created a celebrated collage which employed (as did Max Ernst later) the motif of the transfixed eye, which stands for hallucinatory vision (fig. 25), and Luis Buñuel and Salvador Dalí gave central importance to the motif in their film *Un chien andalou* (1929).

Fig. 20 Otto Freundlich
Ecstasy, 1917–18
(from *Die Aktion* 1/2, 1918)
HvW 443
Woodcut
13 x 11.4 cm

Fig. 21 Otto Freundlich
Vision, 1917–18
(from *Die Aktion* 25/26, 1918)
HvW 447
Woodcut
14.7 x 15.5 cm

The Dadaist Baargeld, who like Freundlich was involved in *Bulletin D*, used trivial visual material and worked in printed letters, and in this distinguished himself from Freundlich's narrative, which is in the tradition of "activistic Expressionism." But in Freundlich's *Dedication to Die Aktion* (HvW 456, p. 75), he ventures out into similar peripheral areas of the medium. Drawing on Guillaume Apollinaire's calligrammes,

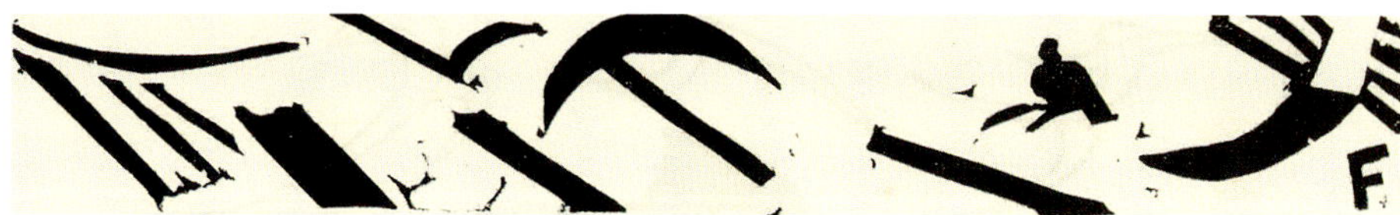

Fig. 22 Otto Freundlich
Landscape, 1918
(from *Die Aktion* 13/14, 1918)
HvW 445
Linocut
3 x 19.6 cm

the letters in the title are reinterpreted as ambiguous ciphers with hints of landscapes and physiognomies. They turn "Aktion" into an eloquent title in which the "o"—representing an open mouth—mutates into a sign for the origin of the new language, in analogy to Raoul Hausmann's sound poems.

Dialectics of the Line

What we have seen for his art prints likewise applies to the drawings Freundlich did in his Cologne period, if slightly modified: they were also done under the dictate of decomposition. But the greater formal flexibility of the medium, including sketches and drafts, corresponds to the differentiation of the means: it consists in the modification of the line.

Jugendstil in Munich has been connected with Freundlich's early work due to the movement's importance as a precursor to abstraction. Freundlich's formal signature, the liberated wavy line, also dominates the pencil drawing *Cosmic Composition* from 1910 (HvW 264, p. 89).[5] Three silhouettes are caught in expressive motion within the eddying planar strips. But their integration into the continuum of spatial motion is not wholly consistent. Done in a combination of dissonant styles, the synthetic structures relating to Freundlich's later work can be understood as a call for Picasso's plurality of styles.[6] As if to confirm the contrast model in *Cosmic Composition*, the antithetical possibilities for expression in the line are presented separately in two studies of heads. While the two parallel wavy lines—sometimes thicker, sometimes thinner—in the ink drawing *Head* (HvW 269, p. 94) show the facial forms dissolving into streams of energy that extend out over the edge of the paper, the other drawing, titled *Protruding Figure II*, works with the expressive potential of the line with firm strokes and perspectival foreshortening (HvW 267, p. 78).

On his return to the motif of the head in 1917, both possibilities of the line were looked at in separate works. In the etching *Head* (p. 82, right), the long curved lines that meet together as cross-hatching have developed a rhythmic life of their own. Extending out across the entire sheet, they set the latter in vibration. By contrast,

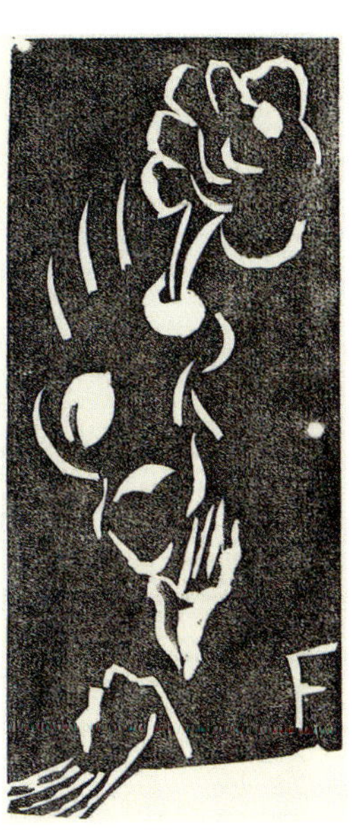

Fig. 23 Otto Freundlich
The Dagger, 1918
(from *Die Aktion* 27/28, 1918)
HvW 448
Woodcut
20.5 × 9 cm

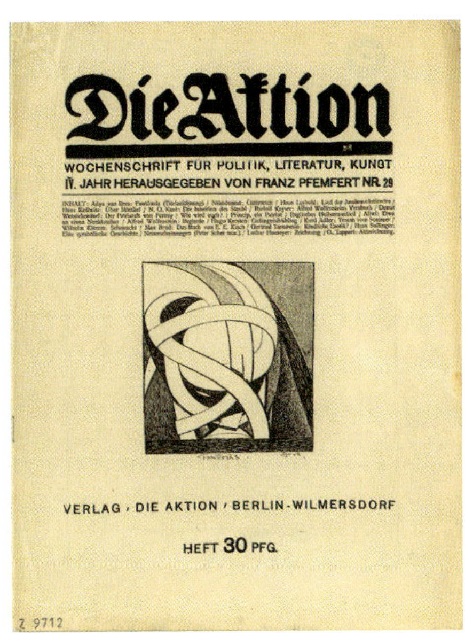

Fig. 24 Adya van Rees
Fantômas, 1914
(from *Die Aktion* 29, 1914)

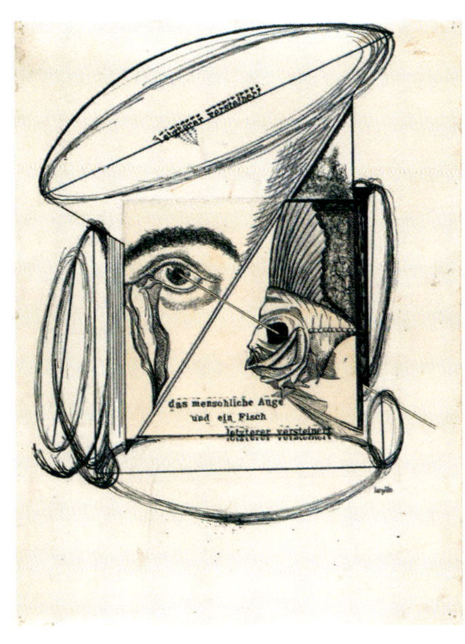

Fig. 25
Johannes Theodor Baargeld
The Human Eye and a Fish, The Latter Petrified, 1920
Paper collage, ink, and pencil on paper
31.1 × 23.9 cm
Museum of Modern Art, New York

a pen and ink drawing has fragmented the facial forms into curved elements—to the extent that they seem to assume an independent existence through their eccentric actions (HvW 295, fig. 28, p. 60).[7] The distance between the lines expands to become energized space.

As regards Freundlich's constructivist methods, it is worth making a comparison between the themes of the head and the figure. *Man and Vegetation* of 1916 (HvW 440, p. 105), for example, borrows one figure from the 1910 work *Four Parallel Figures* (HvW 103, p. 87), joined together by a shared movement in a harmonious atmosphere. Freundlich takes the last of these bowing forms with expressive mien and places it before a picture field opening upwards at an acute angle and containing, in keeping with the title, vertical tiers of leaf forms.

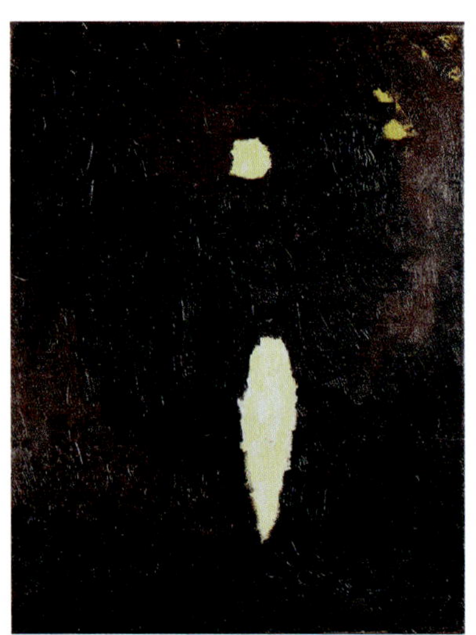

Fig. 26 Otto Freundlich
Composition I, 1916
HvW 121
Oil on canvas
70.5 × 61 cm
Private collection

Fig. 27 Otto Freundlich
Composition II, 1916
HvW 122
Oil on canvas
65 × 50 cm
Private collection

Already the older picture, a drawing in watercolors, explores the possibilities of isolating the figure from the rhythmic continuum. In contradistinction to Ferdinand Hodler's method of parallelism, Freundlich links up each of two neighboring figures as pairs. Reduced to their structures, not only the contrast between architecture and nature in *Man and Vegetation* is brought into focus in the figure, but also the antithetical behavior of space between concentration and expansion.

Likewise in the twinned paintings *Composition I, II (Sun and Moon Picture)* (HvW 121, fig. 26, and HvW 122, fig. 27), the lanceolate shape of the leaves triggers associations with nature. Prompted by autumnal impressions from the park of Versailles,[8] he developed here an almost monochrome, richly structured style of painting. Finely nuanced nature studies, an ongoing interest in cosmologies, light metaphors, and the influences of anthroposophy—one recalls his friendship with the Cologne anthroposophist Friedja Schugt-Maus—are intimately connected.[9] Without any concrete representational details, our powers of vision are induced to feel their way into the seemingly melancholy moods of the colors. At the same time the choice of making cycles of paintings, which he returned to later in life, reflects a penchant of Symbolism for paraphrasing an idea for a painting in a suite of works rather than pinning it down in one. In this way the mental compass is expanded.

The confrontation between or indeed transformation of organic into architectural forms, such as the figure into nature in *Man and Vegetation*, finds its continuation in *Composition* from 1918–19 (HvW 126, p. 104). In *A Tree* (HvW 293, p. 108), the ascent of a trunk towards the light is followed. Comparable to this, the elements in *Composition* all participate in a constant flow of linear movement. This runs continuously from bottom left upwards via a loop-shaped constriction before embarking on a spiraliform ascent—a basic form in Jugendstil. Dynamic spatial poetry, intensified by a hidden light source, maintains a balance with stabilizing forces. The draw of the depths is enhanced by a frame with a pronounced profile that the artist devised, an element that suspends the boundaries.

Freundlich came up with a complex image of nature ranging between the poles of Earth and cosmos. Creating a link between Symbolism and Jugendstil, nature proves amenable to the analogy of creativity. Echoes of Freundlich's visual constructions are to be found in Fritz Winter's *Inner Springs of the Earth* from 1944, a suite of pictures which became a key work of postwar abstraction, not least because it was done towards the end of World War II as a symbol of "inner emigration."

The union of inside and out also applies to a variation on *Opera Scene* done with the same motif, which Freundlich returned to after a gap of ten years (HvW 260, p.99, and HvW 270, p.98). The spatial and scenic nexus in the early drawing is cut up into discrete sections. In order to underline the autonomous qualities in the drawing of the segments, the dividing lines have been expanded into flat strips. With either straight or curved edges, they pick up on the aforementioned dialectic of the lines. Against this, *Landscape* from 1918 places the accent on the interaction between the signs, which stimulates the imagination (HvW 292, p.93). In one further ink drawing (HvW 277, p.92), the boundaries between figure and landscape dissolve to the point of pure abstraction.

While an early pencil drawing suggested a concrete topological setting (*Marne Landscape*, HvW 268, p.92) by the contour lines it depicts, on the pen and ink sketch *Landscape* from 1918 the signs for sky (half moons), clouds, and earth are placed loosely one above the other (HvW 292, p.93). Areas of straight hatching juxtaposed with one another not only emphasize the formal independence of the signs, but also create atmospheric transitions through intermediate shades of gray. In its encoding of objective forms as poetic symbols (hieroglyphs), the drawing recalls the visual dialogue between the painter Franz Marc—like Freundlich, a multi-talent—and the poet Else Lasker-Schüler,[10] who were bonded by the deep exchange of ideas, by the way they superimposed images.

1 Biographical details are taken from Joachim Heusinger von Waldegg, *Otto Freundlich und die rheinische Kunstszene mit Briefen an Herwarth Walden und Wilhelm Niemeyer*, ed. Verein August Macke Haus, exh. cat. August Macke Haus (Bonn, 2006).

2 See Raoul Hausmann, "Die neue Kunst," *Die Aktion* 19/20 (1921), column 281–285 (with reference to the neo-Kantian Ernst Marcus, 1856–1928), reprinted in Hausmann, *Bilanz der Feierlichkeit: Texte bis 1933*, vol. 1, ed. Michael Erlhoff (Munich, 1982), pp. 179–185.

3 Otto Freundlich, "Die Verwandlung der sichtbaren Welt" [1921], in Uli Bohnen, ed., *Otto Freundlich: Schriften. Ein Wegbereiter der gegenstandslosen Kunst* (Cologne, 1982), pp. 118–119.

4 Otto Freundlich, "Zur Synthese Architektur—Plastik—Malerei" [1919], in Bohnen, *Otto Freundlich: Schriften*, op. cit. (note 3), p. 109.

5 Erich Franz, "Otto Freundlich—Dynamischer Raum," in *Freiheit der Linie: Von Obrist und dem Jugendstil zu Marc, Klee und Kirchner*, ed. Erich Franz, exh. cat. Landesmuseum für Kunst und Kulturgeschichte, Westfälisches Landesmuseum Münster (Bönen, 2007), p. 242.

6 Otto Freundlich, "Was wollt ihr von Picasso?" [1922], in Bohnen, *Otto Freundlich: Schriften*, op. cit. (note 3), pp. 128–129.

7 *Otto Freundlichs Kopf-Plastiken: Stufen der Verwandlung*, ed. Joachim Heusinger von Waldegg, published on the occasion of the exhibition *500 Skulpturen für den Frieden—5.500 km quer durch Europa*, Museum St. Wendel (St. Wendel, 2014), pp. 11–15.

8 Letter from Freundlich to Friedja Schugt-Maus, Cologne, November 2, 1916, in Heusinger, *Rheinische Kunstszene*, op. cit. (note 1), p. 252.

9 See the letters from Friedja Schugt-Maus to Freundlich from November 2, 1916, to February 8, 1917, ibid., pp. 252–256.

10 For Freundlich and Else Lasker-Schüler see Heusinger, *Rheinische Kunstszene*, op. cit. (note 1), p. 78.

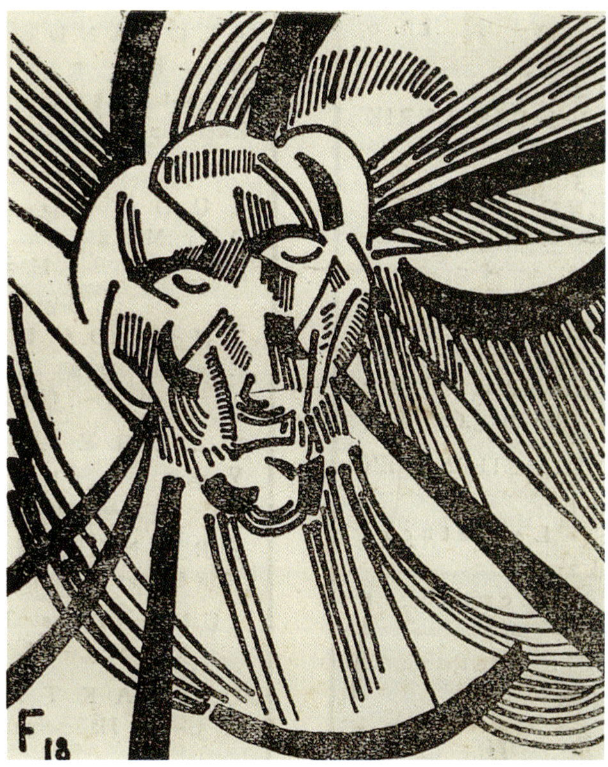

Fig. 28 Otto Freundlich
Head, 1918
(from *Die Aktion* 33/34, 1918)
HvW 295
Ink on paper
Lost

Fig. 29 *Die Aktion* 37/38,
Special issue on
Otto Freundlich, 1918
with the woodcuts:
Self-Portrait, 1918
HvW 449
Cello Player, 1918
HvW 453
Dedication to Die Aktion,
HvW 456

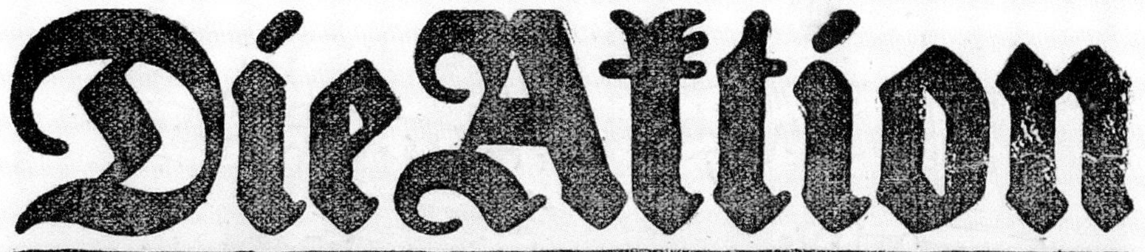

WOCHENSCHRIFT FÜR POLITIK, LITERATUR, KUNST

VIII. JAHR. HERAUSGEGEBEN VON FRANZ PFEMFERT NR. 37/38

SONDERHEFT OTTO FREUNDLICH. INHALT: OTTO FREUNDLICH: SELBSTPORTRÄT (TITELBLATT) / OTTO Freundlich: Welt-Urwelt / Otto Freundlich: Drei Federzeichnungen und sieben Holzschnitte (vom Stock gedruckt) / Alfred Gruenwald: Dominanten zu Herrn Hillers „Herrenhaus“ / Johannes Urzidil: Klage des Erdgerechten / Pol Michels, Heinrich Fischer, Georg Kulka, Werner Hahn, Camill Hoffmann, Arnold Berney und Edith Rényi: Lyrische Anthologie / Carl Figdor-Wien: Der Dichter / F. P.: Ich schneide die Zeit aus; Kleiner Briefkasten / Beilage zur Büttenausgabe: Otto Freundlich: Original-Holzschnitt

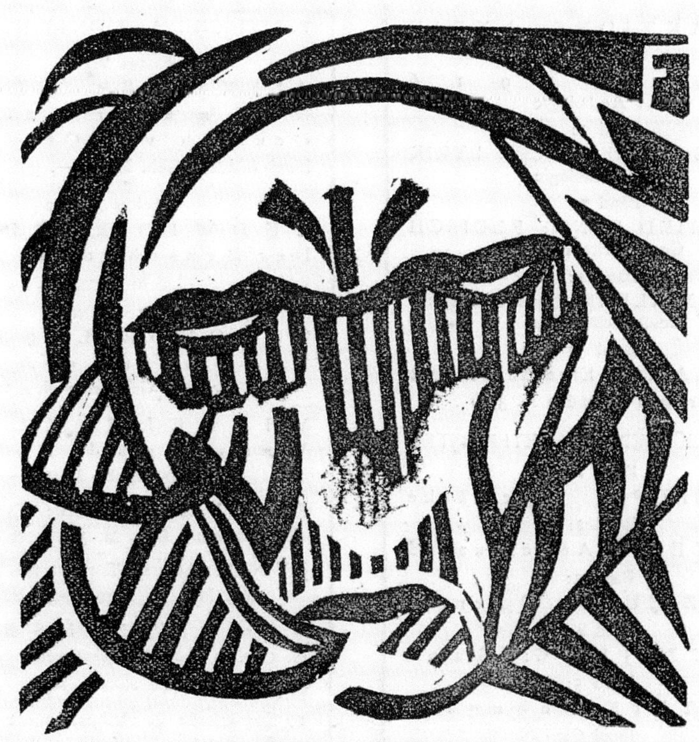

Von dieser Büttenausgabe sind 100 Exemplare gedruckt worden. Dieses Exemplar trägt die Nummer

75

VERLAG · DIE AKTION · BERLIN-WILMERSDORF

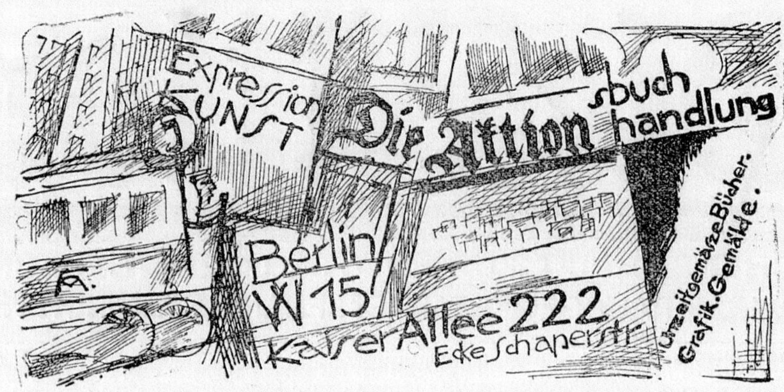

September: IX. Sonderausstellung: J. v. Hulewicz
Wochentags geöffnet von 10 bis 1 und von 4 bis 7 Uhr. Eintritt frei.

DIE AKTIONS-LYRIK

Band 1:
1914—1916
Eine Anthologie

Band 2:
JÜNGSTE TSCHECHISCHE LYRIK
Eine Anthologie

Band 3:
GOTTFRIED BENN: FLEISCH
Gesammelte Lyrik

Band 4:
WILHELM KLEMM: Aufforderung
Gesammelte Verse

Band 5:
DER HAHN. Eine Anthologie

Jeder Band gebunden M. 3,60

AKTIONS-BÜCHER DER AETERNISTEN

Band 1:
HARDEKOPF: Lesestücke

Band 2:
EINSTEIN: Anmerkungen

Band 3:
FRANZ JUNG: Opferung

Band 4:
FRANZ JUNG: Saul

Band 5:
EINSTEIN: Bebuquin

Band 6:
PÉGUY: Aufsätze

Band 7:
JUNG: Sprung aus der Welt

Band 8:
HEINRICH SCHAEFER: Gefangenschaft
Roman

Band 1, 2 und 4 kosten gebunden je M. 2,40
Band 3, 5, 6 und 7 kosten gebunden je M. 3,60
Band 8 (nur auf Subskription) geb. M. 20,—

POLITISCHE AKTIONS-BIBLIOTHEK

Erstes Werk:
ALEXANDER HERZEN
Erinnerungen
Deutsch von Otto Buek
Zwei Bände. Geb. M. 15,—, geh. M. 10,—

Zweites Werk:
LUDWIG RUBINER
Der Mensch in der Mitte
M. 3,—

Drittes Werk:
THEODOR LESSING
Europa und Asien
M. 3,— Gebunden M. 4,50

WILHELM KLEMM
Verse und Bilder
Luxusausgabe M. 15,—

FRANZ JUNG: Sophie
Ein Roman. Geb. M. 3,60, geh. M. 2,40

JUNG: Das Trottelbuch
Geh. M. 3,—, Leinenband M. 4,50

Das AKTIONSBUCH
M. 3,—, in Halbpergament gebunden M. 6,—

EXPRESSIONISTISCHE KUNST
10 Sonderhefte in Halbpergament M. 10,—

DER ROTE HAHN
Jeder Band kostet 80 Pf., Doppelband M. 1,60

Bisher erschienen 28 Bände: Victor Hugo, Hedwig Dohm, Tolstoi, Goll, Otten, Lassalle (Doppelband), Benn, Hilde Stieler, Mehring (Doppelband), Lyrik-Anthologie, Sternheim, Heinrich Schaefer, Pfemfert (Doppelb.), Otto Freundlich, Jakob van Hoddis, Claire Studer, Heinrich Stadelmann (Doppelb.), Josef Capek (Doppelb.), Alexander Herzen, Ludwig Bäumer, Kurd Adler (Doppelb.), Jules Talbot Keller.

DIE AKTION

8. JAHRGANG HEFT 37/38 21. SEPTEMBER 1918

WELT — URWELT

Von Otto Freundlich

Die schönen Farben der Vögel sind ihren Augen vielleicht grau. Und die Gesänge der Nachtigall! Wissen wir denn, ob Vogelohren die Kaskaden, Wirbel, Leitern, Ketten, Tropfen von Tönen ebenso empfinden, wie Menschenohren? Vielleicht ist die Schönheit keine ewige Idee und kein ewiger Wille, sondern nur eine menschliche Deutung; und auch die Vollkommenheit keine ewige Idee, sondern nur eine menschliche, so menschliche Hoffnung. — Ein Abgrund winkte mir einen Augenblick, als ich hörte: die Farben, die uns beglücken, sollten denen unempfindlich sein, die sie tragen? Berührt hier die ganze Welt menschlicher Ästhetik und Ethik den wirklichen Hintersinn der schaffenden Kraft nur wie der Schaum das Meer? Müssen wir einmal diese Grenze fühlen und unsre Erwartungen ändern? Und wenn wir diese Grenze fühlen, wenn wir fühlen, Menschengeist dringt nicht ein in den Sinn, für den die Haut und Oberfläche des Leibes kaum etwas anderes sind als die Bronce, vom Regen grün geworden. Noch mehr; alle Formen der Körper und Erscheinung sind nicht mehr für diesen Sinn als die Verwitterungserscheinungen, als oxydiertes Kupfer.

Wie wunderbar und den menschlichen Hochmut verletzend ist diese Erkenntnis, daß der eigentliche Schöpfungstrieb, der Geist Gottes, sich um kein individuelles und kein soziales Fazit kümmert; er geht daran vorbei, durch es hindurch, wie der Lichtstrahl durch das Prisma.

Wie beschämend für alle Bemühungen des menschlichen Geistes ist es, daß sie unfruchtbar für das Diesseits und Jenseits sind, daß er keinen Weg zu finden weiß, zum Beherrscher der Welt, und dieser, seit Beginn der Weltgeschichte, kalt an allen Bemühungen vorbeisieht und keinen Rat erteilt.

Dieser Geist, dieser Menschengeist ist es, der, ausbeuterisch von Anbeginn, die Erzschächte, Kohlengruben, Silber- und Goldadern in dem geistigen Erdreich dieses Planeten durchwühlte und verschwendete, der dies Erdreich unökonomisch mit Tragen überlastete, und als die für eine lange Dauer bestimmte Kraft durch unrationelle Wirtschaft vor der Zeit versiegte, da machte die Not der Unfruchtbarkeit und der Schuld den gebliebenen Rest des Geistes bösartig und zerstörerisch. Denn was ist geblieben? Geblieben ist weiter nichts als der Mensch. Der Mensch im Stein, der Mensch in Baum, Blatt und Holz, der Mensch in Wolke, Luft, Wasser und Erde. Doch welcher Art Mensch blieb? Fragt nur seine Geschöpfe: diese Steine, diese Bäume und Blätter, diese Wolken, Luft, Wasser und Erde. Seht sie Euch genau an, diese Ebenbilder des Menschen, und wenn Ihr einmal an die Grenze kommt, wo Ihr das Geheimnis jedes außermenschlichen Wesens ahnt; ahnt, daß aus ihm eine Sprache nach einer anderen Seite gerichtet ist als der menschlichen, jedes von ihnen eine Antwort von dorther vernimmt, nur der Mensch nicht; dann schwört ihr endlich ab diesem armgewordenen Geist und seinen armen Methoden, die nichts deuten können, sondern nur Leichen bestatten.

Ja, was bleibt dem Menschen übrig inmitten einer Natur, die sein mißbrauchter Geist miß-

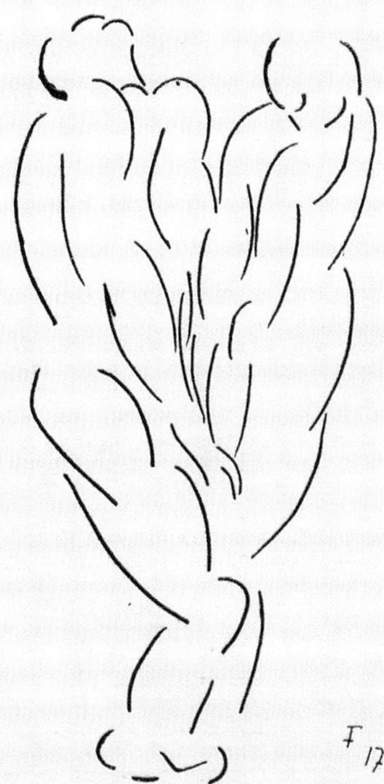

Otto Freundlich *Federzeichnung*

brauchte. Oh, nur eins; aber nichts mehr und nichts weniger. Er versage sich die intellektuelle Masturbation; er versage sich die Ausbeutung der Erde. Er gebe sich und ihr Freiheit und Ruhe. Ein Jahrhundert der Andacht, d. h. mit dem Schwergewicht nicht auf die Seite des Erwerbes, wissenschaftlicher und kaufmännischer Unternehmungen, sondern Zeit, Muße, Eingabe an die Wiederbelebung jener verkümmerten Geisteskraft, die in jedem Wesen lebt und also auch im Menschen, die ihn befähigt, sich in jedes Wesen zu verwandeln, die aus diesen Verwandlungen eine andere Entzifferung des Lebenssinnes mitbringt, als aus der Einschätzung nachwirtschaftlicher Nutzbarkeit. Noch mehr: er lerne es, die angewandten Wissenschaften als subalterne Angelegenheiten des Geistes anzusehen und versage sich ihrer Anwendung, trotzdem ihm die Methoden zur Verfügung stehen. Die banale Diesseitigkeit dieser Methoden, im Grunde ein Kniff unter Gaunern, die geschickt alle Türen verrammelten, damit kein Lichtstrahl hinein könne in ihre obskure Werkstätte, zu der sie schließlich die Erde gemacht haben. Allerdings, Ihr Herren, Eure Diebslaternen dringen auch nicht hinaus aus Eurem Verließe, und wenn Ihr ja einmal hineinleuchten wollt in die Wunder des Kosmos, geschieht es unter dem Gelächter aller derer, die noch eine Vorstellung vom großen Licht bewahrt haben.

So kündet sich also der Bankerott der Anthropomorphismen an, gesprengt werden sie durch die eindringenden Wogen des kosmischen Meeres; hoch gehen sie, und höher werden sie gehen. Einige alte Steindämme brausen schon; Tagelöhner, unzählige Sklaven flicken sie Tag und Nacht. Aber woher die Hände nehmen: schon wieder kracht's, ein neuer Damm zerbrach, eine neue Woge stürzt ins Land, alle Bleienten zittern. Zu lange preßtet Ihr die Welt in Eure Kuchenformen, Ihr — Genießer, Ihr Bäcker und Konditoren; doch Ihr selbst seid nicht süß, nur für Euch soll alles süß schmecken, damit es auf Euren Tafeln prangen kann für Eure unersättlichen Bäuche. Doch man muß Euch kennen, Ihr Liebhaber von Süßigkeiten, wie bitter Ihr seid, wenn — wenn der Teig nicht so willfährig sein will, wie die Gier Eures Gaumens ihn will: denn in einer Hand habt Ihr die Kuchenform, in der andern — das Schwert, den Dolch; Kanonen, Gift, Gase und Martern stehen bereit, um den widerspenstigen Teig klein zu kriegen. Wehe, sagt Ihr, wenn der Odem Gottes sich wieder seines Stoffes bemächtigt: Wehe Gott und wehe dem Stoff. Jahrhunderte, nein, seitdem es Despoten gibt, ringt Gottes Odem mit den Usurpatoren seines Thrones. Aber schließlich macht er es wahr, daß tausend Jahre vor ihm sind wie ein Tag und er bläst sie weg.
Wohlan! es muß hinaus in die Welt, daß ein falscher Geist die Geschichte gemacht hat und Geschichte macht, die nämlich, die eine Kette von Kriegen ist. Ein falscher Geist war es, der die

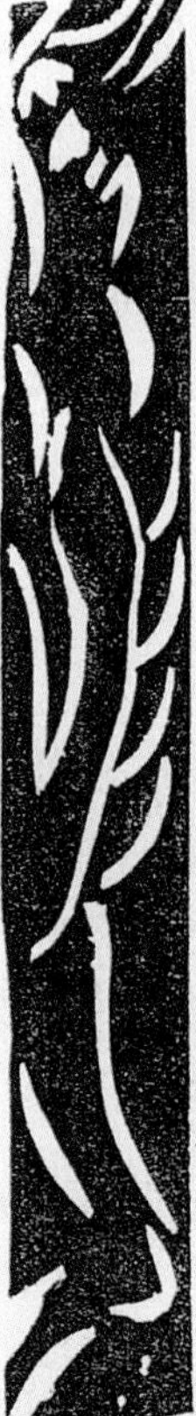

Freundlich: Akt

Wissenschaften schuf, die nämlich, die die Blutsbrüderschaft der Dinge löste, Verbindungsadern durchschnitt und ein Nebeneinander von lauter blutleeren Larven erzielte. Ein falscher Geist war es, der den Bau erschuf, den nämlich, der seinen Bestand mit dem Unglück und der geistigen Verarmung seiner Untertanen bezahlte. Ein falscher Geist war es, der die Familie erschuf, die nämlich, die die Moral des Staates nach Unterdrückung und Übervorteilung als geheime Vorbehalte in sich aufnahm. Ein falscher Geist war es, der die Natur erschuf, die von Menschen gesehene, den ausbeuterischen, deren Schwärmen noch ein Triumph gelungenen Todschlags an ihr ist, deren eiserner Griff die Dinge würgt, sobald ihr göttlicher Odem die Grenzen der Körperhaft nicht achten will und nach anderem Willen als dem menschlichen sich zur Unendlichkeit desavouiert.
Wie aber sähe die Welt aus, wenn nicht alle Sinne, durch tausend Schleusentore zerbrochen, als kleine Wässerchen sich in die Welt stehlen müßten; wenn nicht ihre geheime Kraft und Selbstsicherheit, sich ihrem Gefälle zu überlassen, zurzeit wehrloser Kindheit durch operativen Eingriff zeitlebens geschwächt wäre. Dann würden wir die Vögel nicht lieben, weil sie schöne Federn haben, schwach sind, harmlos zirpen, oder Nachtigallentöne in heller Mondnacht unsre Liebe verewigen: Nein, wir würden sie lieben mit blindem Auge, taubem Ohr, fern von unserm Getast; wir würden sie lieben und uns durch diese Liebe unsres Menschtums entäußern und durch die Pforte jeder Kreatur eingehen in ihr großes Reich; wir würden sie lieben, wie wir die Wunder der Meerestiefen lieben, obwohl wir sie nicht sehen. Jedes Ding aber schwimmt über seinem unergründliches Meere; jedes Ding hat seine Tiefe nicht zum Menschen hin: auch der Mensch hat seine Tiefe nicht zum Menschen hin. Aber wer wagte es noch einen Menschen zu töten und seine Tiefe zu enthaupten. Würde nicht ein Schrei des Entsetzens aus den Mündern aller derer ihn strafen, die ihre Tiefe wie den einzigen Weg zur Gottheit hegen und ihn schützen und niemand das Recht zugestehen, ihn davon zu trennen? Würde nicht seine Hand und sein böser Sinn zittern vor der Tat, wenn er wüßte, daß der Tod eines Menschen dem Leibe Gottes selbst eine Wunde schlägt? Würde die Heiligung der Welt nicht dadurch entstehen, wenn wir die der Welt abgewandte Seite jedes Dinges liebten und sie verehrten, wie alles Sein sie als die tiefste Liebe zu seinem Ursprung verehrt? Würde unser Intellekt noch die scharfen Quälereien unternehmen, Ursachen und Wirkungen ausfindig zu machen, die doch nur eine Wissenschaft von Unheil und Gift erzeugen können; denn diese Gesetzmäßigkeit, diese Ursache und Wirkung ist nicht die Kausalität, berührt durchaus nicht den Logos des Kosmos, sondern sie ist die krankhafte Wirkung eines seines kosmischen Nährbodens beraubten

Gewächses. Im Denken wie im Tun schaffen wir Vernichtung — nie etwas anderes — wenn wir unser und alles Geschaffenen Ursinn nur als ein Wort und nicht als die dauernd notwendige Begleitschaft für unsre sittliche Kraft verstehen und verehren.

Was bleibt dem Gelehrten ohne seine angewandten Wissenschaften? Oh, es bleibt ihm davon genug, um sie mit Maß auszuüben. Aber einer anderen Wissenschaft wird seine beste Kraft gehören; das ist die Wiederherstellung der Bindungen, die er einst zerschnitt. Und sollte er es sich immer versagen wollen, jenes andere Gebiet der Erfahrung zu begehen, für das jenes Auge des Mikroskopes allerdings nicht genügt?

Wir kommen dahin, uns der Not zu entäußern, die die ersten Kinderschritte begleitete. Denn was ist das Gefühl der plastischen Form anderes als die Angst, überall von Ungewißheit umgeben zu sein, die Befriedigung, den umschrittenen kaum als Sicherheit erkannt zu haben. Was ist die Perspektive anderes als die Abstraktion unseres Hingehens in die Ferne, die theoretische Befriedigung daß wir dort hingehen könnten. Wie sklavisch muß aber alles, zwischen dem Hier des Beschauers und dem fernen Zielpunkt, dieser Begierde dienen, dorthin zu gelangen. Alles Zwischenleben in der Luft und auf der Erde wurde nur anthropomorphisch gedeutet, also mißdeutet, so wenig fand der Geist seine Freiheit von den ersten leiblichen Gehversuchen. Die Optik scharf abgegrenzter Körper oder Flächen entspricht dem Beamtentum und Bureaukratismus im Staate: alles hat seine Rubrik auszufüllen, im übrigen ist sein Leben, seine Neigung und gar sein Freiheitsbedürfnis gleichgültig und wird unterdrückt. Wenn der Künstler die ersten Taten vollzogen hat, die Natur aus diesem Beamtentum zu befreien, so tat er es darum, weil ihr ganzes Beieinander durchtränkt war von dem Geiste der Sklaverei, und nicht brach er ihre Ketten, weil ihn Beispiele aufmunterten, weil sein Auge belehrt worden wäre durch die Gegenstände, nein: hier gebot der Geist und sein unabhängiger Sinn, die Freiheit sichtbar zu machen, und strafte den Hang des Sehens fertiger Werte Lügen. Die Prüfung dieser geistigen Gebote durch die atavistische Optik und an ihr wäre geradeso, als wenn man die Bestätigung des freien Menschen unter lauter Uniformen suchen wollte. Wir werden endlich aufhören, Bestätigungen für diese geistigen Forderungen in der Natur sehen zu wollen, diese erstarrte, maskenhafte Natur ist wieder zum Embryo, fast zum Urstoff geworden, hat gar keine Selbständigkeit, geschweige denn Führerschaft, sie beginnt erst wieder jung und schwach zu atmen unter dem Hauche des schaffenden Geistes. Es ist nicht leicht, der Verführung zu entgehen, eine noch sichtbare untergehende Welt, die uns und der Menschheit vor uns Tausende von Jahren vertraut war, mit der aufgehenden, als Gesamtheit noch gar nicht überblickbaren Welt zu vergleichen. Dieser Nötigung sollen wir nicht nachgeben. Hier handelt es sich darum, daß zwei Geistesepochen sich ablösen. Sich in dieses Phänomen zu versenken, es als sein eigenes Leibesschicksal anzusehen, die Klarheit des sich immer mehr auswachsenden Gesetzes zu erfassen, seine ernste Unterscheidung von dem Bisherigen nicht als eine Willkür, sondern eine Notwendigkeit zu ergründen, seine Freiheitsverheißung als auf der persönlichen Leistung jedes einzelnen aufgebaut zu verwirklichen: Es ist kein Kunstgesetz, das hier zur Welt will; es ist der Schöpfungsprozeß neuer Leibes- und Naturforschung; eines neuen Leibes, der alte, unbrauchbar gewordene Organe verliert und dem dafür neue wachsen. Für diesen Vorgang gibt es sonst nur prähistorische Parallelen, und sicher ist die Entstehung der Fauna und Flora auf der Welt kein Schöpfungsprozeß höherer Ordnung als dieses jetzt vollziehende neue Mittelsverhältnis des Menschen zwischen Kosmos und Welt.

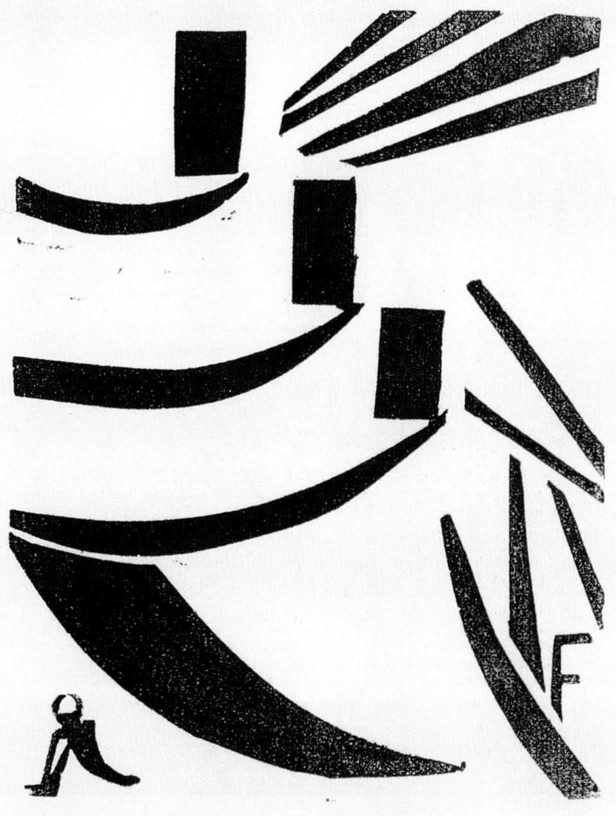

Otto Freundlich *Der Mensch in der Landschaft*

DOMINANTEN ZU HERRN HILLERS „HERRENHAUS“

Von Alfred Gruenwald

„fängt ‚dort‘ auch Geist erst an, wo Sonderung zu einem deutschen Herrenhaus entworfen wird, so ist es doch schon dieses Hauses Geist, der es entwirft.“ (zu S. 4 der Schrift.)

S. 4. „Geist bricht aus Erde, lebt — der gesetzmäßige — verwoben mit Zufälligem, objektiviert sich nie anders als durch ein Subjekt . . .“ in gefälligem Besitzverhältnis treudienert er Apostaten. Nun — seltenster Vorgang — durch Konsolidierung ersichert sich Beidem Funktion, endliche Statik: der Sprung in die Verfassungsurkunde des Deutschen Reiches.

S. 7. „Empörung ‚des Volks‘ sagen wir . . . und vergessen leicht, daß sie ihren Ursprung allemal im Bewußtsein Weniger nimmt . . .“

darum sieh, schaudernd hackige Grimasse der Ohnmacht, doch kurz vor der Macht, stumpframmige Stirn Vergewaltigter, die Gewalt wittert, kurz noch, der vor seinem Aufgellen noch, grade noch verschäumende Krampf der All-Schmach —, Oligos! „in dessen Existenz und Wirken die d u n k l e (?) Einheit ‚Volk‘ sich zur Sicherheit ballt“; Gelegenheitskipper am Bröckelrand der Eruptionen!

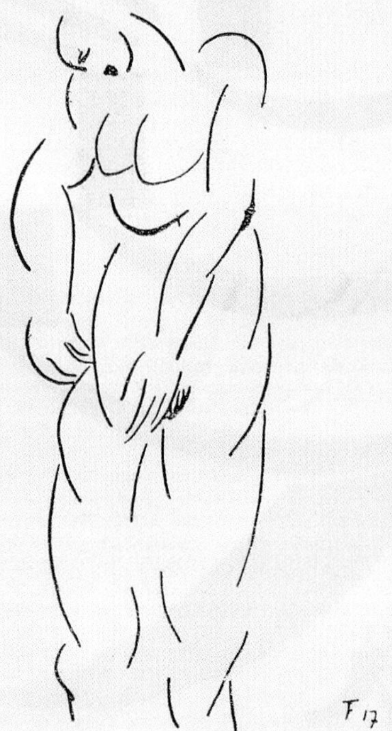

Otto Freundlich *Federzeichnung*

S. 8. „Das Volk lebt um seiner selbst willen . . . Auch ‚um des Staates willen‘ lebt es nicht“ — . . . aus Schmerzen der Jahrhunderte Volk erblutet Geist, darin weitüberwissend es zu Brudertat auftaumelt: SIND A u f e r s t e h u n g e n, nicht von Spenderkabinets des Geistes angeahnt, und seit Ungedenken vergebliches Bemühn um Einzeiten der Aufruhre, wo Seele, dem wundgeprellten Urstoff aufschreiender Epochen, der Zukunft Allelement, sich zu geben zu arm, verklammt: Schöpfung schließt auch die Klerisei aus, doch ihr Verderb wird erst der Kleinglaube. Von ursprünglicher Notwendigkeit, von fanatisierender Reinheit ist es, wo Botschaft — epochales Mal! — n i c h t erträumt, nicht verweg beflekt werden kann.

S. 12. „Umgekehrt werden edle Mengen, werden Gefolgschaften stets das Produkt ihres Führers sein. Masse schwitzt Funktionäre aus; der Führer stampft Armeen aus der Erde.“

Der Einzelne und sein Weg? Funktionär, Führer, Einzelner, gelte! —: Und ER beginnt entsteilend aus wahrhaft und von allenthalben ‚dunkler‘ Schichtung seines Bluts — — Wo aber reißen, die seiner Sendung Schwung erschleudern, darin das schwere Geblüt der Abertausend sich aufringt, die ‚dunkeln‘ Fasern seiner Werdung; ist dort die Scheidung, wo wechselgehärmter Erde er das Kinn hebt einmal zum Blick in die sengende Ewigkeitstatik des Schöpferschoßes? Wo apostrophiert der „ausgeschwitzte“ Funktionär zum Freiballon der Oligoi?

S. 13. „in eine Klasse, in eine Rasse hineingeborensein berechtigt zu keinem Privileg; in eine Klasse, in eine Rasse hineingeborensein verpflichtet zu keinem Leiden.“

. . . ‚einer‘ aber sah es, unter wimmelnden, getretenen, tretenden, nach Auskommen schnappenden Heloten: den aderfeinen, den pulsierenden Spalt im Heerweg der Heloten, vom Pulverschlag seines ringenden Nackens, und stets wieder wußten es diese ‚Einen‘: Geschenk des Atlas, wo einmal sphärische Totalität die Erde in eine Stirne dröhnte, einmal, da behalten die Sais'schen Bilder ihr Unrecht, da ist grenzenlosere Empfängnis, tellurisches Austragen — oder Verkümmerung, schwerer Schuld ob ihres doppelten Betrugs, ist Schmerzumarmung, bis Erde Erde zurückgegeben wurde. — Der ‚Einen‘ Geburt ist von dem Atlasraub, und gellt zurück, woher sie kam: Ist vom Menschentum, allen Wassern entwaschen, ist markendes Kristall aller dunkelfiebernden Möglichkeiten, ist vom Scheidewasser der Schickungen und Flüche, das nach den Hoffnungslosigkeiten und Toden, den entseelenden Retouchen des Leids leckt, markend im Zerfunken, übergeistend in seinen Katastrophen, verschleudernden Aufgehens: Aufgabe, Umgeburt, Volk!

Ausklang: S. 33 u. a.: „Ein Bund entsteht. Er gibt sich Satzungen“ (??) — „Aristoi“ (?) „Ein letzter Schritt: Der Arbeitsausschuß des Bundes wird unter genauer Abgrenzung seiner Kompetenzen in die Verfassungsurkunde des Deutschen Reiches als Oberhaus aufgenommen.“ (???)

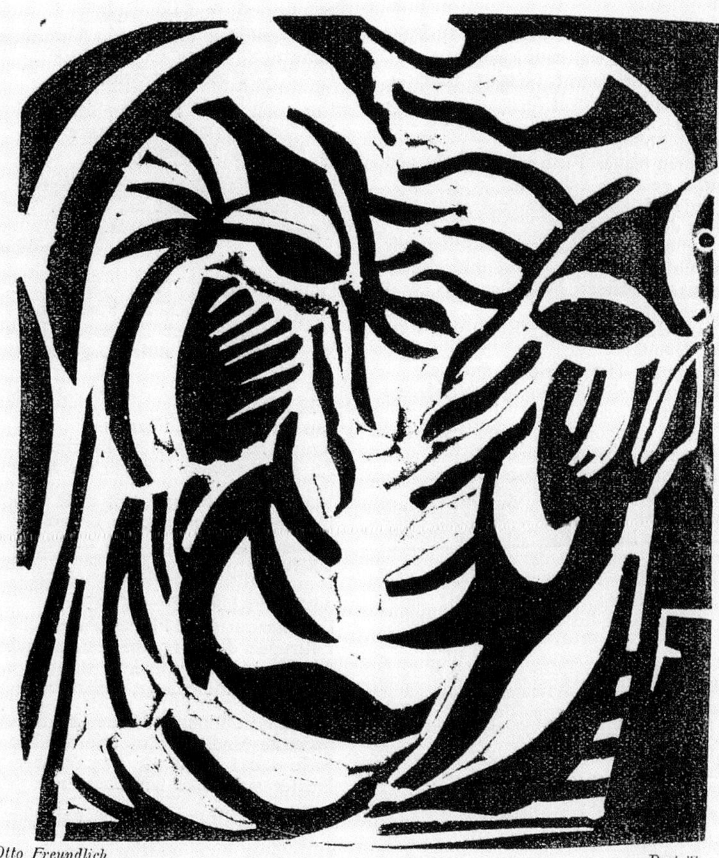

Otto Freundlich *Porträt*

KLAGE DES ERDGERECHTEN

Ich entfuhr den Klüften zerborstener Träume
beschwert mit dem Erbgut verworfner Gestaltung.
Ich wandle seither, ein weher Verkünder
der tödlichen Grenzen und der Gesetze.
Ich teilte mir Gott in Gewässer und Klippen
süß-bittere Landschaft ließ er sich nieder.
Ich trage den Maßstab erdachter Entscheidung
und spalte das Leben.

Doch sah ich den Pilger,
verschränkt in Geburten und Tode,
den Wanderer wahrhaft um Süße der Wanderschaft willen.
Leicht wiegt ihm das Leben, wie Atem der Schwalben im Sturme,
ist Strom oder Mantel von zehntausend Strömen des Herzens.
Allseitig sein Walten, der Einfalt des Lichtes vergleichbar,
doch selten erglühend, wie leidenschaftlicher Kaktus,
ihm tönen die Hände von Wohllaut und Glanz der Erkenntnis
das Antlitz des Weltalls durchschwebt Katakomben des Hauptes.

Es raffen die Sterne das Maß des stürzenden Lichtjahrs
und stocken den Lauf, wo rauschend sein Blick sich entfaltet.
Wir aber durchsausen in zischenden Liften den Abgrund
durch Wahnsinns Etagen und branden in dunkle Bedrängnis.
Und alle Gestirne, darein er kristallen verschmolzen,
der schmerzlose Segler im Windstrahl des Göttlichen sind uns
längst toter Systeme kaum schwankende fahle Reflexe,
die magisch verbrüdert hintanzen durch Raumlosigkeiten.

Johannes Urzidil

KNABEN

Blind langten Knaben über schnöde Wirklichkeit
nach brennend weichem Kosmorama,
Doch diese Hand Sehnsucht beladen zauderte,
welk prallte rückwärts.
O dann war unser Taumeln träg Zickzack sich
bäumend ohne Unterlaß
Und heller Frauen blauer Tanz erregte nicht von
Wucht getanzte Schenkel.
Nie warfen federnd hin wir uns dem Flug zum
Golde der Ekstasen
Nie tönte Lachens hohe Kuppel, krochen wir
Knaben alt daher, verglast und stumm
Mit der Grimasse blasser Menschen aus dem
Zirkus nur
Die traurig nach dem Leichnam blinzeln und stets
sehr demütig
gleich ihrem dünnen Tier krepieren möchten.
Wir brachten Opfer sinnvergessen, schleuderten
los den Rest von Scham
Ein Freund (dies Trugbild) lockrufte huschend
über trüber Augen Vision
Empor wir ranken wollten am Entschluß der un-
umschränkten Unterwürfigkeit
Kein zärtlich Wort stellte sich ein, ja keine
Schwesterstirn kühlte vernarbte Elends-
wangen
(. . . und immer enger kerkerte das Gitter, und
immer heftiger
Zerhieb so Strähnenluft die Einfalt der Gefühle).

Pol Michels

SCHMERZLOSES OPFERN

Winter schneit meine Seele,
Die Herbe der Flocken, auf einer Wange zu
schmelzen.
Meines Fallens Feld,
Dieses Lebens verlaufene Wege
Sind euch ein Spielplatz, ihr Knaben,
Die meine Kälte nicht friert,
Euren Herzen unverspürt;
Ach, ihr werdet noch auf mich, linkische Schnee-
dame,
Mit Fingern zeigen.

Und doch: ich bin es.
Seht den Zwang dieses Gewordenen
Und glaubt, ihr Spieler, diesem Sterben nicht.
Denn meine Reue noch seimt einen Honig,
Satt sich daran zu trinken;
Ich blühe Himmel und Erde und Wiese,
Haus und Wald
Und alles, was Knaben lieb ist.

Schmerzloses Opfern der Güte!
Unschmerzliches Grünen der Bäume!
Wahrlich, ihr Knaben, nichts tut weh — — —

Edith Rényi

NARCISS

Narciß, vor Sehnsucht blaß,
Begehrt das Sternbild seiner Fahrt zu schauen,
Der Himmel voller Prunk und Grauen
Stürzt klirrend fremden Haß
Jäh aus den Scheuen, daß
Die Brust ihm stockt. Mit Untierklauen
Zerfetzt Entsetzen sein Vertrauen.
Der Knabe sinkt ins Gras.

Der erste Wind rührt an den Knaben Hüfte,
Der aus verworrnem Traume fährt
In Morgens Nelkendüfte.

Und wie Narciß nicht ohne Zagen
Nun aufblickt, stiebt auf steilem Weg verklärt
Apolls demantner Wagen.

Camill Hoffmann

HOLZSCHNITT: DER KINDLICHE WERTHER

Häuser singen süßeste Kantaten,
Plätze erfüllen sich in Deinem Blick
Meine Gedanken schlagen große Serenaden
Zu Dir zurück.

Will es beenden.
Aus der bleichen Phantasei
Knüpf' ich mich auf mit knöchernen Händen
Zu einer weißen lächerlichen Melodei.

Vor Deinem Fenster, mit toten Sinnen,
Flatternde Pose in roten Linnen — —
Meinen himmlischen Tod zu beginnen,
Olietta!

Arnold Berney

ABEND AUF DER HÖHE

Der flammenden Flotte letzte Schaluppen
Enttrugen den Tag auf schimmernden Pfaden,
Wie Sargtuch umdunkeln dämmrige Schwaden
Blondblühende Hänge, umkränzte Kuppen.

Talwärts ertrinken Türme im Schatten.
Bunteste Vielheit wird schwärzestes Meer.
Stille starrt rings wie geschliffener Speer.
Weitesten Wolken will Ebene sich gatten.

Leben liegt irgendwo fern, ganz fern.
Namenlos ängstet die Seele ein Bangen:
Starbst Du, den Süchte endlich ersangen? —
Wie Heiland ersteht der erste Stern.

Heinrich Fischer-Karlsbad

STOSS

Unter der riesigen Landschaft
Brechen fast die tragenden Schläfen.
Zum Ende die stoßende Leidenschaft —
Blick, fall nieder in Ebenen, in Häfen.

Es tragen Reiterinnen in der Truppe,
Die mich zieht, mein Augenweißes den Horizont
hinab.
Ich allein dränge meine drehende Schaluppe
Immer nach Mündung, nach offenem Arme ab.

Trennungen bröckeln mich ab, Namen fallen,
Singende Sterne, um mich tief ins Meer —
Ewiges tönt im Straßenlärm verloren; es krallen
Ins purpurne Haar sich Frauliche. Gottheit brich
her.

Fritz Heckerling

SEHEN

Das Fahle haftet unbewegt in bunteren
Vom Schein verseuchten Bahnen.
Einmal vergeht die Wollust
Des Ablaufs: Wölbungen sind mild erlöst.

Zum Kreise münden Stadien der zersplitterten
Noch unvollkommnen Nähe,
Verharren zackig stechend:
In Kegeln Büschel aufgeblähtes Licht.

Was schauernd ausging schleicht einst matt zurück.
Die Schluchten des Gesichtes
In Strahlungen gestaltet
Umfließt behütend und durchsprüht der Schmerz.

Werner Hahn

HELLER TROPFEN MOND

Heller Tropfen Mond Säule über Zeiten
Sind wir, wir sind nicht in Zeitlichkeiten.

Von der letzten Kindheit spitz verraten,
Müssen wir die Dämmerung durchwaten.

Erst wenn Ebene den Abend weggezogen,
Liegt geglättet Seele, hohler Bogen.

Keines Raumes bedürftig, dazusein und zu haften.
Steigen Sterne zu seligen Brüderschaften.

Georg Kulka

DER DICHTER

Der Dichter beharrt:

Beten
daß aller Gnaden Glaubens Träume / über das Spiel wogender Kräfte dahingeflossen / in ein Ziel schießen.
Starrheit / vor fiebererttrinkenden Augen / der Dinge spröde gewordene Formen in dem Glutatem der blinden eigenen Anspannung / davor Risse reißen und Sprünge klüften.
Vor der flammenden Forderung den Willen zersprühend / neigt sich nur Haß nicht / den zu hassen ich jauchze / gegen spießbürgerliche Gaukler und Schöpfer / in der Eingebung eines Augenblickes oder im Sechstagewerk / für ein Königsdasein oder einem jüngsten Tag zuliebe.
Ich bin glücklich und biege mich in meinem Hasse.
Beten
denn hinter mir lagert Elend und Angst / und im Gesicht springt vor mich / mit Augen darin, die schwören, daß sie sehen können wie die meinen.

Der Dichter betet:

Ich schaue in den Glanz deines Reiches und das Irrlichtern einer Menschenseele zu Füßen deines Thrones ist erstarrt / Seit der Ahnung deines Ingrimms Fragen gegen mein verhärtetes Herz gerollt sind, habe ich in Demut die Knie gebeugt / Seit die Ströme deines Willens vor das Neigen meiner Hände geschäumt sind, lagert der Gedanken vom letzten Tag vor der Weltenschöpfung / Seit das Jauchzen deiner Heerscharen ob der Milde deines Antlitzes vor mein Ohr gewogt ist / flammt meine Liebe zu dir, Herr!
O Herr, wie strahle ich in Schönheit / seit in den Wogen des Glanzes deines unendlichen Himmels ich meine Seele wiege / seit in den Posaunen von Ewigkeit zu Ewigkeit mein Ohr bebt / und meine Hände unter Segnungen gebreitet sind.
O Herr, wie liebe ich dich, meine Kraft und mein Gebet vom Anfang bis zum Ende / Vor der Unendlichkeit deiner Klarheit strahlt dein Licht bis in die Verwirrung des letzten Stäubchens / Du liebst mich, Herr / du lässest mich nicht verzagen, wenn Feinde wider Feinde sind.
Zu euch ihr Brüder neige ich mich / wes Freund und Feind ihr seid / und fasse eure Hände / euch meiner Segnungen zu segnen und eures Gottes Kraft in meine Arme zu gießen.

Carl Figdor-Wien

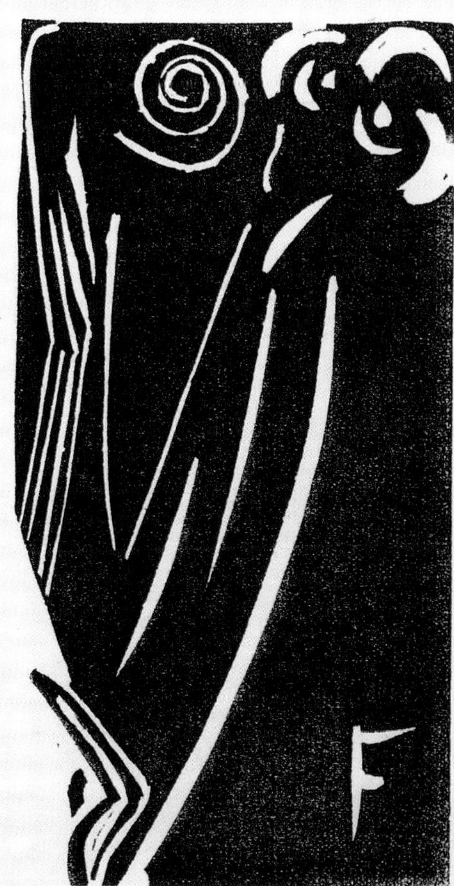

Otto Freundlich *Cellospieler*

ICH SCHNEIDE DIE ZEIT AUS
LXXVI

Kinderfest im H-H-Park, Stellingen. Nur das Kind ist glücklich, das die ganze Süßigkeit des Wortes „Spiel" voll und ganz auskosten darf. Diesen Grundsätzen hat die Hugo Haase A.-G. in ihrem Vergnügungspark sorgfältig Rechnung getragen, indem sie ihn zu den Mittwoch-Nachmittagen zu einem Kindergarten umgestaltete, in dem der Jugend Gelegenheit gegeben ist, sich nach Herzenslust auszutoben. Der Zeit entsprechend, finden natürlich auch patriotische Umzüge unter Musikbegleitung statt, bei denen die Kleinen, militärisch eingekleidet, unsere tapferen Feldgrauen wie auch den Feind darstellen. Beim Terrassen-Café werden unter Gewehr- und Geschützsalven Kampfspiele abgehalten und Schlachten geschlagen, bei denen es sogar ohne „Verwundete" nicht abgeht. Also: Auf in den „H-H-Park" in Stellingen!

„Hamburger Nachrichten", 14. 8. 1918.

Erlösung von allem heutigen **Erden-Elend**

durch ein neues, naturgemäßes Staatssystem, das allen Menschen ungeahntes Glück verbürgt.

Preis geh. M. 3.–.

Inhaltsauszug:

Der Weltkrieg — Fürsorge für die heimkehrenden Krieger — Grundzüge einer neuen Staatseinrichtung — Der Staat zahlt jedem Menschen ein ausreichendes Gehalt auf Lebenszeit — Nur täglich dreistündige Arbeitszeit für alle — Eine Weltverkehrssprache — Mehr Lebensfreuden für jung und alt — Ehe oder freie Liebe und Naturehe — Das Heiraten der Mädchen wird immer schwieriger — Mit Einführung der Naturehe wird es besser — Frauenemanzipation — Naturgemäße Kindererziehung. Vermeidung von Krankheit und Siechtum aller Art, und vieles andere mehr.

Buchanzeige (verkleinert) von F. E. Bilz, Verlag, Leipzig.

KLEINER BRIEFKASTEN

Freunde. Der Nachfolger des Herrn v. Kühlmann, Staatssekretär v. Hintze, hat, nach dem Telegramm des „B. T." vom 7. 9. 18, vor Repräsentanten der österreichischen Presse neben anderen Worten dieses Neue gesagt:

> Ebenso wie im Osten der Friede gekommen ist, so wird er auch im Westen kommen. Wenn es vielleicht auch noch einige Zeit dauern wird. Es können nicht immer Rosen blühen. Der Krieg ist kein Rosengarten, in dem man spazieren geht. Wenn man Rosen pflücken will, muß man auch einen Dornenstich gewärtigen. Ebenso braucht uns der Siegestaumel unseres Feindes nicht zu entmutigen. Sie wissen besser als ich, daß die Presse unserer Feinde weit mehr in dem Sinne entwickelt ist, als ihr Ziel ist, ihre Tätigkeit dem Staate und der Politik unterzuordnen. Wir in Deutschland und Österreich-Ungarn halten an einer freien Presse selbst unter dem Zwange des Krieges fest. Bei unseren Gegnern dagegen stehen die Journalisten unter der Kontrolle des Staates. Ein Zeitungsschreiber, der nicht die Regierungsstimme vertritt, wandert bei ihnen einfach ins Zuchthaus. Das aber widerstrebt unserer Auffassung. Solche Maßnahmen sind für andere Länder geeignet, aber nicht für uns Deutsche. Es ist besser, daß Regierung und Presse miteinander arbeiten. Wir wollen die öffentliche Meinung nicht knechten. Nur so verspricht die Politik einen Erfolg. Dies sage ich nicht, um Wohlwollen zu erringen, sondern es ist meine innerste Überzeugung.

Die ewige Wahrheit, daß der Krieg kein Rosengarten sei, schließt die beiden anderen ewigen Wahrheiten aus: daß Rosen nicht immer blühen könnten und daß keine Rose ohne Dornen. Ist der Krieg kein Garten der Rose, so blüht sie dort eben nie und gibt auch keine Pflückgelegenheit mit Dornenstichen. Wahrscheinlich hat der Tageblattjournalist den blühenden Vergleich aus Eigenem gedrahtet. Dagegen muß ich glauben, daß der Herr Staatssekretär v. Hintze geäußert habe: „Wir in Deutschland und Österreich-Ungarn halten an einer freien Presse selbst unter dem Zwange des Krieges fest. Bei unseren Gegnern dagegen stehen die Journalisten unter der Kontrolle des Staates. Ein Zeitungsschreiber, der nicht die Regierungsstimme vertritt, wandert bei ihnen einfach ins Zuchthaus. Das aber widerspricht unserer Auffassung. Solche Maßnahmen sind für andere Länder geeignet, aber nicht für uns Deutsche. Es ist besser, daß Regierung und Presse miteinander arbeiten. Wir wollen die öffentliche Meinung nicht knechten. Nur so verspricht die Politik einen Erfolg."
Dies zitiere ich, trotzdem ich es wenige Zeilen vorher zitiert habe; man kann nicht oft genug wiederholen, daß es innere Überzeugung eines deutschen Staatssekretärs ist, Deutschland und Österreich-Ungarn hätten eine freie Presse, die Gegner dagegen kontrollierte, geknechtete, vom Zuchthaus bedrohte Zeitungsschreiber. Nun, auch innere Überzeugungen müssen ja nicht immer richtig sein. Darüber, ob Hintzes innere Überzeugung, Deutschland besitze eine freie Presse, richtig ist, kann ich mich mit dem Herrn Staatssekretär gegenwärtig nicht unterhalten. Soweit sich aber die innere Überzeugung auf die „gegnerische" Presse bezieht, müßte der Herr Staatssekretär eigentlich wissen, daß Zeitungsschreiber Frankreichs, die nicht die Regierungsstimme vertreten, weder ins Zuchthaus noch ins Gefängnis noch in den Schützengraben wandern müssen, sondern meist frei bleiben und manchmal sogar (Clemenceau!) in die Regierung eintreten; daß kriegs- und regierungsfeindliche Zeitungsschreiber Englands (schon während der ersten fünf Monate dieser endlosen Zeit) in den sichtbarsten Zeitungen und Zeitschriften unbehelligt Aufsätze veröffentlichten, deren Schärfe nachzueifern deutsche Zeitungsschreiber doch mal versuchen sollten! Wenn aber Herr v. Hintze in einem Nebensatz die Freiheit, die er meint, deutet: „Es ist besser, daß Regierung und Presse miteinander arbeiten", — so ist das eine Ansicht, die alle Regierungen der Welt haben dürften und die mit dem Begriff von der freien öffentlichen Meinung, wie ich sie auffasse, nichts, gar nichts zu tun hat.

Uli. Herr Professor Schücking, Völkerrechtslehrer in Marburg, macht in einer Schrift „Internationale Rechtsgarantien" echt pazifistische Vorschläge:

> Die Staaten verpflichten sich sämtlich, in ihr nationales Strafgesetzbuch eine Bestimmung einzuführen, wonach beleidigende Äußerungen gegen fremde Völker oder Staaten in einer Druckschrift strafbar sind.
> Sollten die zuständigen Behörden es pflichtwidrig ablehnen, wegen solcher Preßvergehen auf den Antrag des betreffenden Staates bzw. seines diplomatischen Vertreters die Ver-

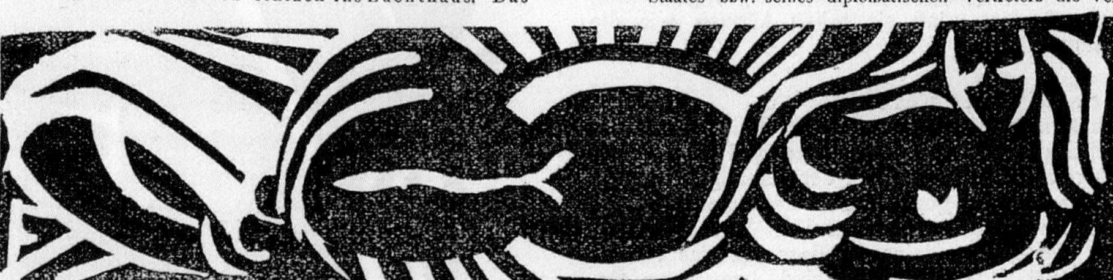

Otto Freundlich *Akt*

folgung einzuleiten, so kann dieser Staat eine Entscheidung der Cour de justice arbitrale im Haag darüber herbeiführen, ob in dem fraglichen Fall eine Strafverfolgung zu geschehen hat.
Außerdem legen die Staaten sich wechselseitig die Verpflichtung auf, daß sie tatsächliche Berichtigungen auf Antrag eines Staates in gewissen vorher festzusetzenden Presseorganen ihres Landes amtlich mitteilen wollen. Die Zufertigung dieser Berichtigung erfolgt im Streitfalle nach eingetretener Vorprüfung durch eine Haager Instanz an die einzelnen Regierungen. Die Berichtigungspflicht gilt auch im Kriege.

Herr Professor Schücking sagt ferner:

Eine besondere Gefahr für den Weltfrieden bildet ohne Zweifel die völkerverhetzende Tätigkeit zahlreicher Preßorgane. Auf zwei Wegen arbeiten sie, oft durch frivole Politiker oder sogar kapitalistische Interessenten, wie die Rüstungsindustriellen, gekauft, der Völkerverständigung entgegen. Einmal wird durch beschimpfende und beleidigende Äußerungen über fremde Völker und Staaten gegen diese planmäßig Stimmung gemacht, dann werden fortgesetzt falsche oder entstellte Nachrichten verbreitet, um bei der Regierung und dem Volk des einen Staates gegen den anderen zu wühlen. Nach den bitteren Erfahrungen dieses Weltkrieges gilt es, für die Zukunft nach beiden Richtungen hin vorzubeugen.

Hier haben wir einen Pazifisten in Reinkultur. Schaffet Schiedsgericht und ein erweitertes nationales Strafgesetzbuch — und der Friedensengel ist gegen Beunruhigung geschützt. Alles Heil kommt von der Willigkeit der Staaten: die Staaten verpflichten sich, fremde Staaten zu schützen, die Staaten müssen Berichtigungen amtlich mitteilen, die Staaten haben, die Staaten müssen — und wenn nicht, dann — Haag. Eiapopaia, was raschelt im Stroh? Nein! Herr Professor, das wird nicht wieder, dieses Ammenmärchen vom Haag und der Einsicht der Staaten. Anderes, Gültigeres muß und wird werden! Aber wenn ich Ihnen den Gefallen tue, Ihren Vorschlag zu diskutieren: welche „zahlreichen" Preßorgane meinen Sie? Die paar alldeutschen Papiere können von Ihnen doch nicht derartig überschätzt werden?! Wenn Sie aber auf die wirkungsvollsten Blätter anspielen, d. h. auf die im Volke verbreiteten, weshalb dann nicht Namen nennen? Und dann: worin unterschieden sich im August 1914 der „Vorwärts", das „Berliner Tageblatt" und alle demokratischen, pazifistischen Zeitungen von den Blättern der Kriegslustigen? In nichts! Oder doch: in der Beständigkeit, in der Männlichkeit, in der Ehrlichkeit! Lesen Sie die Nummern des Mosseblattes (oder der Ullsteinpapiere) aus dem ersten Monat dieser Zeit! Wie würdig wirkt, damit verglichen, etwa die alldeutsche „Post"! Die ist sich treu geblieben, die war nicht den 31. Juli für Tolstoi und den 1. August für Bernardi. Und, das Wesentliche!, ihre Wirkung auf Massen existiert gar nicht! — Also bitte: keine neuen nationalen Strafgesetzbücher gegen einzelne Blätter: die Presse als Geschäftsunternehmung ist überhaupt zu beseitigen, und damit wäre nur eine Friedensgarantie gegeben.

Liebe Nina. Ein anderer Professor, Dr. Josef Kohler, der sich professionell mit den Rechtswissenschaften auseinanderzusetzen hat, veröffentlicht den 18. August 1918 durch die Zeitung, was er zum Thema „Belgien als Pfand" zu denken beliebt. Der berühmte Herr Professor beginnt:

Als der Reichskanzler kürzlich von dem Pfandrecht an Belgien sprach, wußte jeder nur einigermaßen mit dem Völkerrecht Vertraute, wie dies zu verstehen ist und wie tief diese Idee im Rechte wurzelt; allein unter den Gegnern gibt es immerhin Leute, die entweder vom Völkerrecht keinen Begriff haben, oder sich so gebärden, als ob es kein Völkerrecht gäbe, oder ein Völkerrecht für sich zimmern wollen, ganz abgetrennt von aller geschichtlichen Grundlage und von allen ethischen Vorstellungen, auf denen das Völkerrecht schon seit Jahrhunderten beruht. Man will den Krieg und alle die Kriegsereignisse als eine Null betrachten! Es soll eine Null sein, was wir im Kriege unter unendlicher Fülle von Geist, Arbeit, Hingabe und Opfern erzielt haben!

Nach diesem Anlauf erwartete ich Manches. Meine Erwartungen wurden übertroffen:

Das Pfandrecht ist ein Begriff, der allerdings im bürgerlichen Rechte seine erste Quelle hat, der aber schon Jahrhunderte lang auch in das Recht der Völker übergegangen ist. Wie ein Recht des Eigentümers an seinem Grundstück, so besteht ein Recht des Staates öffentlich rechtlicher Art an dem Staatsterritorium; und wie neben dem Eigentum am Grundstück ein Pfandrecht bestehen kann, so können pfandrechtliche Erscheinungen auftreten im Verhältnis zwischen einem Staat und zwischen dem Territorium eines anderen Staates. Diese Erscheinungen haben im Völkerleben eine außerordentliche Rolle gespielt.

Dann, nach historischen Streifzügen, äußert sich Herr Kohler über Belgien (die Sperrungen im Text habe ich veranlaßt):

Unser Eigenrecht am besetzten Territorium benutzen wir zugleich als Pfand, d. h. als Druckmittel, um von dem Feinde die Bedingungen zu erlangen, die wir als sachgemäß und unseren Interessen wünschenswert erachten. Das ist unsere völkerrechtliche Befugnis; denn was wir durch Genie und Kraft in unsere Eroberungsgewalt gebracht haben, das dürfen wir völkerrechtlich verwenden, um den Feinden die Bedingungen aufzuerlegen, die uns als die richtigen erscheinen. Nicht, daß wir darob unsere Staatspflichten in dem besetzten Lande vernachlässigten: wir werden sie weiterhin erfüllen, aber wir bleiben hier als die Herren, bis man uns die geeigneten Friedensbedingungen gewährt.
Wollte man dies für unberechtigt halten, dann müßte man die ganze Lehre vom Völkerrecht und vom Kriege einfach umkrempeln. Man müßte etwa zu der Anschauung gelangen, daß die im Kriege erworbene Gewalt überhaupt keine rechtliche Gewalt wäre und daß die Benutzung dieser Gewalt gegen die Rechtsprechung verstieße, so daß alles nur dem vertragsmäßigen Belieben der Beteiligten oder etwa gar dem Plebiszit unterworfen wäre! Dann führt man eben überhaupt die Kriege für nichts, und alle kriegerischen Errungenschaften verschwinden wie eine Seifenblase! Man hat im Kriege lediglich das erzielt, daß ein paar Millionen Menschen das Leben verlieren, damit es nachher weiter gehe wie vorher!

Hier bitte ich gehorsamst um die Erlaubnis, eine Atempause machen zu dürfen! Auf welchem Stern lebt solche siebzigjährige Berühmtheit, daß sie im fünften Jahre des namenlosen Grauens noch ein Triumphlied auf die Eroberungsgewalt an-

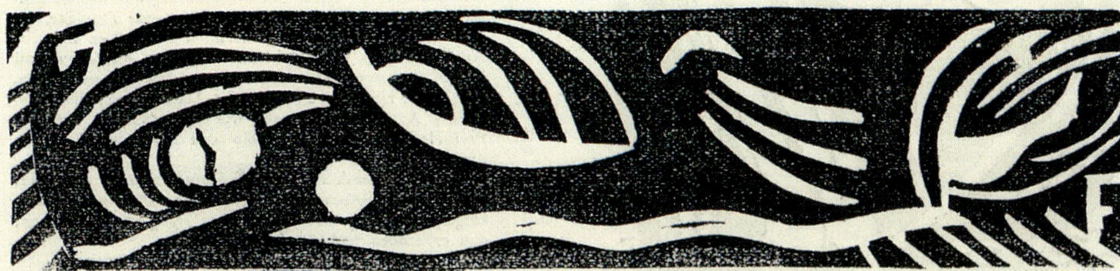

Otto Freundlich *Liegender Akt*

stimmt? Wenn heute mein Urgroßvater aus dem Grabe aufstehen würde, er könnte vor dem Telephon und der elektrischen Straßenbahn nicht die Furcht haben, die Herr Kohler vor der Umkremplung „der ganzen Lehre vom Völkerrecht und vom Kriege" hat. Aber diese Furcht, Herr Professor, wird die Lehre vom Völkerrecht und vom Kriege, die eine Irrlehre war, nicht vom Untergange retten können. Die Menschheit muß und wird zu der Anschauung kommen, daß die im Kriege erworbene Gewalt überhaupt keinen Rechtsanspruch sichern darf; die Menschheit wird, will sie sich nicht ausrotten, die Eroberungsgewalt (die ja nie ihre eigene Angelegenheit war!!!) verwerfen müssen, trotz allen Professoren.

Doch Herr Kohler rede weiter:

> Und doch ist es eben gerade das Wesen des Krieges, daß Herrschaft und Macht auch für das Recht maßgebend sind und daß das Recht sich der Machtstellung fügt, die der siegreiche Staat erworben hat. Betrachtet man den Krieg als ein Gottesurteil, so ist zu sagen, daß das waltende Schicksal uns diese Machtmittel in die Hände gelegt, unser Schwert geschärft und uns die Möglichkeit verschafft hat, durch Zurückhaltung von Gebieten dem Feinde die Bedingungen abzutrotzen, die ihm nicht genehm sind und die er sehr gern uns versagen wollte!

Das ist reine Rechtswissenschaft, liebe Nina.

> Und wenn ein belgischer Minister mit der Behauptung auftrat, daß der Gedanke eines Faustpfandes an Belgien etwas Verletzendes habe, so hat er damit nur gezeigt, daß er sich im Völkerrecht auch nicht einmal die ersten Grundlagen angeeignet hat.
>
> Besetztes Gebiet und Pfand sind Begriffe, die im Völkerrecht so lange eine Rolle spielen werden, als es Kriege gibt, und solange als es Menschen gibt, die in der Lage sind, die rechtlichen Erscheinungen zu konstruieren und juristisch zu kennzeichnen.

Soll ich nachzählen, wieviel deutsche Zeitungen die Wissenschaft des Professors Kohler zustimmend aus den im Kriegspresseamt bearbeiteten „D. K." nachgedruckt haben? Zwei Tage später — doch davon in der nächsten Notiz.

Hermann B. In der „Deutschen Gesellschaft 1914", jener Zeitgründung „zur Erhaltung des patriotischen Geistes von 1914", der die Herren Presber, Heinrich Mann, Reventlow, Wilhelm Herzog, Helfferich, Kammerherr v. Behr-Pinnow, Fendrich, Lensch, Südekum, Theodor Wolff, Rud. Mosse, Paul Cassirer, Ullstein, S. Fischer, Herbert Eulenberg und viele andere verdiente Deutsche als Mitglieder zugehören, hat der Staatssekretär des Kolonialamts, Dr. Solf, den 20. August 1918 eine Rede vorgelesen, die der unvermeidliche „Vorwärts" „klug" und „trefflich stilisiert" nennt, aus der das „Berliner Tageblatt" die „Sprache der praktischen Vernunft" herausklingen hört, die aber von nicht so genügsamen Hörern einfach als die Kandidatenansprache eines der nächsten deutschen Reichskanzler gewertet werden wird. Herr Dr. Solf hat nichts gesagt, was uns überraschen, nichts, was nicht auch Herr Hertling gesagt haben könnte. Ein paar unverbindliche Redensarten, einige Klischeesätze aus dem Phrasenarsenal unserer Sonntagspazifisten, eine sparsame Auswahl selbstverständlicher Wahrheiten, — so wenig genügt heute, um unsere Demokraten ins Entzücken zu treiben. Herr Solf redet also:

> Balfour behauptet, das intellektuelle Deutschland sei von einer unmoralischen Gewaltlehre beherrscht. Meine Herren, hüben und drüben gibt es Chauvinisten und Jingos. Hüben und drüben gibt es Leute, die das Ewig-Gestrige anbeten und mit Angst und Unverstand den herannahenden Morgen einer neuen Zeit erwarten.

Es geschehen merkwürdige Dinge unter der Sonne! Der Leser vergleiche, welche Stellen aus Kohlers Aufsatz zufällig auf der Spalte nebenan Raum gefunden haben!

> Vor dem Kriege bildeten diese Leute bei uns eine kleine Gruppe, ohne Geltung in der Politik und ohne Einfluß auf die Regierung, die sie dauernd bekämpften. Während des Krieges ist ihre Zahl in der Tat gewachsen, nicht etwa, weil das Streben nach deutscher Vorherrschaft in der Welt bei uns tiefer Wurzel geschlagen hat, sondern weil sie Zuzug bekamen aus weiten Kreisen besonnener und besorgter Patrioten. Unter ihnen sind viele, die vor dem Kriege die Ideale der Völkerverständigung, des guten Willens und des Fairplay in den internationalen Beziehungen hochhielten, deren politische Glaubenslehre aber durch die Erfahrungen des Krieges zusammengebrochen ist.

Daß unserer Intellektuellen „politische Glaubenslehre" nicht erst „durch die Erfahrungen dieses Krieges zusammengebrochen" ist, läßt sich leichter als wahr erweisen, als die Behauptung, vor dem Kriege bildeten „diese Leute" (die Chauvinisten) bei uns eine kleine Gruppe, ohne Geltung in der Politik und ohne Einfluß auf die Regierung, die sie dauernd bekämpften. Aber unsere Scheidemänner fühlen sich geschmeichelt und rufen mit Solf:

> „Wer trägt die Schuld? Niemand anders als die Gesinnung unserer Feinde. Dieselbe Gesinnung, die den großen Gedanken des Völkerbundes durch die gleichzeitige Forderung des Handelskrieges gegen Deutschland entwertet und zu einer Spottgeburt gemacht hat. ‚Können wir euch nicht militärisch vernichten, so vernichten wir euch durch den Völkerbund.'"

Herr Dr. Solf gibt den letzten Satz in Gänsefüßchen; darf man fragen, wen er da wörtlich zitiert? Ich bin diesem Satz in keiner Kundgebung begegnet. Herr Dr. Solf hat auch den Brest-Litowsker Frieden gegen Rußland gepriesen (der jetzt neu bearbeitet worden ist):

> Die zweite Anklage Balfours geht gegen unsere Ostpolitik.
>
> Ich antworte ihm darauf: Der Brest-Litowsker Frieden kam zustande auf Grund der einen großen Übereinstimmung zwischen der russischen und der deutschen Regierung, daß die jahrhundertelang unterdrückten Fremdvölker Rußlands das von ihnen erstrebte nationale Eigendasein erhalten sollten. Diese Übereinstimmung über das Schicksal der Randvölker ist eine weltbedeutende Tatsache, die sich aus der Geschichte nicht mehr auslöschen läßt. Nicht über das Ziel, wohl aber über die Methoden und Wege, die zum Eigendasein der Völker führen sollten, gingen die russische und deutsche Auffassung auseinander. Unsere Auffassung ist nach wie vor, daß der Weg zur Freiheit nicht über Anarchie und Massenmord führen darf. . . .
>
> Der Brest-Litowsker Frieden ist ein Rahmen; das Bild, das darin entstehen wird, ist erst in seinen ersten Anfängen entworfen. Die deutsche Regierung ist entschlossen, den erbetenen und gegebenen
>
> Schutz nicht zu einer gewaltsamen Annexion zu mißbrauchen,
>
> sondern den bisher unterdrückten Völkern den Weg zur Freiheit, Ordnung und gegenseitigen Duldung zu öffnen.

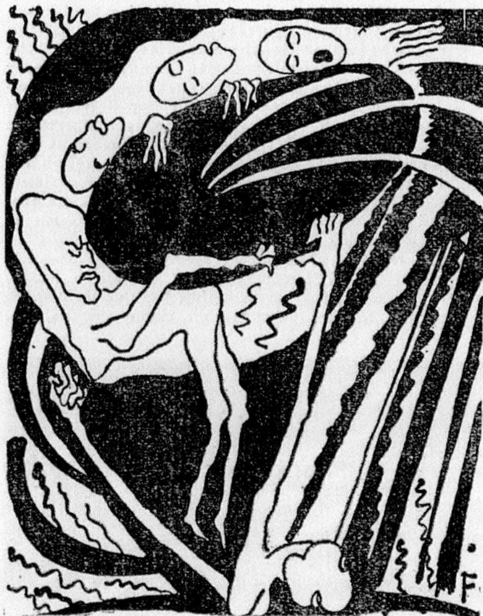

Otto Freundlich *Zeichnung*

Daß die Verhandlungen von Brest-Litowsk begannen, nachdem die russische Revolution den „jahrhundertelang unterdrückten Fremdvölkern Rußlands" das Selbstbestimmungsrecht gesichert hatte, ist aus der „trefflich stilisierten" Rede nicht klar zu erkennen. Trotz dem Stil weiß ich ferner nicht, ob die russischen Revolutionäre in Brest-Litowsk die Auffassung hatten, über „Anarchie und Massenmord" zur Freiheit zu wollen. Nach den Worten Solfs muß es aber so gewesen sein! Und das Echo aus dem Scheidemannpapier am 21. August?

> Aber da kommt der Staatssekretär auf Brest-Litowsk zu sprechen und man muß wieder aufrichtig die Geschicklichkeit bewundern, mit der er das tut.

Herr Dr. Solf, Reichkolonialamtes Staatsekretär, hat, natürlich, auch über die Kolonien gesprochen. Dabei hat er dann diese Fragen an den englischen Staatssekretär Balfour gerichtet:

> Hat er sich bei seinen Kollegen vom englischen Kolonialamt erkundigt, was es bedeutet, mit Eingeborenen gegen Eingeborene Krieg zu führen? Hat er eine Ahnung von dem
> unermeßlichen Schaden für die koloniale Sendung aller Kulturvölker,
> der daraus entstehen muß, daß man Schwarze im Kampf gegen Weiße verwendet und nach Europa bringt? . . . Hat er vergessen, daß Deutschland die einzige kriegführende Macht ist, die die
> Abschaffung des Militarismus in Afrika
> ausdrücklich unter ihre Kriegsziele aufgenommen hat?

Aber die „Abschaffung des Militarismus in Afrika" ist ja wohl nur zu beschließen durch die Abschaffung des Militarismus überhaupt? Und sind Weiße gegen Weiße nicht „Eingeborene gegen Eingeborene?"

Aus dem Schluß der Solfschen Verlesung diese Sätze:

> Meine Herren, in allen Ländern gibt es heute Gruppen und Menschen, die man als
> Zentren des europäischen Gewissens
> bezeichnen kann. Denken Sie nicht an einzelne Namen, weder bei uns, noch im Feindesland. In diesen Zentren regt sich so etwas wie eine Erkenntnis, daß der Weg ins Freie nur gefunden werden kann, wenn die kriegführenden Nationen zu dem Bewußtsein ihrer gemeinsamen Aufgaben zurückerwachen.
> Wie vermeiden wir künftige Kriege? Wie erzielen wir die Wirksamkeit internationaler Abmachungen auch bei einem neuen Kriege? Wie stellen wir die Nichtkombattanten sicher? Wie ersparen wir es den neutralen Staaten in Zukunft, daß sie für ihre Friedfertigkeit büßen müssen? Wie schützen wir nationale Minderheiten? Wie regeln wir unsere gemeinsame Ehrenpflicht gegenüber den minderjährigen Rassen dieser Welt?
> Meine Herren, das sind alles brennende Menschheitsfragen. Hinter ihnen steht die Stimmung von Millionen, hinter ihnen steht unsägliches Leid, stehen unerhörte Erlebnisse.

Die Antworten auf diese brennenden Menschheitsfragen sind vor dem Ausbruch dieser Zeit dagewesen, Herr Staatssekretär Dr. Solf. Wissen Sie, womit die Antworten damals beantwortet wurden?

Nachdem Herr Dr. Solf die Begeisterung der fürs Demokratische engagierten Schreiber in Bewegung gebracht hatte, nahm, den 22. August, der Prinz von Baden sich ihrer an. Wieder rief uns Fettdruck zu: „Achtung vor der Menschenwürde und der persönlichen Freiheit des Einzelnen", „Zusammenarbeit der Völker", und zwischendurch, nicht fett hervorgehoben:

> Noch ist Krieg. In England, Frankreich und Amerika hebt schamloser denn je der Vernichtungswille sein Haupt. Ihre alten, längst zusammengebrochenen Illusionen tauchen wieder auf. Sie werden wieder zusammenbrechen. Wir haben es nicht nötig, uns zur Einigkeit zu ermahnen. Jede Handlung, jede Rede der feindlichen Regierungen ruft uns zu: Schließt die Reihen!

Und die sogenannte Deutsche Friedensgesellschaft hat, wie sie mir soeben mitteilt, sowohl Herrn Dr. Solf wie dem Prinzen Max ihre Zustimmung ausgesprochen.

L. R. Die Petersburger Telegraphen-Agentur, Filiale Berlin, also das Sprachrohr der Joffe-Bolschewisten, sendet diese Meldungen in die Welt:

Moskau, 29. August (P. T.-A.). Das Organ der Narodniki-Kommunisten teilt mit, daß aus dem Kremlgefängnis die linken Sozialrevolutionäre Mstislawsky und Ismailowitsch freigelassen worden sind. Spiridonowa und Sablin sind im Gefängnis belassen worden.

Petersburg, 28. August (P. T.-A.). Die außerordentliche Kommission zum Kampfe gegen die Gegenrevolution beschloß 20 Mann standrechtlich erschießen zu lassen.

In der „Voss. Ztg." vom 1. September 1918 wird gedruckt:

Moskau, 31. August. Das Volkskommissariat hat bekannt gegeben, daß 5000 verhaftete Sozialrevolutionäre zum Tode verurteilt worden sind. Das Urteil wird jedoch nur dann vollstreckt, wenn die sozialrevolutionäre Partei neue Putschversuche gegen die Sowjetregierung unternimmt.

Und diese P. T.-A., die solches verbreitet, verbreitet auch dieses:

Moskau, 26. August (P. T.-A.). Die Presse der Ententeländer ist Tag für Tag voll von Lügen und Verleumdungen gegen das revolutionäre Rußland und gegen die Arbeiter- und Bauernsowjets.

Aber können denn auch die tollsten Lügen und Verleumdungen schärfer gegen die Leninisten wirken als die trockenen Originaldepeschen der P. T.-A.?

Renate. Ein Journalist des „Berliner Tageblatts" hatte das Glück und die hohe Ehre, von dem ukrainischen Ministerpräsidenten Lysogub eine Unterredung gewährt zu erhalten. Ein Bruchstück:

> Auf die Frage nach dem Parteileben in der Ukraine, von dem man hierzulande nicht viel wisse, antwortete der Ministerpräsident, daß es ganz frei und durch keinerlei Kautelen eingeschränkt sei. Sofern freilich bemerkt würde, daß sich aufrührerische Gruppen bildeten, die direkt gegen die Regierung agitieren und ihre Stellung zu untergraben suchten, müsse man sich zur Wehr setzen und ihre Zusammenkünfte verbieten. Doch herrsche im Reiche nicht nur absolute Meinungsfreiheit, sondern auch uneingeschränktes Versammlungsrecht.

Da rede nun noch einer, die Ukraine sei nicht befreit. Wer nicht gegen die Regierung agitiert, dem ist die Freiheit unbeschränkt, für die Regierung zu wirken.

Lieber Leser, wo du ihn anpackst, ist er interessant, der

Vorwärts-[illegible]

Freitag, den 30. August 1918, schreit das „Stampferblatt":

> Kaisertreue Arbeit.
> Ein neues Verleumder-Flugblatt.
> Nachdem die „Kaisertreuen" jüngst behauptet hatten, die Sozialdemokratie sei von Amerika bezahlt, verkünden sie jetzt in einem neuen Flugblatt, daß der „Vorwärts" von der deutschen Regierung gekauft sei. Es wird darin gesagt:
> „Die sozialdemokratische ‚Münchener Post' spricht vom kaisertreuen Skandal. Unser Wirken ist kein Skandal, aber ein Skandal ist es, daß die oben genannten Zeitungen und ihr Troß unsere ehrliche Arbeit derart begeifern, und ein noch viel größerer Skandal ist es, daß diese Blätter von der Regierung bezahlt werden. Daß die ‚Norddeutsche Allgemeine Zeitung' ohne die Staatsunterstützung keine drei Tage erscheinen könnte, das weiß jedermann. Daß aber der ‚Vorwärts' jährlich von der Regierung eine viertel bis eine halbe Million erhält und das ‚Berliner Tageblatt' gar $2^1/_4$ Millionen — nach amtlichen Quellen —, das wissen die wenigsten. Rudolf Mosse erhält für seine Zeitungen insgesamt vom Reich jährlich $3^3/_4$ Millionen! Seit Beginn des Weltkrieges 15 Millionen!"
> Diese blödsinnige Verleumdung ist bekanntlich schon einmal von einem gewissen Dr. Hopfen verbreitet worden. Die Vereinigung Großstädtischer Zeitungsverleger hat daraufhin festgestellt, daß es sich um die teilweise Rückvergütung der Papierpreissteigerung handelt, die allen Zeitungen ohne Unterschied der Richtungen, den ‚unabhängigen' ebensogut wie den alldeutschen, nach Maßgabe ihres Papierverbrauchs zusteht. Mit seinen (übrigens willkürlich gegriffenen) Zahlen will aber der ‚Bund der Kaisertreuen' den Anschein erregen, als ob ‚Vorwärts' und ‚Berliner Tageblatt' von der Regierung irgendwelche Extravergütung erhielten."

Das will er sicherlich gar nicht. Aber vielleicht müßte man erst mal versuchen, auch der AKTION jene „teilweise Rückvergütung der Papierpreissteigerung" zu zahlen, die, nach dem revolutionären „Vorwärts", allen Zeitungen zusteht, um mir begreiflich zu machen, daß die Kaisertreuen tatsächlich „verleumden", wenn sie Tatsachen feststellen, die weder vom „Tageblatt" noch vom „Vorwärts" bestritten werden können. Denn so simpel, wie der herzigreine „Vorwärts" die Entrüstung deichselt, ist die Sache nicht! Schließlich werden der xfache Millionär Mosse und das streng kapitalistisch rechnende Unternehmen „Vorwärts" wissen, daß diese „Rückvergütung" („Rückvergütung"? hat der Staat von Mosse zu viel erhalten?) nicht aus überfüllten Reichssäckeln erfolgt; schließlich könnte der auf Proletarier spekulierende „Vorwärts" sich sagen, es gäbe heut andere Wunden zu heilen als den verletzten Profit „kriegswichtiger" Zeitungen. Wenn es als „Verleumdung" verrufen ist, die Wahrheit auszusprechen, dann will ich dem „Vorwärts" gegenüber gern als „Verleumder" gelten. Wer aber nicht als Beleidigung empfindet, die „Rückvergütung" angeboten zu erhalten, wer sie jahraus, jahrein nimmt, der wird mir schon erlauben müssen, daß ich feixe, wenn er die Mitteilung, er habe genommen, eine Beschimpfung nennt.

Heute, den 3. September, orakelt irgendein Redaktionshelfer über den Terror und sagt dann:

> Die Untersuchung wird lehren, welche Motive den Tätern die Waffe in die Hand gedrückt haben. Die Vermutung liegt nahe, daß das Gefühl nationaler Demütigung durch den Brester Frieden, seine weitherzige Auslegung seitens Deutschland und die eben geschlossenen Zusatzverträge die Springfeder der unheilvollen Entschlüsse gewesen ist. Wie die Anschläge auf Eichhorn und Mirbach die Vertreter Deutschlands traf, so hätten die neuen Attentate Männer vernichten sollen, die der Nationalismus des Verrats des eigenen Volkes an Deutschland zeiht.
>
> Eine unbegreifliche Torheit. Lenin war nur in der Phantasie der Entente das willige Werkzeug, der feile Agent Deutschlands. Er ist durch feindliches Gebiet in seine Heimat gefahren und hat den Brester Frieden geschlossen. Das ist wahr. Aber nicht minder wahr ist, daß er die proletarische Revolution nach Deutschland tragen und die deutsche Regierung mit der schlimmsten Gefahr bedrohen wollte. . . .
>
> Wie immer man über die praktischen Möglichkeiten dieser Theorie denken mag, sicher ist, daß sie einen großen Zug hat, und, mag sie auch falsch sein, sich doch vorteilhaft von dem kläglichen Fortschreiten und Fortwursteln der gelernten Diplomaten unterscheidet. (Nanu? Palastrevolution gegen Scheidemann?)
>
> Die deutsche Sozialdemokratie lehnt die Leninschen Gedanken ab. Sie hat nicht den Mut, das eigene Land dem Belieben des Siegers in Hoffnung auf eine Revolution im siegreichen Staat oder Staatenbund preiszugeben. . . .

Und so weiter. Auf der Spalte nebenan heißt es

> Branting dementiert.
>
> Wie die „Wiener Arbeiterzeitung" mitteilt, hat Branting nach seiner Rückkehr Erklärungen des Inhalts abgegeben, daß er die am meisten beanstandeten Äußerungen gar nicht getan habe.

Welche Äußerungen Branting nicht getan haben will, ob die gegen den „Vorwärts" oder andere, die Mitteilung der „Wiener Arbeiterzeitung" läßt das nicht erkennen. Dem „Vorwärts" aber genügt die Notiz, um im üblichen Jargon loszuhetzen:

> Diese sind danach das Phantasieprodukt gewissenloser Journalisten und ein neuer Beweis der von den offiziösen Entente-Nachrichtenbureaus systematisch betriebenen internationalen Verhetzungsarbeit. Ein Beweis, der Branting in seiner Ententefreundschaft nachdenklich stimmen könnte.
>
> Wir können im Augenblick nicht feststellen, ob sich das Dementi Brantings auf alle oder nur auf einige hier bekannt gewordenen Äußerungen bezieht. Jedenfalls bleibt die Tatsache seiner Reise an die französische Westfront bestehen, die selbst den Tadel eines so zurückhaltenden Beurteilers wie des Genossen Troelstra gefunden hat.

Weshalb sollte Branting nicht reisen, wo doch diesseits auch Herr Scheidemann gereist ist und Herr Genosse Fendrich?

Den 5. September lese ich im „Vorwärts" diese Selbstverständlichkeiten:

> Ein (internationaler [F. P.]) Sozialdemokrat ist gewohnt, ein Flugblatt, das ihm in die Hände fällt, nicht nur auf seinen Inhalt zu lesen, sondern auch zu fragen: Wer steckt dahinter, und was wird damit bezweckt? Bei Aufrufen, die von Feindesseite kommen, wird er sich ohne weiteres sagen, daß ihr Zweck kein lauterer ist, daß ihre Verbreitung nicht im Interesse Deutschlands oder des deutschen Volkes, sondern im Interesse der feindlichen Kriegführung geschieht. Mit der Durchschauung dieses Zweckes ist auch der Inhalt für ihn erledigt. Er wird weder fragen, ob das Gesagte an sich wahr oder falsch ist, sondern er wird es in seinen Erwägungen außer acht lassen, weil es nicht aufrichtig gemeint ist. Man behandelt derartige Flugblätter etwa wie anonyme Briefe, die man in den Papierkorb wirft, ganz gleichgültig, ob ihr Inhalt wahr oder falsch ist. Denn es ist natürlich möglich, daß sich die feindliche Propaganda hier und da auch an sich richtiger Gedanken zu ihren Zwecken bedient . . .

Auch der Feuilletonteil des „Vorwärts" ist nicht ohne. Da hat irgendwo irgendein Robuster von seinen Experimenten mit kleinen Stubenfliegen erzählt. Der „Vorwärts", dem die Stichmarke naheging, greift die Erzählung auf:

> — Die rotblinde Fliege. Nach einer Beobachtung ist die kleine Stubenfliege völlig rotblind. In einem Dunkelzimmer, das von einer dunklen Rubinglasbirne erhellt wurde, konnten die Fliegen den sich nähernden Finger des Beobachters oder dessen Schatten nie bemerken, sondern ließen sich zerdrücken. . . .

Wie gemütvoll! Aber auch: wie unbedacht vom „Vorwärts"-Redakteur, dies zu drucken! In der Dunkelkammer der Zeit steckend, reagiert etwa der Scheidemann auf Rot? Er wird den sich nähernden Finger des Beobachters oder dessen Schatten nie bemerken, sondern sich hochbeglückt zerdrücken lassen.

J. M. Herr Parvus-Helphand scheint endlich zu ahnen, daß sein kriegswichtiger Dr. Lensch doch nicht die rechte Zugnummer der „Glocke" ist. Eine Zugnummer aber braucht diese hinreichend belanglose Zeitschrift, und da hat Herr Parvus sich jetzt einen Antisemiten aus Wien verschrieben (oder er ist Wiener Antisemit geworden, was dem Verwandlungskünstler nicht unähnlich sein würde). In Heft 23 tritt die neue Attraktion zum ersten Male auf und wird, wie jene maskierte Löwendompteuse, als X annonciert. „Österreichischer Katzenjammer" betitelt sich die erste Darbietung, aus der ich einen Prachtsatz wiedergeben will:

> „. . . Der Bolschewistenwahn wühlt unter einer Arbeiterschaft, deren politische Bildung so dünn ist, daß sie alle theoretischen Diskussionen, fast wie in Rußland, einer kleinen Gruppe meist jüdischer Rabulisten überliefert, während aus dem deutsch-österreichischen Proletariat selbst fast keine selbständige Begabung erwachsen ist."

Es hat eine Zeit gegeben (es war Helphands scheinrevolutionäre Vergangenheit), da wühlte der russisch-jüdische Rabulist Parvus (meist vom Ausland aus) unter der Arbeiterschaft Rußlands, deren politische Bildung „so dünn" war, daß sie alle Phrasen des Parvus ernst nahm.

Renate. Beim Durchblättern gesammelter Zeitdokumente springt eine Titelüberschrift fett hervor:

„Kinder werden aufs Land gebracht." Der Lokalreporter, der die Ausreise fürs „B. T." zu schildern hatte, muß wohl ein Kriegsreporter sein:

Die vom Vaterländischen Frauenverein für den Kreis Insterburg bestimmten 539 Berliner Kinder, Knaben und Mädchen, traten gestern nachmittag ihre Ausreise an. Versammlungsort war der Schulhof der Gemeindeschule in der Langen Straße. Die Lehrerschaft, Stadtschulrat Wacke an der Spitze, hielt die letzte Musterung ab. Die einzelnen Gruppen sammelten sich um ihre Fahne. . . Auf das Abmarschzeichen setzten sich die Kinder mit Gesang in Marsch nach dem Bahnhof.

So das „Tageblatt" vom 28. Mai. Anders machen wir's nicht. Und da es noch immer Eltern gibt, die das Ungeheuerliche begehen: der Zeitung die Kinderseele auszuliefern, so ist anzunehmen, daß der Abreisebericht in den Kreis Insterburg drang.

K. Z. Die Pressenotizen, denen Sie begegnen, sind meist Waschzettel, die der Herr v. Weber selbst verfaßte. „Das Heft erfreut wie seine Vorgänger durch seinen frischen und offenen Ton, geißelt Lauheiten und Schiefheiten, bringt witzige Beiträge vom Tage" — das hat keine Zeitung, das hat der Weber geschrieben. Daß dieser Weber allmählich vom Zeitgemäßen abzuschwenken scheint, darf Sie nicht irre machen: seine mit besonderem Hinweis der Presse anempfohlenen Stilübungen: „Der Feind im Lande", „Europäertum im Kriege" (mit dem Untertitel „Absage an literarische und Künstler-Kreise, die auch in dieser Zeit den Internationalismus pflegen") zeigen den „Zwiebelfisch" in bengalischer Beleuchtung. Also, bitte, nicht mehr darüber! Sie haben ja in München eine saubere, mutige, gut von Karl Kraus beeinflußte Zeitschrift „Der Ziegelbrenner", die ich Ihnen sehr empfehlen kann.

Anatole. Durch die deutschen Zeitungen ging folgende Nachricht:

> Einer Einladung der „Concordia" und der Deutsch-Österreichischen Schriftstellergenossenschaft Folge leistend, werden reichsdeutsche Pressevertreter aus Berlin, Dresden, Frankfurt, Hamburg, Köln, Königsberg und München zu einem Besuche nach Wien kommen.

Die Einladung trug das Motto „In der Heimat da gibt's ein Wiedersehen", doch waren auch Nichtwiener als Reichsdeutsche zugelassen. Leider war die Leitung des Festes nicht Karl Kraus übertragen worden, der die Stefan Großmann, Stampfer usw. würdig empfangen haben würde.

E. T. In einer „Gegenerklärung", die Herr Mühsam im April 1918 drucken ließ und die ich jetzt, im September 1918, zugesandt erhalte (Rudolf Großmann-Wien hatte unnötigerweise den Ton beanstandet, den der beliebte Anarchist mir gegenüber riskierte) . . in dieser Gegenerklärung lügt Herr Mühsam aufs neue, ich hätte hier als Ganzes ausgegeben, was ich als Bruchteil aus seiner berühmten Erklärung zitierte. Herr Mühsam lügt das dreist in die Welt hinaus, obwohl er weiß, daß jeder Leser meiner Glossen ihn auslachen muß. Doch nun zum Erfolg der Erklärung. In den Augusttagen 1914 war in den verschiedensten deutschen Blättern zu lesen:

> „Wie sehr alle Kreise ohne Unterschied der Parteirichtung das gemeinsame Schicksal aneinanderkettet, beweist folgende Erklärung des bekannten Anarchisten und Weltfriedensapostels Erich Mühsam, der soeben das Erscheinen seiner Zeitschrift „Kain" sistiert, an seine Leser:
>
> „Die über Länder und Völker hereinbrechende Katastrophe ist nicht mehr aufzuhalten. In diesem Augenblicke wäre es müßiges Tun, Kritik zu üben oder Schuld auszuteilen. Die Ereignisse nehmen mir, der ich um der Menschlichkeit willen meine Zeitschrift geschaffen habe, die Feder aus der Hand. Die Leser, die in vierzig Monaten mein Wollen erkannt haben, werden meine Stellung verstehen und billigen. In dieser Stunde, wo es um das Schicksal aller geht, gibt es nichts Wesentliches und nichts, was eine Zeitschrift für Menschlichkeit angehen könnte. Deshalb habe ich mich entschlossen, die Herausgabe des „Kain" während der Dauer des Kriegszustandes zu unterbrechen. Nachher werde ich wieder auf dem Plane sein, um die Wege zu Frieden und Glück suchen zu helfen. Möge es bald sein. Vorerst ruhe im Lande aller Zwist. Das Grundsätzliche meiner Überzeugungen wird durch die gegenwärtigen Ereignisse nicht berührt. Aber ich weiß mich mit allen Deutschen einig in dem Wunsche, daß es gelingen werde, die fremden Horden von unseren Kindern und Frauen, von unseren Städten und Äckern fernzuhalten."

Auch dieser Jubel über die Entschließung des bekannten Weltfriedensapostels (der nachher, wie die Lissauer, Klabund, Fulda, wieder „auf dem Plane" sein wird), gab dessen „Erklärung" nicht ungekürzt. War aber Wesentliches weggeblieben? Herr Mühsam hatte vor dem Satz: „In dieser Stunde usw." noch offenbart: ihm bliebe nur die Wahl, ganz zu schweigen oder zu sagen, „was jetzt niemandem frommt" und was unter dem Ausnahmerecht seine persönliche Sicherheit gefährden könne (!); ein Drittes sei unmöglich, da Herr Mühsam seine Überzeugung nicht verleugnen noch frisieren könne; auch den Ausweg, belanglose Kleinigkeiten zu glossieren oder sich auf kunstkritische Betrachtungen zu beschränken, verschmähe er, Mühsam. Nach diesen (von den erfreuten Blättern zu Recht als nebensächlich gestrichenen) Offenbarungen schwieg der Erklärer nicht, noch sagte er „was niemandem frommte", sondern es folgte der Satz: „In dieser Stunde, wo es um das Schicksal aller geht, gibt es außerdem nichts Wesentliches usw." und schließlich, — was den Zeitungen sehr wohl frommte —, die von mir gesperrt zitierten Worte. Ist deren reine Wirkung durch die Kürzungen irgendwie beeinträchtigt worden? Nur Herr Autor Mühsam wird das behaupten.

E. E. Die AKTION kommt mitunter kuriosen Leuten in die Hand! Es ist doch wahrlich nicht meine Erfindung, wenn ich die Notizen des Kleinen Briefkasten mit Adressen versehe. Überdies ist für Fremde in jedem Inhaltsverzeichnis ausdrücklich F. P. als der Verfasser der Notizen genannt. Tut nichts! Immer wieder schreiben Diskussionslustige gegen F. B. oder H. L. usw., selbst gegen Nina werden erhebliche Klagen geführt. Und alle Protestler (oder auch Beifallspender) warten mit der bitteren Frage auf: „Weshalb verschweigen Sie Ihren Namen?" E. E. (auch einer der Kuriosen) wird, trotz diesen Zeilen, nun glauben, diese Notiz habe ein gewisser E. E. geschrieben . . .

B. B. Für die Oktober-Ausstellung der AKTION bestimmte Werke (Gemälde, Graphik) müssen den 28. d. M. in den Ausstellungsräumen sein. Nur Mitarbeiter sind zugelassen!

DER BÜTTENAUSGABE DIESES HEFTES liegt bei: eine Originalgraphik Otto Freundlichs, vom Künstler numeriert und signiert. Diese Beilage gelangt nicht in den Handel.

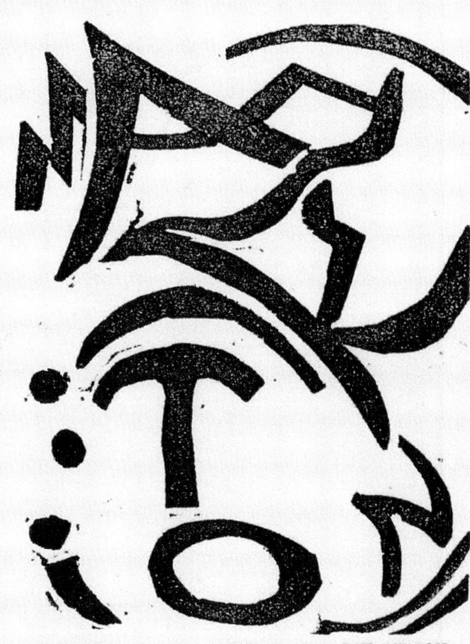

Otto Freundlich *Widmungsblatt DIE AKTION*

Large Head, 1912
HvW 63
Plaster
Lost

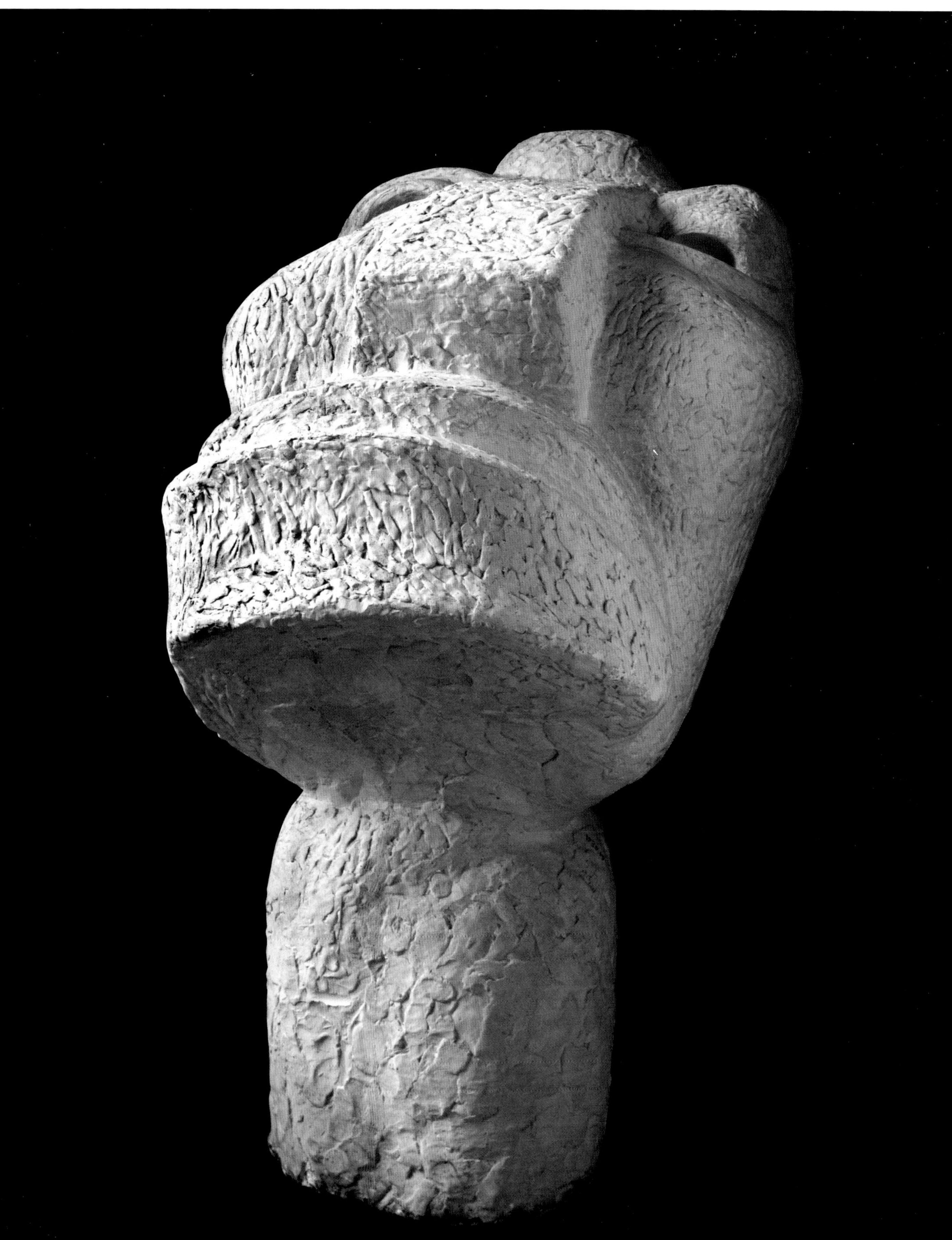

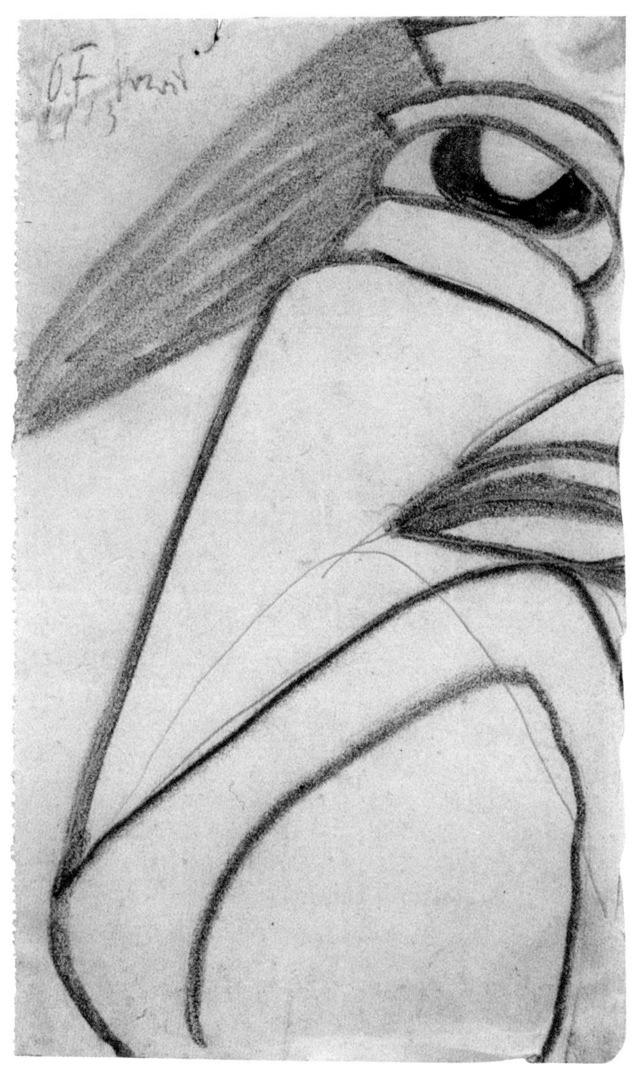

Protruding Figure II
(Study of Head), 1913
HvW 267
Pencil on paper

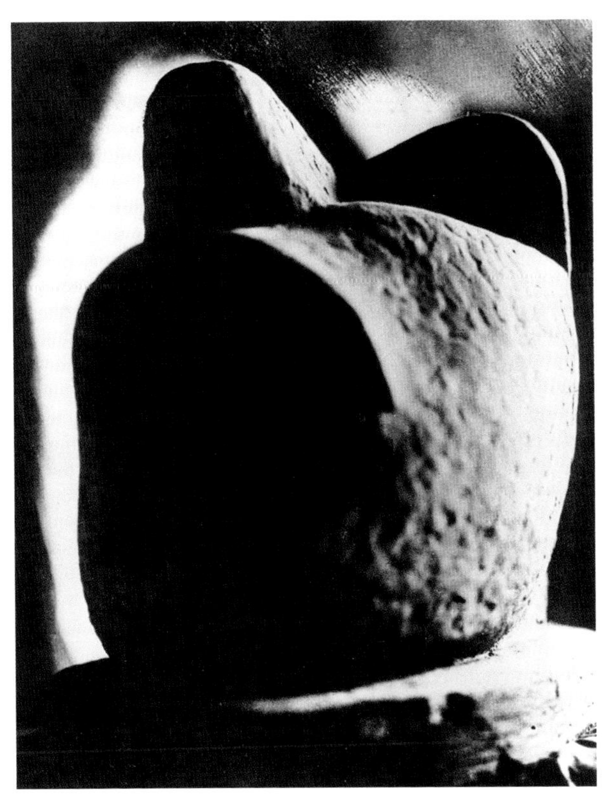

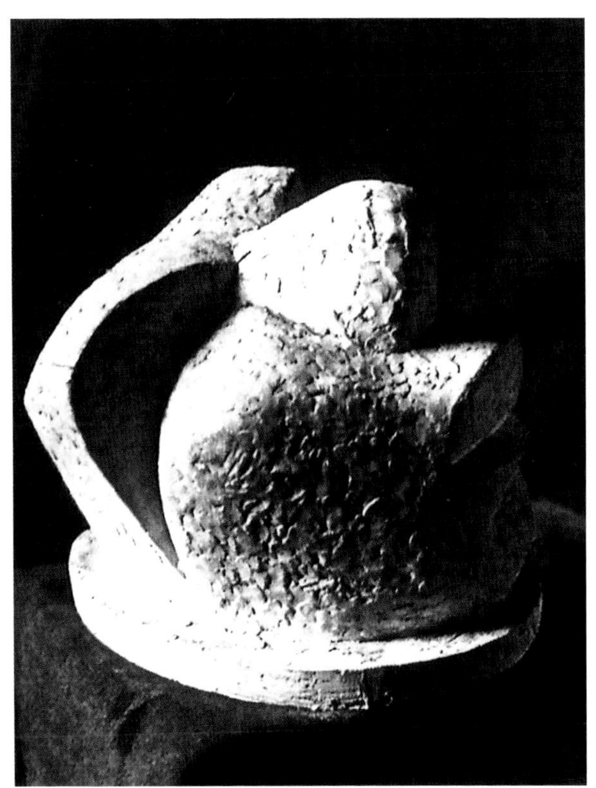

Head, ca. 1915/1922
Front and side view
Plaster
Lost

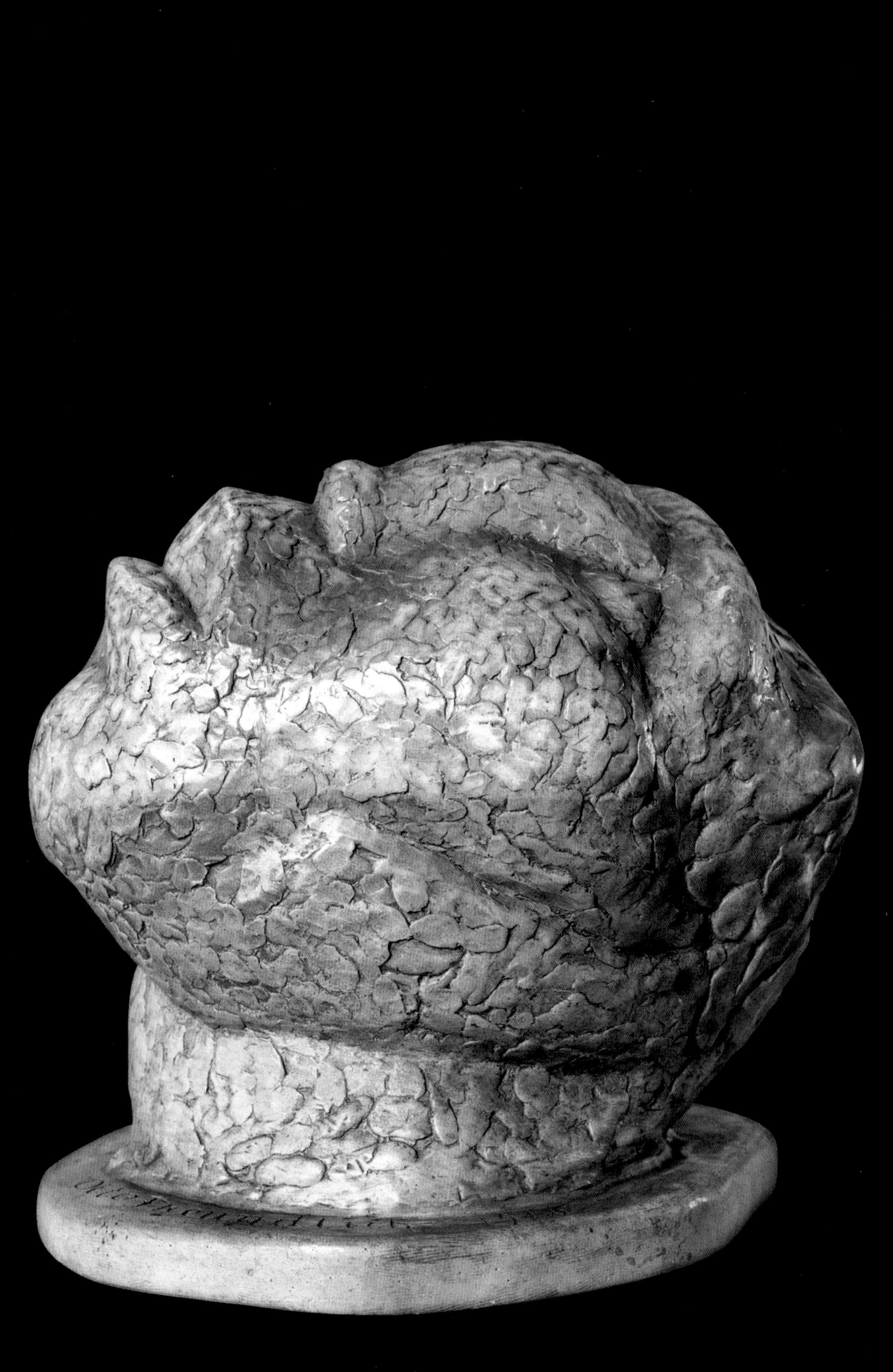

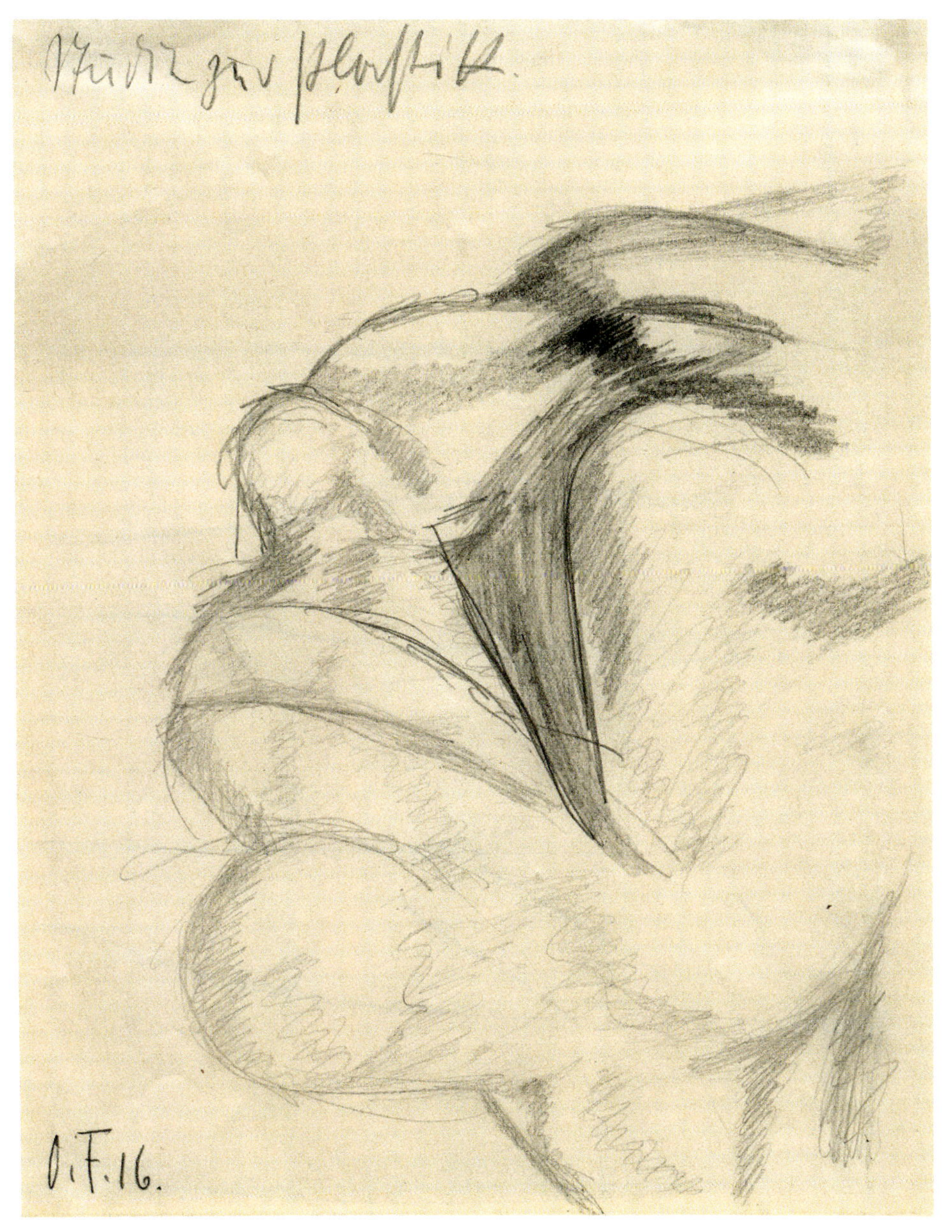

Head, 1916
HvW 65
Lacquered plaster
Lost

Sketch for Sculpture, 1916
Pencil on paper

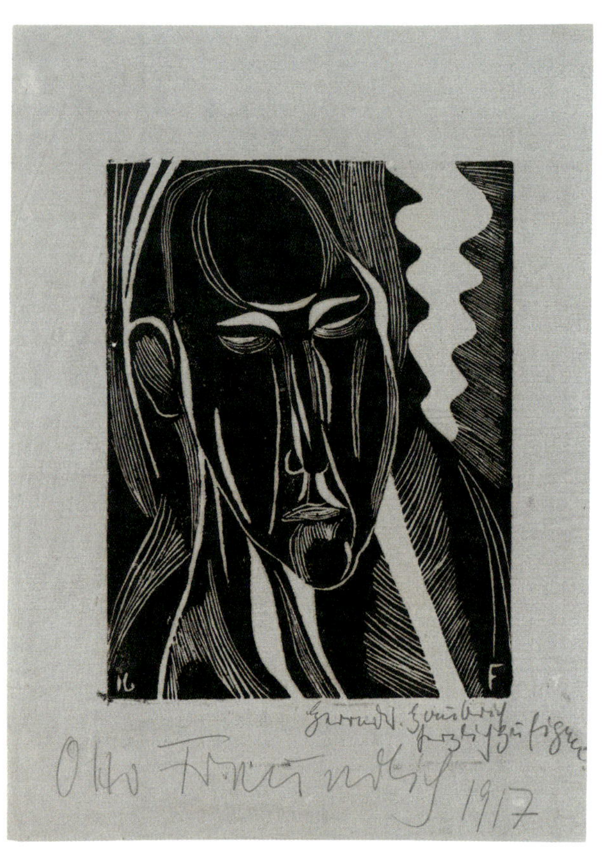

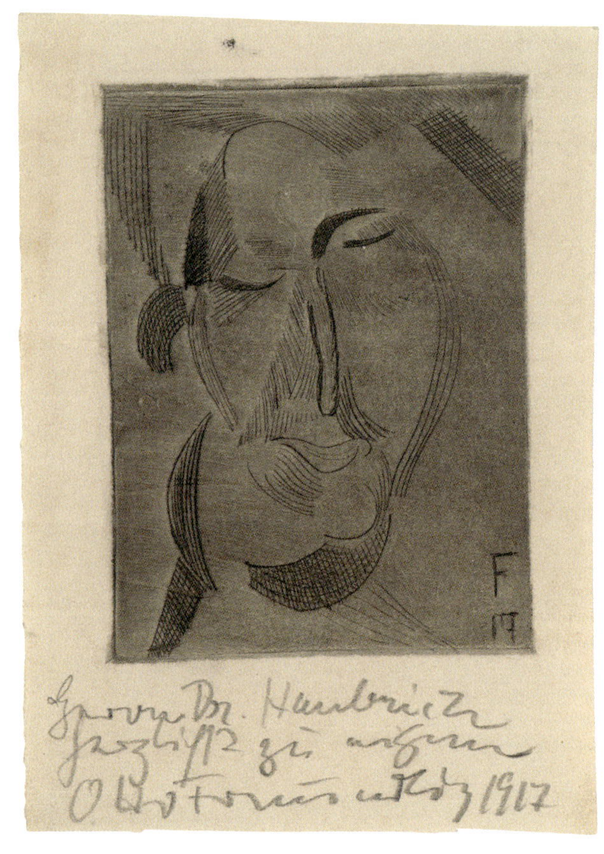

Head, 1916
HvW 441
Woodcut on gray paper

Head, 1917
Etching on paper

Head, 1925
Terracotta with black glaze

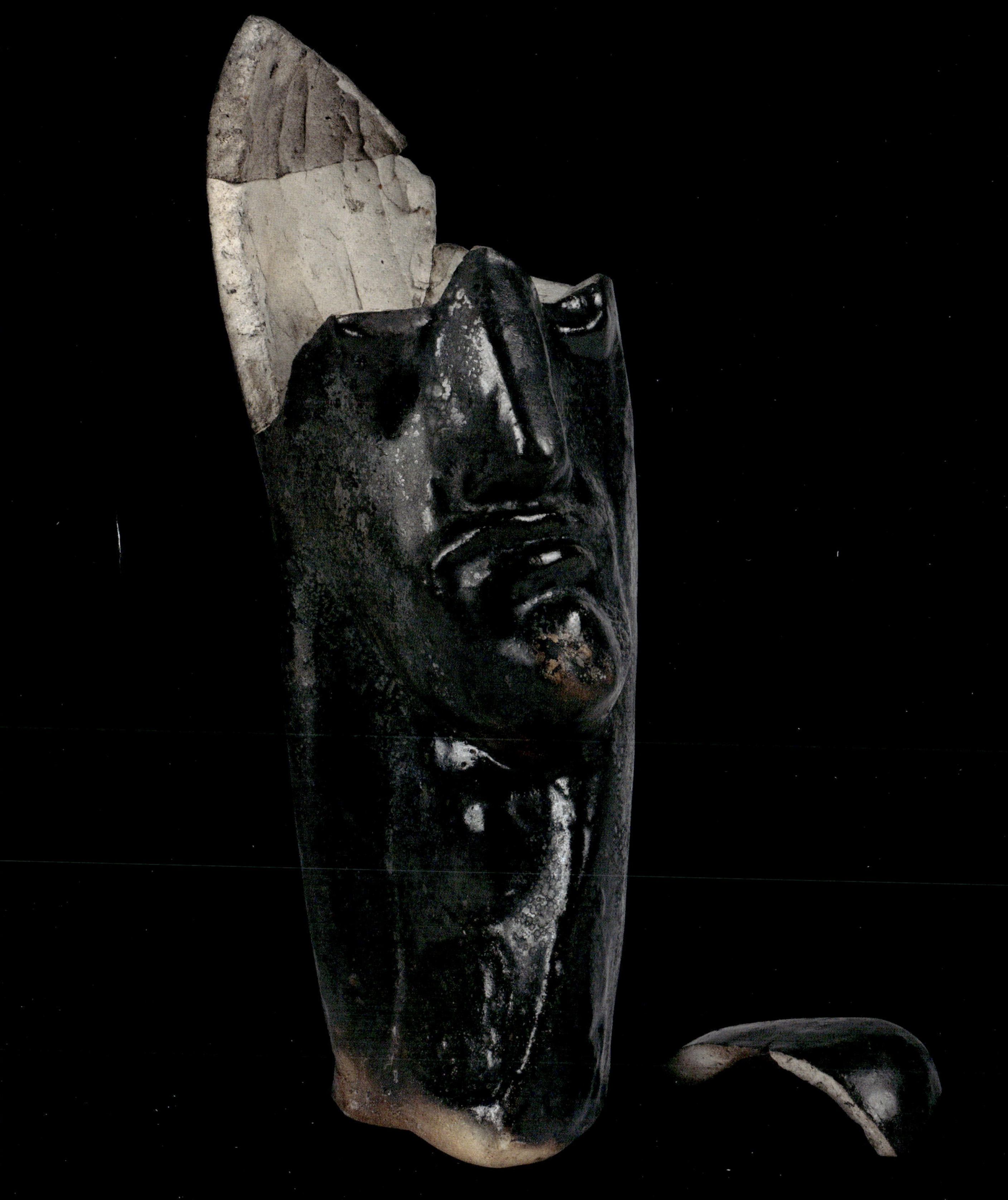

83

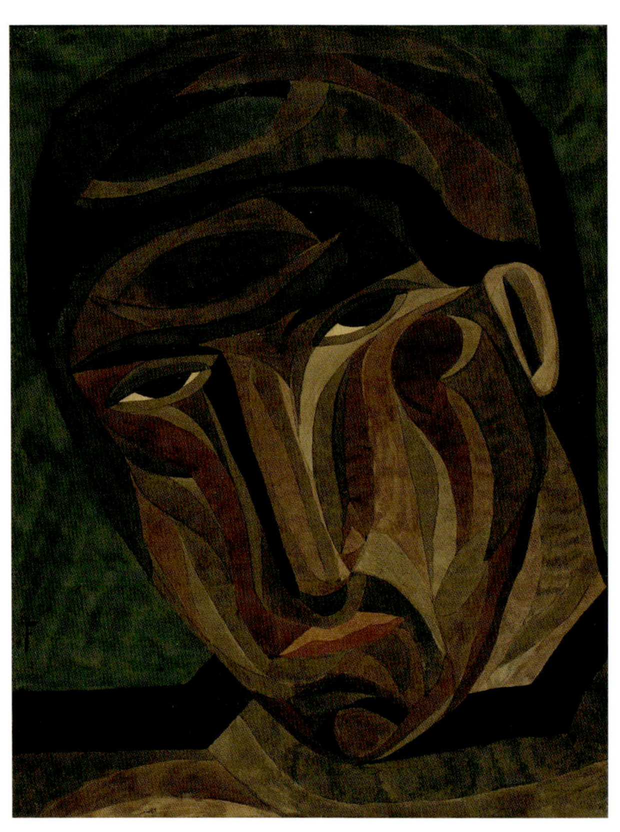

Head, 1911
HvW 109
Watercolor and ink on paper

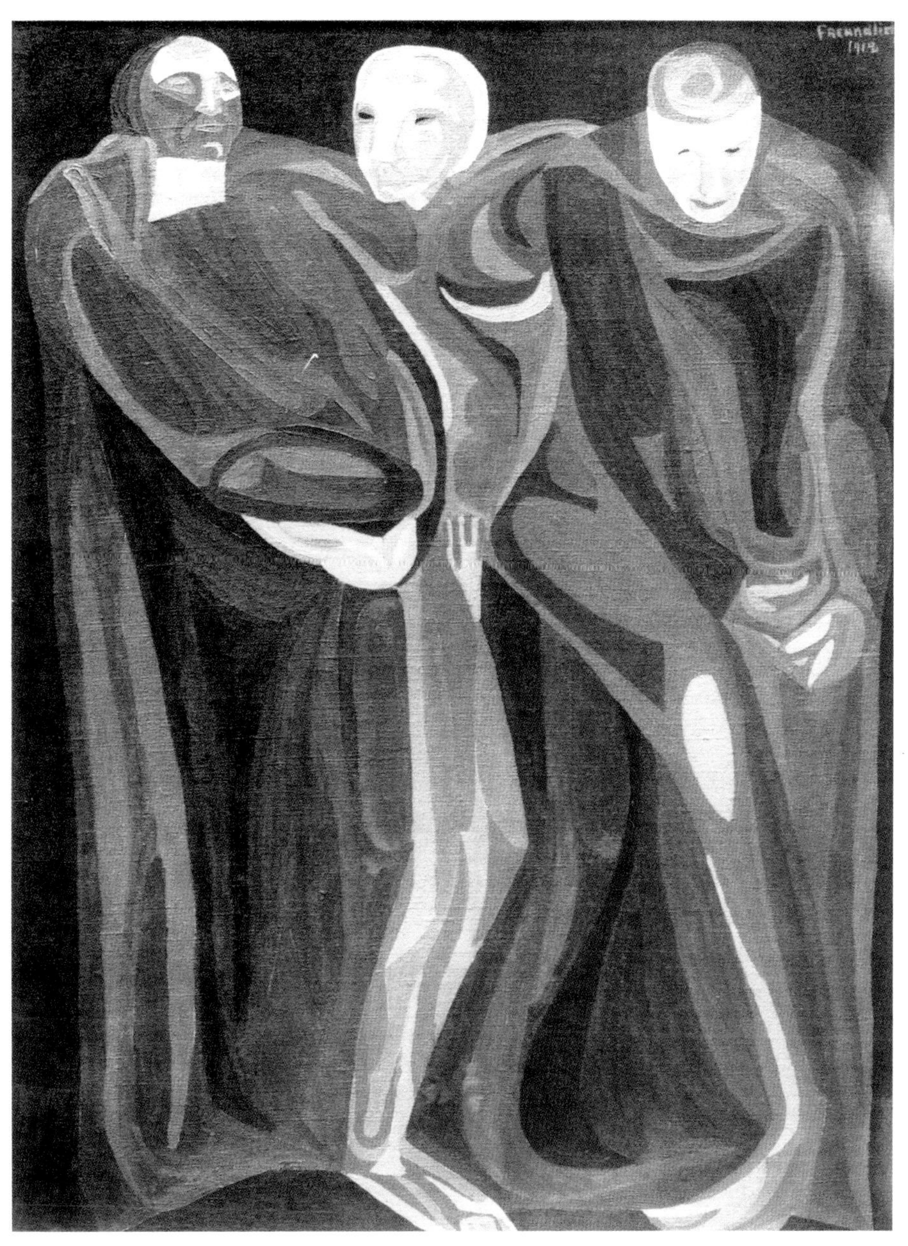

The Sick Man, 1912
HvW 116
Oil on canvas
Lost

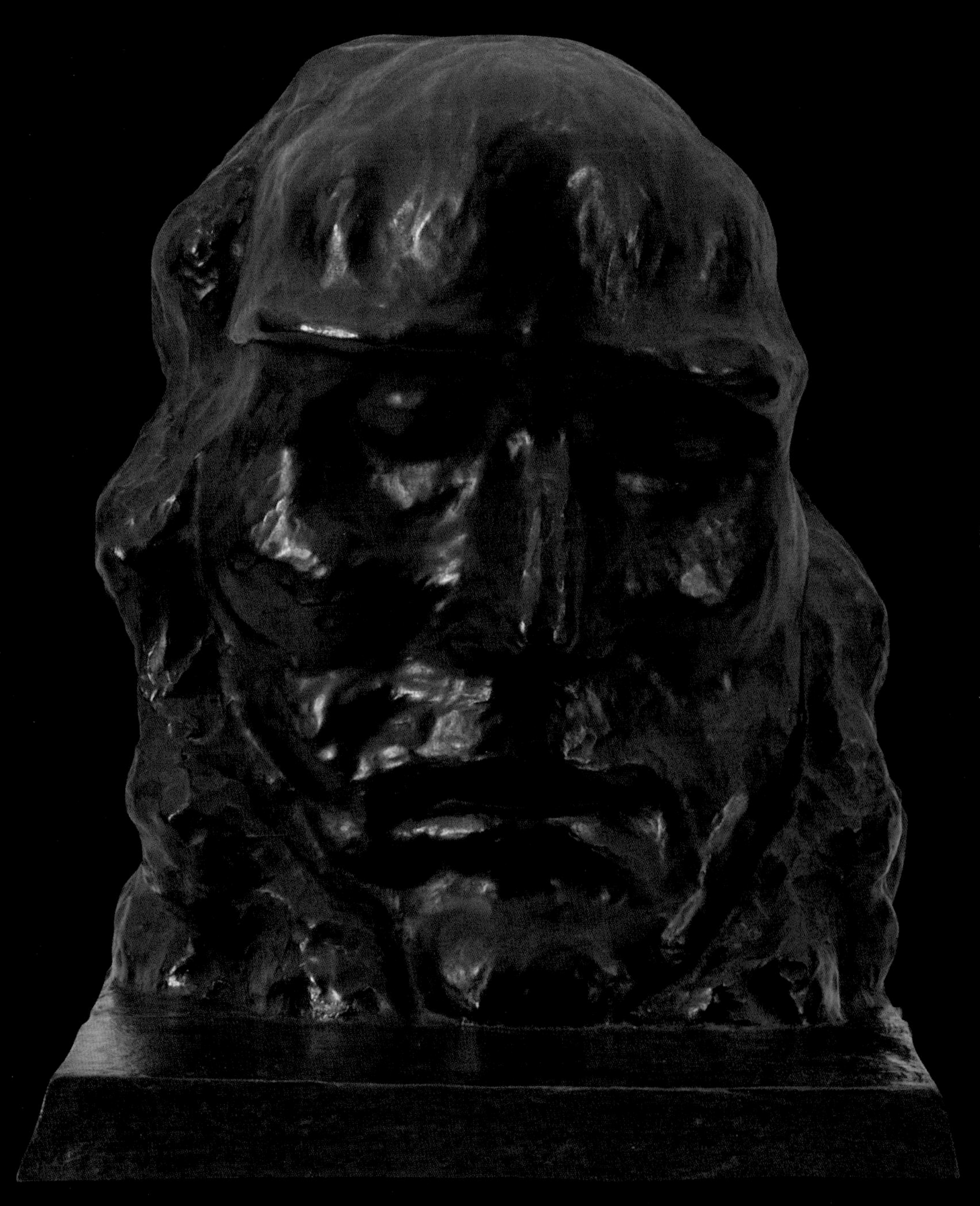

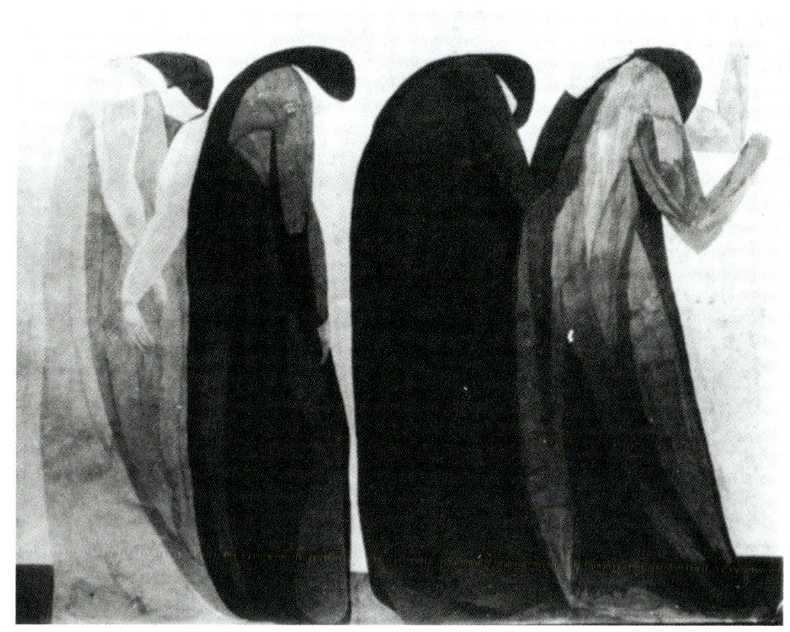

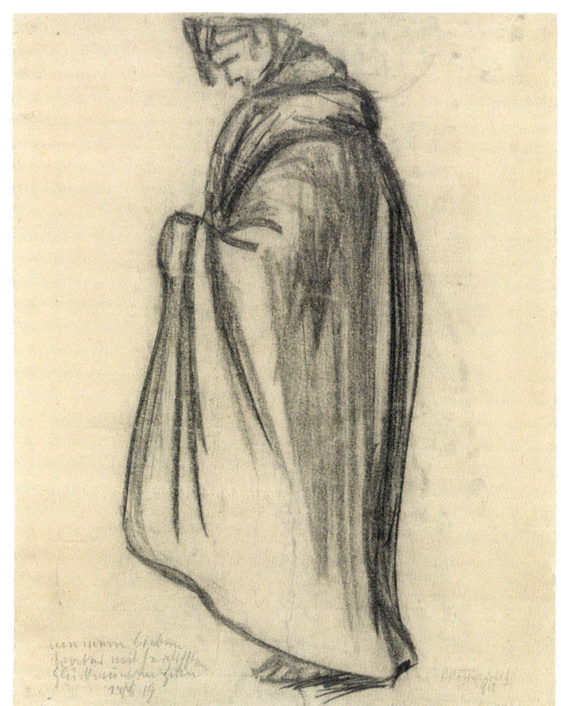

Standing Mask, 1909
HvW 55
Bronze

Four Parallel Figures, ca. 1910
HvW 103
Watercolor
Lost

Robed Figure with Bowed Head, 1910
HvW 263
Charcoal on paper

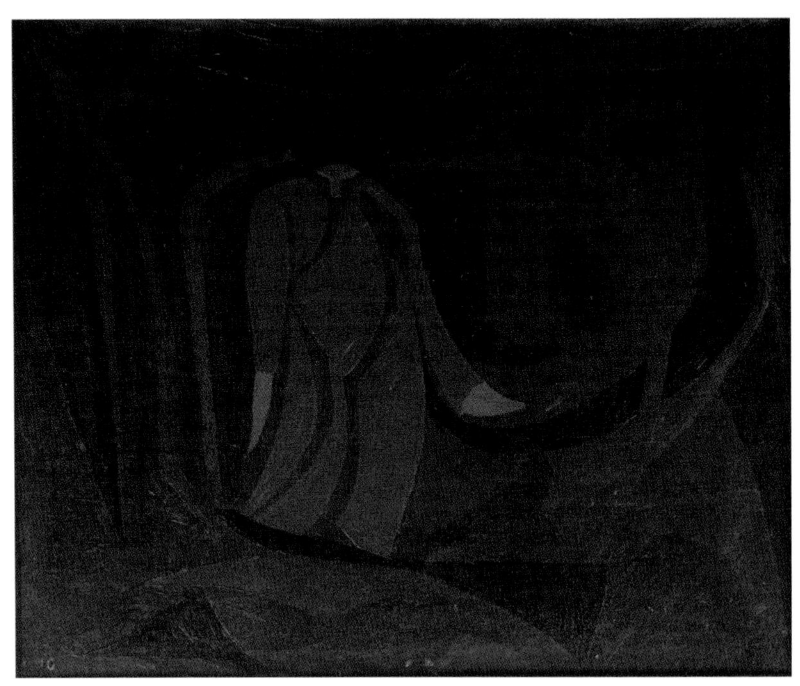

Composition with Figure, 1911
HvW 108
Oil on canvas

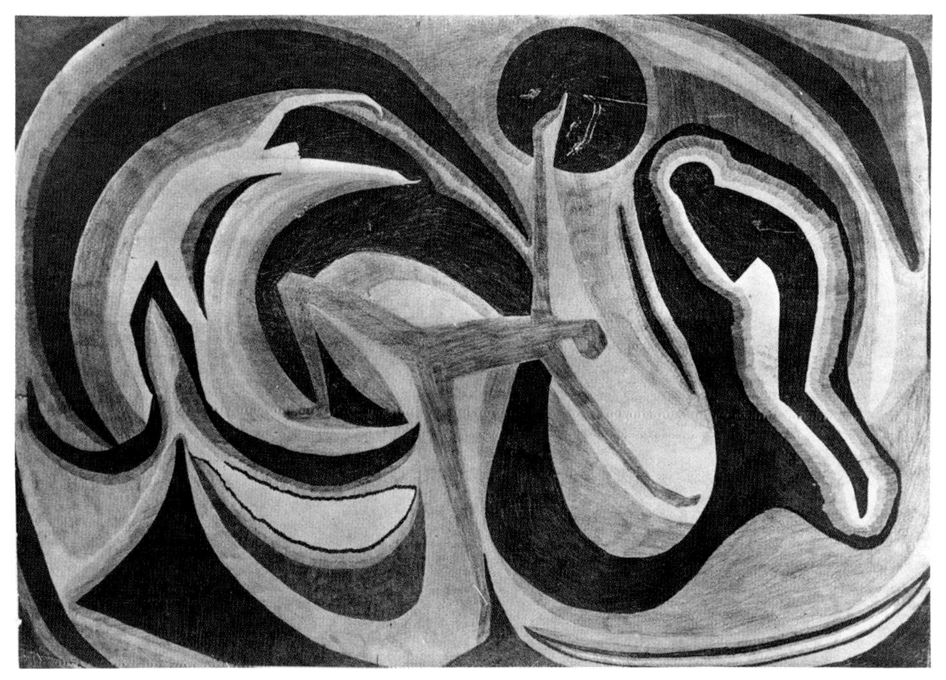

Cosmic Composition, 1910
HvW 264
Pencil on paper
Lost

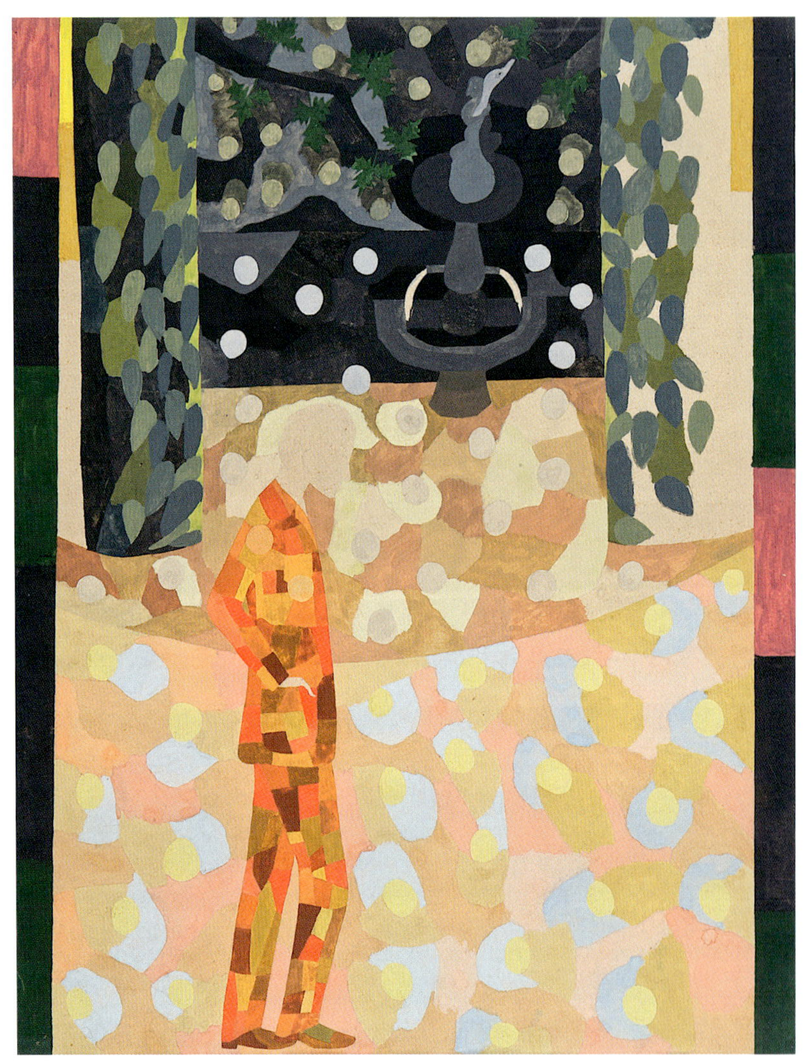

Man in Front of a Fountain, 1911/1942
HvW 105
Gouache on paper

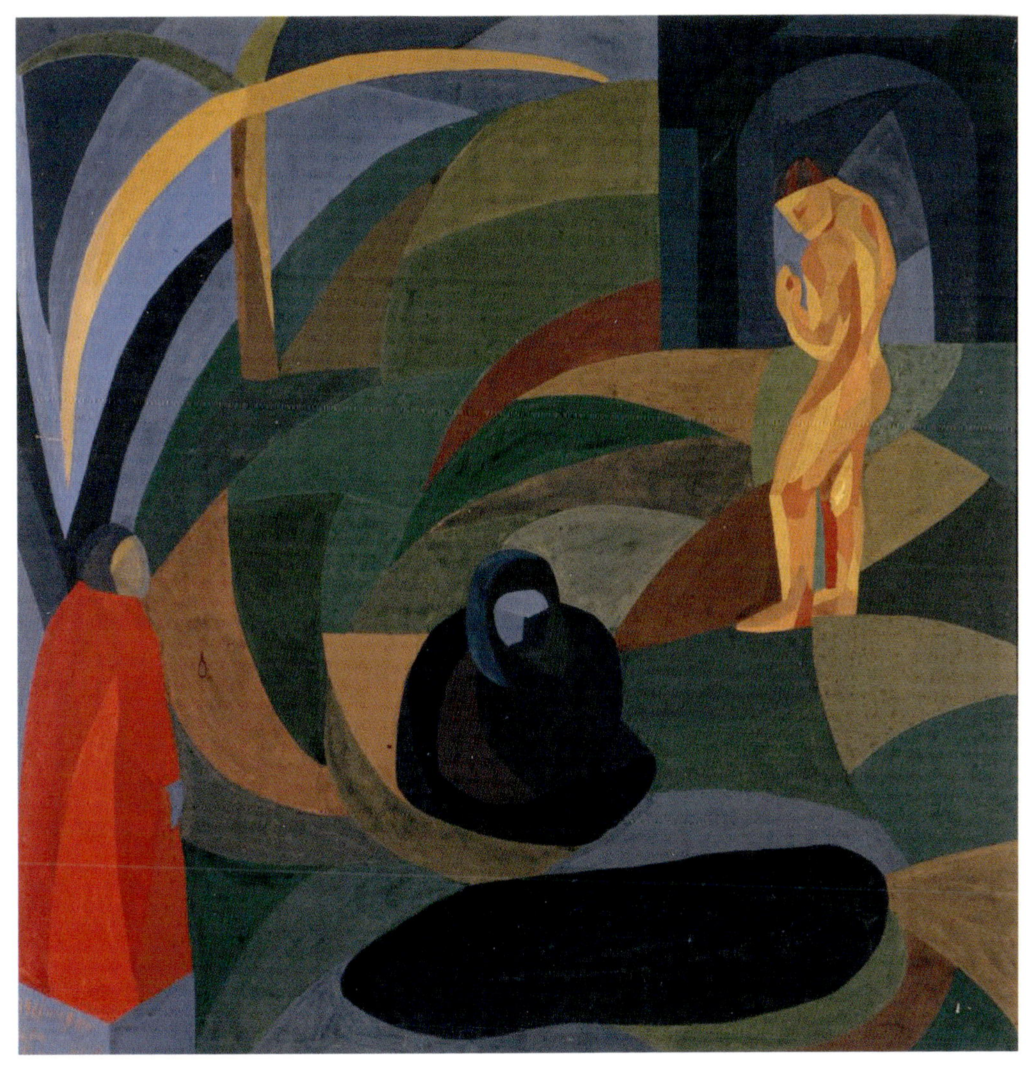

Composition with Three Figures, 1911/1941
HvW 111
Gouache on cardboard

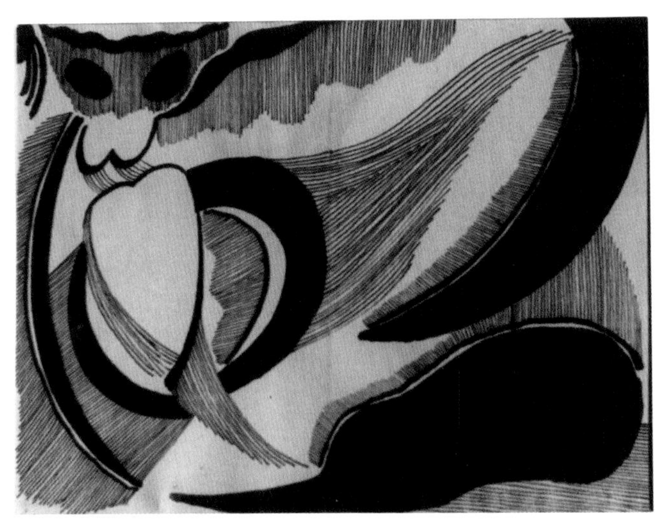

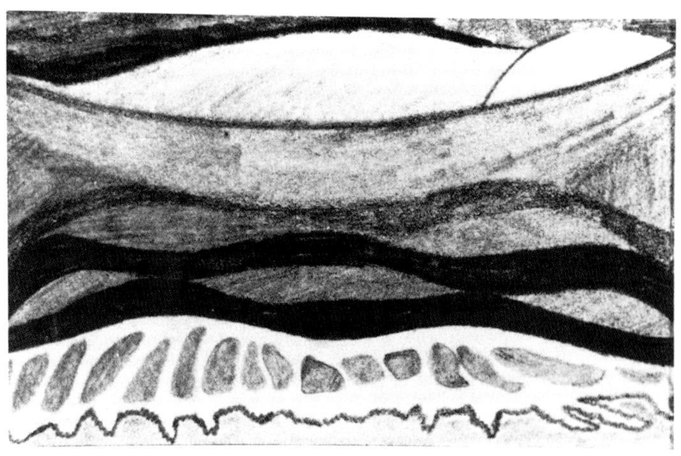

Composition, 1917
HvW 277
Ink on paper

Marne Landscape, 1913
HvW 268
Pencil on paper
Lost

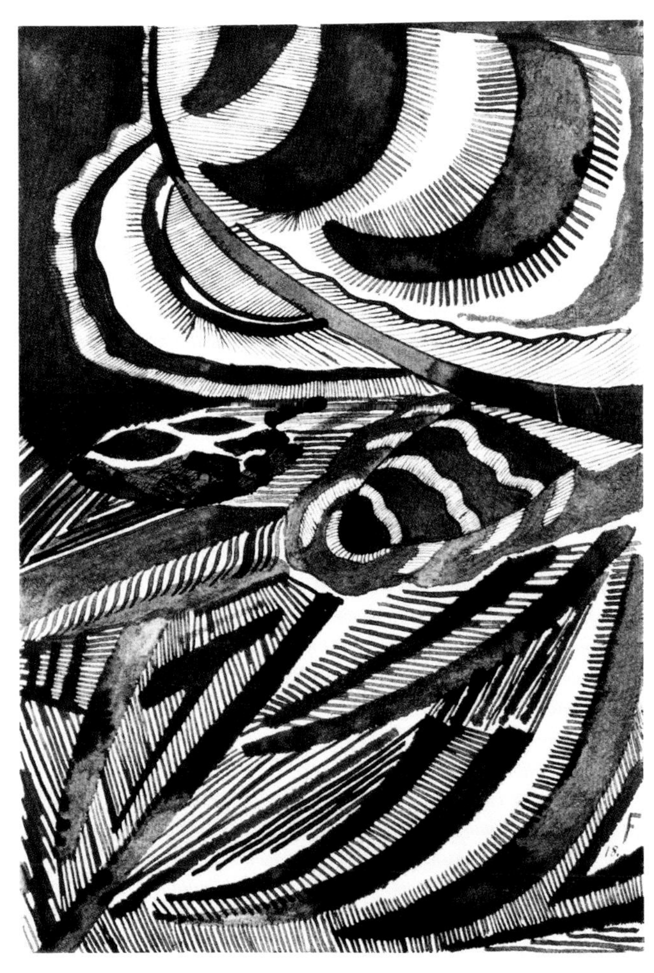

Landscape, 1918
HvW 292
Ink on cardboard

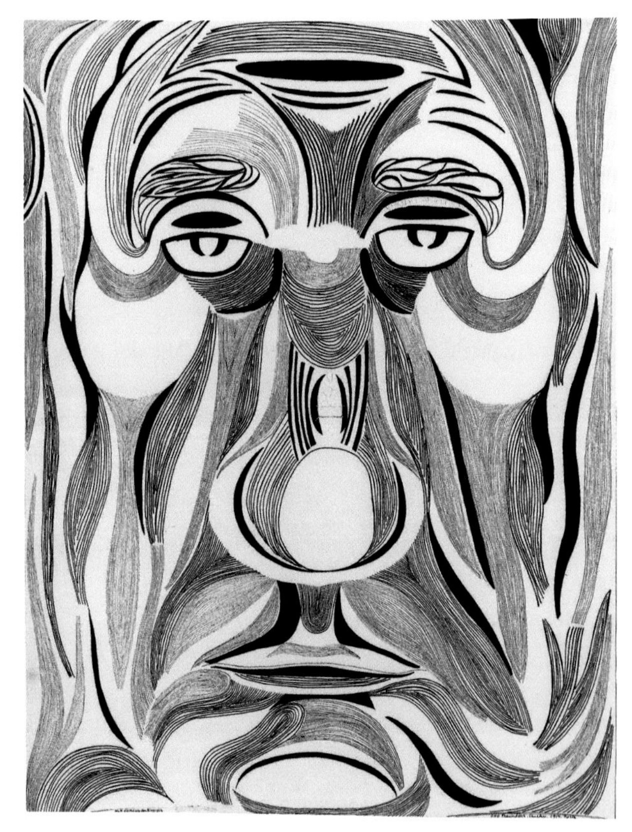

Head, 1914
HvW 269
Ink on cardboard

Head, 1925
HvW 75
Plaster
Lost

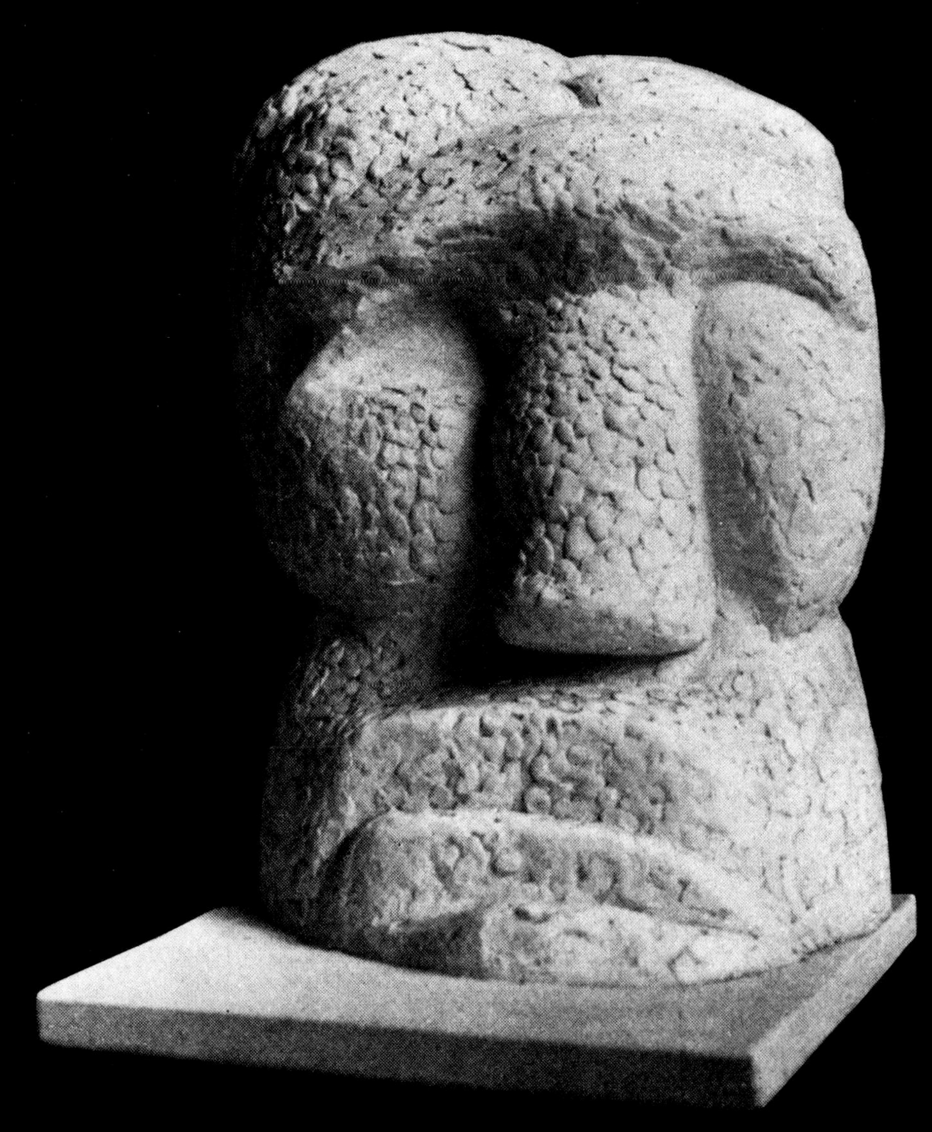

95

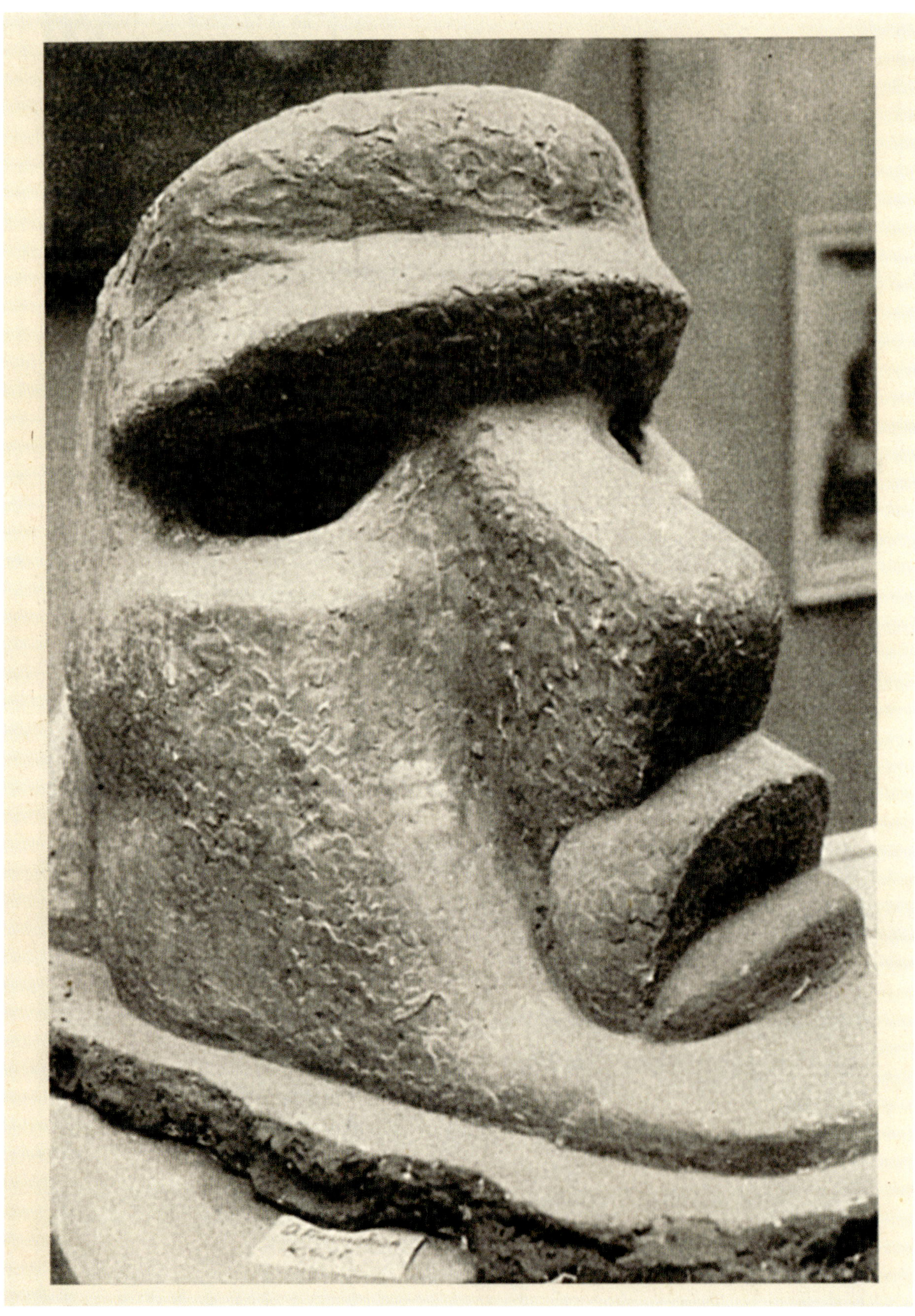

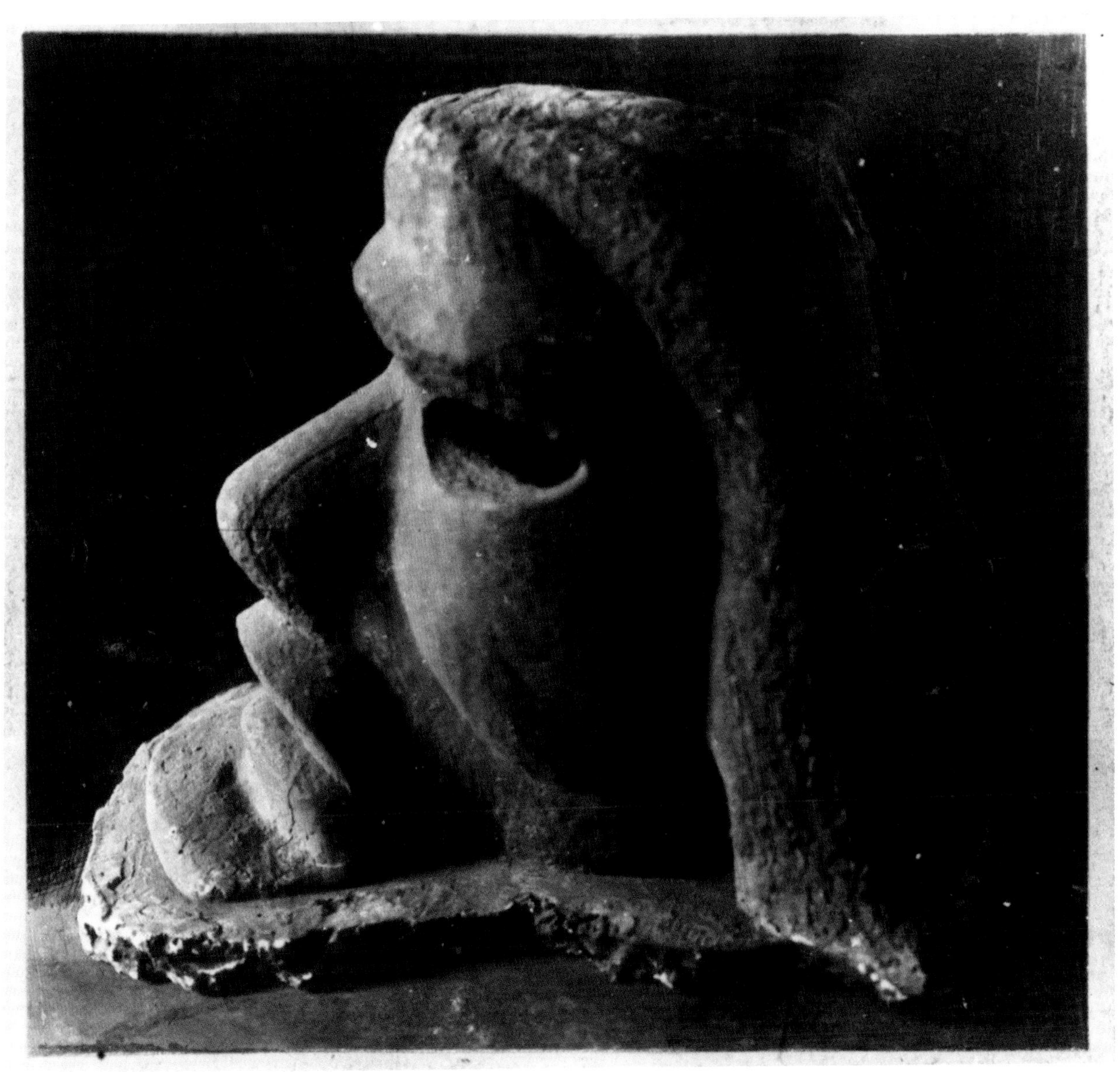

Male Mask, ca. 1910/1920
Right and left sides of the face
HvW 58
Plaster
Lost

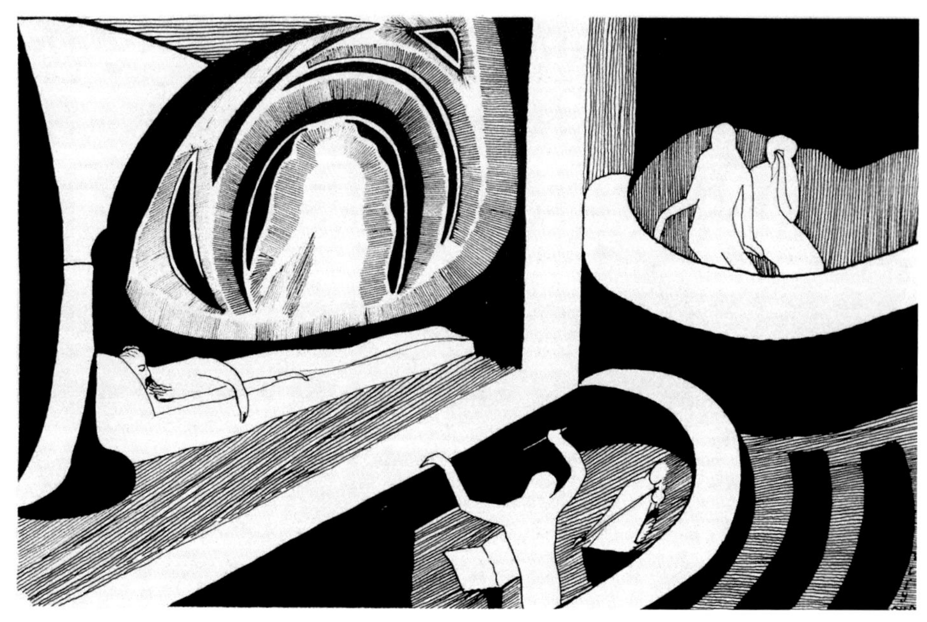

Egmont's Dream, 1915
HvW 270
Ink on paper on cardboard

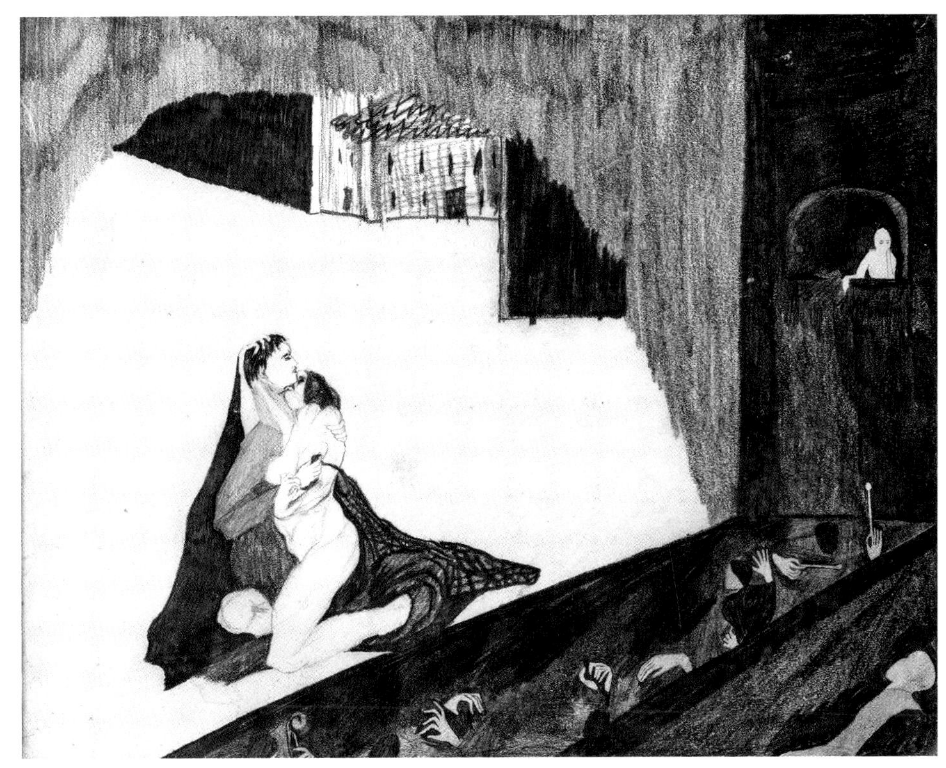

Opera Scene, 1905
HvW 260
Pencil on paper

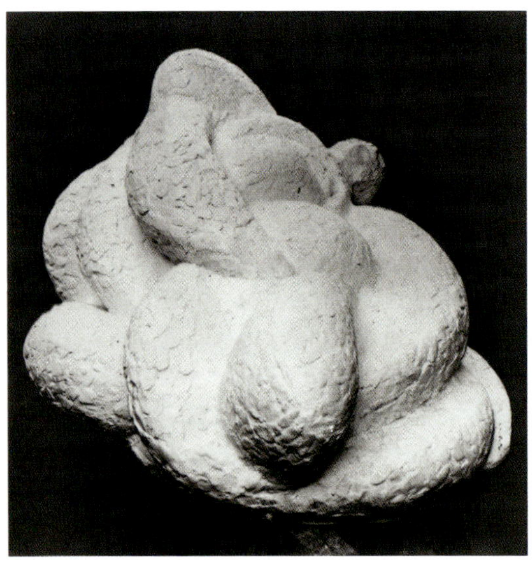

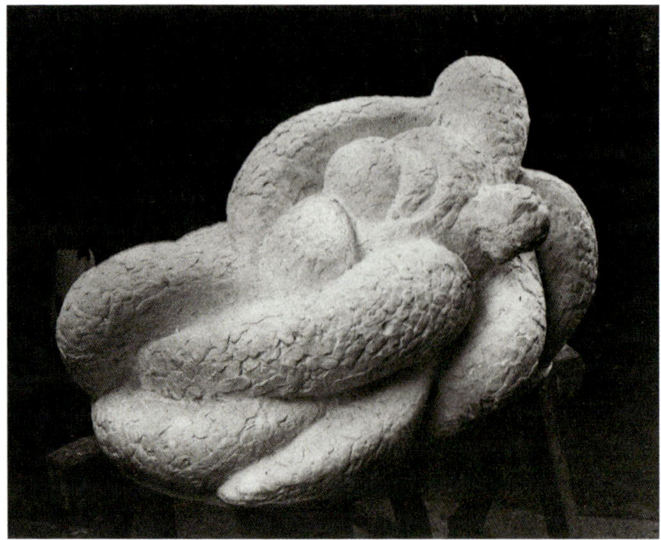

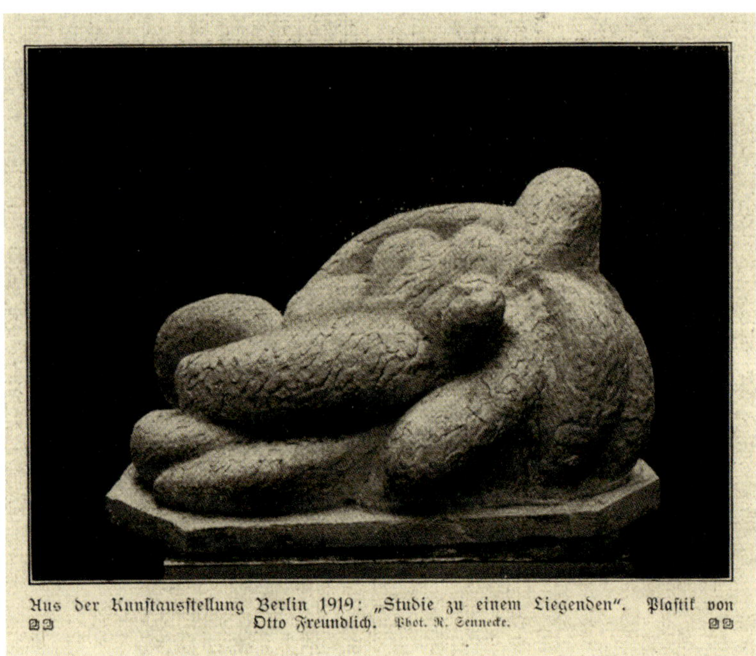

Aus der Kunstausstellung Berlin 1919: „Studie zu einem Liegenden". Plastik von Otto Freundlich. Phot. R. Sennecke.

Reclining Figure/Study for a Reclining Woman, ca. 1917
HvW 67
Plaster
Lost

Male Mask, 1915
HvW 64
Colored plasticine
Lost

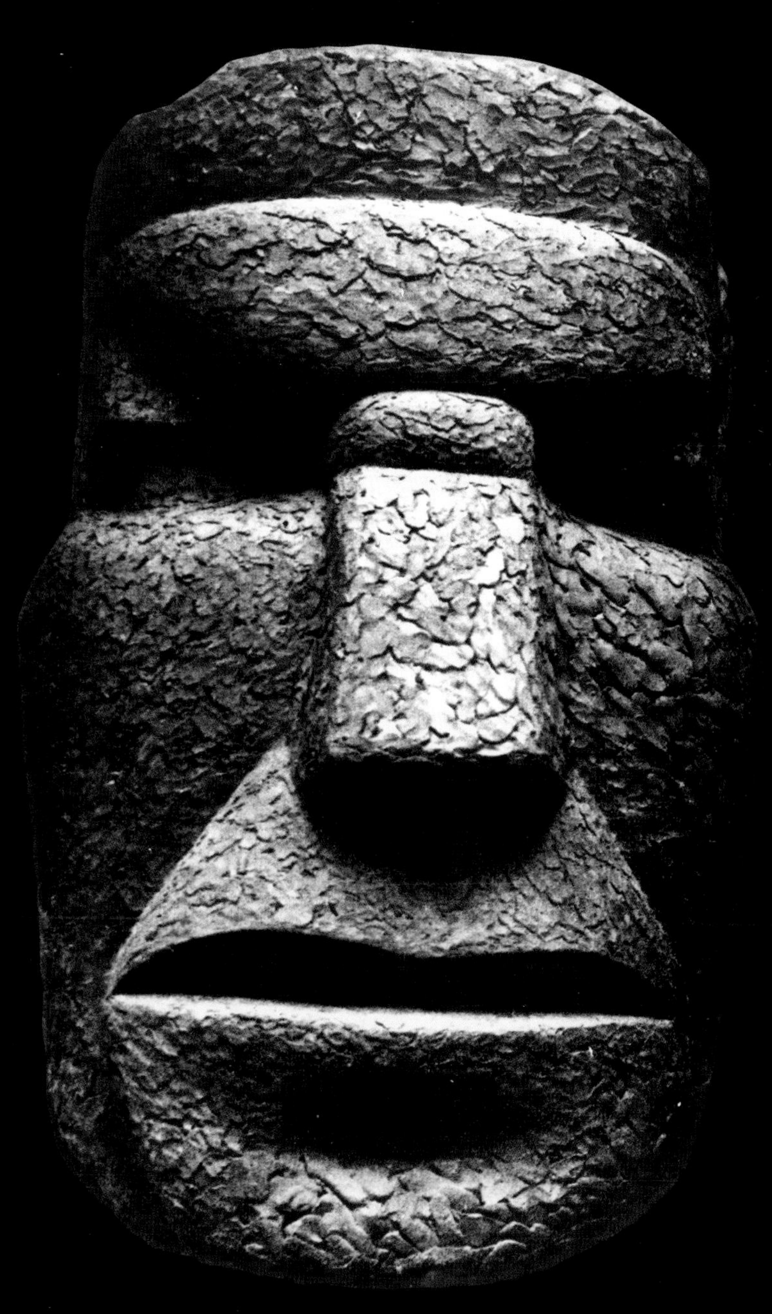

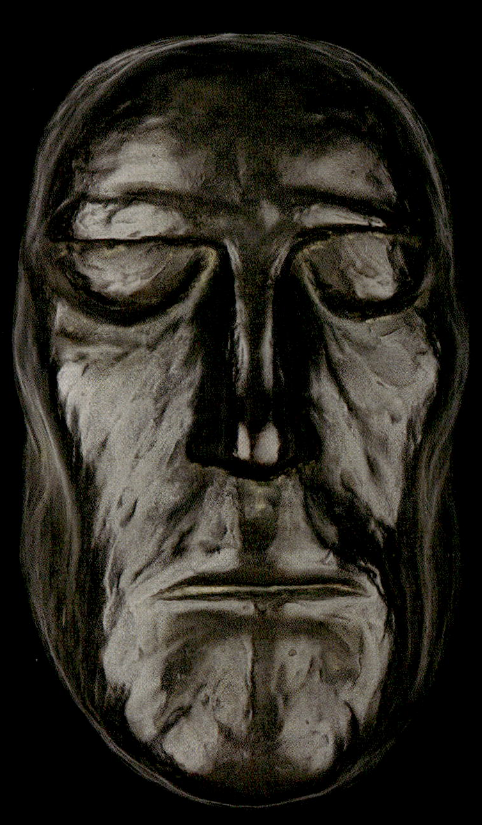

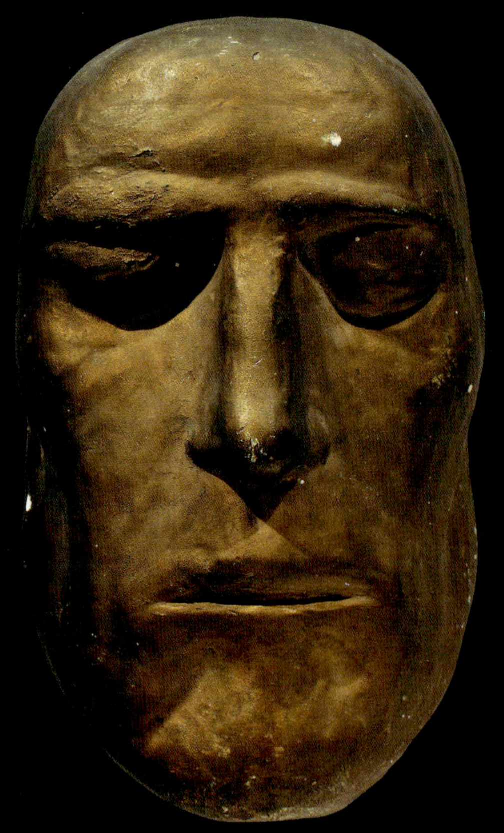

Mask, 1909
HvW 54
Left: bronze
Right: plaster, painted golden-brown

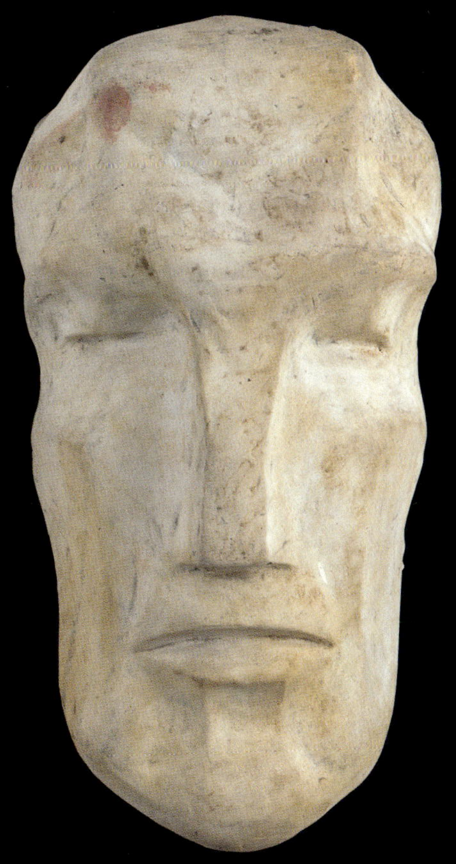

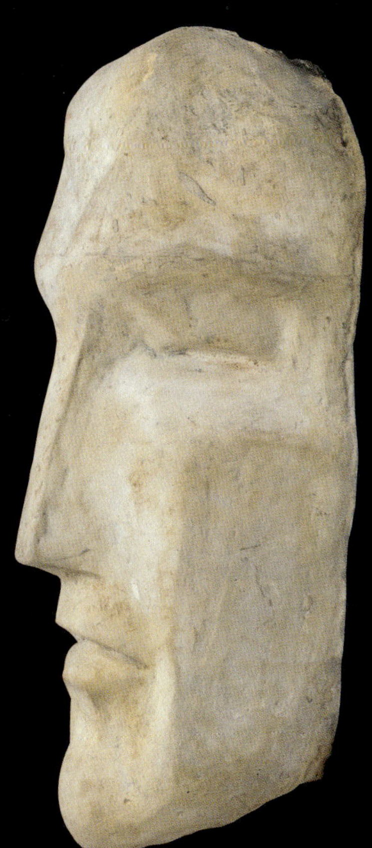

Male Mask, 1911
Front and side view
HvW 61
Plaster

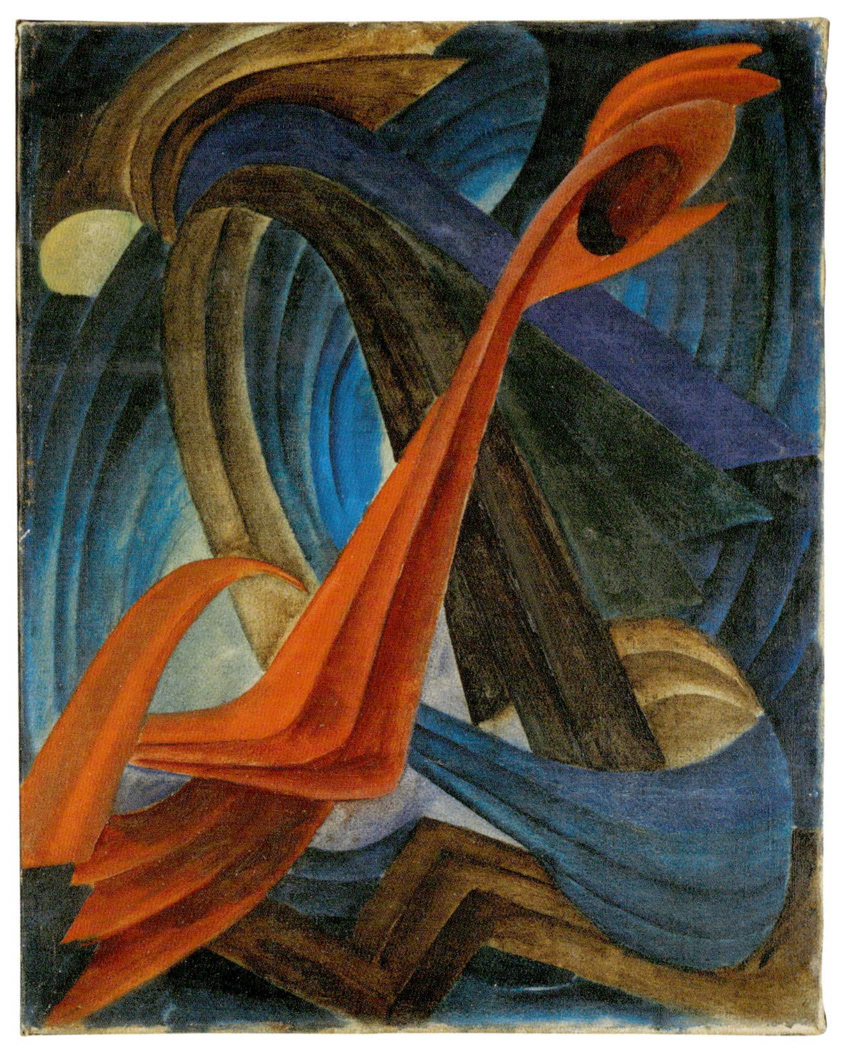

Composition, 1918–19
HvW 126
Oil on canvas

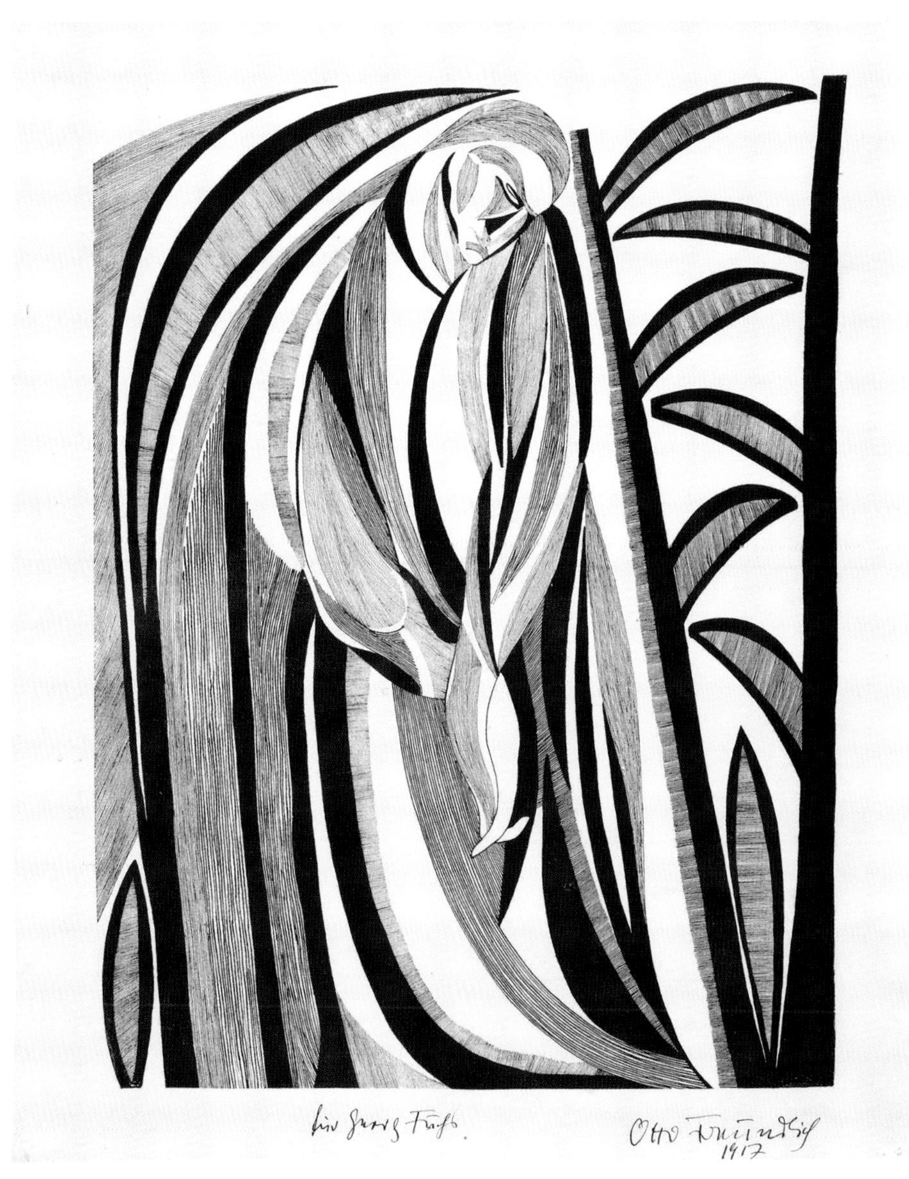

Man and Vegetation, 1916
HvW 440
Zinc engraving on paper

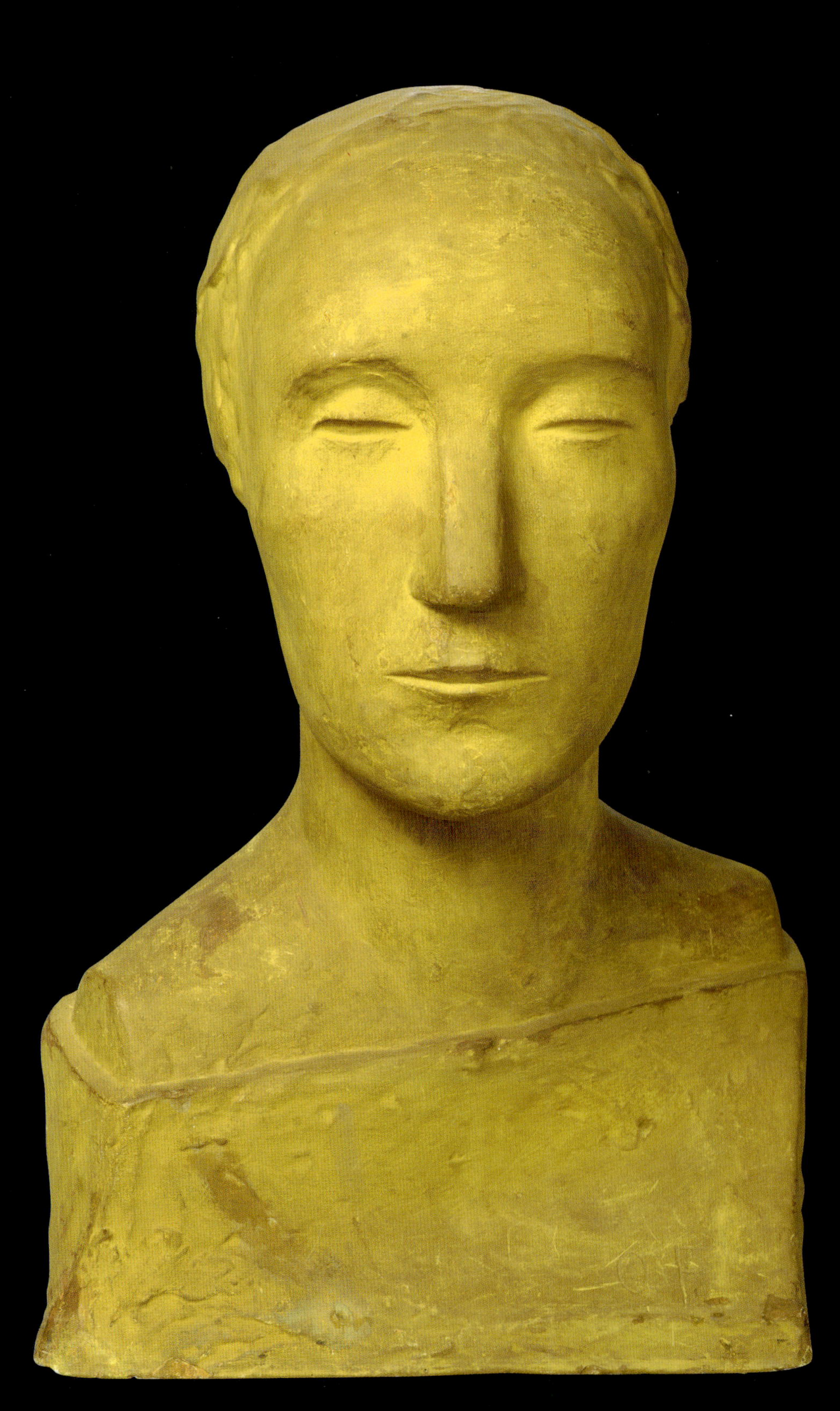

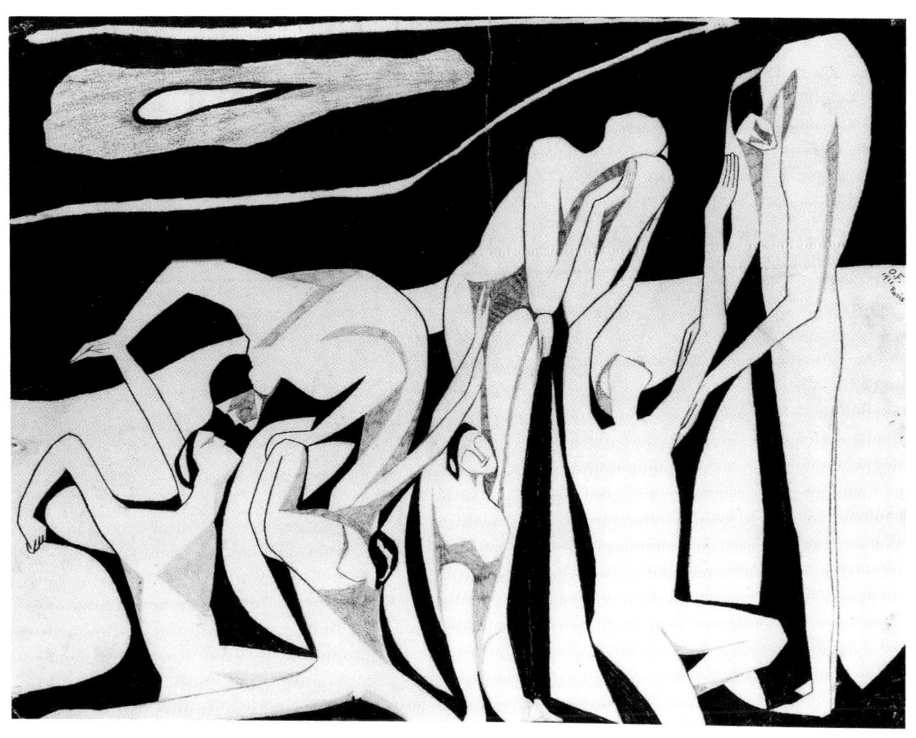

Bust of a Woman, 1910
HvW 56
Plaster, painted yellow

Group, 1911
HvW 265
Pencil on paper

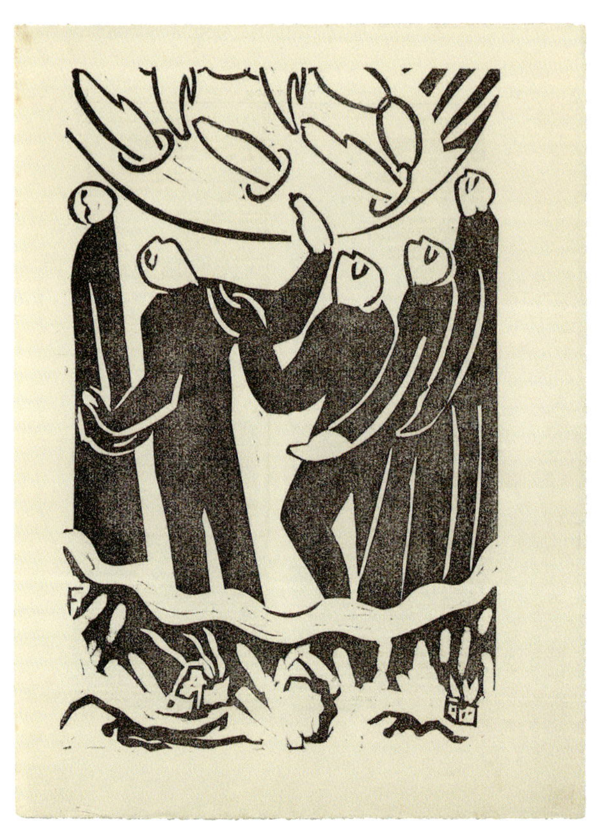

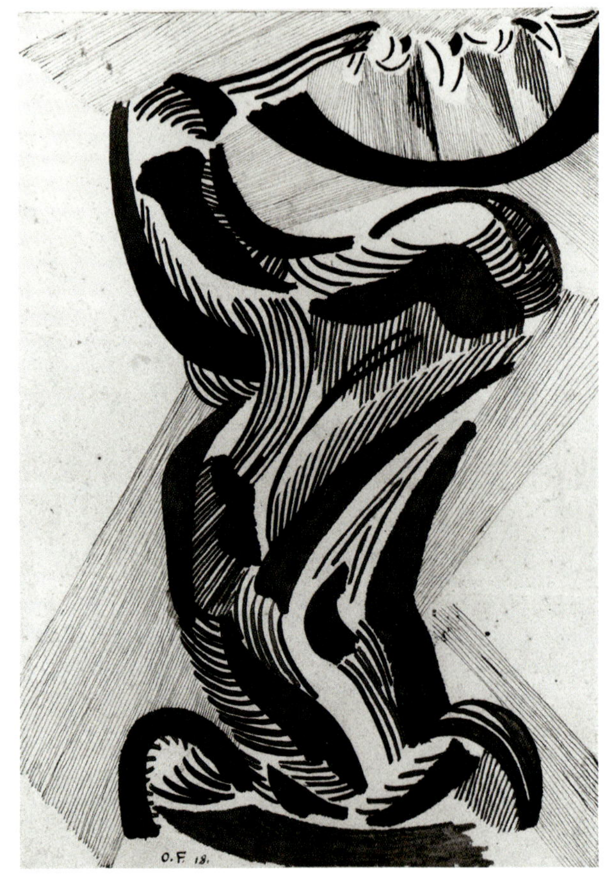

Leaflet on the Communist Manifesto, 1918
HvW 446
Linocut

A Tree, 1918
HvW 293
Ink on Bristol paper

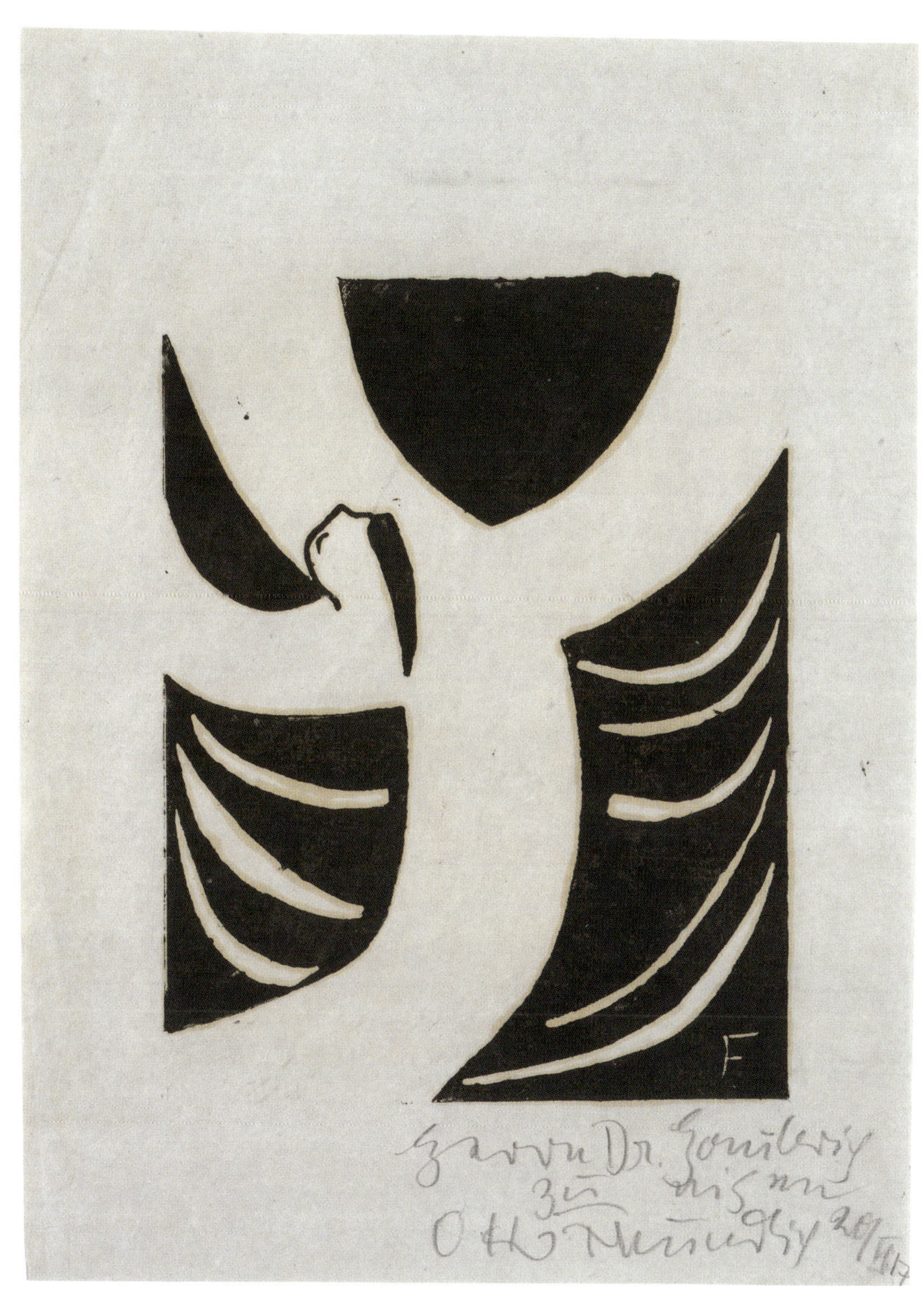

Upsurge, 1917
HvW 442
Woodcut on gray paper

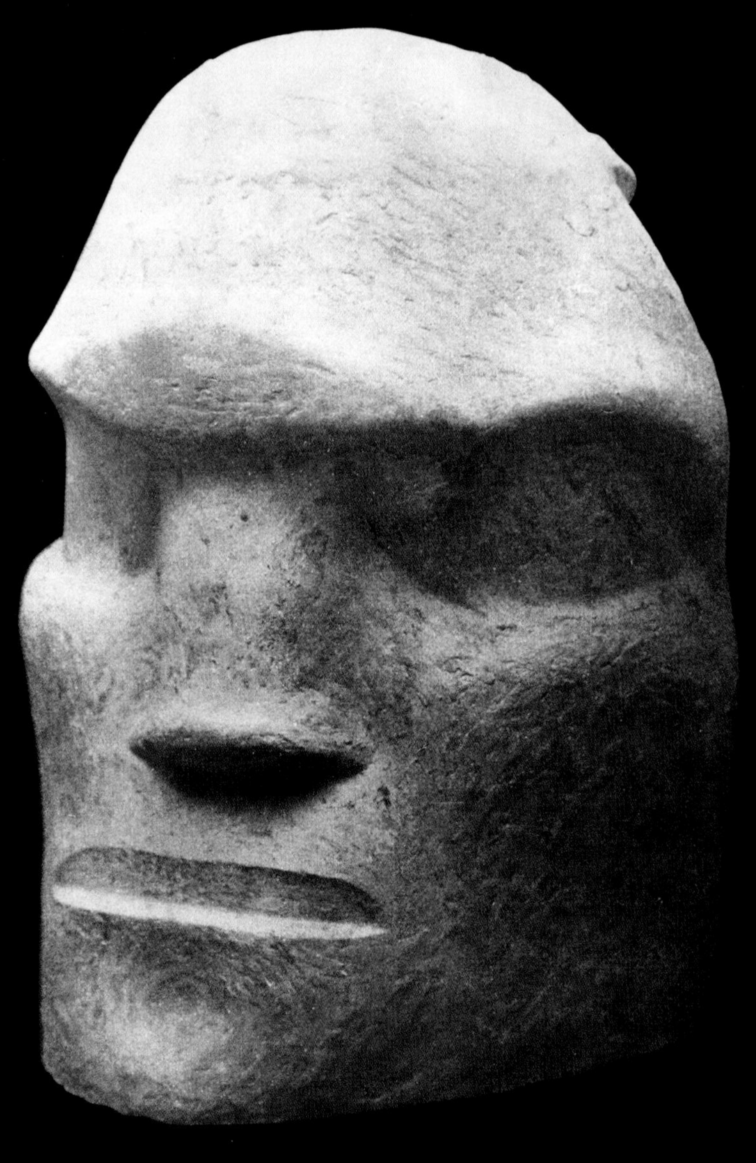

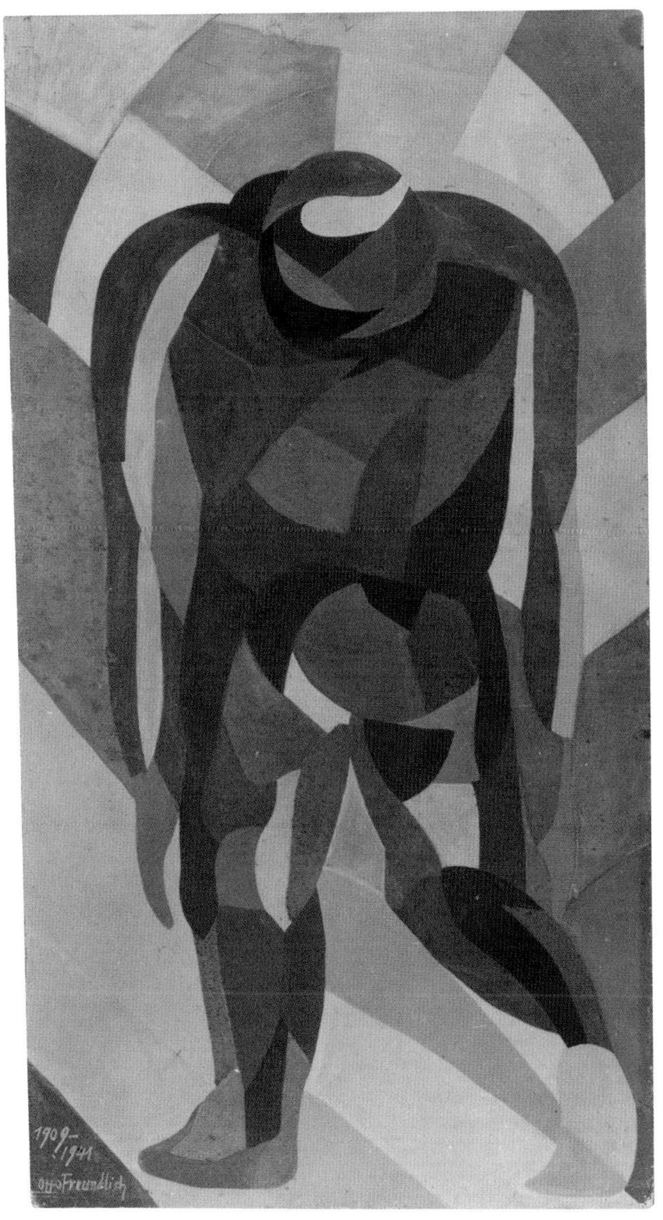

Head, 1912
HvW 62
Plaster
Lost

Striding Figure
(*From Behind*), 1909/1941
HvW 101
Gouache
Lost

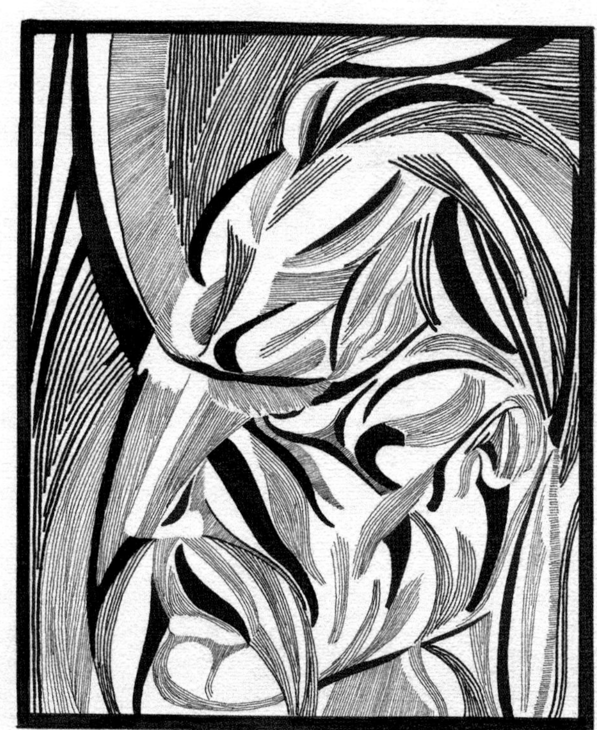

Nietzsche, 1916
Ink on paper

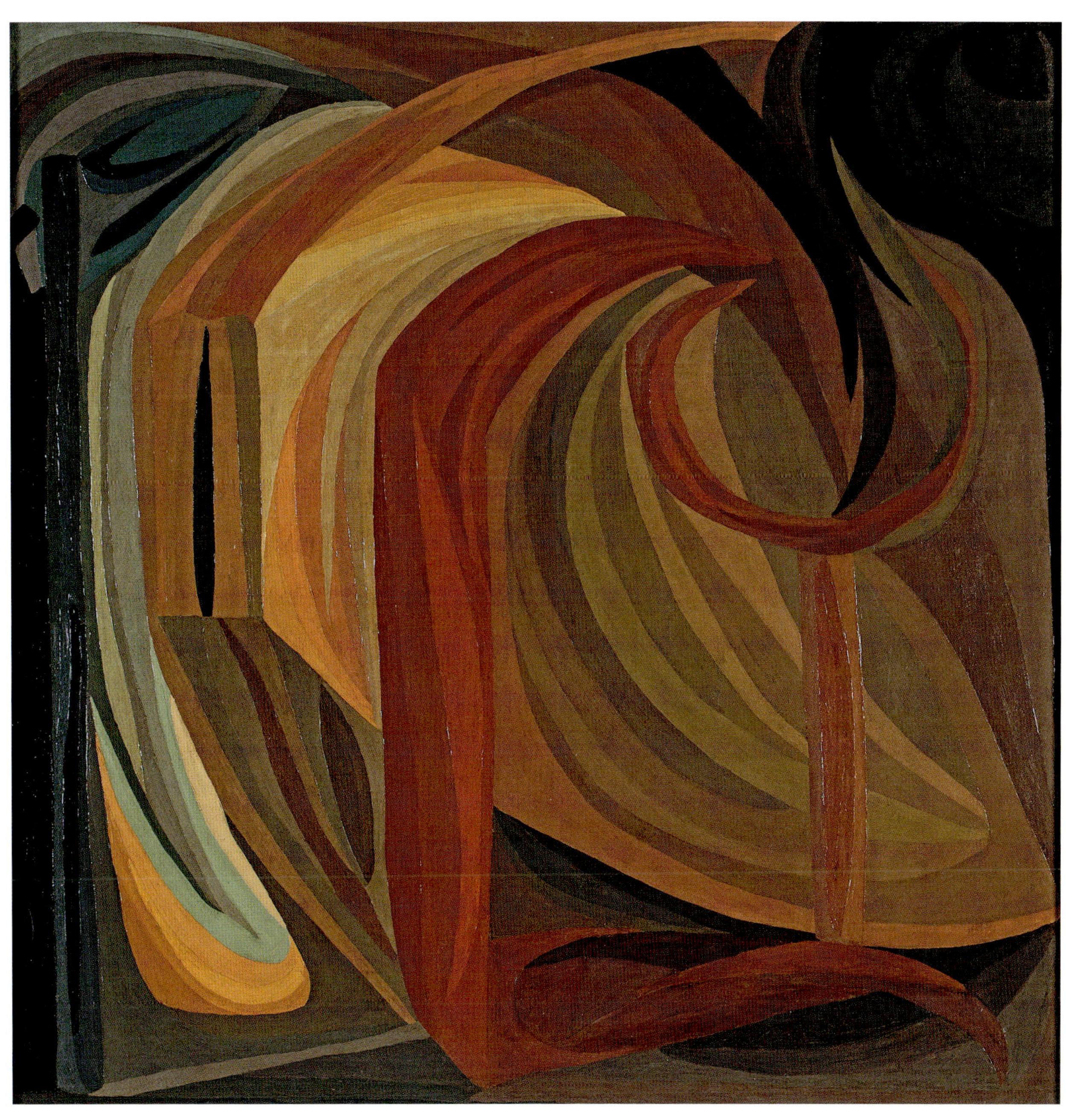

Composition, 1911
HvW 107
Oil on canvas

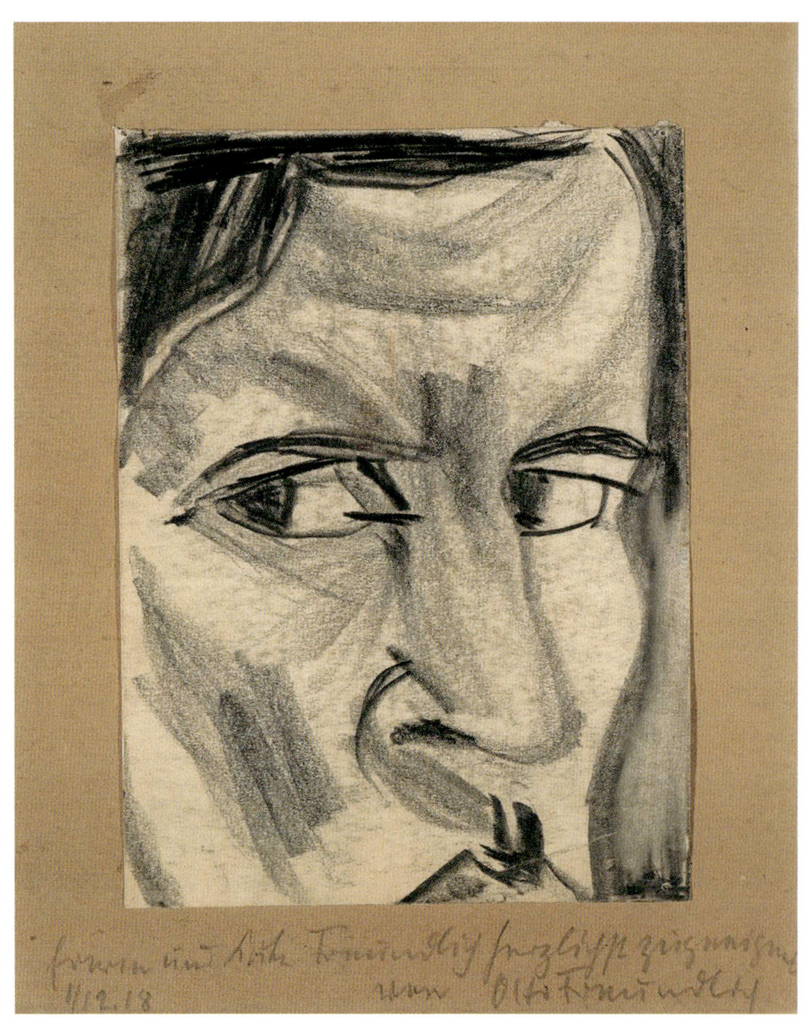

Self-Portrait, 1918
HvW 296
Chalk on paper on mount

Geneviève Debien

The Sound and Color of Cosmic Architecture

November 1918: The armistice and then a revolution led to the Weimar Republic, and with that to art groups who demanded new changes. Otto Freundlich was actively involved, not least by the thirteen articles which he published in 1919 alone. He was a member of the newly founded Arbeitsrat für Kunst (Workers' Council for Art) and took part on December 3, 1918, at the first meeting of the Novembergruppe.[1] The consolidation of the arts was supposed to bring about a new society. Freundlich for his part was concerned with a "plain and simple architecture of juxtaposition."[2] In his essay "Zur Synthese Architektur—Plastik—Malerei" ("On the Synthesis of Architecture—Sculpture—Painting") from April 1919 he demanded that "painters, sculptors and architects come together" so as "to create not the artwork, but first the prerequisite for that: the person."[3] He coined here the term "cosmic communism,"[4] which foresees the dissolution of the individualistic "ego"[5] in the "heaving seas of the whole cosmic body."[6] His Communist convictions were accompanied by a religion of the spirit aimed at coalescing the new society.[7] Because "space" or the cosmos consists not only of "physical force[s],"[8] but spiritual ones, too. In order to describe these spiritual forces, Freundlich employed around 1919 the term "architecture," as in "sociable-human architecture,"[9] and already by 1913 in the phrase "invisible architecture,"[10] as well as "the supra-organic structure."[11]

The task of constructing this "architecture" was to be assigned to the artist who has realized the "truth" and "is able to impregnate materials with spirit." This "spiritual crystallization" was to be achieved with the aid of the eye.[12]

The eye is central to the process of perception. Inspired by the neo-Kantian philosopher Ernst Marcus, Freundlich was convinced that perception occurs by the eye projecting a mental image outward[13] and with that creating the world: "Apperception is a power of resurrection."[14] When this process of perception manifests in an artwork, it should give the beholder new insights and make him a joint constructor of the new society. It was in this context that Freundlich also investigated colored light.

Already in 1916 he evinced an interest in the technique of mosaic: "Sch[midt]-R[ottluff] has had so much opportunity to do stained glass and mosaics. I had to sigh, although without any envy, because I couldn't dismiss the thought of how much I would have had to say in the two media."[15] Shortly after, he received his opportunity. Before the war he had met Josef Feinhals, a tobacco merchant and patron of contemporary art.[16] On Feinhals's recommendation, Gottfried Heinersdorff, Berlin partner of the Vereinigte Werkstätten für Mosaik und Glasmalerei Puhl & Wagner–Gottfried Heinersdorff,[17] went in 1916 or 1917 to Freundlich's studio in Cologne: "I had an encounter there which for me, too, was one of the most curious and, I don't mind saying, most beautiful that I have ever experienced with an artist."[18] Heinersdorff came up with the idea that Feinhals should join him in giving Freundlich a commission.[19] The order to design a mosaic was placed in January 1918.[20] At latest in April 1918, after being relocated to a position as medical NCO in a Berlin military hospital, Freundlich embarked on a "preliminary study." The design was finally finished in early March 1919, done on cardboard that Heinersdorff had provided him with specially.[21] The actual execution commenced in April 1919;[22] Feinhals planned to put the ultimately 215 × 305 centimeter mosaic "on the rear wall of a small garden house that has yet to be built"; it proved, however, to be too large.[23] As a result, it was sent on his suggestion to be shown at exhibitions, first in 1919 at Galerie Fritz Gurlitt in Berlin,[24] and then on to Cologne, where it was shown at the Kölnischer Kunstverein.[25]

A male figure made up of reflecting shards is shown inside an elliptical space, in a posture indicating upward movement. The figure is flanked by two more figures nestling against the curves, which were interpreted by critics as female entities.[26] Freundlich gave the work the title *The Birth of Man* (HvW 8, fig. 31, p. 118), which provides us with a key to interpretation. The dividers in the figure's hand denote him as being an architect, and strongly recall "On the Synthesis of Architecture—Sculpture—Painting." But what is actually depicted? The genesis of a New Man through "a new artwork," a new "architecture," or the origin of this architecture by the New Man—or both? Is it possible that here "painter, sculptor and architect come together"? That Freundlich has created a manifesto as one of the artist-prophets, in the Nietzschean sense, such as he had announced?[27] The architectural component would be represented then by the mosaic as a wall element, as well as by the figure of the architect, and the sculptural component by the mosaic technique and the design of the elliptical picture space. As Rita Wildegans has conjectured,[28] this depicts the curvature of space, the theory of which Freundlich most likely came to know from his cousin, Erwin Finlay-Freundlich, a colleague of Albert Einstein;[29] Finlay owned the gouache in which the mosaic was designed (HvW 127, p. 130).[30] And finally the painterly components can also be seen in the colors and the color theories that painter Freundlich mastered.

The color scheme inside the elliptical space corresponds strongly with Goethe's theory of colors. The primaries (yellow, blue, red) dominate and are supported by their intermixtures (violet, orange, green).[31] Light and shade are depicted with fine nuances, the figures' eyes are yellow and blue and thus correspond to the two "pure elementary" polarities from which the "color wheel" and with that the universe came into being.[32] This color rhetoric can already be recognized in his *Composition with Figure* from 1911 (HvW 108, p. 88) featuring a red figure with hands of yellow and blue flames. In the mosaic, blue, yellow, and red strips meet up beneath the form in the center, which also becomes redder towards the top and with that evokes what Goethe describes as the "constant progress or augmentation in yellow and blue ... to redness."[33] Further, the three figures form a trinity, as if in accordance with color theory, while at the same time with their Goethean eyes they themselves seem to create an architecture of color around them. The rays link them with the outer regions and prompt thoughts of a sacral event. The New Man architect is holding a pair of dividers in his right hand like some divine figure.

He is located at the center of a dispute between various color theories, because on the right-hand margin, structured rainbow-like curved colors are shown rising up from a chaos of dark, bluish shapes, all pointing to Newton's color theory and its scale of colors. Freundlich's 1919 essay "Der Raum" ("Space") and the manuscript "Der raumlose Himmel" ("Heavens without Space") from 1925 show that he had occupied himself with the similarities between painting and music.[34] The upper surface on the facial axis of the man-architect points in turn to the color theory of Michel Eugène Chevreul, one of the sources employed by Robert Delaunay.[35] The complementary colors red and green and their slightly diverging tones orange and lemon yellow have been placed in slices on a gray background to form simultaneous contrasts. These colors agree exactly with the color theory that Vincent van Gogh describes using in his *Night Café* (fig. 30). Van Gogh had moved at that time towards Chevreul's complementary colors and simultaneous contrasts through the influence of art critic Charles Blanc.[36] In this connection the "second frame" planned on the preliminary sketch for Freundlich's mosaic (HvW 297, p. 130) is of interest. It is reminiscent of a sunflower, a symbol of the light-giving sun, and also a metaphor alluding to Van Gogh; from 1922 onward, this image is regularly encountered in Freundlich's texts.[37] In his view,[38] the spirit residing in the artist produces the light, which is to say the world, with the instrument of the eye. Here the New Man has been composed at the center using Goethe's color theory, while surrounded by the theories of others. Could one see in this New Man the "crystallization" of the spirit called for in "On the Synthesis"? In that case, this New Man–architect would be the crystallized spirit of the artist, the prerequisite for the creation of the new society.

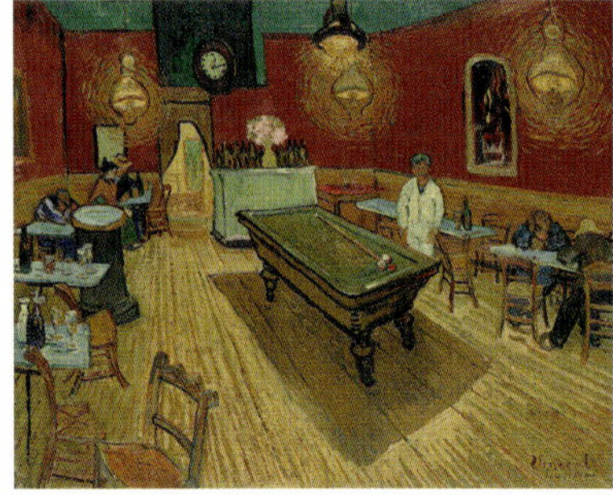

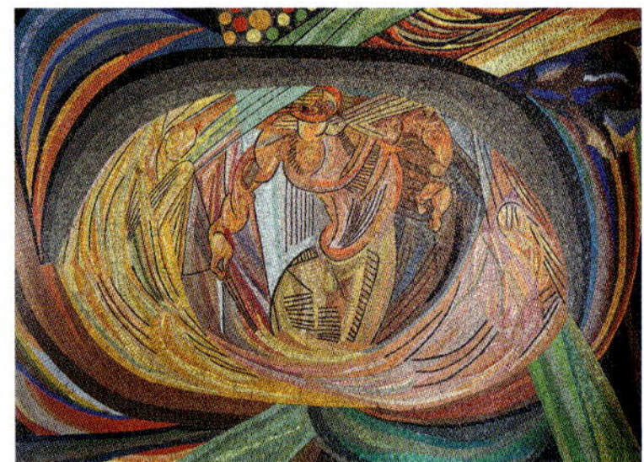

Fig. 30 Vincent van Gogh
The Night Café, 1888
Oil on canvas
72.4 × 92.1 cm
Yale University Art Gallery

Fig. 31 Otto Freundlich
The Birth of Man, 1919
HvW 8
Mosaic
215 × 305 cm
Bühnen Köln–Cologne Theatre

The color design in this composition is linked with the terms of architecture, as a practical and spiritual structure in society. In the opening years of the Weimar Republic, Freundlich was closely connected with the architects of the Gläserne Kette (Glass Chain),[39] not least through the artist groups mentioned earlier—the gouache of the mosaic was reproduced, for instance, in the 1919 program of the Arbeitsrat.[40] In 1922–23, Freundlich was involved in the work on the Wissinger tomb and designed a sculpture that rose up above the tombstone amid an architectural structure by Max Taut made of Gothic arches (p. 195).[41] During this period Freundlich constructed his color compositions as an architecture of colored light, as in the painting *The Mother* (HvW 129, p. 142) from 1921.

Here the central figure merges with the space through the juxtaposition of the colors. The concentric curves intensify this and can also be interpreted as depicting the curvature of space. Here, too, the over-dimensional eyes shaped in spirals are reminiscent of galaxies and tinted yellow and blue, which brings Goethe's color theory to mind. And once again rays are built up from the primary colors and their mixtures. Even more fascinating is the division of the image into two areas by a diagonal running from lower left to top center. Dominating the right hand side is the play of transparency, as described by Goethe[42]: in the upper right-hand corner the yellow ray changes to orange, while the blue rays below turn to shades of violet, and the hand in the blue ray into reddish shadows. Finally, at the "acme" inside the upper left red ray "neither yellow nor blue is to be detected," as in Goethe's "culmination."[43] Two other central passages from Goethe[44] also come to mind here: In the left eye we can observe a "drifting apart of yellow and blue" which "produces green below and red above." These four colors are also to be seen on the left ankle, around the diagonal dividing line in the composition. In keeping with this, a rainbow opens out on the left, whose colors according to Newton correspond to the "seven tones of the octave."[45] The woman's left hand is covering her ear, as if she does not wish to hear Newton's tones. The right might be performing the *mudra* of teaching (although the Buddhist tradition uses the left hand), thereby indicating the reconciliation of the two color theories.

Like his friend Stanisław Kubicki, Freundlich worked with Buddhist and Christian iconography during this period in Berlin. Through Goethe the color scheme can be linked to the "earthly [and the] heavenly creations of Elohim."[46] Thus, with the title *The Mother*, Freundlich points to a divinity which on the one hand exists as colored light on the actual painting, and on the other hand gives birth, as a mother, to light. Once again this is a de-individualized figure, in this case female, which could also represent the crystallized spirit of the artist as one who masters the theory of colors and therefore the perceptual world.

This metaphorical representation combines here the two seemingly antithetical color theories of Goethe and Newton in a harmonious and unified space. A curved space, light, and cosmos spring into being within the crystalline color-architecture from the cosmic eyes, which are an instrument of the mind. So once again "cosmic communism" is made manifest in this image. A few years later, in 1924, Freundlich used a similar iconography when he returned to the same thematic complex in the pastel *Composition* (HvW 230, p. 141).

The subject of an architecture of colors and a deep examination of the color doctrines emerges once more in *Composition* from 1926 (HvW 134, p. 157).[47] The thickly applied paint creates numerous reflections. There seems to be a reference on the upper surface to the cycle of day and night—from the appearance of the moon to the rising of the sun. At the same time the primary colors and their combinations dominate once again, as do the contrasts between brightness and darkness in the tones, all of which are Goethean aspects. Prompting thoughts of Newton, the largest surface in the composition is represented by a series of slender stripes, which are rounded off somewhat like piano keys. At the same time their formation is distantly reminiscent of František Kupka's musically composed verticals. In the lower section the play of colors allows once again a curvature to manifest. Is this also a form of cosmogenesis here? Are Goethe's colors playing on the piano of Newton's chromatic chords? In 1924, two years before working on this painting, Freundlich wrote: "[The] visible world will no longer consist of the rigid coexistence of things and forms, but instead a movement will enter the appearances, much like an acoustic one, which today is invisible to the enslaved eye and unimaginable to the likewise enslaved mind."[48]

1 *15. Europäische Kunstausstellung Berlin 1977: Tendenzen der zwanziger Jahre—Die Novembergruppe. Teil I—Die Maler*, ed. Peter Hopf, exh. cat. Kunstamt Wedding (Berlin, 1977), pp. 8, 14. Otto Freundlich was, however, to publish his repudiation to the Deutscher Werkbund, the Arbeitsrat für Kunst, and the Novembergruppe on December 25, 1919, see *Arbeitsrat für Kunst 1918-1921*, ed. Manfred Schlösser, exh. cat. Akademie der Künste (Berlin, 1980), p. 113, reprinted in Uli Bohnen, ed., *Otto Freundlich: Schriften. Ein Wegbereiter der gegenstandslosen Kunst* (Cologne, 1982), pp. 116–118.

2 Otto Freundlich, "Zur Synthese Architektur—Plastik—Malerei," *Die Erde* 8 (1919), pp. 233–237, here p. 233. Abbreviated in Bohnen, *Otto Freundlich: Schriften*, op. cit. (note 1), pp. 109–111.

3 Ibid., pp. 233, 236.

4 Otto Freundlich, "An die Novembergruppe (Brief, Berlin-Wilmersdorf, 11. Februar 1919)," *Kunst der Zeit*, special issue "Zehn Jahre Novembergruppe," 1–3 (1928), pp. 33–34. Reprinted in *Otto Freundlich: Monographie mit Dokumentation und Werkverzeichnis*, ed. Joachim Heusinger von Waldegg, exh. cat. Rheinisches Landesmuseum Bonn et al. (Cologne, 1978), p. 251, and in Bohnen, *Otto Freundlich: Schriften*, op. cit. (note 1), pp. 108–109.

5 Otto Freundlich, "Es wird Ernst," *Die Erde* 5 (1919), pp. 129–135, here p. 135.

6 Otto Freundlich, "Die namenlose Welt," *Der Strom* 1 (1919), pp. 14–16, here p. 16.

7 Freundlich, "Es wird Ernst," op. cit. (note 5), pp. 129–135.

8 Otto Freundlich, "Der Raum," *Die weissen Blätter* 2 (1919), pp. 82–87, here p. 86. Reprinted in Heusinger, *Otto Freundlich: Werkverzeichnis*, op. cit. (note 4), pp. 254–257 and abbreviated in Bohnen, *Otto Freundlich: Schriften*, op. cit. (note 1), pp. 106–107.

9 Freundlich, "Zur Synthese," op. cit. (note 2), p. 233.

10 Letter from Freundlich to Wilhelm Niemeyer, Paris, March 8 [1913], in Joachim Heusinger von Waldegg, *Otto Freundlich und die rheinische Kunstszene mit Briefen an Herwarth Walden und Wilhelm Niemeyer*, ed. Verein August Macke Haus, exh. cat. August Macke Haus (Bonn, 2006), p. 159.

11 Freundlich, "Der Raum," op. cit. (note 8), p. 86.

12 Freundlich, "Zur Synthese," op. cit. (note 2), pp. 234–235.

13 Otto Freundlich, "Über eine unveröffentlichte Schrift," *Die weissen Blätter* 9 (1916), pp. 297–300; Rita Wildegans-Krollpfeiffer, "Otto Freundlichs Werk im Kontext naturwissenschaftlicher und gesellschaftlicher Erkenntnisse," PhD diss., Universität Hamburg (Hamburg, 1989), pp. 18–23.

14 Freundlich, "Der Raum," op. cit. (note 8), p. 86.

15 Letter from Freundlich to Niemeyer, Cologne [after July 17, 1916], in Heusinger, *Rheinische Kunstszene*, op. cit. (note 10), p. 236.

16 Peter Springer, "Blauer Dunst für die Moderne. Der Sammler und Mäzen Josef Feinhals," in Andreas Beyer, Vittorio Lampugnani, Gunter Schweikhart, eds., *Hülle und Fülle*, Festschrift for Tilmann Buddensieg (Alfter, 1993), pp. 535–556.

17 *Wände aus farbigem Glas: Das Archiv der Vereinigten Werkstätten für Mosaik und Glasmalerei Puhl & Wagner, Gottfried Heinersdorff*, exh. cat. Berlinische Galerie im Martin-Gropius-Bau (Berlin, 1989), p. 217.

18 Letter from Heinersdorff to Feinhals, November 28, 1922. The cited correspondence between Feinhals, Heinersdorff, and Freundlich comes from the Archiv Puhl & Wagner–Gottfried Heinersdorff, Berlinische Galerie.

19 Letter from Heinersdorff to Feinhals, January 14, 1918.

20 Letter from Freundlich to Niemeyer, Trier, January 23, 1918, and January 31, 1918, in Heusinger, *Rheinische Kunstszene*, op. cit. (note 10), pp. 241 and 243.

21 Letter from Freundlich to Heinersdorff, Wilmersdorf, April 10, 1918; Freundlich to Heinersdorff, Wilmersdorf, March 14, 1919.

22 Letter from the Vereinigte Werkstätten to Freundlich, April 9, 1919.

23 Letter from Feinhals to Heinersdorff, Cöln-Marienburg, August 13, 1919.

24 Letter from Freundlich to Heinersdorff, July 10 [1919, according to entry of receipt].

25 Letter from Feinhals to Heinersdorff, September 12, 1919. The mosaic is currently in the Cologne Opera.

26 Max Creutz, "Ein Mosaik: Ausstellung des Cologneer Kunstvereins," *Westdeutsche Wochenschrift* 30 (1919), p. 473.

27 Otto Freundlich, "Janthur als Graphiker," *Der Cicerone* 11 (1919), pp. 510–518, here p. 514. Abbreviated in Bohnen, *Otto Freundlich: Schriften*, op. cit. (note 1), pp. 113–116.

28 Wildegans-Krollpfeiffer, "Otto Freundlichs Werk im Kontext," op. cit. (note 13), pp. 18–23.

29 Ibid. and Bohnen, *Otto Freundlich: Schriften*, op. cit. (note 1), p. 27 and p. 49, footnote 11.

30 Heusinger, *Otto Freundlich: Werkverzeichnis*, op. cit. (note 4), HvW 127.

31 Johann Wolfgang von Goethe, *Theory of Colours*, translated by Charles Lock Eastlake, R.A. (London, 1840), paras. 551 & 552, pp. 212–213. Freundlich's admiration of Goethe's work can be demonstrated from as early as 1904 (cf. Heusinger, *Rheinische Kunstszene*, op. cit. [note 10], p. 82) and is manifest in the manuscript "Goethe" (ca. 1930) (archive Association Les Amis de Jeanne et Otto Freundlich (AAJOF), IMEC, FRN 20.14).

32 Goethe, *Theory of Colours*, op. cit. (note 31), paras. 695, 696, p. 276, and para. 707, p. 280.

33 Ibid., para. 794, p. 314.

34 Freundlich, "Der Raum," op. cit. (note 8), p. 83; manuscript "Der raumlose Himmel," archive Association Les Amis de Jeanne et Otto Freundlich (AAJOF), IMEC, FRN 20.8, excerpted in Bohnen, *Otto Freundlich: Schriften*, op. cit. (note 1), pp. 148–149. Freundlich first remarked directly on Newton in 1927, see his letter to Max Sauerlandt, July 5, 1927, Max Sauerlandt Estate, Staats- und Universitätsbibliothek Hamburg Carl von Ossietzky.

35 On Otto Freundlich's connections with Robert Delaunay see Heusinger, *Rheinische Kunstszene*, op. cit. (note 10), p. 42.

36 Vincent van Gogh, *The Night Café,* 1888, oil painting, 70 × 89 cm, Yale University Art Gallery; letter from Vincent van Gogh to Theo van Gogh, Arles, September 8, 1888, in *The Letters of Vincent van Gogh* (Harmondsworth, 1997), p. xviii, and Klaus Stromer, Ernst Peter Fischer, *Die Natur der Farbe* (Cologne, 2006), p. 142. In 1912 Otto Freundlich saw the large Van Gogh retrospective at the Cologne *Sonderbundausstellung,* see Heusinger, *Rheinische Kunstszene*, op. cit. (note 10), pp. 37–38.

37 Anne Ganteführer-Trier, "Zeitgenossen," in *Zeitgenossen: August Sander und die Kunstszene der 20er Jahre im Rheinland*, exh. cat. Josef-Haubrich-Kunsthalle Cologne (Göttingen, 2000), p. 41; cf. Heusinger, *Rheinische Kunstszene*, op. cit. (note 10), p. 62.

38 Otto Freundlich: "' . . . durch äonenlange Erfahrung.' (Marcus, Kants Weltgebäude)," *Die Aktion* 15/16 (1918), col. 183–185, here col. 183.

39 Annette Menting, *Max Taut: Das Gesamtwerk* (Munich, 2003), pp. 60–69.

40 *Ja! Stimmen des Arbeitsrates für Kunst in Berlin* (Berlin-Charlottenburg, 1919), fig. 9.

41 The sculpture met with objections, was removed in 1923, and has been considered lost since then. See Christoph Fischer, Volker Welter, eds., *Frühlicht in Beton, Das Erbbegräbnis Wissinger von Max Taut und Otto Freundlich in Stahnsdorf: Geschichte und Hintergründe der Entstehung. Dokumentation der Restaurierung 1987/88* (Berlin, 1989). On Freundlich's closer relations with the architect see Heusinger, *Rheinische Kunstszene*, op. cit. (note 10), pp. 306–307.

42 Goethe, *Theory of Colours*, op. cit. (note 31), para. 518, pp. 212–213. Here and passim, some modifications have been made to the historic translation [translator's note].

43 Ibid., para. 523, pp. 214–215.

44 Ibid., para. 919, p. 352, and paras. 695–701, pp. 276–277.

45 Werner Spillmann, ed., *Farb-Systeme 1611–2007: Farb-Dokumente in der Sammlung Werner Spillmann* (Basel, 2009), p. 16.

46 Goethe, *Theory of Colours,* op. cit. (note 31), para. 919, p. 352

47 Heusinger, *Otto Freundlich: Werkverzeichnis*, op. cit. (note 4).

48 Otto Freundlich, "Die gesehene Form," *Die Aktion* 13/14 (1924), col. 687–688, here col. 688. Reprinted in Bohnen, *Otto Freundlich: Schriften*, op. cit. (note 1), pp. 146–148, here p. 147.

Julia Friedrich

The Chartres Experience
Otto Freundlich's Stained Glass Paintings and Pastels from the 1920s

It has often been observed that glass works played an important part in Otto Freundlich's artistic development,[1] yet they are scarcely known. Although Freundlich tried time and again to land commissions in this field, it was mostly in vain, and of the few works he realized just one sole example still exists that can be said with certainty to have been made during his life.

Just how important glass pieces were to him was often emphasized in his letters and texts, and can also be seen from a biographical detail. When he moved in 1924 to Paris shortly after finishing two windows, he registered in the French capital with the job title "stained glass artist."[2] The following year he wrote to Max Sauerlandt, the director of the Hamburg Museum für Kunst und Gewerbe: "But if a new opportunity were to arise where I could teach stained glass, mosaic or sculpture, I would take it without a second thought."[3] Of the three arts he names, Freundlich placed stained glass first.

Where did this penchant for stained glass come from? And why did Freundlich manage to make so few works in the medium? The first question at least is easily answered. In 1914 he spent five months in Chartres. He took a studio in the north tower of the cathedral, whose windows left a deep impression on him. Later he was to sum up the experience, saying: "For about five months I fell under the spell of the world of Chartres and as I left I was marked for life."[4]

Already in Chartres he did a *Study for a Glass Window (Mary)* (HvW 120, now lost), which was exhibited in Fritz Gurlitt's Berlin gallery.[5] In 1916 he drew a *Blossoming Branch of Chartres* (HvW 272, lost) for the art historian Wilhelm Niemeyer, and that same year he described to a friend of his, Friedja Schugt-Maus, the "pure blue of the sky" in the "ancient stained glass"[6] at Chartres. He also gave her one of his window designs (HvW 276, p. 154), whose animated circles may well have been inspired by the rosette in the cathedral.

But many years were to pass before the Chartres experience was to have its real effect on his art. These were telling years: through war and revolution and his own politicization, the artist arrived at his concept of a total interconnectivity, of cosmic communism, from which he derived his principles for a collective, anti-individualistic, and, with that, planar and non-representational art.

His style changed during this period from the Expressionism and Symbolism of his early work to a prismatically split-up abstraction. The basic element in this art, as he named it in a retrospective review written in 1935, was "trapezoidal surfaces."[7] These surfaces, which became typical of his paintings and works on paper from the mid-1920s onward, came however from his involvement with glass as a material. While working on his first window,[8] he learnt from a master glazier that trapezoidal surfaces can "be easily cut from glass," unlike curved surfaces, which have to be divided up into numerous pieces and thus broken up.[9] At the same time he also pointed to Chartres: "Instinctively, and informed by my studies of old stained glass painting from the XII and XIII century," he painted not only curved but also trapezoidal surfaces in his designs.[10]

Freundlich gives a detailed account of the meaning these surfaces were to assume in his painting. He tells us that while designing the next window and "painting [the surfaces] directly next to one another," he was "seized by a feeling of excitement . . . as if from a new life in painting." This new life only "truly revealed" itself to him, though, later on: "The intimate connection between all the surfaces on one picture, in which like a cell in an organism each passes the energy on to the next cell until there is but an unbroken circulation of these energies throughout the entire organism, this could first be realized by the accumulation of all colors in one picture. And this was the one goal that I strived to attain, because it tallied with my social convictions: with Socialism."[11] However, the "accumulation" of directly bordering colors, the "dialectical language of the picture,"[12] not only points to Socialism as a conviction, Freundlich also attributes to it—at least in retrospect—a specific class origin: among the guild craftsmen of the Middle Ages, as the master glaziers indicated to him.

His first window (HvW 9) was done in 1922 in a studio in Naumburg.[13] Freundlich was commissioned to design it by his friend and patron Julius Wissinger, who had it installed in his home. Since 1933, all trace of it has vanished. According to Wissinger's son Detlev, it had "colored vibrations and circles,"[14] which indicates an abstract composition.

This first commission for a glass piece was followed by just two more that were demonstrably realized.[15] Both were done in 1924 in the Berlin studio run by the glass construction manufacturer Gottfried Heinersdorff, in which Freundlich had already had his mosaic *The Birth of Man* (HvW 8, p. 131) made in 1919. As co-founder of the Deutscher Werkbund (German Association of Craftsmen) in 1907 and the Berliner Künstlerbund für Glasmalerei und Glasmosaik (Berlin Artists' Association for Stained Glass and Glass Mosaic) in 1910, Heinersdorff made a decisive contribution to establishing the medium of glass in the avant-garde. Expressionists such as Max Pechstein, César Klein, and Adolf Hölzel worked in his studio, which merged in 1914 with the studios run by Puhl & Wagner.[16] Heinersdorff wanted to replace "painting on glass," as was practiced in his view by the Jugendstil and Historicism movements, by "painting with glass."[17] He knew and admired the glass works of the Middle Ages. Freundlich found the right partner in him, a person who not only had a similar artistic background—Heinersdorff visited Chartres for the first time in 1912 and wrote about it[18]—but also had the technical possibilities to realize his artistic ideas.

The window for the Münster publisher and printer Johannes Bredt (HvW 11, p. 140)was one meter by two in size. A black and white photograph still exists of the window. In its composition it is reminiscent of the painting *The Mother* from 1921 (HvW 129, p. 142) and the pastel *Composition* from 1924 (HvW 230, p. 141). It was probably done in dark colors, with apparently green and brown tints in the lower section.[19] Freundlich emphasized that he had introduced a technical innovation: he

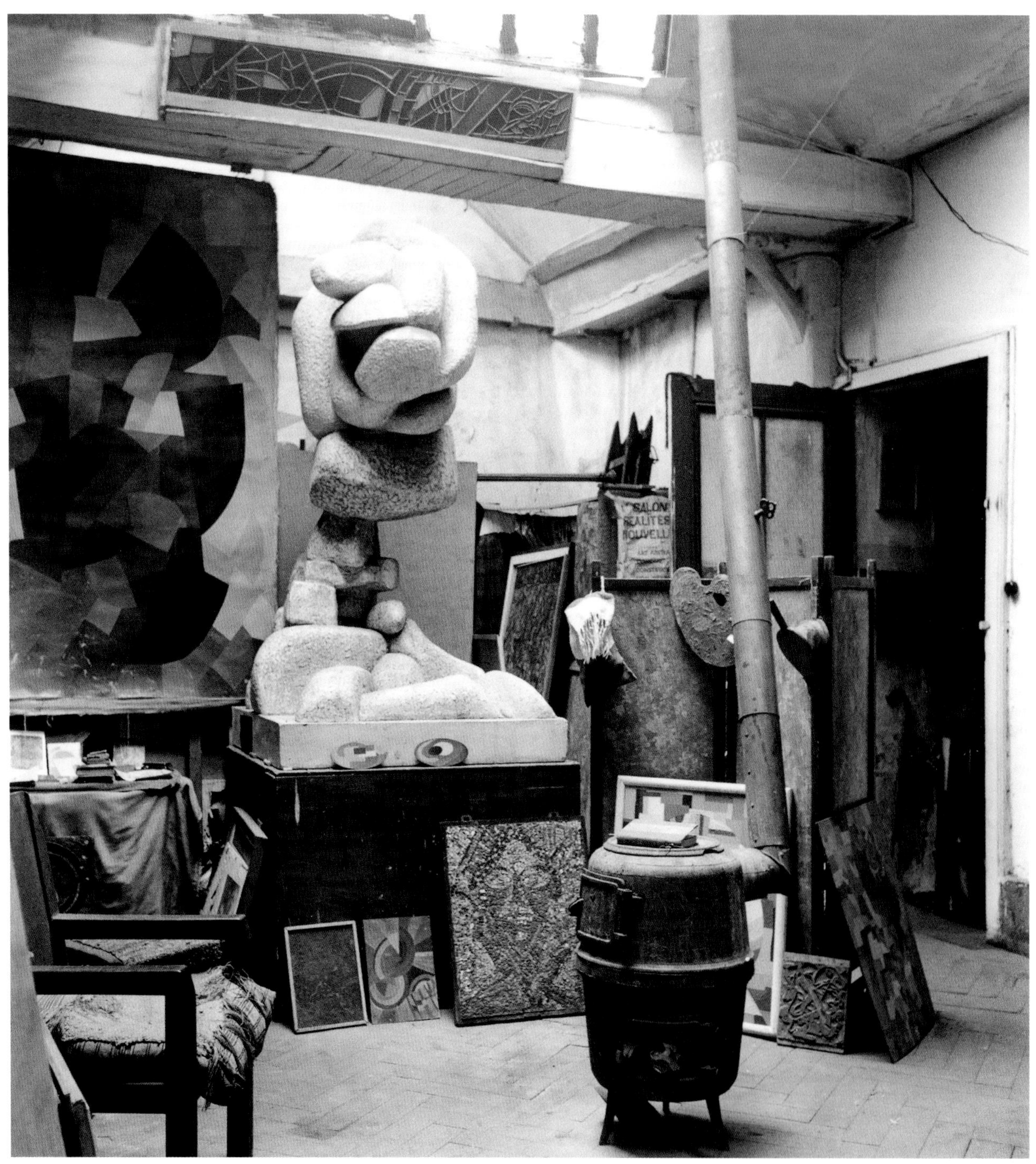
SALON

backed the glass pieces two- or even three-fold so as to be able to dispense with black enamel.[20] This technique of placing a number of pieces of glass one behind the other may have been taken from Adolf Hölzel, who had developed it for his Bahlsen Windows (1915–18) in Heinersdorff's workshop.[21]

This renunciation of black enamel distinguished Freundlich from Expressionist friends such as Max Pechstein and Karl Schmidt-Rottluff, who employed the varnish to heighten the chromaticity of the glass, in keeping with medieval techniques, or even to give them an old patina (fig. 32).[22] This kind of historifying use of the technique was alien to Freundlich. The medieval methods only interested him for their artist effect, and he had no reservations about dropping them when a comparable or even stronger effect could be achieved by contemporary means. Heinersdorff recommended in 1924 that he should view the medieval windows in the Trocadéro collection in Paris. After his visit Freundlich wrote to him: "The red is flamed and reminds me of the glass pieces in our window backed with opal [semi-transparent glass]. And I am convinced that the old masters would have used opal if they had known it."[23]

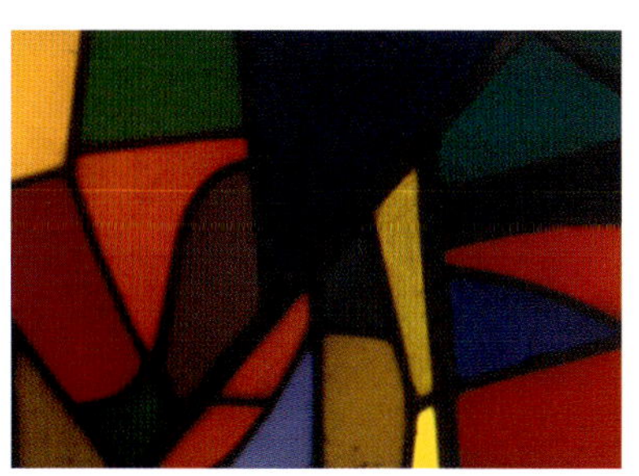

Fig. 32 Karl Schmidt-Rottluff
Head of Christ, ca. 1919
Stained glass
65.5 × 51.1 cm
Brücke Museum, Berlin

Fig. 33 Otto Freundlich
Reclining Woman (detail), 1924
HvW 10
Stained glass
24 × 163 cm
Donation Freundlich – Musées de Pontoise

Fig. 34 Willy Maywald
Otto Freundlich's studio with *Ascension*, *Reclining Woman*, and *Rosette I*, together with works by Jeanne Kosnick-Kloss, 1948
Association Willy Maywald

Freundlich's window for the photographer Henri Martinie (*Reclining Woman*, HvW 10, p. 145) has survived. Its extreme horizontal format resulted from its intended location in the client's house in Paris. Why it was never installed there remains unclear. Freundlich kept it in his studio in Paris, whence it entered his estate (fig. 34). For the format he returned to the woodcuts that appeared in the magazine *Die Aktion* in 1918: *Reclining Nude* and *Nude* (HvW 454, p. 144). He described the figure in a letter as a "sleeping woman."[24] Much more so than in the preliminary drawing (p. 144), her form has been dissolved in the window and divided up into sections of rays and circles. This is also due to technical considerations; the stained glass maker has to work with segments that are divided up by lead strips. The result shows the figure broken up prismatically in a way almost reminiscent of Cubism, although Freundlich rejected the latter as a non-planar art bound to three-dimensional plasticity.[25]

In August 1924, shortly after finishing the second window, Freundlich went to Paris. Just how seriously he remained with the job description of "stained glass painter" he chose there can be seen from a letter he wrote in December 1926 to Heinersdorff from Chartres: "As I entered the cathedral the afternoon sun flooded through the west window. This golden yellow was ablaze and dominated the other colors. A yellow like egg yolk, without the slightest trace of green or brown!! What a summation of boldness and beauty in these windows. If only we had the assignments we could simply lavish out our treasures."[26]

In order to pay off his debts to Heinersdorff, in the same letter he offered him a business partnership: He wanted to produce colored lampshades. "I got the idea directly from my windows."[27] His plan was to create mixed colors from light by overlapping pieces of glass in various shades.[28] He writes that he has established the "correctness of this principle" with the aid of a model: "tackled in grand manner, the result could lead to an international revolution in the lighting industry."[29] The idea, he further relates, had been filed a year before at the patent office but the 550 francs were lacking to pay for the actual patent, which had been promised.

Heinersdorff considered the technical implementation to be too complicated and costly and rejected it as "having no future."[30] A recently discovered design[31] shows how Freundlich envisaged the glass lampshades (p. 147).

Also in December 1926 he complained in a letter to Sauerlandt that "despite his great enthusiasm at the beginning," Bredt hadn't done anything about his window. "I find that sad, because I have given my best to the piece & was occupied with it for 4 whole months. Every piece of glass was chosen by me & all the backing layers [were] pieced together by me—work that made me happy but nevertheless was long and arduous. . . . If only it had been reproduced or reviewed at least in the art press . . . I would have had the chance of getting new contracts. But nothing of the kind, a reign of silence fell on me, as with my mosaic."[32] He asked Sauerlandt to take up the sale of the window. But nothing became of it.[33]

So no sooner did Freundlich see himself as a glass painter than he found it impossible to be one. He concentrated instead on another medium closely related to stained glass: pastels. The first pastels were done in 1919. Later they accompanied his work on the windows and window designs, and in the following years they actually had to deputize for the medium he had lost. He probably felt much like Hölzel, who on completing his Bahlsen windows only ever did pastels and, unlike Freundlich, even turned his back on oils.[34]

With pastels the pigments are largely applied to the paper without any binding agent, so that they radiate brightly. Unlike the works with glass, Freundlich could dispense here with lead strips. The colors have been placed directly side by side, often smudging the contours of the surfaces, or with one color deliberately slurred into the next. An impression arises of transparency and gleaming light (HvW 234, p. 162). The circles, vibrations, and rays that are shown reflect Freundlich's vision of a cosmic order that can be depicted through a grand harmony of colors.[35] The dark blue in many of the pastels is clearly not just the blue of the sky but of heaven, as he had already seen in the windows at Chartres and described in 1916 to his anthroposophical friend Friedja: "In the glorious cathedral at Chartres . . . the pure blue of the heavens is to be found in the ancient stained glass. [It] manifests floating, unearthly, radiantly inspirited, and even though the entire heavens live above us as something uniformly seeing, our enraptured eye always lands presciently on another and enters into dialogues in the populous firmament with countless blue stars, blue starry eye-stars."[36] Even the radiant yellow in the pastels goes back to Chartres, to the " yellow like egg yolk, without the slightest trace of green or brown!!" or the "golden yellow ablaze" in the afternoon sun that he described in 1926 in that letter to Heinersdorff. Quite a number of the pastels also recall heavenly bodies, one for instance a gleaming comet (HvW 227, p. 169), another a full moon (HvW 234, p. 162).

Just how close glass and pastel were connected for Freundlich is also shown in *View from the Window* (HvW 231, p. 160) from 1924–25, whose title is not necessarily from him.[37] In the pastel, a frame can be distinguished that seems to look onto a tripartite landscape. The inwardly splintered steps differ with the incidental light, growing brighter from top to bottom. Striking here are the driplike elements, which resemble polished crystals. A similar form can be found in the window for Martinie, which also resembles this pastel in its prismatic fragmentation. Perhaps Freundlich is showing here not a view *out* of a window but a view *of* a window—a look at the variously tinted and polished glass facets of a stained glass painting whose color dynamics and blue tinged sky point once again to a cosmic reality.

It may be seen from his correspondence with Heinersdorff, Sauerlandt, and Franz Wilhelm Seiwert that Freundlich tried to drum up new commissions for glass works in the late twenties.[38] That he continued to be preoccupied with this medium right into his later years is attested to not only in his letters but by drawings in his estate (HvW 371, p. 155; HvW 346, p. 155, and HvW 415, p. 154). With one exception from 1936–37, he was not to do any more pastels after 1931. The oil paintings and gouaches of his later years are not so closely related to glass, even if Freundlich attributes the "accumulation of all colors on one picture" to the master glazier's trapezoidal segments.

As late as 1941 he designed another glass window (HvW 210, p. 280). The gouache bears the title *Rosette II*. He mentions it in a letter to Picasso which however he never sent. As may be read in the letter, it took him back to the starting point in his glass art: "I have worked on a design for a glass piece which is intended to be done on the scale of a rosette in a cathedral."[39]

1 Günter Aust, *Otto Freundlich. 1878–1943* (Cologne, 1960), pp. 28–29; Maria-Katharina Schulz, *Glasmalerei der klassischen Moderne in Deutschland* (Frankfurt am Main et al., 1987), pp. 165–185; Thorsten Rodiek, "Glasgemälde und Mosaiken als Metaphern des Universalen," in *Otto Freundlich: Ein Wegbereiter der abstrakten Kunst*, ed. Thorsten Rodiek and Gerhard Leistner, exh. cat. Ostdeutsche Galerie Regensburg et al. (Regensburg, 1994), pp. 33–39; Joachim Heusinger von Waldegg, *Otto Freundlich und die rheinische Kunstszene mit Briefen an Herwarth Walden und Wilhelm Niemeyer*, published by Verein August Macke Haus, exh. cat. August Macke Haus (Bonn, 2006), pp. 42–43.

2 Joachim Heusinger von Waldegg, "Otto Freundlich—Leben und Werk," in *Otto Freundlich: Monographie mit Dokumentation und Werkverzeichnis*, ed. Joachim Heusinger von Waldegg, exh. cat. Rheinisches Landesmuseum Bonn et al. (Cologne 1978), pp. 11–43, here p. 27.

3 Letter from Freundlich to Sauerlandt, December 26, 1925, Archiv Museum für Kunst und Gewerbe (MKG), Hamburg.

4 Letter from Freundlich to Heinersdorff, December 22, 1917, Archiv Puhl & Wagner–Gottfried Heinersdorff (APWGH), Berlinische Galerie.

5 Cf. Heusinger, *Otto Freundlich: Werkverzeichnis*, op. cit. (note 2), p. 86. The remaining works that he made during the five months in Chartres belong more to Freundlich's early symbolist period.

6 Letter from Freundlich to Schugt-Maus, January 2, 1916, cited in Heusinger, *Rheinische Kunstszene*, op. cit. (note 1), p. 252.

7 Otto Freundlich, "Bekenntnisse eines revolutionären Malers" [1935]; Eng. trans. "Confessions of a Revolutionary Painter," in the present volume, pp. 4–16, here p. 9.

8 Glass window for Julius Wissinger, HvW 9, lost.

9 Freundlich, "Bekenntnisse," op. cit. (note 7), p. 9.

10 Ibid., p. 9.

11 Ibid., p. 9.

12 Ibid., pp. 9–10.

13 It was not possible to learn which studio was used in Naumburg for the stained glass picture.

14 "Freundlich designed a glass window for my father's study in our house, and he really loved it. It consisted of colored vibrations and circles. When we moved in 1932 to Charlottenburg the window remained in the house. The new inhabitant was the painter Bruno Krauskopf, who set up his studio in that room. But since the window distracted him, he took it out and stored it away in the building. In 1933 Bruno Krauskopf had to leave the country, and since then nothing is known of the window's whereabouts." Letter from Detlev Wissinger to Joachim Heusinger von Waldegg, July 31, 1979, private archive of Heusinger von Waldegg, whom I thank for granting me access to it.

15 The catalogue raisonné contains two designs for glass windows on which Freundlich noted that he had executed them in 1934 and 1937 (HvW 346 and 371, both p. 155). No further information could be found on either. The window HvW 371 based on HvW 28 was made posthumously in 1956, as were windows HvW 42 and 43 (cf. Heusinger, *Otto Freundlich: Werkverzeichnis*, op. cit. [note 2], pp. 78–79). The small round window HvW 27 may have been made during his life (cf. letter to Heinersdorff dated March 6, 1925: "I am taking my little window with me to Paris where it is anticipated with joy," APWGH, Berlinische Galerie), but cannot be attested to before 1960. HvW 12 was made posthumously in August Wagner's studio in Berlin. (Cf. the letter from Jeanne Kosnick-Kloss to Hans Wagner, February 7, 1955, APWGH, Berlinische Galerie. The pane was destroyed in transport to Paris and presumably replaced.) Maria-Katharina Schulz assumes that a number of the dalle-de-verre glass windows in his estate were done during his lifetime. According to her, Freundlich saw the new technique at the world exposition in Paris 1937 and was among the first to use it. (Cf. Schulz, *Glasmalerei*, op. cit. [note 1], pp. 181 and 248.) While conceivable, there are no certain dates for these glass works. The dalle-de-verre glass windows HvW 16 (p. 153), HvW 33 (p. 152), and HvW 45 are signed and dated on their frames. It is doubtful, though, whether the signatures are by Freundlich's own hand.

16 Heinersdorff at first took over his father's workshop before merging his firm in 1914 with Puhl & Wagner to become the Vereinigte Werkstätten für Mosaik und Glasmalerei Puhl & Wagner—Gottfried Heinersdorff. Cf. Jutta Dresch, "Gottfried Heinersdorff und Johan Thorn Prikker: Zwei Protagonisten der Glasmalerei der klassischen Moderne in Deutschland," in *Glasmalerei der Moderne: Faszination Farbe im Gegenlicht*, ed. Jutta Dresch, exh. cat. Badisches Landesmuseum (Karlsruhe, 2011), pp. 21–29, here p. 21.

17 Ibid., p. 22. Cf. also Kai Habermehl, "Einführung: Lichtsteine Gottfried Heinersdorff und die Erneuerung der Glasmalerei in Deutschland," in *Farblicht: Kunst und Künstler im Wirkungskreis des Glasmalers Gottfried Heinersdorff (1883–1941)*, ed. Burkhard Leismann, exh. cat. Kunstmuseum Ahlen; Edwin Scharff Museum Neu-Ulm; Clemens-Sels-Museum Neuss (Hagen, 2001), pp. 7–13, here p. 8., and Schulz, *Glasmalerei*, op. cit. (note 1), pp. 27–38.

18 Cf. Gottfried Heinersdorff, "Die Glasmalereien der Notre-Dame von Chartres," in *Kunst und Künstler* 10 (1912), pp. 589–594.

19 Cf. letters from Freundlich to Sauerlandt, July 8, 1924, Archiv MKG, published in part in Heinz Spielmann, ed., *Max Sauerlandt: Ethos des Kunsturteils. Korrespondenz 1909–1933* (Hamburg, 2013), p. 210, and from November 24, 1924, Archiv MKG.

20 Cf. letters from Freundlich to Heinersdorff, May 2, 1924 (APWGH, Berlinische Galerie), and Freundlich to Sauerlandt, December 9, 1926, Archiv MKG, published in part in Spielmann, *Sauerlandt*, op. cit. (note 19), pp. 221–222.

21 Cf. Schulz, *Glasmalerei*, op. cit. (note 1), p. 168.

22 Cf. ibid., p. 32. Black varnish was also employed to give visibility to the structure of hand-blown antique glass. Cf. Dagmar Schmidt, "Expressionistische und konstruktive Tendenzen in der profanen Glasbildkunst," in Leismann, *Farblicht*, op. cit. (note 17), pp. 15–41, here p. 21.

23 Letter from Freundlich to Heinersdorff, August 24, 1924, APWGH, Berlinische Galerie.

24 Letter from Freundlich to Henry Poulaille, October 31, 1924: "J'ai fini le projet pour le vitrail Martinie. Je l'ai changé tout à fait, c'est maintenant devenu 'la dormeuse,' une femme qui dort." Archive Association Les Amis de Jeanne et Otto Freundlich (AAJOF), IMEC, FRN 9.1.

25 Cf. Otto Freundlich, "Was wollt ihr von Picasso?" [1922], in Uli Bohnen, ed., *Otto Freundlich: Schriften. Ein Wegbereiter der gegenstandslosen Kunst* (Cologne, 1982), pp. 128–129, here p. 128.

26 Letter from Freundlich to Heinersdorff, December 1926, APWGH, Berlinische Galerie.

27 Ibid.

28 Letter from Freundlich to Sauerlandt, December 28, 1925, Archiv MKG, partly published in Almut Klingbeil, "Zur Korrespondenz Otto Freundlich—Max Sauerlandt," in *Jahrbuch des Museums für Kunst und Gewerbe Hamburg* 9/10, 1990–1991 (Hamburg, 1993), pp. 141–152, here pp. 144–145.

29 Letter from Freundlich to Heinersdorff, December 1926, APWGH, Berlinische Galerie.

30 Letter from Heinersdorff to Freundlich, January 29, 1927, APWGH, Berlinische Galerie.

31 Rediscovered by Geneviève Debien, on whose advice the Jüdisches Museum Berlin acquired the draft.

32 Letter from Freundlich to Sauerlandt, December 9, 1926, Archiv MKG, printed partly in Klingbeil, "Zur Korrespondenz," op. cit. (note 28), p. 146, and in Bohnen, *Otto Freundlich: Schriften*, op. cit. (note 25), p. 151.

33 Sauerlandt corresponded about the window with Bredt. After an exhibition at Fritz Gurlitt's in August and September 1924, it found its way to him at the Hamburg Museum. Whether it was ever at Bredt's in Münster is unclear. At the end of December 1926, Bredt wanted to take it with him, but did not contact the artist after January 1927. Cf. correspondence between Sauerlandt and Bredt and also Sauerlandt and Freundlich, December 1926 to July 1927, Archiv MKG.

34 Dresch, *Glasmalerei*, op. cit. (note 16), p. 38.

35 Cf. Uli Bohnen, "Otto Freundlich—Entwürfe zum kosmischen Kommunismus," in Bohnen, *Otto Freundlich: Schriften*, op. cit. (note 25), pp. 9–51, here pp. 41, 48.

36 Letter from Freundlich to Schugt-Maus, January 2, 1916, in Heusinger, *Rheinische Kunstszene*, op. cit. (note 1), p. 252.

37 The Wuppertal lawyer Emil Grobel, who received the pastel from Freundlich as a present in the 1920s, divulged this title to Günter Aust during the preparations for the exhibition at the Wallraf-Richartz-Museum in 1960. Cf. exhibition documents in the Archiv Museum Ludwig. No title is given on the rear of the pastel.

38 In November 1927 Freundlich hoped for a commission to design the window of a Protestant church in Paris, but it was never executed and the correspondence with Heinersdorff petered out (cf. letter from Freundlich to Heinersdorff, November 9, 1927, APWGH, Berlinische Galerie). Schulz presumes that HvW 301–305 comprise the designs for the window. Cf. Schulz, *Glasmalerei*, op. cit. (note 1), p. 248. In the file from Puhl & Wagner in the archive of the Berlinische Galerie are four sketches of various sizes showing religious scenes. It is possible that they are connected with the hoped-for commission. Max Sauerlandt took pains to see that Freundlich could execute a kindred work in the new building for the *Hamburger Fremdenblatt*, but this commission likewise fell through (cf. letter from Freundlich to Sauerlandt, January 31, 1927, Archiv MKG, partly published in Klingbeil, "Zur Korrespondenz," op. cit. [note 28], p. 148). Franz Wilhelm Seiwert drew Freundlich's attention as late as 1930 to a competition which Irene With, wife of the director of the Kunstgewerbemuseum Köln, Karl With, wished to organize for designs in a Cologne church. This likewise came to naught (cf. letter from Seiwert to Freundlich, December 15, 1930, archive AAJOF, IMEC, FRN 14.24).

39 Letter from Freundlich to Picasso, undated, but written in the Pyrenees, and thus after June 1940. Archive AAJOF, IMEC, FRN 9.1.

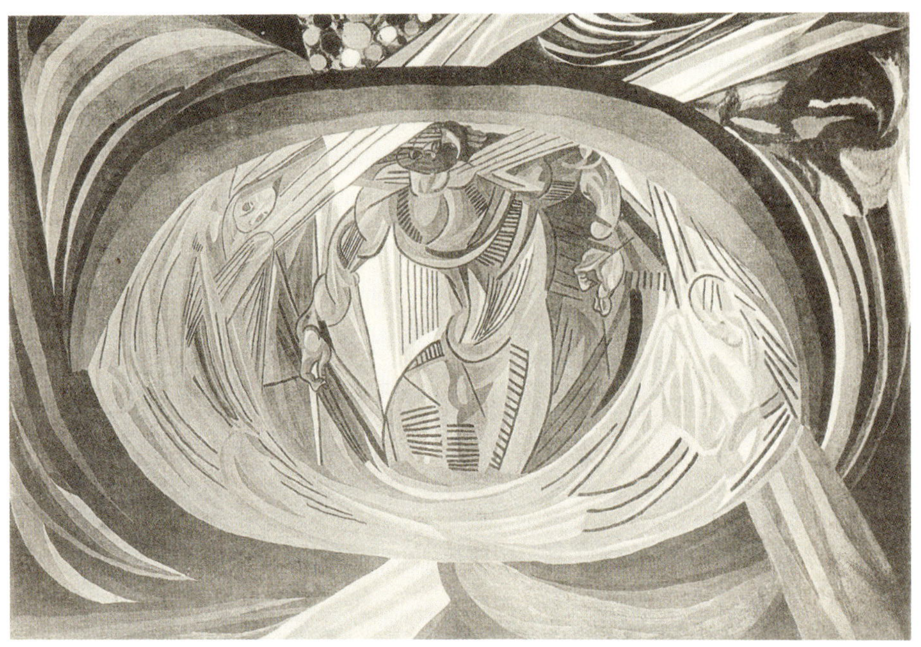

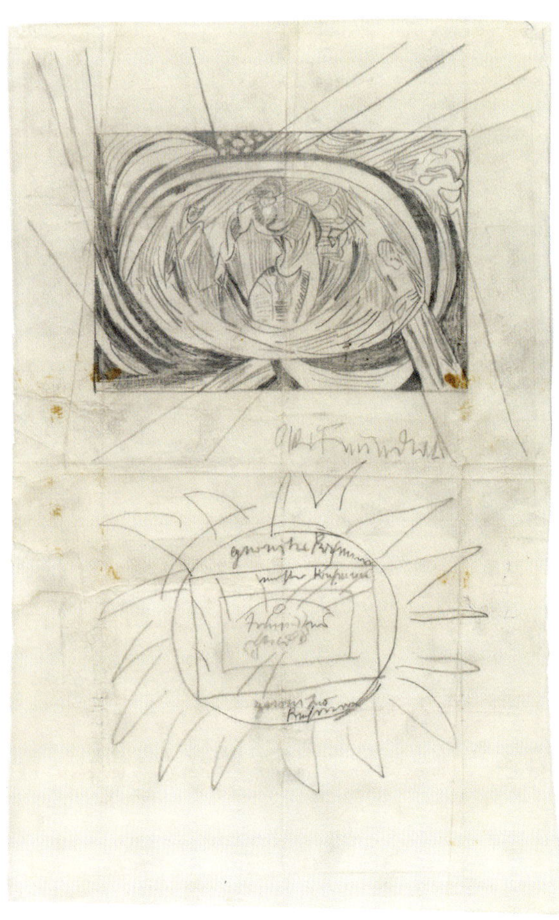

The Birth of Man, ca. 1918–19
HvW 127
Gouache
Lost

Sketch for the mosaic The Birth of Man, 1919
HvW 297
Pencil on tracing paper

The Birth of Man, 1919
HvW 8
Mosaic

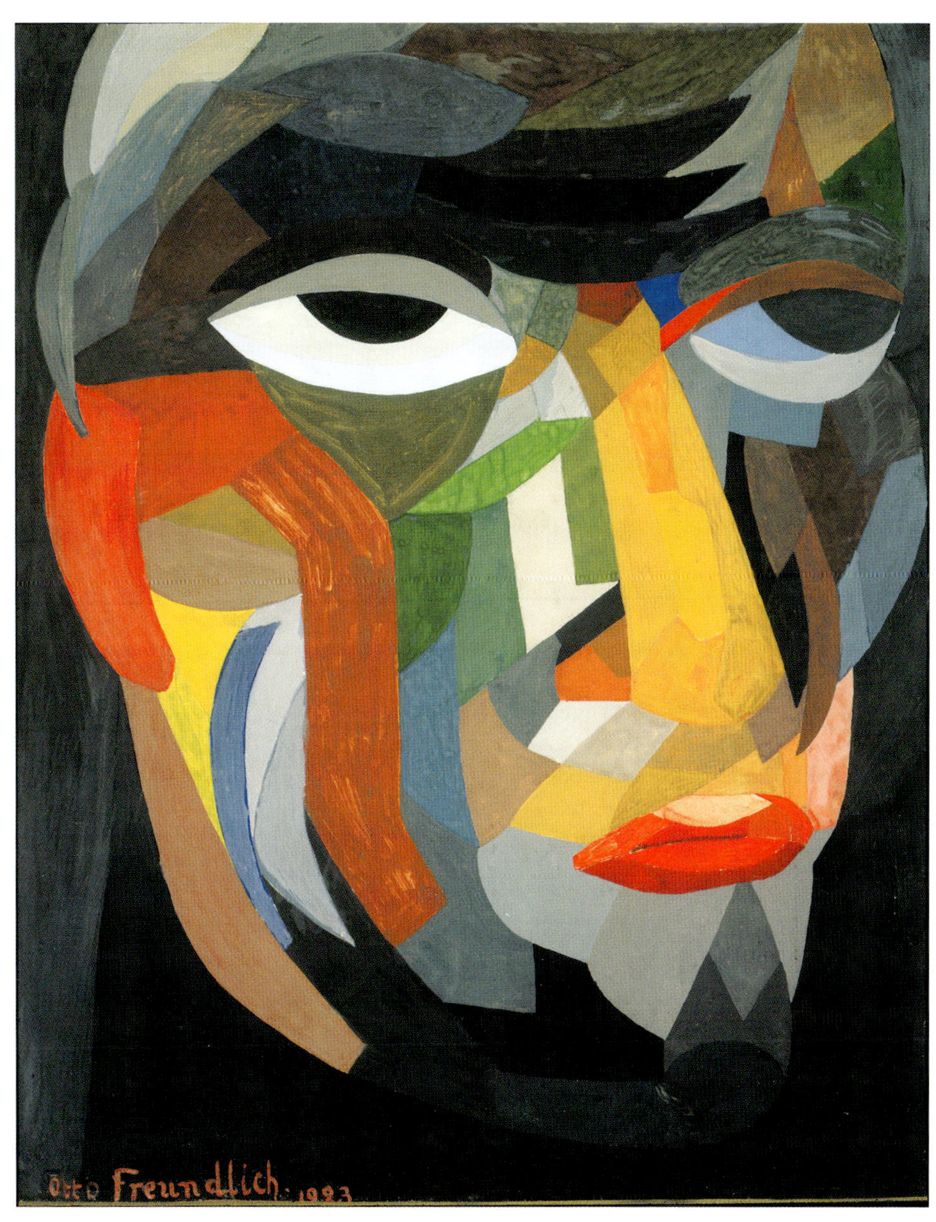

Head (Self-Portrait), 1923
HvW 131
Gouache on paper

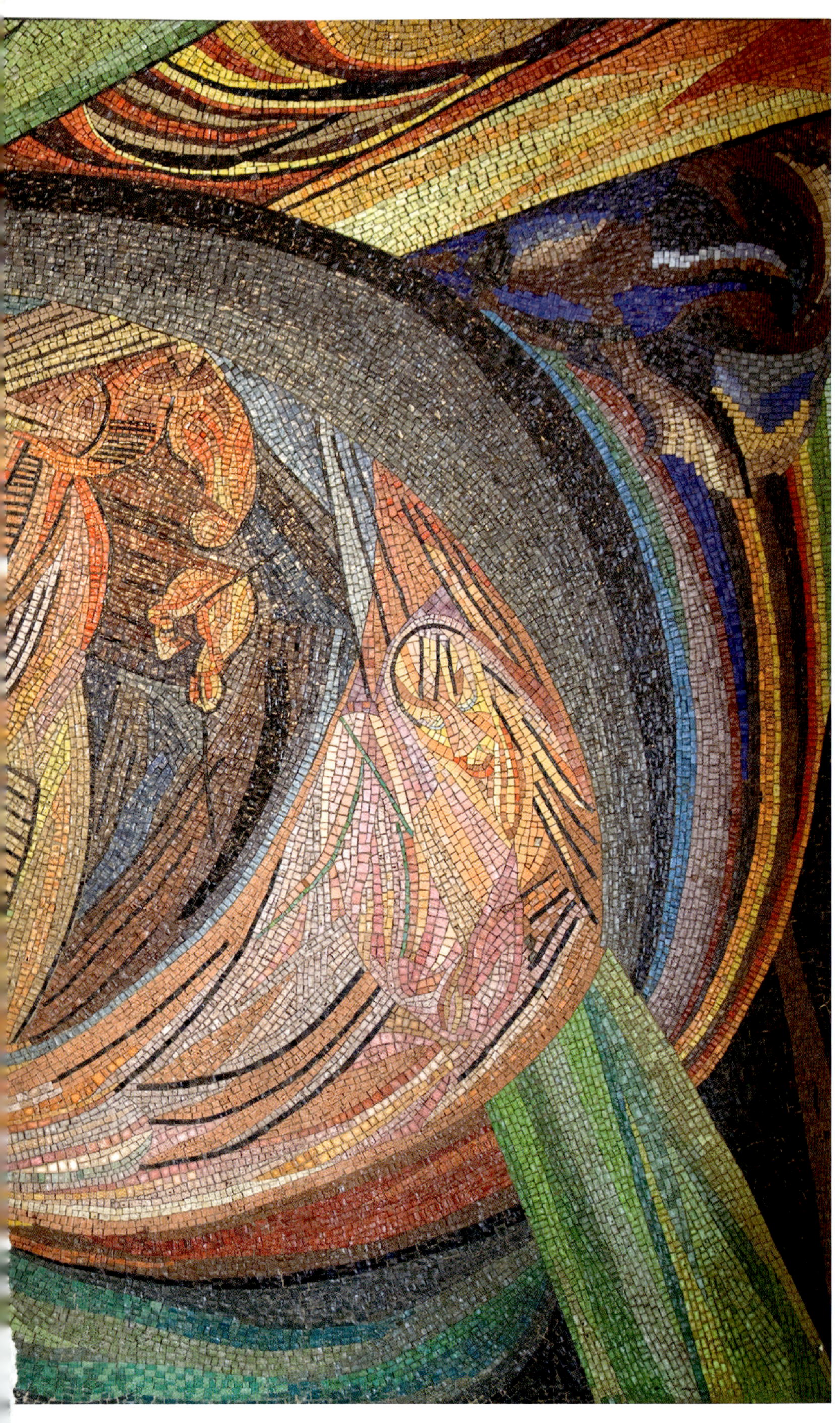

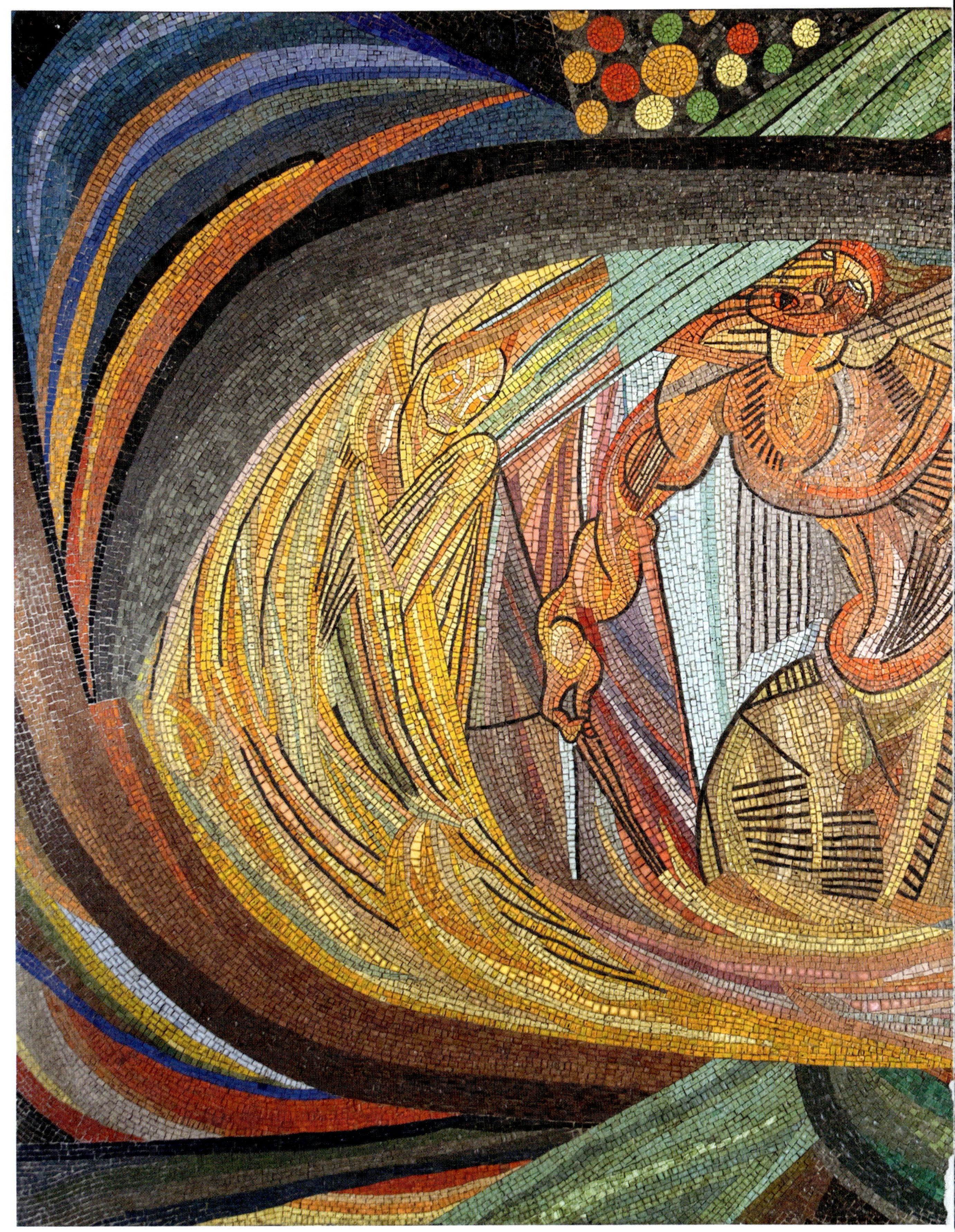

DENN DAS IST DIE LETZTE MATERIE.
SO EIN DING ALLEIN IN IHM SELBST STEHET
UND JUBILIERET IN SEINER EXALTATION.
MEISTER ECKEHARD.

DIE ZEICHEN

OTTO FREUNDLICH

MEINEM LIEBEN FREUNDE
COLLOFINO
IN DANKBARKEIT.

Für [illegible] und [illegible]
in herzlicher Freundschaft.

Köln Febr. 1920 Otto Freundlich

KAIROS-VERLAG · KÖLN AM RHEIN 1920.

DRUCK GEORG LUTZ, KÖLN.

The Signs, 1919–20
Title page of the folio

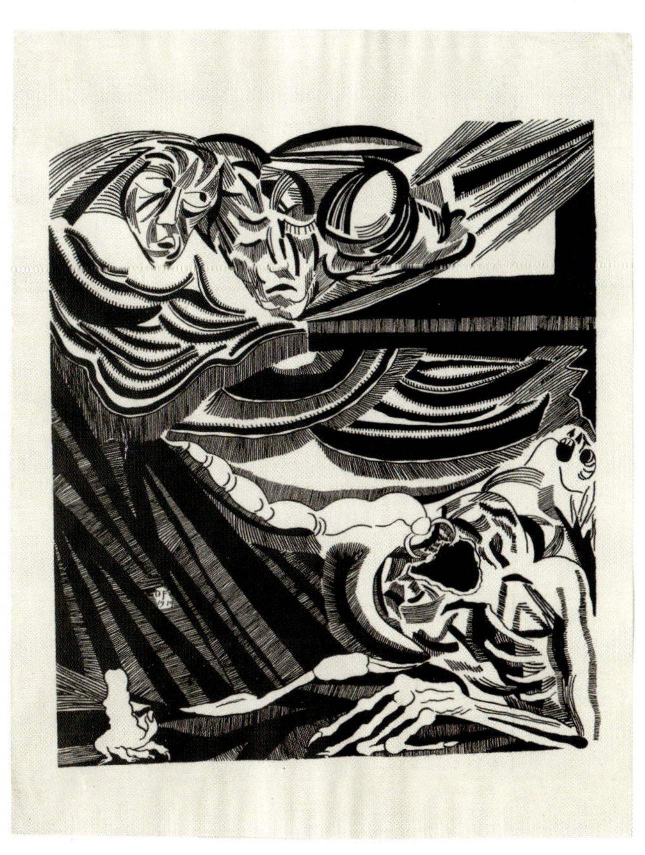

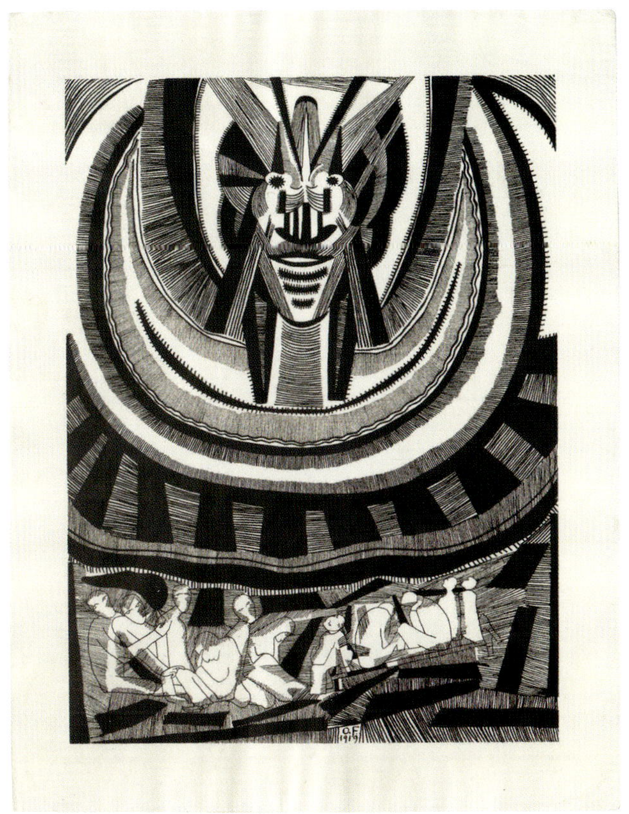

The Signs, 1919–20, sheet 1
HvW 461
Zinc engraving on paper

The Signs, 1919–20, sheet 2
HvW 462
Zinc engraving on paper

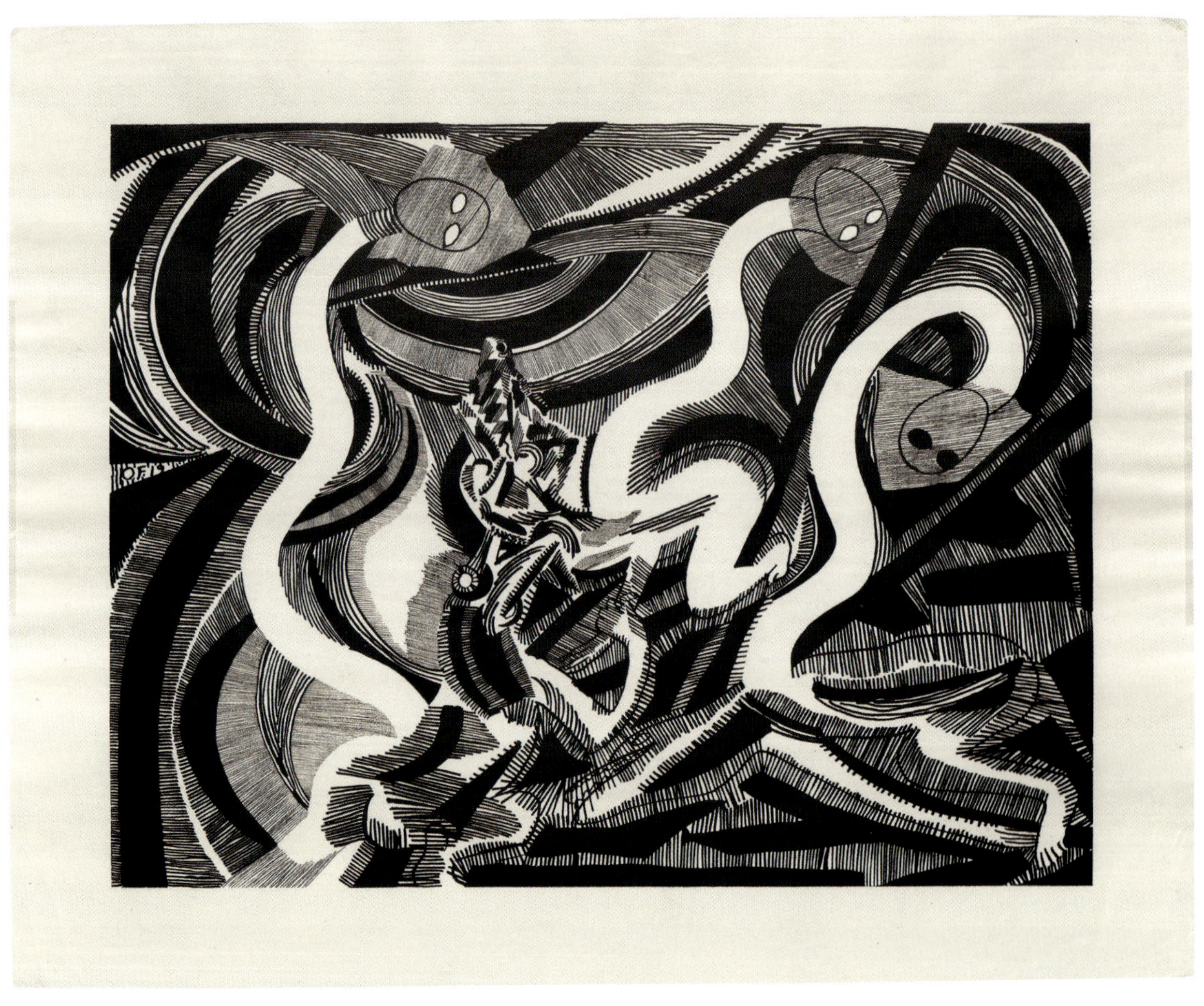

The Signs, 1919–20, sheet 3
HvW 463
Zinc engraving on paper

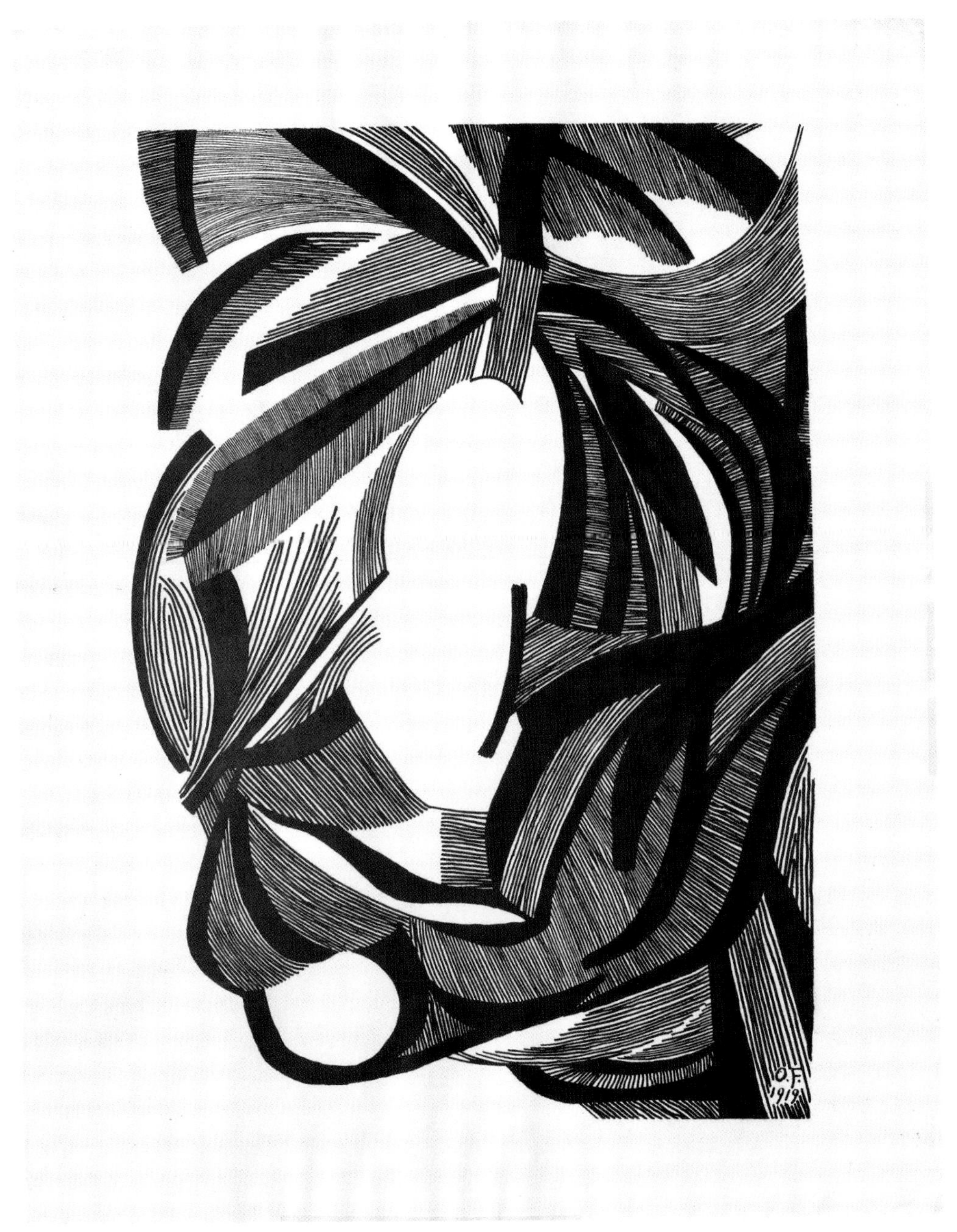

The Signs, 1919–20, sheet 4
HvW 464
Zinc engraving on paper

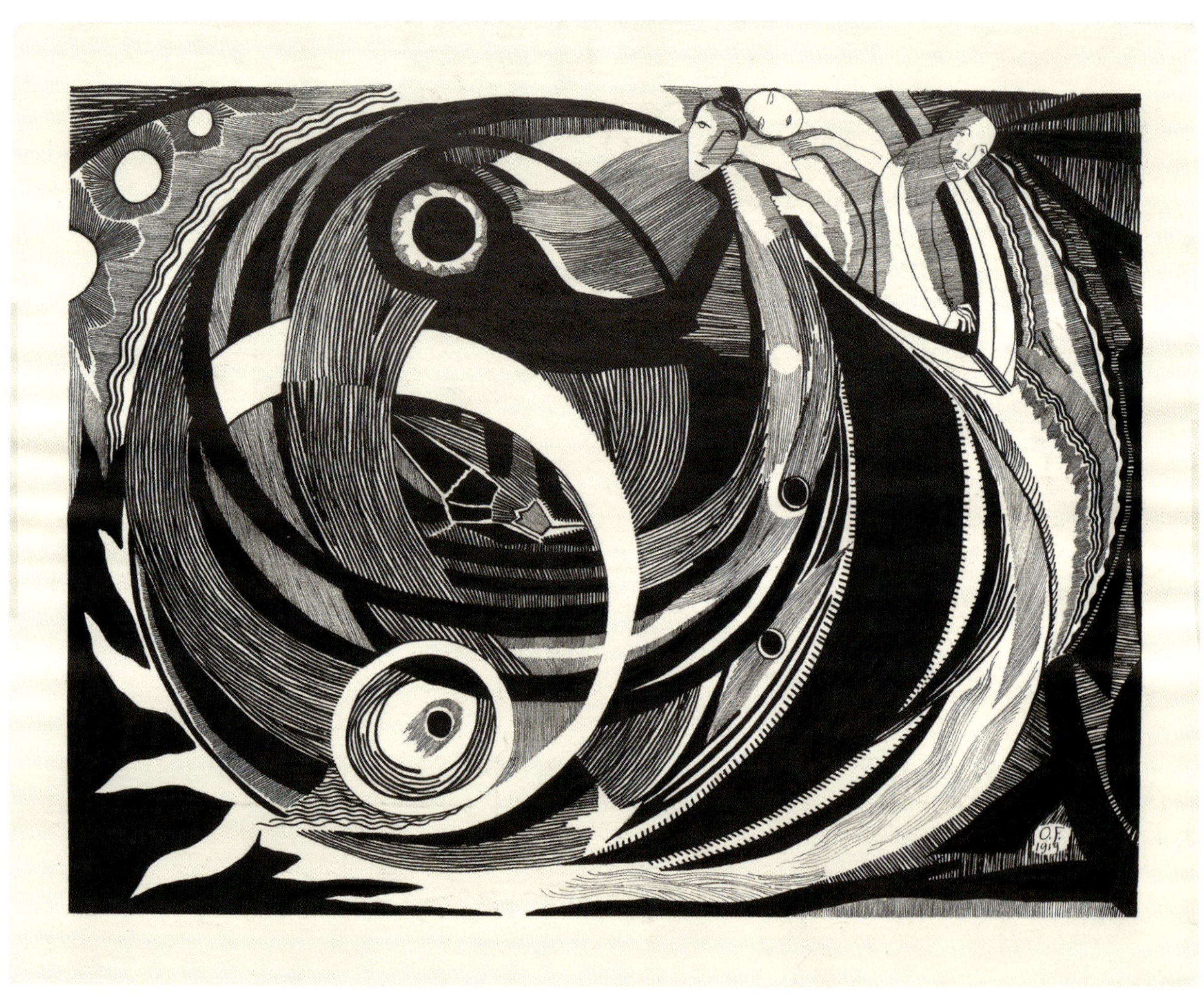

The Signs, 1919–20, sheet 5
HvW 465
Zinc engraving on paper

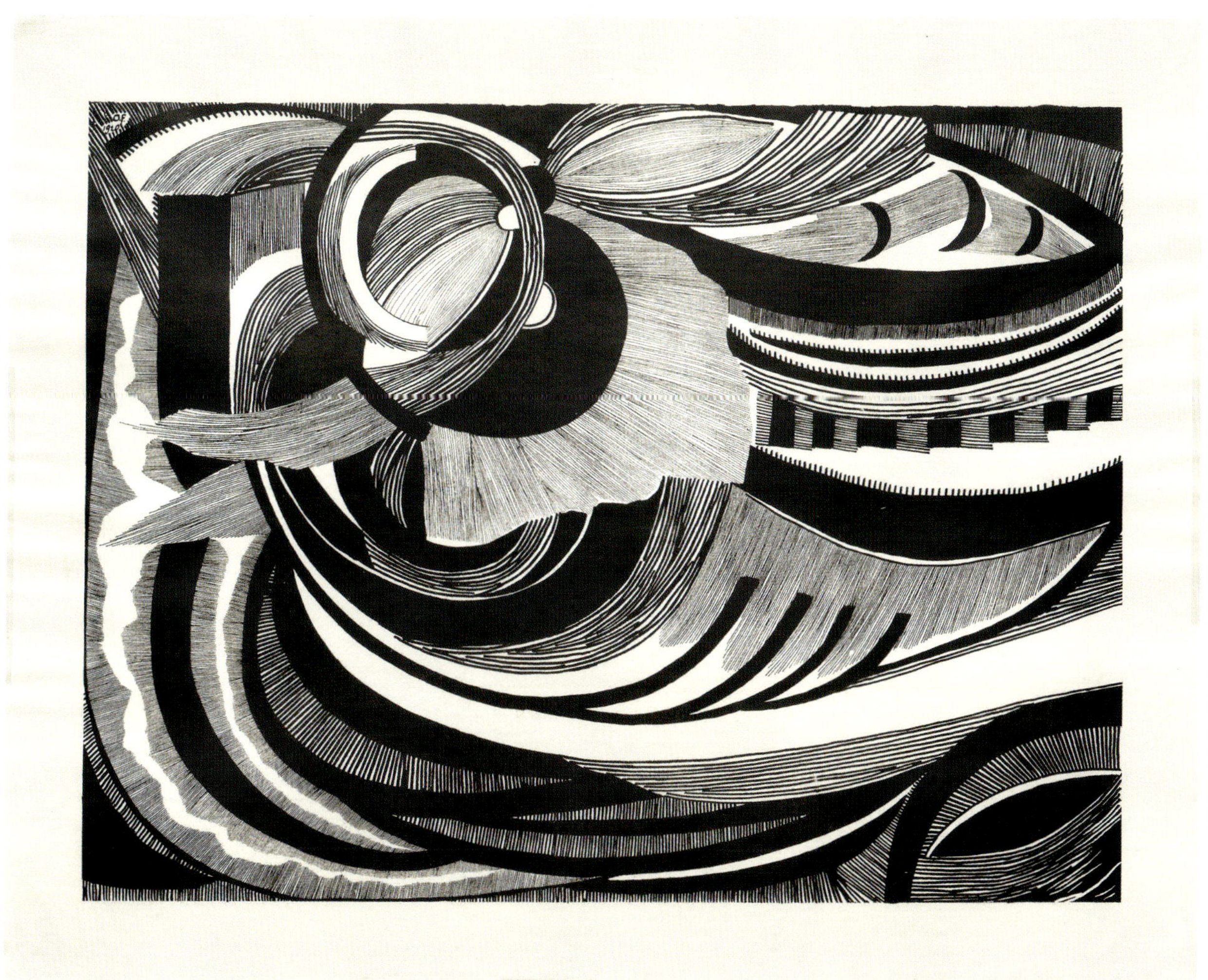

The Signs, 1919–20, sheet 6
HvW 466
Zinc engraving on paper

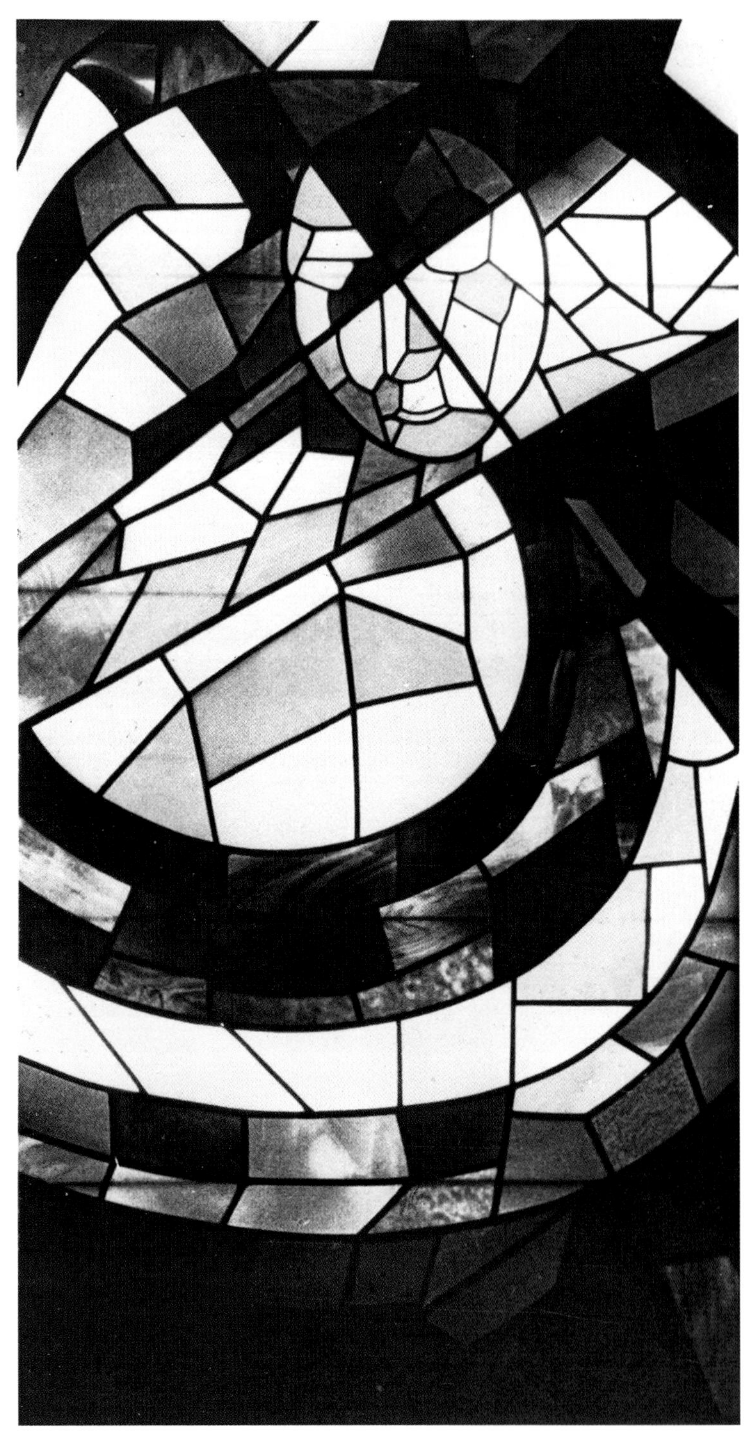

Composition, 1924
HvW 11
Stained glass painting
Lost

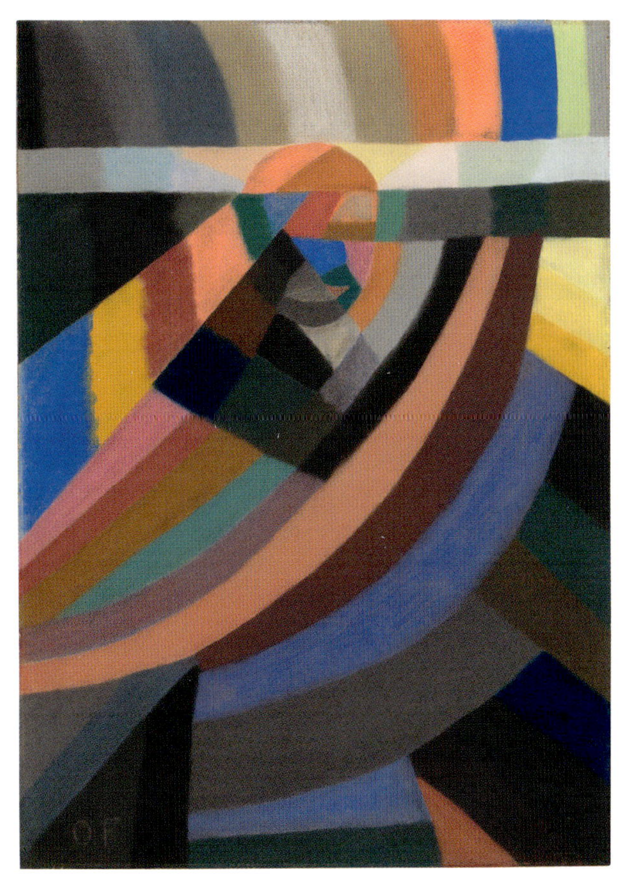

Composition, 1924
HvW 230
Pastel on paperboard

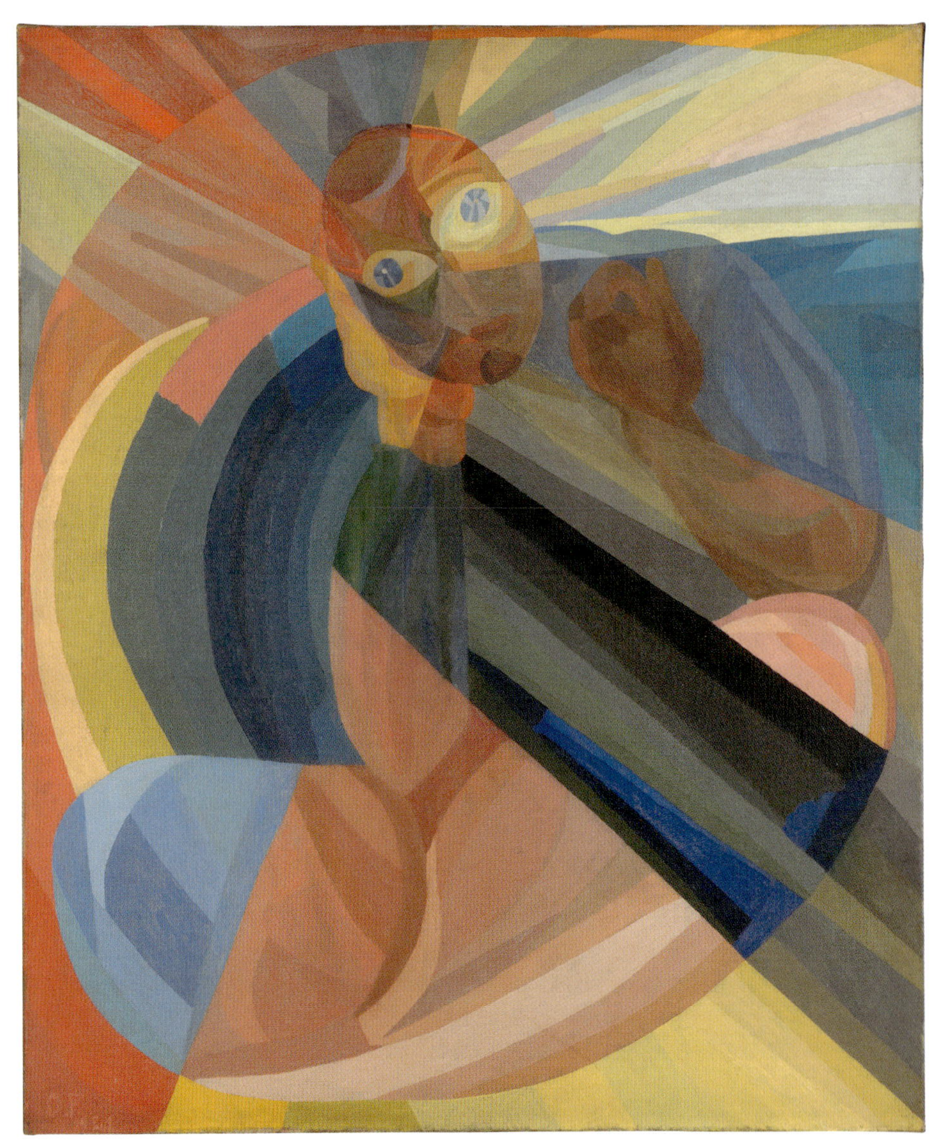

The Mother, 1921
HvW 129
Oil on canvas

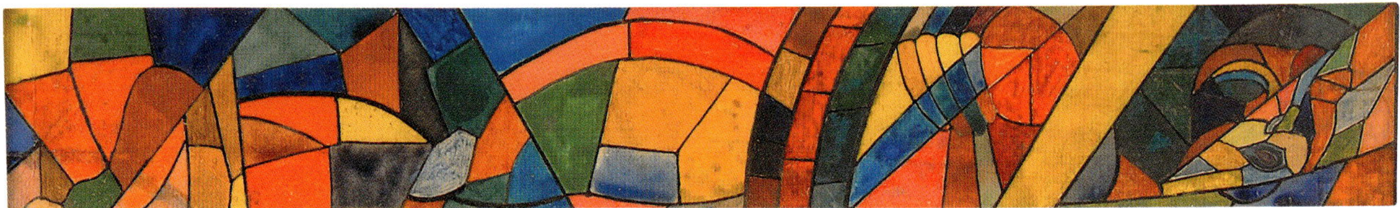

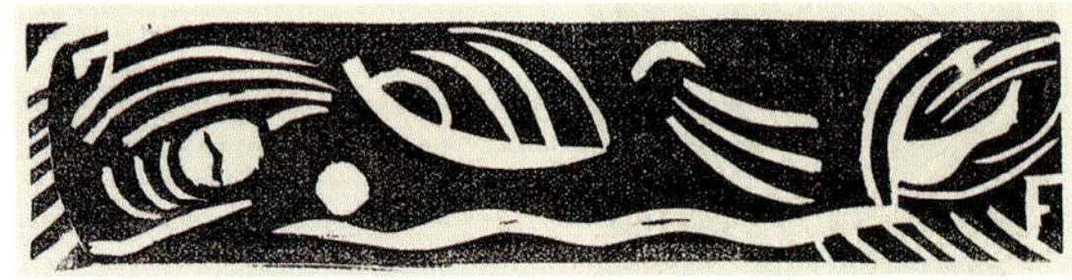

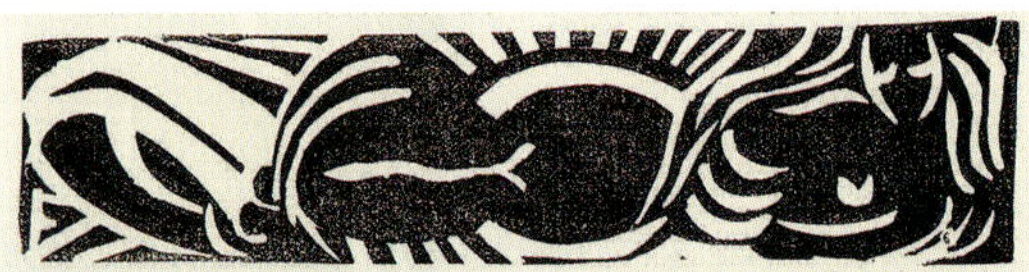

Reclining Woman, 1924
Watercolor on paper

Reclining Nude, 1918
HvW 455
Woodcut

Nude, 1918
HvW 454
Woodcut

Reclining Woman, 1924
HvW 10
Stained glass painting

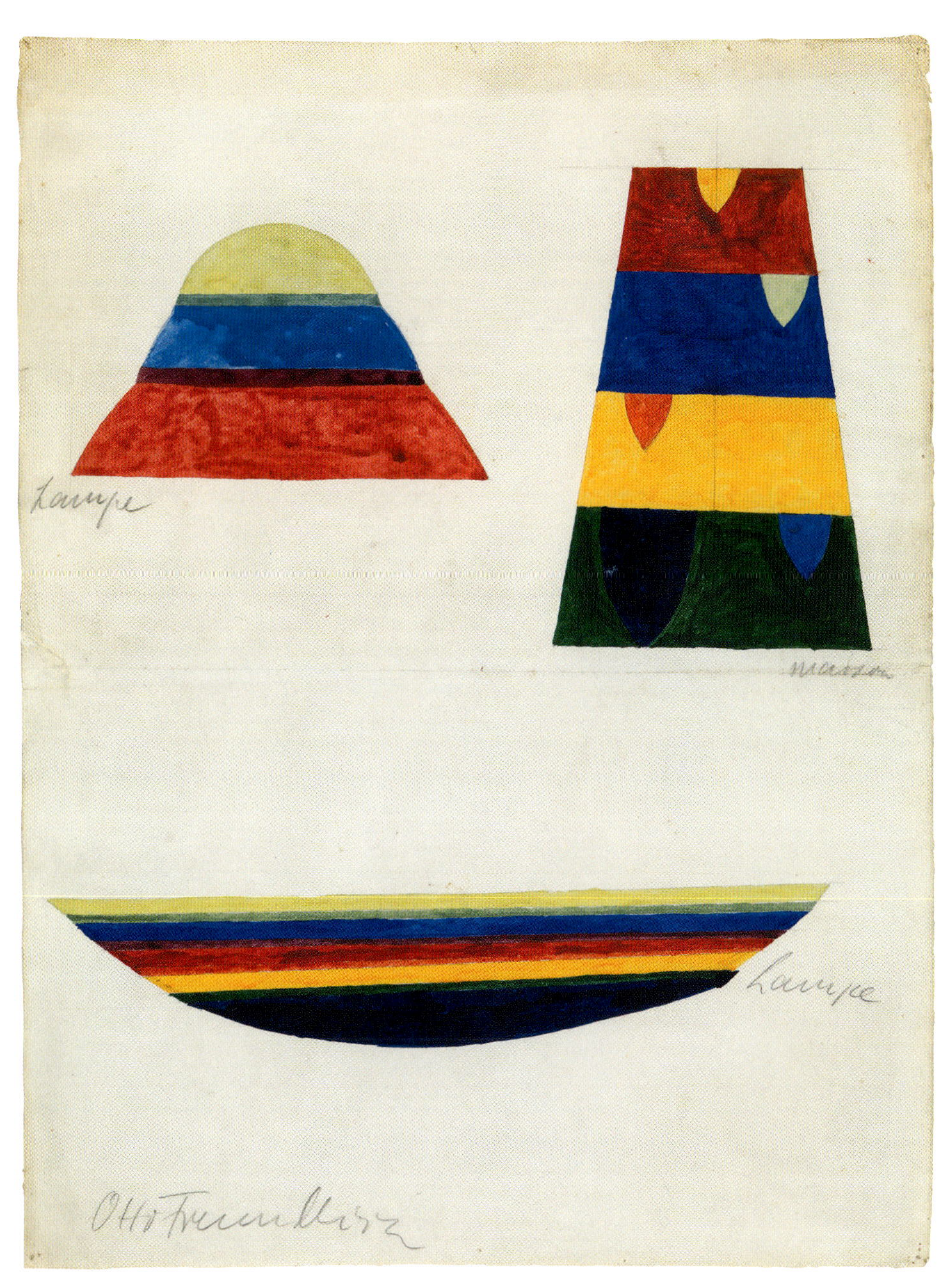

Designs for Lamps, ca. 1927
Watercolor and pencil on paper

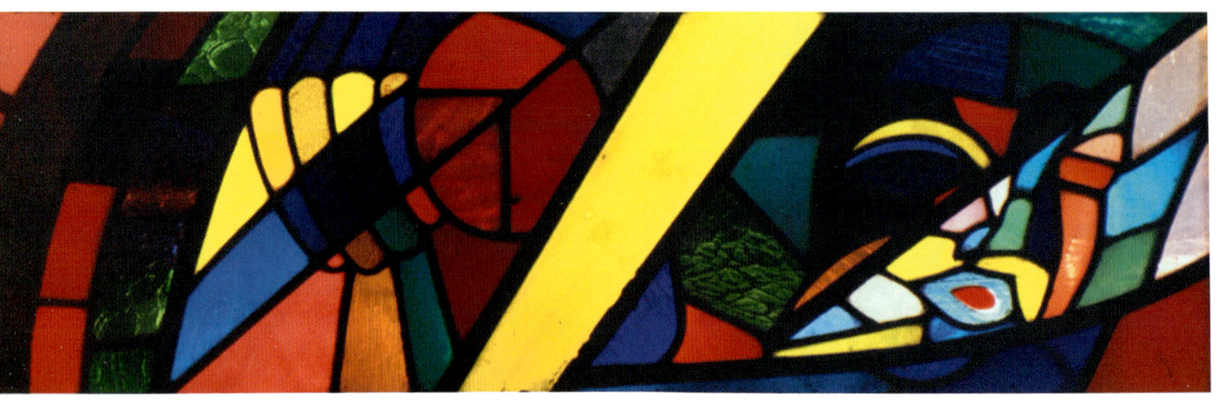

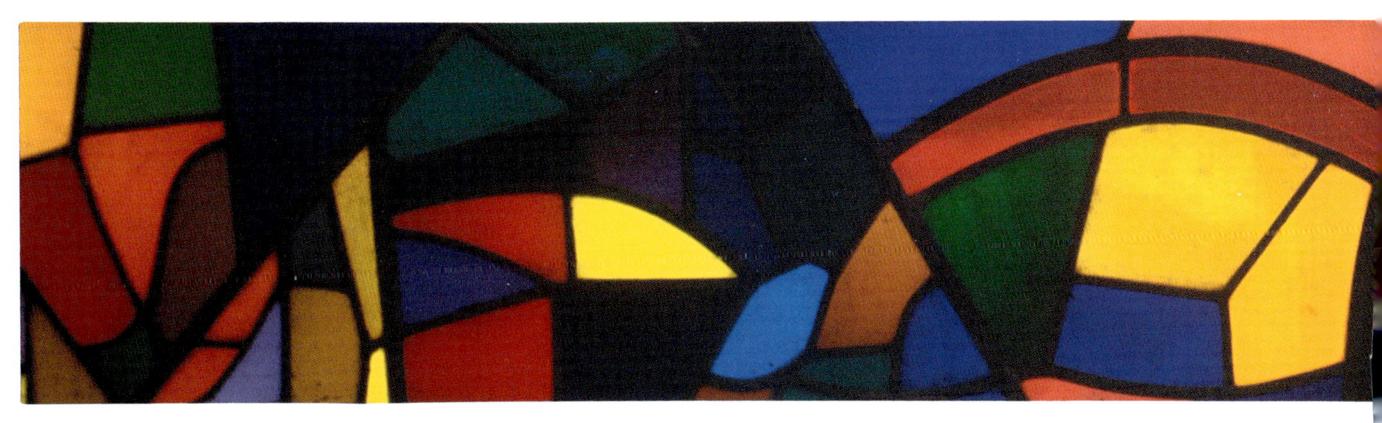

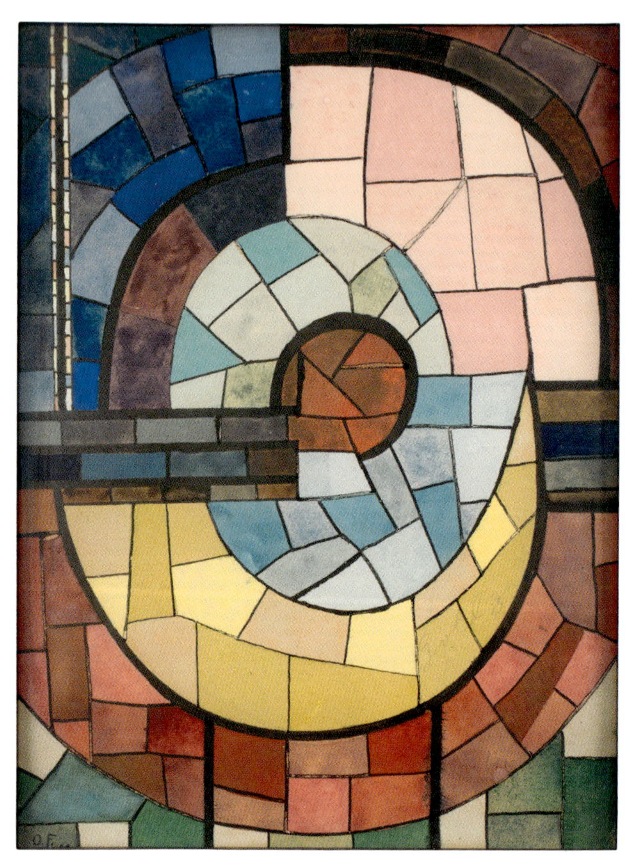

Composition I (Stained Glass Window Design), 1929
HvW 146
Gouache on paper

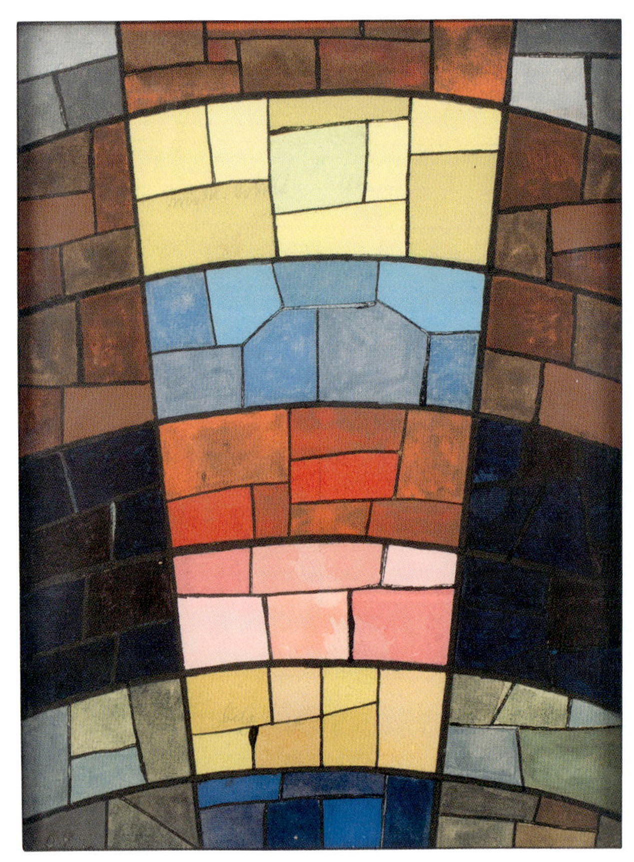

Composition II (Stained Glass Window Design), 1929
HvW 147
Gouache on paper

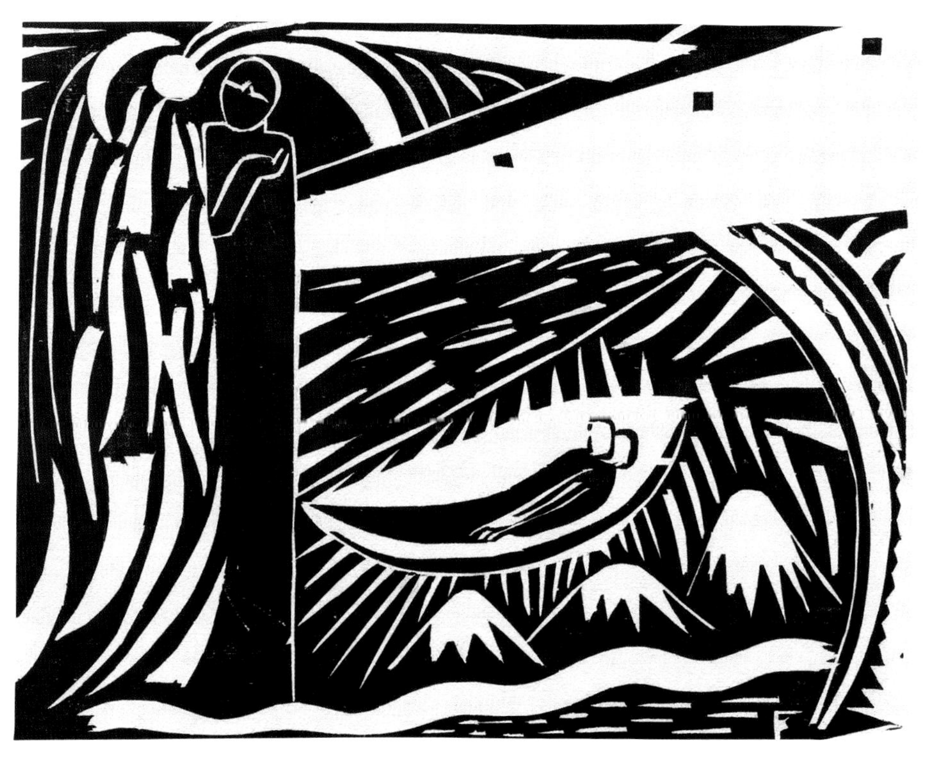

Figural Composition, ca. 1918
HvW 444
Woodcut on paper

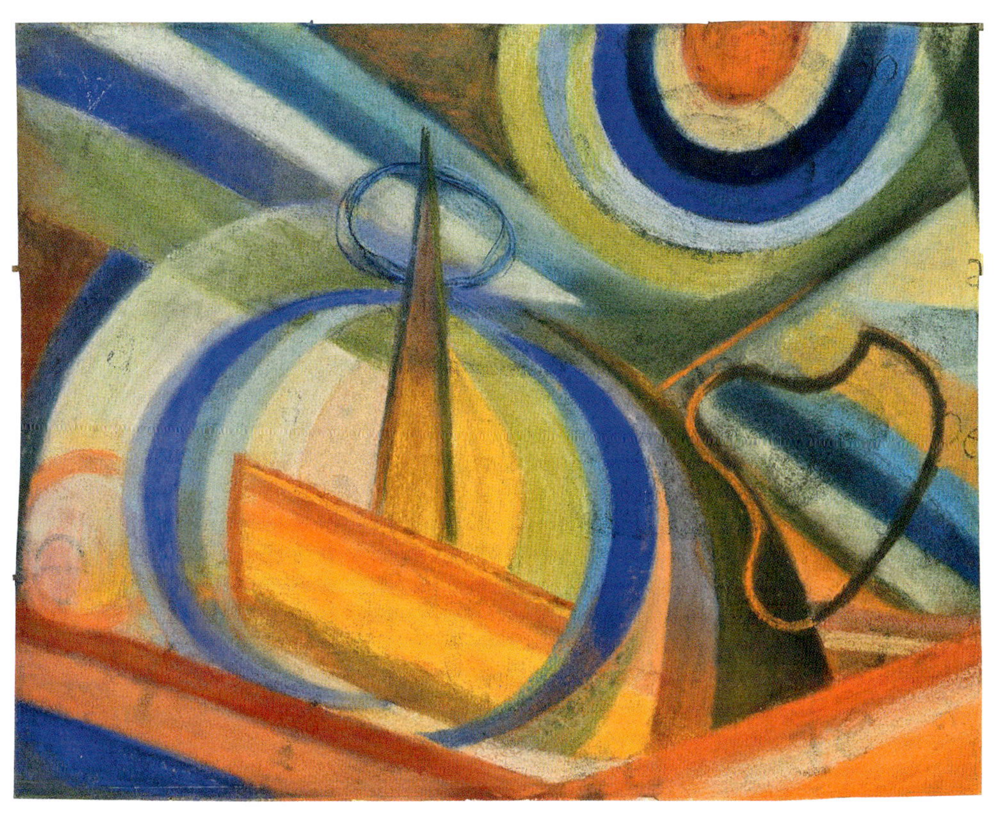

Composition with Ship, ca. 1918–19
HvW 219
Chalk pastel on wove paper

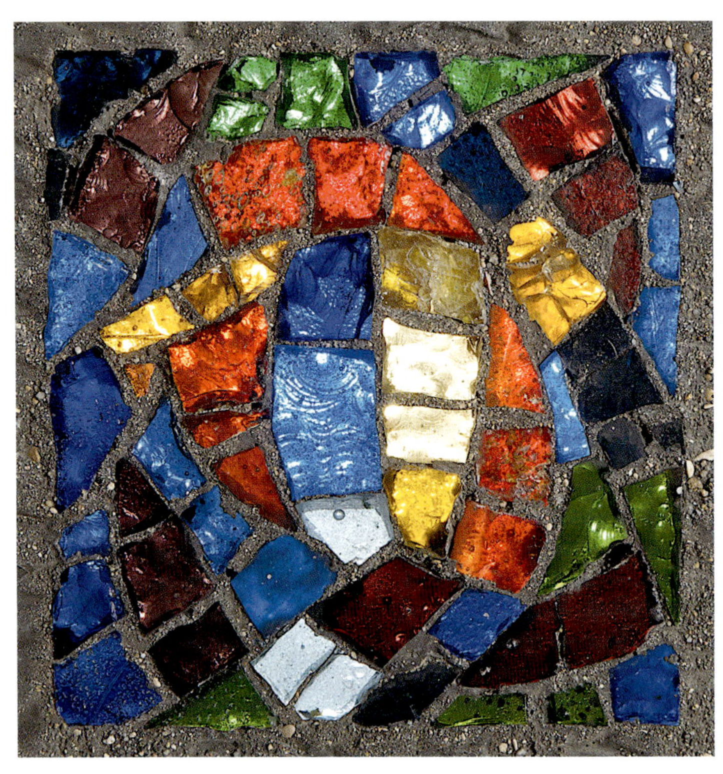

Composition, 1938?
HvW 33
Dalle-de-verre glass

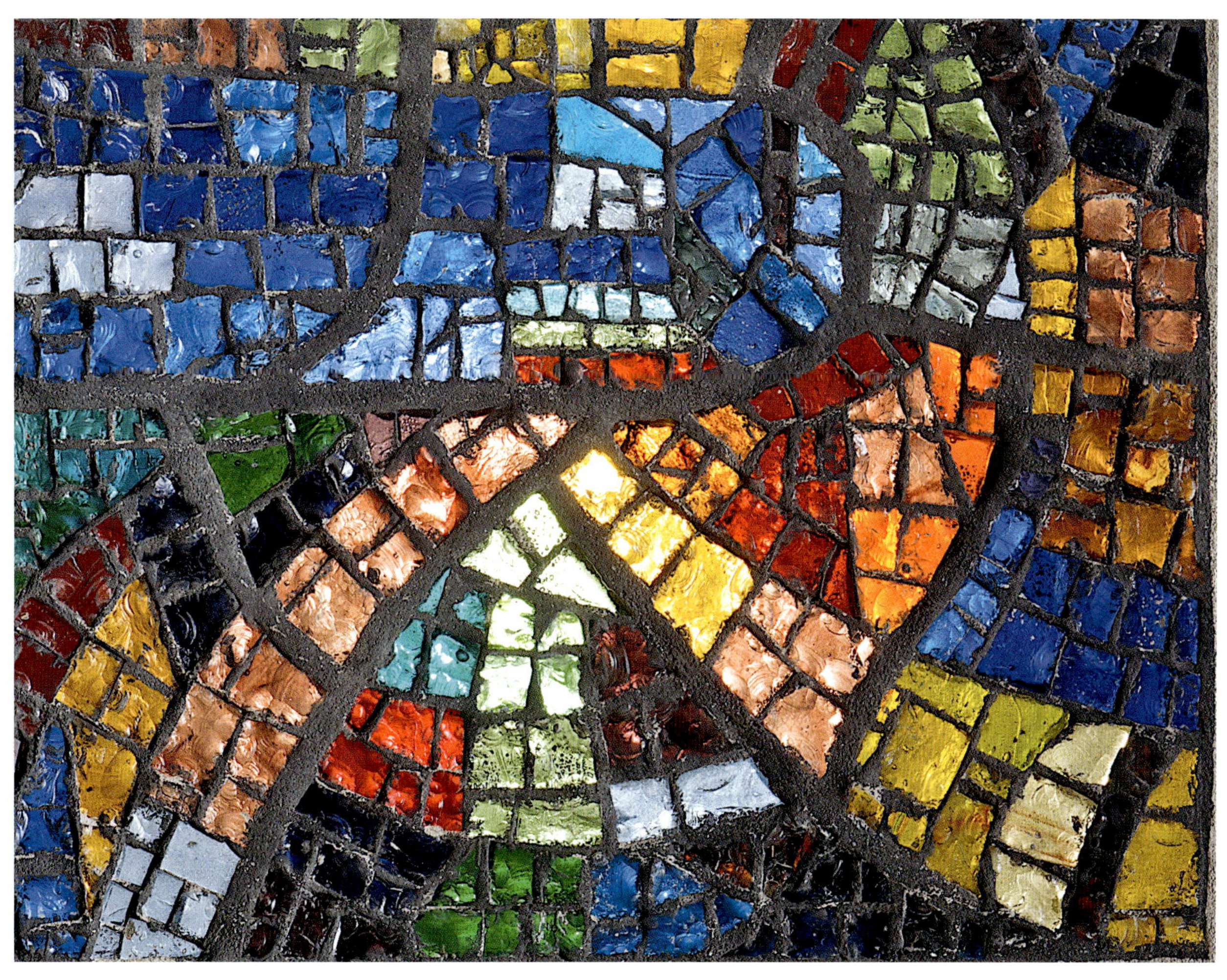

Composition, ca. 1938,
or posthumous
HvW 16
Dalle-de-verre glass

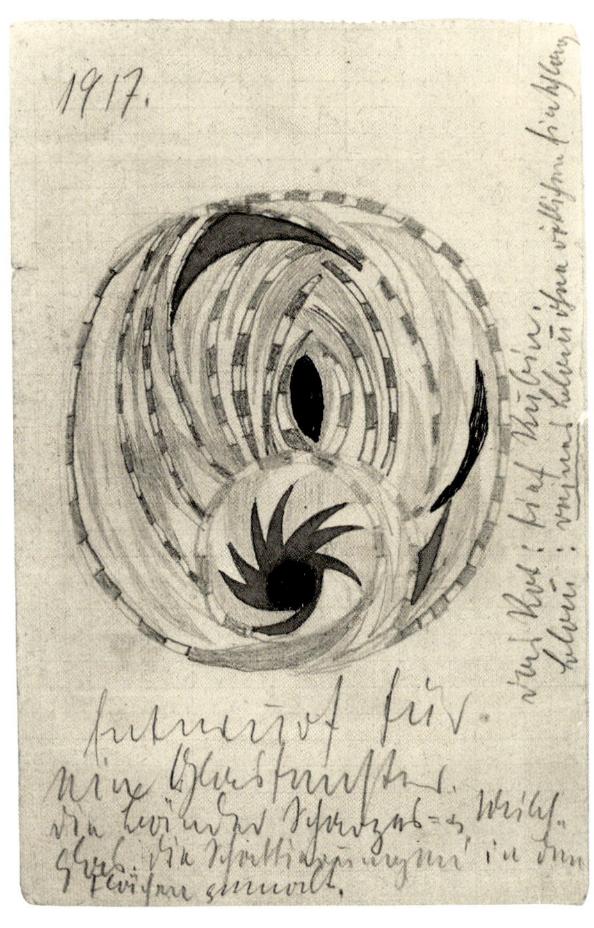

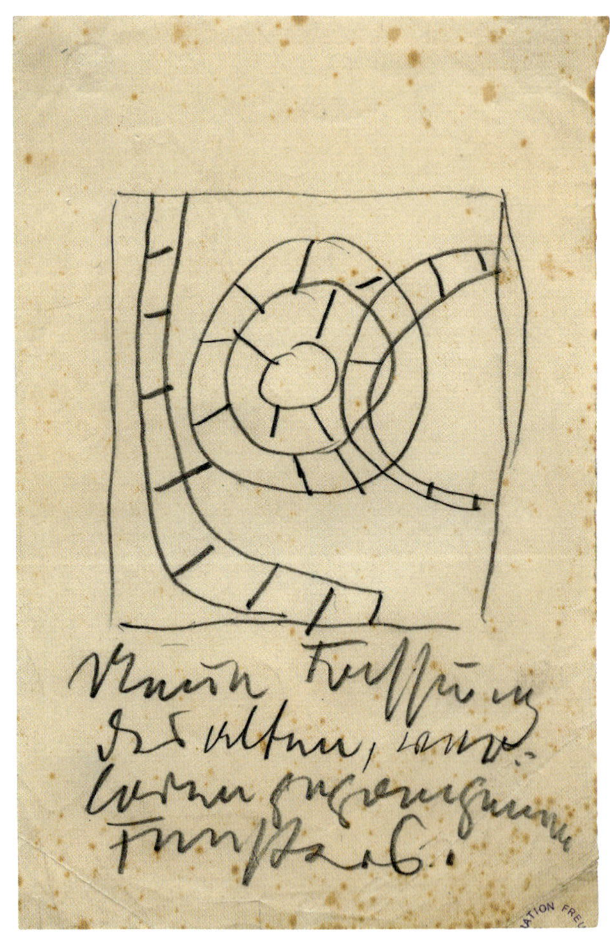

Design for a Stained Glass Window, 1917
HvW 276
Pencil and watercolor on paper

Design for a Stained Glass Window, ca. 1941
HvW 415
Pencil on Ingres paper

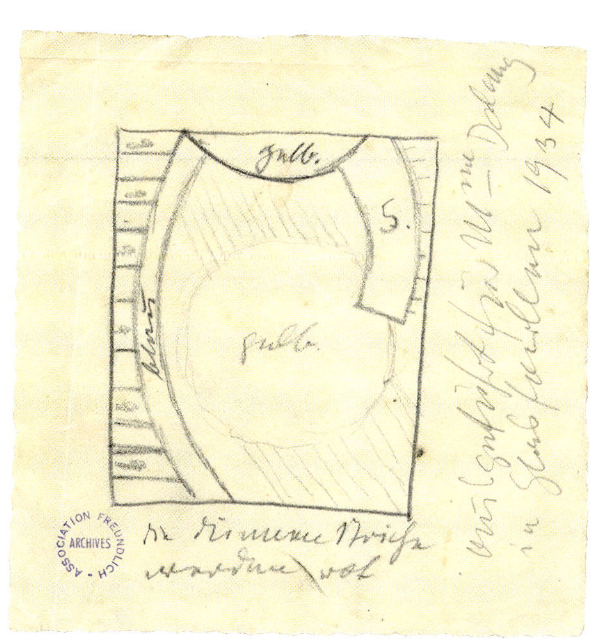

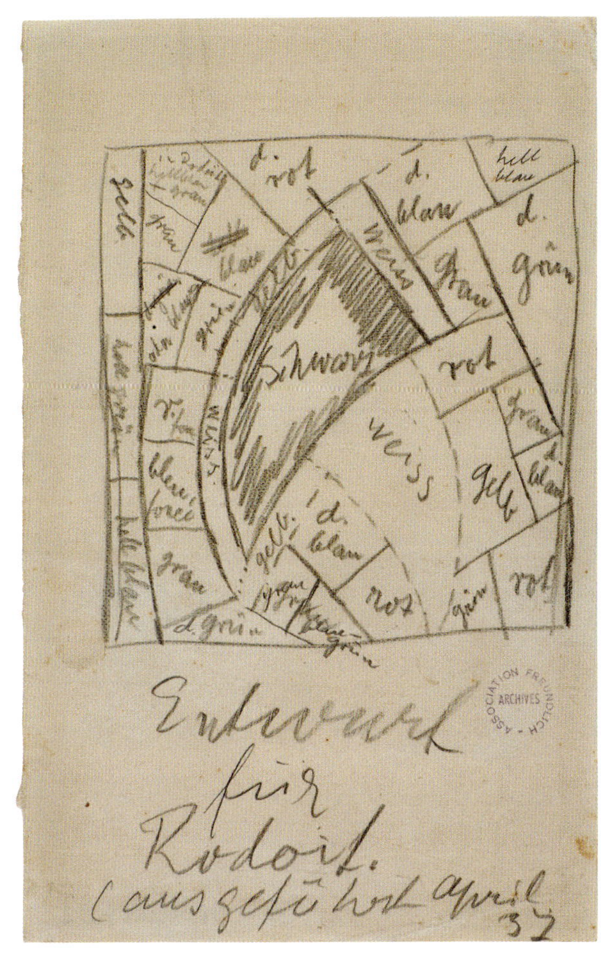

Composition, ca. 1934
HvW 346
Pencil on paper

Composition, 1937
HvW 371
Pencil on paper

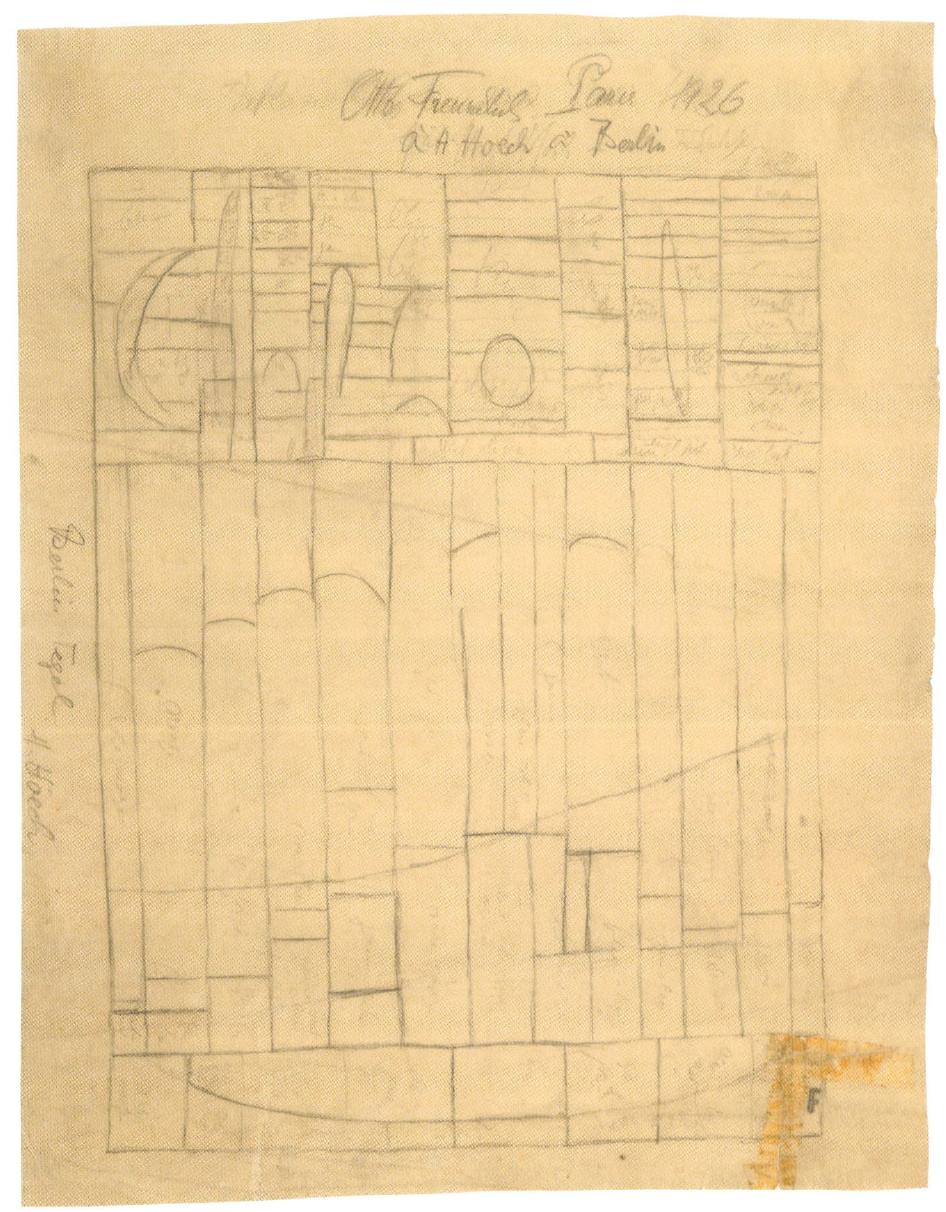

Design sketch for the painting Composition, 1926
Pencil on vellum

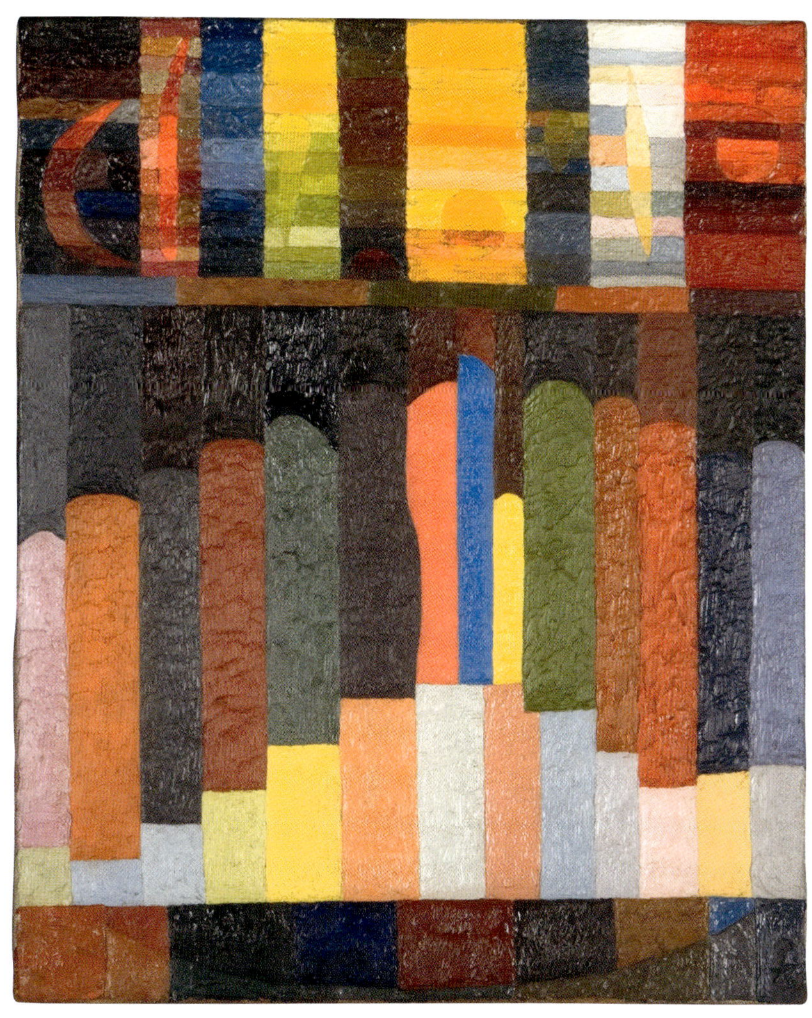

Composition, 1926
HvW 134
Oil on canvas

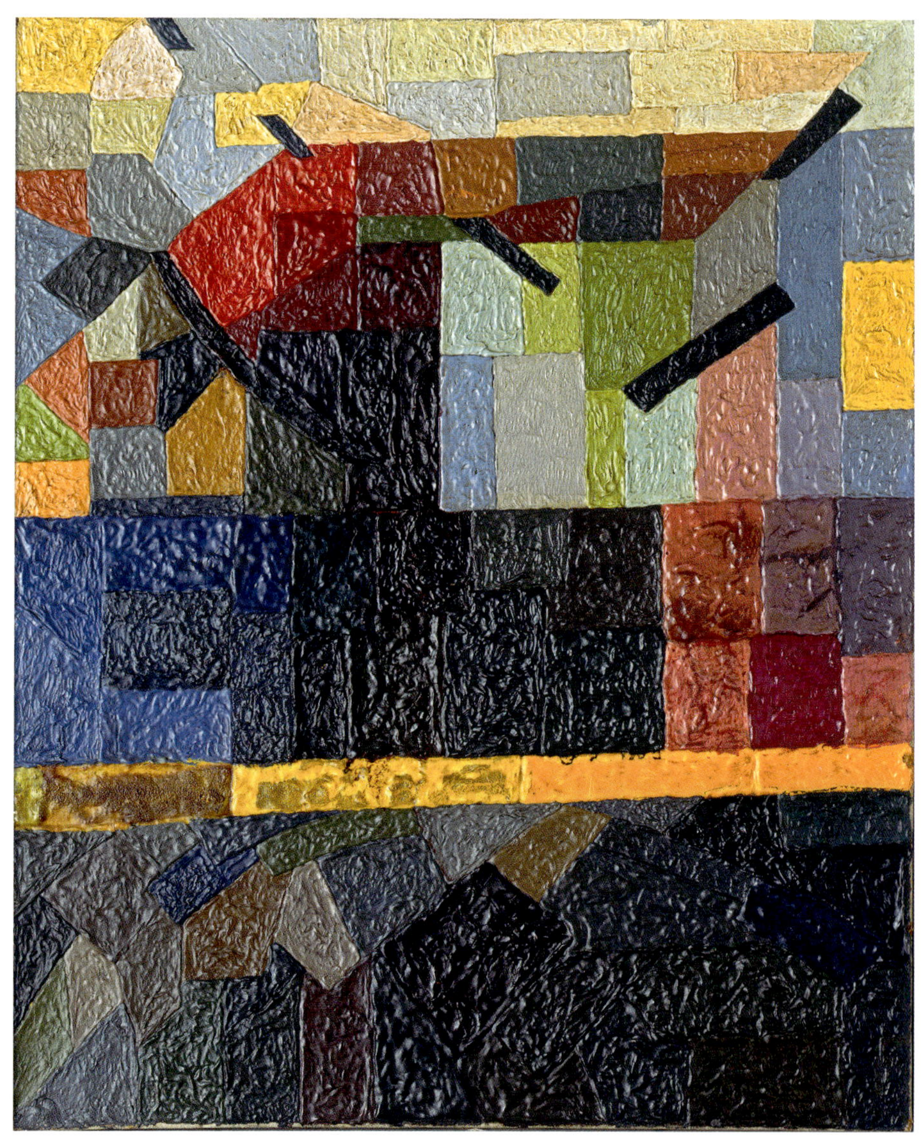

A Tree, 1927
HvW 137
Oil on canvas

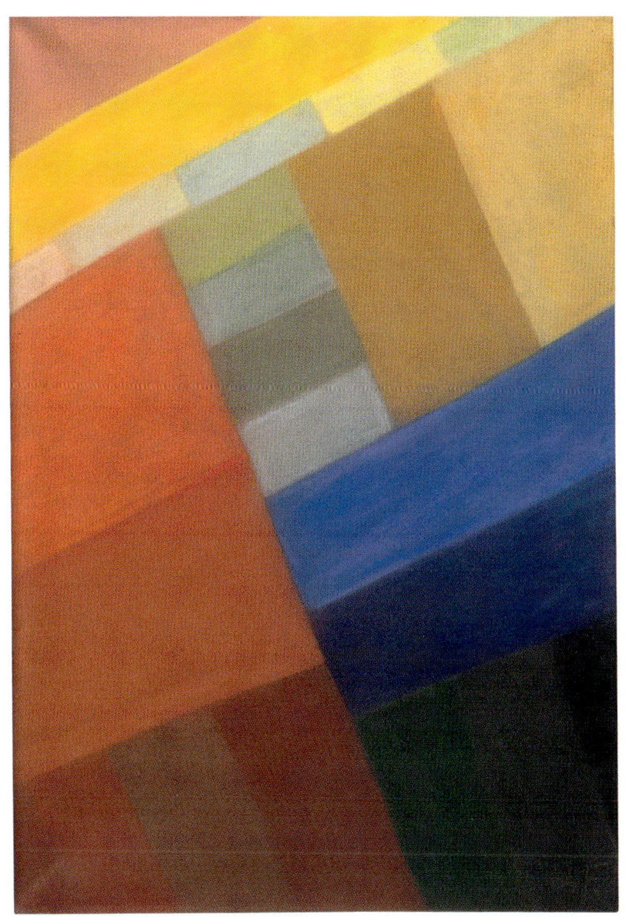

Composition, ca. 1931
HvW 256
Pastel on velvet paper

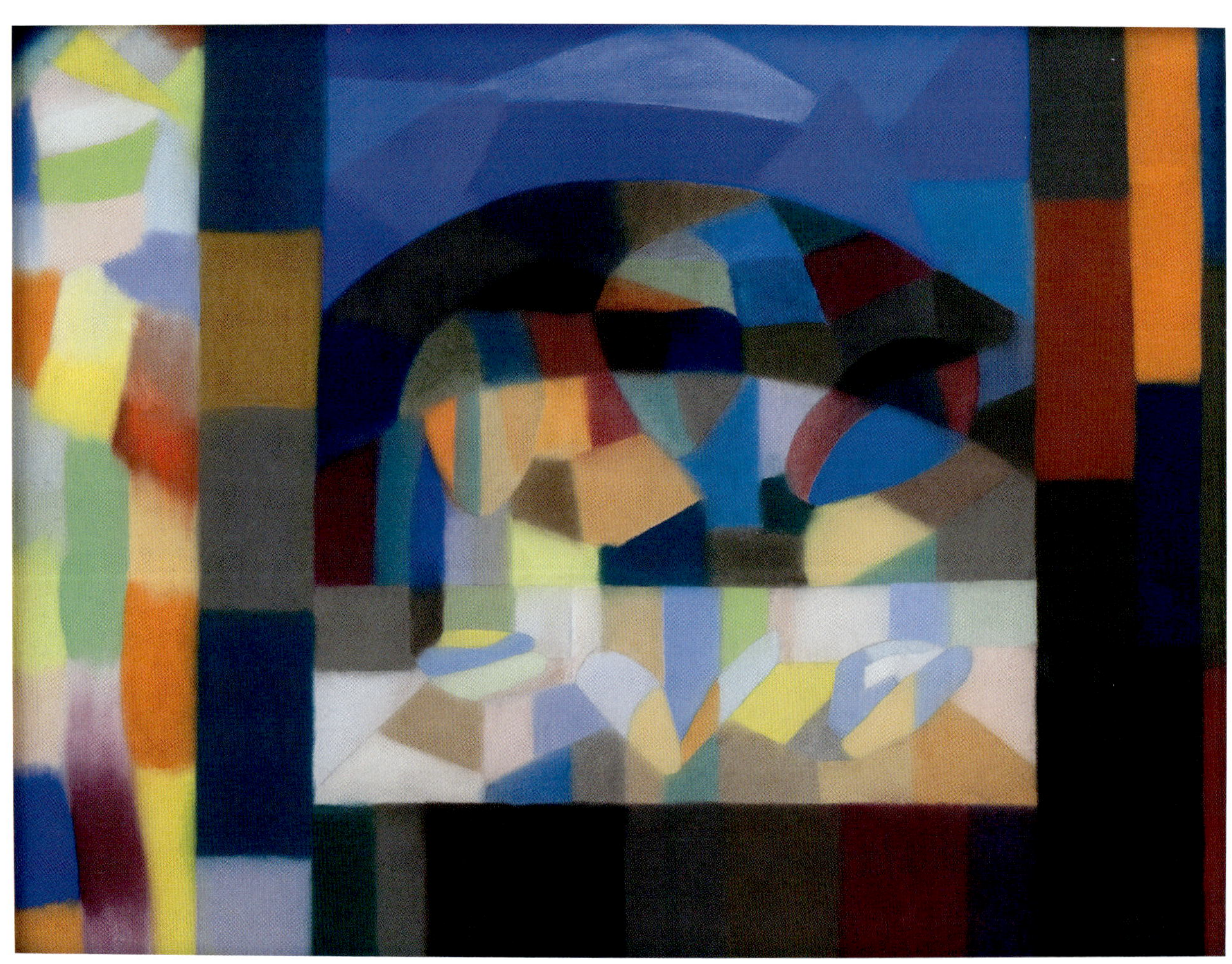

View from the Window,
ca. 1924–25
HvW 231
Pastel on paper

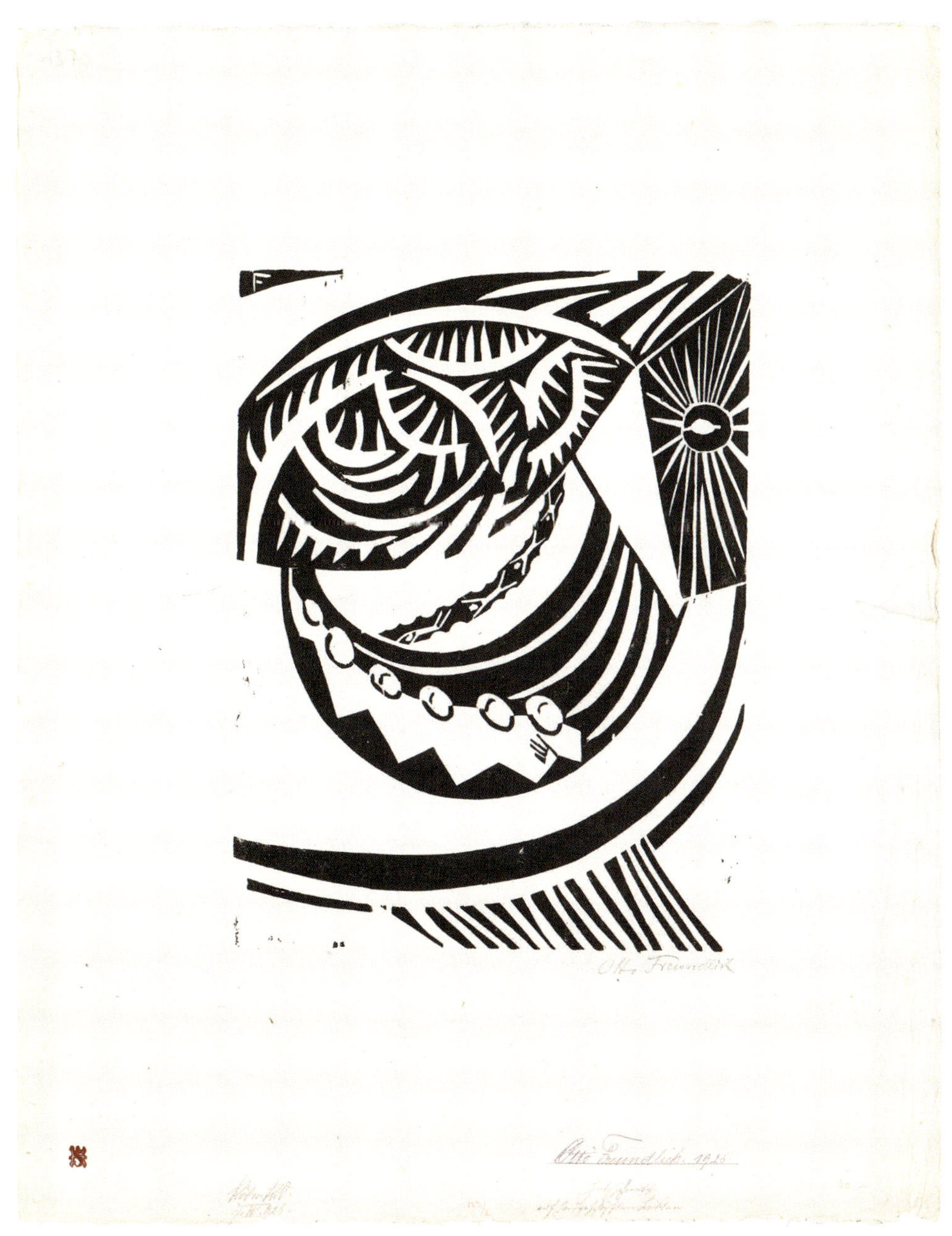

Composition, 1921
HvW 470
Woodcut on paper

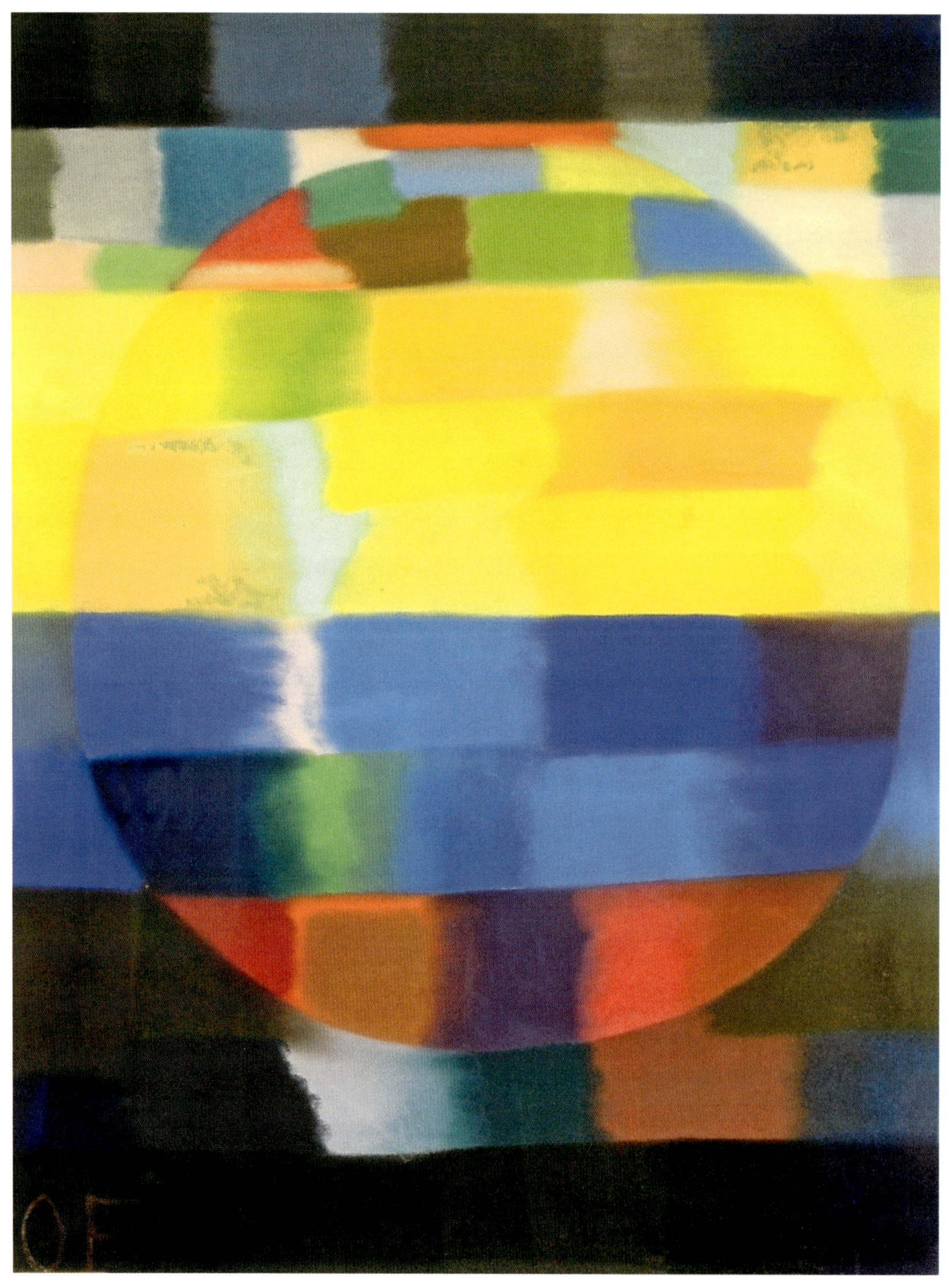

Spherical Bodies, 1925
HvW 234
Pastel on paper

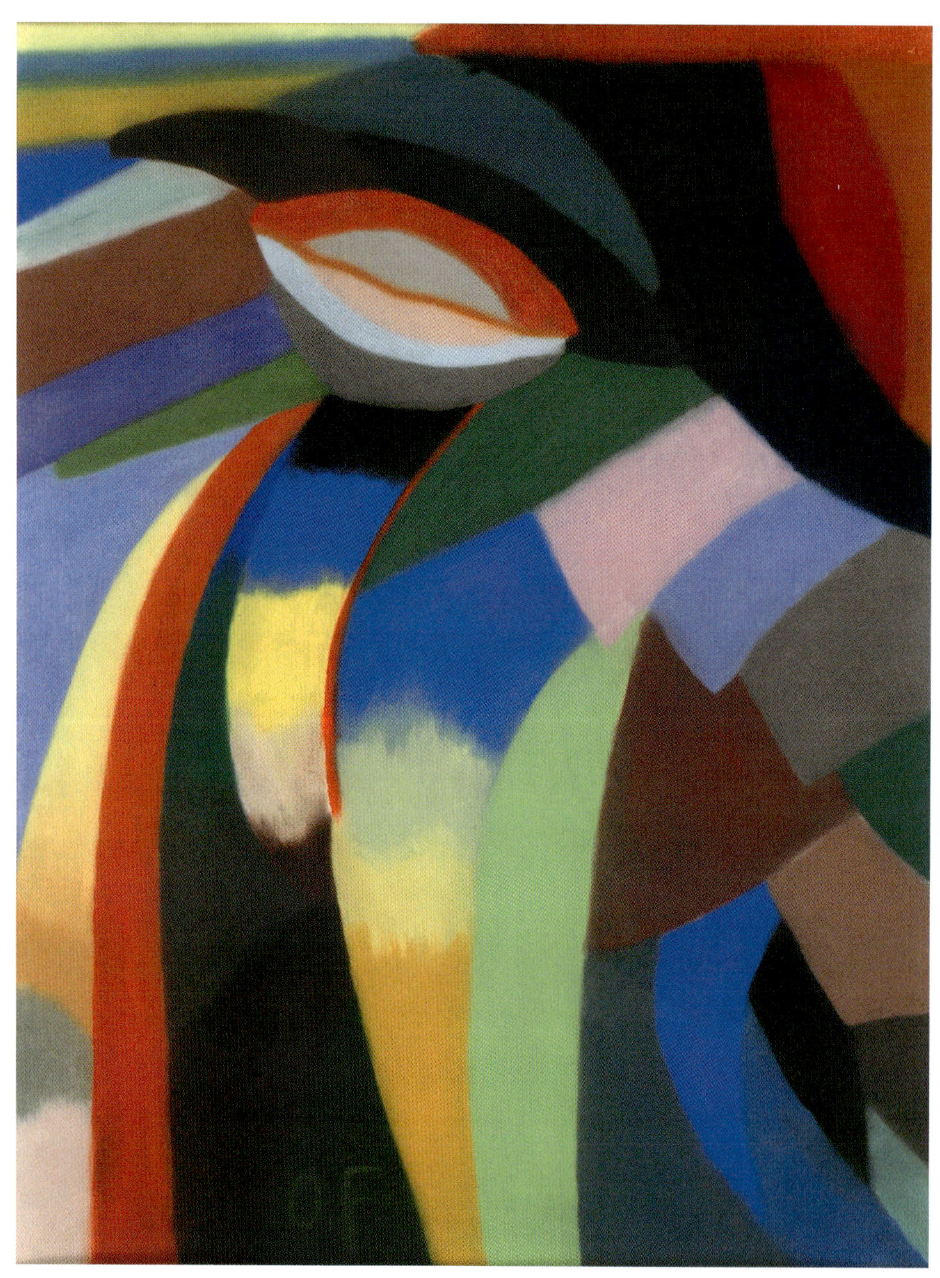

Composition, 1919
HvW 223
Pastel on paper

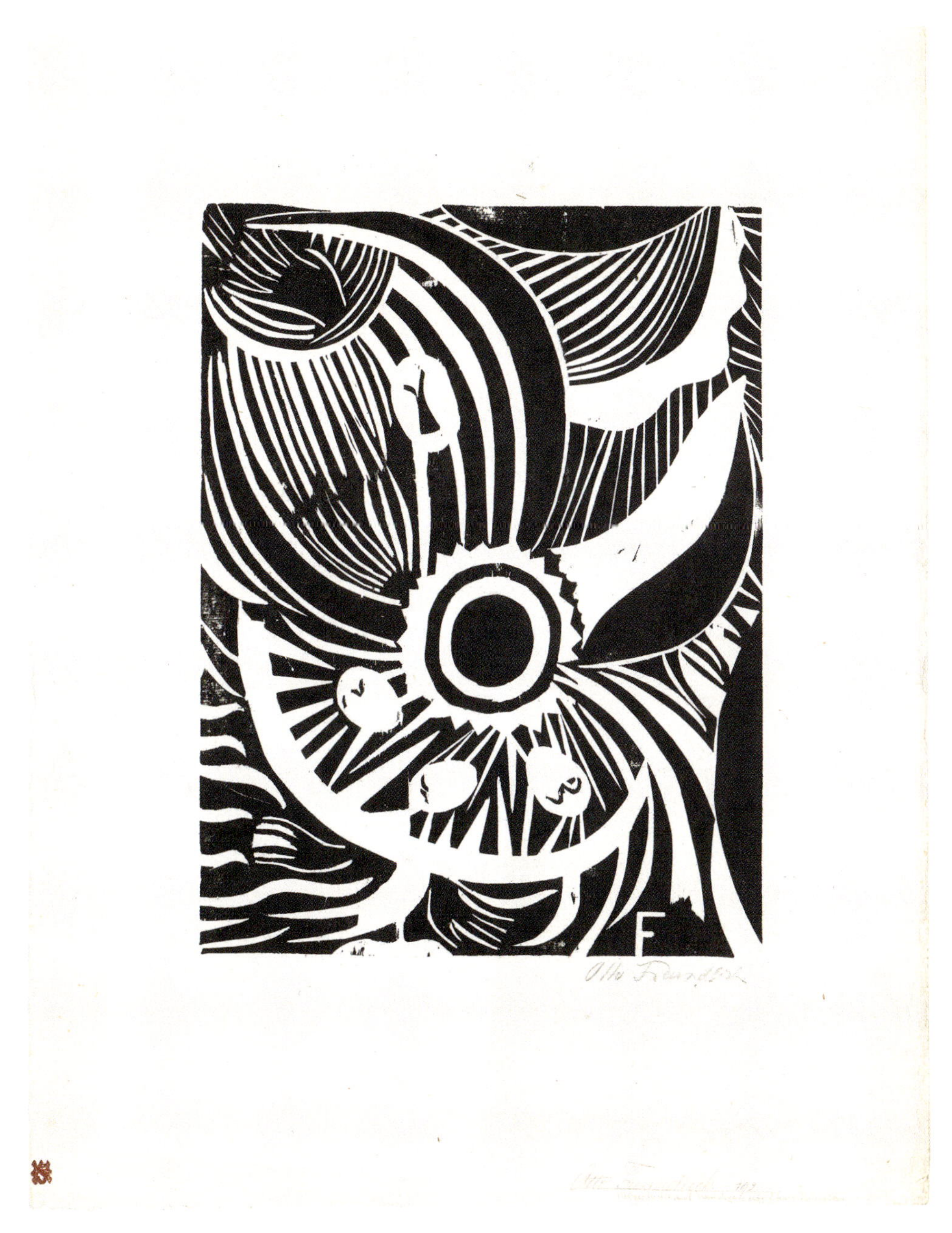

Composition, ca. 1920–21
HvW 469
Woodcut on handmade laid paper

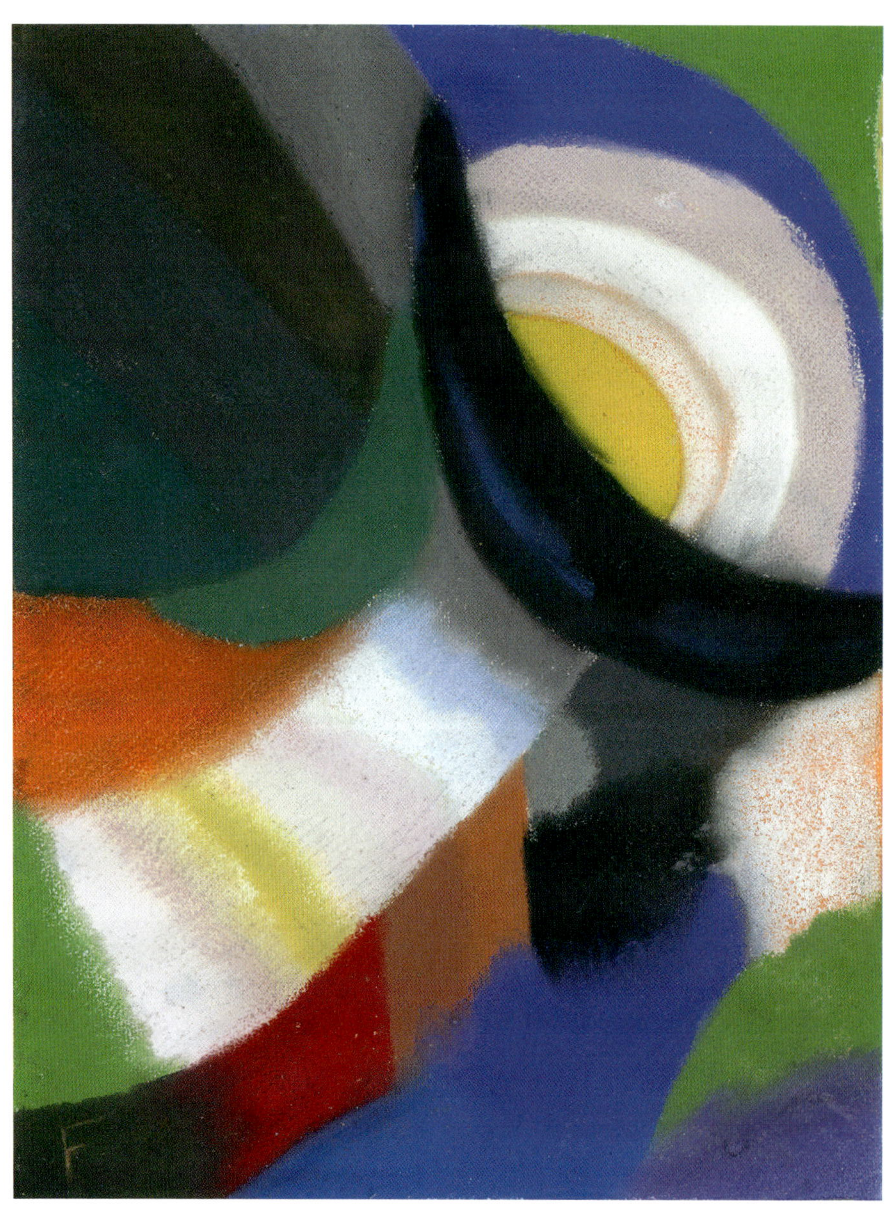

Cosmic Composition, ca. 1922
Pastel on paper

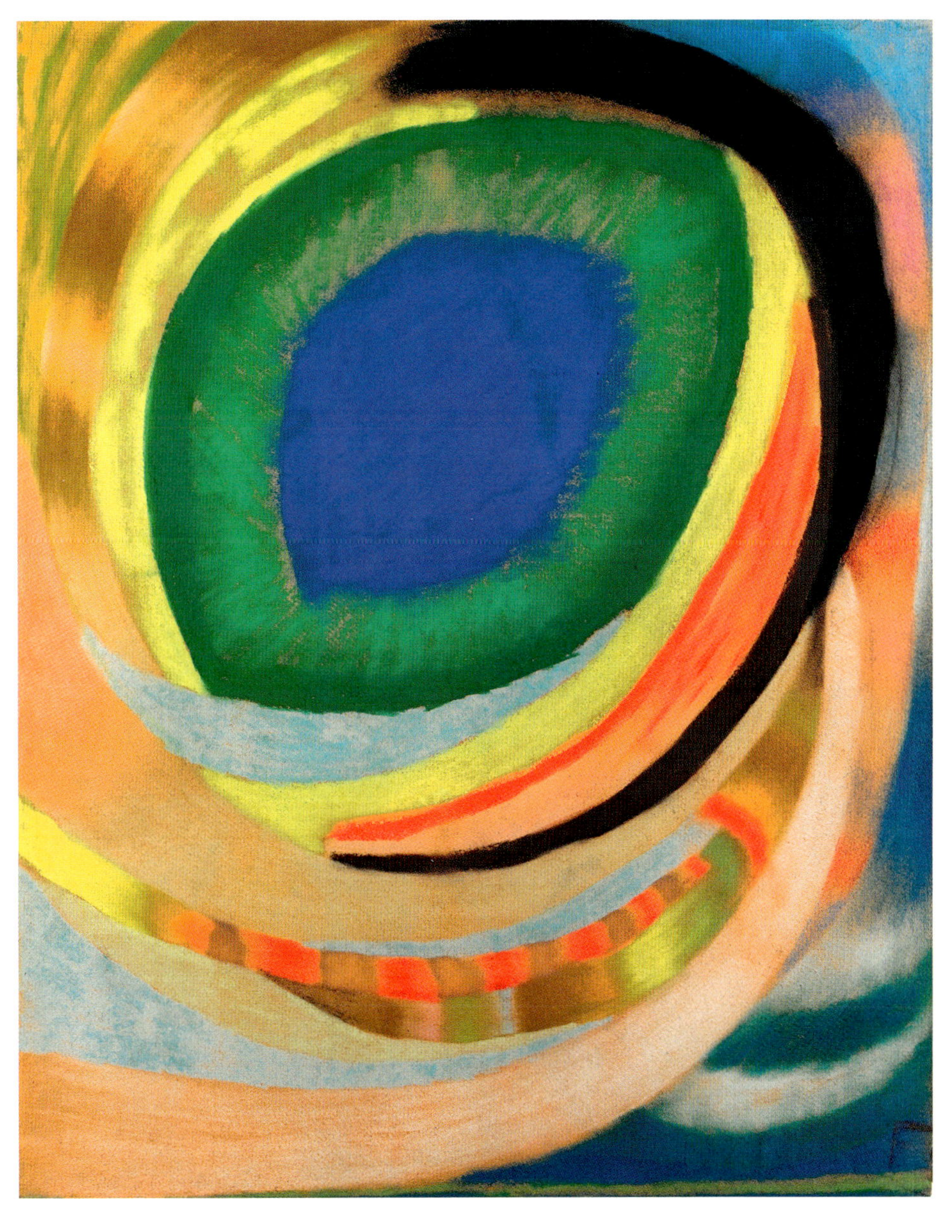

Cosmic Eye, 1921–22
HvW 229
Pastel on paper

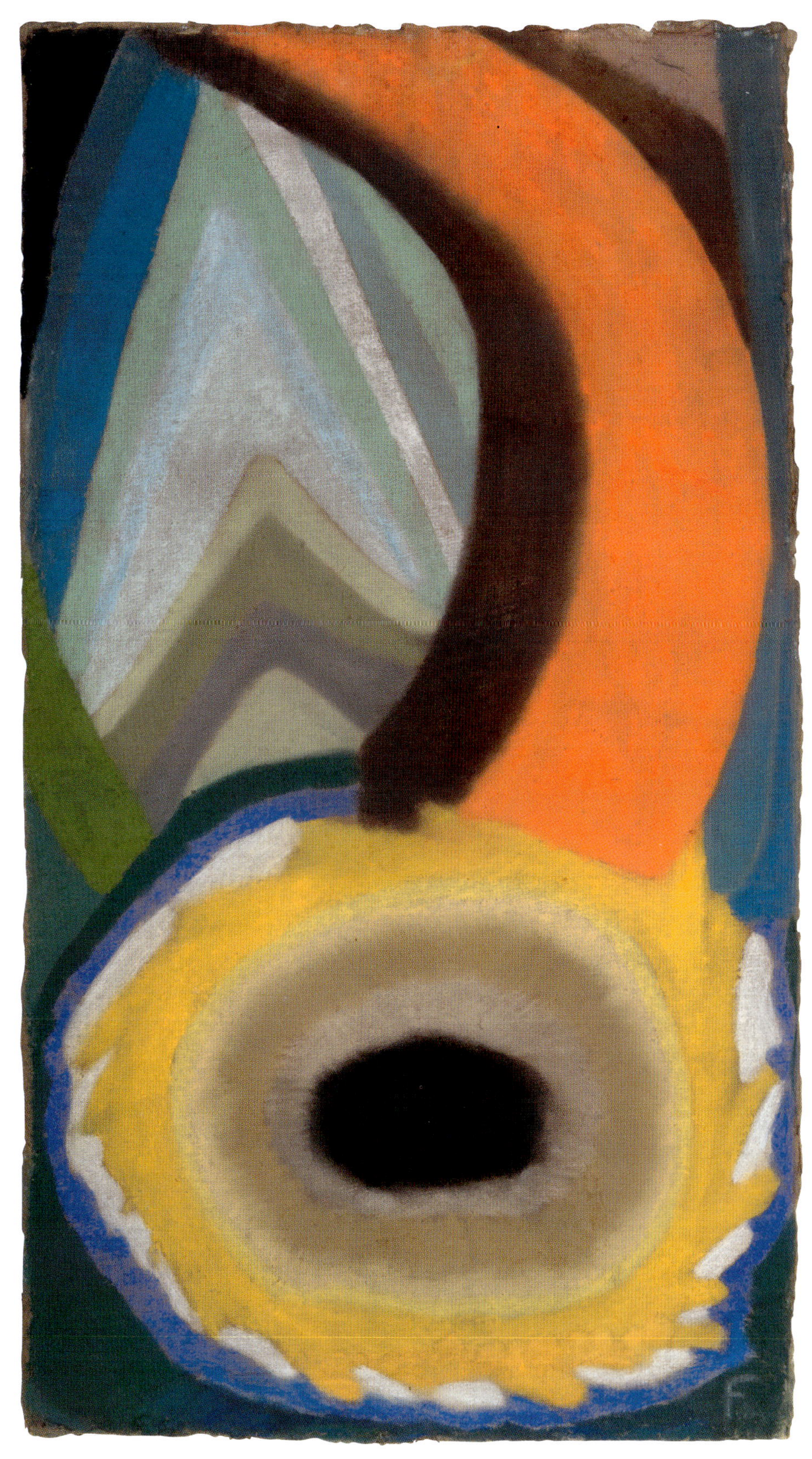

Composition, 1921
HvW 227
Chalk pastel on paper

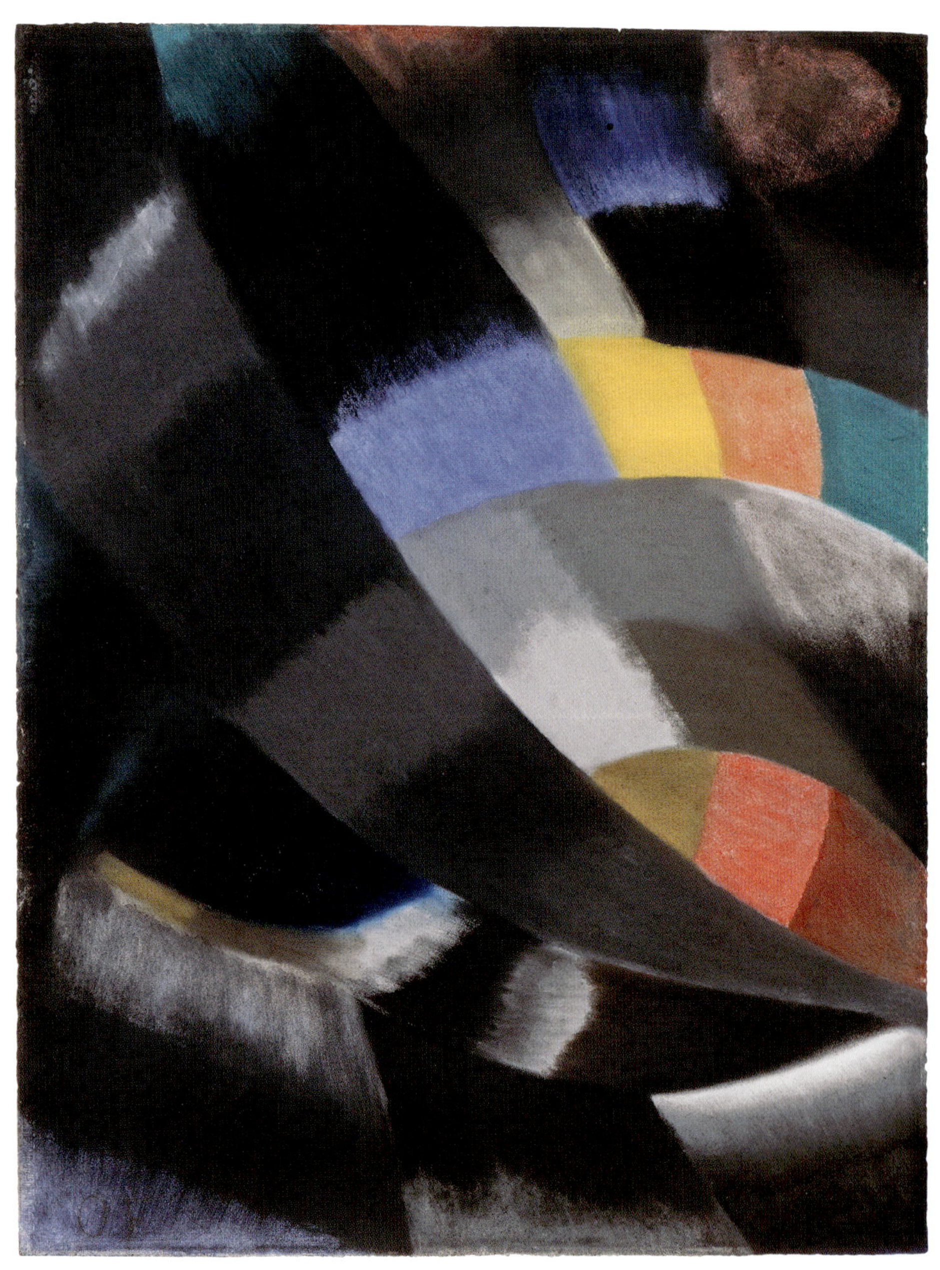

Ship in a Storm, 1924
HvW 232
Pastel on wove paper

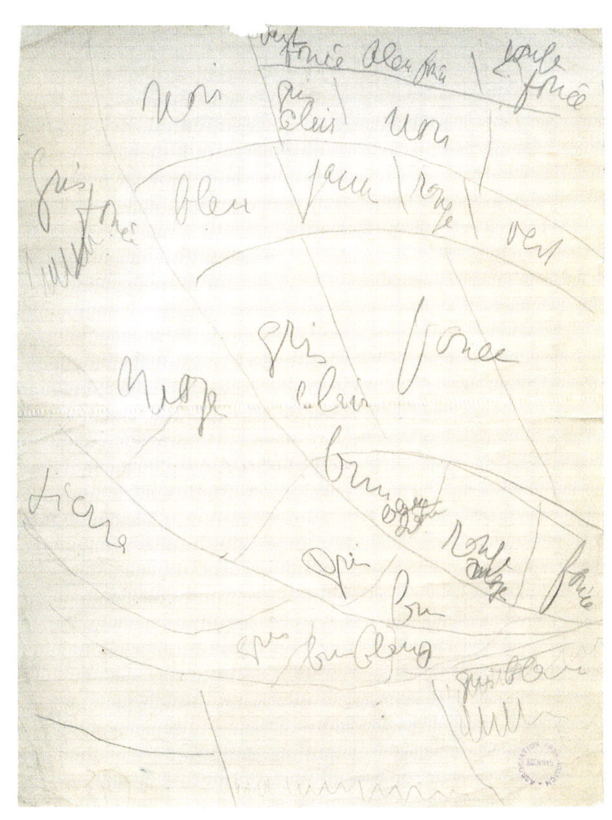

Ship in a Storm, 1924
HvW 307
Pencil on graph paper

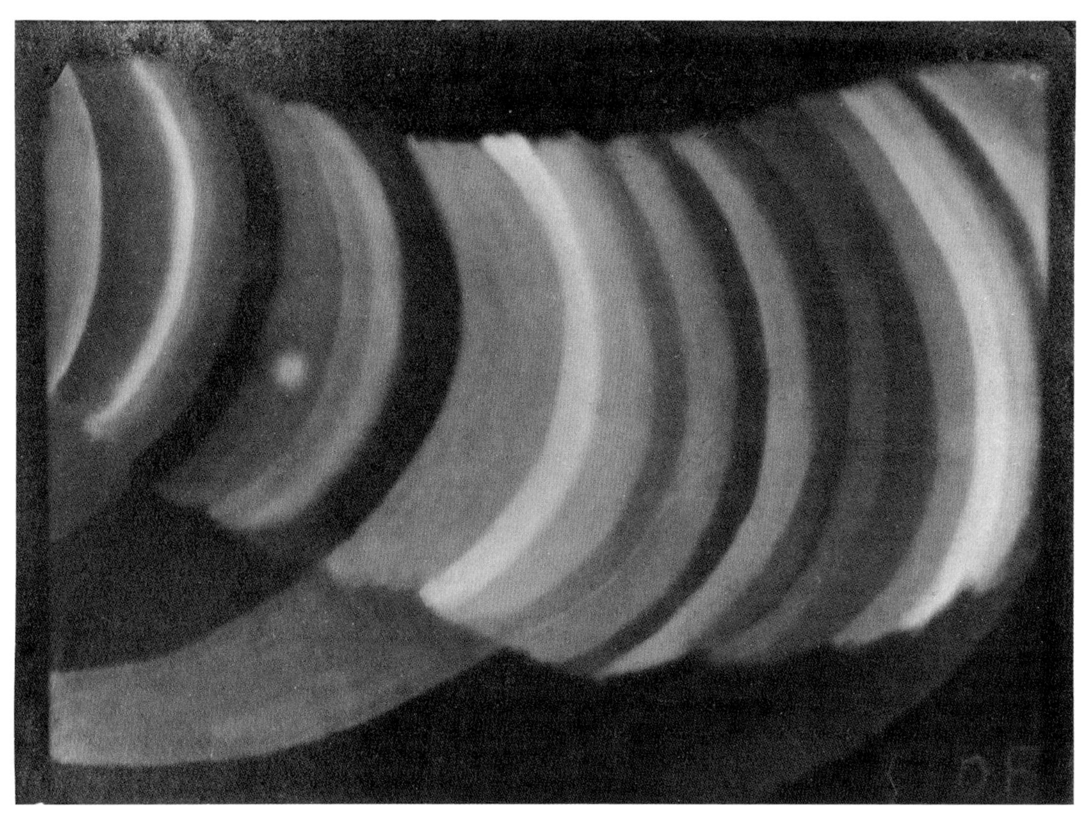

Composition, 1921
HvW 226
Pastel on paper
Lost

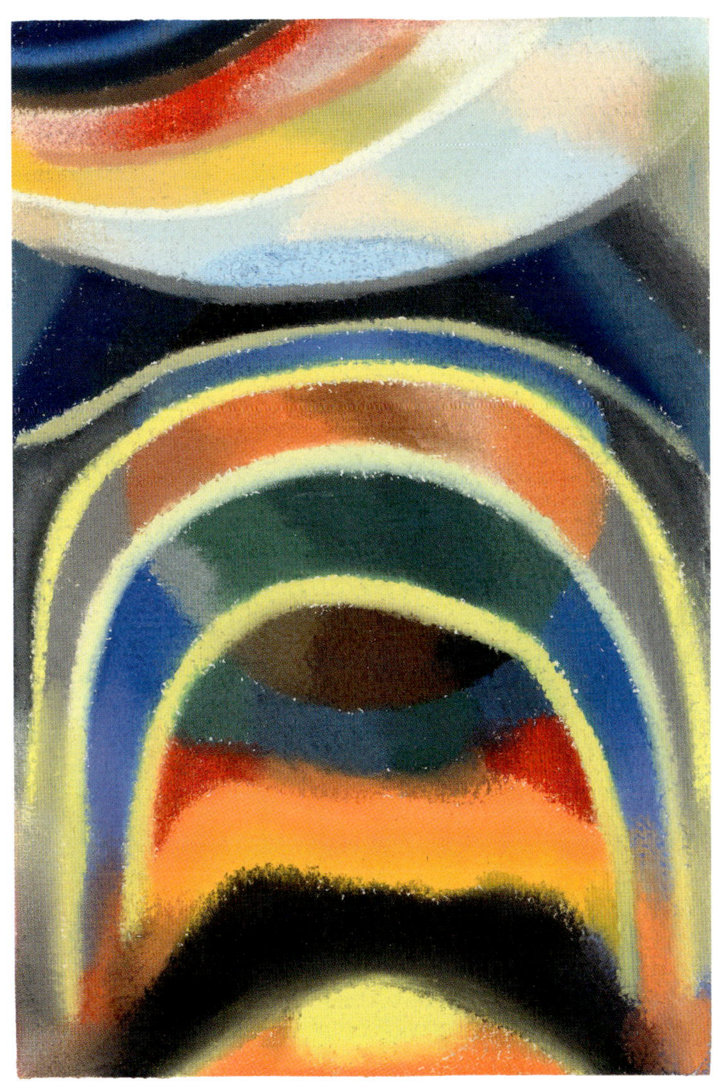

Circles of Light
(Cosmic Rainbow), 1922
HvW 228
Pastel on paper

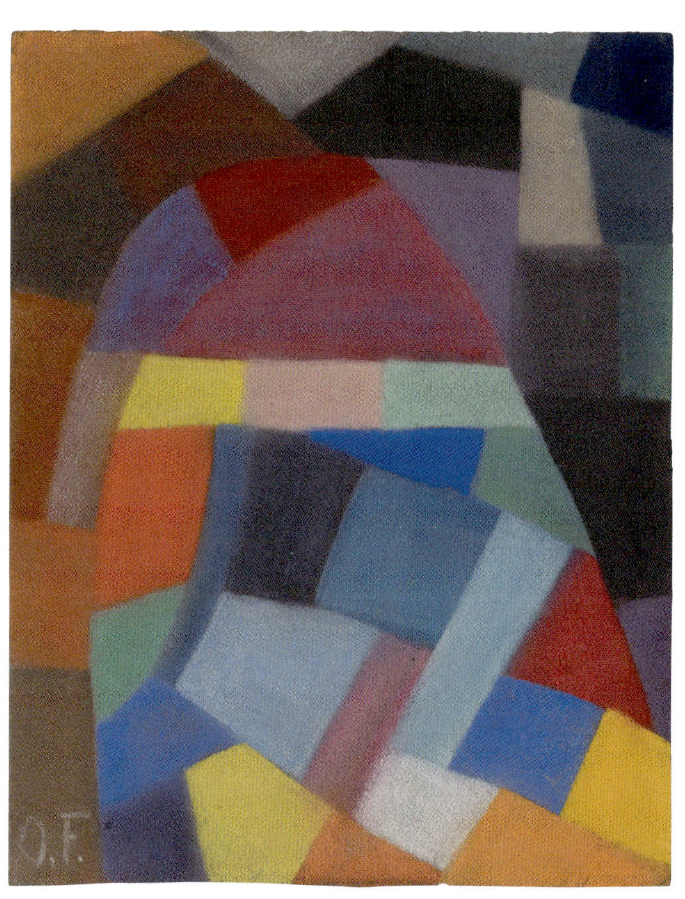

Composition, ca. 1929
HvW 252
Pastel on mottled paper

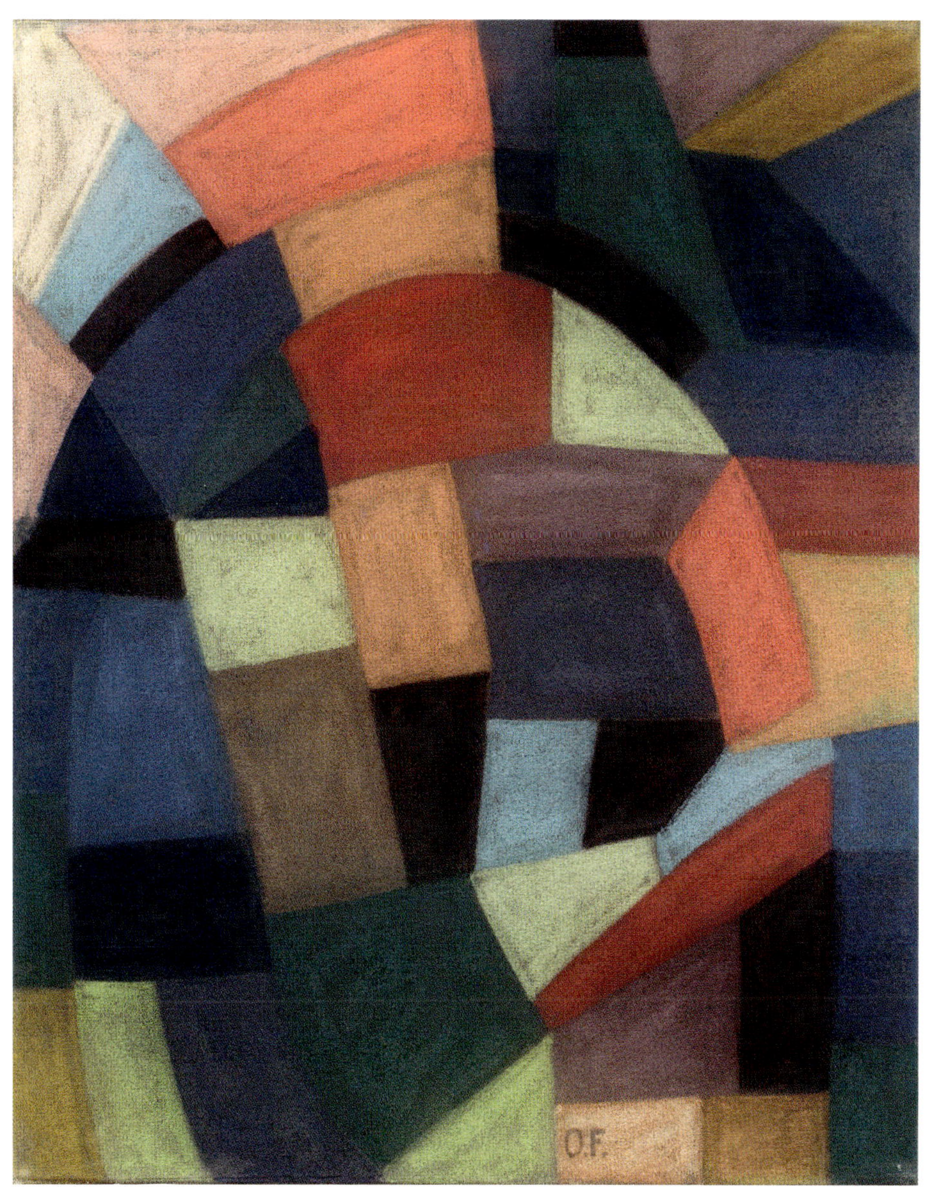

Composition, 1928
HvW 246
Pastel on canvas

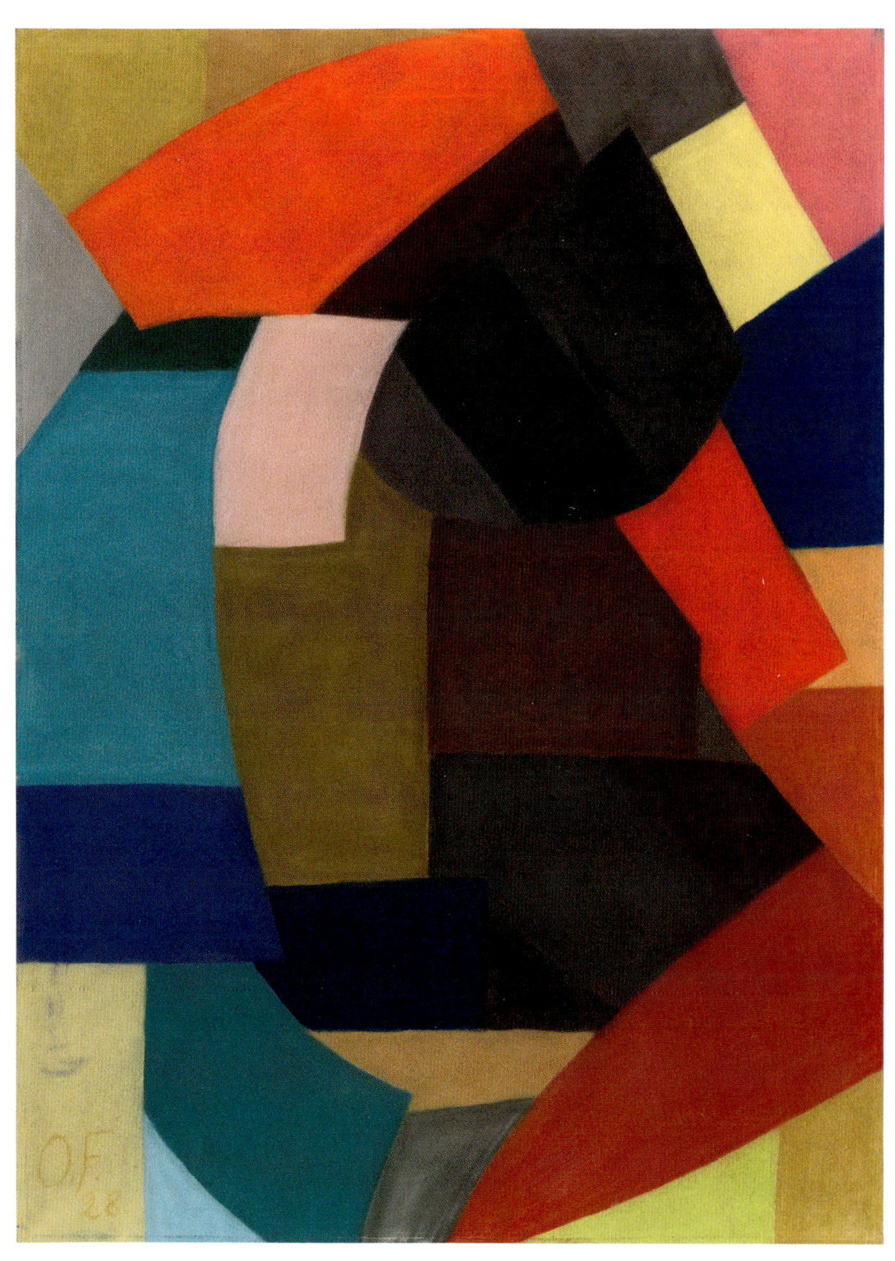

Composition, 1928
HvW 247
Pastel on paper

Nina Schallenberg

Eliminating the Boundaries
Otto Freundlich's Abstract Sculptures

Otto Freundlich's largest art project was never realized: two roads of sculptures designed to criss-cross Europe from north to south and east to west. According to his companion Jeanne Kosnick-Kloss, he planned a *Road of Human Fraternity* from the Netherlands via Provence to the Mediterranean Sea, while the *Road of Human Solidarity in Remembrance of the Liberation* was to stretch from the English Channel across Belgium to Russia.[1] The point where the two roads crossed was set to be in Auvers-sur-Oise, the place where Vincent van Gogh died and where Freundlich spent the summer in 1930. A *Lighthouse of the Seven Arts* (HvW 81, p. 193) was to be erected here, based on the interaction of the seven arts.[2] Setting out from this point, Freundlich wanted to place seven sculptures done in concrete and measuring between about twenty and thirty meters in height along the four sections of the sculpture roads. In a text he wrote in 1936, he described the *Sculpture-Mountains* as abstract monuments that would form vertical markers on the horizontal planes of the landscapes.[3] Freundlich envisaged the *Sculpture-Mountains* equipped with strong light projectors at their uppermost tips, such that they could be used not only as observation decks, but also as orientation beacons for nighttime aviation.

The utopian spirit that inspired Freundlich's project from the beginning resulted in part from the political situation, which made the realization of such a venture right across Europe quite impossible in the 1930s. It was further hampered by the fundamental difficulty of actually rendering an abstract sculptural concept in such monumental dimensions. While sculptures had for a long time been assigned fixed locations and functions in public space in their role as monuments, this changed when sculptors turned their backs on academic traditions. It is in this sense that Rosalind E. Krauss discerned a "fading of the logic of the monument" in the sculptural developments from the late nineteenth century onwards, because many designs for modernist monuments were either rejected or only accepted after numerous revisions.[4] The lack of public place for modernist art that this led to, especially for abstract sculpture, must have been quite unacceptable for an artist like Freundlich, who vehemently championed the social relevance of art. Before setting out into utopian dimensions with his *Sculpture-Mountains* and sculpture roads, he reflected on the social relevance of modern sculpture through his abstract works *Ascension* (1929; HvW 76, p. 186), *Composition* (1933; HvW 78, p. 190), *Architectural Sculpture* (1934–35; HvW 79, p. 192), and the relief *Composition* (1936; HvW 80, p. 194).

Dialectics

At first sight the renunciation of the figural motif seems to indicate that the artist was distancing himself from outer and thus social reality. The concentration on the importance of formal means that came with abstraction enabled Freundlich, however, to draw analogies between the structure of his works and dynamic processes in both nature and society. This, to his mind, was closely connected with a revaluation of visual and tactile perception. As he understood it, the sense of touch that dominates when looking at three-dimensional objects encourages an awareness of the separateness of person and world. Against this, the faculty of vision enhances the feeling of connectivity and unity, because here it has no physical boundaries to overcome. In the journal *Die Aktion*, Freundlich linked the dynamism he saw in the optical with the effectiveness and significance of abstract forms: "Since the dogma of the delimited form no longer exists for the visible world freed of the sense of touch, these boundaries that have as yet been inviolable for my eye can be broken by inner or outer forces. And with ongoing liberation, we see that a joy and something voluntary lives in these forms, undergoing constant change through the inner and outer forces, i.e. permitting themselves to be deformed or dissolved. In this state of freedom, something which almost always was regarded as the sole motor behind artistic creation begins to lose more and more in importance: the motif disappears."[5]

When Freundlich published this text, his sculptures differed from his paintings in that they were still figurative, even though he had already abandoned the dictates of mimesis in the 1910s as he modeled the individual parts of the sculptures. Thus the regions of the forehead, nose, cheeks, and mouth of the now lost sculpture *Large Head* (HvW 63, p. 77) seem committed first and foremost to the rhythmic interplay of surfaces and angles, to protrusion and depression, to light and shade, and not so much to the outward replication of a human head. During the following period, Freundlich's sculptural forms became increasingly autonomous, although he never actually abandoned all reference to figures. Even the abstract sculptures permit associations with figural motifs. Thus for instance the three-part construction in *Ascension* recalls an upright standing body with a large, powerful head, and the ensemble of smaller elements in *Architectural Sculpture* a leaning figure. Freundlich did not view the relationship between abstraction and figuration as a matter of either–or. He was interested rather in visualizing dynamic processes in both that eliminated the boundaries. "All that is procreative in them must step out of the rigid boundaries of abstract and egocentric formulation so as to renew itself in the unity that arises from the counter-movements of abstraction to form and form to abstraction."[6]

In these words Freundlich reveals a basic figure that shaped his thoughts, especially in the 1930s, the period in which he made his abstract sculptures: the dialectical principle in which the union of opposites allows something new to arise on a higher level. For Freundlich, not only the relationship between abstraction and figuration had a dialectical potential, but also, as he noted in an undated manuscript on dialectics that was possibly from 1937, the relationship between unshaped and shaped material.[7] A linocut done in 1937 can be interpreted as a vivid rendering of this dialectical process (HvW 473, p. 275). According to Freundlich, the "unshaped matter acts as the basis"; in this print it is in all likelihood depicted by the black-and-white-striped rectangle on the lower picture margin. He may then have visualized the "shaped matter" above this in the form of the black and white areas, which in part have curved lines running around them. At the very top, the cross-hatched surface demarcated by a curved line must depict "material as a new unity."[8] The interplay between unshaped and fashioned material, which determines the compositions in his abstract paintings and drawings, is also found in his sculptures. Translated into three dimensions, the unshaped matter assumes amorphous forms, while block-like elements visualize shaped matter, and ultimately their interactions lead to forms that unite geometrical and organic elements. In *Ascension*, the upward surging layering of this dialectical triad has been rendered in an especially vivid way.

Surface

A world view that took as its point of departure the elimination of all boundaries, as well as the processuality of life, seemed to pose great difficulties when attempting to square it with sculpture—because the prevailing opinion since the nineteenth century had been that, unlike painting, sculpture is literally bound to reality.[9] Freundlich responded to this dilemma by bringing together contrasting formal principles to create a dynamic tension in his compositions. In addition to which, already by the 1910s he had developed a highly idiosyncratic approach to the surface design of his sculptures which involved coating them with flat modeled platelets. Depending on the material, their effect changed with the light. When placed on the pale grounds of the plaster versions, for instance, the shadowy areas create fine but striking linear structures. In the case of the bronze versions, either the material and the shaded spaces merge to form dark surfaces occasionally lightened by reflections, or the relationship between work, angle of the light, and the viewer's position generates the impression of a bright, busy surface. In any case, these dynamic structures reduce the hardness of the contours that bound the sculptures. Thus a description that Freundlich gave as regards the overall composition of his sculptures also applies to the surfaces with their small component parts: "There where the sculptor has created a deep cavity or undercut, a protruding mass simultaneously ensues and assumes the character of a function: of an outward striving from the center of the stone. The simple fact that three-dimensional material can be differentiated of its own accord, so as to destroy the sense of closure in its contours, leads us to the possibilities that dwell within the three-dimensional material for its self-liberation."[10]

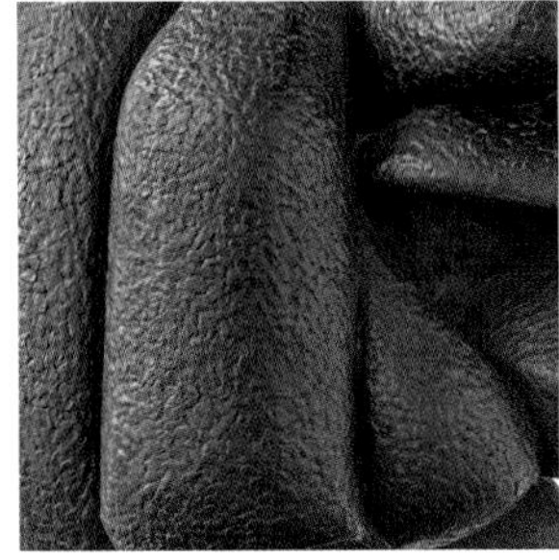

Fig. 35 Otto Freundlich
Ascension (detail), 1929
HvW 76
Bronze

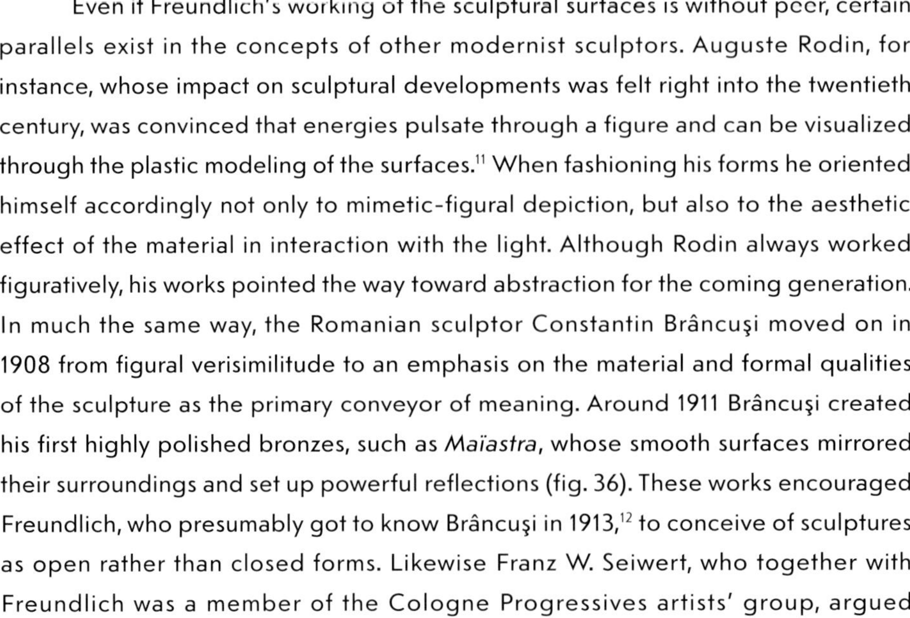

Even if Freundlich's working of the sculptural surfaces is without peer, certain parallels exist in the concepts of other modernist sculptors. Auguste Rodin, for instance, whose impact on sculptural developments was felt right into the twentieth century, was convinced that energies pulsate through a figure and can be visualized through the plastic modeling of the surfaces.[11] When fashioning his forms he oriented himself accordingly not only to mimetic-figural depiction, but also to the aesthetic effect of the material in interaction with the light. Although Rodin always worked figuratively, his works pointed the way toward abstraction for the coming generation. In much the same way, the Romanian sculptor Constantin Brâncuşi moved on in 1908 from figural verisimilitude to an emphasis on the material and formal qualities of the sculpture as the primary conveyor of meaning. Around 1911 Brâncuşi created his first highly polished bronzes, such as *Maïastra*, whose smooth surfaces mirrored their surroundings and set up powerful reflections (fig. 36). These works encouraged Freundlich, who presumably got to know Brâncuşi in 1913,[12] to conceive of sculptures as open rather than closed forms. Likewise Franz W. Seiwert, who together with Freundlich was a member of the Cologne Progressives artists' group, argued along these lines in his article "extensive und intensive plastik" published in 1930 (fig. 37, p. 182). Taking as his examples Freundlich's *Head*, and a bronze version of *Princesse X* by Brâncuşi, he classified the work of the first artist as inwardly directed and that of the latter as outwardly radiating.[13] Despite these antitheses, Seiwert came to the conclusion that both sculptors were concerned with a "dialectic of formal development" in which "intensive" and "extensive" aspects act together. Inside and outside act here not as two separate regions whose boundary lies on the surface of the sculpture. Rather the sculptors managed in their different ways to make their works appear as objects whose forms were the constantly varying result of inner and outer forces. As late as 1939 Freundlich wrote: "An artwork is then true when the inner and outer forces join to form a whole. The *whole* inner life, the *whole* outer life are the worlds that strive for unity in the artwork."[14]

Architecture

The central importance that Freundlich's concept of sculpture attached to the relationship between inside and outside leads to the question of whether and how he staged the relationship of his sculptures to their respective settings. This in fact was one of the largest challenges for a modern sculptural practice, because only rarely were the works conceived for specific locations.

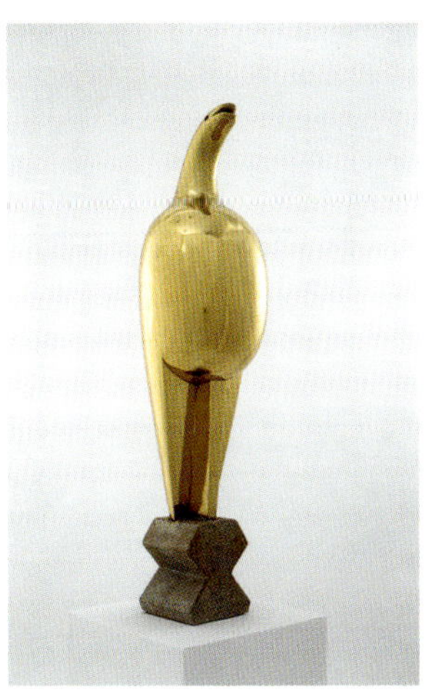

Fig. 36 Constantin Brâncuşi
Maïastra, 1912 (?)
Polished brass
H. 73.1 cm
Peggy Guggenheim Collection, Venice
(Solomon R. Guggenheim Foundation New York)

Freundlich achieved a unity of sculpture and surrounding architecture in a single instance: the funeral vault for the Wissinger family, which Max Taut built in 1922–23 at Stahnsdorf Cemetery in Berlin[15] (p. 195). Set in the middle of an open arcaded structure that reflected Taut's ideal of a crystalline, transparent style of architecture, Freundlich placed a cast concrete slab on the grave of Hermann Otto Julius Wissinger. Set on top was a reclining figure whose amorphously shaped forms attain a degree of autonomy that is echoed in the heads Freundlich made at that time. The closeness of the sculpture to the ground was qualified by the way the arcades open up above. Because just like this architecture, the "interstices," as Freundlich wrote in the year the ensemble was made, these "doorless chambers of eternity, open with *one* great window up above."[16]

But how did Freundlich manage to achieve spatial embedment in the case of sculptures that lacked any fixed architectural context? Sadly there are scarcely any documents that give us an idea of how his works were presented in temporary exhibitions. There are two photographs of *Ascension* taken in 1938 in the garden at Galerie Jeanne Bucher (fig. 47, p. 198), and roughly ten years later in his studio. They show the work on a conventional cubic plinth, whose surface more or less corresponds to the statue's base (fig. 34, p. 124). The height of the plinth allows the beholder to view the work from slightly below, which underlines the effect of upward aspiration. Presumably Freundlich preferred a location for this work that allowed it to be viewed from all sides. Because only on circumambulating it can one see the true dynamism of the forms as they leap out and in again, and of the changes in the light and shaded sections. A number of images taken during the sculptor's lifetime capture this (p. 186).

The plinth as well as the positioning and illumination of the sculptures were among the means of staging the works that were determined by the facilities available at the location where they were presented. Since the possibilities for presentation in

a bis z 10

organ der gruppe progressiver künstler
köln august 1930
herausgeber heinrich hoerle

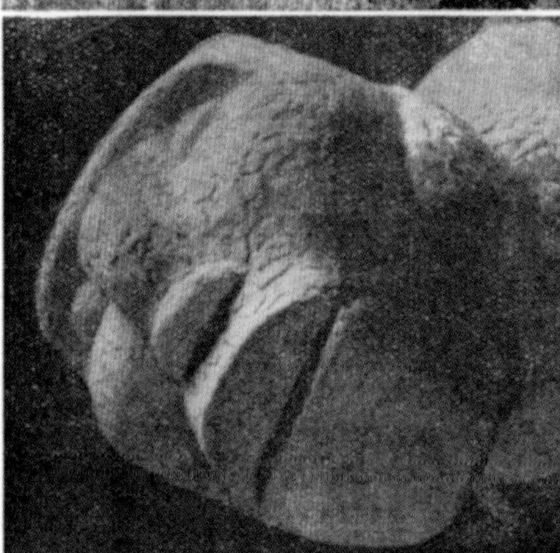

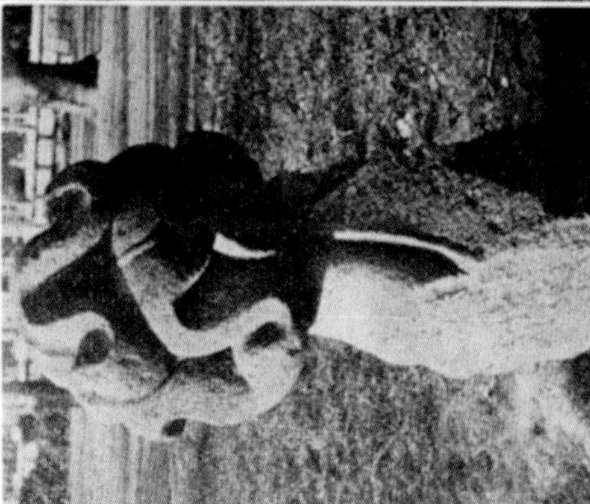

rolf ubach-paris:
krisis des französischen intellektualismus

das wirre suchen der nachkriegsjugend nach einem geistigen halte jenseits der erkenntnis, ihre ablehnung jeder tradition bedeutet für uns die tatsache des zerfalls traditioneller bürgerlicher kontinuität. diese jugend, die durch das versteckspielen mit sich selbst der entscheidung ausweicht, mußte die zersplitterung ihrer weltanschauung sowie die auflösung ihrer kultureinheit herbeiführen. in frankreich erhielt die allgemeine ethische verwirrung ihren notwendigen ausdruck in verschiedenen bewegungen, deren nih lismus sich am meisten in ästhetischen spielen mit unheimlichen hohne gegen den traditionellen bürgerlichen aufbau entwickelt hat; ohne jedoch diese rein destruktive äußerung ihrer sentimentalen verzweiflung durch eine konstruktive bejahung der zeit auszugleichen. ihre absolute weigerung, jemals die haltbarkeit eines wertes anzuerkennen, verwarf ebensogut die verbindung individueller anschauung mit der einheitlichen lösung der kulturfrage als die neugestaltung des lebens durch soziale revolution. darum führte ihre negative haltung zu der geistigen unruhe der nachkriegsjugend, deren gründe zum teile in der umwälzung des ökonomisch-politischen und sozialen gesellschaftsprozesses liegen. der verlust des gleichgewichts zwischen ökonomischer und intellektueller struktur war der grund zur bildung zeitgemäßer kräfte, denen heute der individualismus höherer schichten weichen muß. die allgemeine konzentration des menschenmaterials im modernen produktionsrythmus, wo das individuum nur als glied eines riesigen mechanischen körpers fungiert, besonders die ungeheuere wirkung der maschine auf das gemüt, hat im innern der kapitalistischen produktion ein neues zeitgefühl gebildet, von dem walter stern sagt, daß es den menschen nur noch durch die vervielfältigung seiner selbst sichtbar werden läßt.

dieses wahre kollektive wesen unserer epoche muß durch künstler und intellektuelle fühlbar gemacht werden, als dynamisches kampfmittel zur zerstörung der letzten stellungen des bürgerlichen individualismus. seine heutige revolutionäre bedeutung hat der kollektive gedanke im wissenschaftlichen sozialismus und in einer steigerung des klassenkampfes gefunden. seine einheit kann nur durch den ausbruch einer politischen revolution zum ausdruck gelangen. gegenüber ihrem sozialistischen gestaltungsziele muß sich daher die heutige zeitepoche als übergangsperiode betrachten, wenn sie nicht den grund ihres strebens im nichts der bürgerlichen verzweiflung verlieren will. vorbereitung politischer revolution durch aktive stellungsnahme des intellektuellen und künstlers auf ihrem gebiete ist eine forderung, die für jeden gilt, der die irrende, weltfeindliche haltung vor dem leben infolge des zusammenbruchs seines alten spirituellen inhalts überwunden hat.

1. gotischer stein aus heisterbach; 2. otto freundlich: kopf; 3. barockstein aus heisterbach; 4. brancusi: princesse x. text nächste seite.

temporary exhibitions often scarcely met the aesthetic demands of the individual piece, modern sculptors began to incorporate architectural elements into their compositions and thus supplied the work directly with its connection to space—as for instance in the form of a base. Freundlich picked up on this trend in his abstract sculptures. In *Architectural Sculpture* (HvW 79, p. 192), the title already points to a shift in focus to the architectural context. The compositional dominance of the tall stele is correspondingly great. The plastic elements at its foot recall the cubic and conical forms of the monumental sculpture *Composition* (HvW 78, p. 190). It is as if with *Architectural Sculpture*, Freundlich had added an architectural support to a smaller version of *Composition*. Through the ground-level arrangement of the stele and the sculptural ensemble, he shifted the customary vertical arrangement of sculpture and pedestal onto the horizontal.

Fig. 37 *a bis z* 10, August 1930, with Constantin Brâncuşi *Princesse X*, 1915–16 H. 61.7 cm and Otto Freundlich *Head*, 1916 HvW 65 Lacquered plaster H. 32 cm Lost

In the relief he made shortly after, *Composition* (HvW 80, fig. 38), he took this development a step further by straightening out the cubic and conical elements and placing them before a uniform background. Although they touch in places, each element nevertheless stands on its own. In this way Freundlich moved from a plastic figure to a plastic, architectural ensemble. There are various examples of a shift of this kind in the sculptural ideas we see in his environs in Paris. In the reliefs by Jean Arp, we find abstract forms placed in relationship to one another in a similar manner (fig. 39). In the field of sculpture, Alberto Giacometti used the same principle in the early 1930s in a number of Surrealist pieces, such as in his *Project for a Plaza* (1930–31) (fig. 40). Finally Brâncuşi must be named again, because he already began in 1917 to group individual sculptures as temporary ensembles. He offered, for instance, the collector John Quinn the works *The Child in the World*, *Cup II*, and *The Endless Column* together under the title *The Child in the World, "mobile group"* (fig. 41, p. 185). Sculptural and framing architectural elements were conceived of here as a whole. This kind of approach to opening up sculpture in the direction of architecture was realized twenty years later by Brâncuşi in urban space. Commissioned by the National League of Romanian Women of Gorj, in 1937–38 he created a monument in memory of the people of the city of Târgu Jiu who fell in World War I. Along a roughly one-and-a-half-kilometer west-east axis, he placed monumental versions of *The Table of Silence* (fig. 43, p. 185), *The Gate of the Kiss* (fig. 44, p. 185), and *The Endless Column* (fig. 42, p. 185) While the gate took its form from the sculpture *Le Baiser*,

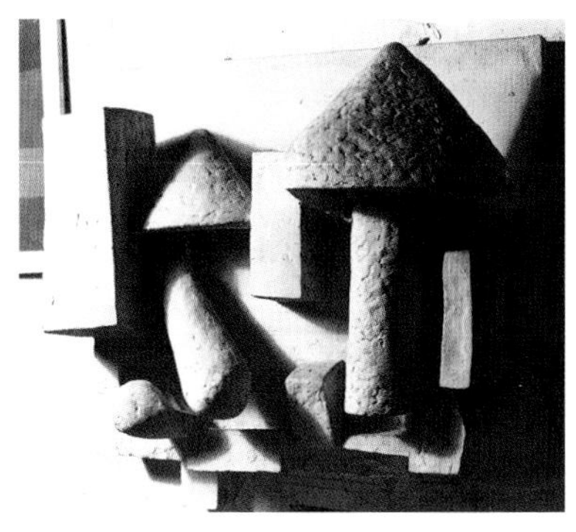

Fig. 38 Otto Freundlich *Composition*, 1936 HvW 80 Plaster 67 × 77 × 14 cm Donation Freundlich – Musées de Pontoise

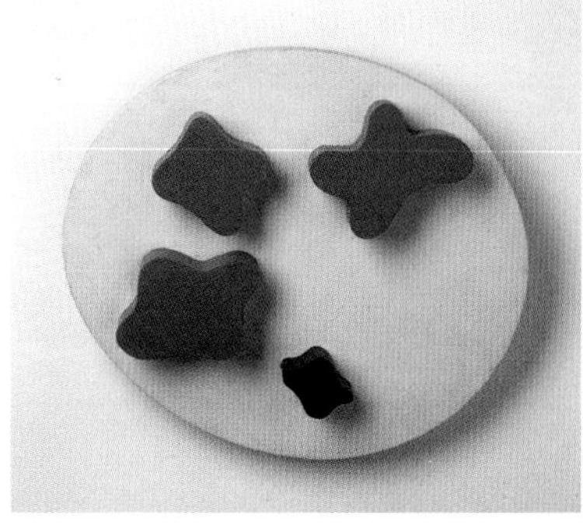

Fig. 39 Jean Arp *Leaves IV*, 1930 Wood, painted 33 × 32 × 2.5 cm Stiftung Arp e.V., Berlin/Rolandswerth

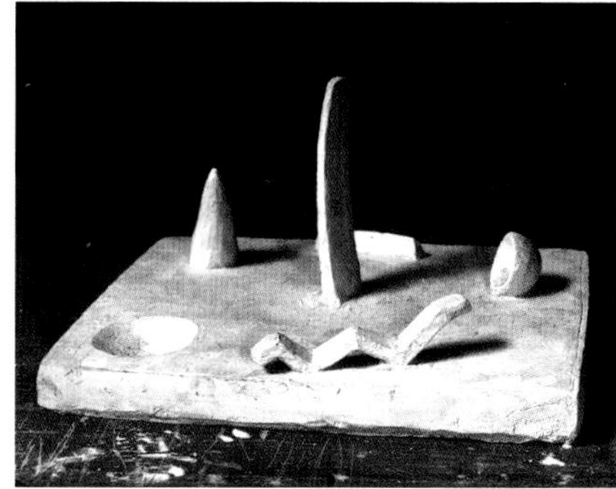

Fig. 40 Alberto Giacometti *Project for a Plaza*, 1930–31 Plaster 16 × 126 × 42 cm Destroyed

the table and the column were based on plinth elements. With that, Brâncuşi dispensed with the traditional division into sculpture, plinth, and architecture in favor of a juxtaposition of plastic-architectural elements.

More or less at the same time, Freundlich was working on his concept of the road of sculptures with the *Sculpture-Mountains* and *Lighthouse of the Seven Arts*. In a similar way, these works conceived of as walk-in sculptures resisted the distinction between sculpture and architecture, between utility and freedom of purpose. Had this project been realized as Freundlich had envisaged, it would have allowed us to experience his dream of eliminating all boundaries, from the tiniest surface detail to the overriding architectural function.

1 See Jeanne Kosnick-Kloss [Jeanne Otto Freundlich], [untitled], Paris, 1959. Note published in *Otto Freundlich: Monographie mit Dokumentation und Werkverzeichnis*, ed. Joachim Heusinger von Waldegg, exh. cat. Rheinisches Landesmuseum Bonn et al. (Cologne, 1978), p. 261. The sculptor Leo Kornbrust began work on a *Straße des Friedens* in 1971 in St. Wendel, Saarland, which picked up on Freundlich's idea of a "street of sculptures" uniting the nations. See http://www.strasse-des-friedens.net (accessed July 2016).

2 Freundlich refers here to the division of the arts in Hegel's *Lectures on Aesthetics* (1835–38) into architecture, sculpture, painting, music, performing arts, and literature, to which film was added at the beginning of the twentieth century. For a considered look at this project see Joachim Heusinger von Waldegg, *Otto Freundlich (1878–1943). Leuchtturm der sieben Künste: Ein utopisches Denkmal*, exh. cat. Stadtmuseum St. Wendel et al. (St. Wendel, 2007).

3 Otto Freundlich, "Sculptures-Montagnes," brochure from the Association Les Amis de Jeanne et Otto Freundlich (Paris, undated [1959]), reprinted in Heusinger, *Otto Freundlich: Werkverzeichnis*, op. cit. (note 1), p. 261.

4 Rosalind E. Krauss, "Sculpture in the Expanded Field," in *The Originality of the Avant-Garde and Other Modernist Myths* (Cambridge, MA, 1986), pp. 277–289, here p. 279.

5 Otto Freundlich, "Die gesehene Form," *Die Aktion* 13/14 (1924), col. 687f., here cited in Uli Bohnen, ed., *Otto Freundlich: Schriften. Ein Wegbereiter der gegenstandslosen Kunst* (Cologne, 1978), pp. 146–148, here p. 147.

6 Freundlich, "Der bildhafte Raum" [1938], unpublished manuscript, cited in Bohnen, *Otto Freundlich: Schriften*, op. cit. (note 5), pp. 211–220, here p. 216.

7 Freundlich, "Dialektik" [undated], published and linked with the print by Bohnen, *Otto Freundlich: Schriften,* op. cit. (note 5), pp. 207–208.

8 Ibid., p. 208.

9 See here Alex Potts, *The Sculptural Imagination* (New Haven and London, 2000), pp. 2–3.

10 Otto Freundlich, "Ideen und Bilder: Aufzeichnungen eines Malers" [1940–42], typescript from the estate, published in excerpts in Bohnen, *Otto Freundlich: Schriften*, op. cit. (note 5), pp. 221–249, here p. 241.

11 See here Nina Gülicher, *Inszenierte Skulptur: Auguste Rodin, Medardo Rosso und Constantin Brancusi* (Munich, 2011), p. 33.

12 In an article published in 1930, Otto Freundlich describes his first contacts in Montparnasse and mentions Brâncuşi. Otto Freundlich, "Modigliani," *a bis z* 6 (1930), pp. 21–22, here p. 21. Freundlich was on sufficiently good terms with the Romanian sculptor to recommend him to Franz W. Seiwert in a letter dated July 17, 1926. The polite, distanced tone in this and another letter to Brâncuşi on January 9, 1930, suggests that the artists were quite familiar with each other, but not close friends. The two letters are in the keeping of the Fonds Brâncuşi at the Bibliothèque Kandinsky in Paris. For the reception of Brâncuşi's works in the circles of the Cologne Progressives see Nina Gülicher, "Der rheinische Blick nach Paris: Brâncuşi, Seiwert und die Suche nach dem 'abc der form,'" in Gülicher, Julia Friedrich, and Lynette Roth, eds., *Form & Gesellschaft: Symposium zur Ausstellung* köln progressiv 1920–33 (Cologne, 2008), pp. 19–29.

13 Franz W. Seiwert, "extensive und intensive plastik," *a bis z* 10 (1930), p. 38.

14 Freundlich, "Der bildhafte Raum," op. cit. (note 6), p. 213.

15 For greater depth see Christoph Fischer, Volker Welter, eds., *Frühlicht in Beton, Das Erbbegräbnis Wissinger von Max Taut und Otto Freundlich in Stahnsdorf: Geschichte und Hintergründe der Entstehung. Dokumentation der Restaurierung 1987/88* (Berlin, 1989).

16 Otto Freundlich, "Der Raum," *Die weissen Blätter* 2 (1919), cited in Heusinger, *Otto Freundlich: Werkverzeichnis*, op. cit. (note 1), pp. 254–256, here p. 254 [italics in the original].

Fig. 41 Constantin Brâncuşi
View of studio with the mobile sculpture group *The Child in the World*, before Dec. 27, 1917
Photo: Adam Rzepka
Silver gelatin print
30.1 × 23.9 cm
Centre National d'Art et de Culture Georges Pompidou, Paris

Fig. 42 Constantin Brâncuşi
Endless Column in Târgu Jiu, 1938
Silver gelatin print
24 × 18 cm
Centre National d'Art et de Culture Georges Pompidou, Paris

Fig. 43 Constantin Brâncuşi
Table of Silence in Târgu Jiu, 1938
Silver gelatin print
24 × 29.8 cm
Centre National d'Art et de Culture Georges Pompidou, Paris

Fig. 44 Constantin Brâncuşi
Gate of the Kiss, front view, ca. 1938
Silver gelatin print
17.8 × 22.7 cm
Centre National d'Art et de Culture Georges Pompidou, Paris

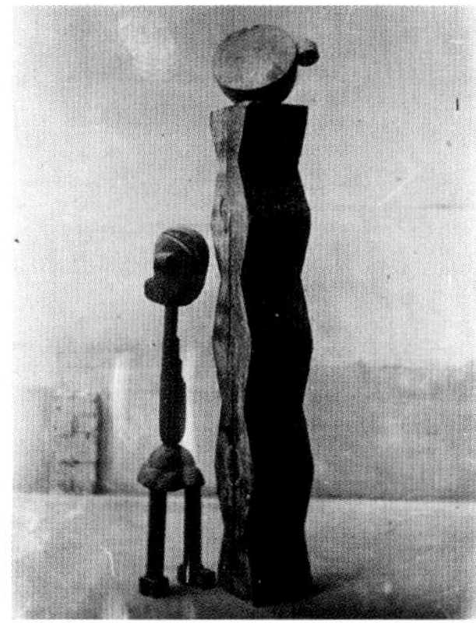

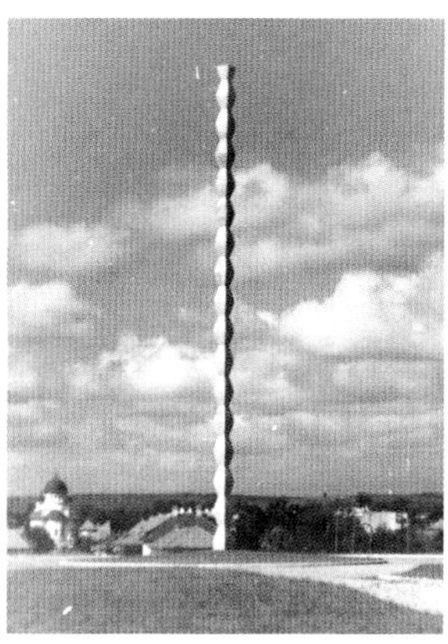

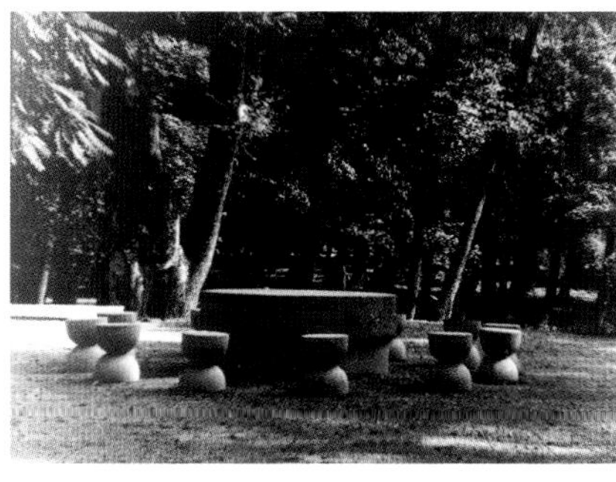

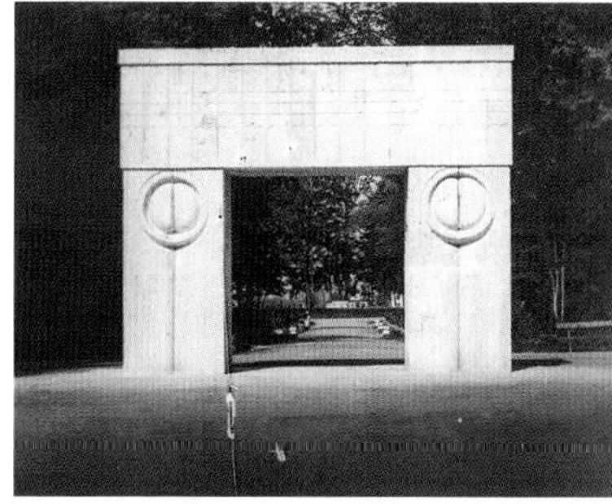

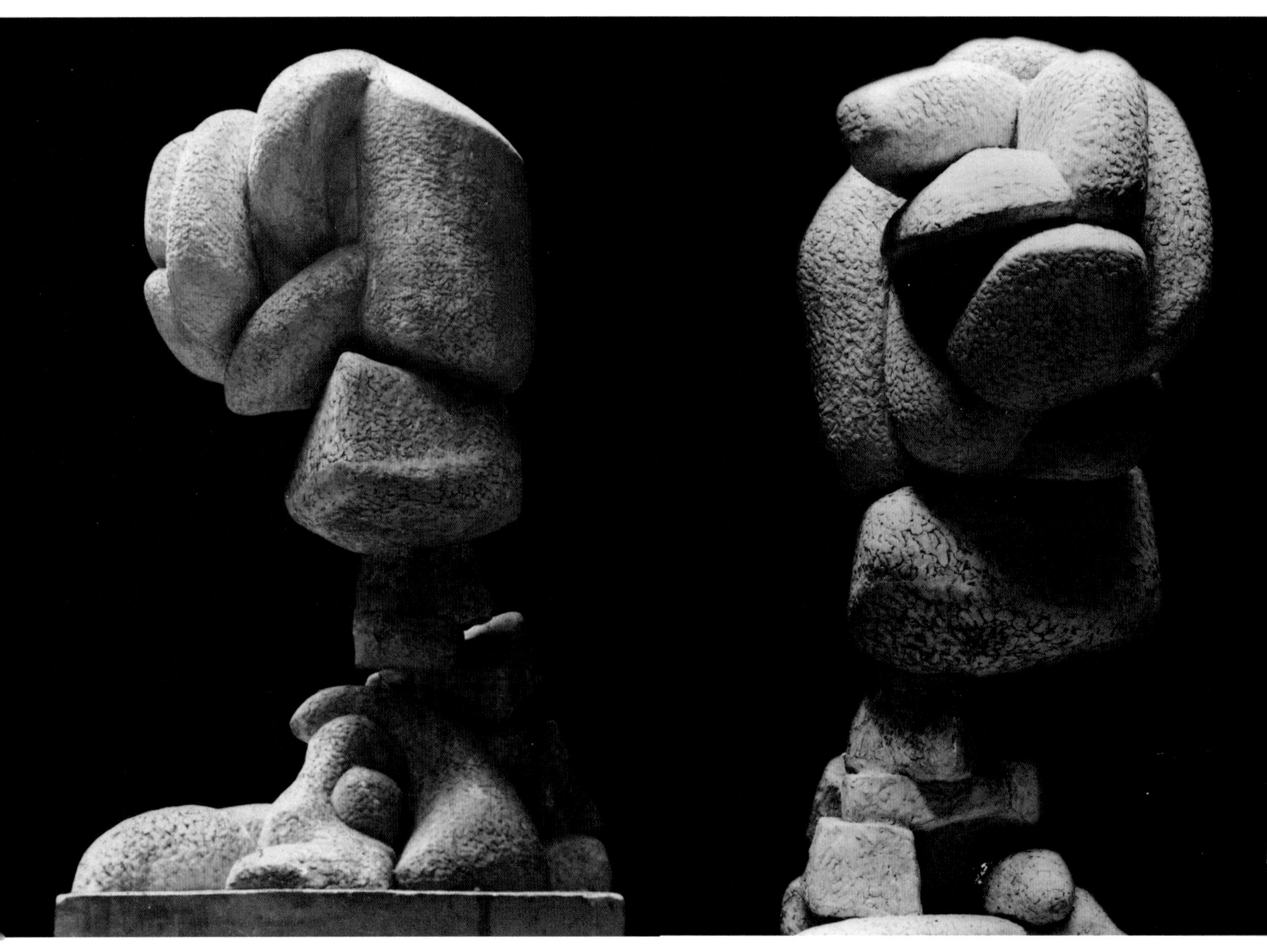

Ascension, 1929
HvW 76
Plaster

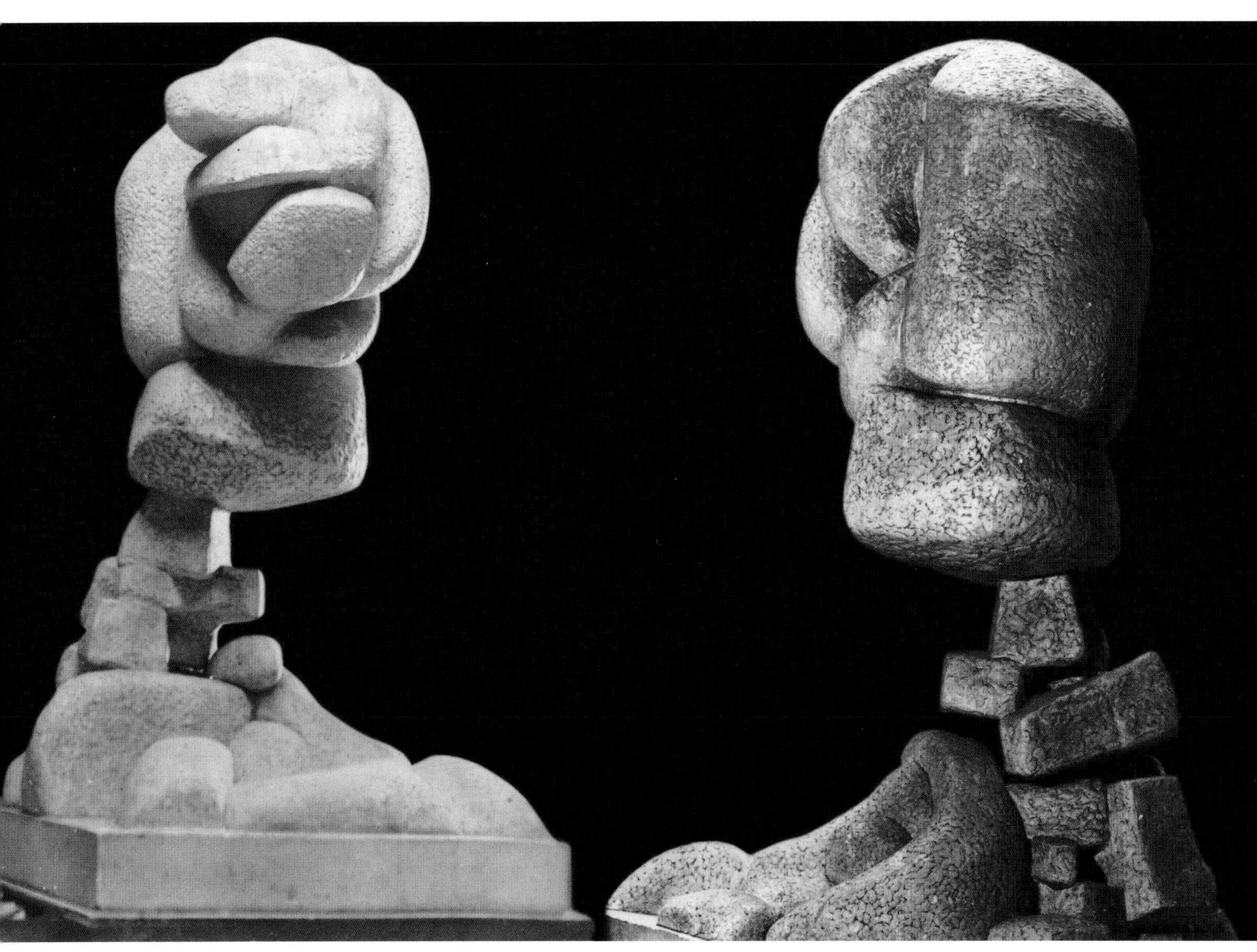

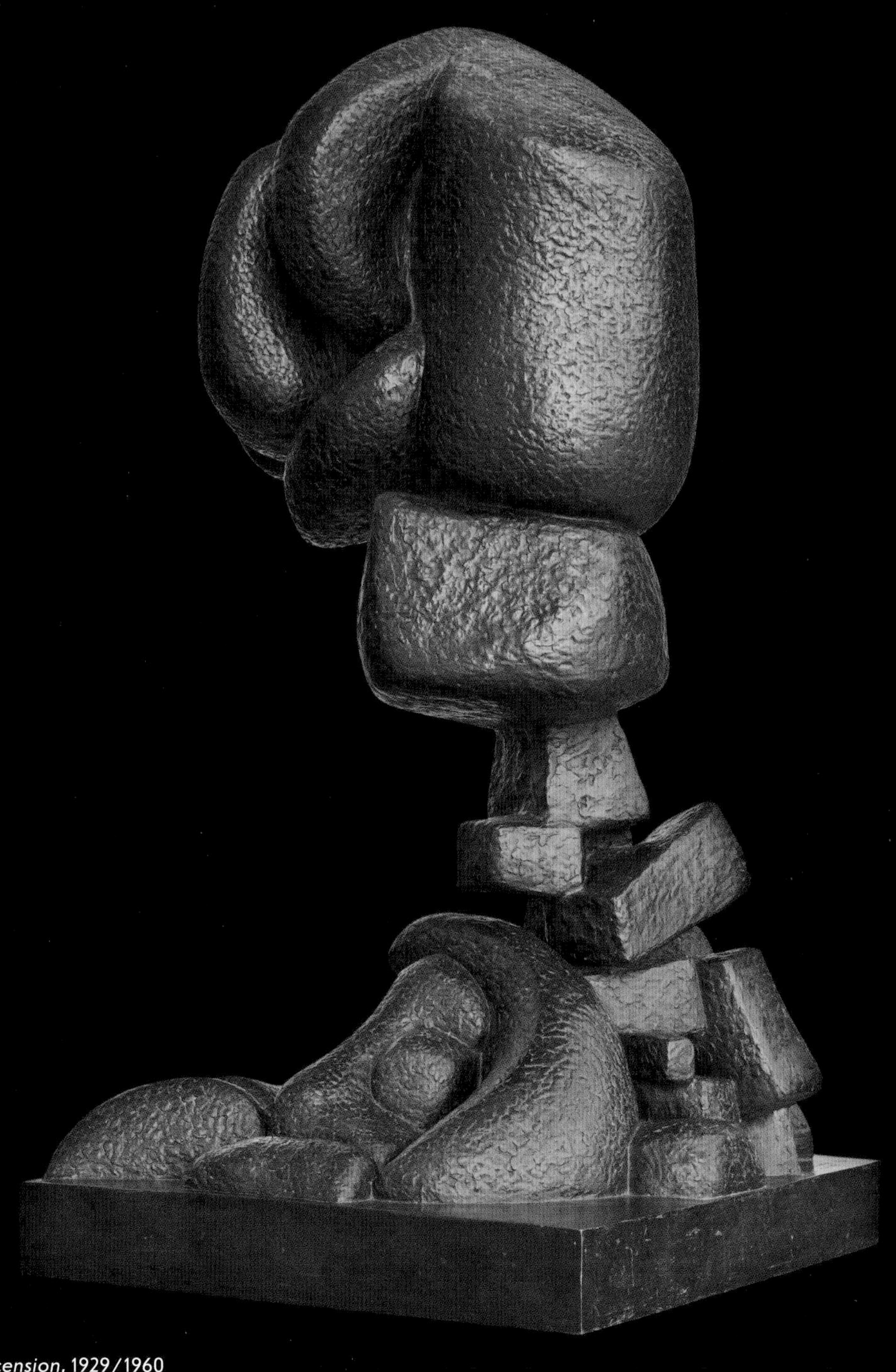

Ascension, 1929/1960
HvW 76
Bronze

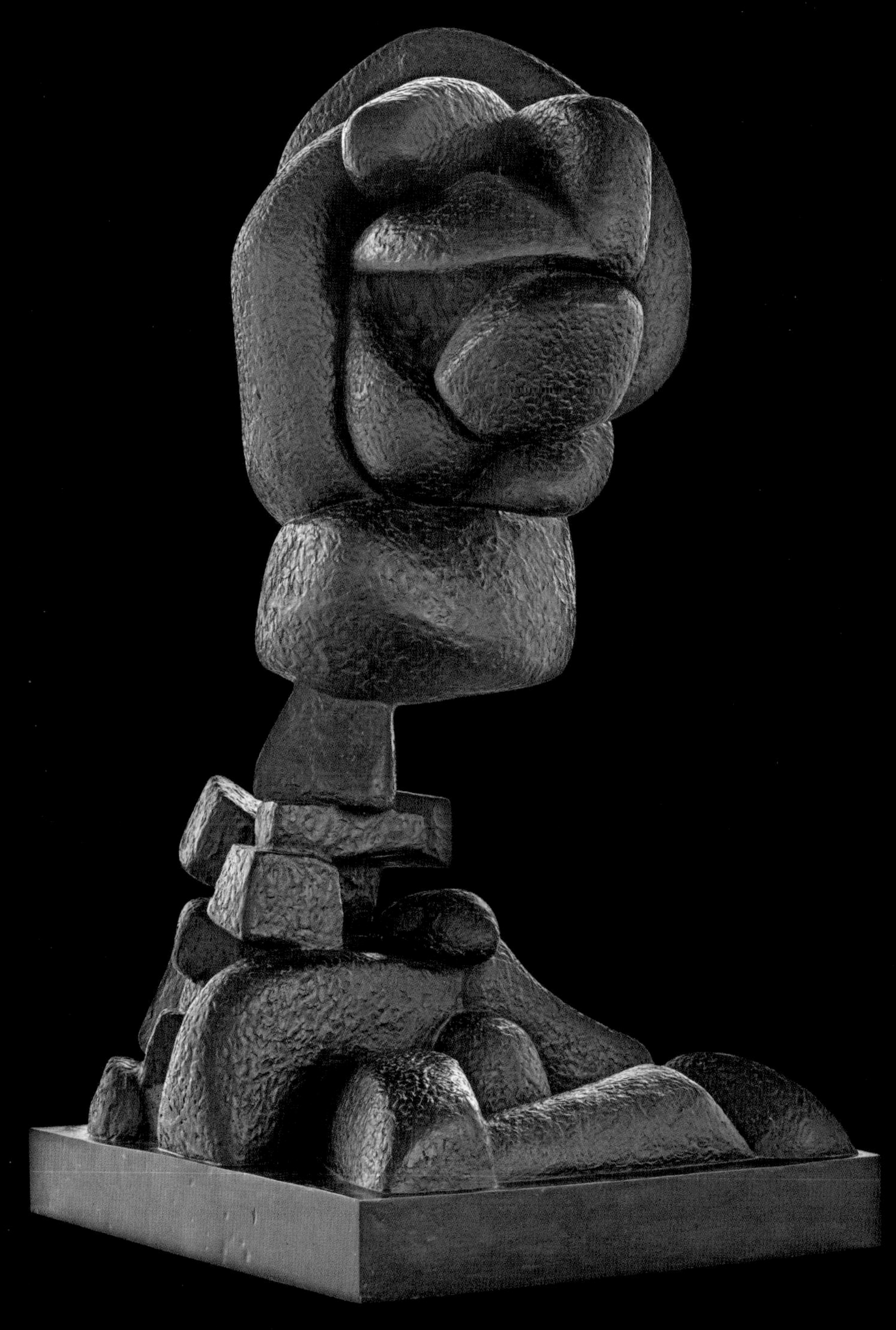

189

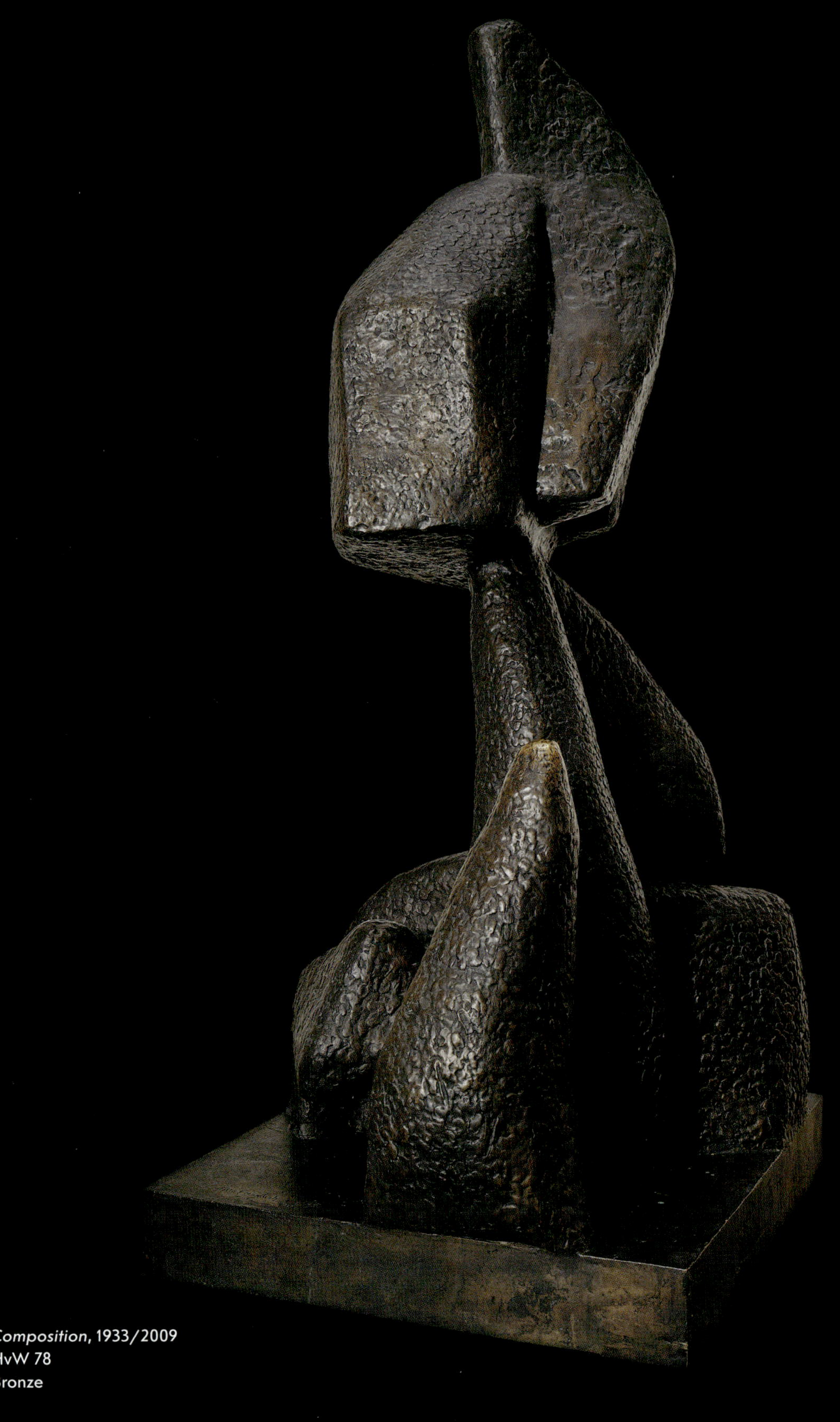

Composition, 1933/2009
HvW 78
Bronze

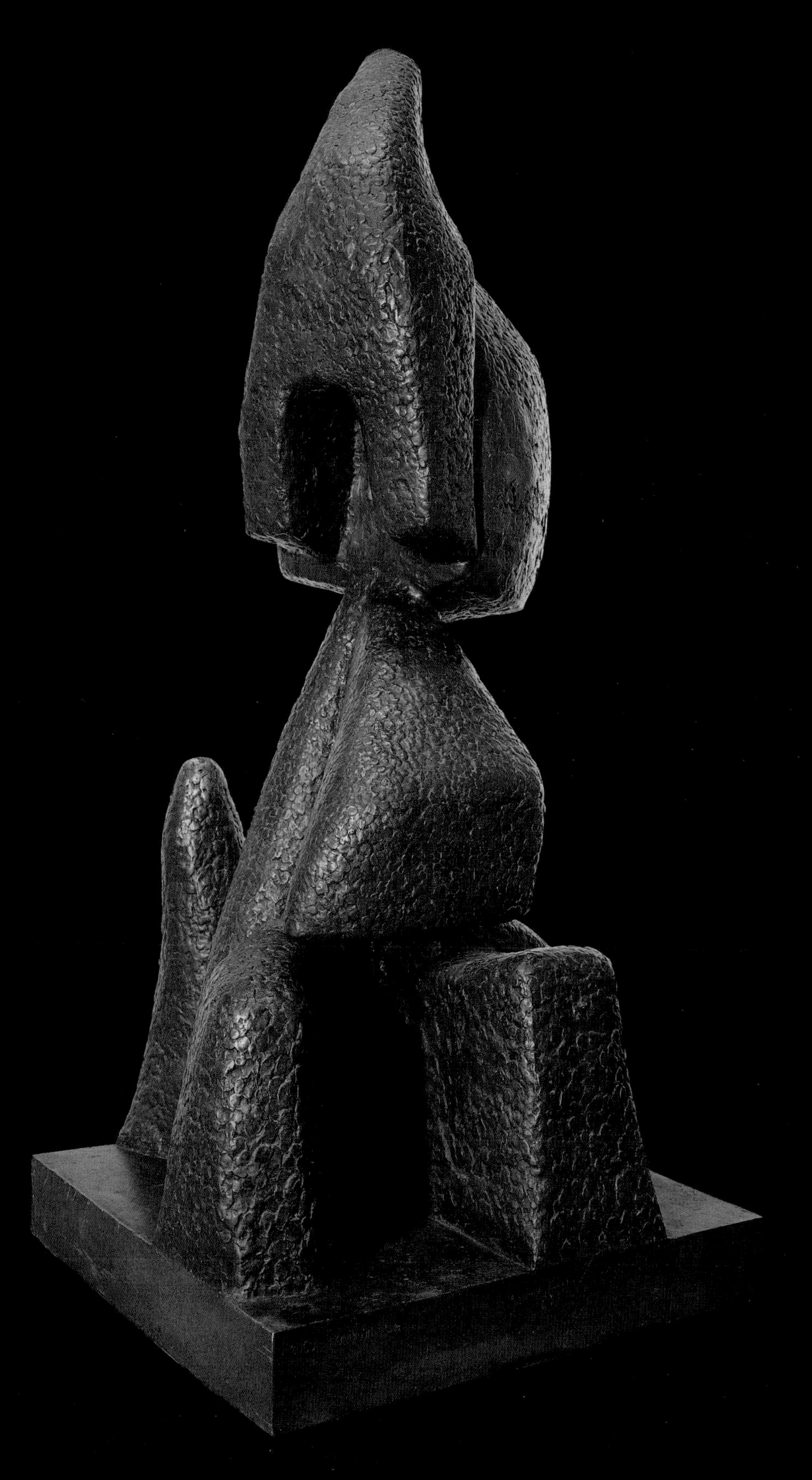

191

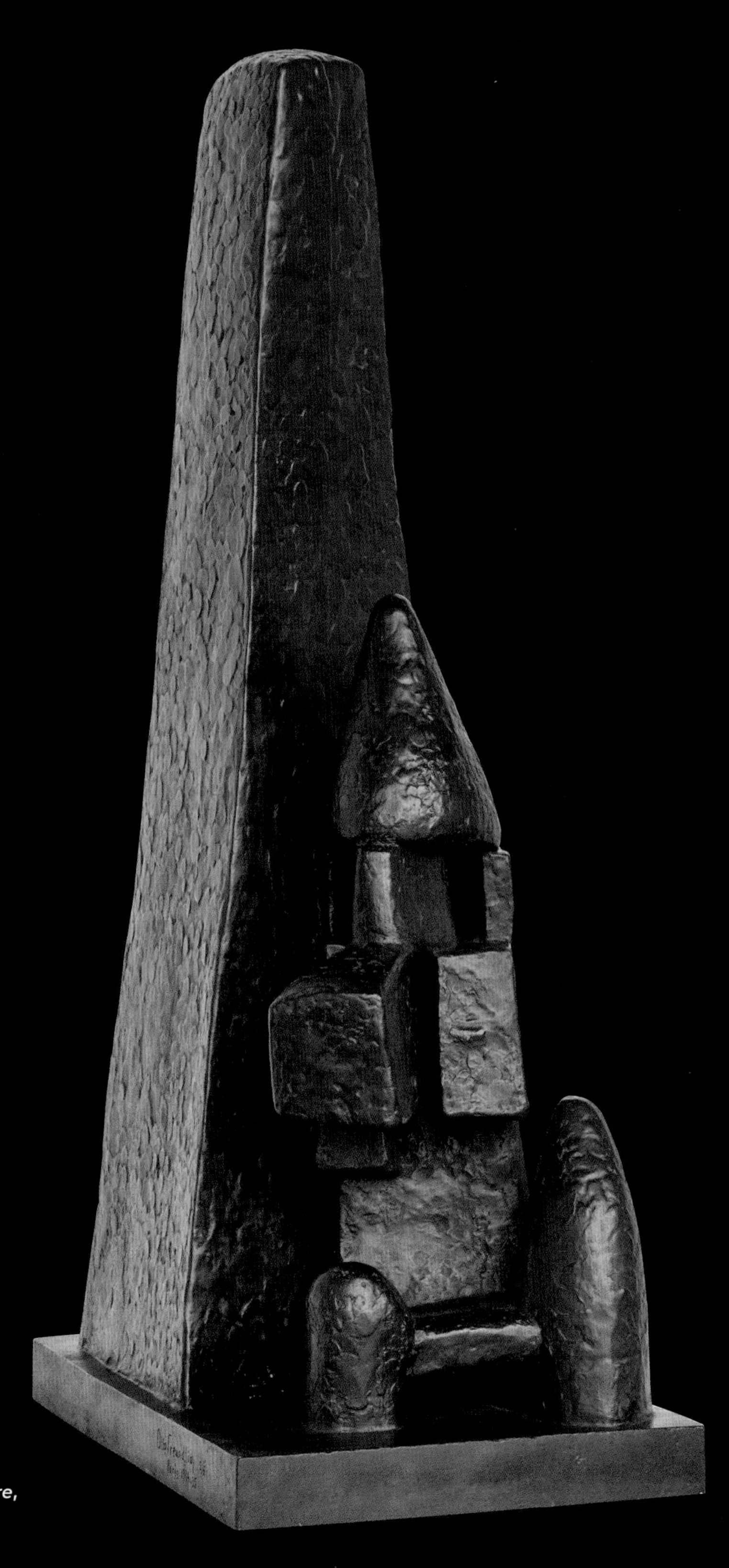

Architectural Sculpture,
1934–35/1988–89
HvW 79
Bronze

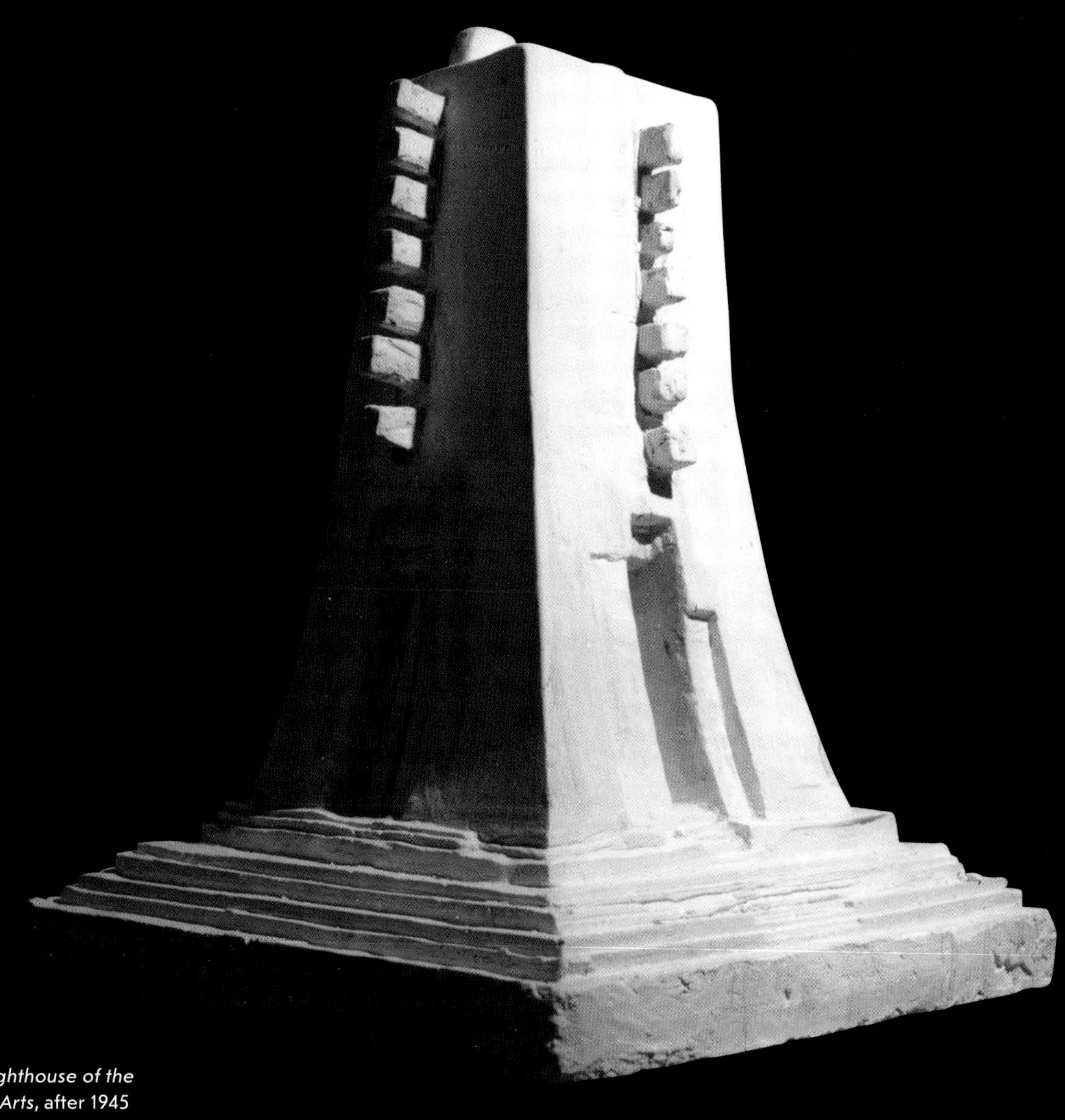

The Lighthouse of the Seven Arts, after 1945
HvW 81
Plaster

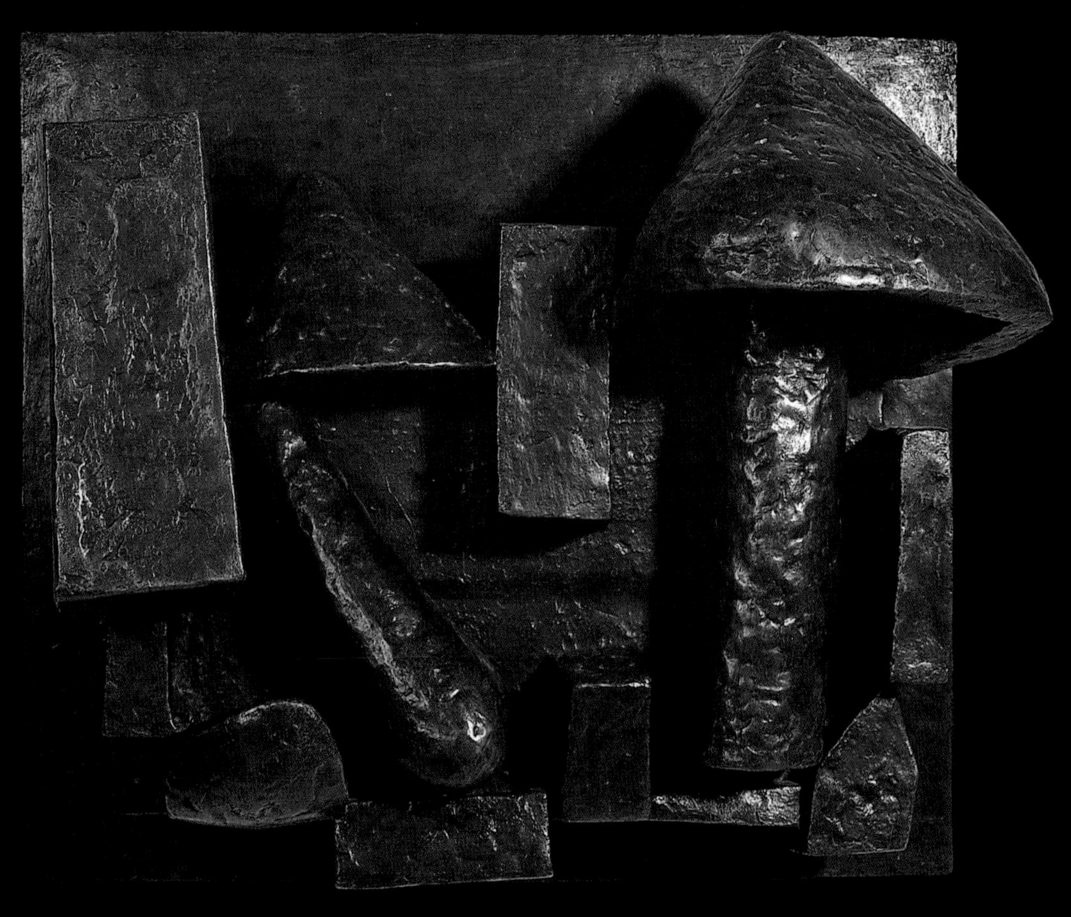

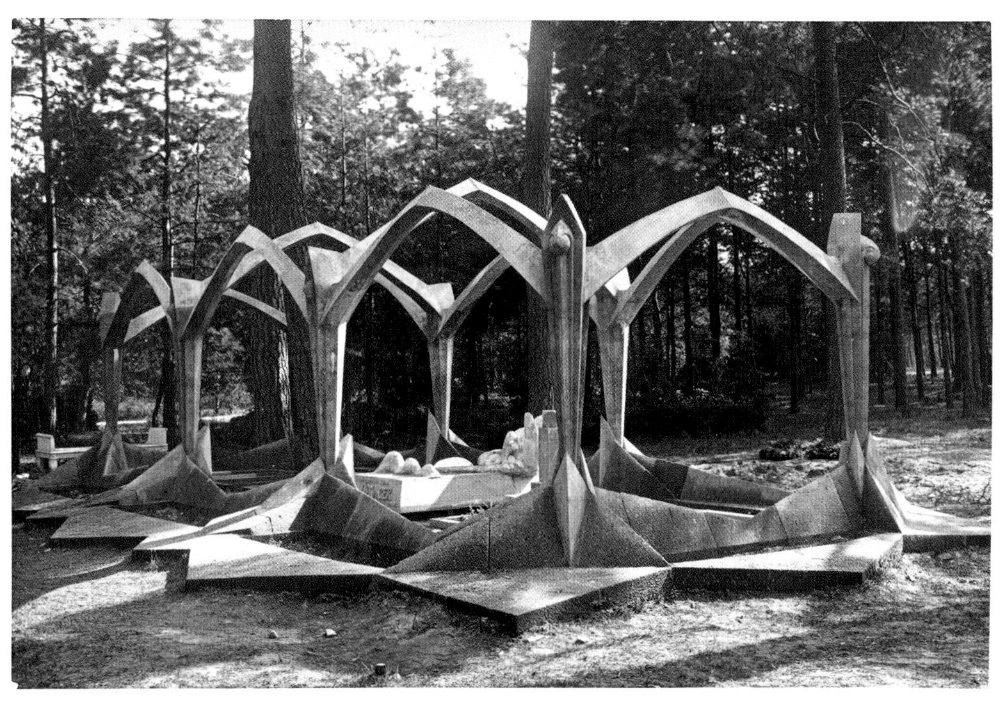

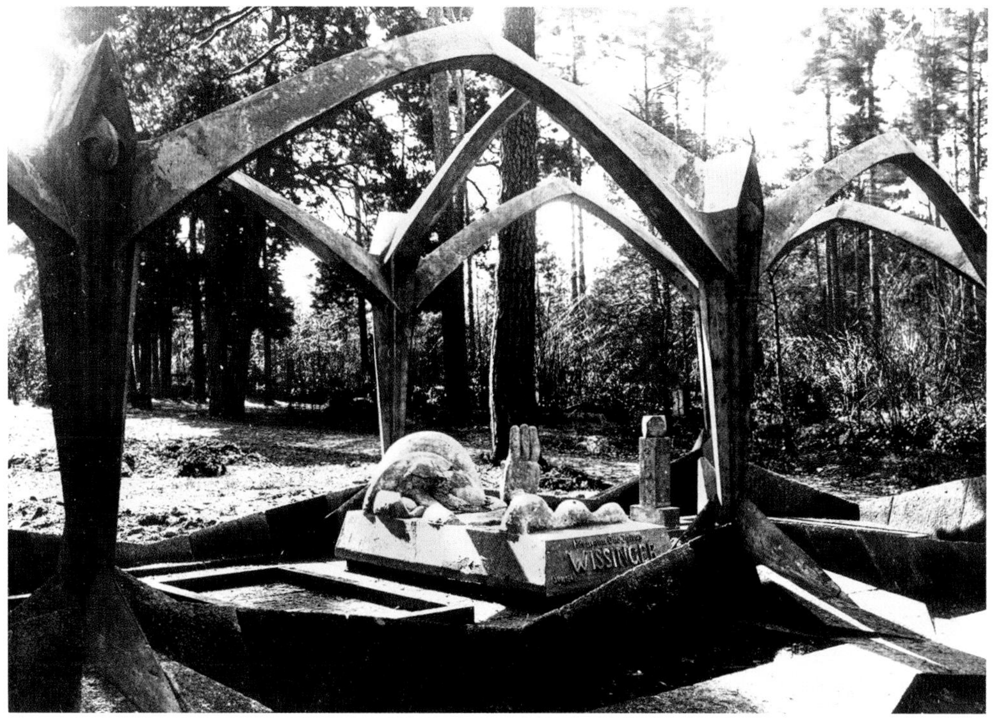

Composition, 1936
HvW 80
Bronze relief

Ground Sculpture for the Wissinger Family Tomb, Berlin-Stahnsdorf, 1922–23
Destroyed

Denise Vernerey-Laplace

Otto Freundlich between Light and Twilight Galleries, Friendships, and Solidarity

The *Large Head* (HvW 63, p. 77), a sculpture by Otto Freundlich, stares from the cover of the catalogue for the exhibition *Degenerate Art*, which opened in Munich on July 19, 1937. The Nazis had seized fourteen of Freundlich's works from the museums where they were displayed. Yet at the same time that he was being pilloried in Germany, the artist wrote to Paul Westheim on July 14, just four days before the exhibition's opening, full of confidence and optimism: "Recognition is a fine and beautiful thing, but when it recognizes the essence of goodness in the artist's efforts, its value is beyond the beautiful."[1]

The reason for Freundlich's optimism was that, since the opening of the Paris World's Fair on May 25, 1937, three galleries in France alone had accorded him the recognition he was hoping for. Moreover, the German photographer Willy Maywald[2] was exhibiting paintings by friends who had emigrated in his Paris studio. Among them were the couple Jeanne Kosnick-Kloss and Otto Freundlich (fig. 45/46). Maywald later wrote that Freundlich was one of "the very first abstract painters. Thanks to the Hitler regime, he lost contact with German museums and galleries."[3]

In 1938, the young painter René Breteau opened his gallery Matière et Forme[4] and invited the painter Hans Reichel,[5] a close associate of Freundlich's, to participate. The following year, Breteau presented photographs by Maywald, "embroideries" by Kosnick-Kloss, and *Compositions* by Freundlich in a show entitled *Art Décoratif*. Despite the events of that period, the works remained on display throughout the summer.

One year later, Berthe Weill, the "little gallerist of the avant-gardes,"[6] invited Freundlich and Kosnick-Kloss to participate in the exhibition *Peintures et Sculptures du groupe éclectique*.[7] Weill was the first woman to open a gallery in Montmartre in 1901. It was she who brought Pablo Picasso, Henri Matisse, Amedeo Modigliani, and the École de Paris to the attention of a wider public.

The Exhibition at Jeanne Bucher's Gallery Of all Freundlich's exhibitions during those years, his show at the Jeanne Bucher Gallery in 1938 was far and away the most important. Since 1935, when Bucher had begun to collaborate with Marie Cuttoli, her gallery at 9 boulevard du Montparnasse had borne the name Bucher-Myrbor.[8] Freundlich had been a regular visitor to Bucher's galleries since 1926. On February 16, 1938, she asked his permission to visit his studio with Wassily Kandinsky. Together, the three selected works by the artist to exhibit on the occasion of his sixtieth birthday,[9] an event announced by Bucher in the journals *Beaux-Arts* and *Cahiers d'Art*.[10]

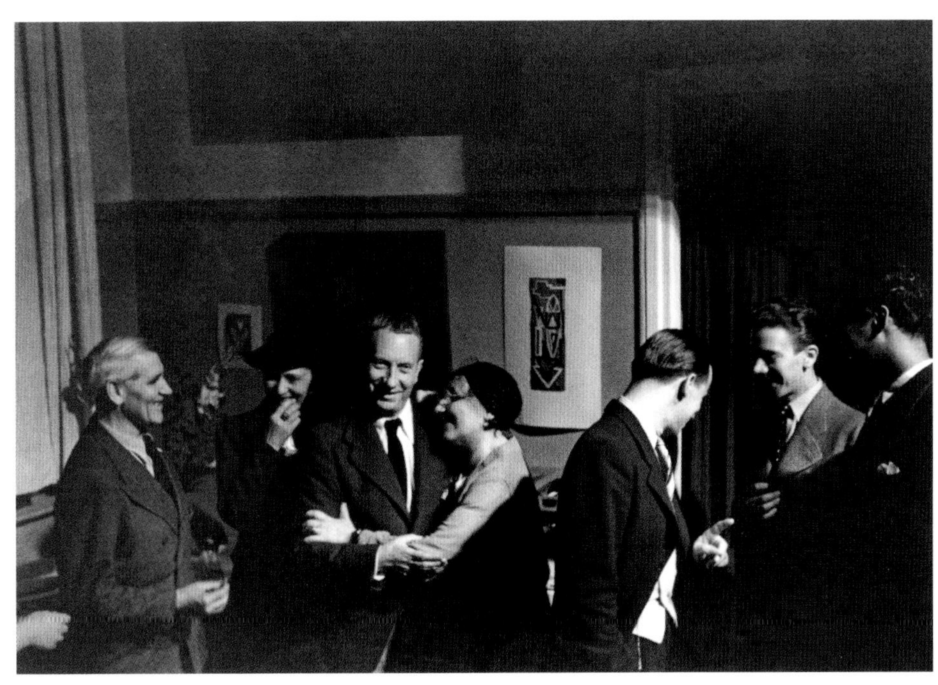

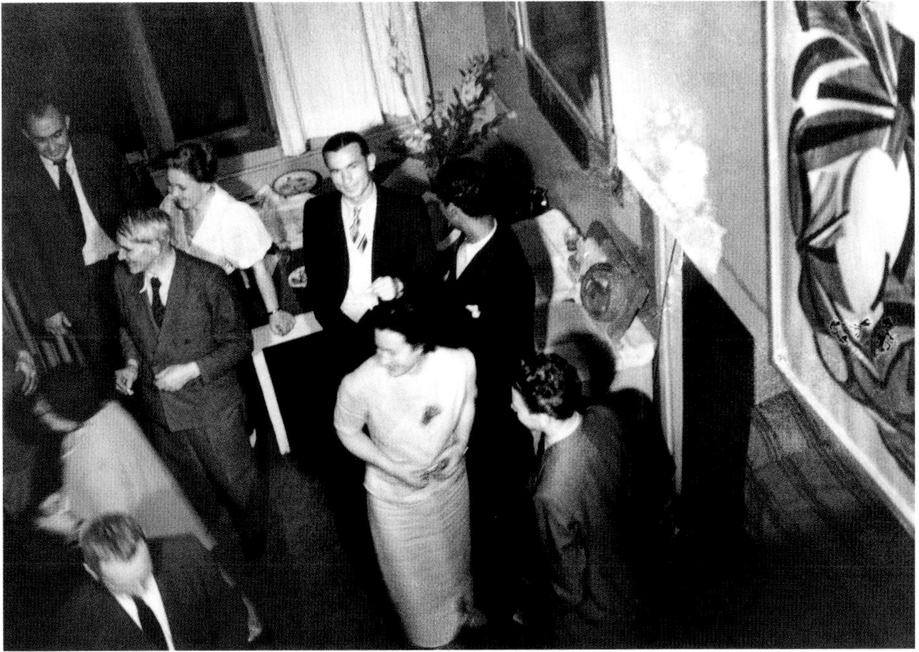

Fig. 45/46 Willy Maywald
Opening of exhibition Otto Freundlich and
Jeanne Kosnick-Kloss in Atelier Maywald, July 2, 1937
Above, from left to right: Otto Freundlich,
Sophie Taeuber-Arp, Jean Arp, and Jeanne Kosnick-Kloss
Association Willy Maywald

On June 3, 1938, at four o'clock in the afternoon, the exhibition was officially opened by Georges Huisman, then director general for fine arts at the Ministry of Education, and André Dézarrois, director of the Jeu de Paume. The exhibition's visitors' book contains the signatures of Alfred H. Barr Jr., director of the Museum of Modern Art in New York, and the gallerist Pierre Loeb, among others. Old friends came as well, including Charlotte and Rudolf Gutmann and the artist's boyhood friend Richard Gottschalk, as did artists in droves: Sophie Taeuber-Arp and Jean Arp, Maurice Estève, Raoul Hausmann, Jean Hélion, the Kandinskys, Félix Del Marle, Piet Mondrian, Picasso, Alfréd Réth, and Georges Vantongerloo. Peggy Guggenheim came with Samuel Beckett.[11]

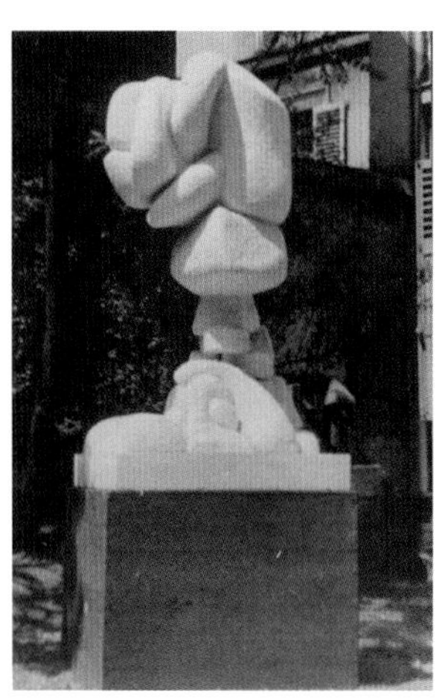

Fig. 47 Otto Freundlich
Ascension
Plaster
In the garden of Galerie Jeanne Bucher, 1938

What works were exhibited? The "Appeal on behalf of Otto Freundlich" (fig. 48, p. 200) refers to "sculptures, paintings, pastels, and drawings." A certain Mr. Segond, a collector from Draguignan, purchased a *Composition* from 1938 (HvW 195, p. 248). In his review of the exhibition,[12] Géo-Charles mentions a plaster *Head* from 1925 (HvW 75, p. 95).[13] Bucher wrote to Freundlich on an undated card: "Tomorrow, Saturday, I'll be talking with a workman about the possibility of showing the paintings in the garden. Can you give me the exact dimensions of the 2 x 2 m and tell me roughly how much it weighs?"[14] Yet there is no indication in the gallery's archive that paintings were actually presented in the garden. While he regards it as possible that they were, since the garden could accommodate fifty to a hundred people, Emmanuel Jaeger of Galerie Jeanne Bucher Jaeger feels it isn't something Jeanne Bucher would be likely to have done. The dimensions cited by Bucher suggest the abstract *Composition* of 1911 (HvW 107, p. 113), which was purchased by the Lüttich-based collector Fernand Graindorge, a regular visitor to the gallery.[15] Be that as it may, there is a photograph in which the sculpture *Ascension* (1929; fig. 47) can be seen in the gallery's garden; Beckett considered the work to be "very beautiful."[16]

An Appeal on Freundlich's Behalf The tradition of artists banding together for philanthropic purposes dates back to World War I.[17] After 1933, committees were formed in many countries to come to the aid of refugee artists and intellectuals. But the "Appeal on behalf of Otto Freundlich" was something genuinely new, since it took a phenomenon that had hitherto been collective and gave it an individual focus. The organizers set up a subscription to enable the purchase of a "representative" work by Freundlich. No other artist had ever been shown this kind of solidarity.

The "Appeal" was signed by more than just the "Action Committee" consisting of Cuttoli, Alfred Döblin, and Max Ernst.[18] While some of the donors wished to remain anonymous, there are many well-known names on the list. With regard to artists, in addition to those already mentioned there were the Arps, Georges Braque, Gio Colucci, Alberto Giacometti, Kandinsky, Moïse Kisling, Jacques Lipchitz, Jean Lurçat, Alberto Magnelli, Louis Marcoussis, Joan Miró, Picasso, Marie Raymond, Alfréd Réth, Hans Richter, Maria Helena Vieira da Silva, Árpád Szenes, and Georges Vantongerloo. Each one made a small individual contribution, with donations ranging from ten to a thousand francs (fig. 49–51, p. 202). Hélion wrote on July 10, 1938: "I deeply regret not being able to do more."[19]

Paul Klee explained his refusal to contribute: "I am afraid, however, that I am unable to comply with your accompanying request, since I must consider the well-being of people who are close to me. Spare me the need for a more detailed explanation, and excuse me, since I can assure you that despite appearances, I am justified in a human sense in not contributing to something that might look like an act directed against the Germany of today."[20] Oskar Kokoschka, in exile in London, signed the appeal and made a donation. Nor did the artist's friends hold back: Géo-Charles, Jean Gacon, the Gutmanns, Maria and Eugene Jolas, and Max Jacob. Also among the participants were collectors and dealers, including Henri Laugier, Tristan Rémy, and Wilhelm Uhde. Additionally, there were positive responses from Alfred Barr, Albert Eugene Gallatin, Galerie Simon de Paris, and the French-Scandinavian Gallery in Stockholm. Peggy Guggenheim sent a private check and later a second one from the Guggenheim Jeune Gallery in London.

The work the group ultimately decided to purchase was Freundlich's large gouache of 1935 (HvW 178, p. 244), that Beckett called "a very fine one, far and away the best in the show"[21] and that paved the way for a mosaic completed in 1938, the *Homage to the Peoples of Color* (HvW 36, p. 245). The mosaic is a visual manifesto for the cosmic or universal communism which Freundlich had embraced at least since 1919: "The painters, sculptors, and architects who hurry ahead and accompany the development and never make compromises with impunity must dig ever deeper into the laws of collectivity and universalism."[22]

A Powerful Supporter The opening of the Guggenheim Jeune Gallery in London in January 1938 created a sensation. That same year, the new gallery was joined by Nelly van Doesburg. "Her passion for abstract art was fanatical," Peggy Guggenheim recalls, "which was why she had come to me."[23] From then on, the two women were inseparable. Doesburg persuaded Guggenheim to support Otto Freundlich and his wife. Nelly had been close friends with Freundlich since her marriage to Theo van Doesburg.[24] The two couples lived through the years of artistic creativity together but also through those of Theo van Doesburg's illness.[25]

Guggenheim promised Freundlich a "place of honor" at the exhibition *Modern German Art*, which she was planning, together with Herbert Read, to mount at the New Burlington Gallery in July 1938. Freundlich exhibited his *Universal Synthesis* there (HvW 170, now lost). Later, a number of Freundlich's paintings were included in the exhibition *Abstract Art* at Guggenheim Jeune: *Universal Synthesis, Transfiguration* (HvW 175, lost), *Open Contours* (HvW 189, lost), and a *Composition* from 1939 (HvW 196, p. 267). Guggenheim expressed interest in purchasing an India ink work by the artist, his *Composition* of 1938 (HvW 376, p. 247). *Open Contours* and *Transfiguration* were included in the show's stopover in Paris at Galerie de Beaune, presumably together with the *Composition* from 1939.

Right from the beginning, however, business was bad at Guggenheim Jeune. In March 1939, even before the gallery was forced to close in June, Guggenheim brought up the idea of creating a "modern museum."[26] Read was to be its director. But after September 3, when France and Great Britain declared

UN APPEL EN FAVEUR DE OTTO FREUNDLICH

Le 10 Juillet 1938 OTTO FREUNDLICH, peintre et sculpteur aura 60 ans; il doit être considéré comme un des précurseurs les plus importants de l'art "abstrait" et comme un chercheur infatigable des voies nouvelles.

Les musées de l'Allemagne démocratique, Hambourg et Cologne en particulier, reconnurent jadis le rôle primordial joué par FREUNDLICH dans l'évolution de l'Art Moderne et acquirent plusieurs de ses oeuvres. L'Allemagne hitlérienne ne vit naturellement dans l'art contemplatif de FREUNDLICH qu'une dégénérescence. Mais, en plaçant la reproduction d'une sculpture de FREUNDLICH "L'Homme Nouveau" sur la couverture du catalogue de l'exposition organisée récemment à Berlin, sous le titre : "l'Art dégénéré" les Allemands rendirent - à leur insu - un hommage à OTTO FREUNDLICH.

Cet artiste vit à Paris dans des conditions si pénibles et douloureuses qu'il lui arrive de ne pouvoir acquérir les couleurs indispensables à la réalisation de son art. Plusieurs artistes et critiques voudraient essayer de lui fournir la possibilité de poursuivre son oeuvre loin de tels soucis. Leurs premières démarches ont rencontré l'accueil le plus chaleureux dans les milieux de l'art moderne.

Une première décision a été prise : celle d'acquérir, par souscription un des tableaux de FREUNDLICH, celui qu'on considère généralement comme le plus représentatif de son art, et de l'offrir au Musée du Jeu de Paume.

La Galerie Jeanne Bucher-Myrbor fera le 3 Juin 1938, une exposition de FREUNDLICH comprenant des sculptures, des peintures, pastels et dessins. Cette exposition sera inaugurée par Monsieur G. Huisman, Directeur des Beaux Arts, et par Monsieur Dézarrois, Directeur du Musée du Jeu de Paume.

Les soussignés s'adressent à vous, Monsieur, en vous priant de bien vouloir coopérer par un don personnel au mouvement entrepris en faveur d'OTTO FREUNDLICH et de son art. La banque Hugo Simon, Paris 2e, 6, rue d'Antin, recevra les dons d'argent.

Jankel Adler, H. Arp, G. Braque, J. Cassou, A. Derain, P. Dermée, R. et S. Delaunay, J. Gacon, Géo-Charles, L. de Gonzague-Frick, A. Gleizes, W. Gropius, A. Herbin, Max Jacob, W. Kandinsky, Kokoschka, Laurens, Léger, Lhote, G. Linze, Lipchitz, Picasso, M. Raynal, H. Read, S. Täuber-Arp, W. Uhde, P. Westheim.

Pour le Comité d'Action:

Marie Cuttoli, A. Döblin, Max Ernst.

Fig. 48

An Appeal on Behalf of Otto Freundlich

On July 10, 1938, the painter and sculptor OTTO FREUNDLICH will turn sixty years old. He deserves to be seen as one of the most important precursors of "abstract" art and as a tireless seeker of new paths.

The museums of democratic Germany, in particular those of Hamburg and Cologne, have already recognized the essential role played by FREUNDLICH in the development of Modern Art and have acquired a number of his works. Needless to say, Hitler's Germany sees FREUNDLICH's contemplative art as nothing but a symptom of degeneracy. Yet by placing the reproduction of one of FREUNDLICH's sculptures, *L'Homme Nouveau* [*The New Man*], on the cover of the catalogue for the exhibition recently organized in Berlin under the title *Degenerate Art*, the Germans unwittingly paid tribute to OTTO FREUNDLICH.

This artist is currently living in Paris in such difficult and painful conditions that he is sometimes unable to purchase the paints he needs to practice his art. A number of artists and critics would like to attempt to make it possible for him to pursue his work without facing concerns like these. Their initial efforts have been met with an extremely warm response in modern art circles.

A first decision has been taken: to launch a subscription to purchase one of FREUNDLICH's paintings—the one that is generally regarded as the most representative of his work—and donate it to the Museum of the Jeu de Paume.

Galerie Jeanne Bucher-Myrbor will hold an exhibition of FREUNDLICH's work on June 3, 1938, including sculptures, paintings, pastels, and drawings. This exhibition will be opened by Monsieur G. Huisman, director of the Beaux Arts, and Monsieur Dézarrois, director of the Museum of the Jeu de Paume.

The undersigned turn to you, dear Sir, in hopes that you will kindly agree to support this movement on behalf of OTTO FREUNDLICH and his art with a personal gift. Monetary donations should be directed to Bank Hugo Simon, Paris 2e, 6, rue d'Antin.

Jankel Adler, H[ans] Arp, G[eorges] Braque, J[ean] Cassou, A[ndré] Derain, P[aul] Dermée, R[obert] and S[onia] Delaunay, J[ean] Gacon, Géo-Charles, L[ouis] de Gonzague-Frick, A[lbert] Gleizes, W[alter] Gropius, A[uguste] Herbin, Max Jacob, W[assily] Kandinsky, [Oskar] Kokoschka, [Henri] Laurens, [Fernand] Léger, [André] Lhote, G[eorges] Linze, [Jacques] Lipchitz, [Pablo] Picasso, M[aurice] Raynal, H[erbert] Read, S[ophie] Taeuber-Arp, W[ilhelm] Uhde, P[aul] Westheim.

For the Action Committee:
Marie Cuttoli, A[lfred] Döblin, Max Ernst.

Raymond
Leiris Kahnweiler gal. Simon 100 – x
Bardon 50 – x
Gutman 50 – x
Louise Janin (20)
Jacques Lipchitz sc 50 frs. x
Géo Colucci 10 frs x
Picasso p 500 – x
Schaefers 15 – x
Miró p 100 x
Peggy Guggenheim, gal. Gugg. j. Londres 1000 x
Gallatin p 100 x
Mme Guggenheim, Peggy, un chèque 1000
Mme Eugène Jolas 200 – Ecole bilingue à Neuilly 200 x
Karl Nierendorf gal. N. York (100) –
Charles Vildrac (50) x

Monsieur Tower 200
mécène inconnu (200)
Max Jacob (100)
H. Richter (100)
J. Gacon (50)
Jean Lurçat 50 x
~~Mademoiselle Greiner~~ ~~50~~
Madame Bois 20 x
Miss Elizabeth Curran 20 x
Mr. Kandinsky p 100 x
Mademoiselle Sulzer 100 x
Mr. Alfred Barr, directeur du Musée Moderne, New York 100 x
Melle Rose Adler 100 x
Madame Eve Daniel 20 x
Monsieur Giacometti sc 10 –
Viera da Silva p 10. –
Mr. Mme Arp 100. –
Brill 20 –
Madame Cuttoli reçu x 100 – x
Mr. Desaint Paul 50 –
J. Cherchesky 20
Mr. Borgitz 10
Desnoyer 100
Glass 5
A. et S. Magnelli x 100 –
Henry Valensi p 25
Mr Kiling p 100 r.
Mr Beraco 100 –

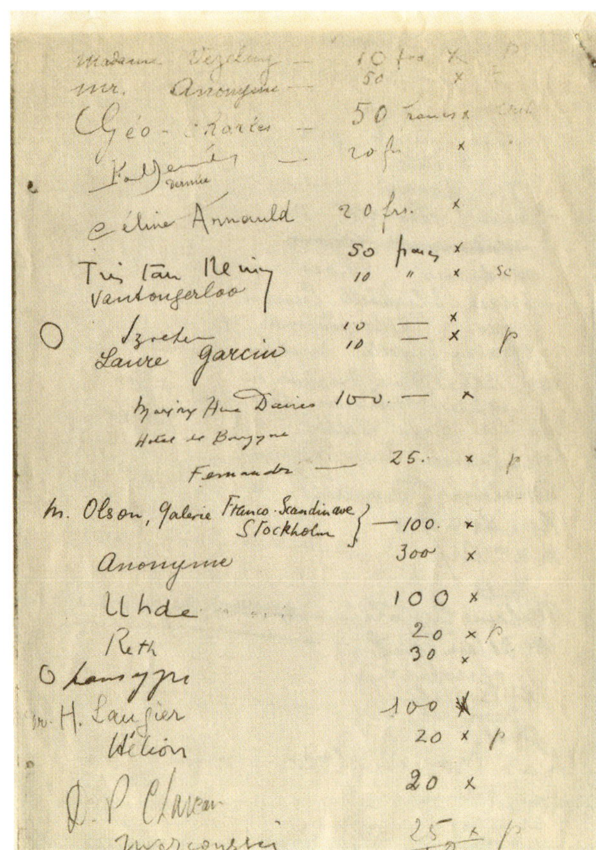
Madame Vézelay – 10 frs x
Mr. Anonyme – 50 x
Géo-Charles – 50 francs x
Kaljenès – 20 fr x
Céline Arnauld 20 fr. x
Tristan Rémy 50 francs x
Vantongerloo 10 " x sc
Szrebe 10 x
Laure Garcin 10 x p
Marey Hue Davies 100. – x
Hotel de Bourgogne
Fernandez – 25. x p
M. Olson, Galerie Franco-Scandinave Stockholm – 100. x
Anonyme 300 x
Uhde 100 x
Reth 20 x p
Lanzagne 30 x
Mr. H. Laugier 100 x
Hélion 20 x p
D. P. Clavan 20 x
Marcoussis 25 x p

Fig. 49 –51 List of subscribers to the Appeal on Behalf of Freundlich

war, she abandoned the plan. Taking advantage of her considerable wealth—her inheritance from her mother—Guggenheim followed Nelly van Doesburg to Paris. "My motto was 'Buy a picture a day' and I lived up to it."[27]

With Freundlich interned at the prisoner-of-war camp in Colombes, Jeanne Kosnick-Kloss did not give up hope. At Van Doesburg's suggestion, Guggenheim had purchased a painting by Freundlich "for the museum in London"[28] and planned to "pay one thousand francs a month for it, in keeping with the price set by Galerie Charpentier. [She] would also be willing to advance the costs associated with becoming naturalized citizens."[29]

Works by Freundlich went everywhere the "crates" did in which Guggenheim kept her collection. Van Doesburg arranged for them to be stored by Andry-Farcy (actually Pierre-André Farcy), a curator at the Museum of Grenoble. But when the Germans extended their occupation to the hitherto "free zone" in the South of France, the collection was forced to emigrate. Guggenheim boarded a ship to New York with it in spring 1941. Once there, she showed it at her newly opened gallery, Art of this Century. As part of the Guggenheim collection, works by Freundlich later traveled to Venice,[30] where the presence of his black-and-white India ink work *Composition* (HvW 376, p. 247) and the oil painting *The Unity of Life and Death* from 1936–38 (HvW 185, p. 240) is attested as late as 1968.

No one did more to support Freundlich's work in these difficult times than his friends Nelly van Doesburg and Peggy Guggenheim. In March 1943, when Freundlich was murdered, a creative force was lost that still had a great deal left to offer. In the great artistic debates of the postwar years, his bluntness, his rigorous theory, and the dynamic equilibrium of his compositions were all sorely missed, and so too were the brilliant colors of his works.

1 Letter from Freundlich to Westheim, Paris, July 15, 1937, Central Special Archives, Moscow, Westheim Papers, document no. 602-1-11/85–86, quoted in Ines Rotermund-Reynard, "The Art Historian Charlotte Weidler: A Lost Voice Speaks from the Moscow Special Archive," in Ines Rotermund-Reynard, ed., *Echoes of Exile* (Berlin, Munich, and Boston, 2015), pp. 104–122, here p. 112.

2 Willy Maywald was born in Kleve, Germany, in 1907 and died in Paris in 1985. In the early 1930s, he settled permanently in Paris, opening his first studio there in 1934. See *Willy Maywald: Portraits und Ateliers. Frankreich 1938–1970*, exh. cat. Heck-Art Galerie (Chemnitz, 2011).

3 Willy Maywald, IMEC (Institut mémoires de l'édition contemporaine), archives of Galerie Breteau.

4 At its opening, the gallery's core collection consisted of works by the artists' group Témoignage: Jean Bertholle, Jean Le Moal, Alfred Manessier, and François Stahly.

5 See the press documents connected with the gallery's exhibition, IMEC, archives of Galerie Breteau.

6 See Marianne Le Morvan, *Berthe Weill 1865–1951: La petite galeriste des grands artistes* (Orléans, 2011).

7 I am grateful to Marianne Le Morvan for allowing me access to the archives of Galerie Berthe Weill.

8 "Myrbor" was the name that Cuttoli gave her own gallery, after her maiden name, Myriam Bordes.

9 Postcards from Bucher to Freundlich, February 16 and 17, 1938, archive Association Les Amis de Jeanne et Otto Freundlich (AAJOF), IMEC, FRN 1.12.

10 *Beaux-Arts* 283 (1938), in the column "Les expositions"; the announcement ran again in issues 284 and 285 (1938). *Cahiers d'Art* 1–2, 1938.

11 I am grateful to Mr. Emmanuel Jaeger for allowing me to inspect the visitors' book. According to him, there is no list of exhibitions in the archives of Galerie Bucher; conversation of June 23, 2016.

12 Géo-Charles (pen name of the poet Charles Louis Prosper Guyot, 1892–1963), "Le 60è anniversaire d'un précurseur de l'art moderne," *Anthologie* 5 (1938), pp. 8–9.

13 Lost; a photograph can be seen in ibid., p. 8.

14 Archive AAJOF, IMEC, FRN 1.12.

15 Conversation with Emmanuel Jaeger, June 23, 2016. Fernand Graindorge wrote to Günter Aust, who presented works by Freundlich at the Wallraf-Richartz Museum in Cologne in 1960, that he had discovered the *Composition* (HvW 107) in "an attic" (Archiv Museum Ludwig). As long as there are no proofs, however, it can neither be documented that paintings were hung in the gallery's garden nor that this *Composition* was among them.

16 Letter from Samuel Beckett to Thomas McGreevy, June 15, 1938, in *The Letters of Samuel Beckett*, vol. 1: 1929–1940, ed. Martha Dow Fehsenfeld and Lois More Overbeck (New York, 2009), pp. 629–633, here p. 630.

17 This according to Claire Maingon in "La Guerre exposée à Paris, 1914–1918. Galeries et salons," in *Les artistes et leurs galeries: Paris-Berlin. 1900–1950*, ed. Hélène Ivanoff and Denise Vernerey-Laplace (Le Havre, 2016).

18 For more on the committee, see archive AAJOF, IMEC, FRN 17.4.

19 Archive AAJOF, IMEC, FRN 10.15.

20 Letter from Klee to Freundlich, archive AAJOF, IMEC, quoted in *Otto Freundlich: Ein Wegbereiter der abstrakten Kunst*, ed. Thorsten Rodiek and Gerhard Leistner, exh. cat. Ostdeutsche Galerie Regensburg et al. (Regensburg, 1994), p. 226.

21 Letter from Beckett to McGreevy, June 15, 1938, op. cit. (note 16), p. 630.

22 Otto Freundlich, "Bekenntnisse eines revolutionären Malers" [1935]; Eng. trans. "Confessions of a Revolutionary Painter," in the current volume p. 15.

23 Peggy Guggenheim, *Out of This Century: Confessions of an Art Addict* (New York, 1979), p. 200.

24 Joël Mettay and Edda Maillet, *Otto Freundlich et la France: Un amour trahi* (Perpignan, 2004), pp., 150 and 154–155.

25 See ibid., as well as the correspondence of Otto Freundlich and Nelly van Doesburg, archive AAJOF, IMEC, FRN 9.15.

26 Peggy Guggenheim, *Out of This Century*, op. cit. (note 23), p. 196.

27 Ibid., p. 209.

28 See Jeanne Kosnick-Kloss's correspondence with Ms. Stern regarding this matter; archive AAJOF, IMEC, FRN 17.21.

29 See the correspondence of Jeanne Kosnick-Kloss and Otto Freundlich from 1938 through October 1939, archive AAJOF, IMEC, FRN 11 19–20, particularly Kosnick-Kloss's letter to Freundlich of October 28, 1939. It has thus far been impossible to determine whether the sale was actually completed.

30 Peggy Guggenheim, *Out of This Century*, op. cit. (note 23), pp. 185, 199, 221, 224, 254, 261–262, 267.

Mandy Wignanek

Faked Icon
The *Large Head* in the Propaganda Exhibition *Degenerate Art*

The *Large Head* (HvW 63, fig. 53) by the Jewish artist Otto Freundlich is still doubtless the best-known work from the *Degenerate Art* exhibition, in which National Socialist Germany ridiculed and condemned modernist art. The monumental sculpture was depicted on the cover of the exhibition guide, and to this day it is mostly known by the title "The New Man"—which the National Socialists invented for it. More about that later. But not only was the title of the plaster sculpture faked under the Nazi regime: it is more than likely that the sculpture itself was faked—and quite crudely so.

On March 11, 1941—just four years after the first *Degenerate Art* exhibition opened in Munich—an article appeared in the *Ostdeutschen Morgenpost* consisting of an in-depth review of a particular stage of the touring exhibition, in this case in the Schlesisches Grenzlandmuseum in Beuthen (now Bytom), Silesia. The text includes a photograph of the *Large Head* (fig. 52) and the caption below states: "This monster spawned by a deranged mind was titled 'The New Man' by its 'creator.' An exhibit from the 'Entartete Kunst' show."[1] The photograph shows the head from the left, set on a plinth with a sign. If one compares this photograph of the *Large Head* with one that was taken from the same angle at the Berlin exhibition in 1938 (fig. 54), certain differences are noticeable. These are most apparent in the area of the mouth: the lips are very narrow and pursed, and the left corner of the mouth does not extend right down to the chin. The chin is also narrower and descends almost parallel to the neck. Likewise the eyes are longer and smaller as a result of a broad eminence on the head, while the cheeks protrude more and diminish the size of the nose. Apart from which, the Beuthen sculpture is for the first time visibly mounted on a plinth. It seems to be much smaller, when one considers the line of the floor and the section of frame in the background of the photograph.

It may be assumed that what we have here is a replica of the *Large Head*. Quite possibly the sculpture was irreparably damaged while being handled. The photograph from Berlin already shows damage to the neck and chin. Perhaps it was no longer possible to transport the sculpture and it was replaced for the Silesian stages of the touring exhibition by a smaller replica. The differences to the original suggest that the replica was commissioned by the exhibition's National Socialist organizers. Nothing remains of Freundlich's artistic intent: the sculpture now looks like a textbook illustration of Nazi ideas of "degenerate art." Indeed, we can read just what this kind of art supposedly looked like: Paul Schultze-Naumburg and Adolf Dresler had outlined the distinguishing marks of "degeneracy" and contrasted these condemned works with "Germanic art."[2] The design of the replica may have received direct input from Wolfgang Willrich's 1937 book, *Säuberung des Kunsttempels* (Purging

Schon 1932 Kunstaufklärung in Beuthen

Gedanken zur Ausstellung „Entartete Kunst" im Grenzlandmuseum

Es ist nicht das erste Mal seit der Machtübernahme, daß die Beuthener Bevölkerung Gelegenheit erhält, noch einmal einen tiefen Blick in den Höllenschlund eines Kulturinfernos zu werfen, von dem es uns heute beinahe unwahrscheinlich dünkt, daß diese krankhafte Daseinsluft des Untermenschentums richtungweisend für den Geisteszustand einer ganzen Nation sein sollte. Als erfreuliches Zeichen der Aufgeklärtheit mag es gelten, daß der Zustrom zu der Ausstellung „Entartete Kunst" im Schlesischen Grenzlandmuseum nicht abreißt, — die Räume dieser Ausstellung setzen damit eine Tradition fort, die 1934 in der Gegenüberstellung der „Schlesischen Kunstschau in Schwarz-Weiß" mit einer Abteilung der „Entarteten Graphik" in den Anfängen einer neuen, öffentlichen Kunsterziehung durch das Anschauungsmaterial einer Ausstellung steckte. Bereits damals bewahrheitete Beuthen die nationalsozialistische These, daß Kunst, als öffentliches Instrument zur Volksführung gesehen, richtig gehandhabt, aufbauend und fördernd wirkt, schlecht benutzt jedoch zur Keimzelle der Zersetzung und Zerstörung werden muß. Denn dieser erste Versuch eines Vergleiches in der „Schwarz-Weiß"-Kunstschau mußte in einer Zeit, in der die reinliche Scheidung der Geister noch die Spuren einer frischen Tat an sich trug, blitzartig den Vorhang zerreißen, den ästhetelnde Wichtigtuer mit hochtönendem Phrasengedresch vor die Entfesselung der niederen und triebhaften Kunstproduktion hängte, um eines Veilchenduft Schlagermelodie „Den haben se mit der Banane aus 'm Urwald gelockt" und andere unter jüdischer Oberhoheit

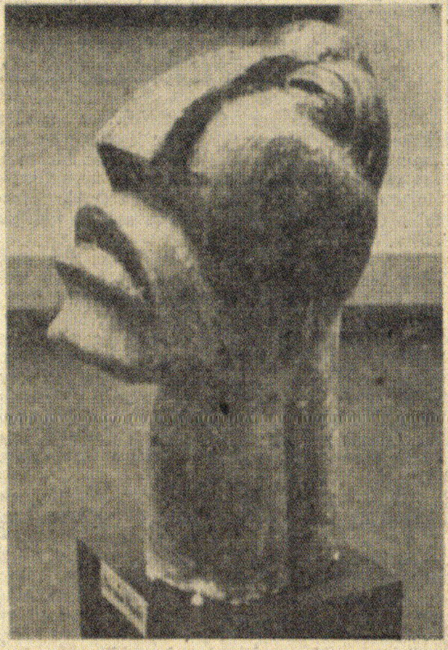

Diese Ausgeburt einer geistesgestörten Phantasie bezeichnete ihr „Schöpfer" mit „Der neue Mensch". Ein Ausstellungsstück aus der Schau „Entartete Kunst". (Aufn.: Mehl)

stehende Sudeleien als „Kunst" auf den Markt und an den damals gar so leichtgläubigen Deutschen zu bringen.

Es darf für den Beschauer der „Entarteten Kunst" nicht allein bei dem Kopfschütteln über die Idiotien eines Kandinski, Schmidt-Rottluff, Otto Dix oder Lionel Feininger oder anderer teils jüdischer, teils innerlich verjudeter Produzenten einer krankhaften Kunst-Zeit bleiben. Sinn der Ausstellung, die mit der jetzigen Deutschland-Fahrt endgültig ihre Pforten schließt, ist nicht die Erinnerung an eine Fülle beunruhigender und selbstzerstörerischer Probleme in Farben und Form und pathologischer Stilentgleisung, über die wir dank der gradlinigen Ausrichtung unseres gesamten Kulturwesens inzwischen längst zur Tagesordnung übergegangen sind; — wir sollen uns gleichzeitig darüber klar sein, daß diese auf dem Müllhaufen marxistisch-mosaischer Glanzzeiten entstandenen „Kunst"-Werke zu jener uns vom Lügenlord Churchill wie sauer Bier angepriesenen Demokratie gehören, mit deren zweifelhaften Segnungen uns England so gerne beglücken möchte, wenn, — ja wenn, um bei dem Thema „Kunst" zu bleiben, Deutschland nicht längst begriffen hätte, daß Kunst und Kultur nur dann bestehen können, wenn sie sich auf die Werte der Persönlichkeit, des Volkes und der Rasse gründen.

Und im engeren Beuthener Raume soll die „Entartete Kunst" uns an die Kleinarbeit in Beuthen erinnern, die notwendig war, um, von der Jugend angefangen, die uralte, deutsche Lebensauffassung der Kunst wieder lebendig werden zu lassen, die das Schaffen den Volksbegriff, den Sinn für Land und Menschen, Heimat und Ueberlieferung und schließlich für die Zusammengehörigkeit des Blutes anerkennt. Und vor den Chronisten einer deutschen Kunsterziehung in Beuthen tritt das Erinnerungsbild der bedeutsamen Kundgebung deutscher Geistarbeit an der damaligen „Kulturgrenze Ost" Beuthen im Jahre 1932, als zur schreckhaften Verwunderung der Parteien und Parteichen die NSDAP. mit zwei großen Abenden den nationalsozialistischen Totalitätsanspruch auch auf dem Gebiet der Kultur anmeldete und eine Kunst- und Buchausstellung sowie die Großveranstaltung „Kultur und Bühne" (mit der durch Vortrag, Bühnenschau und Theater-Ausstellung betonten Scheidung zwischen dem Geist von Bayreuth und Goethe-Weimar und jenen Vertretern um Krenek, Weill, Weinberger usw.) vor stets ausverkauften Sälen starten konnte. Die Breitenarbeit nach der Machtübernahme ging dann über Kunstausstellungs-Führungen und Aufklärungsvorträge zu der „Schwarz-Weiß"-Ausstellung mit der „Entarteten Graphik", um danach in kleineren und großen Kunstausstellungen zu zeigen, daß der politische Sieg des Nationalsozialismus gleichbedeutend mit der Erneuerung und Gesundung der deutschen Kunst war, und daß jene Zeit ausgewirtschaftet hat, die noch Kunstwerke aus den Ausstellungen ablehnen konnte, die heute zum geförderten Kulturbesitz der Stadt Beuthen und des Schlesischen Grenzlandmuseums gehören. Die Schreckenskammer der Kunst, die sich uns nun noch ein letztes Mal in der Ausstellung „Entartete Kunst" öffnet, kann im Besinnen auf die Kulturarbeit in Beuthen nur das stolze Gefühl in uns wecken: — hier haben verantwortungsbewußte Kräfte früh die Verpflichtung erkannt und an ihrer Verwirklichung gearbeitet, die lebendige Gestaltungskraft der Kunst im Dienste echten völkischen Mittlertums zu steigern.

Erich Zabel.

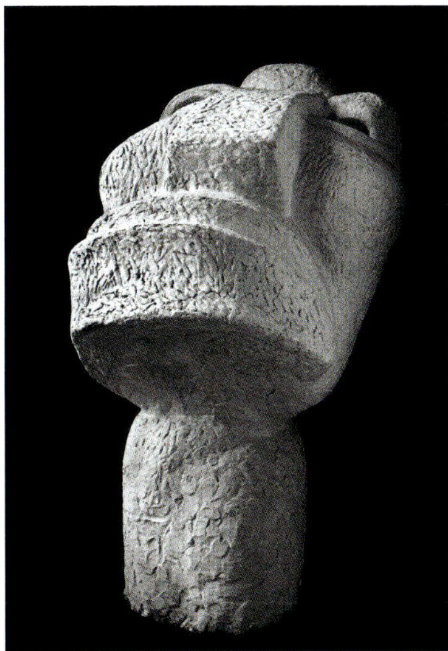

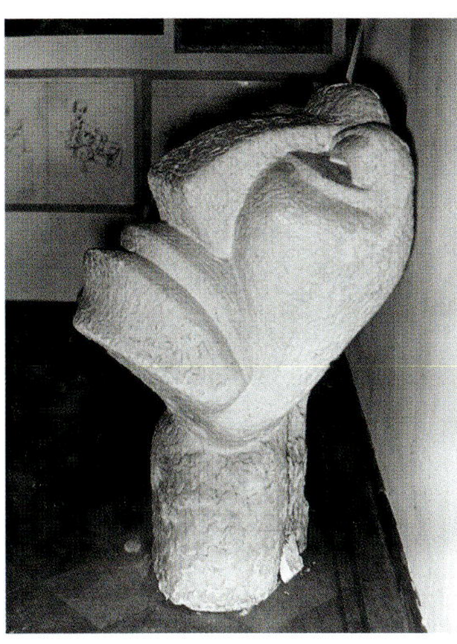

Fig. 52 *Ostdeutsche Morgenpost,* March 11, 1941, with a replica of the *Large Head* in the *Degenerate Art* exhibition, Grenzlandmuseum Beuthen

Fig. 53 Otto Freundlich
Large Head, 1912
HvW 63
Plaster
H. 139 cm
Glass negative plate from 1930, from the Museum für Kunst und Gewerbe, Hamburg

Fig. 54 The *Large Head* in the *Degenerate Art* exhibition at the Haus der Kunst, Berlin, February 24, 1938

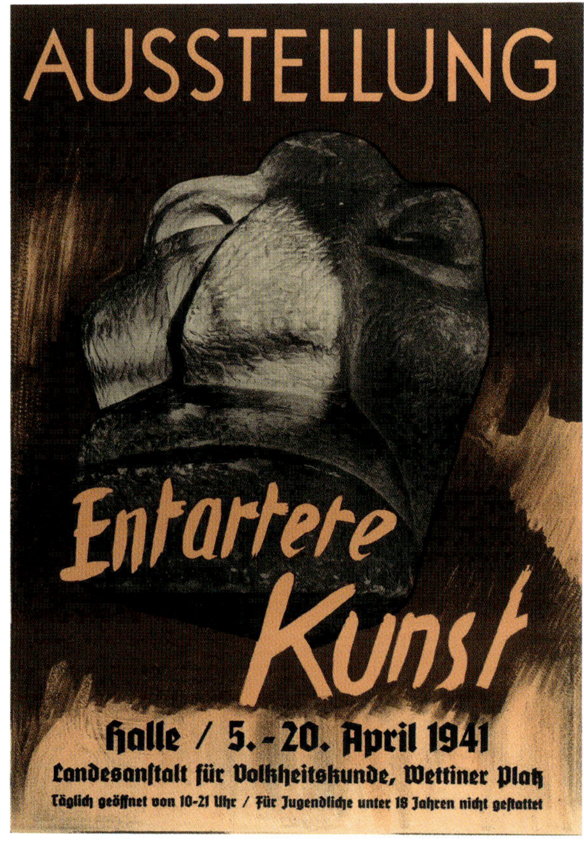

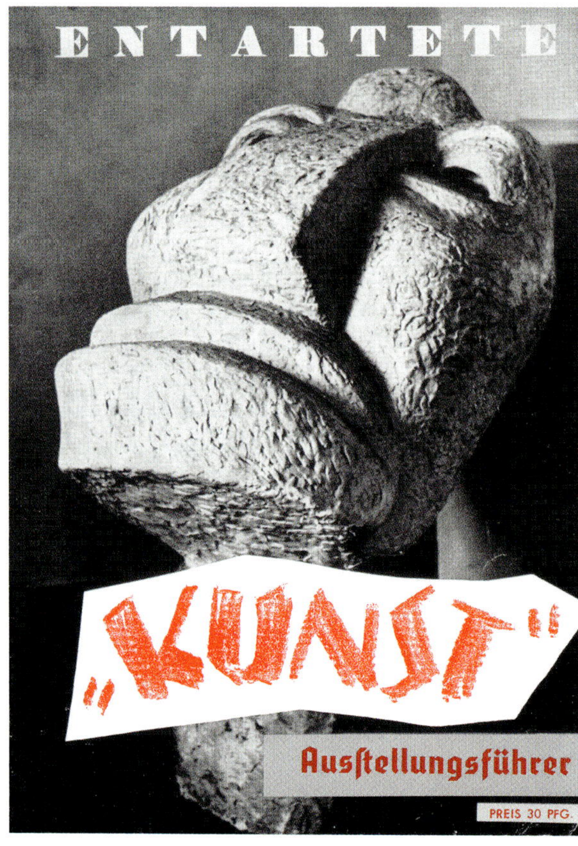

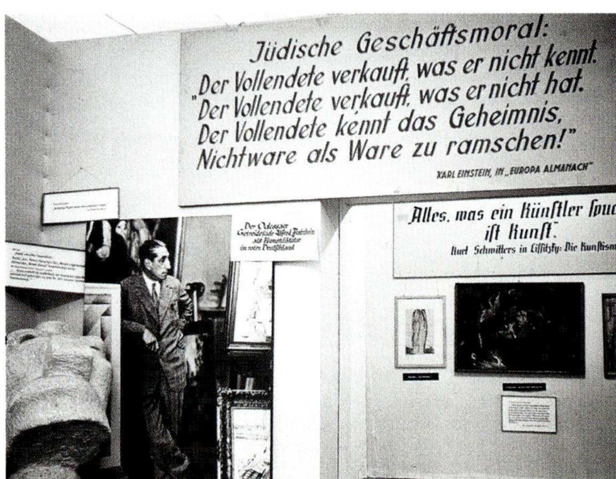

Fig. 55 Poster for the exhibition *Degenerate Art* in Halle, 1941
Lithograph and collaged offset print on paper
59 × 42 cm
Stadtarchiv Halle (Saale)

Fig. 56 Exhibition guide *Degenerate Art*

Fig. 57 View of the *Degenerate Art* exhibition at the Festspielhaus Salzburg with the *Large Head* and a photograph of Alfred Flechtheim, 1938

Fig. 58 The *Large Head* in the *Degenerate Art* exhibition in Munich, 1937

Fig. 59 *Head*, 1916
HvW 65, at the *Degenerate Art* exhibition in Munich, 1937

Fig. 60 *Völkischer Beobachter*, edition for northern Germany, February 26, 1938, p. 3

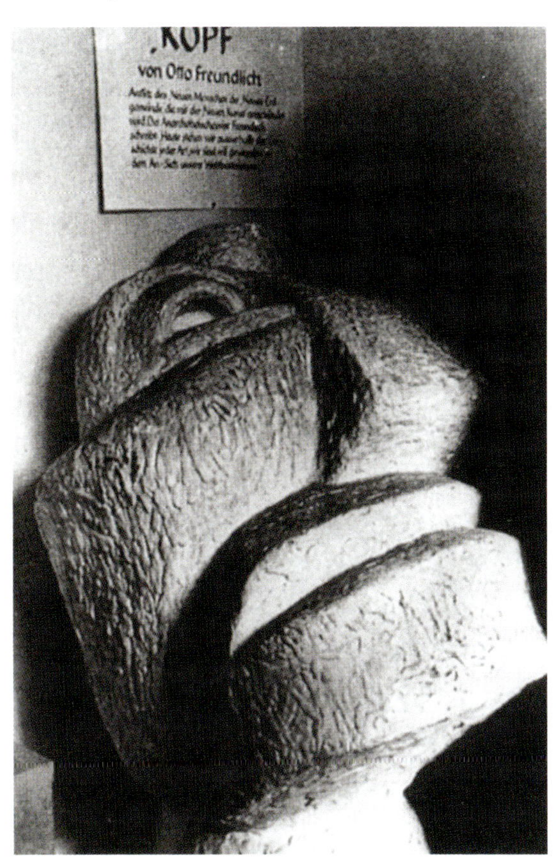

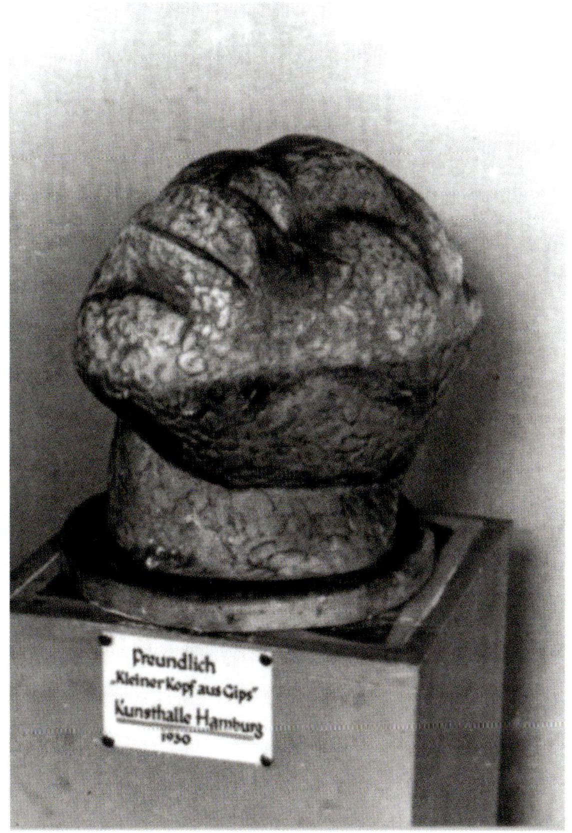

Solche von Juden als Kunst gepriesenen Machwerke sind ausgerottet im Dritten Reich

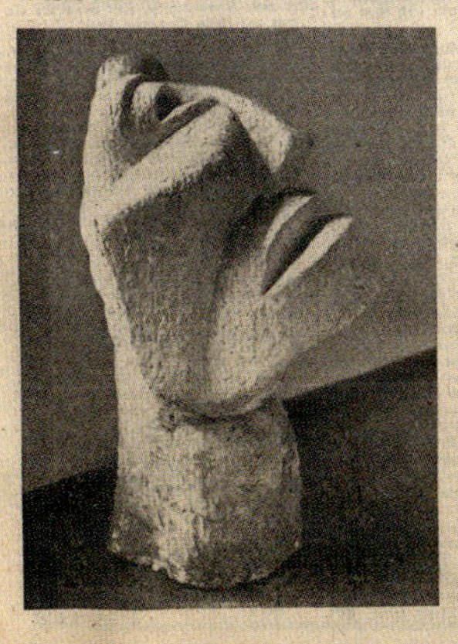

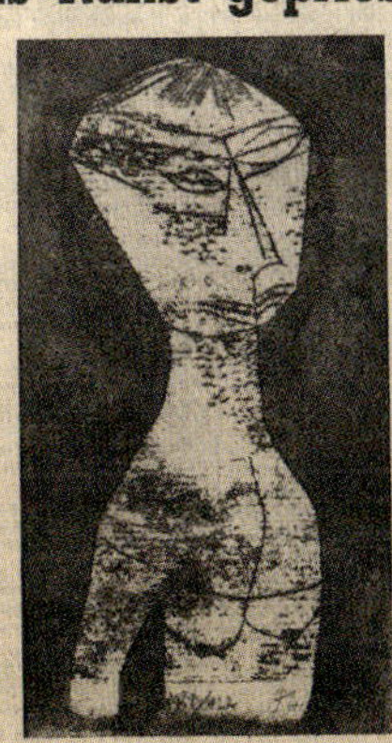

Die Ausstellung „Entartete Kunst" jetzt in Berlin

Ganz links: „Der neue Mensch", wie ihn sich der Jude Otto Freundlich erträumt hat. Wir wollen heute weder solche asiatischen Wüstenträume, die von jüdischer Rabulistik als Offenbarungen höchster Kunst hingestellt und entsprechend hoch verschachert wurden, noch solche orientalischen „neuen" Menschen unter uns sehen

Links: „Die Heilige vom inneren Licht" von Paul Klee ein Beispiel für die religiöse Haltung jenes Kulturbolschewismus, mit denen kirchliche Kreise bei uns in engen Beziehungen standen

Rechts: So durfte einst der Maler Otto Dix ungestraft die deutschen Kriegsverletzten verhöhnen, die opferbereit ihren Leib für deutsche Ehre und Freiheit eingesetzt hatten

Aufnahmen: Presse-Bild-Zentrale (2), Presse-Photo (1), Weltbild (1)

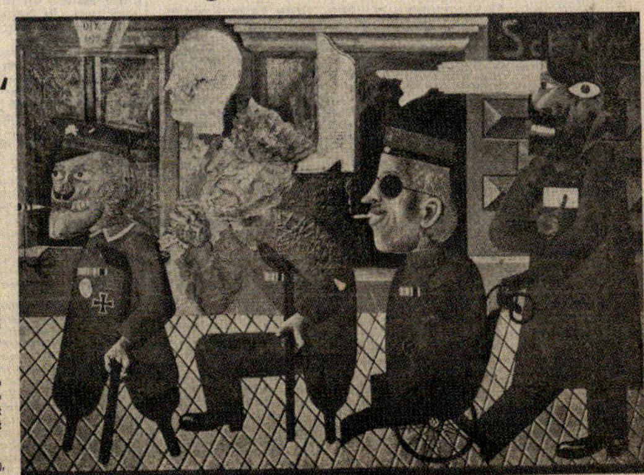

the Temple of Art). Willrich cites here Freundlich's words, which could also be read at the exhibition, and also depicts his *Male Mask* (HvW 58, fig. 61, p. 213), which is described as the "Face of the 'New Man,' of the once again 'primeval' vanquisher of the racial boundaries."[3] The replica resembles the *Mask* in several of its features, such as in the shape of the mouth and the transition to the nose. Apart from which, the modeling of the eyes and forehead in the Nazi version recalls the African masks and sculptures that were familiar in Germany, and not so much the stone heads from Easter Island that Freundlich clearly cited. Perhaps they corresponded more to the idea of a "racially inferior" "creature from the jungle."[4]

The exhibition guide bearing Freundlich's *Large Head* on the cover was published in 1938 for the opening of the first leg of the touring exhibition in Berlin[5] (fig. 56, p. 208). Emblazoned across the sculpture's neck is the legend "KUNST" (art), in quotation marks, done with letters scrawled in red crayon: the artistic value of the work is scornfully denied, and instead dilettantism and "cultural Bolshevism" are pointed to.[6] The cover portrays the *Large Head* as an icon of "degeneracy," and to this day this staging has obscured people's perception of the sculpture. Which is also a reason to look at its past history.

Freundlich probably created the work at the end of 1912 during a stay with the Niemeyer family in Hamburg. The Niemeyers were among Freundlich's first collectors. The art historian Wilhelm Niemeyer had been a lecturer since 1910 at the Hamburg School of Arts and Crafts, where the *Large Head* may have been made.[7]

The monumental, 139-centimeter-tall sculpture recalls in both its form and conception the monolithic sculptures of Easter Island (fig. 8, p. 47). The main visual thrust of these enormous male half-length figures centers on the heads with their broad noses, long earlobes, slender lips, and angular chins. As many of these sculptures originally had a headpiece (*pukao*), the brows are low set and overshadow the dark, empty eye sockets. A number of features in Freundlich's *Large Head* have a great similarity to those of the colossal stone statues, including the empty eyes beneath the broad brow, and the precipitous line of the unworked head at the rear. The lips, however, are large and full; the corners of the mouth are drawn down to the chin; and the head without body rests on a squat, cylindrical neck.[8]

In July 1914, the *Large Head* was purchased by Anna Blumenfeld of Hamburg. She was a cousin of the art historian Aby Warburg. Her son, Hans Blumenfeld, lived with Warburg in Hamburg until he completed his schooling. At that time the Blumenfeld family did not have a permanent home for them all to live in; not until 1920–21 did Hans Blumenfeld rent a farmstead in Brunstorf near Schwarzenbek.[9] In July 1914, which is to say a month after the purchase of the sculpture, Anna Blumenfeld visited Warburg at his house in Travemünde.[10] It is very likely that she talked with Warburg about the *Large Head*, and conceivable that the hefty sculpture was stored at Warburg's until the Blumenfeld family moved to Brunstorf.

Anna Blumenfeld kept the *Large Head* and other works by Freundlich until her death in 1930.[11] Anna's son, Hans Blumenfeld, asked the collector Olga Solmitz[12]—a friend of the family of many years standing—to pass on the works owned by the departed woman to Hamburg's Museum für Kunst und Gewerbe, where they were received by the director Max Sauerlandt.[13]

On August 23, 1933, a good four months after Sauerlandt was placed on compulsory leave, the *Large Head* was transferred along with other modernist sculptures as a permanent loan to the Hamburg Kunsthalle. The works remained there in the depot until they were confiscated by the National Socialists. A committee under the directorship of Adolf Ziegler—president of the Reichskammer der bildenden Künste (Reich Chamber of Fine Art) and organizer of the overall *Degenerate Art* action—chose among other works the *Large Head* on July 5, 1937, for the coming show, and arranged for its transport to Munich.[14]

Initially conceived as a counter-show to the *Große Deutsche Kunstausstellung* (*Great German Art Exhibition*), which opened at the same time in the Haus der Deutschen Kunst in Munich, *Degenerate Art* opened in July 1937 in the arcades in Munich's Hofgarten. Some 600 works by 110 artists were pilloried there until November of that year.[15] The *Large Head* was placed on the ground floor, in the corner of a lobby.[16] Above the work was a sign: "Face of the 'New Man' of the 'New Community of the Earth,' with which the 'New Art' is proclaimed. The anarcho-Bolshevist Freundlich writes: 'Today we are beyond any kind of history, we are mature enough now to face the facticity of our universal destiny'" (fig. 58, p. 209). The sign contained altered and abbreviated quotations from an essay Freundlich published in 1917 in the magazine *Die Aktion*.[17] The name commonly applied to the work, "The New Man," was thus used for the first time in 1937, even though the sculpture simply bore the title "Head" in the Munich exhibition. "The New Man" only established itself as its appellation during the course of the touring exhibition. It is simply a propaganda title; Freundlich's essay, from which it is taken, makes no mention of the sculpture. In various letters and in the catalogue raisonné that Freundlich compiled, it is referred to solely as *Large Head* or *Large Plaster Head* (fig. p. 296).[18]

That the "New Man" title stuck was above all the doing of the exhibition guide. On pages 20 and 21, the sculpture was presented with a picture as part of "Group 8" ("Three Specimens of Jewish Sculpture and Painting").[19] The commentary to the *Large Head* contains the remark: "Here among other things is also 'The New Man,' as dreamt up by Jew Freundlich."[20] The press latched on to the title. Daily papers used the picture to illustrate their articles on the exhibition. And it was used moreover on posters and leaflets, as for instance in Hamburg and Halle (fig. 55, p. 208).[21] Often the caption mentions "The New Man," and mostly asserts that the sculpture depicts a Jew.[22] The *Hamburger Tageblatt* wrote in 1938: "'Countenance of the New German Man.' That is the title of the sculpture above given by the Jew, now emigrated to Paris. It was found in the depot of the Hamburg Kunsthalle—in the 'crazy' department."[23]

The success that the Munich exhibition enjoyed with the public inspired the organizers to take the show on tour.[24] Only a few photographs are known showing the *Large Head* in subsequent exhibitions. Many of them were taken at the first two venues in the tour, Munich and Berlin, and were also used to illustrate subsequent newspaper articles.[25] The Institut für Deutsche Kultur- und Wirtschaftspropaganda gave the visuals to the press for free, so that the newspapers rarely commissioned their own photographs.[26] Exposures of the *Large Head* exist from the exhibition spaces in Salzburg in 1938 and Stettin (Szczecin) in 1939 (fig. 57, p. 208). At both of these locations a photographic portrait of the art dealer and publisher Alfred Flechtheim hung next to the sculpture.[27] Flechtheim had already drawn the hatred of the National Socialists early on as a Jew and champion of avant-garde art. The propaganda made the most of the fact that his features resembled the Nazi cliché of a Jewish physiognomy. The installation in *Degenerate Art* aimed to underscore the resemblance of Flechtheim's supposedly Jewish features to those of the sculpture—and vice versa.

After an interval of fifteen months, the exhibition was also sent in 1941 to smaller towns in present-day Poland. It is known that it was presented at Waldenburg (now Wałbrzych), Liegnitz (Legnica), Oppeln (Opole), and Beuthen (Bytom). The last known leg was Halle an der Saale (April 1941). It can be seen from newspaper reports that in the end the exhibition was divided up and smaller exhibitions put on simultaneously in a number of cities.[28]

Until what point the original *Large Head* was exhibited,[29] what happened to it, and why it was replaced by an altered replica, has yet to be clarified. Doubtless the despised works were not treated tenderly when packed and transported for the touring exhibition. Was it the thought that the public could not be denied the chance of seeing the frequently depicted icon of "degenerate art," even if it had been damaged or perhaps even destroyed? Was Freundlich's original not "degenerate" enough, were the changes aimed at increasing its effectiveness as propaganda? It is impossible to tell at the moment whether the replica was already shown prior to the Beuthen exhibition in March 1941.[30] At the end of the touring exhibition the works were left in the keeping of the Ministry of Propaganda in Berlin. Freundlich's *Large Head* is not noted on the list, not even under then title "Der neue Mensch."[31] All trace of both the *Large Head* and the replica is lost from then on.

1 Erich Zabel, "Schon 1932 Kunstaufklärung in Beuthen. Gedanken zur Ausstellung 'Entartete Kunst' im Grenzlandmuseum," *Ostdeutsche Morgenpost,* March 11, 1941.

2 Cf. Paul Schultze-Naumburg, *Kunst und Rasse* (Munich, 1928); Adolf Dresler, *Deutsche Kunst und entartete "Kunst": Kunstwerk und Zerrbild als Spiegel der Weltanschauung* (Munich, 1938).

3 Wolfgang Willrich, *Säuberung des Kunsttempels: Eine kunstpolitische Kampfschrift zur Gesundung deutscher Kunst im Geiste nordischer Art* (Munich and Berlin, 1938), p. 26.

4 As the sculpture was referred to in the press. Cf. "Pokerspieler der Kunst: Rundgang durch die Ausstellung 'Entartete Kunst'—ihr Besuch wird zur Pflicht," *OS-Tageszeitung*, February 22, 1941: "A sculpture stares at the exhibition-goers, *a hideous gargoyle* that could be a creature from the jungle. But the sculpture is titled 'The New Man.' Nothing needs to be added to that." The same article was previously published for the venue in Waldenburg in the *Neues Tageblatt,* January 31, 1941. Cf. Christoph Zuschlag, *"Entartete Kunst": Ausstellungsstrategien im Nazi-Deutschland* (Worms, 1995), p. 291, fig. 114.

5 Cf. *Entartete "Kunst,"* exhibition guide, Munich and Berlin, 1938, in Peter-Klaus Schuster, ed., *Nationalsozialismus und "Entartete Kunst" Die "Kunststadt" Munich 1937* (Munich, 1998).

6 Cf. Isgard Kracht, "Vom Symbol der Freiheit zum Sinnbild 'entarteter' Kunst: Otto Freundlichs Plastik 'Der neue Mensch,'" in Uwe Fleckner, ed., *Das verfemte Meisterwerk: Schicksalswege moderner Kunst im "Dritten Reich"* (Berlin, 2009), pp. 3–23, here pp. 15 and 22–23.

7 Cf. Joachim Heusinger von Waldegg, *Otto Freundlich und die rheinische Kunstszene mit Briefen an Herwarth Walden und Wilhelm Niemeyer*, ed. Verein August Macke Haus, exh. cat. August Macke Haus (Bonn, 2006), p. 298.

8 Cf. Angela Ziesche, "Otto Freundlich," in Ziesche, *Der neue Mensch: Köpfe und Büsten deutscher Expressionisten* (Frankfurt am Main et al., 1993), p. 108.

9 Cf. Hans Blumenfeld, *Life begins at 65: The not entirely candid autobiography of a drifter* (Montreal, 1987), pp. 74–75, as well as a letter from Freundlich to Niemeyer dated July 24, 1914: "I've just received news from Frau B. in Travemünde." Cf. Heusinger, *Rheinische Kunstszene*, op. cit. (note 7), p. 186.

10 Cf. Blumenfeld, *Life*, op. cit. (note 9), pp. 11–13, 16, and 31.

26 Erster Teil. Kunstbolschewismus und Kunstanarchie

und das Urhafte. Wir werden später auf diese Nolde-Groteske zurückkommen. Das „Urhafte", Ungeistige (im Sinne der Abwesenheit gesundgeistigen und gemütstiefen Ausdrucks), das Wider- und Nieder-Rassische entsprach dem Wunschbild der roten Herren. Das war der Grund zum Erfolg aller derer, die sich darauf verstanden, es sinnfällig zu machen.

Die hochtönenden Redensarten ergänzten solche Machwerke:

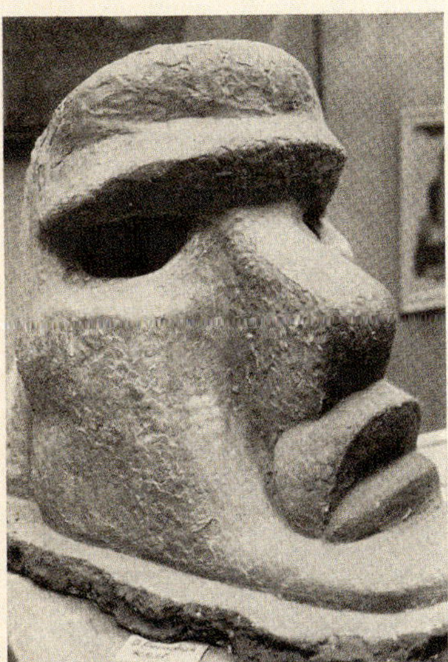

Abb. 8. Antlitz des „Neuen Menschen" des wieder „urhaften" Überwinders der Rassengrenzen – „gestaltet" von O. Freundlich, einem regen Mitarbeiter der Aktion

Die Aktion, 1917, S. 602: Das Kommende Reich, Verfasser Otto Freundlich:

„Heute aber stehen wir außerhalb und über der Geschichte jeder Art. Das müssen wir, denn wir sind reif geworden zu dem An-Sich unserer Weltbestimmung."

A. F. Gruenwald.
(Aktion XII 1919.):

„Schönheit und Edles schlagen wir aus eurer Welt. (Von mir hervorgehoben. W.) Wie wollt ihr denn von Welt sprechen, die ihr zu haben seid wie die Weiber.

. . . .

Wir machen kein Hehl aus der Gewalt, wir sind die rechten Vergewaltiger! Wo wir gingen, kann bloß Neues wachsen, da blieb nichts Altes, das wir schonten.

Ja, bald ist es so weit."

Der Kunstprofessor Georg Biermann, der Herausgeber der üblen „Jahrbücher junger Kunst" und der Monographien daraus, sowie der Zeitschrift Cicerone (allesamt im Verlag Klinkhardt & Biermann, Leipzig), jener stärksten Quellen aller Kunstverseuchung, predigt in gelehrt-dürren Worten denselben Text (Kunstwende. Die neue Kunst als soziologisch-psychologisches Problem, Verf. Georg Biermann, Junge Kunst, 1921, S. 281):

„Diese Kunst, deren Sphinxantlitz vielen noch unfaßbar und geheimnisvoll das Werden dieser Zeit überschattet, ist für uns Ausdruck und Niederschlag all dessen, was an geistig-dynamischen Kräften die Menschheit von innen her bewegt. Sie ist in diesem Sinne ebensosehr soziologisches Phänomen wie Widerschein einer neuen Ethik, die einem sich sichtbarlich vorbereitenden neuen Gemeinschaftsideal der Menschheit die Wege weisen will. Sie ist – mit einem Worte gesagt – seelisch tief verankert in jenem Urgrund menschlich-geistiger Gemeinsamkeiten, aus denen sich heraus auch politisch und sozial einmal in nicht zu ferner Zeit das Bild jener neuen Erdgemeinde entwickeln wird, die vielleicht eines Tages so glücklich ist, Grenzscheiden

Fig. 61 Excerpt from Wolfgang Willrich, *Säuberung des Kunsttempels*, Berlin, 1937, with Freundlich's sculpture *Male Mask*, ca. 1910–20, and citation from Freundlich about the New Man

11 The correspondence between Olga Solmitz and Max Sauerlandt indicates that not only the *Large Head* went from Anna Blumenfeld's possession to the Museum für Kunst und Gewerbe, but also the smaller *Head* (1916, HvW 65, p. 80) and the pen and ink drawing *The Blossoming Branch of Chartres* (1916, HvW 272, lost). Cf. Almut Klingbeil, "Zur Korrespondenz Otto Freundlich–Max Sauerlandt," in *Jahrbuch des Museums für Kunst und Gewerbe Hamburg* 9–10, 1990–91 (Hamburg, 1993), p. 149. Anna Blumenfeld's great-grandson, Tony Plaut, has two works by Freundlich not yet included in the catalogue raisonné (pp. 81, 112).

12 Cf. Sebastian Giesen, "Der Künstler ist der Mikrokosmos des sozialen Lebens: Otto Freundlich in Hamburg," in *Freundlich–Gangolf–Kogan: Drei Künstlerschicksale*, exh. cat. Ernst-Barlach-Haus (Hamburg, 2004), pp. 21–23, in particular p. 21; cf. Heusinger, *Rheinische Kunstszene*, op. cit. (note 7), p. 70.

13 Cf. letters from Max Sauerlandt and Olga Solmitz dated May 9, 1930, and May 10, 1930, Archiv Museum für Kunst und Gewerbe (MKG), Hamburg.

14 Cf. David Klemm, *Das Museum für Kunst und Gewerbe Hamburg: Bd. 1. Von den Anfängen bis 1945* (Hamburg, 2005), p. 367 and p. 397, footnote 197.

15 Cf. Mario-Andreas von Lüttichau, "'Deutsche Kunst' und 'Entartete Kunst': Die Münchner Ausstellungen 1937," in Schuster, *Nationalsozialismus*, op. cit. (note 5), pp. 83–118, here p. 97; on the exhibition guide pp. 100–101.

16 Cf. ibid., p. 111.

17 The same citation is to be found in Willrich, *Säuberung*, op. cit. (note 3), p. 26. In its larger context, the passage reads: "We the new humanity became the new artists; but we smashed the old humanity the way the ploughman ploughs the field at harvest. With this we gained new eyes which create the new body and the new nature. As is our aim.—Anyone unable to read from the true art of all ages that the aim is the progressive, deepening and then leveling comprehension of the same universal problem, can regard himself as a subaltern interpreter of intellectual history. But today we are beyond and above any kind of history. We must, because we are mature enough now to face the facticity of our universal destiny. All that preceded however was relative, between people who had lost free research in the service of intentionality.—*Art however is the freest research*.—A science?—No; not at least in the meaning up to now." Otto Freundlich, "Das kommende Reich," *Die Aktion* 45/46 (1917), cols. 600–602, here col. 602.

18 The Appeal on Behalf of Otto Freundlich (p. 200) in July 1938, shortly before the publication of the guide to the *Degenerate Art* exhibition, names the sculpture *L'Homme Nouveau* (The New Man). It is not recorded who wrote the appeal. Nor are any comments known from Freundlich about the use of his sculpture on the guide.

19 Both title and captions were changed in an amended edition. Cf. Zuschlag, *"Entartete Kunst,"* op. cit. (note 4), pp. 235–236.

20 Cf. *Entartete "Kunst,"* op. cit. (note 5), pp. 20–21.

21 Cf. Kracht, "Symbol der Freiheit," op. cit. (note 6), pp. 15–16.

22 Cf. *Leipziger Tageblatt*, May 14, 1938: "Das Antlitz des Juden in der Kunst—eine jüdische Selbstenthüllung wie sie bezeichnender nicht sein kann."

23 *Hamburger Tageblatt*, November 13, 1938.

24 The touring exhibition was shown in the following cities in the following order, as far as can be established: Berlin, Leipzig, Düsseldorf, Salzburg, Hamburg, Stettin, Weimar, Vienna, Frankfurt am Main, Chemnitz, Wałbrzych, Görlitz, Legnica, Oppeln, Bytom, Halle an der Saale. Cf. Zuschlag, *"Entartete Kunst,"* op. cit. (note 4), pp. 222–299; Cf. Zuschlag, "75 Jahre Ausstellung 'Entartete Kunst,'" in *Der Berliner Skulpturenfund: "Entartete Kunst" im Bombenschutt*, ed. Matthias Wemhoff, exh. cat. Staatliche Museen Berlin, Museum für Vor- und Frühgeschichte Regensburg (Regensburg, 2012), pp. 37–52, here pp. 46–49.

25 Cf. Lüttichau, "Deutsche Kunst," op. cit. (note 15), p. 102.

26 Cf. Zuschlag, *"Entartete Kunst,"* op. cit. (note 4), p. 249.

27 Cf. ibid., pp. 274–275. Flechtheim's photograph was first mentioned in connection with the Düsseldorf showing. Cf. ibid., p. 255.

28 Cf. Zuschlag, "75 Jahre," op. cit. (note 24), p. 46.

29 The original *Large Head* was depicted on advertising material or in reports—apart from Munich and Berlin—marking the exhibitions in Hamburg, Leipzig, Düsseldorf, Chemnitz, and Wałbrzych. Cf. Kracht, "Symbol der Freiheit," op. cit. (note 6), p. 14. These pictures do not prove however that the original was on show at the exhibitions.

30 There is a time gap in which a replica could have been made: there is a span of fifteen months between the prematurely ended station in Chemnitz (August 11–26, 1939), and the commencement of the tour in the Silesian territory in Wałbrzych (January 18–February 2, 1941). For the stops at Chemnitz and Wałbrzych cf. Zuschlag, *"Entartete Kunst,"* op. cit. (note 4), pp. 288–292. Whether the sculpture was shown in Halle an der Saale cannot be reconstructed because no interior shots are known to exist.

31 Cf. Zuschlag, *"Entartete Kunst,"* op. cit. (note 4), pp. 295–297.

Christophe Duvivier

Organic Syntax
Otto Freundlich and Theo van Doesburg—Disparate Paths from Composition to Construction

In 1924, Otto Freundlich returned to France. His departure from Germany came at a time when he was also refocusing his energies on the evolution of his work. While he did not break off relations with his friends or with various journals, with which he continued to collaborate, by settling in Paris he distanced himself from the Dadaists and Surrealists, who were striking out in directions foreign to his own. Although he was beginning to enjoy a certain amount of recognition in his own country, his rejection by the Bauhaus (1920), intellectual misunderstandings with his Communist friends, and the evolution of society under the Weimar Republic, which in his view was not favorable to revolutionary ideas, all contributed to his decision to move to France.

In Paris, Freundlich encountered artists from every country, all of whom were seeking refuge there from the rising tide of nationalisms. Some of those most committed to pursuing a non-representational art had already been living in the city for several years, including exponents of De Stijl such as Piet Mondrian, César Domela, Theo van Doesburg, and Georges Vantongerloo. But in the late 1920s, although they lived and worked close together in Montparnasse, they were still relatively isolated from the French art scene within a larger context of international tensions and economic crises that was less than conducive to the birth of new movements. A small group of non-representational and Constructivist artists that was also frequented by Freundlich attempted to draw attention to these artists by bringing them together in associations designed to organize exhibitions and publish journals. Initially, Michel Seuphor took the lead together with Joaquín Torres-Garcia and Georges Vantongerloo. Beginning in 1921, with his journal *Het Overzicht* (*The Panorama*), which he published in Antwerp at that time with Jozef Peeters and Geert Pijnenburg, Seuphor came in contact with a large number of artists from all over Europe. After settling in France in 1925, he joined the group Cercle et Carré (Circle and Square) in 1929–30 together with Torres-Garcia and Vantongerloo; the group published three issues of a homonymous journal and mounted an exhibition, in which Freundlich participated. In 1930, also in Paris, the movement Art Concret was founded on a more rigorous conceptual basis by Theo van Doesburg, editor of the journal *De Stijl*, in response to Cercle et Carré. Although the movement would go on to acquire broad historical significance following the publication of the *Manifesto of Concrete Art*, the first and only issue of the journal *Art Concret* reached just a small audience of initiates at the time. With Michel Seuphor ill and away from Paris, Theo van Doesburg considered founding a group that would be larger than Art Concret, but he died in April 1931. Both groups disbanded and were superseded in late 1931 by Abstraction-Création, one of the largest associations of abstract artists,

Fig. 62 Theo van Doesburg
Arithmetic Composition, 1929–30
Oil on canvas
101 × 101 cm
Kunstmuseum Winterthur, long-term loan from a private collection, 2001

Fig. 63 Theo van Doesburg
Six Moments in the Development of Plane to Space, ca. 1926
Pencil, ink, enamel paint on transparent paper
150 × 27 cm
Kröller-Müller Museum, Otterlo

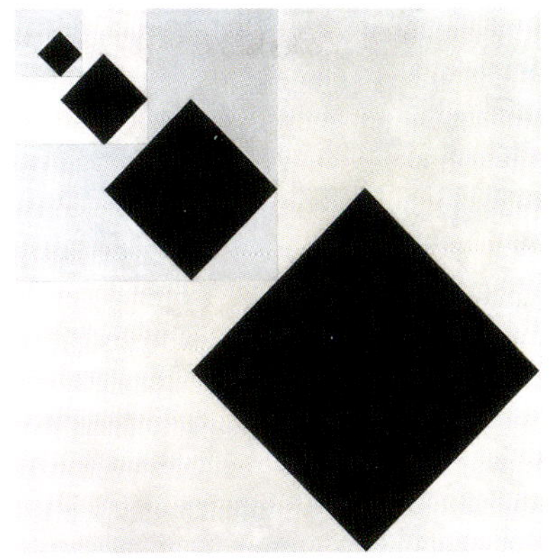

which would live on after 1946 in the Salon des Réalités Nouvelles.[1] Two hundred and seven members of Abstraction-Création have been identified, barely a quarter of whom were French. Indeed, not all the group's members lived in France or in Paris, as evidenced by the fact that the largest national contingent was from Switzerland, whose sixty-eight members heralded that country's burgeoning interest in concrete art.[2]

If Otto Freundlich did not really choose a camp, this was because—with the exception of Art Concret, which was relatively fleeting—none of these groups was really organized around a strong aesthetic or intellectual position. Abstraction-Création was initially designed to serve all non-representational currents, including abstract Surrealism. In 1930 Freundlich participated in the exhibition of Cercle et Carré, and in 1931 in that of the Indépendants; moreover, he was on friendly terms with Theo van Doesburg. It was undoubtedly only van Doesburg who, in his late work, grappled with problems similar to those that interested Freundlich, although with very different consequences, as we will see. In fact, van Doesburg's last works, those linked to his *Arithmetic Composition* of 1930 (fig. 62), represent a crucial step toward controlling the relationships between elements and totality in a work conceived as the unfolding of a process. This work by van Doesburg is a product of the ideas he had put forward in his manifesto "Elementarism," but it is also an expression of his interest in abstract films, that is, in breaking up a geometric shape into sequences. In July 1930, in his article "Elementarism (The Elements of the New Painting)," van Doesburg replaced the older notion of composition with that of construction: "The method leading to universal form is based upon calculations of measure and number. . . . Composition means individual variation of form and color or balanced relationships (the painter functioning as equilibrist). Construction means stabilization and the synthesis of form, color and relationships which is a supra-individual approach."[3] This rational development of a shape in time and space can be seen in the drawing *Six Moments in the Development of Plane to Space* (fig. 63), which van Doesburg published in 1929 in his article "Film als reine Gestaltung,"[4] and which would go on to serve as the basis for his *Arithmetic Composition*. In the drafting of the *Manifesto of Concrete Art*, van Doesburg was probably responsible for article 2, which states: "The work of art should be fully conceived and spiritually formed before it is produced."[5] And yet this proposition was more open-ended and more likely to meet with general agreement than that contained in his article of July 13: "In reference to 'form,' a single element—for instance, the square—is sufficient. The square represents a stable element which must be arithmeticized if it is to be animated."[6]

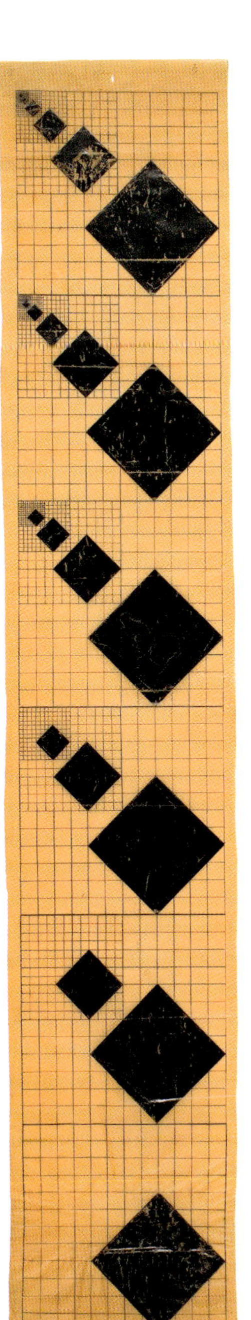

While the reflections of van Doesburg and Freundlich both share a common denominator, they also differ fundamentally. Whereas Freundlich soon concluded that the work is the product of a living totality of autonomous elements, van Doesburg wished to control the development from element to totality within the work, and to this end he searched for modular (geometrically simple) elements, the only ones that could be subjected to strictly arithmetic laws. Logically, this position led him to choose the square. As Peter Lowe has pointed out,[7] van Doesburg's final conception, elaborated shortly before his death, may therefore be seen as anticipating a serial, even systematic artistic method. At this same time, Freundlich was focusing on combinations of organic elements. Behind this fundamental divergence lie opposing conceptions of the function of the artwork and how to perceive it. Freundlich's idea of a cosmic symbolism was indirectly rejected by van Doesburg, who was similarly indifferent to the metaphysical dimension of Mondrian's Neoplasticism. In the same article, van Doesburg had made his position very clear: "To create presupposes, in any case, that we ourselves are opposed to matter, nature and the surrounding environment; otherwise, plastic art would not possess meaning."[8]

Freundlich took the opposite view, writing in 1927: "All our research will be mere patchwork if we do not discover cosmic relationships and their effects in [the realm of] the earthly."[9] Similarly, he writes of color: "As limit values, black and white stimulate the colors to unfold toward the limits. And we human beings, who are placed between the limits of birth and death, understand the all-encompassing nature of this process: an all-encompassing, powerful life, indeed perhaps the symbol of life itself."[10]

The originality of Freundlich's contribution from 1927 to 1929 can best be appreciated by contrasting it with van Doesburg's final explorations. For Freundlich, the work must be perceived as a living totality, which, once completed, preserves the dynamic (and symbolic) dimension of its production. "The artist performs a series of creative acts in his painting, whose synthesis is produced by the viewer who experiences the painting as a living whole."[11] Specifically, unlike van Doesburg, who had been commited to orthogonality for roughly a decade, and despite the fact that he too appreciated the rational possibilities inherent in such an approach, Freundlich remained deeply attached to the expressive power of the curve.[12] In 1925 and 1926, he produced a number of works that seek to reconcile orthogonality and curved lines, including the pastel *Spherical Bodies* (HvW 234, p. 162) and *Composition* (HvW 134, p. 157). And this effort continued in many of his works until his death (HvW 218, fig. 64). A critical point was reached in 1927 and 1928 with the production of two works that share the same title, *Fragments of Figures in a Context of Planes* (HvW 136, p. 236, and HvW 141, p. 237), a phrase that initially seems enigmatic but is illuminated by his writings. Just as in the case of van Doesburg but for very different reasons, for Freundlich controlling the relationships between the work's constituent elements now became the central aim of all his explorations. At the level of composition, *Fragments of Figures in a Context of Planes* of 1927 still contains a circle, a reminiscence of the "cosmic eye" (HvW 229, p. 167) which clashes with the dominant pattern of the shapes surrounding it, all of which are based on freely constructed four-sided geometric elements. More remarkable is the fact that in the 1927 version, two shapes make their appearance, each of which has two parts and is rigorously constructed as a half arch. While they reinterpret the curved forms of the abstract expressionist language the artist had developed after 1911, they also point ahead to his pictorial language of the 1930s, which will employ them systematically. The composition contains a strong architectural dimension which represents a significant break with the Expressionism still present in his pastels of the early 1920s. The space is completely "walled up" by the juxtaposition of the work's constituent elements, while at the outer edges the elements tend to conform to the

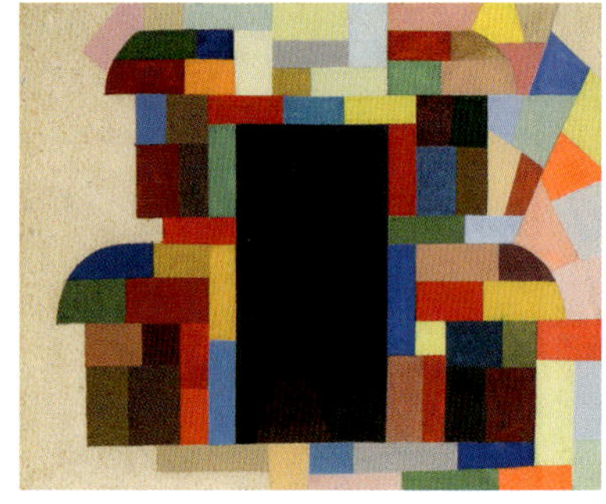

Fig. 64 Otto Freundlich
Composition, 1940–43
HvW 218, unfinished
Gouache and pencil on cardboard
22.5 × 29 cm
Donation Freundlich – Musées de Pontoise

painting's orthogonal format. These works affirm the flatness of the picture plane, even if the overlapping of some elements might seem to contradict this rejection of the third dimension. Also, the use of textural effects in the oil-painted surface enables the artist to give a sense of material solidity to the elements, which thus seem to be braced against one other.

The title *Fragments of Figures in a Context of Planes* makes clear that Freundlich was primarily concerned with transforming a combination of elements (a subjective composition) into a coherent and homogeneous totality. In order for the work to be perceived as a living organism, the principle guiding the combinations must be repeated and transmitted first among the elements within the various subgroups and then among the latter themselves within the work as a whole. In 1935, Freundlich analyzes his new conception in this way: "I combined complexes of kindred colors with one another, which for their part joined up with complexes of other color units, and so on, until the entire picture was covered.... The coexistence of all these color complexes, each of which represents a color individuality, results in the perfect collective of all the colors on a picture surface."[13]

Freundlich soon transposed his new conception to sculpture, where we find it brilliantly realized in the work *Ascension* from 1929 (HvW 76, fig. 65, p. 220). Freundlich had always stressed that sculpture resists the effort to free it from the dimension of Euclidean space: "Euclidean space is space without time. Non-Euclidean space is the union of space-time."[14] While the work's expressive power is initially disconcerting, it soon becomes apparent that an idea has organized this chaos, giving it an upward direction and structure which nevertheless are not contradicted by the massive character of the blocks. Although they are relatively autonomous, the blocks join together to transmit their energy along an axis that expresses the spatial as well as temporal character of the construction. Thus, one can imagine that the individual forms of these elements are a result of their role in a collective movement. Their singularity is a function of the point at which they enter that movement. The slowest elements, which open out at the base of the sculpture, emerge from chaos and already express a direction, coiling around what we perceive as a rising spiral. The intermediate elements, which seem to be entirely focused on their own energy, tend to take the form of cubes, the basic building block. Finally, those at the upper end of the sculpture, which open out again as if freed from the movement that enabled them to rise, are beginning a descent that will give new life to the entire movement. The perception of the temporal or non-Euclidean dimension of the work, to adopt the artist's terminology, thus implies a dynamic reading of the composition, or, if one prefers, its apprehension as an event that is perpetually unfolding. What interests Freundlich is not so much its Euclidean reality as a static, three-dimensional object but rather the fact that it is experienced as a cosmic and metaphysical process: "The painting is the place where two forces meet. One force comes from far away, the other from within ourselves and our community with the earth."[15] Or again: "The forces that are common to humanity and to which the artist gives expression in a material of some kind are the forces of expansion and contraction, attraction and repulsion, not, however, in a physical but in a psychological sense."[16]

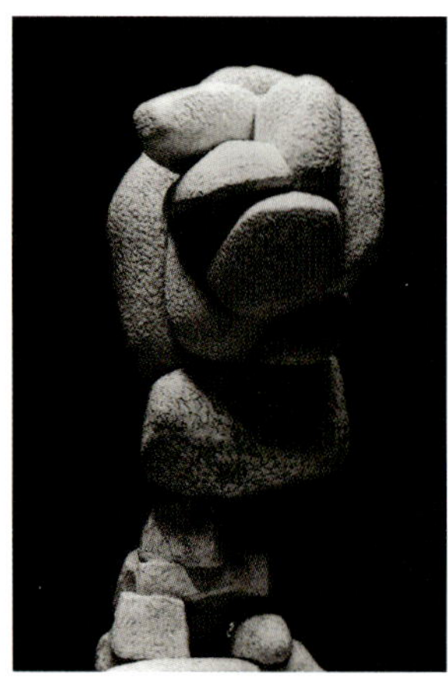

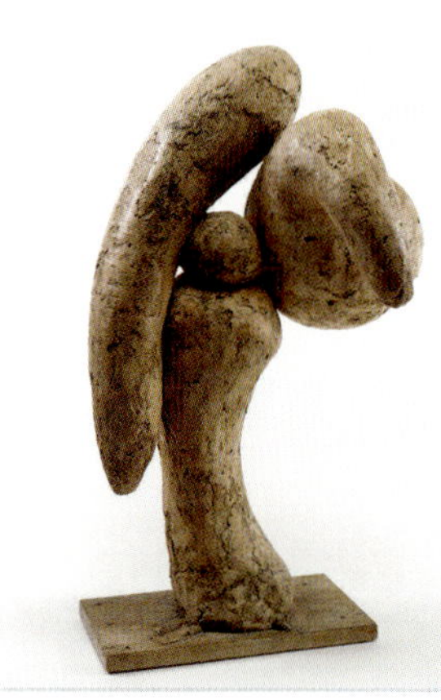

Fig. 65 Otto Freundlich
Ascension, 1929
HvW 76
Plaster

Fig. 66 Pablo Picasso
Head of a Woman,
Boisgeloup, 1931
Plaster
71.5 × 41 × 33 cm
Musée national Picasso-Paris.
Gift from Pablo Picasso

This monumental sculpture attracted the attention of the artist's contemporaries, including Picasso,[17] when it was exhibited after 1929 and reproduced in various publications, including the 1934 almanac of Abstraction-Création, but it was probably not understood beyond its sheer expressive power.[18] Freundlich kept the sculpture in his studio and would take a decade to fully explore its consequences in the medium of painting. The analysis of the painting *Fragments of Figures in a Context of Planes* and the sculpture *Ascension*, considered against the backdrop of the artist's writings and development, provide essential keys for appreciating the originality of his approach in the 1930s. The fact that Freundlich gave them almost programmatic titles underscores the importance he accorded them.

Between 1930 and 1933, Freundlich produced a number of works whose extraordinary artistic quality is widely acknowledged. The arrangement of the elements now evokes the dressing of a wall. The works are organized into chromatically homogeneous subgroups, whose elements are oriented in a way that is consistent with the dominant lines of the composition: "Linearity appears by itself in an image constructed with pure, planimetric color fields. The grouping of these color fields and the directions they point in the image determine the image's force, richness, and character."[19] The artist further emphasizes this coherence by using his brush to deposit the paint in such a way that relief effects are created which highlight the polarization of the various parts. This conception is also at work in the compositions preserved at the Museum of Modern Art in New York (HvW 154, p. 258); the Musée de Saint-Étienne (HvW 149, p. 261); the Musée de Pontoise (HvW 151, p. 259); and the Musée national d'art moderne, Centre Georges Pompidou (*My Sky Is Red*, HvW 168, p. 272). The image is constructed as a flat plane; the elements are primarily four-sided, while three-sided shapes, with or without a curve, are a small minority. The elements form a continuous layer that covers and structures the entire pictorial space. Finally, no single element resembles any other. And yet, although they are autonomous in energetic terms by dint of their individual color and geometry, they contribute to the whole by transmitting those energies to one other. The lines that emerge from the individual elements are only continued one at a time (they do not intersect). The line that continues establishes the direction in which the energy flows, while the line that is interrupted becomes a point of support. This system of opening and closing enables Freundlich to control the polarization of the elements. The process is repeated in the same way among the subgroups up to the level of the work as a whole and conveys the sense of an organizing power indistinguishable from the composition itself.

The powerful but static architectural quality of the 1930 *Composition* (HvW 151, p. 259) soon led Freundlich to go in search of more dynamic solutions. Thus, the two *Compositions* of 1931, one at the Musée de Pontoise (HvW 156, p. 276) and the other at the Von der Heydt Museum in Wuppertal (HvW 159, p. 253), introduce forces that conflict along a roughly diagonal axis. These opposing forces create a tension that seems to hollow out the space. Similar opposing forces can later be seen in a number of the artist's works (HvW 196, p. 267; HvW 203, fig. 67, etc.). Above all, Freundlich will henceforth seek to translate the movements discovered in 1929 in the sculpture *Ascension* into the medium of painting. The most faithful application of the principle can be seen in the *Rosette* of 1938 (HvW 192, p. 279), and then in the large tempera painting of 1939 (HvW 197, p. 277). From this point on, the artist's creative intuitions are rooted in the paradoxical union between a greater visual autonomy of the elements and a powerful expression of the forces that work to weld them into the expression of a living whole.

After 1935, Freundlich began to break up the chromatically homogeneous subgroups. In doing so, he took advantage of the lines produced by the juxtaposition of the elements to organize increasingly complex patterns of visual currents. He took the half-arch shape that had been latent in his work for a long time—consisting of two straight lines and a curve—and applied to it the system he had been employing since 1930: at each of the three extremities of this half arch, he continues one or the other of the lines that intersect there and subdivides the resulting shape into different-colored elements. Remarkably, the visual complexity produced by breaking up the chromatic groupings of the preceding period does not weaken the perception of this shape or of its polarizing power, as evidenced by *Rosette II* (HvW 210, p. 280). From this point on, the subgroups are no longer systematically cast as chromatically homogeneous units.

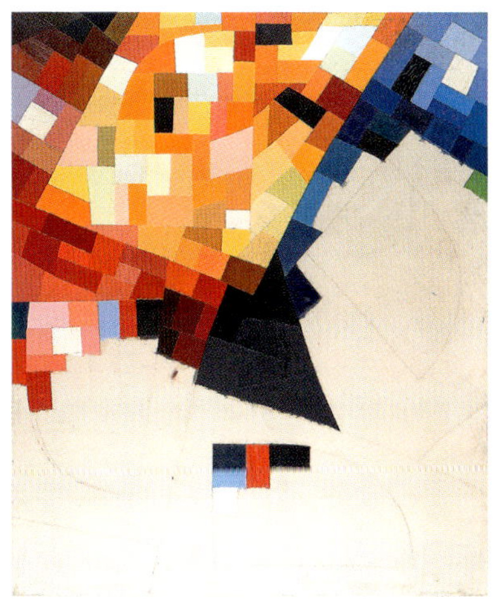

Fig. 67 Otto Freundlich
Composition, 1940
HvW 203, unfinished
Oil on canvas
183 × 154 cm
Donation Freundlich – Musées de Pontoise

What is profoundly original about Freundlich's system is that it seeks to reconcile a flat picture plane completely filled with combinations of elements, originally square, with the presence of polarizing curved forms that explode this geometric organization. While distancing himself from the subjective notion of composition in favor of a conception of the work as the result of a construction and a temporal development, Otto Freundlich conceived an organic syntax which, with its humanist dimension and symbolic possibilities, is radically opposed to the serial and systematic development ushered in by van Doesburg's Elementarism.

1 In 1946, the newly created association Salon des Réalités Nouvelles adopted the title and sequence of the three exhibitions mounted in Paris in 1939 by Galerie Charpentier. Otto Freundlich had participated in the earlier exhibition, contributing a number of works that today form part of the Freundlich donation at the Musées de Pontoise. They included the large tempera painting of 1939 (HvW 197, p. 277) and a pastel from 1919 (HvW 223, p. 164), as can be seen in the photograph of the exhibition's installation (pp. 18–19).

2 See *abstraction création*, exh. cat. Westfälisches Landesmuseum für Kunst und Kulturgeschichte, Münster; Musée d'Art moderne de la Ville de Paris (Münster, 1978), pp. 304–306.

3 Theo van Doesburg, "Elementarism (the Elements of the New Painting)," trans. Joost Baljeu, in Joost Baljeu, *Theo van Doesburg* (New York, 1974), pp. 184–185, here p. 184. Originally published as "Elémentarisme (les éléments de la nouvelle peinture)," *De Stijl. Dernier numéro* (1932), pp. 15–19. [Theo van Doesburg Archive, typescript "Elémentarisme," Paris, July 13, 1930, inv. 475 -mf.94]

4 Theo van Doesburg, "Film as Pure Form," trans. Standish D. Lawder, *Form* 1, no. 1 (Cambridge, UK: Summer 1966), pp. 5–11. Originally published as "Film als reine Gestaltung," *Die Form* 4, no. 10 (May 15, 1929), pp. 241–248. [Theo van Doesburg Archive, typescript "Film als reine Gestaltung," Paris, February 1929, inv. 461 -mf.89].

5 Theo van Doesburg, "Art Concret: The Basis of Concrete Painting," trans. Joost Baljeu, in Baljeu, *Theo van Doesburg*, op. cit. (note 3), pp. 180–181, here p. 180. See also van Doesburg, "Comments on the Basis of Concrete Painting," trans. Joost Baljeu, in ibid., pp. 181–182. Originally published as "Base de la peinture concrète" and "Commentaires sur la base de la peinture concrète," in *Art Concret: Vol. 1, numéro d'introduction* (April 1930), pp. 1 and 2–4. [Theo van Doesburg Archive, typescript "Manifeste de la peinture concrète" ("Manifeste sur l'Art concret"), Paris, January 1930, inv. 471 -mf.92].

6 Theo van Doesburg, "Elementarism," op. cit. (note 3), p. 184 (translation modified); p. 17 in original.

7 Peter Lowe, "La composition arithmétique—un pas vers la composition sérielle dans la peinture de Van Doesburg," in *Theo van Doesburg—Peinture, architecture, théorie* [contributions to a colloquium on Theo van Doesburg held at the University of Dijon in 1982], ed. Serge Lemoine et al. (Paris, 1990), pp. 228–233. An abridged English version of the article is available online at http://www.peter-lowe.com/pl-pdfs/pl-Doesberg.pdf.

8 Theo van Doesburg, "Elementarism," op. cit. (note 3), p. 185; p. 18 in original.

9 Otto Freundlich, "Gedanken des Malers" [1927], in Uli Bohnen, ed., *Otto Freundlich: Schriften. Ein Wegbereiter der gegenstandslosen Kunst* (Cologne, 1982), p. 152.

10 Otto Freundlich, "Ideen und Bilder—Aufzeichnungen eines Malers" [1940–42], in *Otto Freundlich: Schriften*, op. cit. (note 9), pp. 221–249.

11 Otto Freundlich, advertisement for Le Mur art school, archive Association Les Amis de Jeanne et Otto Freundlich (AAJOF), IMEC, FRN 22.3.

12 "The curve is the primordial element of the physical, the three-dimensional; under certain conditions, it very much has a place here. It is the dam of the river without banks, the rock on which it breaks, the arm that points a direction, the echo that follows and the sound that announces the personal, the emissary of the earth in the vastness of space, space's love letter to our life on earth, the symbol of our connection with the cosmos." Otto Freundlich, "Ideen und Bilder," op. cit. (note 10).

13 Otto Freundlich, "Bekenntnisse eines revolutionären Malers" [1935]; Eng. trans. "Confessions of a Revolutionary Painter," in the present volume, pp. 4–19, here p. 9.

14 Otto Freundlich, "Ideen und Bilder," op. cit. (note 10), p. 241.

15 Ibid., p. 225.

16 Ibid., p. 224.

17 Picasso and Freundlich had been friends since meeting at the Bateau-Lavoir in 1908. Their correspondence of the 1920s and 1930s shows that each of them followed the development of the other's work. In June 1930, Picasso spent time at the Chateau de Boisgeloup (near Gisors) and started work on a new series of sculptures, whose forms display a certain kinship with those of *Ascension* (figs. 65 & 66, p. 220).

18 Abstraction-Création organized a series of solo exhibitions. The third—in 1934 at the group's Paris gallery at 44, avenue de Wagram—was devoted to Otto Freundlich and Hans Erni. A reproduction of *Ascension* can be found in the almanac *Abstraction, création, art non-figuratif* 3 (1934), p. 14. Freundlich later also took part in the fifth group exhibition, where his works appeared alongside those of Albert Gleizes, Jean Gorin, and van Doesburg (who had already passed away).

19 Otto Freundlich, "Ideen und Bilder," op. cit. (note 10), p. 232.

Verena Franken

Otto Freundlich's Painting Technique as Represented by His Late Work

The appraisals of Otto Freundlich's painting in this article are based on the findings from technical investigations performed on select works[1] with the aim of learning more about the techniques, origin, and effect achieved by the paintings during his late period. A total of twenty artworks (oils, pastels, gouache, and tempera paintings) were examined.

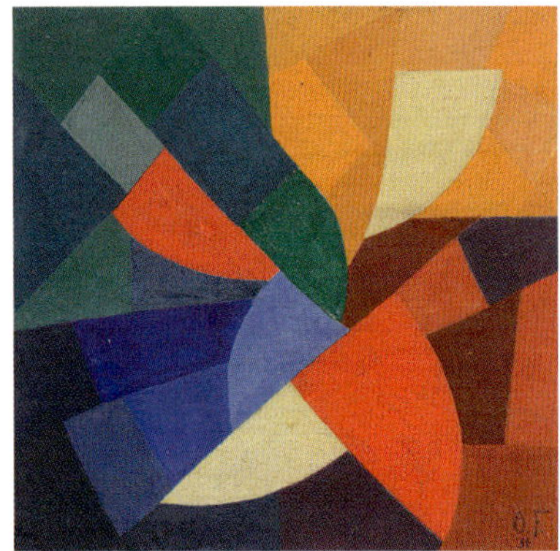

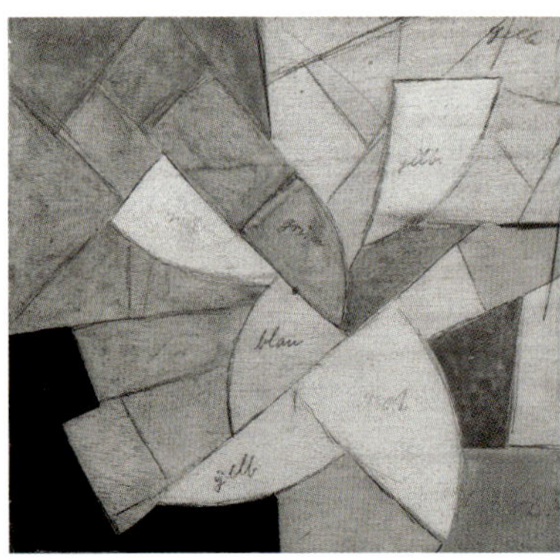

Fig. 68/69 Otto Freundlich
Composition, 1936
HvW 181
Tempera on wood
20.6 x 21.4 cm
Private collection, Switzerland
Below: Infrared reflectogram with underdrawing

The findings from the technological and imaging investigations, such as infrared reflectography, lead us to deduce that Freundlich took a systematic approach in his work. In a good many of the pieces studied, an underdrawing could be ascertained.[2] It served to divide up the picture surface into individual segments and to determine the shape and size of the respective fields. Freundlich did the underdrawings freehand using a dry medium, probably a graphite pencil. The line of the underdrawings differs scarcely from the actual painting and the visible forms. We find just a few minor corrections and lines set next to one another, which in some cases have been corrected (fig. 68/69). This points to a certain resoluteness in the artist regarding the shaping of the figures and design, and reveals that he did not proceed in an experimental or spontaneous way.

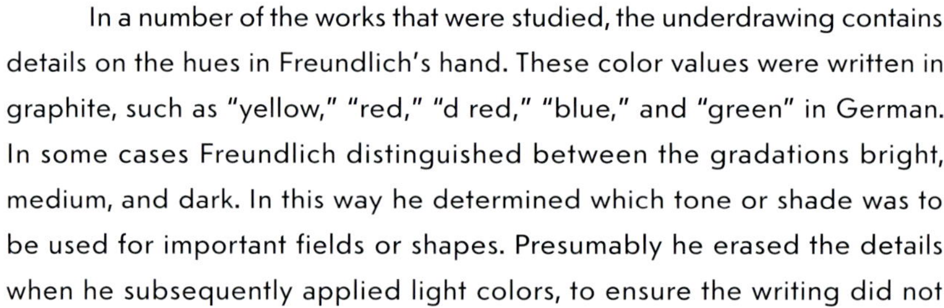

In a number of the works that were studied, the underdrawing contains details on the hues in Freundlich's hand. These color values were written in graphite, such as "yellow," "red," "d red," "blue," and "green" in German. In some cases Freundlich distinguished between the gradations bright, medium, and dark. In this way he determined which tone or shade was to be used for important fields or shapes. Presumably he erased the details when he subsequently applied light colors, to ensure the writing did not show through the paint layer.

In addition he did preparatory sketches and outline plans for the colors, which dictate the picture's structure and color scheme. He sketched out the rough form and noted down individual colors in French or German. His color plans still exist for some works—such as for the pastel *Ship in a Storm*, where the color values were written down in French, such as "jaune," "rouge," "bleu," "vert," "noir," "gris clair," and "foncé" (HvW 232, p. 170; HvW 307, p. 171). These very largely agree with the finished pastel. Freundlich's sketched color plans with their detailed descriptions point to the theoretical side of his work. His work was preceded by careful thought, and clearly he did not leave the choice of colors to chance.

Much as in a mosaic, Freundlich's late work consists of color fields set tightly together to fill the surface. Gouache and tempera pictures distinguish themselves by the opacity of the paint, although the thickness of the paint layer and the

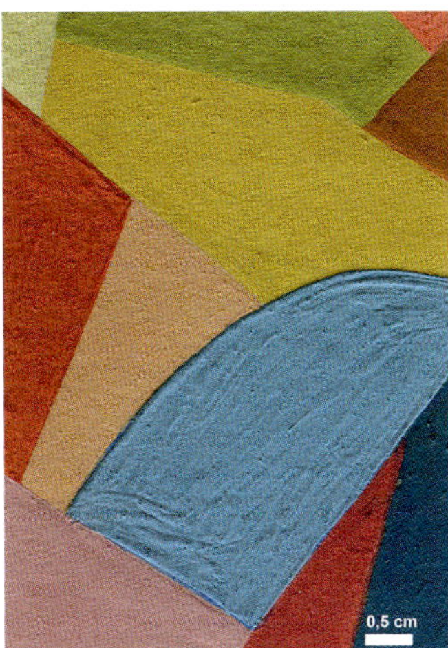

Fig. 70 Otto Freundlich
Detail from *Composition around Two Planes in Black and Gray*, 1942
Staatliche Graphische Sammlung, Munich
(Reproduced in full on p. 255)

structure varies slightly from field to field (fig. 70). Some colors have been applied so thinly that the structure of the support layer is clearly discernible, while others have been done thicker, with a light use of the brush. Freundlich's oil paintings typically employ an impasto style, with the paint laid on with a sweeping brush. The result is a clear relief effect that strongly dominates the composition. The individual color surfaces are delineated from one another by prominences and accretions of paint. Impastoed transitions do not always result in clear-cut edges, but seem at times as if the paint had been ripped at that spot. In the paintings the amount of binding agent in the paint layer varies from one color field to the next, thus allowing him to produce a richly faceted surface structure with a variegated gloss. Some regions distinguish themselves by the use of little binding agent, and with that a hard approach with the brush, and others by a high proportion of binding agents and soft brushwork (fig. 71).

Freundlich often applied the paints at the junctions between the color fields with the greatest care and precision, thus producing a great feeling of quality in the finished painting. In passages where the transitions run in straight lines, it is not impossible that he used a template (fig. 72). Likewise shapes with curves were plotted out with great precision (as for instance in *Composition around Two Planes in Black and Gray* from 1942, fig. 70). The color fields are not delineated from one another by contours, but rather by shapes and colors that augment or rebuff one another. As Freundlich put it: "A colored surface without a linear boundary would thus be a purely mental manifestation, but one that is lost as soon as it unites with the line as a boundary value and outline."[3]

The majority of pictures contain a large number of color fields of different shapes and sizes. Freundlich combined geometrical and freely shaped forms with one another. The supporting framework for the composition and a characteristic element in his painting is the semi-ogive form, which allows various color sections to mesh and interlock (as for instance HvW 196, p. 267).

Fig. 71/72 Otto Freundlich
Details from *Composition Red-Green*, 1939
HvW 199
Left: Section with soft and hard brushwork
Right: Paint applied with great precision at the transitions between the color fields
(Reproduced in full on p. 249)

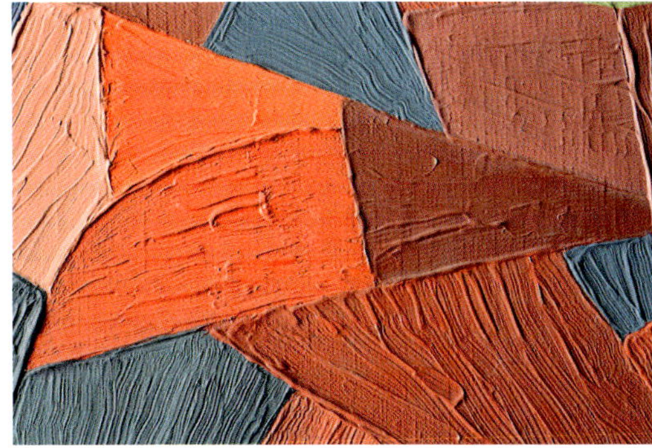

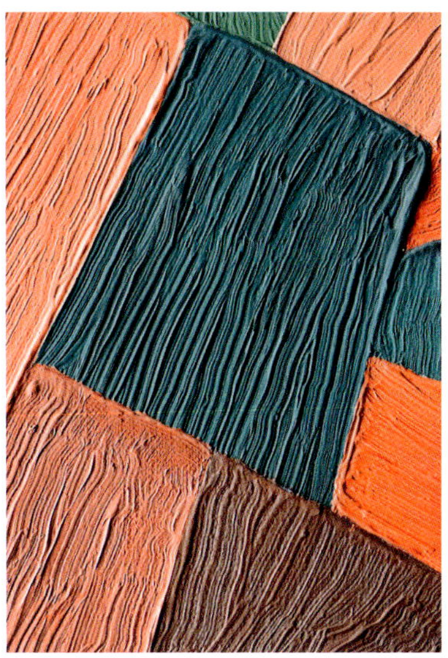

In the majority of the paintings from the late period there is a large variety of colors. Dominant are the primary colors yellow, red, and blue, as well as green in various mixtures of the primaries. Freundlich often combined chromatic hues with achromatic ones, and only rarely did he work solely with monochrome colors (as in HvW 208, p. 243). The colors were mixed—probably on the palette—with differing amounts of white in order to produce gradations between light and dark (e.g. in HvW 151, p. 259, and HvW 196, p. 267). As a result of the precise balancing and nuancing of the tones, scarcely a color in a single composition is the same as another (HvW 199, p. 249). Freundlich created works with light and dark contrasts and with different brightness values. In his gouache *Composition* from 1939 (HvW 197, p. 277), an increasing brightness can be seen extending upwards in the work.

The paint in the examined paintings and works on paper has sometimes been applied in a single layer, and sometimes been built up of several. In the case of a twin layer, often a neighboring color lies beneath the top layer (as in HvW 181, fig. 68, p. 224). On occasion a single tone has been used as a planar substrate for more than one color field (HvW 197, fig. 73). In some works the paint has been laid on in several applications or layers (fig. 74).

The results of the pigment analyses that were conducted permit us to say that Freundlich had a limited number of pigments at his disposal as he worked on the paintings. Microscopic analyses and other investigations into the materials—above all Vis-spectroscopy—demonstrate that often pigments were not used directly but that the works employed more or less complex mixtures of different pigments. Thus violet hues have been made by mixing blue and red pigments, as well as in part black particles (as, for instance, in the painting *Composition around Two Planes in Black and Gray*).

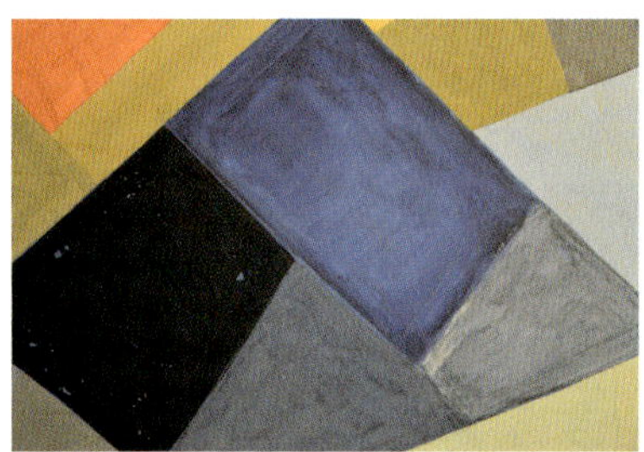

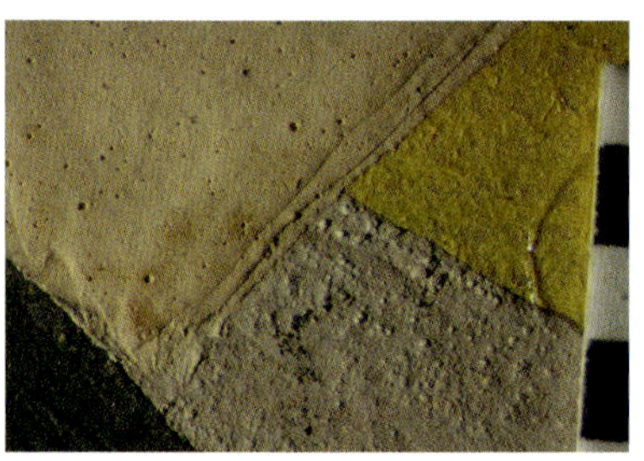

Fig. 73 Detail from *Composition*, 1939 HvW 197, with blue coloring beneath the four fields (Reproduced in full on p. 227)

Fig. 74 Microscope image of *Composition around Two Planes in Black and Gray*, 1942, showing a layer of blue paint applied in at least three coats Staatliche Graphische Sammlung, Munich (Reproduced in full on p. 255)

In the investigated works, both inorganic as well as organic pigments could be identified. Among the inorganic pigments Freundlich mostly used customary colors such as titanium white, carbon black, ultramarine, and various cadmium pigments. But he also painted with organic azo pigments, phthalocyanines, and synthetic madder (anthraquinone PR 83). At times he used toxic pigments containing chrome and lead compounds.[4]

Since he often could not afford artist's materials, they were donated to him by friends such as Renate Goldschmidt, or husband and wife Charlotte and Rodolphe Gutmann.[5] In a letter from Freundlich dated April 14, 1942, he asks friends to get him rose madder, lemon yellow, cobalt blue, and umbra.[6]

He selected his materials with great care. Freundlich preferred flat brushes for oils and round brushes in various sizes for gouaches and watercolors (fig. 75).[7] In a letter dated July 16, 1941, he expresses his wish to Charlotte Gutmann for tubes of paint from the firms Linel[8] or Talens.[9] In a sketch appended to this letter he depicted a small tube of paint from the French manufacturer Bourgeois Aîné[11] (fig. 76, p. 228).[12] Apart from other painting materials owned by Freundlich, a number of tubes of paint from the "Couleur moite" series (Bourgeois Aîné) were discovered in 1983 by art historian Rita Wildegans during her researches.[13] Freundlich had left them some time between 1942 and 1943 in the town of St. Martin de Fenouillet on the hayloft above a disused stable when fleeing from the National Socialists. These paints are important references and documents for his painting. And more than that, they make an important contribution to the research into artist's materials in the twentieth century.

1 In 2015 and 2016, Museum Ludwig commissioned a series of studies into the technical side of Otto Freundlich's artworks and the materials he employed. The investigations into his painting technique were conducted at Museum Ludwig, while the scientific analyses were performed at the Rathgen-Forschungslabor. In addition, the services of the Laboratoire d'Archéologie Moléculaire et Structurale (LAMS) and the Institut für Restaurierungs- und Konservierungswissenschaft (CICS) were enlisted. The work involved microscopic studies, imaging methods (UV examinations, infrared reflectography, radiography), and pigment analyses (x-ray fluorescence analysis, Raman spectroscopy, UV-visible spectroscopy, x-ray diffraction analysis). Also examined were letters in which Freundlich discusses his artistic aims and materials. Cf. Verena Franken, Ina Reiche, Cristina Lopes Aibéo, Sabine Schwerdtfeger, Ellen Egel, "Zur Maltechnik von Otto Freundlich (1878–1943): Maltechnische und materialanalytische Untersuchungen am Beispiel des Spätwerks," *Berliner Beiträge zur Archäometrie, Kunsttechnologie und Konservierungswissenschaft* 24 (2016), pp. 73-92.

2 The canvas painting *Composition Red-Green* (1939, HvW 199, p. 249) lacks an underdrawing in graphite. In all likelihood color glazes were used to roughly map out the composition.

Fig. 75 Letter from Freundlich (also signed by Kosnick-Kloss) to Charlotte and Rodolphe Gutmann, Saint-Paul-de-Fenouillet, dated April 14, 1942, in which he asks his friends to send him various paints and brushes for oils and watercolors

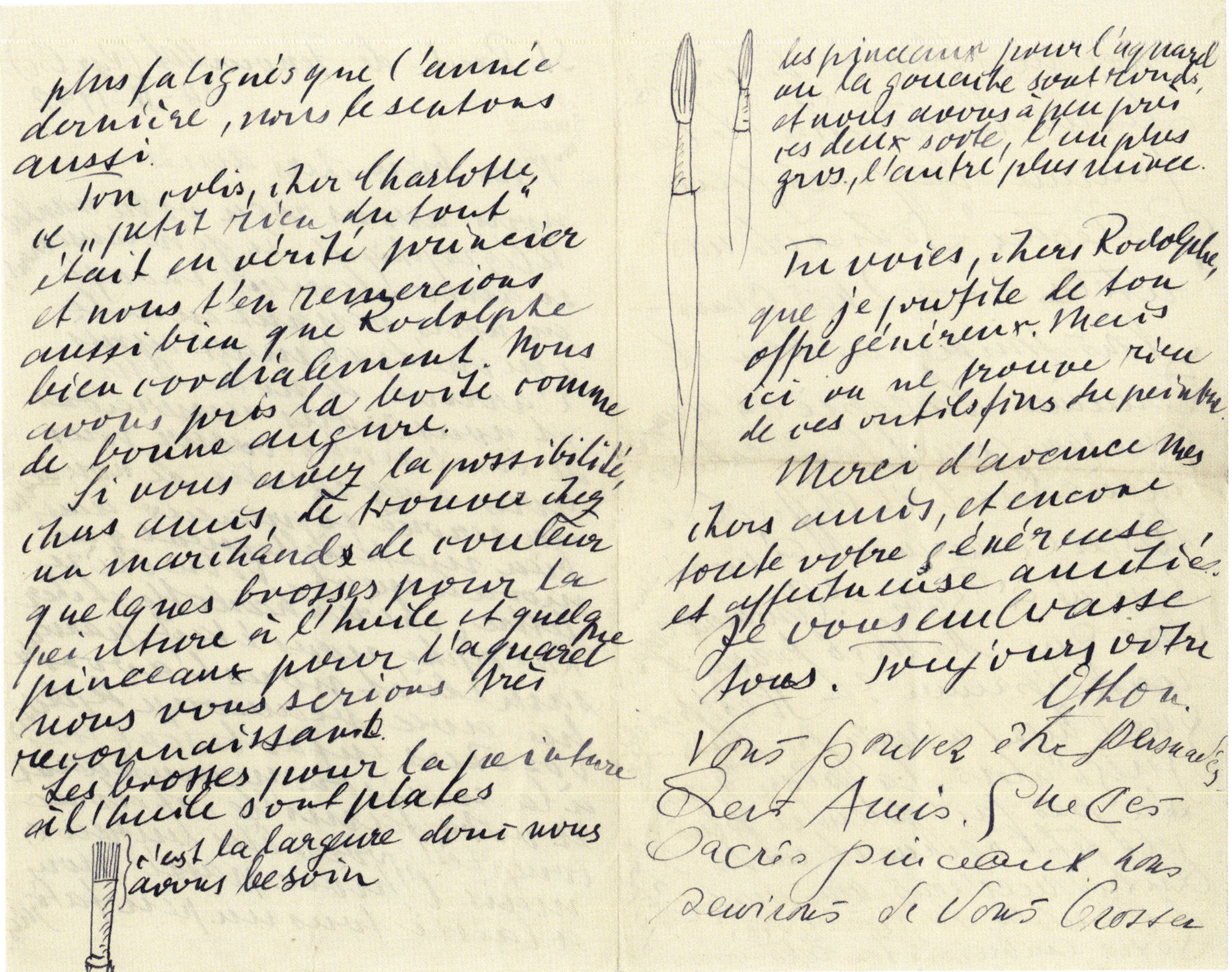

plus fatigués que l'année
dernière, nous le sentons
aussi.
Ton colis, chère Charlotte,
ce „petit rien du tout"
était en vérité princier
et nous t'en remercions
aussi bien que Rodolphe
bien cordialement. Nous
avons pris la boîte comme
de bonne augure.
Si vous avez la possibilité,
chers amis, de trouver chez
un marchand de couleur
quelques brosses pour la
peinture à l'huile et quelques
pinceaux pour l'aquarelle
nous vous serions très
reconnaissants.
Les brosses pour la peinture
à l'huile sont plates
c'est la largeur dont nous
avons besoin

les pinceaux pour l'aquarelle
ou la gouache sont ronds,
et nous avons à peu près
ces deux sorte, l'un plus
gros, l'autre plus mince.

Tu vois, cher Rodolphe,
que je profite de ton
offre généreuse. Mais
ici on ne trouve rien
de ces outils fins de peintre.
Merci d'avance mes
chers amis, et encore
toute votre généreuse
et affectueuse amitié.
Je vous embrasse
tous. Toujours votre
Othon.
Vous pouvez être persuadés
Chers Amis, que ces
sacrés pinceaux sont
devenus de vrais [illegible]

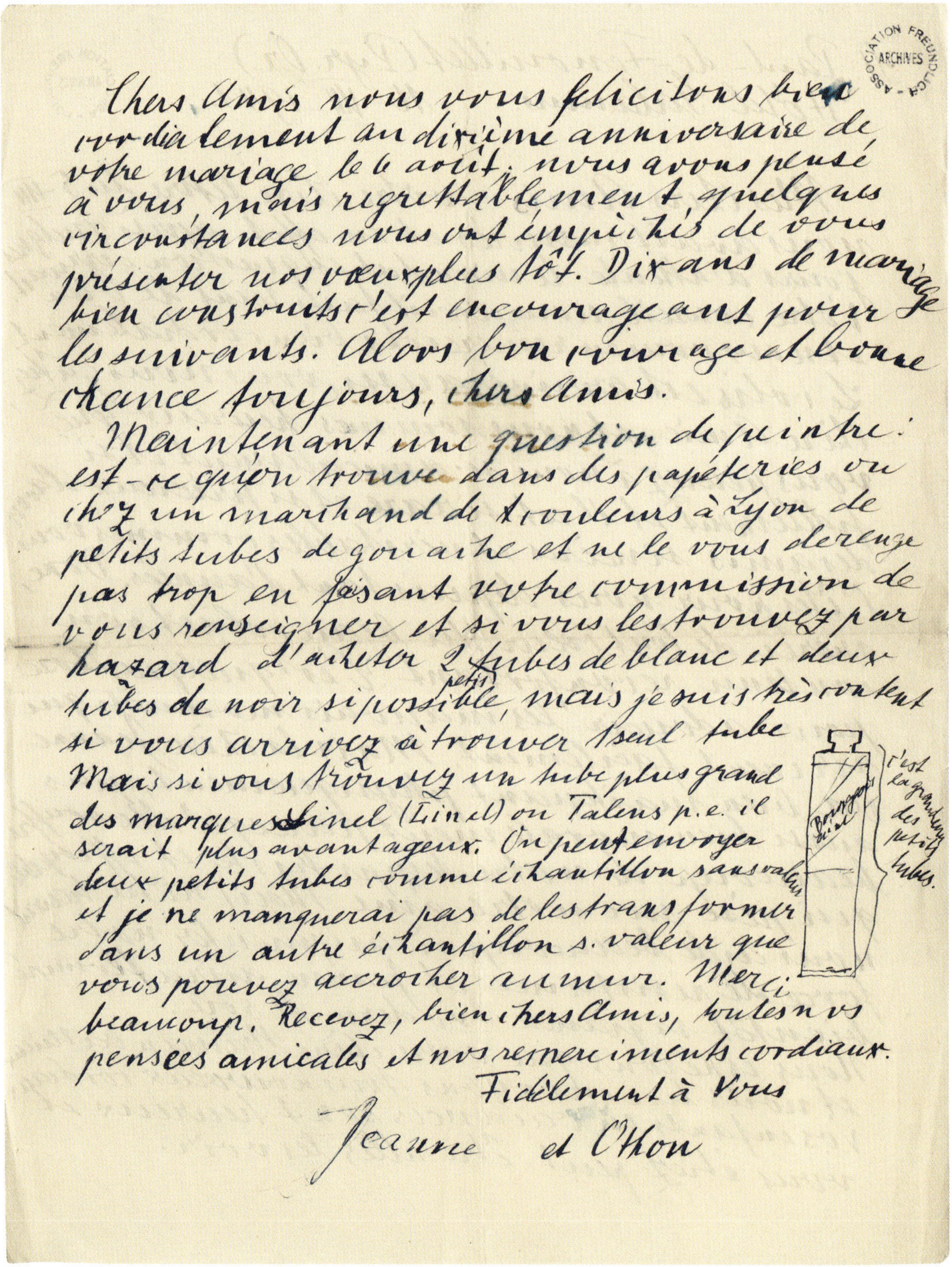

Chers Amis nous vous félicitons bien cordialement au dixième anniversaire de votre mariage le 6 août. nous avons pensé à vous, mais regrettablement quelques circonstances nous ont empêchés de vous présenter nos voeux plus tôt. Dix ans de mariage bien construits c'est encourageant pour les suivants. Alors bon courage et bonne chance toujours, chers Amis.

Maintenant une question de peintre: est-ce qu'on trouve dans des papéteries ou chez un marchand de couleurs à Lyon de petits tubes de gouache et ne le vous dérange pas trop en faisant votre commission de vous renseigner et si vous les trouvez par hasard d'acheter 2 tubes de blanc et deux tubes de noir si possible petits, mais je suis très content si vous arrivez à trouver 1 seul tube Mais si vous trouvez un tube plus grand des marques Linel (Linel) ou Talens p.e. il serait plus avantageux. On peut envoyer deux petits tubes comme échantillon sans valeur et je ne manquerai pas de les transformer dans un autre échantillon s. valeur que vous pouvez accrocher au mur. Merci beaucoup. Recevez, bien chers Amis, toutes nos pensées amicales et nos remerciements cordiaux.

Fidèlement à Vous

Jeanne et Othon

Fig. 76 Letter to Charlotte and Rodolphe Gutmann, Saint-Paul-de-Fenouillet, dated July 16, 1941, with the request to get him some largish tubes of gouache and large tubes from either of the firms Linel or Talens; also a drawing of a small tube from Bourgeois Aîné

3 Otto Freundlich, "Die Verwandlung der sichtbaren Welt" [1921], in Uli Bohnen, ed., *Otto Freundlich: Schriften. Ein Wegbereiter der gegenstandslosen Kunst* (Cologne, 1982), pp. 118–119, here p. 119.

4 These were discovered above all in the pastel *Composition* (HvW 223, p. 164) from his early period, as established by x-ray fluorescence analysis and Raman spectroscopy at the Rathgen-Forschungslabor, Berlin.

5 See the letter by Freundlich to Charlotte Gutmann, August 28, 1941: "Quant à la possibilité de trouver d'autres couleurs que vous nous annoncez, c'est vraiment merveilleux, seulement, les couleurs sont devenus très chères, ce que vous remarqué en acheter les deux tubes." Archive Association Les Amis de Jeanne et Otto Freundlich (AAJOF), IMEC, FRN 3.25.

6 See the letter by Freundlich, September 28, 1941: "Il ne s'agit que de choisir . . . de la liste de couleurs que nous vous avons faite parvenir les 3 ou quatre couleurs dont nous avons besoin maintenant. Ce sont: 1. garance rose 2. jaune citron 3. bleu de cobalt 4. terre d'ombre." Archive AAJOF, IMEC, FRN 3.25.

7 See the letter by Freundlich to Charlotte and Rodolphe Gutmann, April 14, 1942. Archive AAJOF, IMEC, FRN 3.25.

8 Probably referring to gouache paints by the company Linel in France, as used for instance by Henri Matisse. Cf. "Paper Cut Outs (gouaches découpés) [*sic*]" on the website *Henri Matisse*, http://www.henri-matisse.net/cut_outs.html (accessed June 2016).

9 Royal Talens is an important manufacturer of artist's and painting materials founded in 1899 by Marten Talens, which is still in operation. See the company's homepage, https://www.royaltalens.com/about-us (accessed June 2016).

10 The company Bourgeois Aîné was one of the largest producers of artist's and painting materials in France between 1867 and 1965. It was founded by François Alexandre Joseph Bourgeois. See the entry in the *Guide Labreuche: Guide historique des fournisseurs de matériel pour artistes à Paris 1790–1960*: http://www.labreuche-fournisseurs-artistes-paris.fr/fournisseur/bourgeois-aine (accessed June 2016).

11 See the letter by Freundlich to Charlotte Gutmann, July 16, 1941. Archive AAJOF, IMEC, FRN 3.25.

12 Still extant are tubes of watercolors (Bourgeois Aîné, Lefranc, and J.M. Paillard), pans of watercolors, color samples made from pastels, pigments, cardboard palettes (J.M. Paillard), pieces of glass with mixed colors, a small panel coated in animal glue, and a brush. Rita Wildegans entrusted the painting materials to the estate in Pontoise in 1987.

13 Rita Wildegans-Krollpfeiffer, "Otto Freundlichs Werk im Kontext naturwissenschaftlicher and gesellschaftspolitischer Erkenntnisse," PhD diss., Universität Hamburg (Hamburg, 1989), p. 7.

Adolf Muschg

Otto Freundlich as a Family Affair—A Sketch of a Twofold Memory of Hedwig Muschg

It is from my father's first family, none of whom is still alive, that I have inherited my admiration of twentieth-century artists, who all have something in common: their greatness is without question—for those who actually notice them. And the latter must not only show that they are cognoscenti, but also profess their faith—as if it were a matter of standing up for them and their special art in the face of *every* zeitgeist, and against inadmissible oblivion. For Walter Muschg it was the art of writer Hans Henny Jahnn, the "stranded whale"; for Hedwig Muschg that of painter Otto Freundlich. Both were bound to the object of their admiration by personal passion and gave them financial support in times of need; in both cases the Nazis and their barbaric "cultural policies" were the manifest cause of this need, but they were not alone: with the radical claims that both Jahnn and Freundlich laid on their art to change the world, they created their own needy situation which, even under more clement historical circumstances, would have sufficed to make them outsiders. Both grasped their work as a monumental prophetic act for a new order and subscribed to the paradox of militant pacifism. Both were indebted for their greatest inspiration to a period in exile, which initially they chose for themselves, Jahnn in Norway, Freundlich in Paris, but which Hitler's seizure of power then made compulsory for both; with that they forfeited their already slender means of existence. Not until the European tragedy was over did the telling difference become apparent: the "Aryan" Jahnn had survived the Third Reich and was himself able to spread his singular tidings in postwar Germany, if only to a select audience. Otto Freundlich, however, a Jew who had grown up in Pomerania, fell prey to the killing machine, even after his flight to Vichy France: he was deported to an extermination camp, where he found his "grave in the air."

While at secondary school I came across his tracks in the modest apartments rented by my half-sister who, with her sensitivity to uncouth neighbors and to ghostly knockings from the central heating, changed home frequently. And every time she took her paintings, whose strangeness always struck me and whose boldness made a striking contrast to the carefully guarded bourgeois habitus of a retired teacher. In my father's day—he died in 1948 when I was not quite fourteen—there was a family legend about them: the oldest daughter, right from the outset the most delicate of four siblings, had got to know an unworldly and of course penniless artist shortly after taking up her first position in "red" Ober-Winterthur. When she also wanted to marry him she was given the choice: him—or us. For better or worse, the threatened exclusion from the family made her see reason.

That her relationship with Otto Freundlich did not end with their parting, that she continued to cherish the memory of it as a personal treasure, could literally be read from her walls. I remember one painting in particular in which a curved white—or was it black?—trapezium set against a planar mosaic of colors leapt out like a tongue, and that my half-sister treated the pictures as a secret that was not to be discussed. So—I know better now—it was also a way of protecting her own injury. It was from other sources that I learned she must have met her lifelong beloved in the mid-twenties (she herself was just slightly older) during a holiday in Paris, and when shortly after he married, their bond not only remained steadfast but extended to the new couple, literally at her own cost. Because she shared with them her slim teacher's pension to the bitter end, which she tried vainly to forestall for him by immigration to Switzerland: the country preferred, though, to reserve its hospitality for "certified commodities" like Thomas Mann, and had no time for the impecunious avant-garde, especially when, as in Freundlich's case, they raised suspicions of sympathies with world Communism and had been branded "degenerate" in Goebbels's fatal exhibition. The picture on the cover of the catalogue showed of all things a work by Freundlich—a face inspired by the monumental figures on Easter Island—shown at an upward slant: from that brutalizing angle in which modernist art *in toto* was damned to annihilation, before the same fate befell many of its authors.

That the monumentalism of Freundlich's sculptures had been *dared* on the strength of his own premises, that his relationship to figuration had in fact a twist and not very much to do with "abstraction": these observations were reserved for an art-minded world at some future date. Thankfully large portions of his work *reached* this future world, even if it remained an exclusive matter and its scope did not match the universal social utopias that underpinned the art. We only first encounter this in Freundlich's texts. And of all the people who helped transcribe his handwriting for

Fig. 77 Otto Freundlich
Composition, 1926
HvW 235
Pastel on paper
9.7 × 11.8 cm
Private collection, Paris

Fig. 78 Otto Freundlich
Golden Rain, 1927
HvW 240
Pastel on paper
21.5 × 17 cm
Private collection, Munich

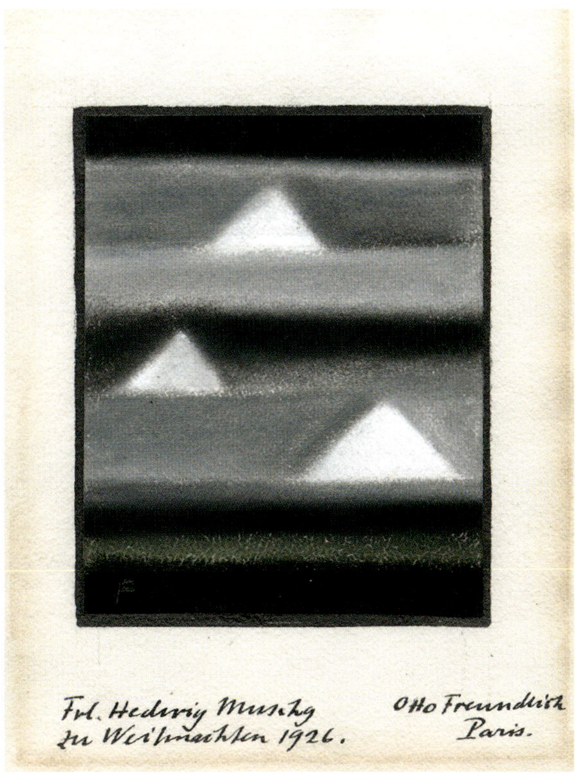

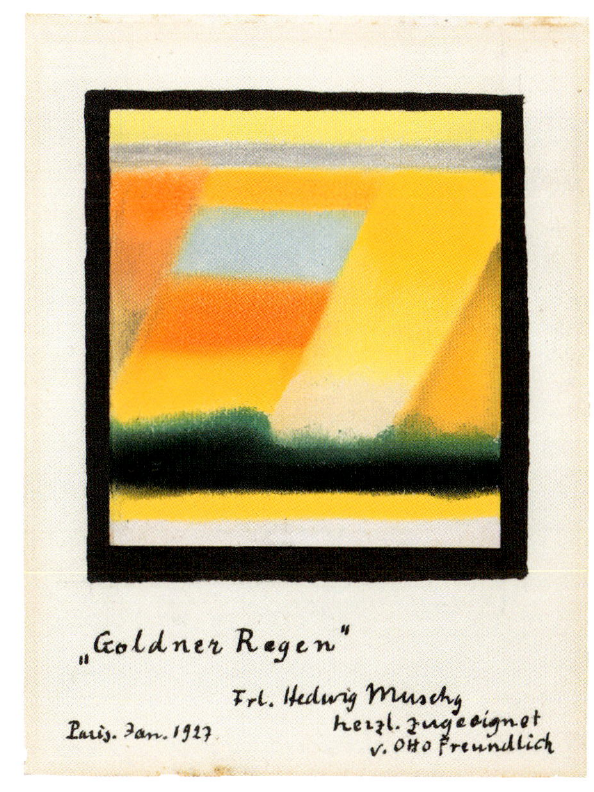

the printed page, my half-sister Hedwig assumed a once again modest yet important place—thus repeating as it were the underlying formula of her relationship with this artist.

At the same time the story of her later years also refuted the disdainful sentiment that selfless deeds never pay. They don't *have* to, but sometimes they do so, perhaps for precisely that reason. With the proceeds from the pictures which Otto Freundlich sent via a mutual friend to Hedwig Muschg in return for her support, she lived a *little* less modestly. As my visits to her became less frequent, I nevertheless noted that her walls grew emptier, but a sense of embarrassment prevented her from giving me the key to understanding: she had handed the public the evidence of her closeness to the artist, choosing the galleries and museums with the greatest care. The more Freundlich's work was allowed to speak for itself, the less it required the private spokeswoman. Her emptying walls were proof that she had not been mistaken in her admiration, nay: her passion. More and more observers began to empathize or sympathize with both, and with increasing age I myself am one. And I miss my sister, who while regarded as particularly timid, was quietly courageous and obstinately sworn to great art. I have never heard her speak more reverently than of Otto Freundlich—*and* of his clever and intrepid wife. Even after his death, the notoriously penniless artist had created just the right position for her, in her early retirement; I will never forget him for that—nor her. I am slightly proud of that, and also look at Freundlich's pictures with new eyes. The tongue that broke out of the colored surface back then has begun to speak: the colored surface, as a binding horizon of the new art, is united there with the revolt against it, the plastic departure into another dimension.

When Hedwig died, she left just one single Freundlich painting to her heirs, a color wheel in watercolors, not totally dissimilar to Goethe's. I gave it then to my publisher on his seventieth birthday, and he hung it over the door to his office, where authors would come and go. Always concerned with the ultimate. I think the little picture was in the right place.

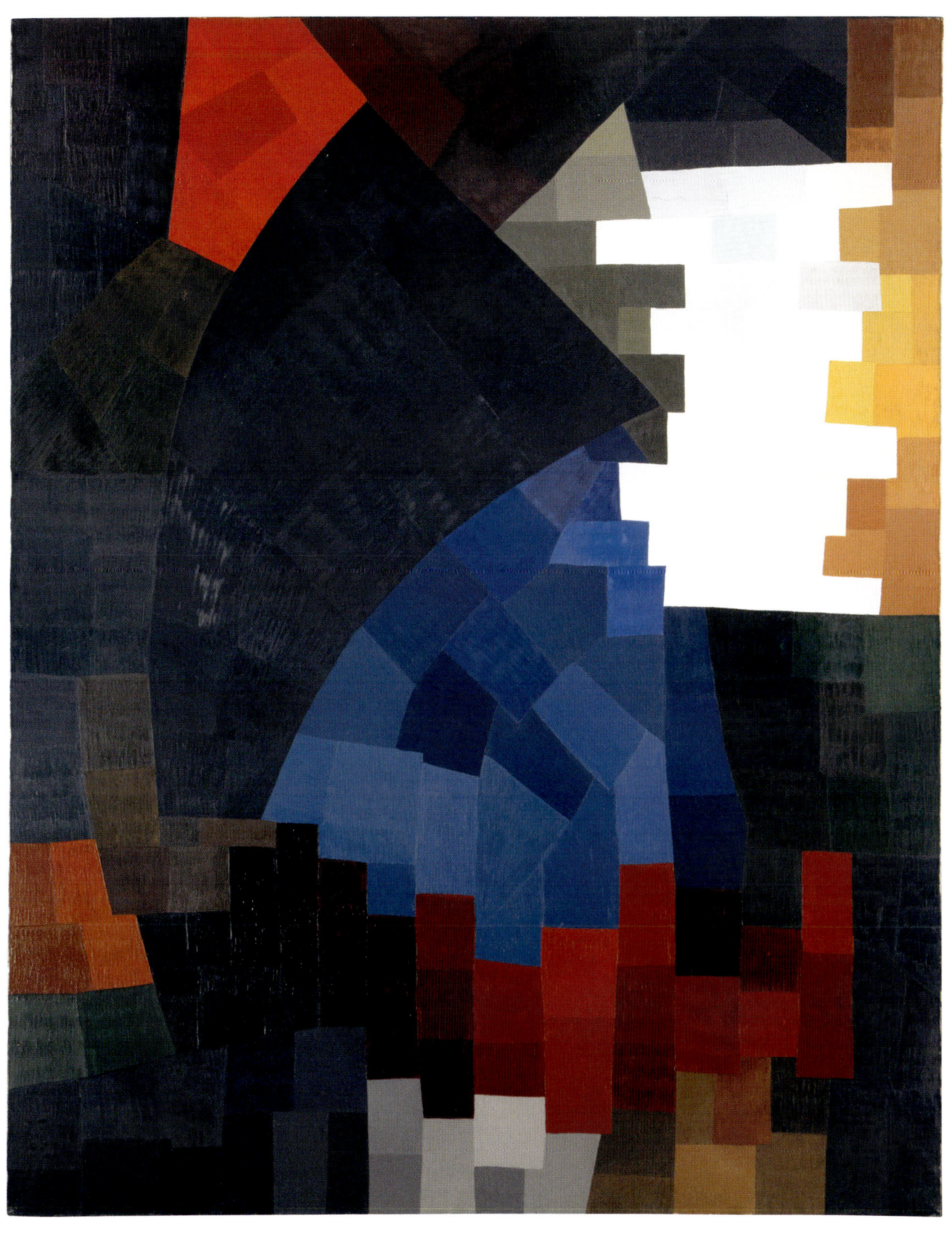

Composition, 1932
HvW 165
Oil on canvas

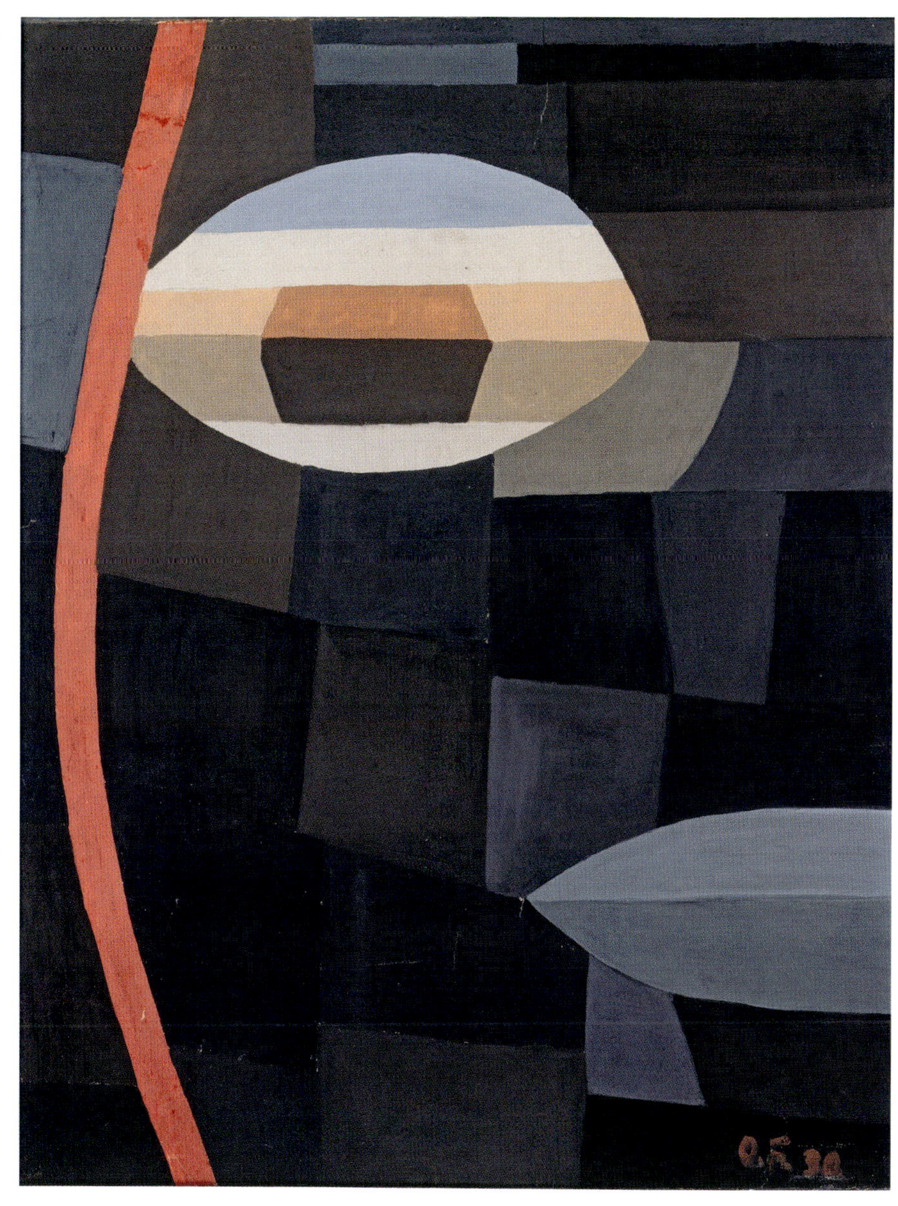

Composition, 1930
HvW 148
Gouache on paper

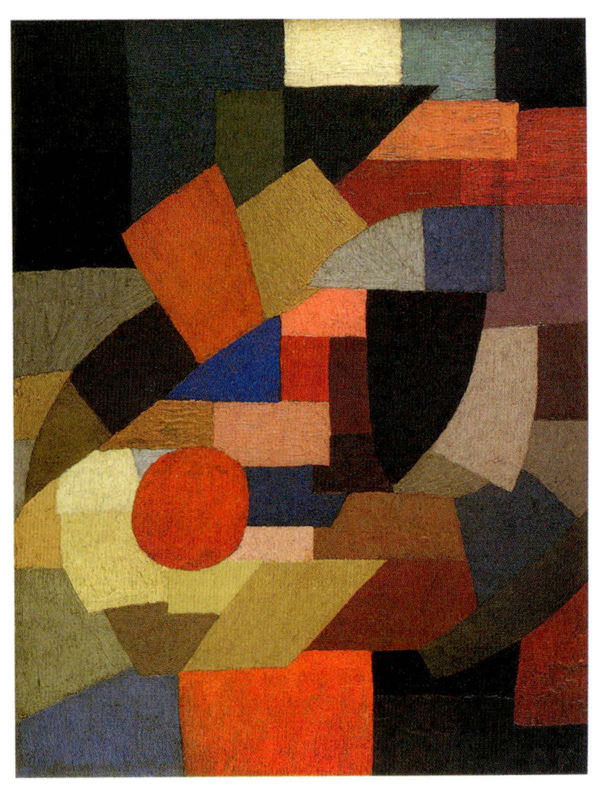

Fragments of Figures in a Context of Planes, 1927
HvW 136
Oil on canvas

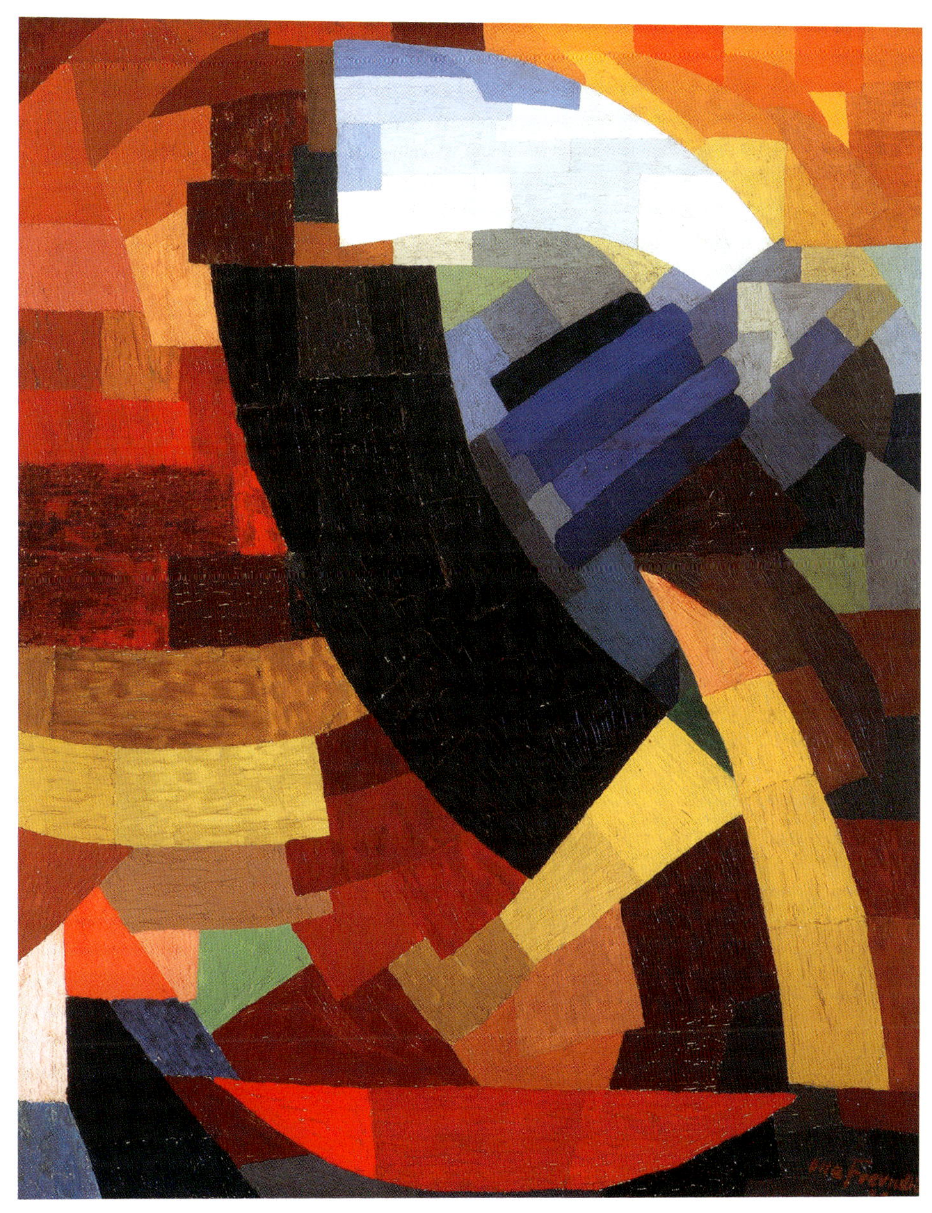

Fragments of Figures in a Context of Planes, 1928
HvW 141
Oil on canvas

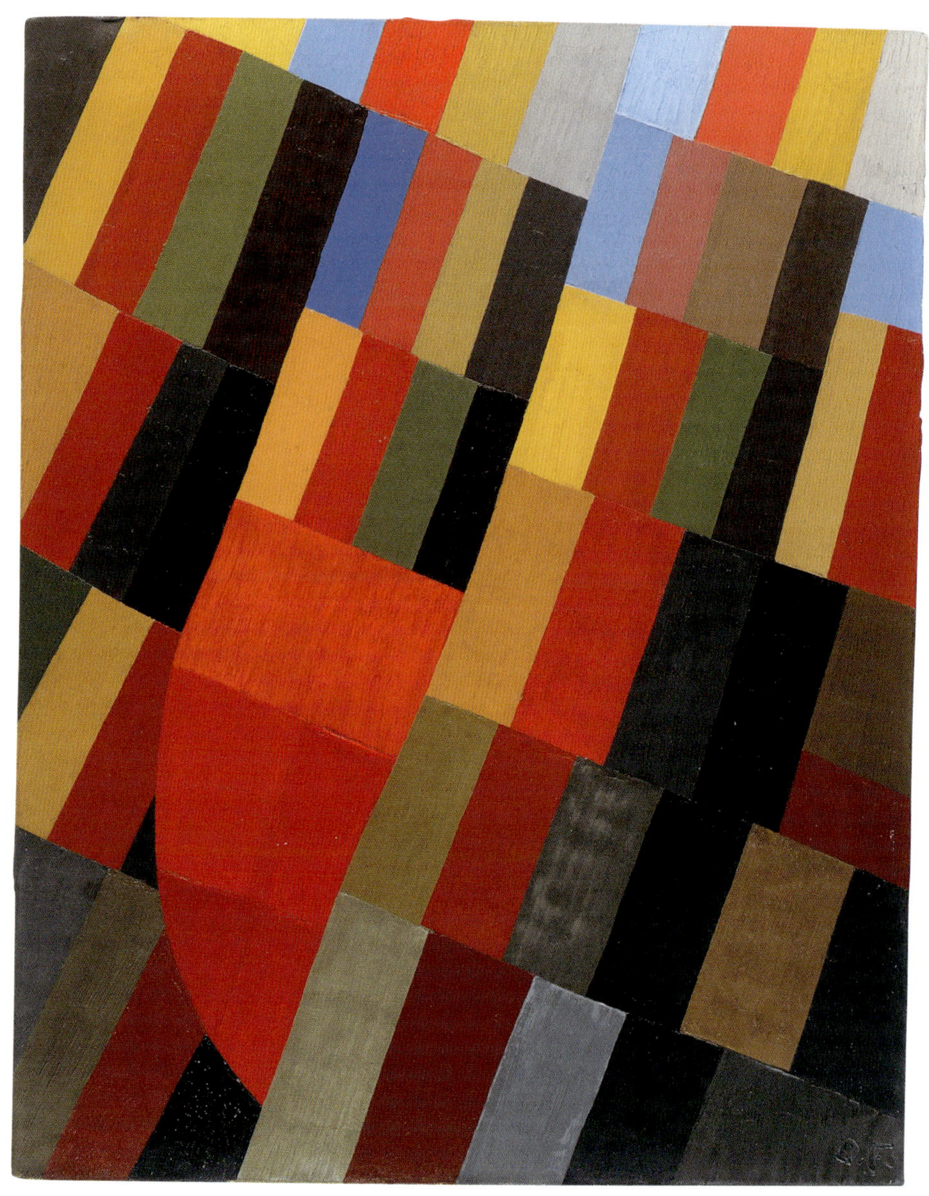

Autumnal Vision, 1935
HvW 174
Oil on canvas

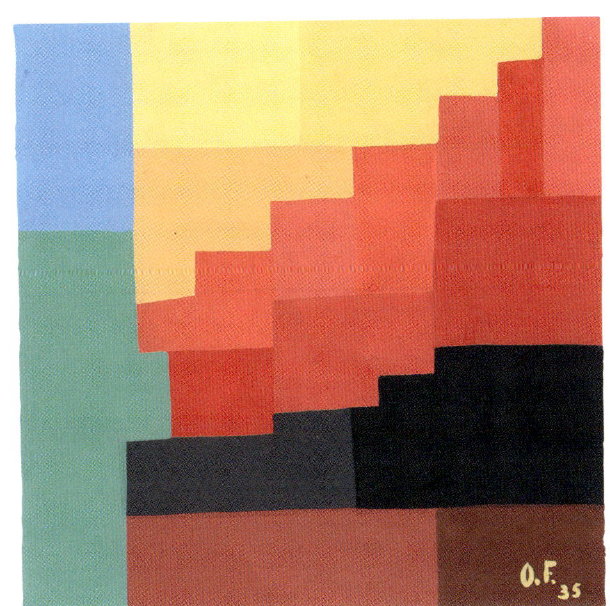

Composition, 1935
Gouache on paper

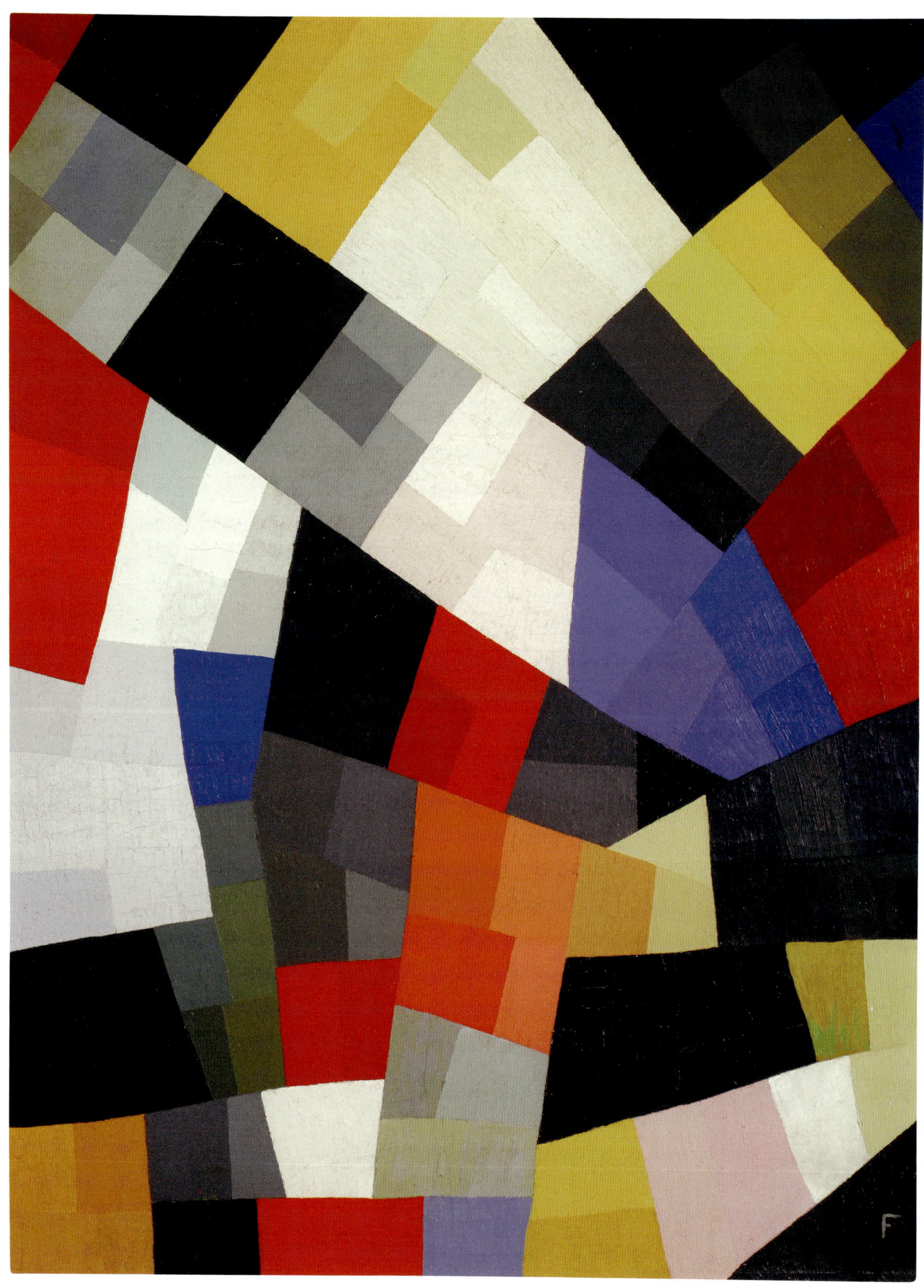

The Unity of Life and Death, 1936–38
HvW 185
Oil on canvas

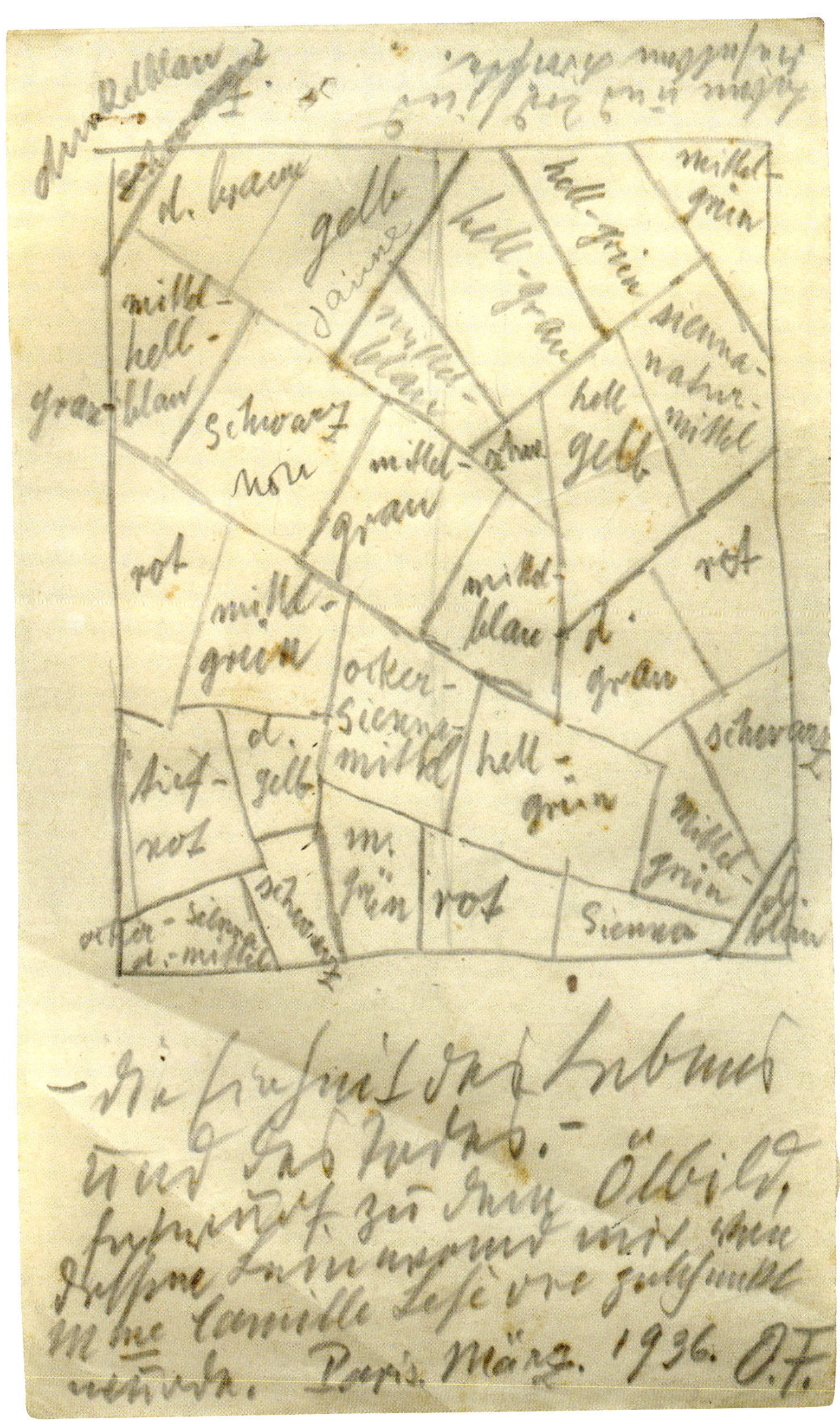

Sketch for the painting The Unity of Life and Death, 1936
Pencil on paper

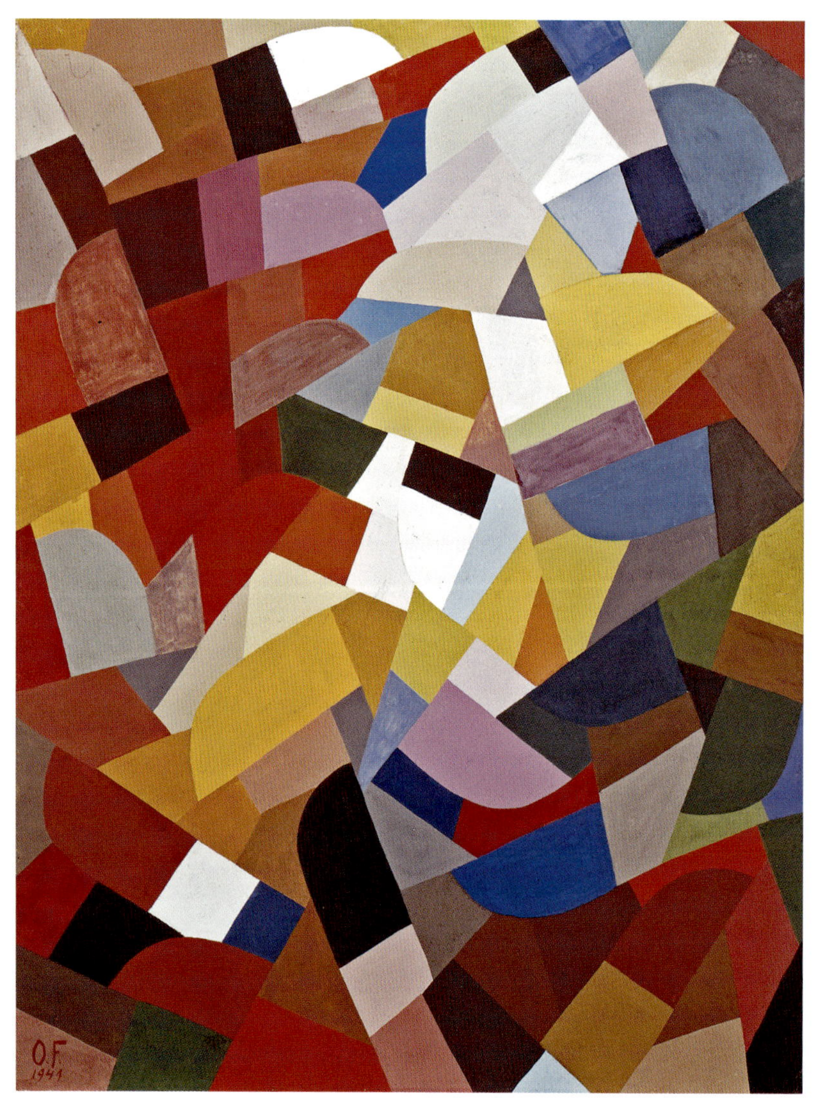

Composition, 1941
HvW 207
Tempera on cardboard

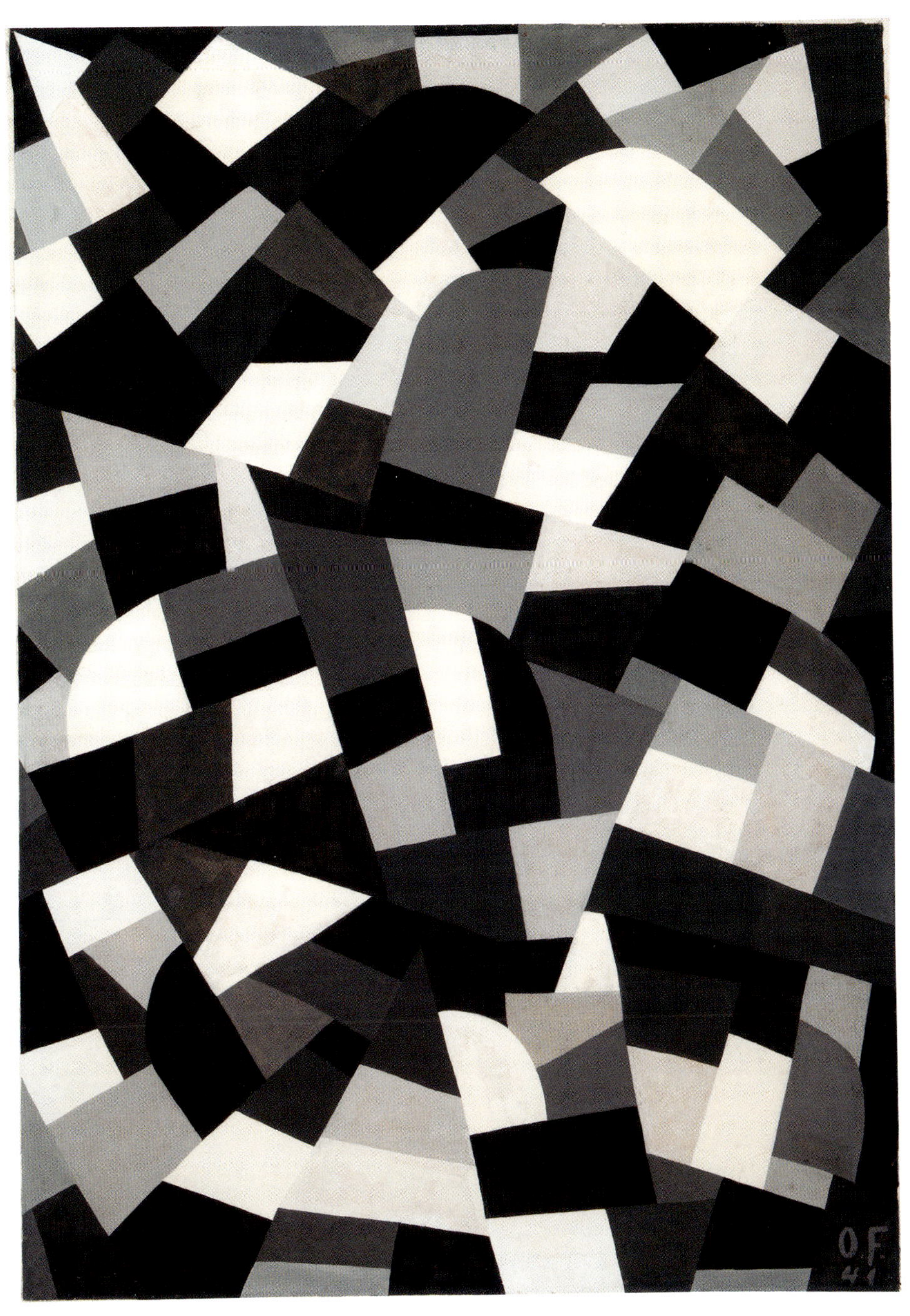

Composition, 1941
HvW 208
Gouache on paper

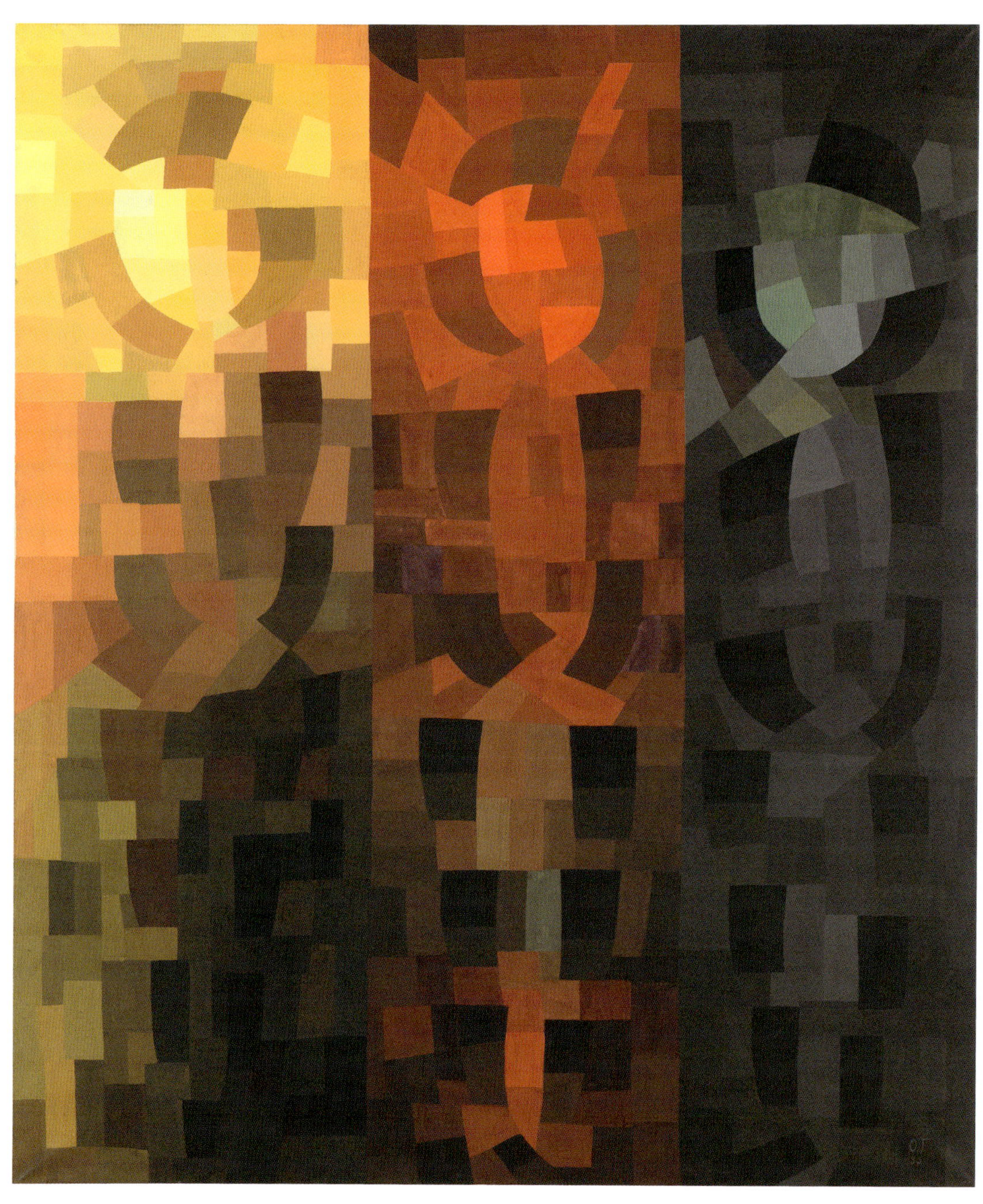

Homage to the Peoples of Color, 1935
HvW 178
Gouache on paper on canvas

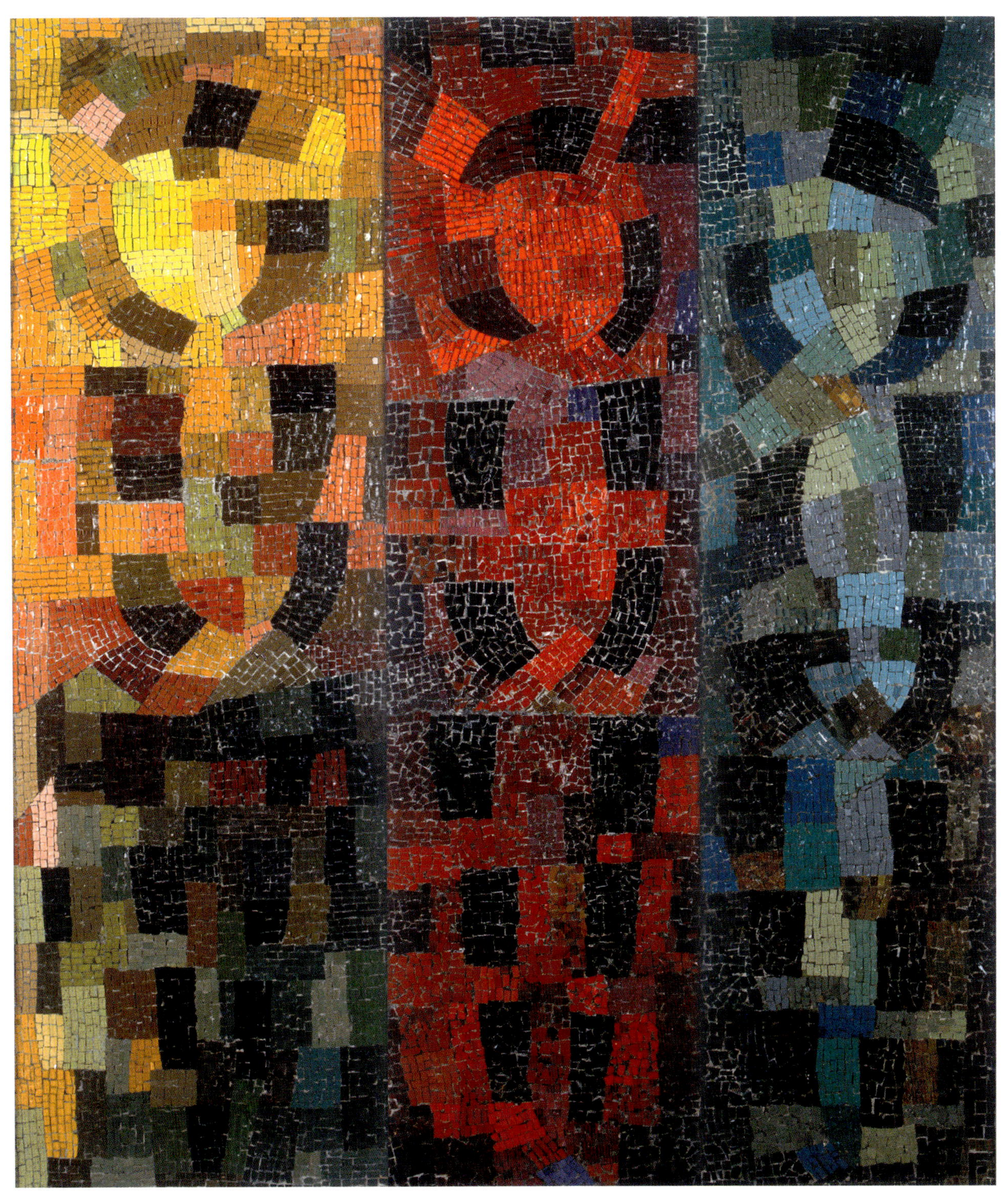

Homage to the Peoples of Color, 1938
HvW 36
Three-part mosaic

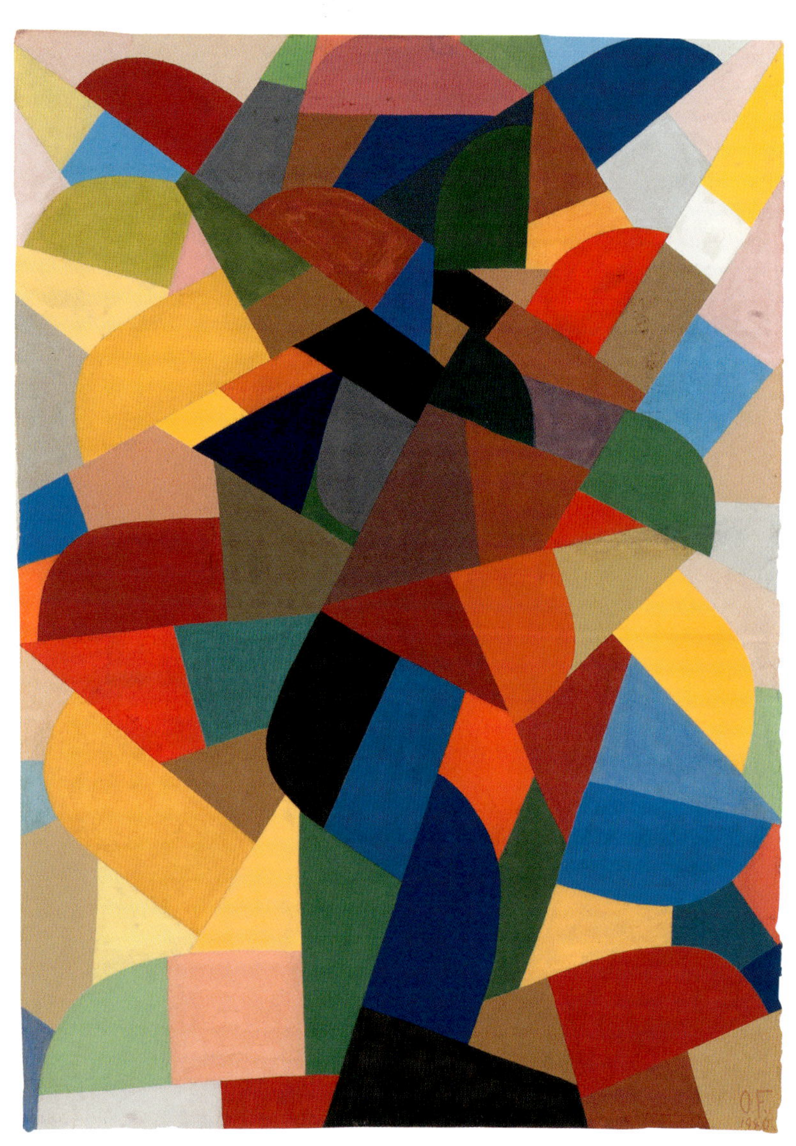

Composition, 1940
HvW 200
Gouache on paper

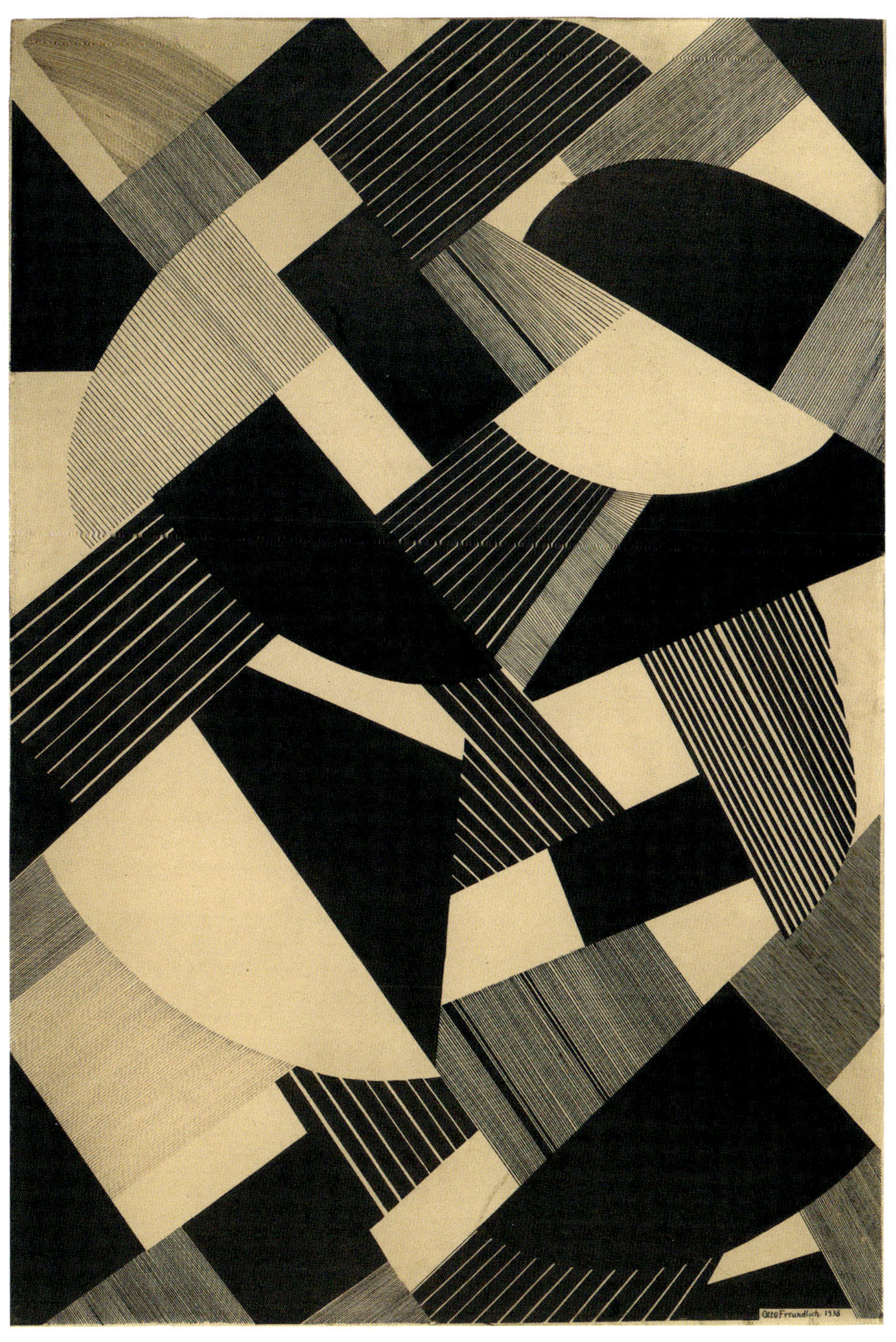

Composition/Geometric Abstraction, 1938
HvW 376
Ink on paper

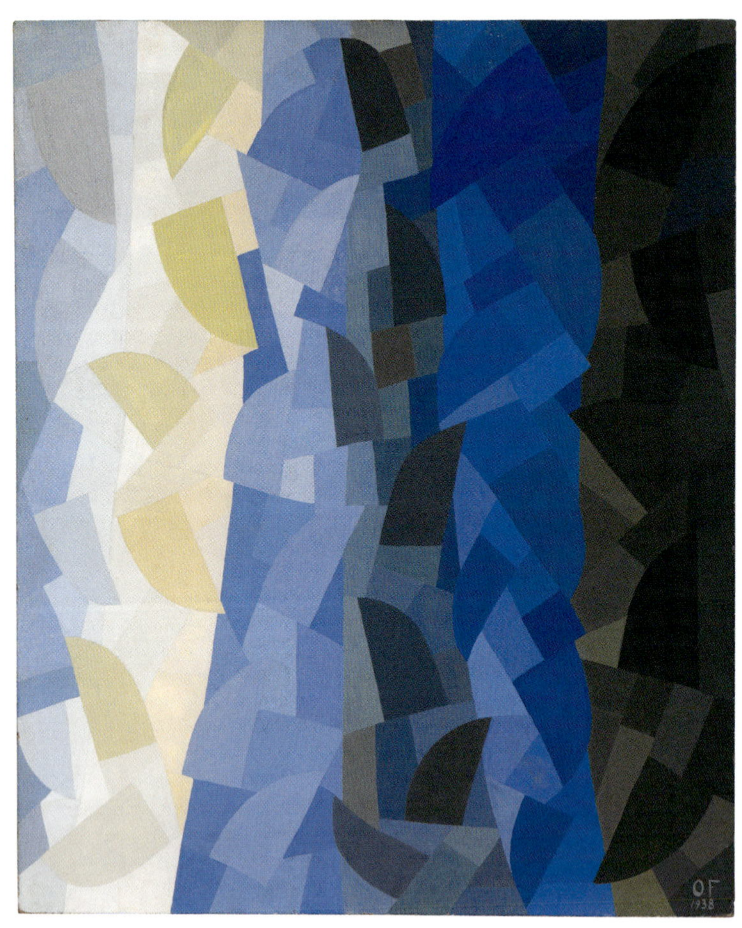

Composition, 1938
HvW 195
Tempera on cardboard

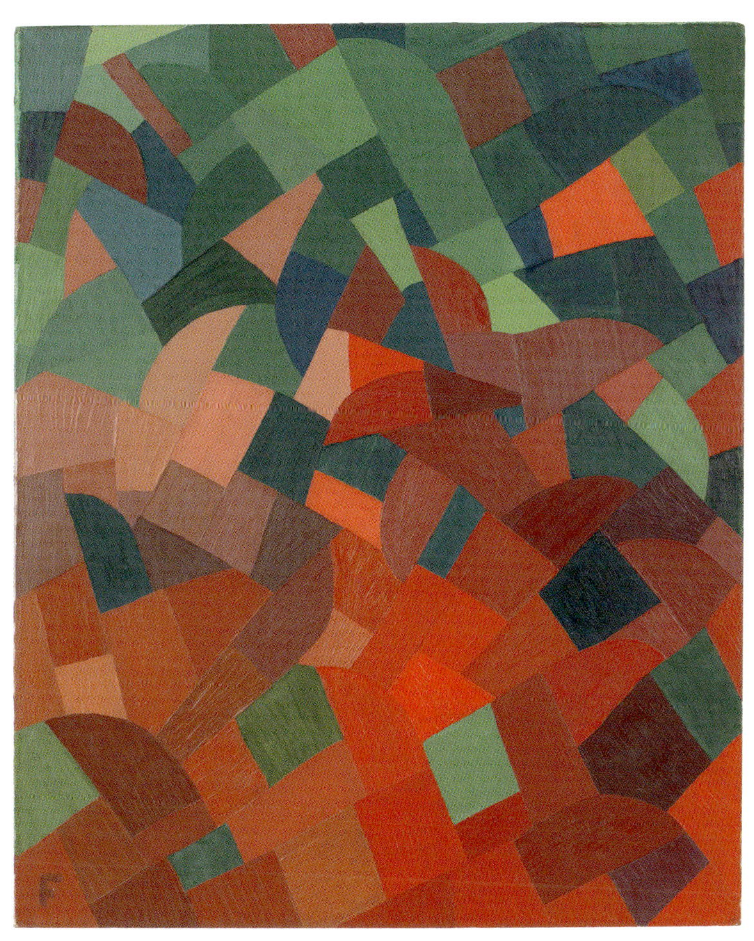

Composition Red-Green, 1939
HvW 199
Oil on canvas

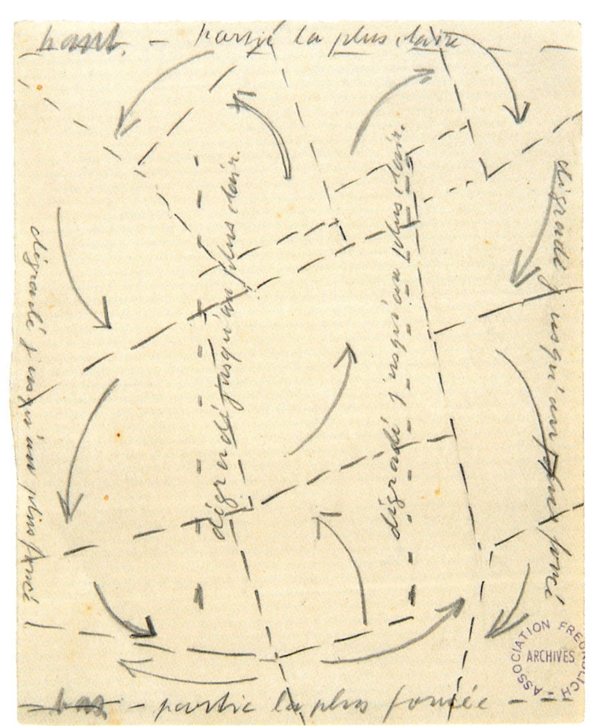

Composition, ca. 1934
HvW 340
Pencil on paper

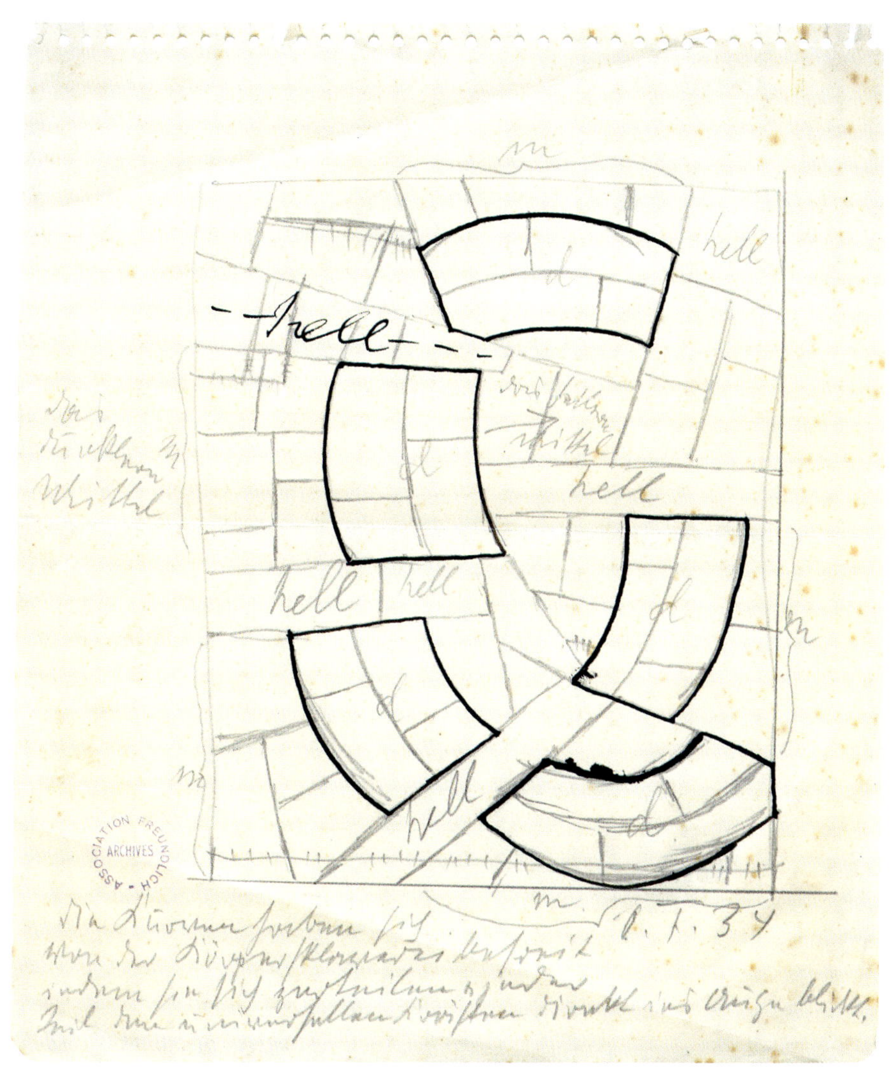

Composition, 1934
HvW 347
Pencil and ink on sketching paper

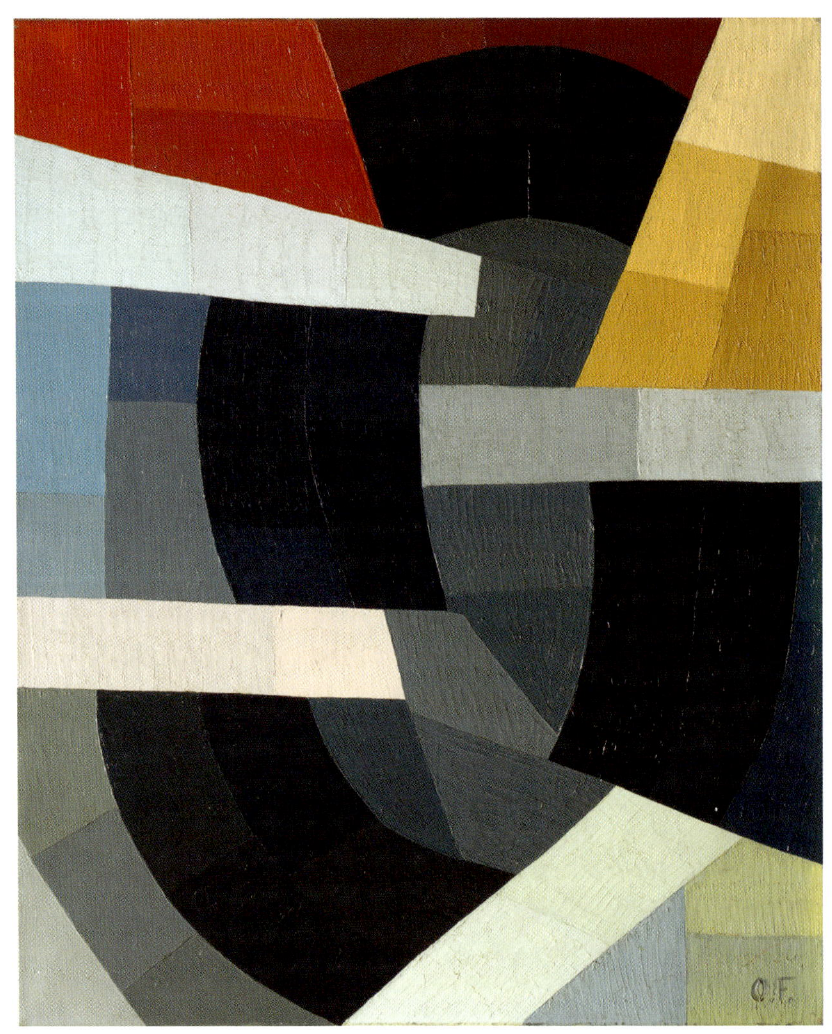

Forces, 1934
HvW 172
Oil on canvas

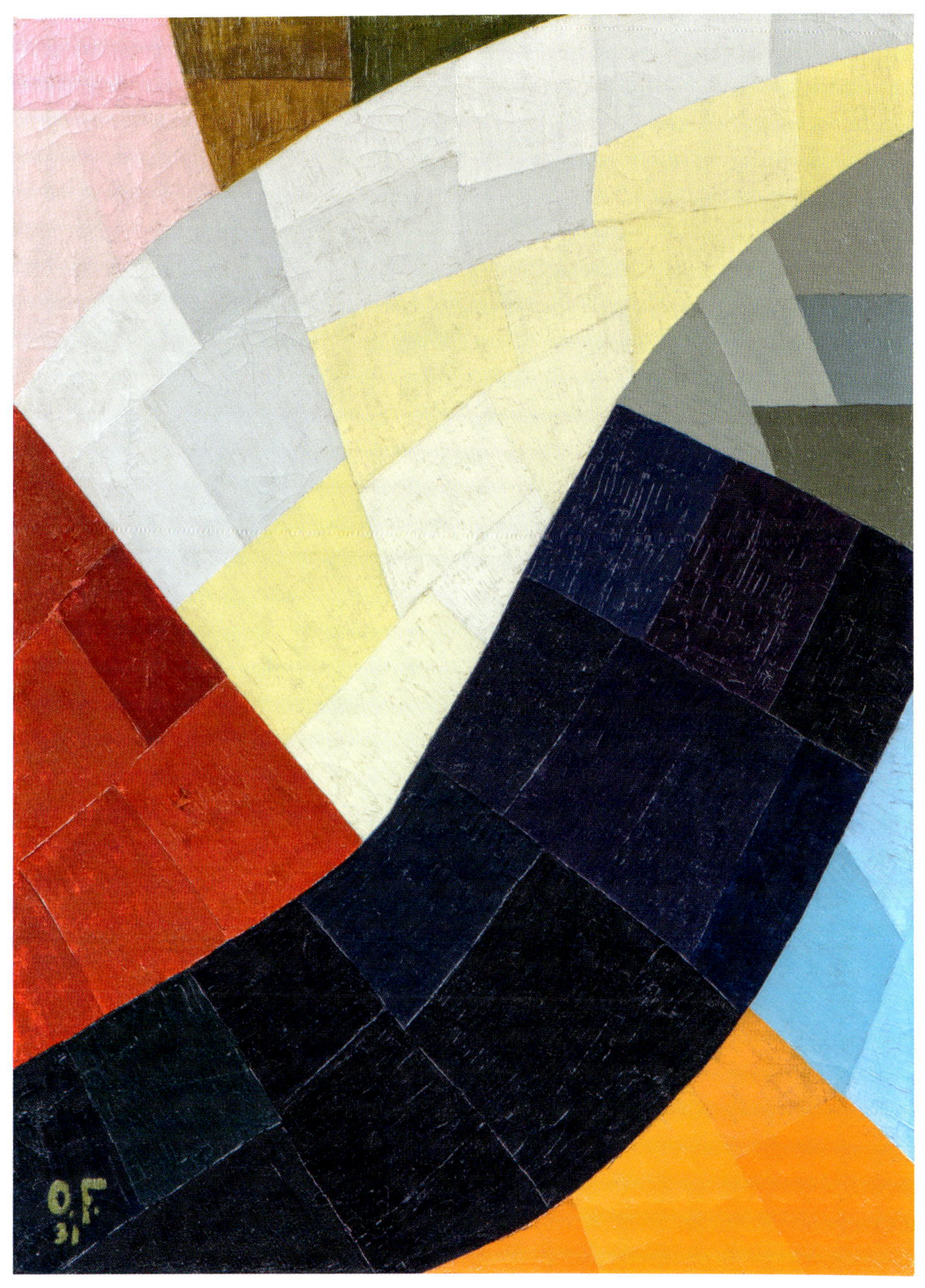

Composition, 1931
HvW 159
Oil on canvas

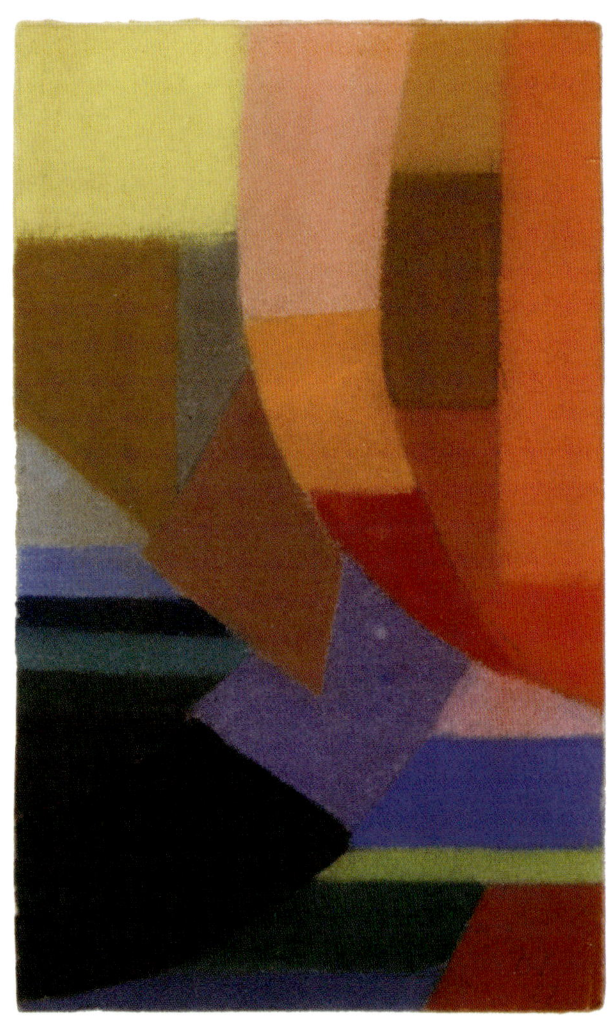

Composition, 1927
HvW 236
Pastel on paper

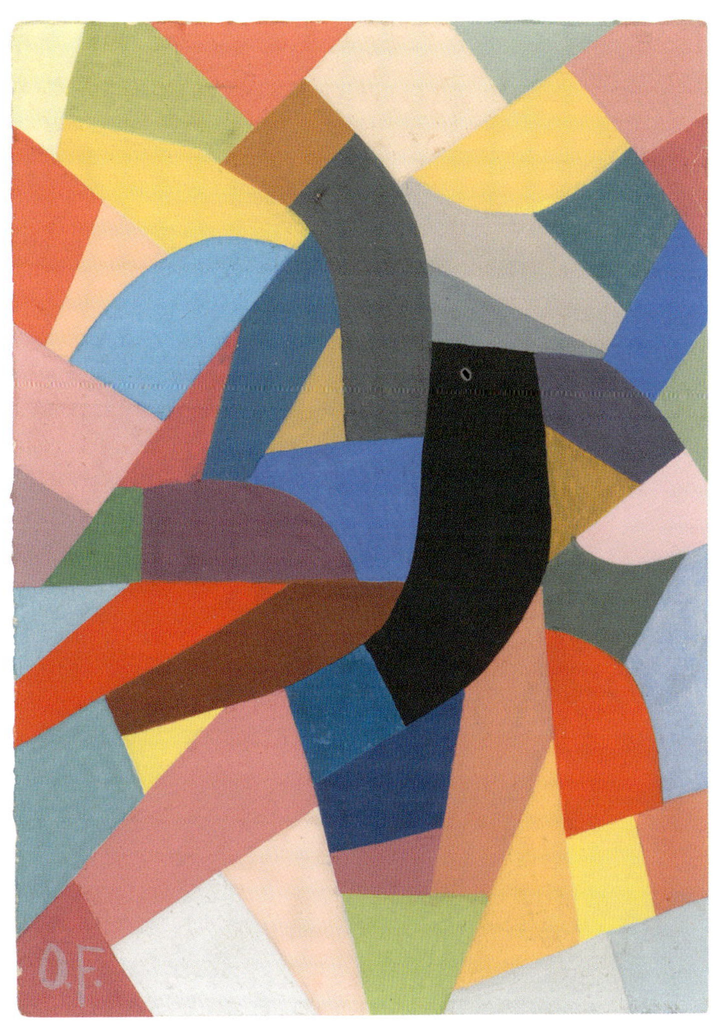

Composition around Two Planes in Black and Gray, 1942
Opaque paint on cardboard

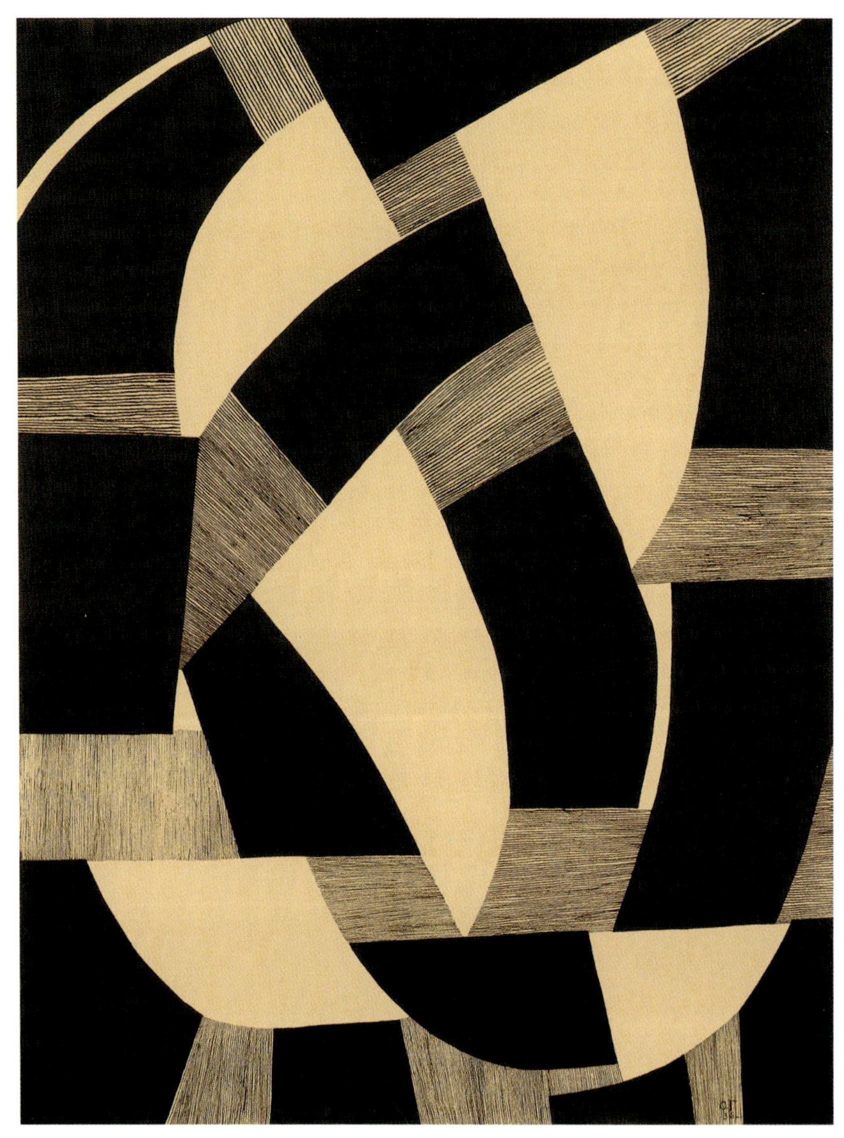

Composition, 1936
HvW 363
Ink on paper

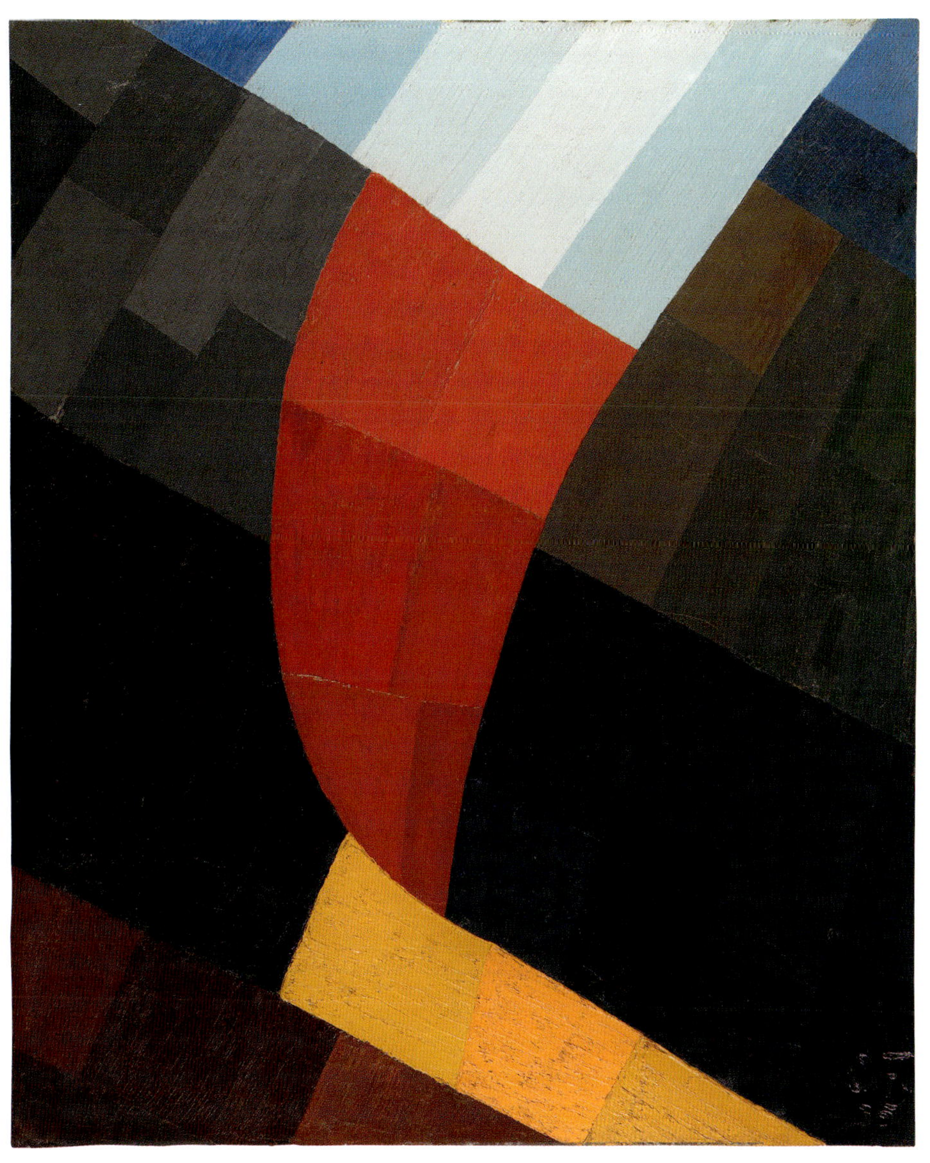

Composition, 1935
HvW 176
Oil on canvas

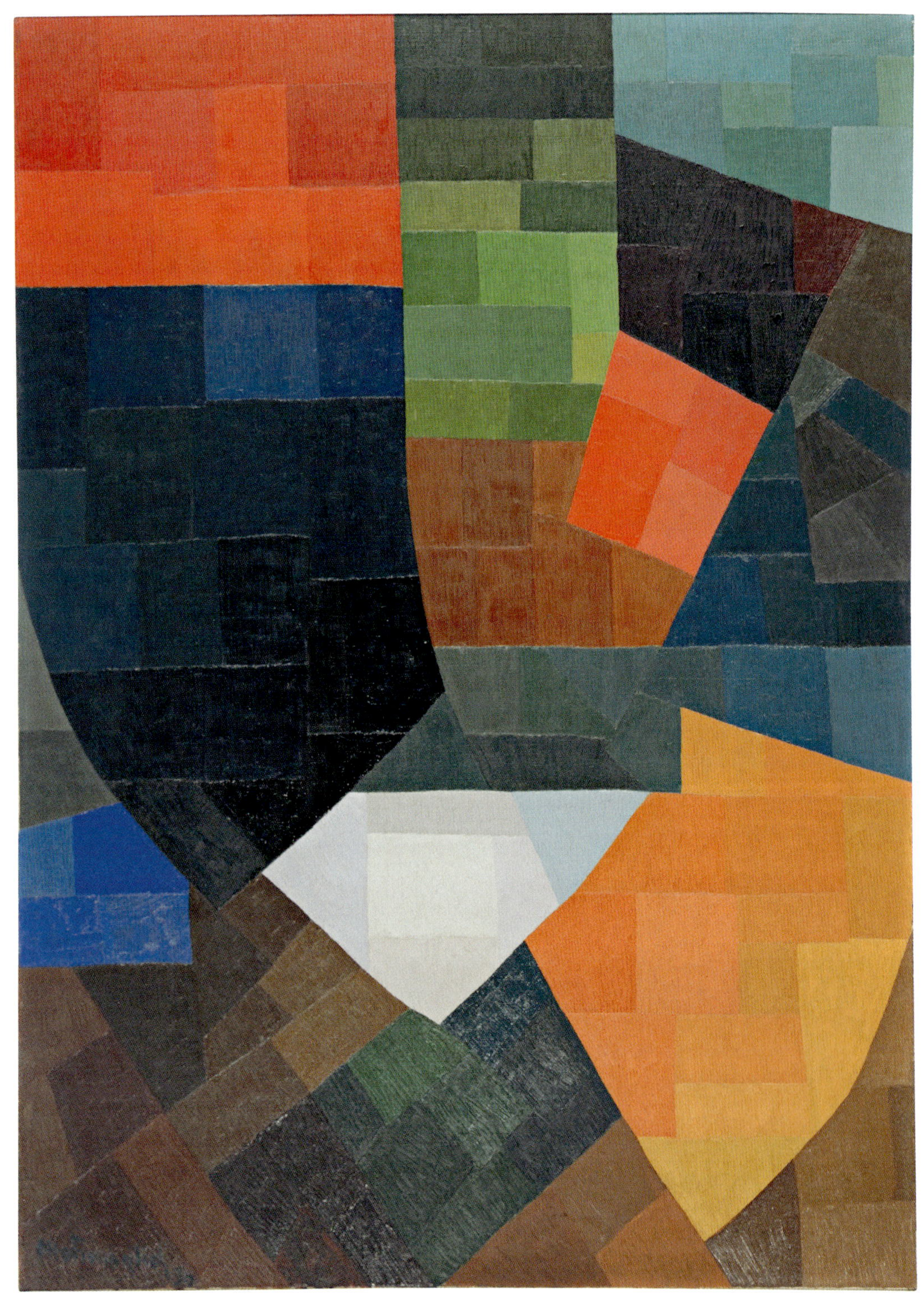

Composition, 1930
HvW 154
Oil on canvas

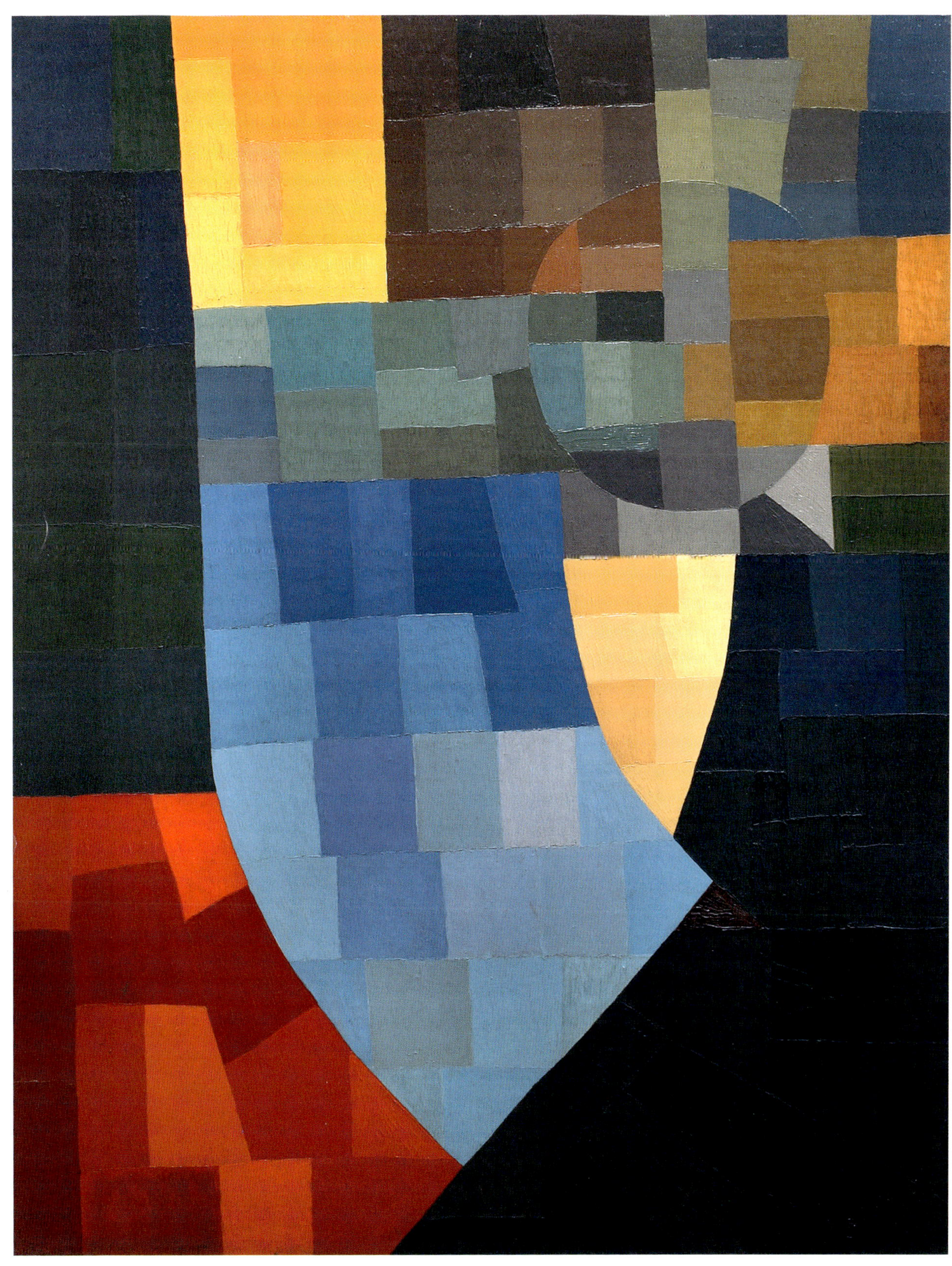

Composition, 1930
HvW 151
Oil on canvas, mounted on plywood

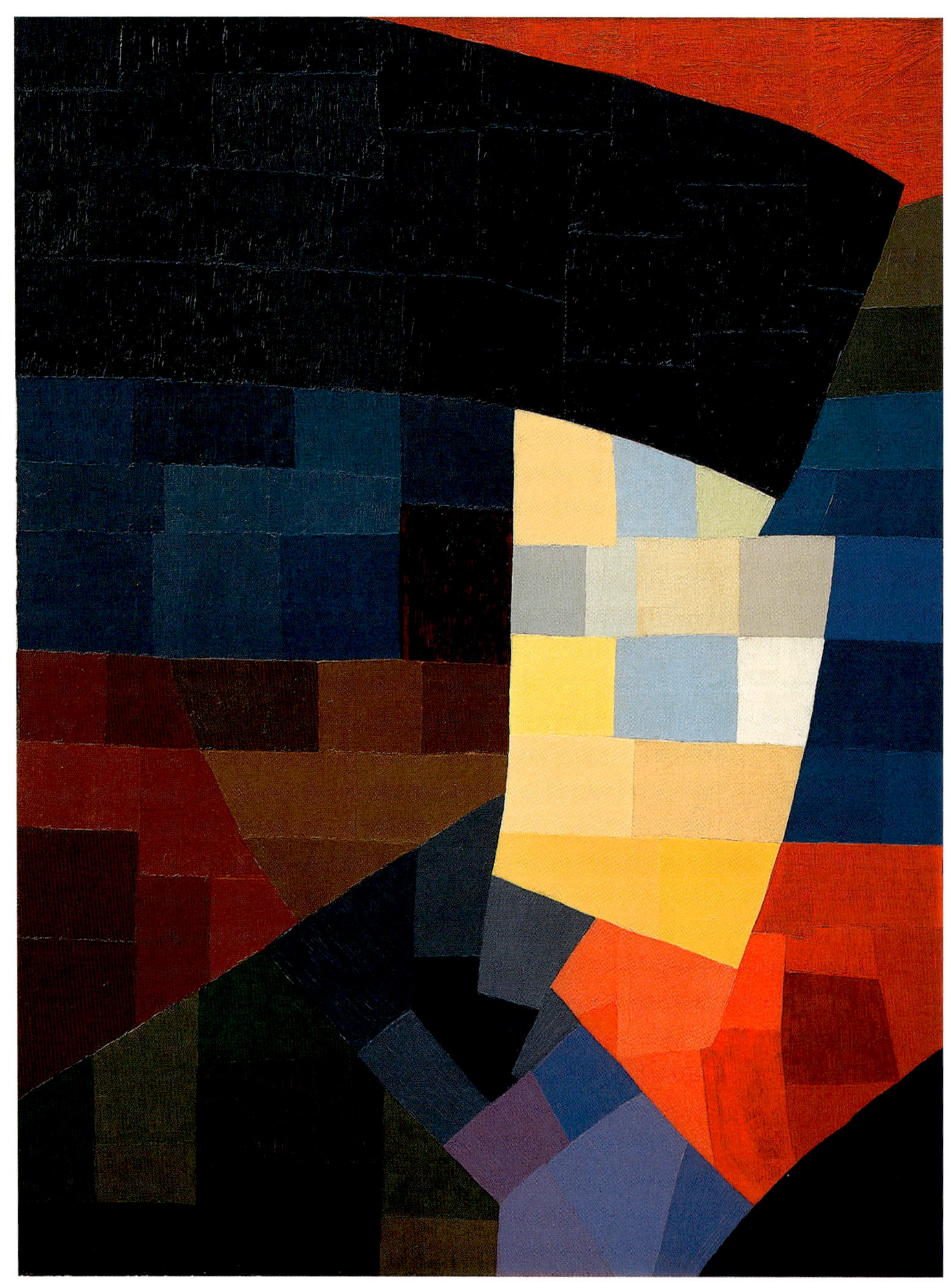

Composition, 1930
HvW 152
Oil on canvas

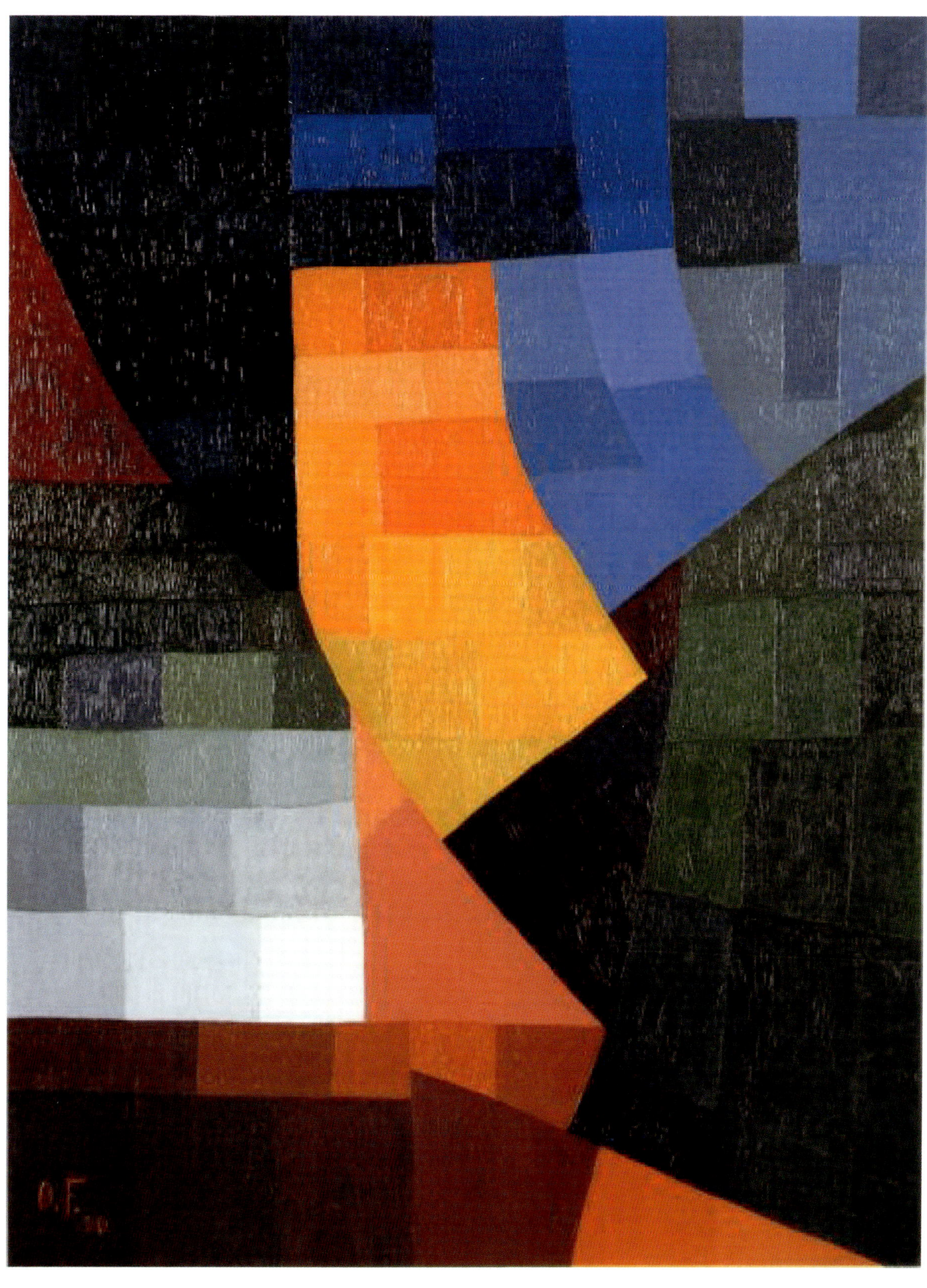

Composition, 1930
HvW 149
Oil on canvas

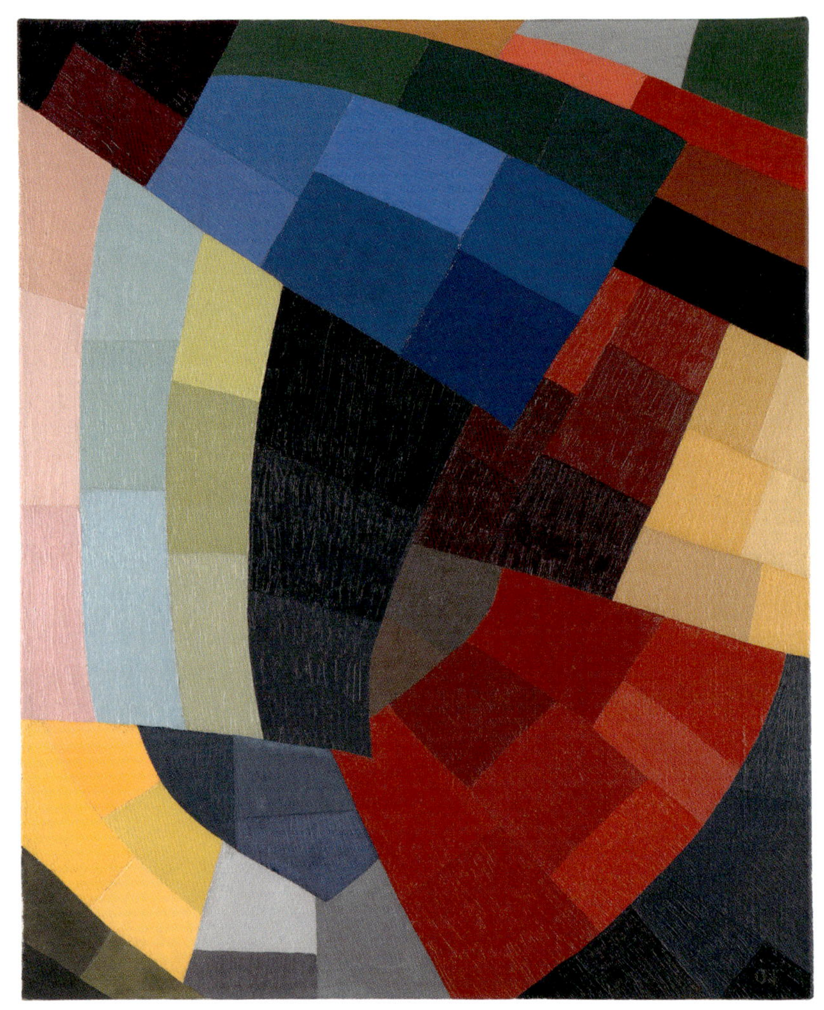

Composition, 1932
HvW 167
Oil on canvas

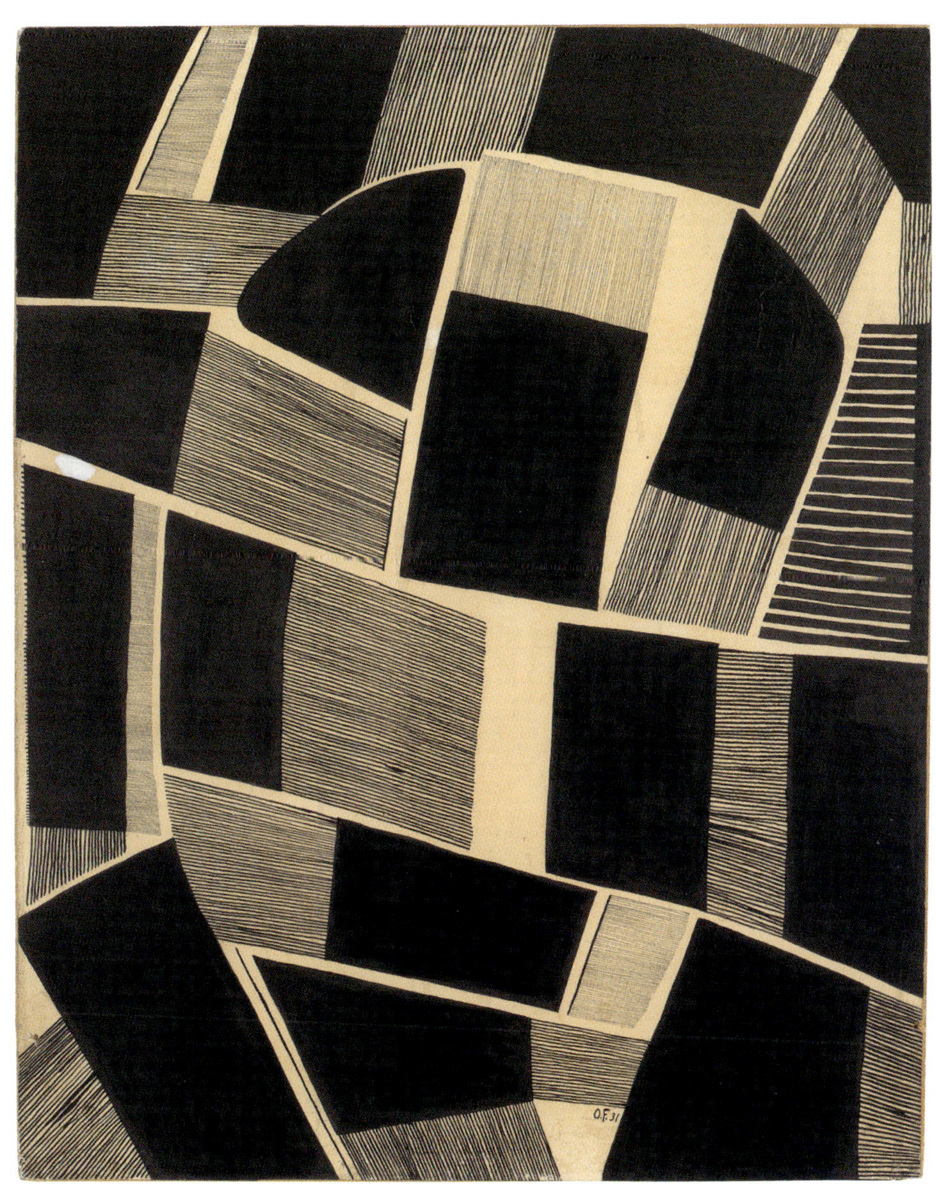

Composition in Black and White, 1931
HvW 322
Ink on cardboard

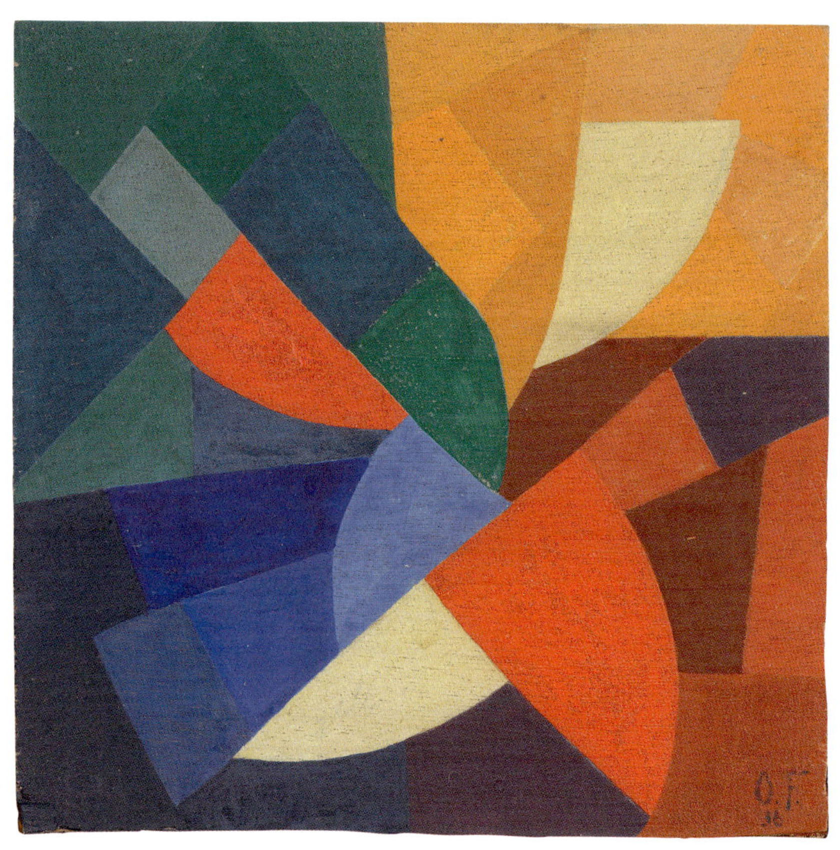

Composition, 1936
HvW 181
Tempera on wood

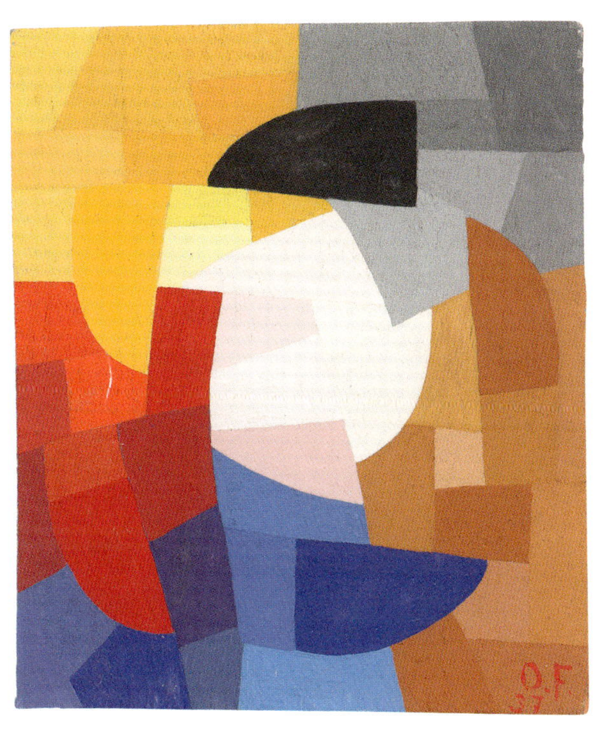

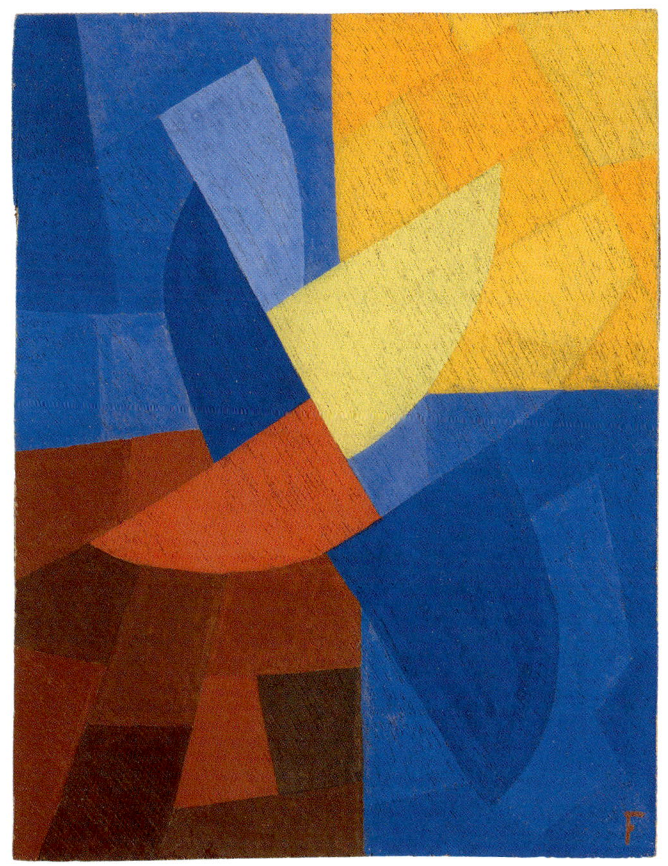

Composition, 1937
Tempera on wood

Composition, ca. 1932
HvW 166
Tempera on wood

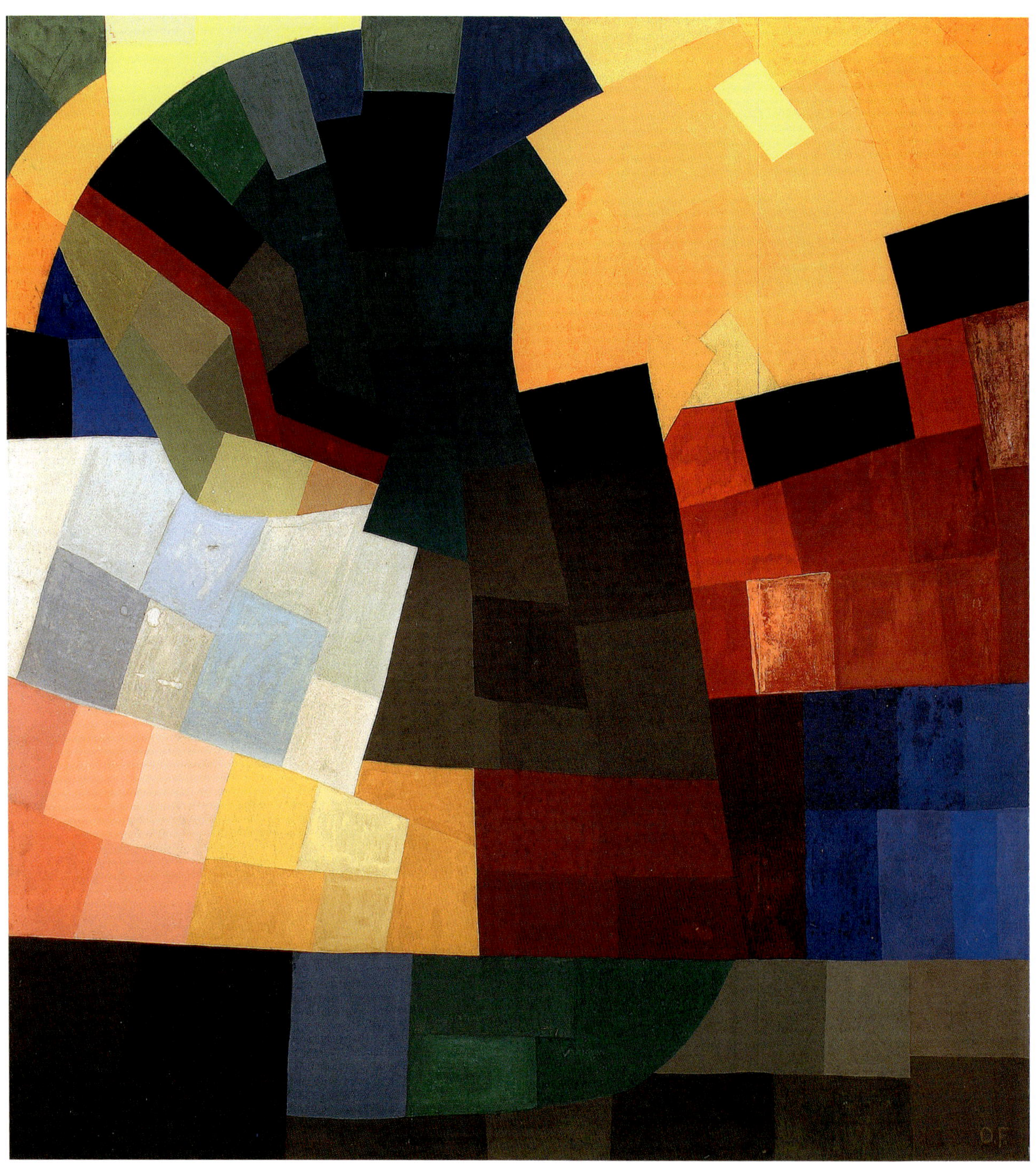

Composition, 1935
HvW 179
Gouache on paper on plywood

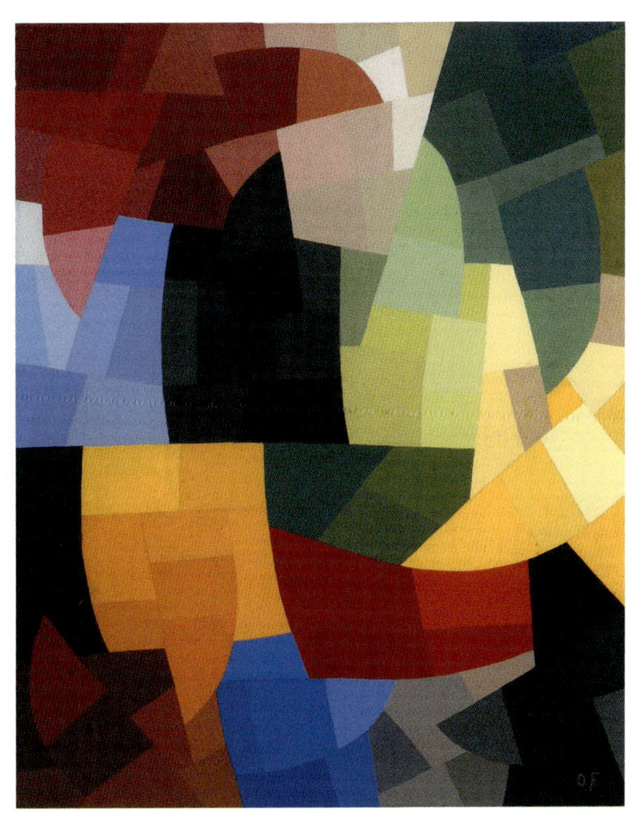

Composition, 1939
HvW 196
Gouache on paper

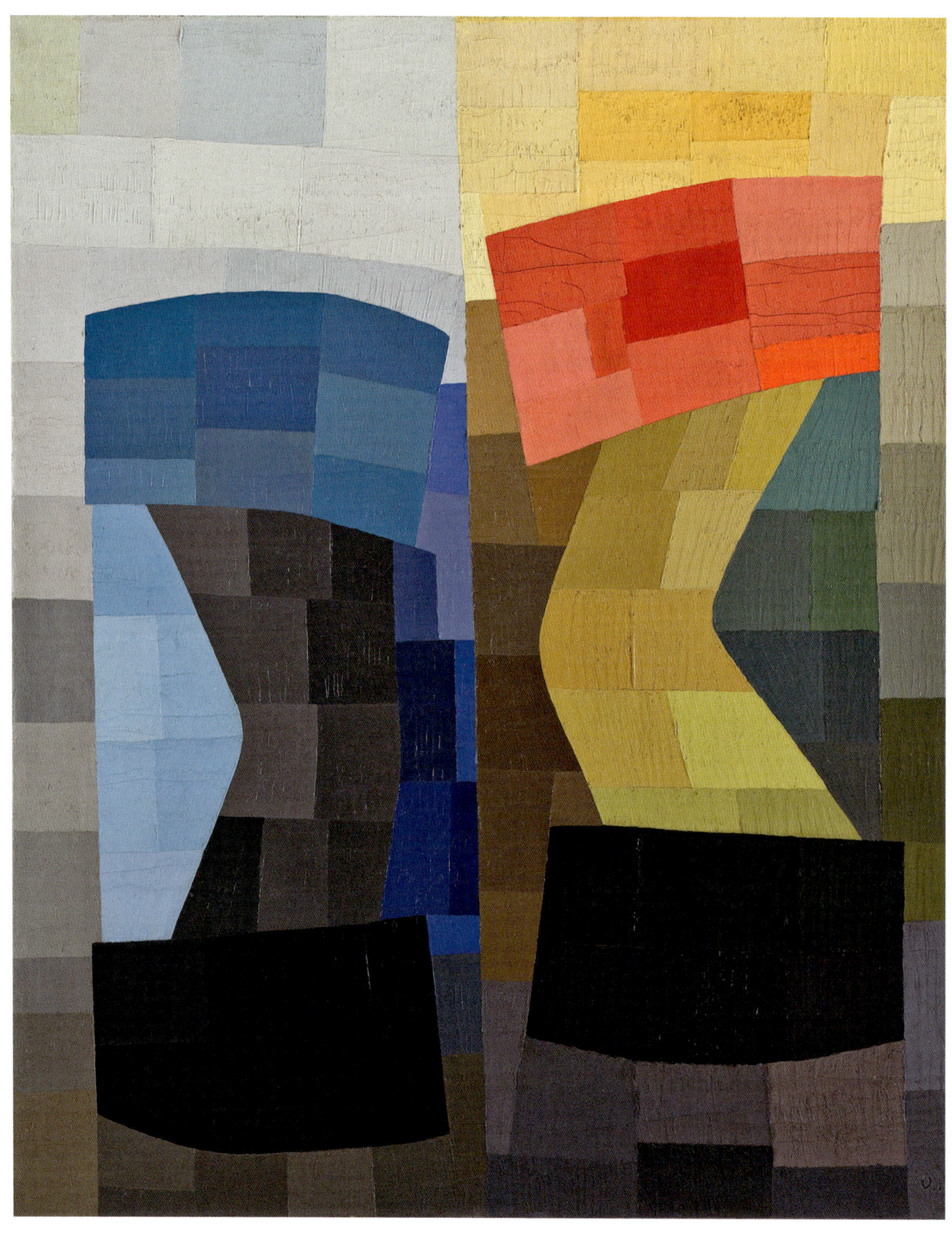

Two Motifs, 1934
HvW 173
Oil on canvas

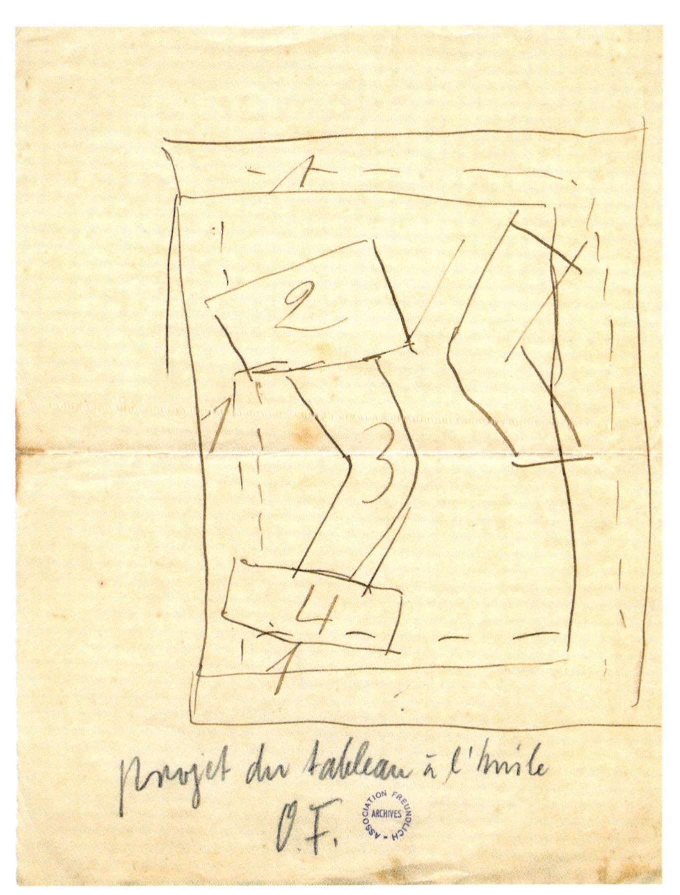

Composition, 1934
HvW 343
Pen on paper

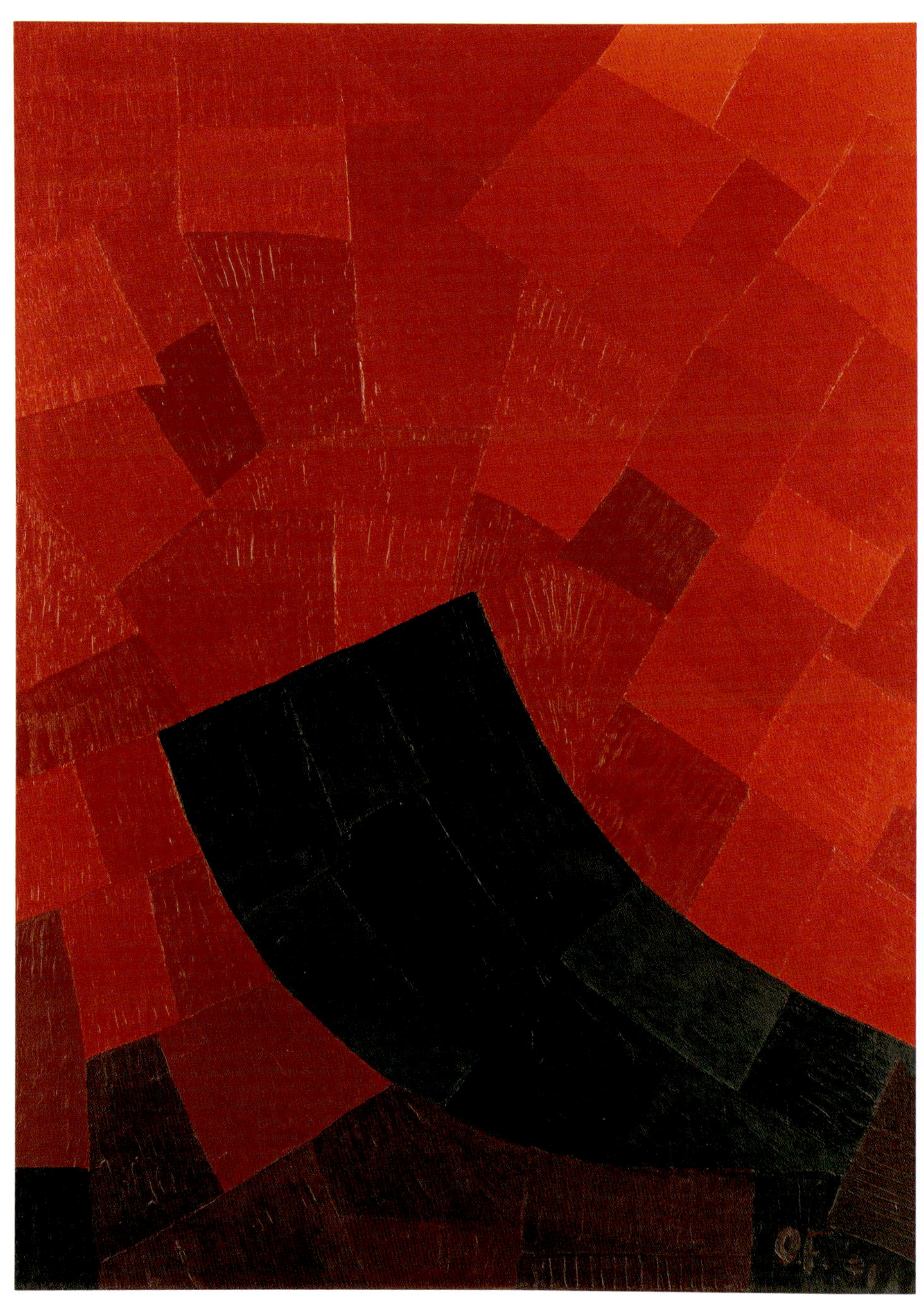

Composition in Red, 1931
HvW 162
Oil on canvas

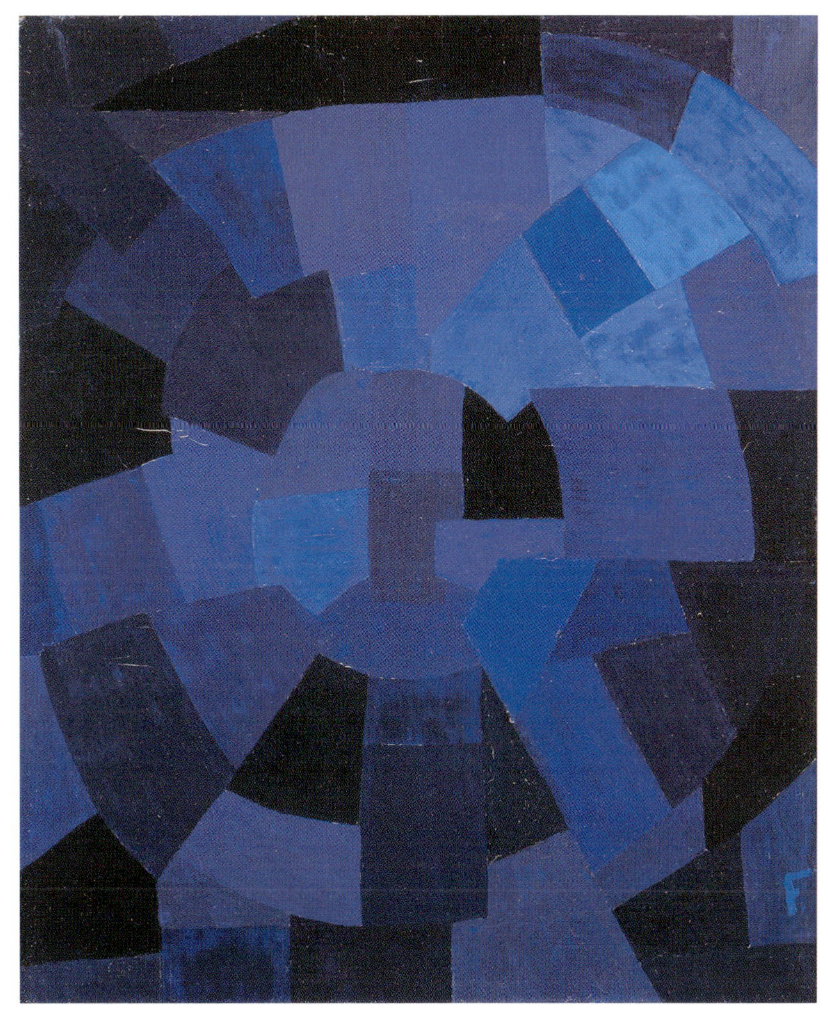

Composition in Blue, 1931
HvW 161
Oil on canvas

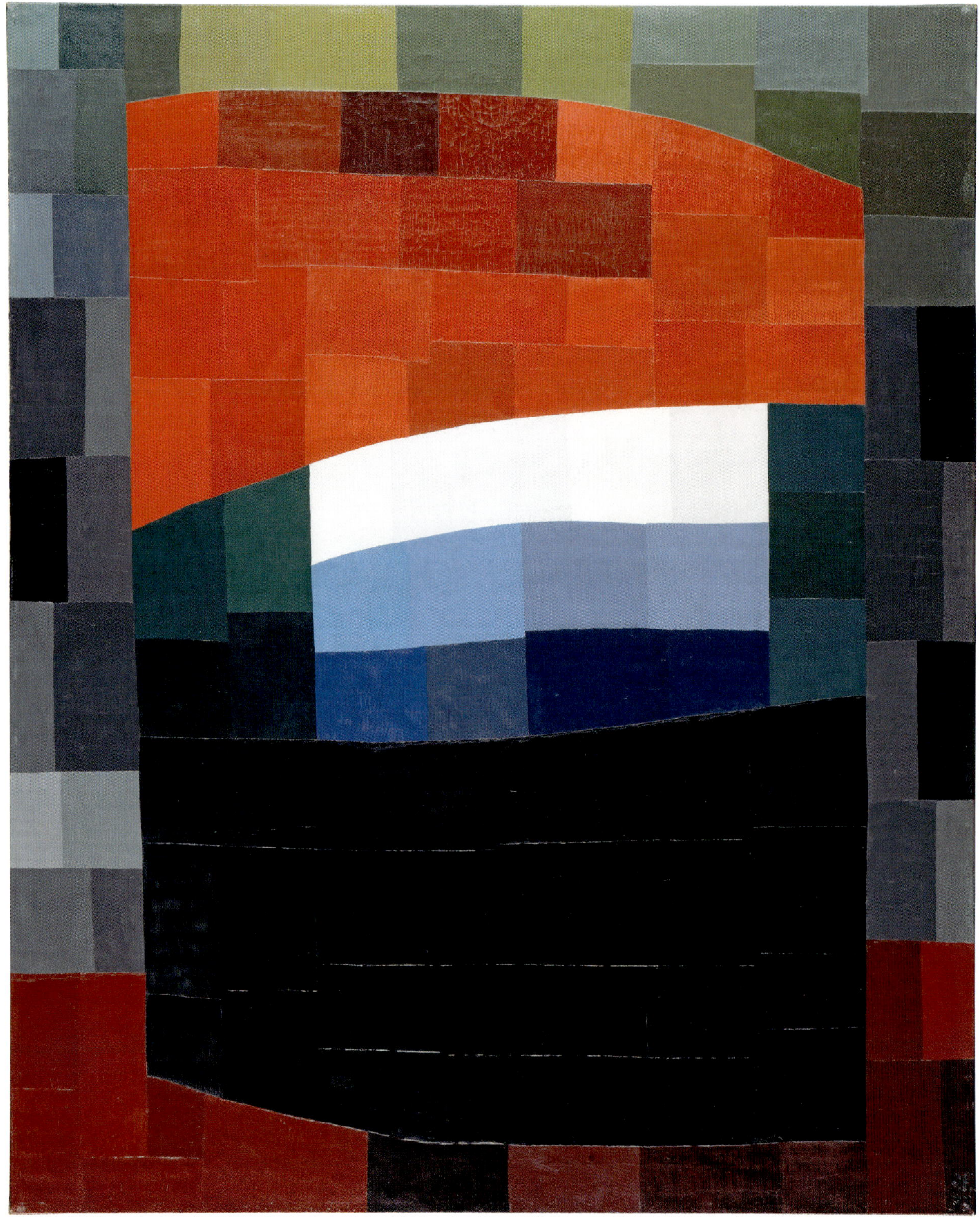

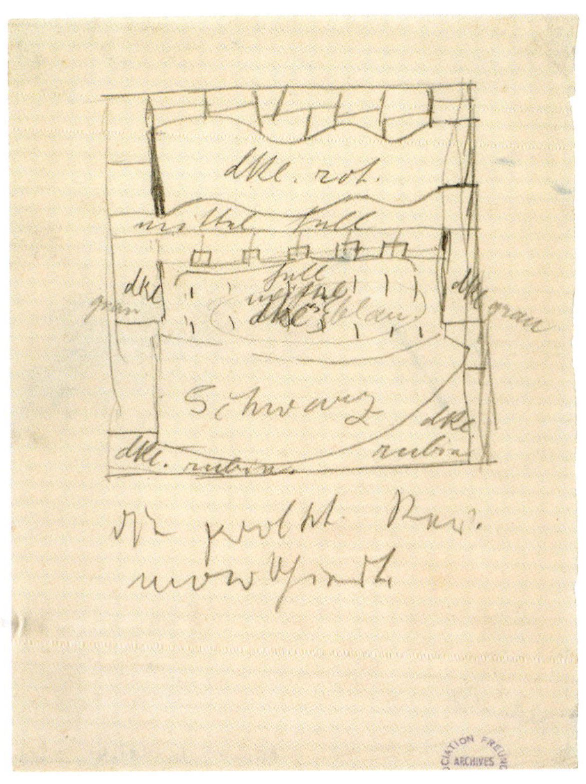

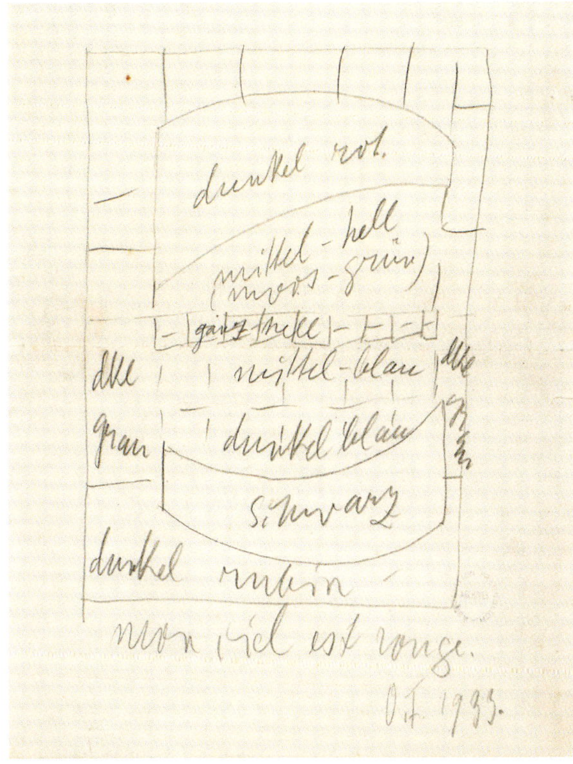

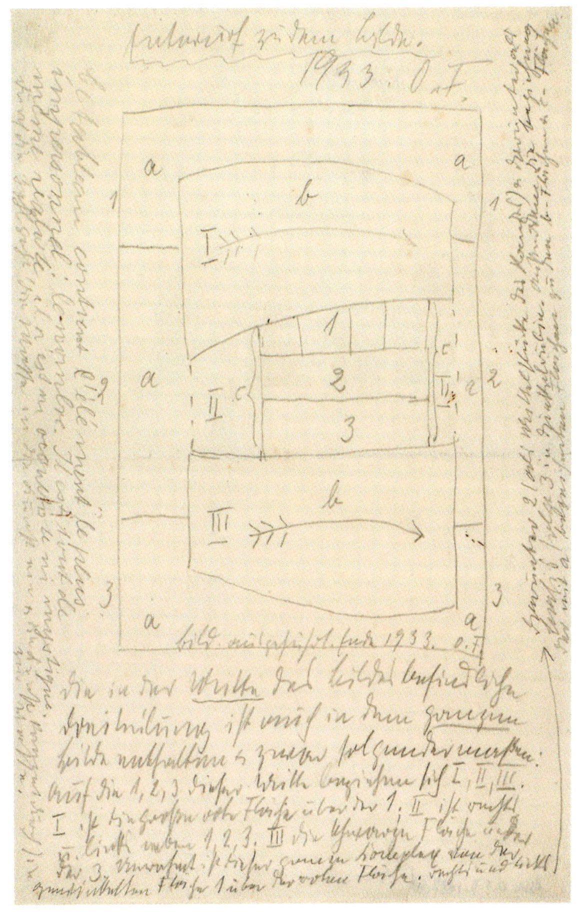

My Sky is Red, 1933
HvW 168
Oil on canvas

My Sky is Red, 1933
HvW 336
Pencil on Ingres paper

My Sky is Red, 1933
HvW 337
Pencil on Ingres paper

My Sky is Red, 1933
HvW 338
Pencil on Ingres paper

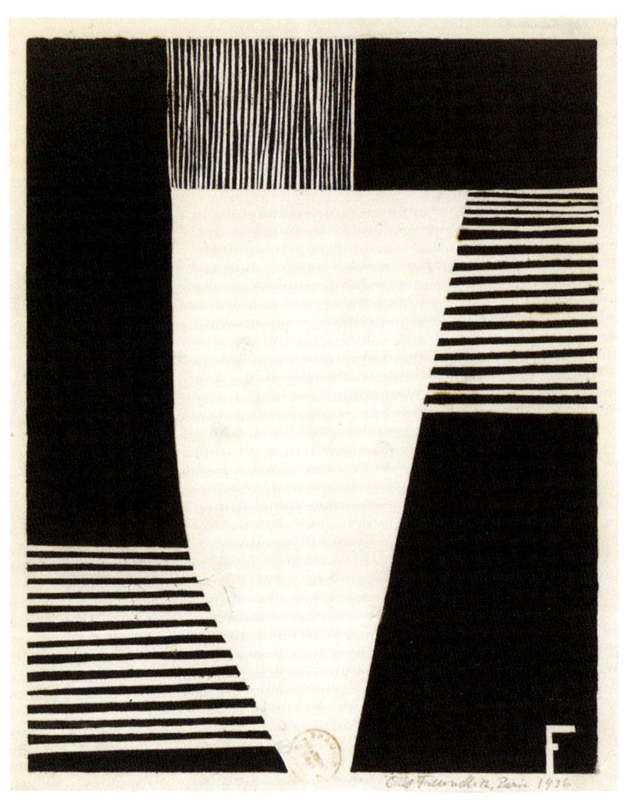

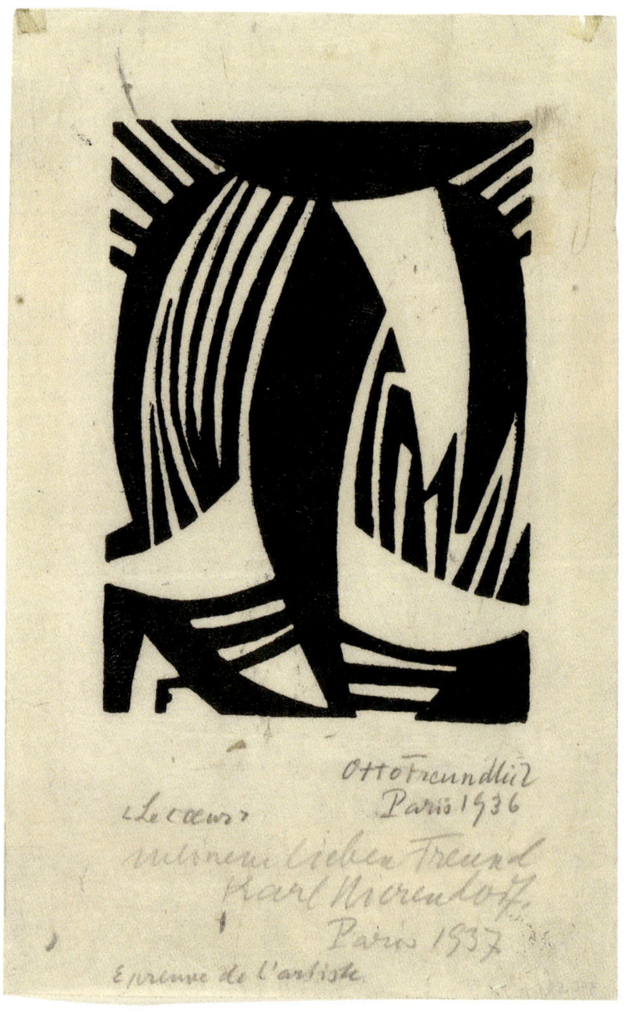

Composition, 1936
HvW 471
Woodcut on laid paper

The Heart, 1936
HvW 477
Linocut on Japanese paper

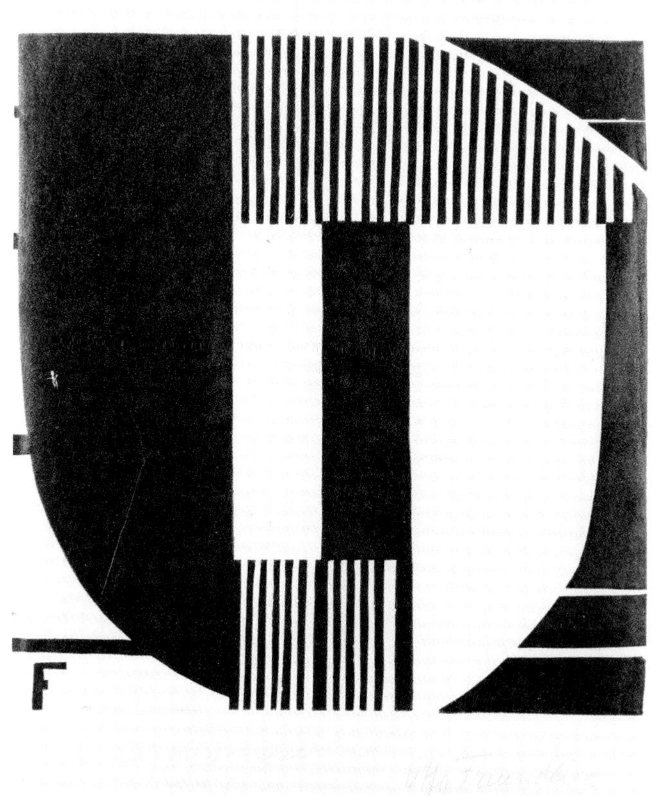

Composition, 1937
HvW 473
Linocut on Japanese paper

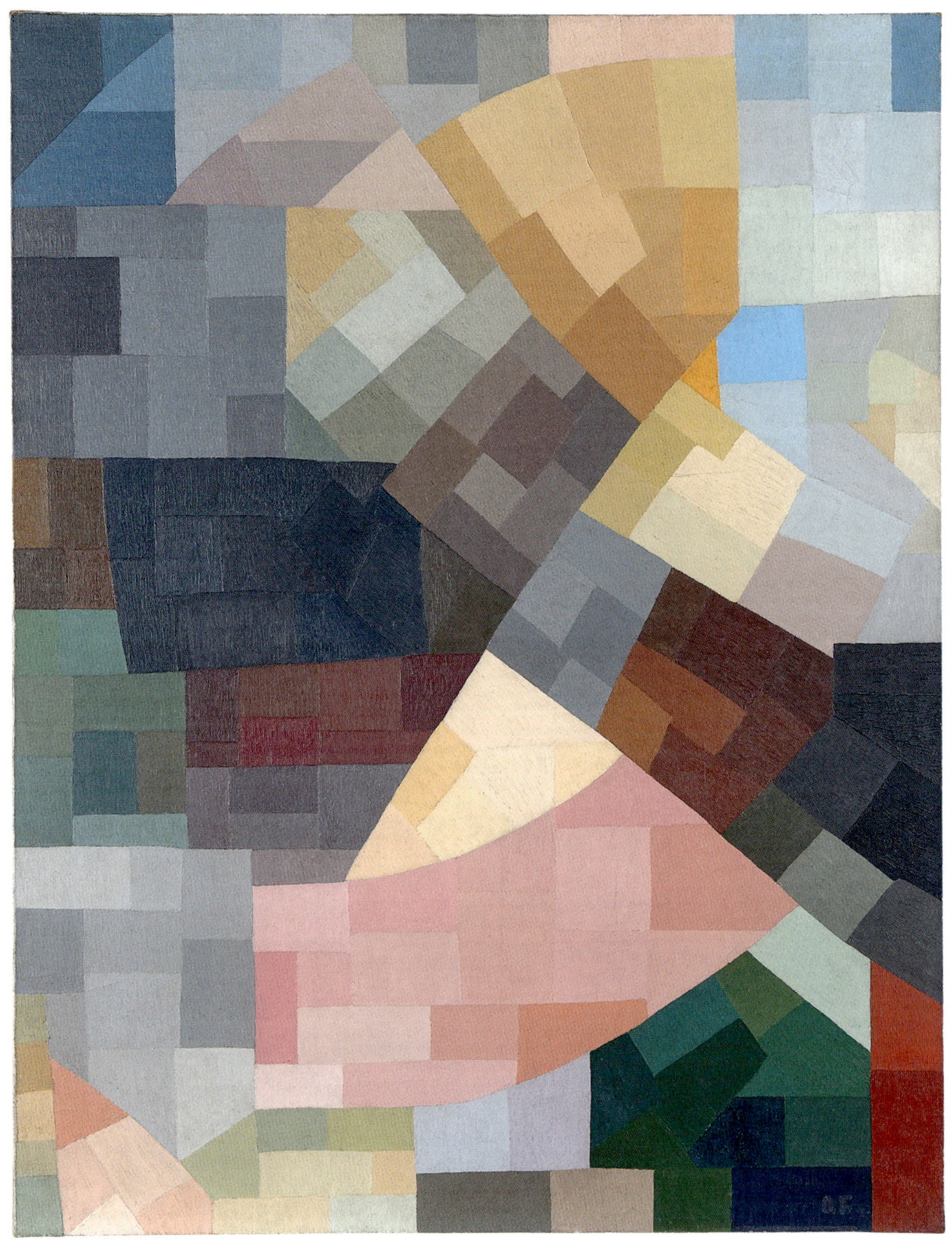

Composition, 1931
HvW 156
Oil on canvas

Composition, 1939
HvW 197
Tempera on paper mounted on canvas

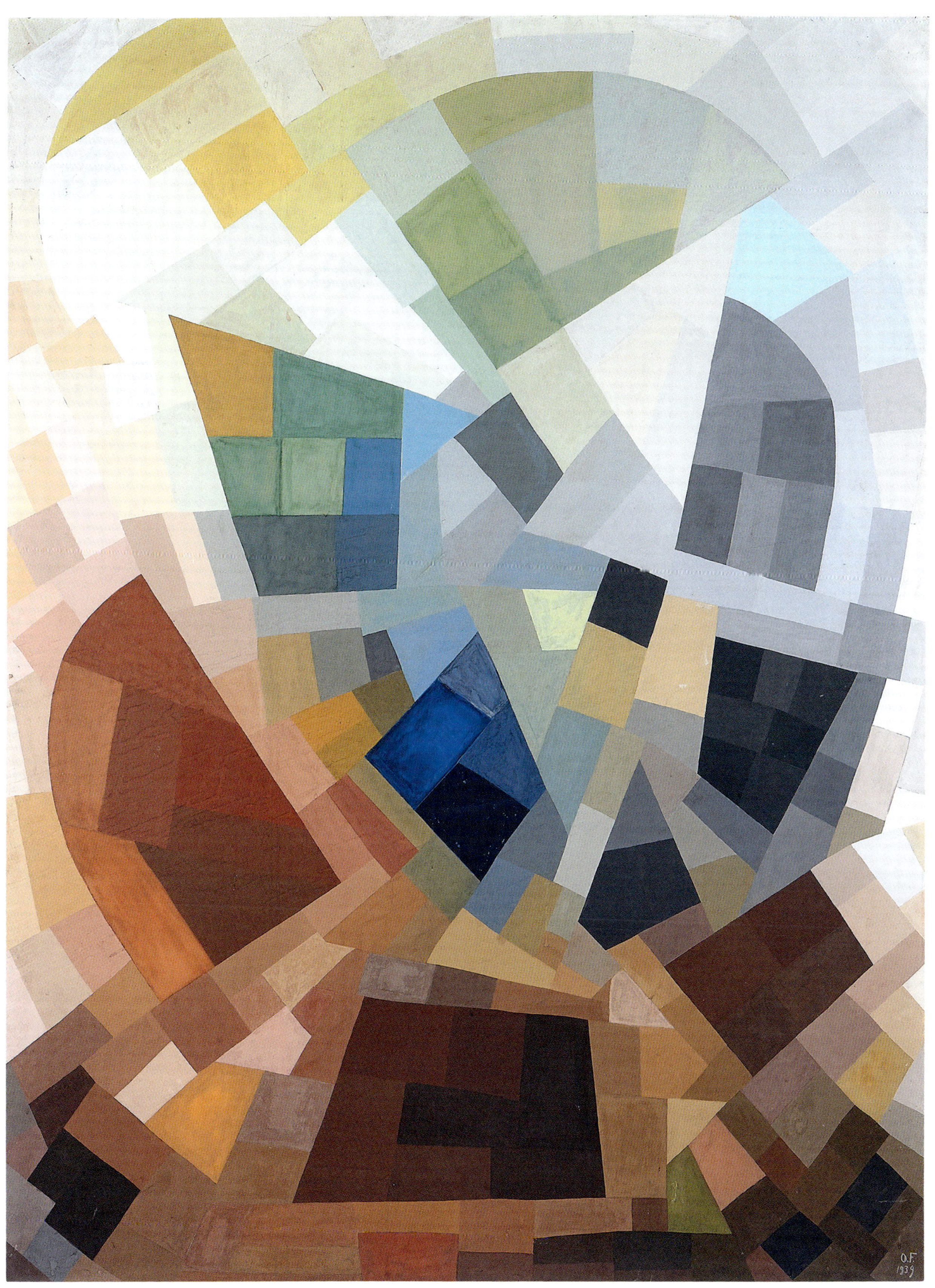
O.F.
1939

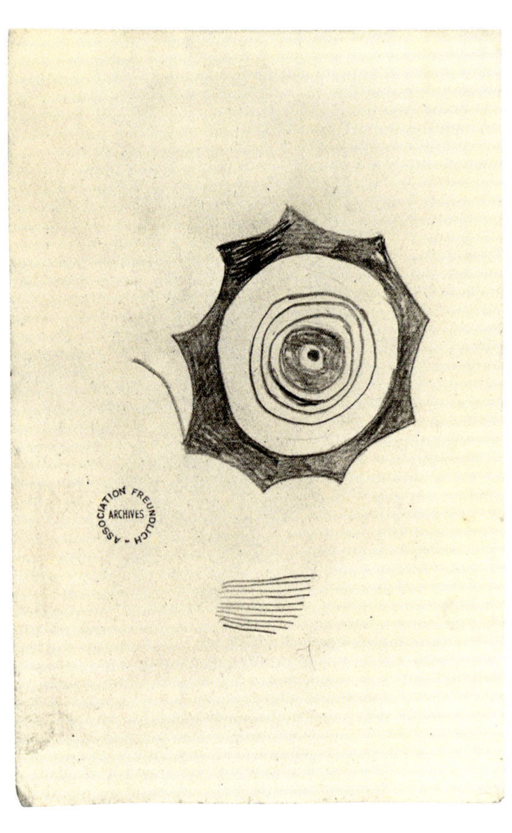

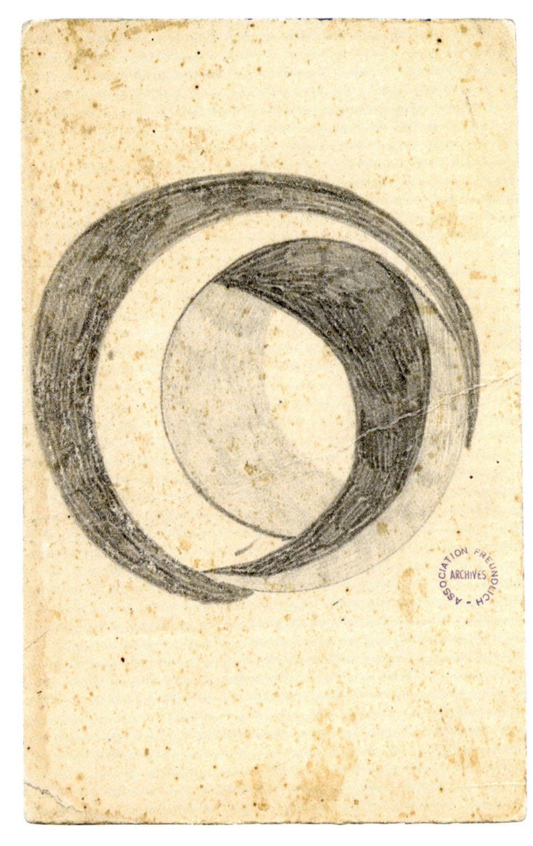

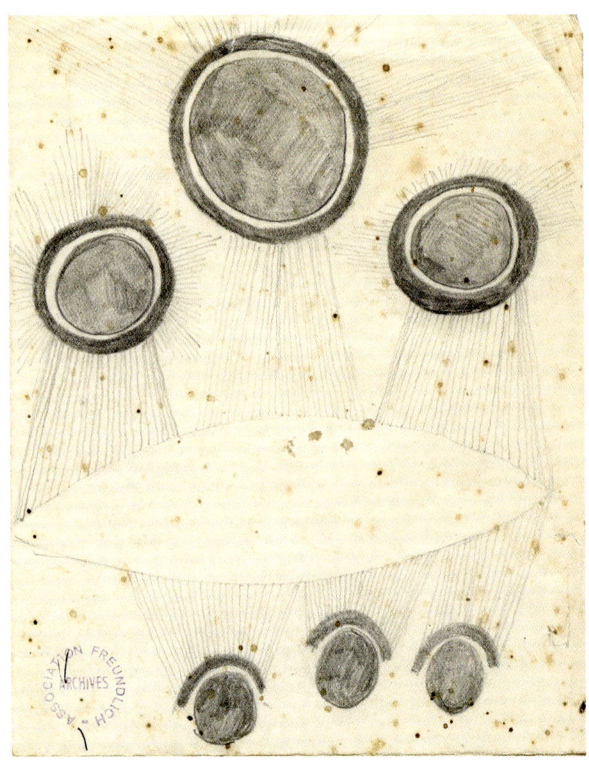

Composition, 1941
HvW 408
Pencil on sketching paper

Composition, 1943
HvW 437
Pencil on cardboard

Composition, 1943
HvW 435
Pencil on sketching paper

Rosette I, 1938
HvW 192
Gouache on paper,
mounted on canvas

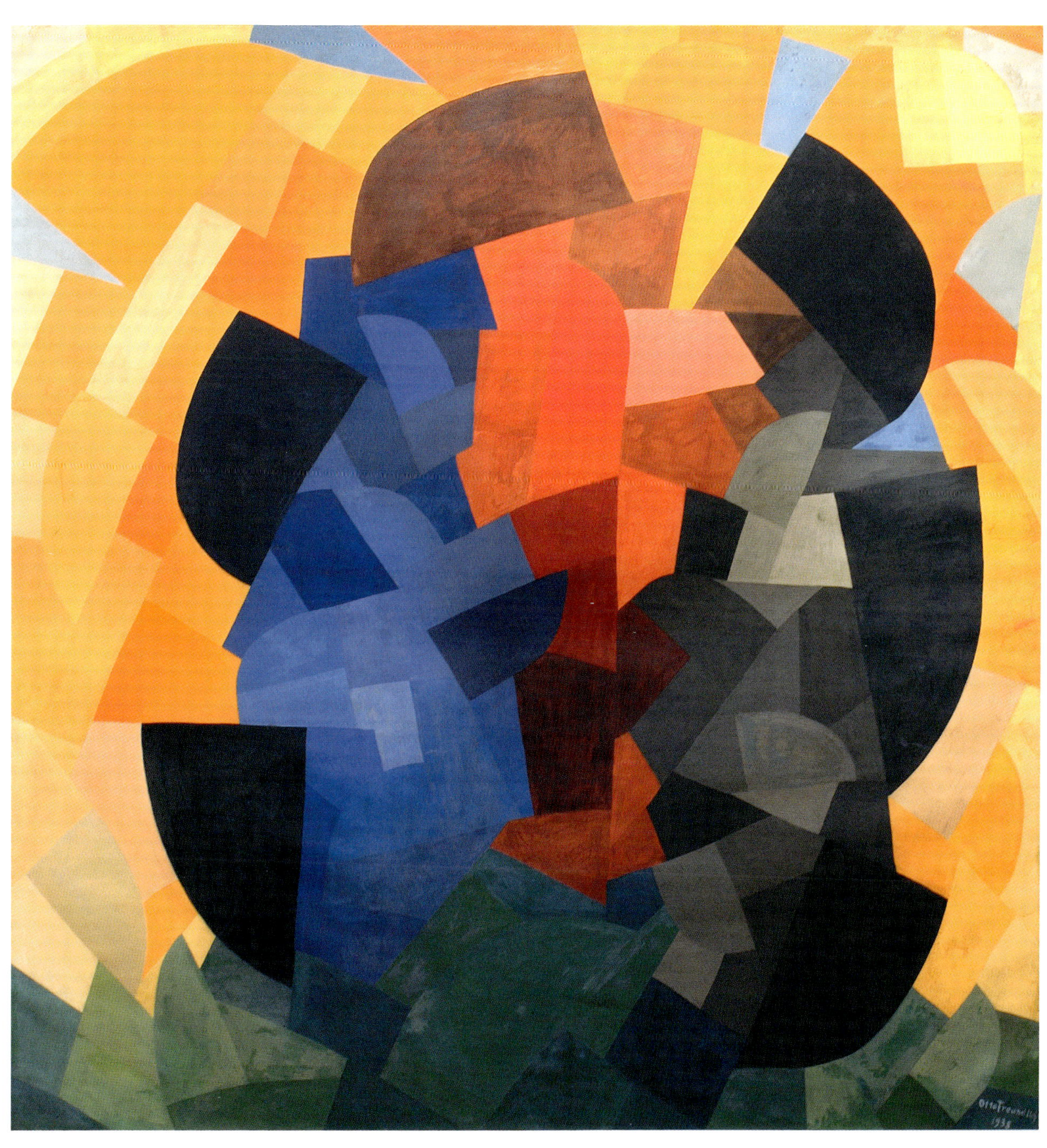

279

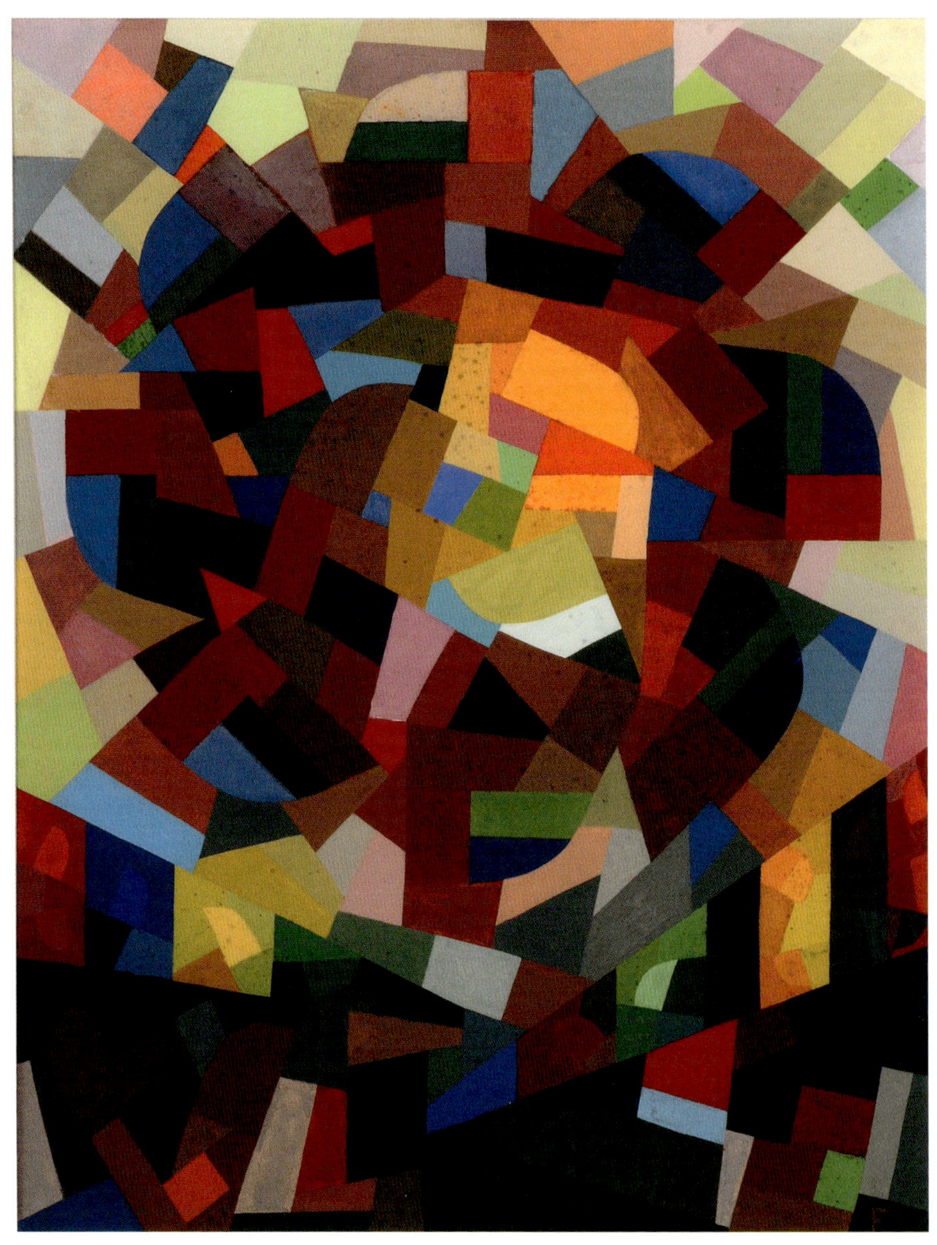

Rosette II, 1941
HvW 210
Gouache on cardboard

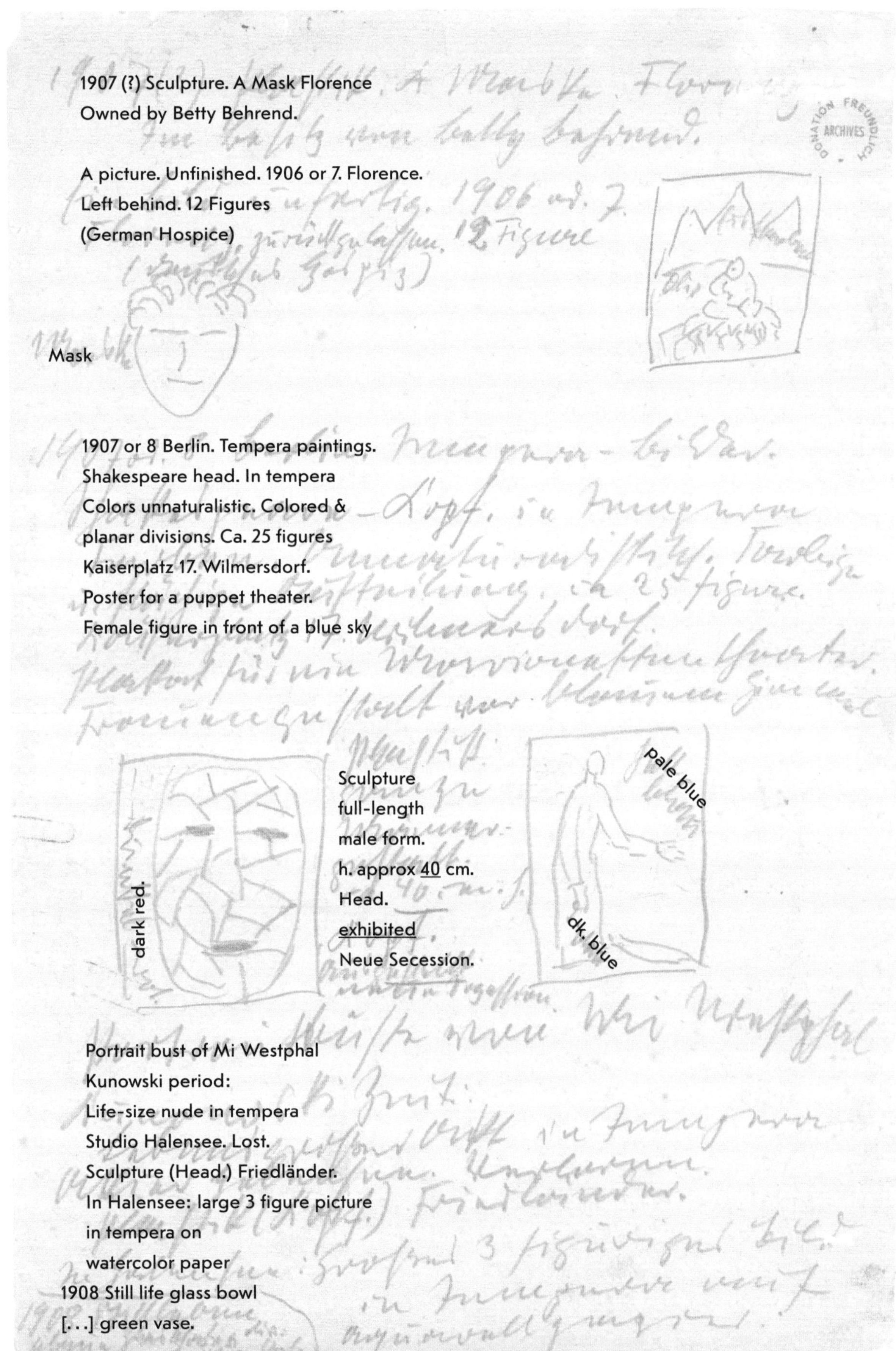
1907 (?) Sculpture. A Mask Florence
Owned by Betty Behrend.
A picture. Unfinished. 1906 or 7. Florence.
Left behind. 12 Figures
(German Hospice)
Mask
1907 or 8 Berlin. Tempera paintings.
Shakespeare head. In tempera
Colors unnaturalistic. Colored &
planar divisions. Ca. 25 figures
Kaiserplatz 17. Wilmersdorf.
Poster for a puppet theater.
Female figure in front of a blue sky
Sculpture
full-length
male form.
h. approx 40 cm.
Head.
exhibited
Neue Secession.
pale blue
dark red.
dk. blue
Portrait bust of Mi Westphal
Kunowski period:
Life-size nude in tempera
Studio Halensee. Lost.
Sculpture (Head.) Friedländer.
In Halensee: large 3 figure picture
in tempera on
watercolor paper
1908 Still life glass bowl
[. . .] green vase.

1907(?) Plastik. A Maske. Florenz

Im Besitz von [illegible] [illegible].

Ein Bild. unfertig. 1906 od. 7.

Florenz zurückgelassen. 12 Figuren

([illegible] [illegible])

Maske

1907 od. 8 Berlin. [illegible]-bilder.

[illegible]-Kopf. in [illegible]

Farben. [illegible] [illegible]. [illegible]

in flüchtiger Aufteilung. ca 25 figuren.

Kurfürstendamm 17. [illegible] [illegible]

Plakat für ein [illegible] Theater.

Frauengestalt vor blauem Himmel

Plastik. Kopf zu Frauengestalt. ca 40. cm. h.

Kopf. ausgestellt [illegible] vergessen

Portrait Büste von [illegible]

[illegible] bis Zeit:

[illegible] [illegible] in [illegible]

[illegible] [illegible]. [illegible].

Plastik (Kopf.) [illegible].

In Gedanken: Großes 3 figuriges Bild in [illegible] [illegible] [illegible].

1908 [illegible] [illegible] [illegible] [illegible]

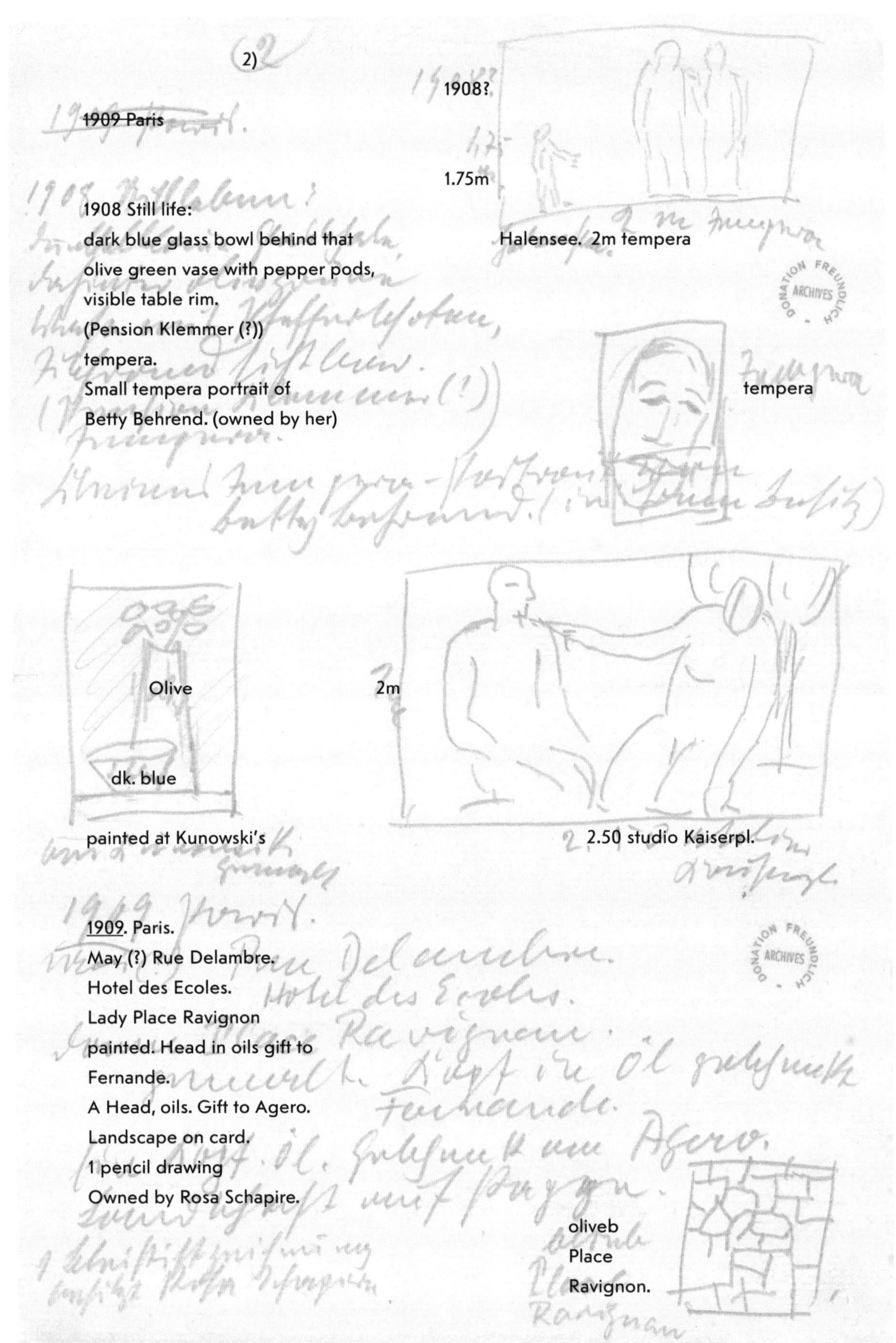

2)

~~1909 Paris~~

1908 Still life:
dark blue glass bowl behind that
olive green vase with pepper pods,
visible table rim.
(Pension Klemmer (?))
tempera.
Small tempera portrait of
Betty Behrend. (owned by her)

1908?

1.75m

Halensee. 2m tempera

tempera

Olive

dk. blue

painted at Kunowski's

2m

2.50 studio Kaiserpl.

1909. Paris.
May (?) Rue Delambre.
Hotel des Ecoles.
Lady Place Ravignon
painted. Head in oils gift to
Fernande.
A Head, oils. Gift to Agero.
Landscape on card.
1 pencil drawing
Owned by Rosa Schapire.

oliveb
Place
Ravignon.

(2)

1908?

~~1909 Paris.~~

1908. Stilleben:
dunkelblaue Glasschale,
dahinter olivgrüne
Vase mit Pfefferschoten,
Hintergrund hellblau.
(Knospen [illegible] (!))
[illegible].
Bildnis Frau [illegible]-Stellwagen [illegible]
[illegible] (in [illegible] Besitz)

1,75 m

2 m

2,50 atelier

1909. Paris.
März (!) Rue Delambre.
Hotel des Ecoles.
Sommer Place Ravignan.
gemalt. Kopf in Öl geschenkt
Fernande.
ein Kopf. Öl. Geschenkt an Agero.
Landschaft mit Pagoden.
1 Bleistiftzeichnung
[illegible]

Atelier
Place
Ravignan

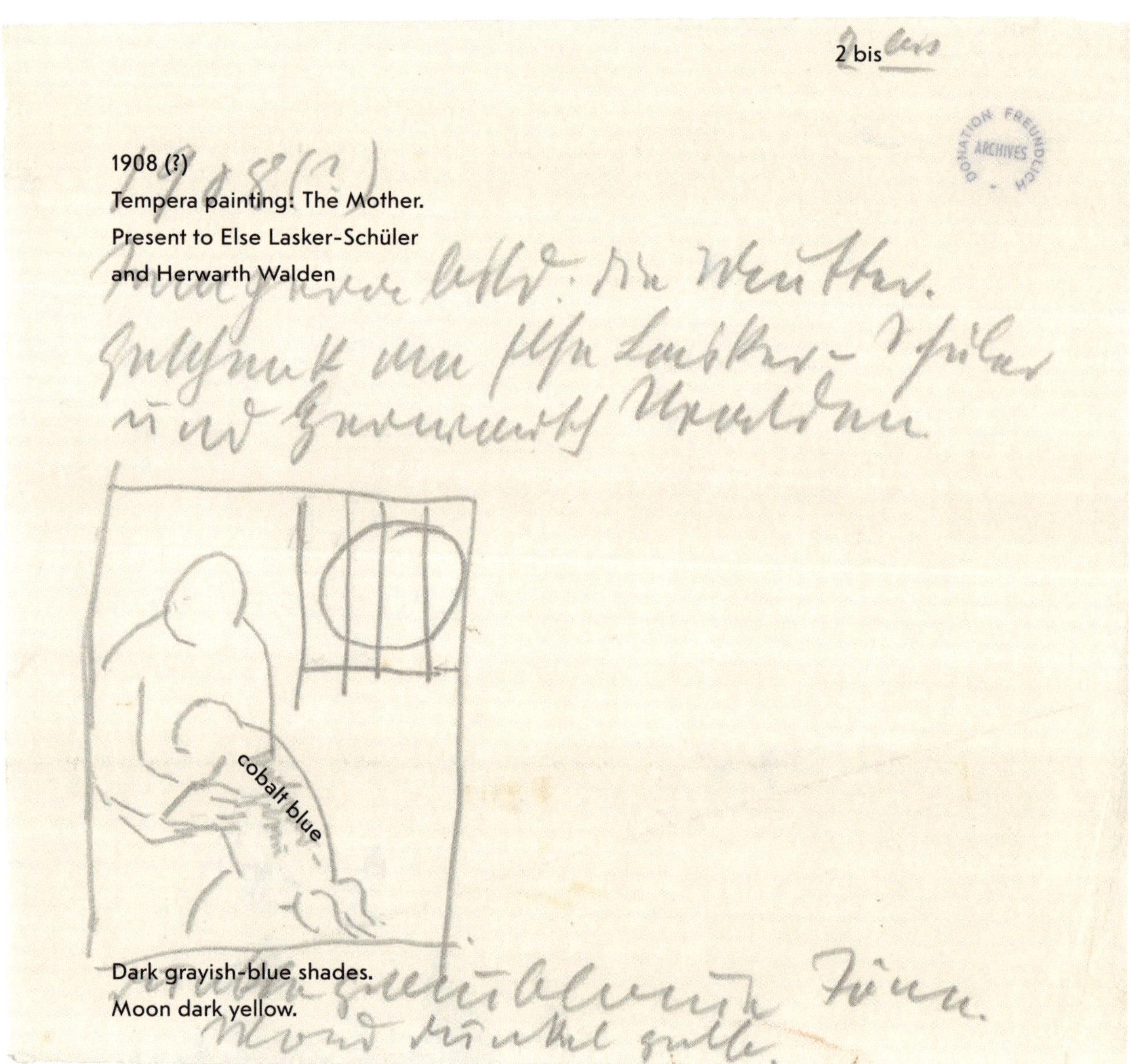
2 bis
1908 (?)
Tempera painting: The Mother.
Present to Else Lasker-Schüler
and Herwarth Walden
cobalt blue
Dark grayish-blue shades.
Moon dark yellow.

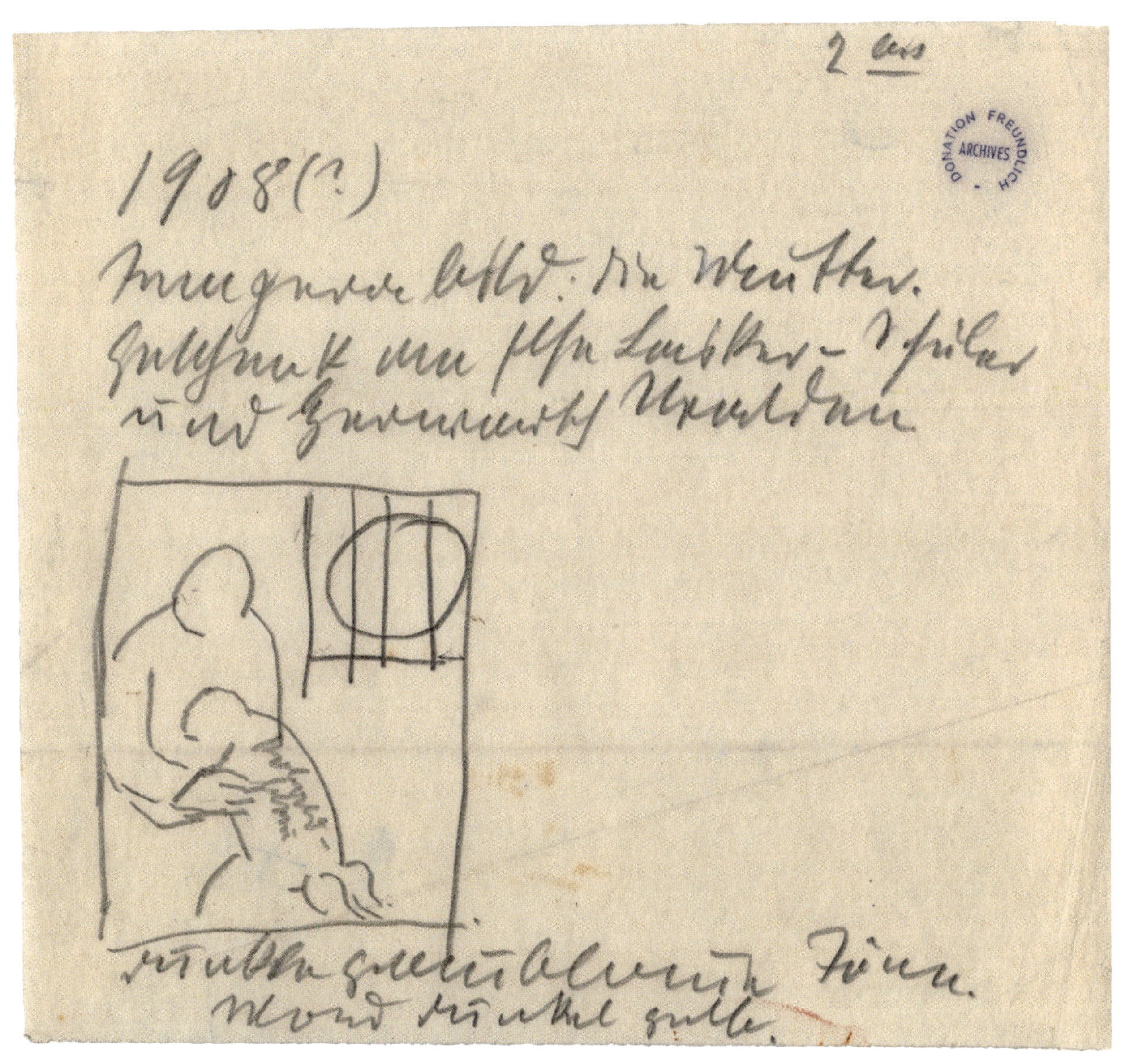
2
DONATION FREUNDLICH
ARCHIVES
1908(?)

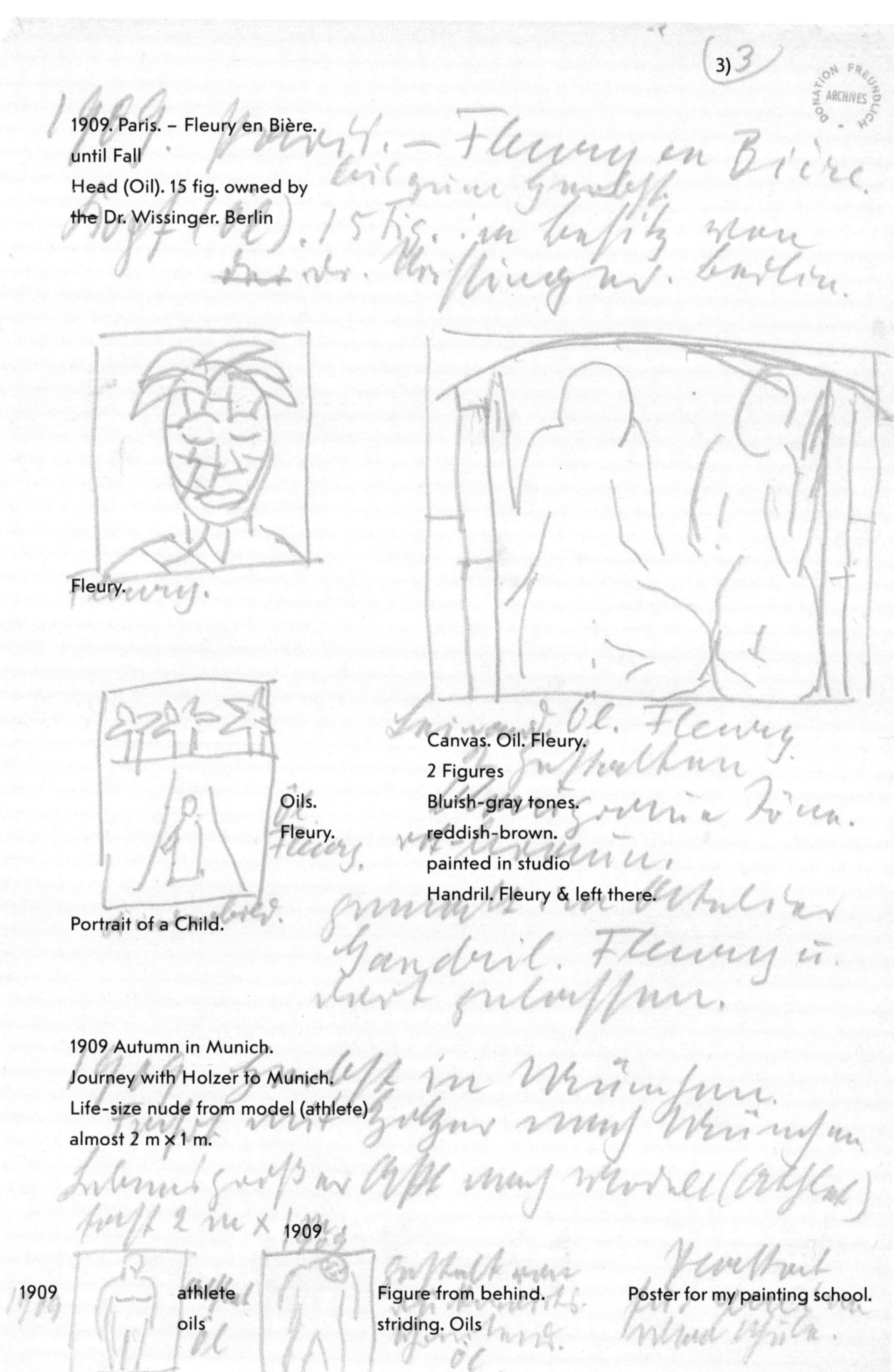

3)
DONATION FREUNDLICH ARCHIVES
1909. Paris. – Fleury en Bière.
until Fall
Head (Oil). 15 fig. owned by
~~the~~ Dr. Wissinger. Berlin
Fleury.
Oils.
Fleury.
Portrait of a Child.
Canvas. Oil. Fleury.
2 Figures
Bluish-gray tones.
reddish-brown.
painted in studio
Handril. Fleury & left there.
1909 Autumn in Munich.
Journey with Holzer to Munich.
Life-size nude from model (athlete)
almost 2 m × 1 m.
1909
1909
athlete
oils
Figure from behind.
striding. Oils
Poster for my painting school.

(3)

1909. Paris. – Fleury en Bière.
[illegible] gemalt.
Kopf (Öl). 15 Fig. im Besitz von ~~Dr~~ Dr. [illegible] Berlin.

Fleury.

Leinwand. Öl. Fleury
2 Gestalten
Ultramarin Tönen.
rot-braunen.

Öl
Fleury.

Kinderbild.

gemalt im Atelier
Gandvil. Fleury u.
dort gelassen.

1909 Gemalt in München.
Fresko mit Holzer nach München.
Lebensgross in Acht nach Modell (Aktfest)
Größe 2 m × 1 m.

1909

Aktfest
Öl

1909

Gestalt einer [illegible]
[illegible].
Öl.

[illegible]
für [illegible]
[illegible] Schüler.

4)

Poster (lithographed)

in the colors yellow, red & black.

poster.

gave 1 print to Walden.

Munich: Mask (Photogr.) Wissinger.

lesson

in pictorial vision (?)

Otto Freundlich

Early 1910 to Berlin.

Kaiserplatz. 17. (2nd time)

Female bust (bronze) Feinhals.

Standing Mask " , Grünwald

Pencil drawings.

(Georg Fuchs has 1 drawing

He likewise has 1 old pen and ink drawing

1 pencil drawing is in the possession of

my niece Bertha Lion.

1910 back to Paris in Fall.

lived in Rue Geoffroy-Marie.

Hôtel des Amériques.

Sculpture (Mask) Waldemar has a cast.

Niemeyer has pencil drawings

from there. Rue des Abbesses. Studio.

55 (?)

4)

Plakat (Lithographisch)
in den Farben gelb, rot u. schwarz

Plakat.

1 Exemplar
Walden
gegeben.

München: [illegible]
(Fotogr.) [illegible]

Unterschrift
Zu bildnerischen Ansichten(?)
Otto Freundlich

Anfang 1910 nach Berlin.
Lützowplatz 17. (2. mal)
Frauenbüste (Bronze) [illegible]
Stehende Gestalt " , Grünewald
Bleistiftzeichnungen.
(1 Zeichnung hat Georg Fuchs.
desgleichen besitzt er 1 alte Federzeichnung)

1 Bleistiftzeichnung besitzt meine
Nichte Berthe Lion.

1910 Herbst zurück nach Paris.
wohnte Rue Geoffroy-Marie.
Hôtel des deux Amériques.

Plastik (Gestalt) Original besitzt Walden.
Bleistiftzeichnungen besitzt [illegible]
wohnte dann Rue des Abbesses. Atelier.
55(?)

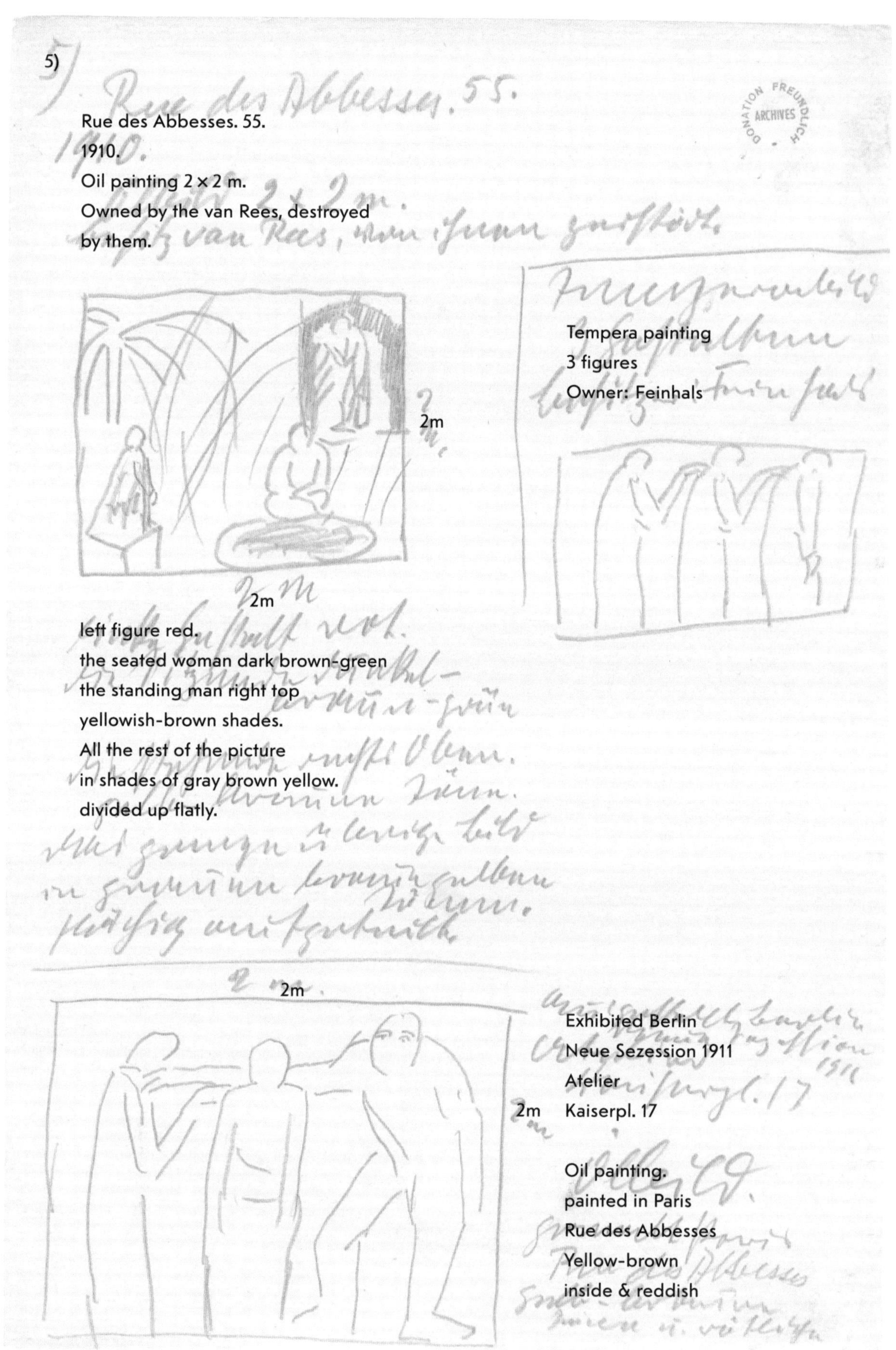

5)

Rue des Abbesses. 55.
1910.
Oil painting 2 × 2 m.
Owned by the van Rees, destroyed by them.

2m

2m

left figure red.
the seated woman dark brown-green
the standing man right top
yellowish-brown shades.
All the rest of the picture
in shades of gray brown yellow.
divided up flatly.

Tempera painting
3 figures
Owner: Feinhals

2m

2m

Exhibited Berlin
Neue Sezession 1911
Atelier
Kaiserpl. 17

Oil painting.
painted in Paris
Rue des Abbesses
Yellow-brown
inside & reddish

5) Rue des Abbesses. 55.
1910.
Ölbild 2 x 2 m.
besitz van Rees, von ihnen zerstört.

2 m.

2 m

linke Gestalt rot.
die Sitzende dunkel-
braun-grün
die Stehende rechts oben.
gelb-braune Töne.
[illegible] u. [illegible] bild
in grünen braun-gelben Tönen.
flächig aufgebaut.

[illegible]
3 Gestalten
besitzer: [illegible]

2 m.

2 m

ausgestellt berliner
Neue Secession
1911
[illegible]
[illegible] 17

Ölbild.
gemalt Paris
Rue des Abbesses
gelb-braune
Töne u. rötliche

6)

Rue Jacob. (1911)

Hôtel Jacob.

1 oil painting (Head) Present to Ludwig &

photo Frieda Rubiner.

1 large oil painting (4 qm), 1911

2 m

2 m

lost.

strictly planar composition

Exhibited in Amsterdam

Kunstkring. (ask Kickert).

head in watercolors (Niemeyer)

Watercolor painting (non-representational)

Niemeyer

1 oil painting (The Sick Man) Sagot.

Photo

1 tapestry design. Oils.

1 " " " tempera } done by Mrs van Rees.

reproduced in catalogue to

the Fall exhibition Walden.

6) Rue Jacob. (1911)
Hôtel Jacob.
1 Ölbild (Kopf) geschenkt an Ludwig u. Frieda Rubiner.
Foto.

---

1 großes Ölbild (4 qm). 1911

verloren.
von flüchtigen Bekannten
ausgestellt im Amsterdamer
Kunstkring. (Kickert fragen).

Aquarellkopf (Erinnerungen)
Aquarell Bild (ungegenständlich) Erinnerungen.
1 Ölbild (der Trunkene) Sagot.
Foto
1 Entwurf für Stickerei. Öl.
1 " " " Zeugdruck. } ausgeführt von Frau van Rees
abgebildet im Katalog der Herbstausstellung Waldens.

---

7)

Rue Boissonade.

1912. after the Sonderbund exhibition in Cologne

Head for Deusser. (photo)
Little oil painting (Rosa Schapire Hamburg)

Oil painting (Niemeyer)
Oil painting (Landscape) Sagot

dark green.
green
green.

Oil painting (Head) Sagot.
Strong yellow shades & blue.

Winter 1912 in Hamburg.
there in the School of Arts and Crafts
large head in clay. owned by
Mrs Blumenfeld. (plaster cast)

1913 Oil painting (Niemeyer) photo
Paris. Rue Boissonade
Large charcoal drawing. (Niemeyer?)

1914. Give up the studio in rue Boissonade
& move to Hôtel rue Delambre
In Mutz's studio in the building of
Café du Dôme I start on a large oil painting
(2 m × 1 m) female figure, which belongs to
Feinhals. March 1914 off to Chartres. the oil
painting finished there & sent to Feinhals.

1915. Cologne. Mask in plasticine.
Cast owned by Mrs Gruenwald.

1916/17 3 pen and ink drawings. 2 originals
owned by Feinhals. 1 Folkwang Museum

7) Rue Boissonade. 1912. nach der Sonderbundausstellung in Köln
Kopf für Deusser. (Foto)
kleines Ölbild (Rosa Schapire Hamburg)

Ölbild (Nimwegen)
Ölbild (Landschaft) vergeb.

Ölbild (Kopf) vergeb.
starke gelben Farben u. Schwarz.

[illegible] 1912 Sammlung.
dort in der Kunstgewerbeschule
großer Kopf in Holz. im Besitz von
Frau Altmannsfeld. (Gipsabguss)

1913. Ölbild (Nimwegen) Foto
Paris. Rue Boissonade
Grosse Kreidezeichnung.
(Nimwegen?)

1914. Gab das Atelier rue Boissonade
auf u. zog in ein Hotel rue Delambre
im Atelier eines Deutsch im Garten des
Hauses des Dôme stellte ich ein großes Ölbild
von (2 m) zusammengestellt, das Feinhals
gekauft. im März 1914 nach Deutschland. dort
Beschädigung des Ölbildes u. von Feinhals
abgeschickt.

1915. Köln. Verwandte im Plastiken
Abguss im Besitz von Frau Grünenberg.

1916/17 3 Kreidezeichnungen. 2 Originale
besitzt Feinhals. 1 Folkwang-
museum.

8)

1916/17. 3 sculptures
Bols in Cologne. Gereonshaus.
1 cast owned by Feinhals.
2 remained in studio in Berlin Kaiserpl. 17
(photos)
2 woodcuts. (blocks in the box of books)

1917. 1 oil painting (Wissinger, Berlin)

1918. Berlin. (Kaiserpl. 17)
Commission for mosaic from Feinhals.
3 m × 2 m. Worked on it till
early 1919. Realized by Puhl &
Wagner, Heinersdorf. Berlin. –
Treptow.

1919. Completed mosaic exhibited at Gurlitt's
then in Cologne at the Kunstverein.
Traveled to Cologne.
In Winter 1919-20 the drawings
for "Die Zeichen" published
by Kairos-Verlag, Nierendorf.

1920/21. Oil painting (remained in studio Kaiserpl.)
Pastels (Feinhals, Wissinger, Mrs [Luise?]
Sophie [. . .]
Journal "Der Strom" by Nierendorf.
Essays.
Pastels: Seiwert. Stiel. Else (?)

1921. 2 sculptures (heads) photo.	} Remained in studio
1 Sculpture (standing forms) photo	Kaiserpl. 17

1922. Oil painting. (The Mother.) Oslo Collection.
Glass window (Wissinger)

8/ 1916/17. 3 Plastiken
teils in Köln. Gereonshaus.
1 Ausguss hat Freundlich.
2 blieben im Atelier in Berlin Kreuzngt. 17
(Fotos)
2 Holzschnitte. (Platten in der Bücherkiste)
1917. 1 Ölbild (Vlissingen, Berlin)
1918. Berlin. (Kreuzngt. 17)
Auftrag für das Mosaik von Freundlich.
3 m x 2 m. daran gearbeitet bis
Anfang 1919. ausgeführt bei Puhl & Wagner, Heinersdorf. Berlin-Treptow.
1919. Fertiges Mosaik ausgestellt
anschließend dann
in Köln im Kunstverein.
Nach Köln gekommen.
Im Winter 1919–20 die Zeichnungen zu „Die Zeichen" herausgegeben
für die Zeichen
neuen Kairos-Verlag Heinersdorf.
1920/21. Ölbild (blieb im Atelier Kreuzngt.)
Pastellen. (Freundlich, Vlissingen, [illegible]) [illegible] Zeitschrift „Die Neue" [illegible] Heinersdorf [illegible]
Pastellen: [illegible] (?).
1921. 2 Plastiken (Köpfe) Foto.
1 Plastik (Stehende Frauen) Foto. } im Atelier geblieben Kreuzngt. 17
1922. Ölbild. (Die Mutter.) Sammlung Oslo.
Glasfenster (Vlissingen)

9)

1922) Pastel (Hausmann)

- *ditto* - (Braun)

4 woodcuts. (blocks in the book box)

Lectures.

1923. Pastels. (Lüttgen. Levin)

1924. Stained glass window for Bret. Photo.

He August to Paris.

1922/ Pastell (Zimmermann)
-do- (Lorenz)
4 Holzschnitte. (Platten in der Bücherkiste)
Vorträge.

1923. Pastelle. ([illegible] Lith. Lorenz)
1924. Glasfenster für Bauh. Foto.
Ansicht verschwund.

Biography

July 10, 1878 Born in Stolp, Pomerania (Słupsk, Republic of Poland), Hospitalstrasse 19, as the fifth of six children. Father Emil Freundlich is a merchant, his wife Bertha (née Levy) dies a year after Otto is born. Both are of Jewish descent, but the family has assimilated. Emil's second wife, Rosa (née Bernhardt), gives birth to a son, Kurt Michael, and raises the children as Protestants.[1]

1888–1892 Attends Stolp secondary school, then quits.

1892–1901 Hamburg. Commercial apprenticeship in the wood trade together with his younger brother, Waldemar,[2] subsequently clerk.

1903

April School finals exam in Bützow (Mecklenburg); the school register notes: "to study medicine."
Moves to Berlin.
Studies art history, philosophy, and literature at the Königliche Friedrich Wilhelms University Berlin (today Humboldt University), under among others Heinrich Wölfflin, Adolph Goldschmidt, Max Dessoir, and Georg Simmel, but abandons his studies after three semesters (August 1904).

1904

February Gets to know the author, publisher, composer and subsequent gallerist and editor of *Der Sturm,* Herwarth Walden, and embarks on a correspondence with him; through this he also comes in contact with Walden's wife, the poet Else Lasker-Schüler.

October Moves to Munich and a flat in the garden house at Kaulbachstrasse 6. Enrolls at the university for dentistry as well as at the faculty of philosophy.[3]
Gets to know Wassily Kandinsky and Paul Klee.

December 23 Writes to Walden that he is engrossed in Hermann von Helmholtz's work *On the Sensations of Tone as a Physiological Basis for the Theory of Music* (1863; Eng. trans. 1875) and is planning a tour of Italy in the first half of 1905.
Quits his studies.

1905

February His essay "Herwarth Waldens Tonlyrik" ("Herwarth Walden's Sound Poetry") is published in *Kampf: Zeitschrift für gesunden Menschenverstand* 18 (1905).

March Meets the critic and writer Ludwig Rubiner.

June Travels to Innsbruck.

September Crosses the Alps by foot.

November Florence.
Intensive study of Italian art history in Florence. Decides to make his own artistic works. First pieces, of which the drawing *Opera Scene* has remained in the family (HvW 260, p. 99).

1906

End of January Returns to Munich.

October Florence (second stay till January 1907).

End of 1906 Brief stopover in Munich.

Exhibitions

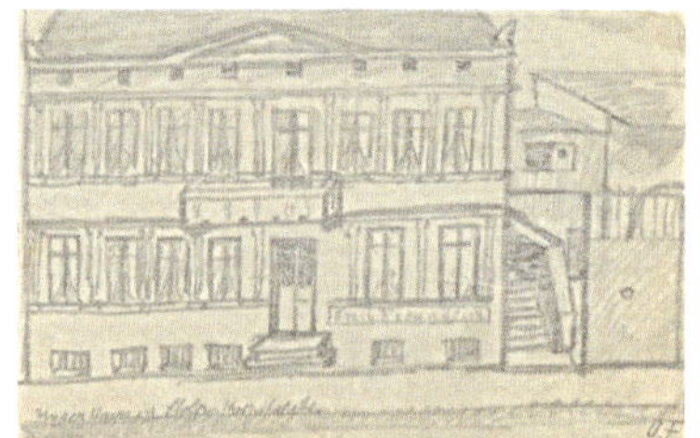

Otto Freundlich
Our House in Stolp, ca. 1919

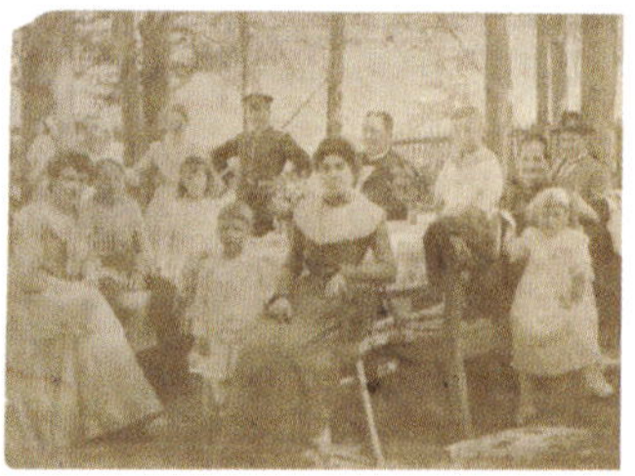

Family photograph with Otto Freundlich standing on the right margin, ca. 1903

Kaufhaus Wertheim, Berlin, March

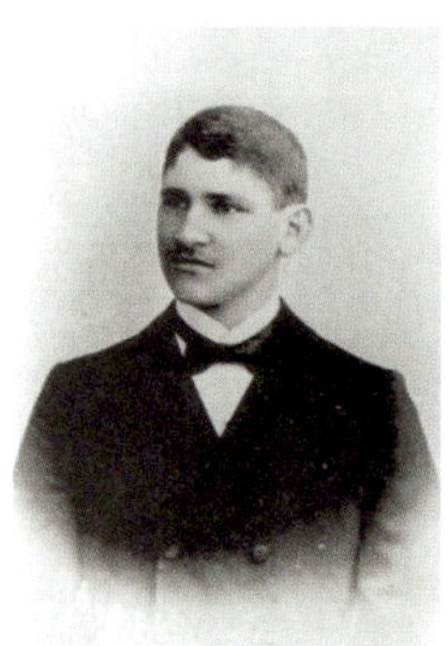

Otto Freundlich, 1900

1907

January
Takes a studio in Via dei Serragli 130a, Florence, "in which I have begun my career as a sculptor & now have no doubt that this is my true and greatest talent."[4]
Returns to Berlin before the end of the year. Studies sculpture in the private schools run by Arthur Lewin-Funcke in Berlin-Charlottenburg and by Lothar von Kunowski. His fellow students include Lothar Homeyer and Heinrich Richter-Berlin.

1908

Early March
Paris, studio in Bateau-Lavoir, 13, rue Ravignan.
Meets among others Pablo Picasso, Auguste Herbin, Georges Braque, Max Jacob, Guillaume Apollinaire, and Robert Delaunay.
Wilhelm Uhde introduces Freundlich to Paris art circles in Montmartre.
Freundlich writes in a letter to Herwarth Walden: "I'm doing fine—acquainted with the fine artists and literati of the martyrs' mount, even if I am not *much* loved by them."[5]
Also becomes friends with the Dutch artist couple Adya and Otto van Rees, who have lived since 1907 in Paris. Presumably he has come to know them through Picasso.[6]

July
Returns to Munich, studio in Theresienstrasse 54.
Plans to open a private art school.
Writes "Polemik ... gegen Lehrer- and Schülertum" ("Polemic ... against the Teacher-Pupil Relationship").

1909

March
Travels to Stolp, then back to Munich.

May
Paris (second sojourn), rue Delambre, Hôtel des Écoles, Montparnasse, round the corner from the artists' haunt Café du Dôme, then to 13, rue Ravignan in the "Bateau-Lavoir."

June
Munich and Berlin.

July–August
Hamburg.

September
Stays with the van Rees in the artists' colony Fleury-en-Bière in the forest of Fontainebleau. This is followed by regular summers there together.

Fall
Munich.
First examples of early works of a symbolist nature, of which two *Masks* (HvW 54, p.102, and HvW 55, p.86) and the drawing of a *Robed Figure* (HvW 263, p.87) have survived.

Galerie Clovis Sagot, Paris, June

Berliner Sezession, Berlin

1910

January
Berlin-Wilmersdorf, studio on Kaiserplatz 17 (today Bundesplatz).
Paints the staircase in his studio.
Becomes a member of the Berliner Secession and Neue Berliner Secession art groups.
Travels to Munich and Hamburg.

Fall
Returns to Paris, rue Geoffrey, Hôtel des deux Amériques.
Draws a first *Cosmic Composition* (HvW 264, p.89), now known only from a reproduction, which he will give to his later friend and patron Wilhelm Niemeyer.

Neue Secession Berlin. I. Graphische Ausstellung 1910, Berlin, 5.15–7.15 (cat.)

1911

March
Takes a studio at 55, rue des Abbesses.
Receives a visit from Heinrich Richter-Berlin.

Summer
Artists' colony Fleury-en-Bière with the van Rees, with whom he also has an intense exchange of ideas about art. Produces his first non-representational *Composition* (HvW 107, p.113). Apart from which, does designs for at least two tapestries that Adya van Rees realizes in wool.

November
Berlin. Makes the acquaintance of Karl Schmidt-Rottluff at the opening of the fourth exhibition of the Neue Secession. A friendship develops that also expresses itself in their closeness as artists. Schmidt-Rottluff puts him in contact with the Hamburg art critic and co-organizer of the *Sonderbundausstellung* (1912) in Cologne, Wilhelm Niemeyer. Niemeyer has worked since January 1910 as an

Neue Secession Berlin e.V., IV. Ausstellung, Berlin, 11.18.1911–1.31.1912 (cat.)

art history lecturer at the Hamburg School of Arts and Crafts.
Contact with the Hamburg art historian Rosa Schapire and the Cologne-based collector Joseph Feinhals, who like Niemeyer purchases works from Freundlich.
In addition, contact with the Expressionists Erich Heckel, Heinrich Campendonk, and Otto Mueller.

November/December — Niemeyer travels to Paris to select works for the *Sonderbundausstellung*. Freundlich takes him to Picasso.

December 31 — Letter to the Neue Berliner Secession announcing his resignation.

1912 — Paris, Hôtel Jacob, 44, rue Jacob.

May — Cologne. Meets Niemeyer during the *Sonderbundausstellung*. Together they visit Karl Ernst Osthaus in Hagen.
Niemeyer arranges the commission for Freundlich's sculpture *Head* (HvW 62, p. 110) for the Cologne painter and co-organizer of the *Sonderbundausstellung*, August Deusser.
Contact with the Cologne artists of the Unist group (members include Max Ernst, Peter Abelen, F[ritz] M[ax] Cahén, Johannes Theodor Kuhlemann, and Franz Henseler).

July — Paris, Montparnasse: studio at 17, rue Boissonnade.[7]
Moves in the circles around the Kikkert group, which the Dutch artist and art dealer Conrad Kickert (aka Kikkert) rallys around him in Paris. Apart from Otto and Adya van Rees, his contacts include Jan F. van Deene and Piet Mondrian. Kickert organizes the *Moderne Kunst Kring* exhibition, which exhibits Freundlich's now lost *Decorative Painting*.

Summer — Makes contact with the sculptors Constantin Brâncuşi and Amedeo Modigliani.

August — Writes a text against naturalism titled "Eine Umrahmung für manche Bilder" ("A Framework for Certain Pictures").

Winter — Hamburg. Fashions the clay model for his monumental sculpture *Large Head* (HvW 63, p. 77) at the School of Arts and Crafts.

Internationale Kunstausstellung des Sonderbundes Westdeutscher Kunstfreunde und Künstler, Städtische Ausstellungshalle am Aachener Tor, Cologne, 5.25–9.30 (cat.)

Moderne Kunst Kring, Stedelijk Museum, Amsterdam, 10.6–11.7 (cat.)

1913

October — Paris. Moves from his studio in rue Boissonnade, lives in a hotel.

December — Hamburg. Stays with Niemeyer, contact with the collector Anna Blumenfeld.
Stays in Cologne over Christmas, visits Feinhals.[8]
Then Paris, Hôtel de Zurich, rue Delambre, where he uses Alfred Mez's studio.[9]

Opening show of Galerie Alfred Flechtheim, Düsseldorf (cat.)

Erster Deutscher Herbstsalon, Galerie "Der Sturm," Berlin, 9.20–12.1 (cat.)

1914

March–July — Chartres. Takes a studio in the north tower of the cathedral.
Studies medieval stained glass and takes part in restoration work in the cathedral. Writes in retrospect that he has "fallen for the world in Chartres" and has "come out of it changed for life."[10] First window designs and a large painting for Feinhals (*Female Figure*, HvW 119), all lost. Filled with enthusiasm for old embroideries.[11]
Writes to the Portuguese painter Amadeo de Souza-Cardoso, on whose recommendation he had traveled to Chartres: "I feel it is important in this context to study the tendency in composition and the tendency of life itself and its beauty. A life of energy comes from the power of decomposition, which means: spiritualizing so that life becomes an eternal flow that streams towards its dissolution [*négation*], but this dissolution must be wished for and cheerful. Congratulate me on this discovery, which is as follows: Decomposition is far more mysterious than composition."[12]

Summer — Last stay with the van Rees in Fleury-en-Bière.

August — Mostly in Cologne and Berlin.
Shortly before the onset of war returns from Paris to Germany, where he enlists as a volunteer. He completes his military training with the Deutz Cuirassiers, Cologne, and is sent to the Western Front.

October 18 — Freundlich appoints Niemeyer as executor of his estate should he die.

Deutsche Werkbundausstellung: Kunst in Handwerk, Industrie und Handel, Architektur, Cologne, May–October (cat.)

1915

Early January — Cologne. Returns from France via Saarbrücken due to ear problems. Alternative service as medical orderly with the rank of corporal/NCO. Friendship with Johannes Theodor Baargeld (Alfred Ferdinand Gruenwald), whom he gets to know at the Deutz Cuirassiers, and whose family takes him in at Breitestrasse 161. Baargeld's mother, Hilla Gruenwald, supports Freundlich by making purchases. She buys among other works the *Standing Mask* (HvW 55, p. 86).[13]

January/February — His hopes rise for a solo exhibition at the Kölnischer Kunstverein, in which he wishes to exhibit works owned by Schapire, Feinhals, and Niemeyer. As Freundlich writes in a letter to Niemeyer on February 17, the exhibition fails to materialize following objections from the member Dr. Paul Seligmann—"Very interesting—but—perhaps some day—group show—more pictures—out of regard for the public—loss of members—!"[14]

October 11 — Announces to Niemeyer poems by Baargeld that he wishes to illustrate: "I shall do the accompanying visual illustrations to them, in black and white."[15]

Acquaintanceship with Hannah Höch.

November — Exhibits collaborative works with Adya van Rees in what is later referred to as a proto-Dada group exhibition at Gallery Tanner. Jean Arp writes in the catalogue on the connection with medieval craftsmanship and non-European art, and years later still underlines the collective spirit of the joint works.[16]

Aktions-Buchhandlung, Berlin

Otto van Rees, Paris, Hans Arp, A.C. van Rees-Dutilh, Paris: Moderne Wandteppiche, Stickereien, Malereien, Zeichnungen, Galerie Tanner Zürich (cat.)

1916

Spring — Cologne. Meets the anthroposophist Friedja Schugt-Maus, Cologne, with whom he discusses Theosophy.

March 23 — Marries the pianist Dore Leeser from Cologne.

Reads Arthur Drews's *Die Christusmythe* (1909).[17]

July — Visits Osthaus in Hagen and the neo-Kantian Ernst Marcus in Essen, where he is able to read the manuscript for *Das Problem der excentrischen Empfindung und seine Lösung* (1918), "whose publication deserves the attention of artists and the artistically minded because it explains visual design in a new light, albeit with Kantian premises."[18] He writes on it in his essay "Über eine unveröffentlichte Schrift" ("On an Unpublished Text") in *Die weissen Blätter* 9 (1916).

Contributes to Ludwig Rubiner's *Zeit-Echo* (article "Der Bau" ["The Building"]) and up to 1924 regularly for Franz Pfemfert's *Die Aktion*.

Gets to know Franz Wilhelm Seiwert.

End of 1916 — His son Berthold is born in Cologne and put in a home early in 1917.[19]

1917

December 22 — Feinhals puts him in contact with Gottfried Heinersdorff, the head of the Vereinigte Werkstätten für Mosaik und Glasmalerei Puhl & Wagner, Berlin. Beginning of correspondence and lively exchange of ideas on the significance and technical possibilities of modern stained glass painting.

1918

January — Freundlich is transferred to a reserve military hospital in Trier. He tries with the aid of Niemeyer, Feinhals, and Heinersdorff to get transferred back to Cologne.[20]

February — Writes a letter to the newly forming Novembergruppe in which he uses the term "cosmic communism" for the first time: "It is my opinion that the whole basis of recent art rests on a feeling of cosmic communism, of which economic communism is a necessary yet subordinate part."[21]

February — Divorce from Dore Leeser.

March — Heinersdorff manages to get Freundlich transferred to Berlin for his hospital duties: "I get up every morning at 5, have to be at roll call at 6:30. Spend till noon with trivial matters, mostly standing. By the time I leave the hospital at 12 I am at the end of my tether."[22]

Mid March — Berlin-Wilmersdorf. Uses his old studio at Kaiserplatz 17.

On commission by Feinhals, starts plans for his mosaic *The Birth of Man* (HvW 8, p. 131) in the Heinersdorff workshops (finished 1919).[23]

Graphikausstellung des Frauenbundes zur Förderung deutscher bildender Künstler, Kölnischer Kunstverein, Cologne, May

Freie Secession Berlin, May–July (cat.)

Der expressionistische Holzschnitt, Galerie Hans Goltz, Munich

May 16 Temporary transfer to Ghent.[24] Again asks Heinersdorff for help to be transferred back to Berlin.[25]

May 26 Berlin. "I returned the day before yesterday from Ghent, the doctor there considered me useless." Assumes duties in Garrison Hospital I in Scharnhorststrasse.[26]

End of May Participates in the artists' group Freie Secession in Berlin.[27]

September A special issue of *Die Aktion* (37/38) appears with texts and woodcuts by Freundlich, as well as volume 13 of the book series published by Pfemfert, "Der rote Hahn": *Otto Freundlich: Aktive Kunst; Das Perpetuum-Mobile*.
Together with Seiwert and Hoerle champions the November Revolution: "not until the last days before the revolution did a social democratic editor reluctantly put us in contact with the spartacus league. but there weren't masses. freundlich devised a poster that was directed equally against wilhelm as against his pseudo-socialist lackeys, it was printed on the back of the red announcements that had been left in the printery proclaiming the governor's fortification of cologne. during the night in which it was supposed to be pasted up, november 7, the sailors appeared in cologne. the revolution took place. the soldiers came back."[28]

December Participates in the first meeting of the Novembergruppe on December 3. Participates in the arts advisory board of the Workers' Council for Art, which is founded parallel to the workers' and soldiers' councils, in the "conviction that the political upheavals must be used to liberate art from decades of patronization."[29] The members of the Workers' Council (incl. Adolf Behne, Gropius, the Taut brothers, Schmidt-Rottluff, Max Pechstein, and César Klein) are partly identical with those of the Novembergruppe and the Deutscher Werkbund (German Association of Craftsmen).

1919

January Friendly contact with Karl Liebknecht's son Robert. Takes part in the funeral after Karl Liebknecht's murder on January 15, 1919.

February "Der Raum" ("Space"), in which he reflects on overcoming Euclidean space, in *Die weissen Blätter* 2 (1919).

March Announcements appear in the journals *Der Einzige* (7–9) and *Die Aktion* (10/11) for an art school that Freundlich is running in his Berlin studio at Kaiserplatz 17.

July Paris (short stay), then Cologne.

September Collaboration on Max Ernst's Dada magazine *Der Ventilator* and on the Expressionist mouthpieces *Das Tribunal*, *Die Erde*, and *Der Strom*. Acts as contact for Wieland Herzfelde and George Grosz as authors for *Der Strom*.
Meets the Cologne-based artists Heinrich and Angelika Hoerle, Hans Schmitz, Franz M. Jansen, Anton Räderscheidt, Marta Hegemann, and has contact with the Kalltal-Gemeinschaft in the Eifel region (incl. Carl Oskar and Käthe Jatho, Franz Wilhelm Seiwert, Beyka and Genya Gusik, Ret Marut, and Irene Merme).

November Collaborates on the Dada journal *Bulletin D*, which is published as a catalogue for the first Dada exhibition put on that November by the Gesellschaft der Künste at the Kölnischer Kunstverein. The catalogue is confiscated by the British occupation authorities on account of Freundlich's essay "Die Lach-Rackete" ("The Laughter Rocket")—a searing critique of the bourgeois family, its oppression of women, and the prostitution of sexuality, not least in marriage.[31]

December With his article "Absage: Eine endgültige Auseinandersetzung mit den drei Instituten: Deutscher Werkbund, Arbeitsrat für art in Berlin, Novembergruppe" ("Farewell: A Final Look at the Three Institutes: German Association of Craftsmen, Workers' Council for Art in Berlin, November Group") published in *Die Erde* 24 (1919), he resigns from all three organizations: "These three institutes resemble one another like triplets, sired in the bed of bureaucracy, baptized with the water of the bourgeois church, steeped in the spirit of snobbery, of upwards elbowing and the whole disease of mercantilism."[32]

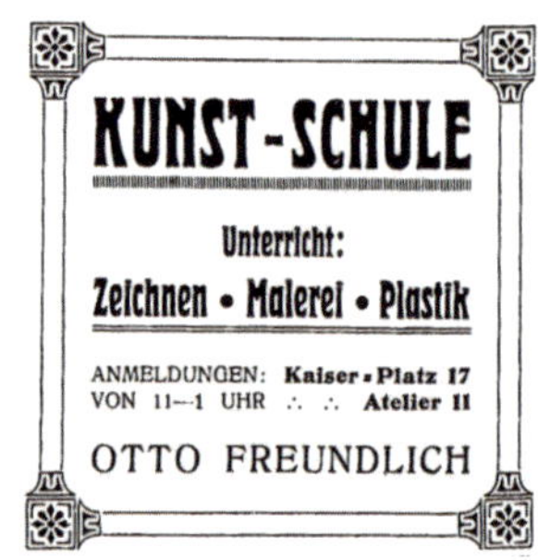

Große Kunstausstellung Berlin, Abteilung Novembergruppe, 7.24–9.30 (cat.)

Group show with Richard Janthur, Erich Heckel, Lene Schneider-Kainer, Willi Jaeckel, Ernst Ludwig Kirchner, César Klein, Heinrich Nauen, and Max Pechstein, Galerie Fritz Gurlitt, Berlin, July–August (cat.)

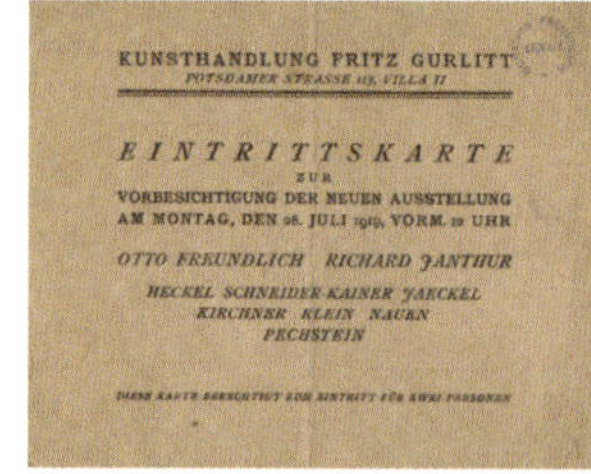

KUNSTHANDLUNG FRITZ GURLITT
POTSDAMER STRASSE 113, VILLA II

EINTRITTSKARTE
ZUR
VORBESICHTIGUNG DER NEUEN AUSSTELLUNG
AM MONTAG, DEN 28. JULI 1919, VORM. 10 UHR

OTTO FREUNDLICH RICHARD JANTHUR
HECKEL SCHNEIDER-KAINER JAECKEL
KIRCHNER KLEIN NAUEN
PECHSTEIN

DIESE KARTE BERECHTIGT ZUM EINTRITT FÜR ZWEI PERSONEN

Künstlervereinigung Der Strom, Kölnischer Kunstverein, Cologne, May

Ausstellung der Gesellschaft der Künste in Köln, Kölnischer Kunstverein, Cologne, 11.1–11.30 (cat.)

1920 Walter Gropius takes pains to find a lectureship for Freundlich at Bauhaus Weimar, but fails because not only the faculty refuses but also Freundlich himself: "In 1919 I was offered a position teaching sculpture at the Bauhaus in Weimar. I declined at the time, because I didn't think I was far enough to impart something really sound to the students."[33]
Start of friendship with Raoul Hausmann, at that time in Berlin, which lasts into the 1930s.
Dedicates his folio *Die Zeichen* (*The Signs*), printed by Kairos publishing in Cologne, to Feinhals.

1921

January — Berlin, studio Kaiserplatz 17.

March 2 — Gives a lecture "Die Verwandlung der sichtbaren Welt" ("The Transformation of the Visible World") at the Graphisches Kabinett J[srael] B[er] Neumann, Berlin.[34]
Publishes "Die schöpferische Macht im Kommunismus" ("The Creative Force in Communism") in *Die Aktion* 39/40 (1921).[35]

Fall — Walter Benjamin considers trying to win over Freundlich as staff member for his journal *Angelus Novus*, but dismisses the idea after visiting his studio: Although Freundlich has in his view "good ideas," he is "incredibly immature."[36]

Graphisches Kabinett J. B. Neumann, Berlin, February

Große Berliner Kunstausstellung, Abteilung Novembergruppe, Berlin, opening 5.14

1922

Since January — Finishes his first stained glass window in a workshop in Naumburg an der Saale. It is exhibited in June at the Graphisches Kabinett J. B. Neumann, then installed in the Berlin study of collector Julius Wissinger.

February 13 — Berthold, Freundlich's son from his first marriage, dies of influenza in Dessau at age three.

March — In protest at the *Erste Internationale Kunstausstellung* planned for May in Düsseldorf, whose organizers Freundlich, Hausmann, and husband and wife Stanislaw Kubicki and Margarete Kubicka accuse of anti-internationalism and mercantilism, he founds together with Jankel Adler and others in Berlin the anarchist art group "Die Kommune." Freundlich is among the signatories of two manifestoes, the first of which appears in the September issue of *Die Aktion*: "We reject the murky opportunism that otherwise prevails in artist groups, and those whose purpose in life consists in such activities. We do not want reconciliation at any price, as preached by those who like to fish in troubled waters. . . . We do not lay down aesthetic laws for ourselves, and have no intention of laying them down for anyone else."[37]

May — Participates with the "Kommune" in the *Erster Kongress der Union internationaler fortschrittlicher Künstler* (First Congress of the Union of International Progressive Artists) from May 29 to 31 in Düsseldorf. The Berlin delegates with Freundlich and Seiwert are unable to get their anarcho-internationalist demands across and leave the plenum in protest. Subsequently the plan is hatched for the joint *International Exhibition of Revolutionary Artists* in the rooms of the Arbeiter-Kunst Exhibition in Petersburger Strasse 39, Berlin.[38]
Freundlich declines Bruno Taut's offer of a teaching post for the sculpture class at the Kunstgewerbeschule in Magdeburg on account of artistic differences with the class director, Rudolf Bosselt.

Summer — Stay at Prerow on the Baltic.

September — In his article "Was wollt ihr von Picasso?" ("What do you want from Picasso?") in *Die Aktion* (33/34) he defends his friend from the critics of Cubism.
Contributes drawings and prints to a lottery for the hungry in Russia (at Kunsthandlung Altmann, Berlin, Lützowufer 13).

December — Visits Niemeyer in Hamburg.

Internationale Ausstellung Revolutionärer Künstler, premises of the Arbeiter-Kunst-Ausstellung, Berlin, 10.22–11.30

1923 Otto Dix does Otto Freundlich's portrait. The litho is published in an edition of around 140 by Karl Nierendorf in Euphorion-Verlag.

Spring Freundlich designs a concrete sculpture for the tomb designed by Max Taut for the Wissinger family at the cemetery in Stahnsdorf near Berlin. Following public protests, the sculpture is already torn down by August 1923, to which Freundlich responds in outrage in a letter to Julius Wissinger: "I am filled with revulsion at the highhandedness with which a work made by an artist with love is simply killed. The main culprit is Max Taut, who as the architect should have had the duty to protect the work . . . As a result of the weakness of character he showed toward them and their likes, who are laymen, he not only destroyed an intellectual protest against bad monumental art, but with the intentionally poor and unclear photograph of the tombstone he did not even leave me with any documentation of my work."[39]

June 25 Married a second time in Berlin-Wilmersdorf. Divorced, however, shortly thereafter by the attorney Theodor Liebknecht, brother of Karl Liebknecht, in Berlin.[40]

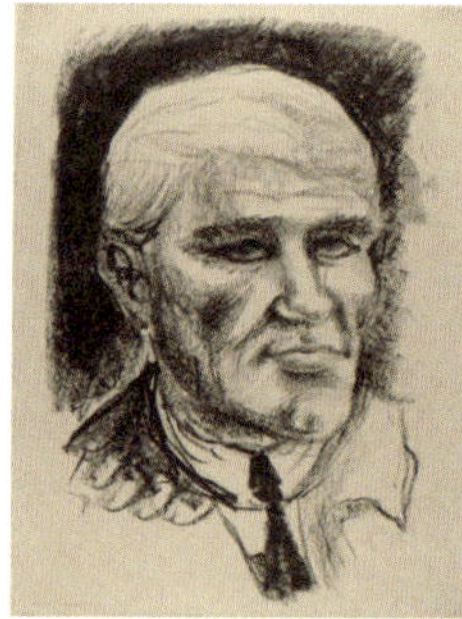

Otto Dix
Portrait of Otto Freundlich, 1923
Lithograph on paper
41.3 x 31 cm
Harvard Art Museums/ Busch-Reisinger Museum, Gift of Louis W. Black

Dance hall in the inn "Engelbert," Remscheid (with, among others, Käthe Kollwitz, Heinrich Hoerle, Franz Wilhelm Seiwert, Jankel Adler, George Grosz, and Otto Dix), opening September 9

1924

March Hamburg. Visits Max Sauerlandt, director of the Museum für Kunst und Gewerbe (Museum of Arts and Crafts).
Visits on March 12 the Ethnographic Museum together with the Hamburg painter Kurt Löwengard and the collector Olga Solmitz, and then visits the sculptor Richard Haizmann to see his works from Paul Klee.

Mid March Visits the publisher Johannes Bredt in Münster, who gives him a commission for a stained glass painting, which Freundlich then has made in the workshops of Puhl & Wagner-Gottfried Heinersdorff, Berlin (HvW 11, p. 140, lost).

July Hamburg. Stays again with Max Sauerlandt.

August Moves to Paris, rue Bonaparte, Hôtel de Paris.
States to the city magistrate in Paris that he is a "glass painter" by profession when applying for his residency permit. Later he names September 9 as the beginning of his stay in France.[41]

September Berlin.

Galerie Fritz Gurlitt, Berlin

Graphisches Kabinett Karl Nierendorf, Berlin (together with Sándor Bortnyik)

Exhibition in the "Neuer Buchladen," Cologne

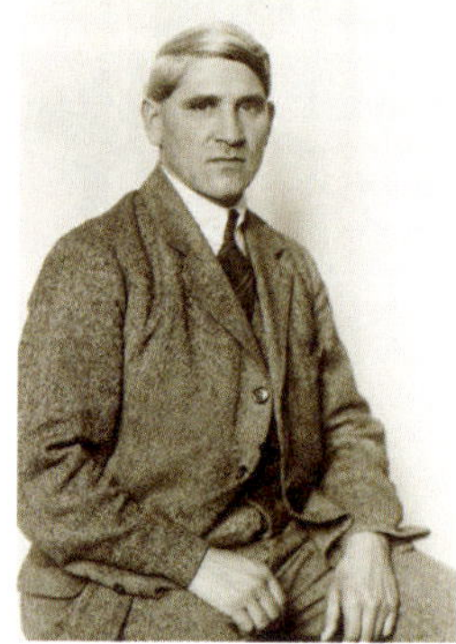

August Sander
Painter and Sculptor (Otto Freundlich), ca. 1925
Vintage silver gelatin print
20.7 x 15.3 cm
August Sander Stiftung, Cologne, courtesy Galerie Julian Sander, Cologne

1925

March Paris, studio in 6, rue Belloni, followed by a studio in rue Bonaparte.

June Visits the abstract filmmaker Viking Eggeling shortly before his death and later mentions their conversation in his 1934 text, "Die Wege der abstrakten Kunst" ("The Paths of Abstract Art").

Fall Invited to the *Revoliytsionnogo Iskusstva Zapada* (*Revolutionary Art of the West*) exhibition in 1926 in Moscow, where he wishes to exhibit a two by two and a half meter stained glass window design (lost), which he hopes August Sander will photograph. He also asks Sander for a print of the portrait he had taken of Freundlich so as to be able to send it to Moscow.[42]

Freundlich's Paris studio, overview of his works, December

1926

July — Visit by Franz Wilhelm Seiwert from Cologne.
Becomes acquainted via the Zurich sculptor Hans Muschg with his sister, the primary school teacher Hedwig Muschg, who subsequently provides him with financial support to the end of his life.

November — Paris, 10, rue de la Sorbonne, Hôtel des Facultés.

December — Visits Chartres again for the first time since 1914.

1927

April and July — Sojourns in Berlin, otherwise Paris.
Visits from Sauerlandt and Haizmann in Paris.

August 12 — Writes to Julius Wissinger: "[Should] anything happen to me through any circumstances, I hereby name you the heir to my artistic and literary estate. In the keeping of the present occupants of my studio on Kaiserplatz are, among other items, 4 large paintings, 2 from the years 1909, one from 1911 (Paris), one from 1921. Apart from which 2 of my sculptures are stored in the building . . . My manuscripts are in the box of books."[43]

1928

June/July — Sojourns in Cologne and Berlin, otherwise Paris.
New companion Lili Ohquist, a Finnish journalist.

September — Paris.
Seiwert tries to get him a commission for a mosaic in Café Namur in Luxembourg, where he himself is installing a glass painting. The commission does not come off.[44]

39e Salon des Indépendants, Grand Palais des Champs-Elysées, Paris, 1.20–2.29 (cat.)

Kölner Kunst 1928, Kölnischer Kunstverein, Cologne, July

Exhibition of mosaic stained glass, Kunstgewerbemuseum, Cologne

1929

January — Olga Solmitz attempts to move Max Sauerlandt to donate 100 Marks to Freundlich so that he can finish his sculpture *Ascension*. Sauerlandt refuses: "His talent lies in the direction of a decorative planar art, and I do not feel I can encourage him in a direction which in my firm conviction is on the wrong track, or leads at best to a dead end."[45]

Summer — Plaster cast of *Ascension*, which is exhibited in October at Kunsthaus Zürich.

October — Becomes a correspondent for the journal *a bis z* (published until January 1933), which is put out by the Gruppe Progressiver Künstler in Cologne.
Member of the artist group Cercle et Carré around Michel Seuphor, Joaquín Torres García, and Georges Vantongerloo.

INVITATION

EXPOSITION D'ART ABSTRAIT

Peintures de JOHN GRAHAM, KAKABADZÉ
SOLLENTO, TORRES-GARCIA, TUTUNDJIAN
ANDRÉAS-WALSER, ZÉRO
Sculptures de OTTO FREUNDLICH
TUTUNDJIAN, VANTONGERLOO

Du 13 Juillet au 2 Août 1929
tous les jours, sauf les dimanches, de 10 à 12 h. et de 2 à 6 h.
Vernissage le samedi 13 Juillet, de 3 à 7 h.

ÉDITIONS BONAPARTE
Tél. Danton 75-91 12, Rue Bonaparte PARIS-VI°

Compagnie de peintres et sculpteurs professionnels, 16e exposition, Brasserie Terminus, Paris, 2.28–end of May (cat.)

40e Salon des Indépendants, Grand Palais des Champs-Elysées, Paris, 1.18–2.28 (cat.)

Prints by the Gruppe Progressiver Künstler Köln, Kroch-Gallery, Chicago, June–July

Art abstrait: 2e groupe, Galerie Bonaparte, Paris, 7.13–8.2

Abstrakte und Surrealistische Malerei und Plastik, Kunsthaus Zürich, Zurich, 10.6–11.3 (cat.)

Galerie Herter, Zurich (cat.)

Expositions Sélectes d'Art Contemporain (ESAC), Stedelijk Museum, Amsterdam (cat.)

1930 Paris, 24, rue Bonaparte, Hôtel de Paris.

January Seiwert tries to find a home for the mosaic *The Birth of Man*, which Feinhals is no longer interested in. On his own initiative he has had it restored and put in a crate for safe keeping at the mosaic workshop Beyer. Karl With, the director of the Cologne Kunstgewerbemuseum, expresses interest in installing it in the entrance to the museum, but nothing comes of it.[46]

May Solmitz acts on behalf of her friend Hans Blumenfeld in the donation of two sculptures and a drawing by Freundlich to the Museum für Kunst und Gewerbe, Hamburg, from the estate of Anna Blumenfeld: *Large Head* (HvW 63, p. 77), *Head* (HvW 65, p. 80), *Blossoming Branch of Chartres* (HvW 272, now lost). Seiwert writes to Freundlich: "There is an announcement in a museum journal that the Kunsthalle in Hamburg acquired the following works from you in 1930: Male Mask (Bronze), Blossoming Branch (pen and ink drawing), Head (watercolor), two Heads (plaster), the latter as a present. Are you aware of this? Perhaps you've been swindled?"[47]

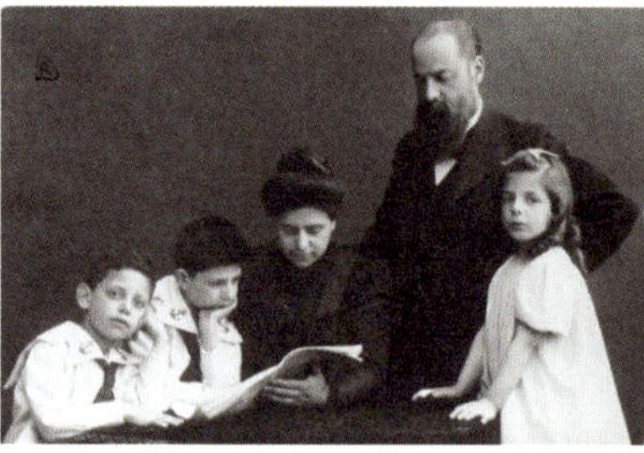

Anna Blumenfeld and family, 1901

Summer Auvers-sur-Oise (several months), together with Theo and Nelly van Doesburg. Here he writes "Zu van Gogh's 40. Todestag" ("On the 40th Anniversary of Van Gogh's Death") and "Ein deutscher Maler in Paris (Erinnerungen an das Künstlerleben in Paris vor dem Kriege 1914)" ("A German Painter in Paris [Memories of Life as an Artist in Paris before the War in 1914]").

Mid September Asks Paul Klee about a position at the Bauhaus, but Klee remains noncommittal.[8]

End of the year Moves together with the German artist and singer Hannah (Jeanne) Kosnick-Kloss.

98. Große Kunstausstellung, Künstlerhaus Hannover, Hanover, 2.23–4.21 (cat.)

La Compagnie de peintres et sculpteurs professionnels: 17e salon, Montrouge, March (cat.)

2e Salon de l'Association Artistique Les Surindépendants, Montparnasse, Paris, 6.7–6.29 (cat.)

3e Salon de l'Art Mural, Paris, opening 6.10

3e Salon de l'Association Artistique Les Surindépendants, Parc des Expositions, Paris, 10.25–11.24 (cat.)

Exhibition of the artists' group Cercle et Carré, Galerie 23, Paris (Otto Freundlich not included in the catalogue), April

Gruppe progressiver Künstler Köln, Weinhaus Deneke, Cologne

Production Paris 1930, Kunstsalon Wolfsberg, Zurich (cat.)

41e Salon des Indépendants, Grand Palais des Champs-Elysées, Paris, 1.17–3.2 (cat.)

1931

Summer The Cercle et Carré disbands, but the protagonists grouped around Georges Vantongerloo and van Doesburg re-form under the name Abstraction-Création. Freundlich is among them.

June Lives in Paris-Montrouge, 18, rue Perrier.[49]

Pens "Der Künstler and die Wirtschaftskrise" ("The Artist and the Economic Crisis") (MS, Cologne, August 1931), published as "Der Künstler in der Krise" ("The Artist in the Crisis") in *Das Kunstblatt* 2 (1932).

October Writes a text that will be published posthumously: "Picasso zu seinem 50. Geburtstag" ("Picasso on his 50th Birthday").

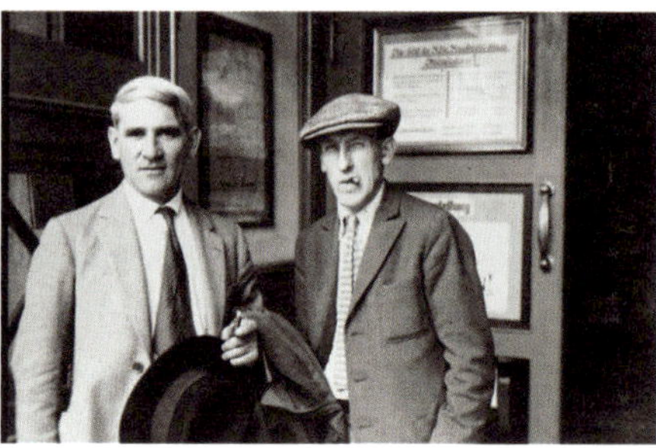

Hannes Flach: *Otto Freundlich and Heinrich Hoerle outside the Kölnischer Kunstverein*, from the series *Painters at work*, ca. 1931

Otto Freundlich, Galerie Dr. Becker und Newman, Cologne, 8.13–9.10

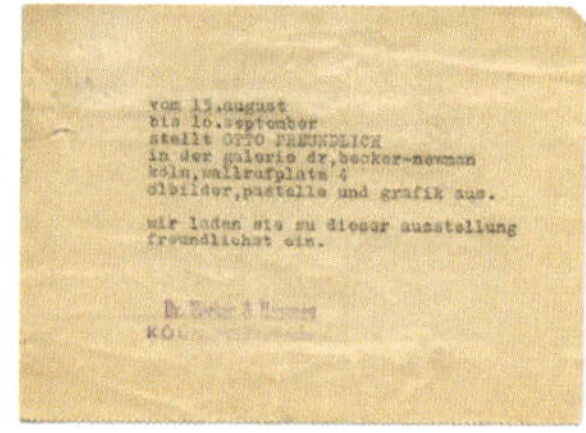

vom 13.august
bis 10.september
stellt OTTO FREUNDLICH
in der galerie dr,becker-newman
köln,wallrafplatz 4
ölbilder,pastelle und grafik aus.

wir laden sie zu dieser ausstellung
freundlichst ein.

Progressive Künstler, Grafik, Galerie Dr. Becker und Newman, Cologne (subsequently in Hamburg, Saarbrücken, Frankfurt/Main)

9x12, Kunsthalle Düsseldorf

Groupe 1940: Première Exposition, Galerie de la Renaissance, Paris, 6.11–6.30 (cat.)

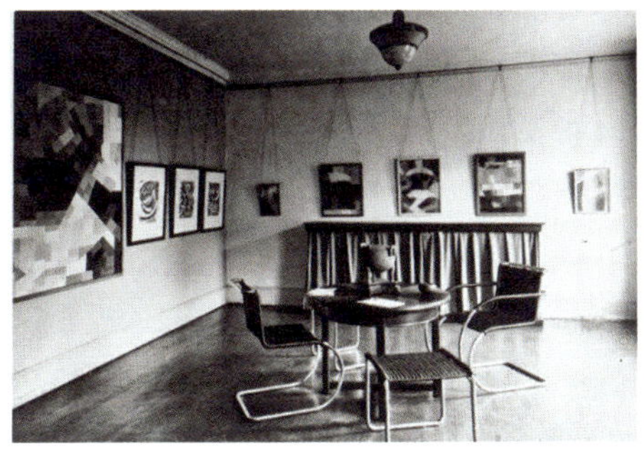

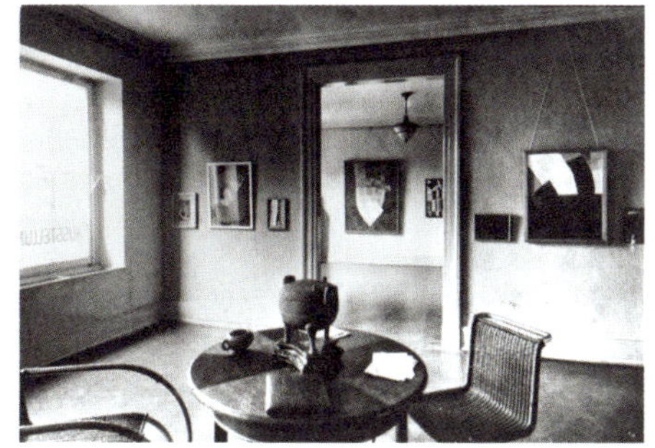

Novembergruppe, Verein Berliner Künstler, neues Haus, Berlin, 7.3–8.3 (cat.)

Kölner Künstler 1931, Kölnischer Kunstverein, Cologne

Solo show in Galerie Dr. Becker und Newman, Cologne, 1931

1932

September Moves to Châtillon-sous-Bagneux, then Clamart (near Paris), 41, rue Fontenay.[50]

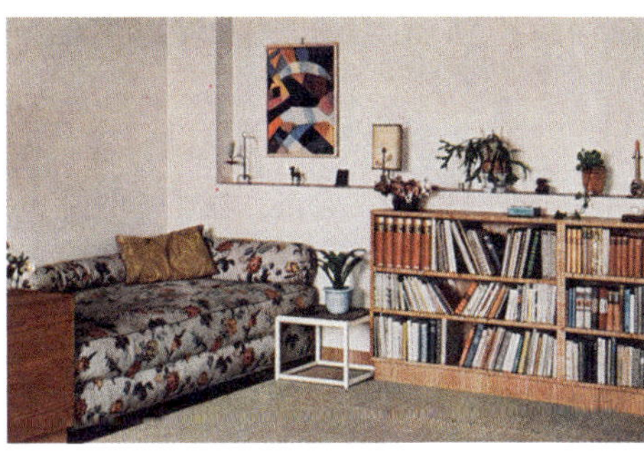

Study of the architect Hans Heinz Lüttgen, 1930s, with the pastel *Composition*, HvW 245

Düsseldorf-Münchener Kunst (Rheinische Sezession, Düsseldorf), Kunstpalast, Düsseldorf, 5.14–8.31 (cat.)

Kölner Gruppe, Galerie Dr. Becker und Newman, Cologne

1e Salon des Artistes Musicalistes, Galerie de la Renaissance, Paris, 12.20.1932–1.19.1933 (cat.)

1933 In Clamart Freundlich produces the sculpture *Composition* (HvW 78, p. 190) and the painting *My Sky is Red* (HvW 168, p. 272).

April Together with Kosnick-Kloss becomes a member of the Association des écrivains et artistes révolutionnaires (A.E.A.R.), which is close to the Communist Party.

Freundlich writes the unpublished text "Für das Bauhaus and gegen die Kulturreaktion" ("For the Bauhaus and against the Cultural Reaction") in response to the repression experienced by professors teaching at academies (dismissals of Otto Dix and Paul Klee) and the closing of the Bauhaus in Berlin on April 11 by the Nazi government.

July Seiwert dies; end of Freundlich's intensive connections with Cologne.

November Announces for the first time that he is leaving Abstraction-Création. He writes to Vantongerloo, saying this is because "the place of a revolutionary artist in these telling times must be solely by the side of the revolutionary proletariat, and since I have taken this place once again my artistic development is inextricably linked with the revolutionary developments and I have no other interests."[51] He changes his mind, though, on Auguste Herbin's insistence.

44e Salon des Indépendants, Grand Palais des Champs-Elysées, Paris, 1.20–2.26 (cat.)

1934 Writes "Die Wege der abstrakten Kunst" ("The Paths of Abstract Art"), in which he describes colored surfaces as an "open commonality" and calls for the conquest of the eye: "Thus the eye is the enemy of the picture because it is a lazy and uncreative organ. The painter does not paint *for* the eye, but *by means* of the eye, so the eye is not a *goal*, but instead a *means*."[52]

May Returns from Clamart to Paris.

November Leaves Abstraction-Création once and for all.

Asks friends like Georges Braque and Auguste Herbin to support him in his bid for naturalization in France. His plan is dashed by the cost involved—1,200 Francs. The offer of handing over a painting in payment is turned down, along with his application.[53]

Special exhibition by the group "abstraction-création" for Otto Freundlich and the Swiss painter Hans Erni, Paris, February

45e Salon des Indépendants, Grand Palais des Champs-Elysées, Paris, 2.2–3.11 (cat.)

1935

March — Holds a lottery of his paintings in his Paris studio in order to improve his financial situation.[54]
Together with Heinz Lohmar, Paul Westheim, and Egon Erwin Kisch and others founds the Kollektiv Deutscher Künstler (KDK) in Paris, a collective of German émigré artists. Further members will include Max Ernst, Eugen Spiro, Gert Wollheim, and Robert Liebknecht.[55]

November — Writes "Bekenntnisse eines revolutionären Malers" ("Confessions of a Revolutionary Painter"), published in full in the present volume.

Invitation to the lottery at Freundlich's Paris studio

Salon de l'Art Mural, Paris (cat.)

46e Salon des Indépendants, Grand Palais des Champs-Elysées, Paris, 1.28–3.3 (cat.)

1936 — Paris, studio at 38, rue Denfert-Rochereau (today rue Henri-Barbusse). Opens Le Mur, a private academy for painting, drawing, sculpture, and woodcuts in his studio at rue Denfert-Rochereau. Gives lectures, but with no financial success.
Visit from Gerd Arntz and Jankel Adler in Paris.

April — Develops the concept of the *Lighthouse of the Seven Arts* (HvW 81, p. 193), which he formulates in the text "Sculptures-Montagnes" ("Sculpture-Mountains"). A short text by Kosnick-Kloss from 1959 reveals that his idea extended to placing the building at the intersection of two large sculpture "streets." These were to run from north to south and from east to west and cross in Auvers-sur-Oise, where the graves of Vincent and Theo van Gogh are located. The axis from the Netherlands to the Mediterranean is designated as the *Road of Human Fraternity,* the one from Belgium across Germany and Poland to Russia as the *Road of Human Solidarity in Remembrance of the Liberation.*

July 3 — Death of Heinrich Hoerle, which prompts Freundlich to write an obituary for both him and Seiwert: "They fulfilled the difficult duty of the artist of combining the revolutionary demands of art with the revolutionary demands of the proletariat."[56]

2e Manifestation de l'Art Mural, Maison de la Culture, Paris, 6.10–6.30

3e Salon des Artistes Musicalistes, Paris (cat.)

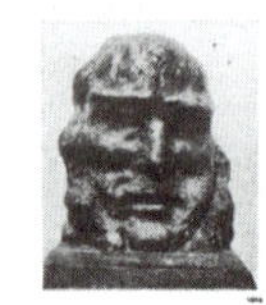

1937

May — Hans W. Wagner from the Puhl & Wagner company travels to Paris in order to realize "a number of sizable works"[57] in the German pavilion at the World's Fair. He has also concealed mosaic stones for Freundlich in the crates for the exhibition, which Freundlich uses for his mosaic *Homage to the Peoples of Color* (HvW 36, p. 245).
Asks Sonia and Robert Delaunay for works for a tombola in Zurich aimed at helping the wives and widows of prisoners in German concentration camps.[58]

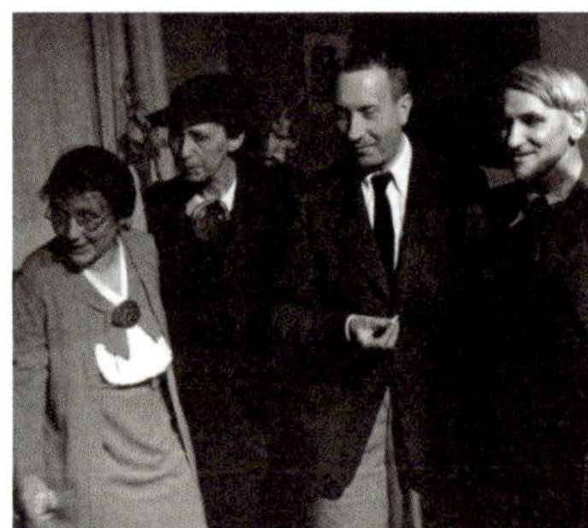

With Jeanne Kosnick-Kloss, Sophie Taeuber-Arp and Jean Arp in Studio Maywald, photo: Willy Maywald (detail)

Studio Willy Maywald, Paris (with Jeanne Kosnick-Kloss)

"Entartete Kunst" [*Degenerate Art*], Hofgarten-Arkaden, Munich, 7.19–11.20.

Konstruktivisten, Kunsthalle Basel, 1.16–2.14 (cat.)

Züricher Kunstgesellschaft, Zurich

Group show, Chicago

48e Salon des Indépendants, Pavillon des Salons, Paris, 3.5–4.4 (cat.)

1937 Exhibition: Unity of Artists for Peace, Democracy and Cultural Development, 41 Grosvenor Square, London, 4.14–5.5 (cat.)

Hans Blumenfeld visits his studio in Paris.
Gets to know the cobbler Gaston Chaissac, who Freundlich encourages to paint. This is the start of a friendship.

July and August — A total of fourteen works by Freundlich are confiscated from public collections by the Reichsministerium für Propaganda und Volksaufklärung (seven works from the Museum für Kunst und Gewerbe, Hamburg/Hamburger Kunsthalle, three from the Hanseatische Hochschule Hamburg, four from the Folkwang Museum, Essen).

10e Salon des Artistes Indépendants Bordelaise, Galerie des Beaux-Arts, Bordeaux, 10.9–11.14 (cat.)

Art réaliste et abstrait, Irmgard Burchard, Z-Haus, No. 18, IV. floor, Zurich, 12.10–12.22 (cat.)

1938

March 5 — Visit from Wilhelm Sandberg, director of the Stedelijk Museum, Amsterdam, in preparation of the *Tentoonstelling Abstracte Kunst* in April.

April — Visit by Raoul Hausmann and Gerd Arntz in Paris.
The influential art historian and editor of the *Burlington Magazine*, Herbert Read, invites Freundlich to participate in *The Exhibition of 20th Century German Art* which Read is mounting at the New Burlington Gallery, London, as a reaction to the Nazi *Degenerate Art* exhibition. Before agreeing, Freundlich asks whether the "notorious Nazi sculptor" Georg Kolbe has been invited, having seen his works in the German Pavilion of the Paris World's Fair. "Out of solidarity with the great and trail-blazing artists who are being oppressed in Germany, it would be impossible for me to take part in the London exhibition if Kolbe was represented."[59] An answer is not known. Although Kolbe's *Head of Paul Cassirer* is exhibited in London, Freundlich is represented with his *Universal Synthesis* (HvW 170, lost)

July — Joint appeal by artists to buy a work by Freundlich, signed by: Jankel Adler, Hans Arp, Georges Braque, Jean Cassou, Marie Cuttoli, André Derain, Paul Dermée, Alfred Döblin, Robert and Sonia Delaunay, Max Ernst, Géo-Charles, Albert Gleizes, Louis de Gonzague Frick, Auguste Herbin, Max Jacob, Wassily Kandinsky, Oskar Kokoschka, Henri Laurens, Fernand Léger, Jacques Lipchitz, Georges Linze, André Lhote, Pablo Picasso, Maurice Raynal, Herbert Read, Sophie Taeuber-Arp, Wilhelm Uhde, Paul Westheim, among others. (fig. 48, p. 200)
Refusals to sign the appeal are documented from Paul Klee and Walter Gropius. Klee fears reprisals against those close to him; Gropius writes from Harvard University, Cambridge, Massachusetts, saying that he is willing to "support Otto Freundlich in every way," but not to "sign an appeal that mingles artistic matters with questions of daily politics to such an extent. I have increasingly come to the conviction that this kind of mingling simply harms cultural affairs without aiding politics, and—for tactical reasons—I am for a strict division between intellectual matters and political ones."[60] His name nevertheless appears in the text of the appeal, probably by mistake.

"Entartete Kunst" (touring exhibition known to have visited 16 cities in the German Reich and territories), February 1938 to 1941 (cat.)

Otto Freundlich: Peintures – Sculptures – Dessins – Gravures, Galerie Jeanne Bucher-Myrbor, Paris, exhibition marking his 60th birthday on July 10, 6.3–7.17

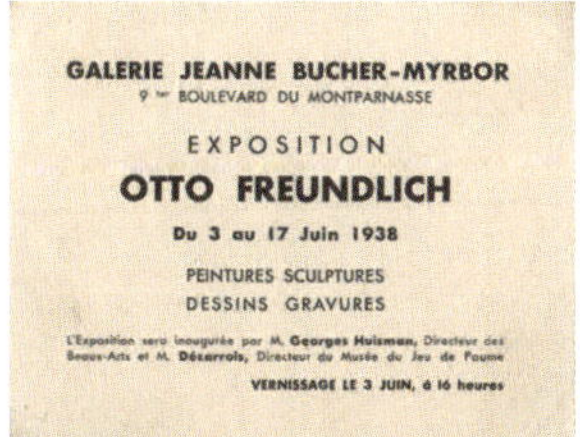
GALERIE JEANNE BUCHER-MYRBOR
9 bis BOULEVARD DU MONTPARNASSE
EXPOSITION
OTTO FREUNDLICH
Du 3 au 17 Juin 1938
PEINTURES SCULPTURES
DESSINS GRAVURES
L'Exposition sera inaugurée par M. Georges Huisman, Directeur des Beaux-Arts et M. Désarrois, Directeur du Musée du Jeu de Paume
VERNISSAGE LE 3 JUIN, à 16 heures

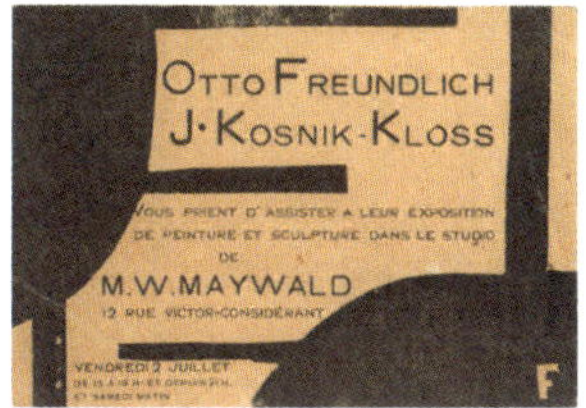
OTTO FREUNDLICH
J·KOSNIK-KLOSS
VOUS PRIENT D'ASSISTER A LEUR EXPOSITION
DE PEINTURE ET SCULPTURE DANS LE STUDIO
DE
M.W.MAYWALD
12 RUE VICTOR-CONSIDÉRANT
VENDREDI 2 JUILLET

Tentoonstelling Abstracte Kunst, Stedelijk Museum, Amsterdam, 4.2–4.24 (cat.)

Exhibition of 20th Century German Art, New Burlington Galleries, London (organized by Sir Herbert Read), 7.8–7.20 (cat.)

Salon de l'Art Mural, Paris

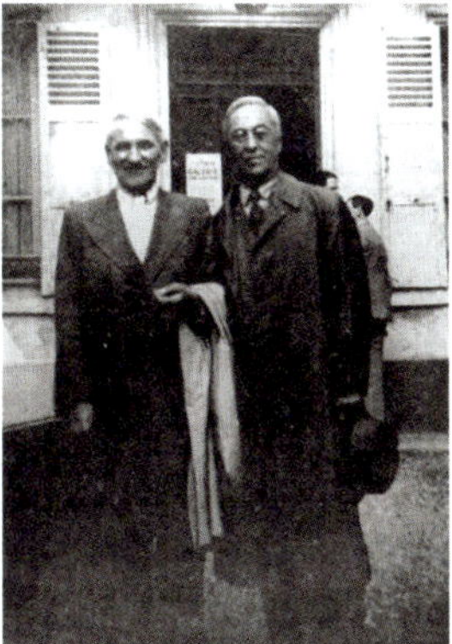

With Wassily Kandinsky, 1938

At St Paul-de-Fenouillet, 1941

With the money collected by the signatories and backers, the large gouache *Homage to the Peoples of Color* (HvW 178, p. 244) can be purchased by public subscription and made over to the Jeu de Paume. "Ehrung für Otto Freundlich!" ("Tribute to Otto Freundlich!") appears on his sixtieth birthday in *Neuer Vorwärts* 266 (1938), where Freundlich is hailed as a "pioneer of absolute painting."
Becomes a member of the Freier Deutsche Künstlerbund which emerges from the Kollektiv Deutscher Künstler in Paris, a non-partisan emigrant organization for German visual artists in French exile founded in 1938 by among others Eugen Spiro and Paul Westheim, which is directed against National Socialist cultural policies.

November — Freundlich is a member of the selection committee for the exhibition *Freie deutsche kunst* mounted by the Freier Künstlerbund at the Maison de la Culture, Paris, but does not exhibit any of his own work. Participating artists include George Grosz, Max Ernst, Paul Klee, Man Ray, Anton Räderscheidt, Robert Liebknecht, and Felix Nussbaum.
To mark his sixtieth birthday he looks back on his life in "Der bildhafte Raum" ("The Pictorial Space"), once again formulating an ethics aimed at bringing people together.

1939

September — After the declaration of war, Freundlich is arrested as a German citizen by the French police.

September 15 — Is detained for around fourteen days at the Colombes sports stadium. From there he is initially brought to Blois (Département Loir-et-Cher), then after a few days to the neighboring village Francillon-par-Villebarou. Kosnick-Kloss sends him pencils and paper so that he can work. Auguste Herbin, Jean Gacon, and gallerists Berthe Weill and Marie Cuttoli attempt to have him released from the camp by giving assurances of his loyalty to France, but to no avail.[61]

Art Décoratif, Galerie d'Art René Breteau, Paris, 5.19–6.8

Peintures & Sculptures du Groupe Eclectique, Galerie Berthe Weill, Paris, opening 4.20

Onze sculpteurs, Galerie Berthe Weill, Paris, 5.18–6.3

Salon des Réalités Nouvelles, Galerie Charpentier, Paris, 6.30–7.15

Abstract and Concrete Art / Art abstrait, Galerie Guggenheim Jeune, London, 5.10–5.27 (the catalogue is in the *London Bulletin*, 14, 1939); Galerie de Beaune, Paris

16e Salon des Tuileries, Palais de Chaillot, Paris, 6.2–7.9 (cat.)

Salon des Réalités Nouvelles, Galerie Charpentier, Paris

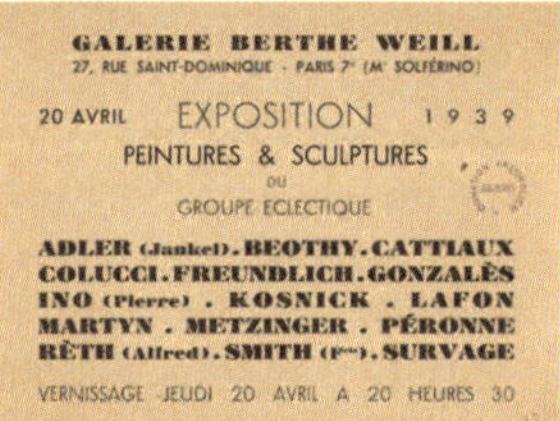
GALERIE BERTHE WEILL
27, RUE SAINT-DOMINIQUE - PARIS 7e (Mt SOLFÉRINO)
20 AVRIL EXPOSITION 1939
PEINTURES & SCULPTURES
DU
GROUPE ECLECTIQUE
ADLER (Jankel). BEOTHY. CATTIAUX
COLUCCI. FREUNDLICH. GONZALÈS
INO (Pierre). KOSNICK. LAFON
MARTYN. METZINGER. PÉRONNE
RÊTH (Alfred). SMITH (Fme). SURVAGE
VERNISSAGE JEUDI 20 AVRIL A 20 HEURES 30

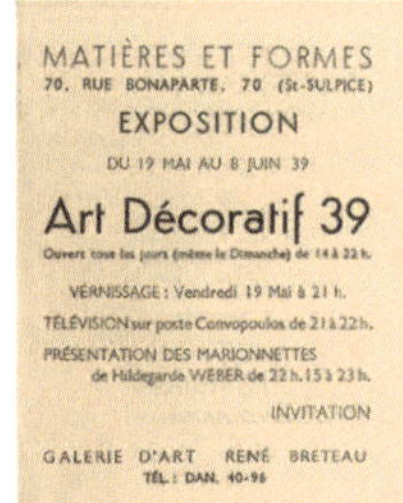
MATIÈRES ET FORMES
70, RUE BONAPARTE, 70 (St-SULPICE)
EXPOSITION
DU 19 MAI AU 8 JUIN 39
Art Décoratif 39
Ouvert tous les jours (même le Dimanche) de 14 à 22 h.
VERNISSAGE : Vendredi 19 Mai à 21 h.
TÉLÉVISION sur poste Convopoulos de 21 à 22 h.
PRÉSENTATION DES MARIONNETTES de Hildegarde WEBER de 22 h. 15 à 23 h.
INVITATION
GALERIE D'ART RENÉ BRETEAU
TÉL. : DAN. 40-96

1940

January — Transferred to a camp in Marolles (Département Loir-et-Cher), then to Fossé (Département Loir-et-Cher).[62] Paul Westheim presses for his release.

February — Freundlich is brought for a few days to the internment camp Cepoy (Département Loiret), before being released at the beginning of February.

February/March — Once back in Paris he submits a new application for naturalization.

End of May — Renewed detention (with, among others, Franz Pfemfert) in the Buffalo Stadium close to Paris. After two weeks he is taken to Bassens (Département Gironde).[63]

June 20 — Discharged from Bassens, he catches the last train to Perpignan. He finds refuge in Hotel Galamus in Saint-Paul-de-Fenouillet (eastern Pyrenees), but is placed under house arrest and police observation.[64]

51e Salon des Indépendants, Palais de Chaillot, Paris, 3.1–3.25 (cat.)

August — Tries to acquire an exit visa for the United States, which fails on account of the costs and because he does not want to leave Jeanne Kosnick-Kloss behind.

End of September — Kosnick-Kloss joins him in Saint-Paul-de-Fenouillet.[65]
His last large text, "Ideen und Bilder" ("Ideas and Images"), which he writes right into 1942.

1941 — Writes his memoirs in a "Biographischen Notiz, von ihm selbst verfasst" ("Biographical Note, Written by Himself"). Draws up a catalogue raisonné from memory and begins to repaint a number of works he considers lost (HvW 101, p. 111; HvW 105, p. 90; HvW 111, p. 91).

October — Turns in vain to refugee organizations for help in his plans to emigrate to the United States.

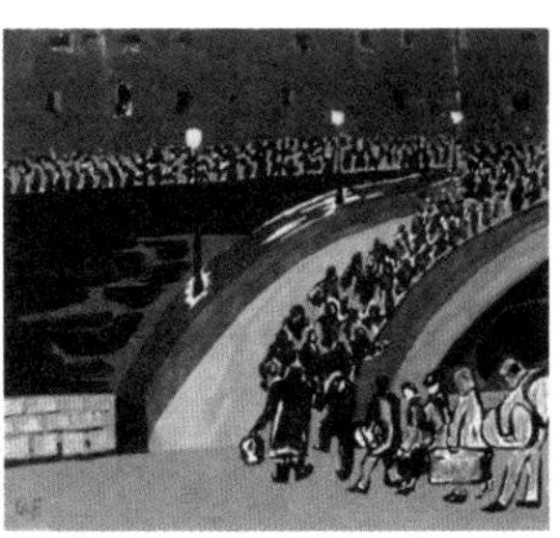

Otto Freundlich
The Inmates from Colombes Crossing a Bridge While Being Transferred, 1942
Gouache

1942

December — The deportation of Jews from France forces Freundlich to go into hiding. A farming family in the village of Saint-Martin-de-Fenouillet above Saint-Paul takes him in. He lives there in a stable hayloft, in which the art historian Rita Wildegans was to find his painting utensils in the early 1980s.

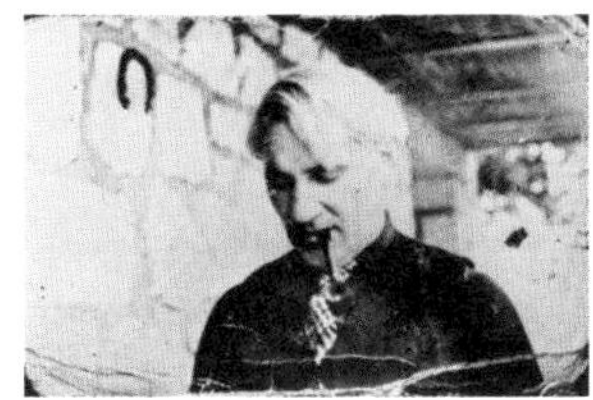

Shortly before his arrest in the Pyrenees, 1942–43

1943

February 23 — After an attack on two German officers, the German authorities instruct the French police to arrest 2,000 Jews in Vichy France.[66] Freundlich is arrested by two gendarmes after being denounced by a neighbor in Saint-Martin.
Brief internment in the camp at Gurs (western Pyrenees), then moved on to the transit camp in Drancy (near Paris).

March 4 — Deportation to Poland. The train, which departs from Drancy at 9:15 a.m., arrives around March 10 at the extermination camp Sobibor.[67] After a selection process, forty men from the 1,003 occupants of the train are taken to Majdanek.[68] Since Freundlich's name is not on the lists of the victims at Majdanek,[69] in all likelihood he was murdered directly on arrival[70] in Sobibor (where no lists were kept[71]), if not already during transportation. The exact date of his death is unknown.

1944 — *Konkrete Kunst*, Kunsthalle Basel, 3.18–4.16 (cat.)

1945 — *Art Concret*, Galerie René Drouin, Paris, 5.15–7.13 (cat.)

1946 — *Premier Salon des Réalités Nouvelles – art abstrait, concret, constructivisme*, Palais des beaux-arts de la Ville de Paris, 7.19–8.18 (cat.)

1947 — *Retrospektive*, Salon des Indépendants, Paris

1949 — *La Collection Guggenheim*, Palazzo Reale, Milan, June; Palazzo Strozzi, Florence/Venice
Do Figurativismo ao Abstracionismo, Museu de arte Moderna São Paulo, March (cat.)
L'art abstrait: ses origines, ses premiers maîtres, Galerie Maeght, Paris (cat.)
1. Préliminaires à l'art abstrait, end April–5.23; *2. Épanouissement de l'art abstrait*, 5.27–6.30

1951 — *Surréalisme + Abstraction: choix de la collection Peggy Guggenheim/ Surrealisme + abstractie: keuze uit de verzameling Peggy Guggenheim*, Stedelijk Museum, Amsterdam; Palais des Beaux-Arts, Brussels (cat.)

1952 — *Otto Freundlich: Un des précurseurs de l'art abstrait*, Galerie Colette Allendy, Paris, 3.1–3.15
Salon 52, Société Royale des Beaux-Arts, Luick
4e Salon de la Jeune Sculpture, Paris

1954 *Otto Freundlich*, Galerie Rive Droite, Paris, 6.22–7.24 (cat.)
Collection Graindorge, Stedeljik Van Abbe Museum, Eindhoven (cat.)

1955 *Œuvres d'artistes juifs morts en déportation*, Musée d'art juif; Galerie Zak, Paris, 2.28–3.12 (cat.)
Ausgewanderte Maler, Städtisches Museum Morsbroich/Leverkusen, 9.23–10.22 (cat.)
20th Century Painting and Sculpture from the Collection of Mr. and Mrs. Harry L. Winston, University of Michigan Museum of Art, Ann Arbor, 10.30–11.27 (cat.)

1956 *100 Sculptures des Peintres, de Daumier à Picasso / Skulpturen von Malern – von Daumier bis Picasso*, Hôtel de Ville d'Yverdon, August–September (cat.); Kunsthaus Zürich, Zurich, 10.26–11.30 (cat.)

1957 *Cinquante ans de peinture abstraite*, Galerie Creuze, Paris, 5.9–6.12 (cat.)
Art abstrait: Les premières générations (1910–1939), Musée d'Art et d'Industrie de Saint-Etienne (cat.)
Malerei des 20. Jahrhunderts in Kölner Privatbesitz, Kölnischer Kunstverein, Cologne
Collecting Modern Art – Paintings, Sculpture and Drawings from the Collection of Mr. and Mrs. Harry Lewis Winston, The Detroit Institute of Art, 9.27–11.3; Virginia Museum of Fine Arts, Richmond, 12.13.1957–1.5.1958; San Francisco Museum of Art, 1.23–3.13.1958; The Milwaukee Art Institute, 4.11–5.12.1958 (cat.)

1958 *Deutsche Maler in Paris*, Pfalzgalerie, Kaiserslautern
Musée de Verviers, Belgium
Otto Freundlich, Retrospective on his 80th birthday, Galerie St. Germain, Paris (with Jeanne Kosnick-Kloss), 6.17–7.12

1959 *Kunstsammler an Rhein und Ruhr, Malerei 1900 bis 1959*, Städtisches Museum Leverkusen, Schloss Morsbroich
Galerie René Drouin, Paris

1960 *Construction and Geometry in Painting: From Malevich to "Tomorrow,"* Galerie Chalette, New York, March (cat.)
Cent sculptures de Daumier à nos jours, Musée d'Art et d'Industrie de Saint-Etienne, 3.26–5.29 (cat.)
Hommage à Jeanne Bucher 1925–1960, Galerie Jeanne Bucher, Paris, May–June (cat.)
Expressionismus, Literatur und Kunst, 1910–1923, Deutsches Literaturarchiv im Schiller-Nationalmuseum, Marbach, 5.8–10.31 (cat.)
L'art moderne Pontoise, l'art sacré Auvers-sur-Oise: Peintures, sculptures, vitraux, gemmaux, céramiques, tapisseries, Musée Tavet de Pontoise, Église et Mairie d'Auvers-sur-Oise, 5.15–7.10 (cat.)
Otto Freundlich. 1878–1943: Gemälde – Graphik – Skulpturen, Wallraf-Richartz-Museum, Cologne, 5.21–7.10 (cat.)
Modern Masters in West Coast Collections: An exhibition selected in celebration of the twenty-fifth anniversary of the San Francisco Museum of Art 1935–1960, San Francisco Museum of Art, 10.18–11.27 (cat.)
Konkrete Kunst: 50 Jahre Entwicklung, Helmhaus Zürich, Zurich, 6.8–8.14 (cat.)

1961 Studio Maywald, Paris

1962 *Deux sculptures monumentales de Otto Freundlich*, Galerie Claude Bernard, Paris, in collaboration with Galerie René Drouin, Paris, and Otto Gerson Gallery, New York, March–April (cat.)
La Sculpture contemporaine, Musée Maison de la Culture du Havre, 5.6–6.17 (cat.)
Monumental Sculpture, Otto Gerson Gallery, New York, June–July (cat.)
Mosaïques contemporaines, Musée des Arts Décoratifs, Paris
Berliner Bildnisse aus drei Jahrhunderten, Städtische Galerie München, Munich, 6.1–7.1 (cat.)

Europäische Kunst 1912: Zum 50. Jahrestag der Ausstellung des Sonderbundes Westdeutscher Kunstfreunde und Künstler in Cologne, Wallraf-Richartz-Museum, Cologne, 9.12–12.9 (cat.)
Moderne Kunst in Köln, Verkehrsamt Köln, Cologne

1963 *Otto Freundlich*, foyer of the Freie Volksbühne Theater, Berlin, 10.1–10.31
Formes Mathématiques: Peintres, sculpteurs contemporains, Université de Paris, Palais de la Découverte, Paris, 1.20–2.17 (cat.)
Wilhelm Lehmbruck and other German Sculptors of his Time, Otto Gerson Gallery, New York, 2.5–3.2 (cat.)
Kunstdiktatur Gestern und Heute, Galerie Ben Wargin, Berlin, 6.16–7.10 (cat.)

1964 *Documenta III, International Exhibition*, Alte Galerie, Museum Fridericianum, Orangerie, Kassel, 6.27–10.5 (cat.)
14e Salon d'Art Sacré, Musée d'Art Moderne, Paris (cat.)

1965 *Berlin – Zwanziger Jahre, Malerei, Grafik, Plastik*, Stadt Bad Godesberg
Traum – Zeichen – Raum: Benennung des Unbenannten. Kunst in den Jahren 1924–1939, Wallraf-Richartz-Museum, Cologne, 10.23–12.12 (cat.)
Galerie de l'Université, Paris
Panathénées de la sculpture mondiale, Athens, 9.8–11.8

1967 *Vom Bauhaus bis zur Gegenwart: Meisterwerke aus deutschem Privatbesitz*, Kunstverein Hamburg, 5.20–7.9 (cat.)
Spektrum der Farbe: Eine Züricher Privatsammlung, Kunsthaus Zürich, Zurich, 3.9–4.23 (cat.)
Kunst des 20. Jahrhunderts aus rheinisch-westfälischem Privatbesitz, Städtische Kunsthalle Düsseldorf, Kunstverein für die Rheinlande und Westfalen, 4.30–6.18 (cat.)
Sammlung Marguerite Arp-Hagenbach, Kunstmuseum Basel, 11.4.1967–1.7.1968 (cat.)

1968 *Otto Freundlich, Jeanne Kosnick-Kloss: Exposition commémorative avec le concours de l'Association des amis d'Otto Freundlich*, Centre Culturel Allemand, Goethe Institute, Paris, 1.9–2.10 (cat.)
Jewish Artists Who Perished in the Holocaust, Tel Aviv Museum, April–May (cat.)

1969 *La Donation Freundlich au Musée de Pontoise, Exposition de vingt-deux œuvres de Otto Freundlich et treize œuvres de Jeanne Kosnick-Kloss* (cat.)
Opening of the Freundlich Foundation
Attraction 1924–1969, Centre Culturel Allemand, Goethe Institute, Paris, 1.15–2.11 (cat.)
Sammlung Wilhelm Hack: Kunst der Römer- und Völkerwanderungszeit, Kunst des Mittelalters, Kunst des 20. Jahrhunderts, Kunsthalle Düsseldorf, Kunstverein Frankfurt am Main, 4.23–6.29 (cat.)
Depuis Rodin, Musée Municipal de Saint-Germain-en-Laye, 11.14.1969–1.15.1970 (cat.)

1970 *Die Zwanziger Jahre (I): Deutsche Kunst von 1914–1923*, Galerie Nierendorf, Berlin, 4.6–8.24 (cat.)
Verzameling Marguerite Arp-Hagenbach, Rijksmuseum Kröller-Müller, Otterlo, 6.28–8.16 (cat.)
L'Art en Europe autour de 1925, L'Ancienne Douane de Strasbourg, 5.14–9.15 (cat.)
Hoerle und sein Kreis, Kunstverein Frechen, December 1970–January 1971 (cat.)

1971 *Non-Objective World 1924–1939*, Galerie Jean Chauvelin, Paris, 6.1–6.30; Annely Juda Fine Art, London, 7.7–9.30; Galleria Milano, Milan, 10.15–11.15
Deutsche und französische Künstler des 20. Jahrhunderts, Galerie Großhenning, Düsseldorf
Kunst des 20. Jahrhunderts: Freie Berufe sammeln. Malerei, Plastik, Objekte, Graphik, Städtische Kunsthalle Düsseldorf, 6.25–8.15 (cat.)

1972 *Weltkulturen und moderne Kunst: Die Begegnung der europäischen Kunst und Musik im 19. und 20. Jahrhundert mit Asien, Afrika, Ozeanien, Afro- und Indo-Amerika*, Haus der Kunst, Munich (on the occasion of the 20th Olympics, 1972), 6.16–9.30 (cat.)
Die gegenstandslose Welt 1939–1955, Annely Juda Fine Art, London, 7.6– 9.8; Galerie Liatowitsch, Basel, 9.20–10.26; Galleria Milano, Milan, 11.14–12.30 (cat.)

1973 *Sculptures de peintres*, Musée Rodin, Paris (cat.)
The Non-Objective World 1914–1955, Annely Juda Fine Art, London, 7.5–9.22; University Art Museum Austin, TX, 10.14–12.15 (cat.)
Kunst in Deutschland 1898–1973, Hamburger Kunsthalle, Hamburg, 11.10.1973–1.6.1974; Städtische Galerie Lenbachhaus, Munich, 2.1–3.11.1974 (cat.)
Futurism: A Modern Focus. Selection from the Lydia & Harry L. Winston Collection, Dr. and Mrs. Barnett Malbin, Solomon R. Guggenheim Museum, New York (cat.)

1974 *Abstraction-Création – Art Non-Figuratif 1932–1936, 30 artistes*, Dépôt 15, Paris (Otto Freundlich not in the catalogue), March–April

1975 *Vom Dadamax bis zum Grüngürtel: Köln in den 20er Jahren. Bildende Kunst, Fotografie, Rundfunk, Architektur, Musik, Theater, Literatur*, Kölnischer Kunstverein, Cologne, 3.15–5.11 (cat.)
Versuch einer Rekonstruktion: Internationale Ausstellung Revolutionärer Künstler 1922 in Berlin, Neuer Berliner Kunstverein, Artothek Berlin, 6.16–7.11 (cat.)
Otto en Adya van Rees, levenen werk tot 1934, Centraal Museum, Utrecht, 4.30–6.22; Gemeentemuseum, The Hague, 7.12–8.24 (cat.)
Art abstrait 1910–1940: Dessins, Musée national d'art moderne, Paris, July–September (cat.)
Die Progressiven, Galerie Brockstedt, Hamburg, 5.15–6.8. (cat.)
Politische Konstruktivisten: Die Gruppe "progressiver Künstler" Köln, Neue Gesellschaft für Bildende Kunst, Akademie der Künste, Berlin, June–July
Le Bateau-Lavoir: Berceau de l'art moderne, Musée Jacquemart-André, Paris (cat.)
Fondation Veranneman, Kruishoutem

1976 *Die reine Form: Von Malewitsch bis Albers*, Kunstmuseum Düsseldorf, 10.15–11.28 (cat.)

1977 *Tendenzen der Zwanziger Jahre, 15. Europäische Kunstausstellung*, Neue Nationalgalerie Berlin; Akademie der Künste (Berlin West); Große Orangerie des Schlosses Charlottenburg, Berlin, 8.14–10.16 (cat.)
Die Novembergruppe, Kunstamt Wedding, Berlin
Die Dreißiger Jahre: Schauplatz Deutschland, Haus der Kunst, Munich; 2.11–4.17; Museum Folkwang, Essen, 4.30–7.3; Kunsthaus Zürich, Zurich, 7.15–9.18 (cat.)
Aspekte konstruktiver Kunst: Sammlung McCrory Corporation New York, Kunsthaus Zürich, Zurich, 1.14–2.27 (cat.)
Aspects historiques du constructivisme et de l'art concret: La McCrory Corporation et sa collection, Musée d'Art moderne de la Ville de Paris, 6.3–8.28 (cat.)
Wem gehört die Welt? Kunst und Gesellschaft in der Weimarer Republik, Neue Gesellschaft für bildende Kunst, Staatliche Kunsthalle Berlin, 8.21–10.23 (cat.)
Hommage à Max Jacob, 1876–1944, Musée de Montmartre, Paris, 10.25.1976–1.30.1977 (cat.)

1978 *Otto Freundlich (1878–1943): Retrospektive*, Rheinisches Landesmuseum, Bonn, 12.19.1978–2.4.1979; Kunstverein Braunschweig, 2.16–3.25.1979; Neuer Berliner Kunstverein, Berlin 4.4–4.28.1979 (cat.)
Hommage à Otto Freundlich à l'occasion du 100ième anniversaire de sa naissance, Goldman-Schwartz Gallery, Jerusalem; The Israel Museum, Jerusalem, September–October (cat.)
Hommage à Otto Freundlich, Musée de Pontoise, 5.27–7.30 (cat.)

L'Art moderne dans les musées de province, Grand Palais, Paris, 2.3–4.24 (cat.)
Abstraction-Création 1931–1936, Westfälisches Landesmuseum für Kunst und Kulturgeschichte Münster, 4.2–6.4; Musée d'Art moderne de la Ville de Paris, 6.16–9.17 (cat.)
Chemins de la création: Dessins de peintres, dessins de sculptures, Château d'Ancy-le-Franc, 6.10–9.17 (cat.)
Le Bateau Lavoir, Museum voor Schone Kunsten, Ghent, 10.6–11.12 (cat.)
Paris–Berlin 1900–1933: Rapports et contrastes France–Allemagne, Centre Georges Pompidou, Paris, 7.12–11.6 (cat.)
McCrory Corporation, Tel Aviv Museum
Franz W. Seiwert – Leben und Werk, Kölnischer Kunstverein, Cologne 1.27–3.27; Westfälischer Kunstverein, Münster, 4.28–6.4; Kunstamt Kreuzberg, Berlin, 6.16–7.30; Städtische Kunstsammlung Ludwigshafen/Rhein, 8.6–9.17 (cat.)
The Non-Objective World: Twenty-Five Years 1914–1939, Annely Juda Fine Art, London, 6.28–9.30 (cat.)

1979 *Éloge du petit format: Peintures – sculptures – dessins – collages – pastels – estampes*, Collection Pierre Bourut, Musée de Pontoise, 2.17–4.15 (cat.)
L'art dans les années 30 en France, Musée d'Art et d'Industrie de Saint-Etienne, March–May (cat.)
Célébration en bleu, Manège Royal, Saint-Germain-en-Laye

1980 *Montparnasse. La Revue de Géo Charles: La collection complète de 1914 à 1930, ses poèmes sur le sport, ses portraits, les œuvres de ses amis peintres*, Musée de Pontoise, 2.9–3.9 (cat.)
Exposition Résistance, Déportation: Création dans le bruit des armes, Chancellerie de l'Ordre de la Libération, Paris, 4.24–6.20 (cat.)
Max Ernst in Köln: Die rheinische Kunstszene bis 1922, Kölnischer Kunstverein, Cologne, 5.7–7.6 (cat.)
Arbeitsrat für Kunst 1918–1921, Akademie der Künste Berlin, 6.29–8.3 (cat.)
Van Gogh bis Cobra: Holländische Malerei 1880–1950, Württembergischer Kunstverein, Stuttgart, 11.30.1980–1.18.1981 (cat.)

1981 *Westkunst: Zeitgenössische Kunst seit 1939*, Messehallen Köln, Cologne, 5.30–8.16 (cat.)

1982 *Otto Freundlich et Jeanne Kosnick-Kloss, les œuvres retrouvées*, Musée de Pontoise, 3.13–4.30 (cat.)
Otto Freundlich, Leben und Werk, Westfälisches Landesmuseum für Kunst und Kulturgeschichte, Münster
Accrochages, peintures, sculptures, dessins, Galerie Thomas Borgmann, Cologne
Enrichissements recents, Musée national d'art moderne, Centre Georges Pompidou, Paris
Les dessins et ses techniques, Musée de Pontoise

1983 *28 artistes de la collection Pierre Bourut*, Mairie d'Auvers-sur-Oise
Verfolgt und verführt: Kunst unterm Hakenkreuz in Hamburg. 1935–1945, Hamburger Kunsthalle, Hamburg, 5.12–7.3 (cat.)
Résistances et Créations, Chapelle du Collège Diderot, Langres
Sammlung Theo Wormland, Haus der Kunst, Munich, 7.23–9.11 (cat.)
Maler bauen Barrikaden: Grafik der 20er Jahre, Haus der Kultur und Bildung Neubrandenburg; Kunsthalle Rostock (cat.)
De l'art juif aux artistes israéliens, continuité ou ruptures, Centre Culturel Thibaud de Champagne, Troyes
Verboten, verfolgt: Kunstdiktatur im Dritten Reich, Wilhelm-Lehmbruck-Museum, Duisburg, 4.10–5.23; Kunstverein Hannover, Hanover, 6.5–8.14; Kunsthalle Wilhelmshaven, 9.24–10.31 (cat.)
German Expressionist Sculpture / Skulptur des Expressionismus, Los Angeles County Museum of Art, 10.30.1983–1.22.1984; Hirschhorn Museum and Sculpture Garden Smithsonian Institution Washington, DC, 4.4–6.17.1984; Josef-Haubrich-Kunsthalle, Cologne, 7.12–8.26.1984 (cat.)

1984 *Skulptur im 20. Jahrhundert*, Merian Park, Basel
Schwebend-Heiter: Gemälde, Aquarelle, Zeichnungen, Drucke, Skulpturen und Objekte, Galerie Pels-Leusden, Berlin, 1.30–4.24 (cat.)
Lesser-known Masters of the Avant-Garde, Helen Serger/La Boetie, Inc., New York
Un siécle, cent chefs d'œuvres, Paris, Grand Palais (celebrating the centenary of the Salon des Indépendants)
Artcurial, Un Art autre – Un autre Art, les années 50 (1945–1955), Paris
Der deutsche Holzschnitt im 20. Jahrhundert, Institut für Auslandsbeziehungen, Stuttgart

1985 *Otto Freundlich: Malerei und Graphik*, galerie contact, Böblingen
Otto Freundlich: La donation Freundlich au Musée de Pontoise, Goethe Institute, Brussels, 2.6–3.5 (cat.)
A un œil et demi, Galerie Franka Berndt, Paris
La Donation Pierre Bourut, Pavillon de la Restauration, Vichy
Vom Klang der Bilder: Die Musik in der Kunst des 20. Jahrhunderts, Staatsgalerie Stuttgart, 7.6–9.22 (cat.)
Contrasts of Form: Geometric Abstract Art, 1910–1980. From the Collection of the Museum of Modern Art, including the Riklis Collection of McCrory Corporation, The Museum of Modern Art, New York (cat.)
Kandinsky in Paris: 1934–1944, The Solomon R. Guggenheim Museum, New York (cat.)
Masterpieces of the Avantgarde: Three Decades of Contemporary Art, The Sixties – The Seventies – The Eighties, Annely Juda Fine Art/Juda Rowan Gallery, London (cat.)
The Sixties: 9.17–10.19; *The Seventies:* 10.22–11.23; *The Eighties*: 11.26–12.20
De la Bible à nos jours: 3000 ans de l'art, Société des Artistes Indépendants et le Comité Français Terre d'Israel in the Grand Palais Paris, 6.6–7.28 (cat.)
Noir et Blanc, Musée de Pontoise
Delaunay und Deutschland, Bayerische Staatsgemäldesammlung – Staatsgalerie moderner Kunst im Haus der Kunst, Munich, 10.4.1985–1.6.1986 (cat.)

1986 *Un regard sur l'art d'aujourd'hui*, Musée Promenade, Marly-le-Roi, 5.16–6.29
Europa-Amerika: Die Geschichte einer künstlerischen Faszination, Museum Ludwig, Cologne, 9.6–11.30 (cat.)
Formen auf weißem Grund: Konstruktivismus und geometrische Kunst, Galerie Stolz, Cologne, September–November (cat.)
Contrastes de forma, abstracción geométrica, 1910–1980 de la colecciones del Solomon R. Guggenheim Museum y The Museum of Modern Art de New York, Museo de Arte Contemporaneo de Caracas, November–December (cat.)
Les modernes classiques, Galerie Franka Berndt, Paris
L'Art et la couleur, Musée des Arts, Cholet, 12.12.1986–3.2.1987

1987 *Modernes for ever*, Galerie Franka Berndt, Paris
Meister des 20. Jahrhunderts, Galerie Gmurzynska, Cologne
The Cologne Progressives 1919–1933, Rachel Adler Gallery, New York (cat.)
1912: Break up of Tradition, Winnipeg Art Gallery, 8.7–10.4 (cat.)
Le eredità sconosciute di Peggy Guggenheim: Da Max Ernst a Jackson Pollock, Solomon R. Guggenheim Museum, New York, March–May 1987; Collezione Peggy Guggenheim, Venice, October 1887–January 1888 (cat.)
"Entartete Kunst": Dokumentation zum nationalsozialistischen Bildersturm am Bestand der Staatsgalerie Moderner Kunst in München, Staatsgalerie moderner Kunst im Haus der Kunst, Munich, 11.27.1987–1.31.1988 (cat.)
"... und nicht die leiseste Spur einer Vorschrift" – Positionen unabhängiger Kunst in Europa um 1937, Kunstsammlung Nordrhein-Westfalen Düsseldorf, 12.4.1987–1.31.1988 (cat.)

1988 *Otto Freundlich*, Musée départemental de Rochechouart, 6.9–8.31
De La Fresnaye à Kandinsky, Galerie Franka Berndt, Paris
The Non-Objective World Revisited, Annely Juda Fine Art, London, 7.1–10.15 (cat.)
German Expressionism: The Second Generation 1915–1925 / Expressionismus: Die Zweite Generation 1915–1925, Los Angeles County Museum of Art, 10.9–12.31.1988; Fort Worth Art Museum, 2.2–4.9.1989; Kunstmuseum Düsseldorf, 5.18–7.9.1989; Staatliche Galerie Moritzburg, Halle (Saale), 8.9–9.30.1989 (cat.)

1989 *Bilderstreit, Widerspruch, Einheit und Fragment der Kunst seit 1960*, Museum Ludwig in den Rheinhallen der Kölner Messe, Cologne, 4.8–6.28 (cat.)
Der Traum einer neuen Welt, Berlin 1910–1933, Museum Altes Rathaus, Ingelheim am Rhein, 4.23–5.4 (cat.)
Abstraction-Création 1931–1936 – Réalités Nouvelles 1946–1956, Galerie Franka Berndt, Paris
Corps-Figures: La figuration humaine dans la sculpture du XXe siècle, Artcurial, Centre d'art plastique contemporain, Paris, May–June (cat.)
Max Jacob et les artistes de son temps, de Picasso à Dubuffet, Musée des Beaux Arts d'Orléans, 6.1–9.30 (cat.)
Les modernes classiques à la Bastille, Galerie Franka Berndt Bastille, Paris
Graphisches Kabinett Kunsthandel Wolfgang Werner, Bremen/ Helen Serger / La Boetie, Inc., New York, Fall (cat.)

1990 *Otto Freundlich*, Galerie Franka Berndt Bastille, Paris, 5.16–6.23 (cat.)
Hommage à Otto Freundlich, Galerie d'Art Moderne Feigel-Pfenniger, Basel
Lambert Rucki et les modernes classiques, Galerie Franka Berndt Bastille, Paris, 9.13–10.31 (cat.)

1991 *Otto Freundlich zum Gedächtnis*, Hamburger Kunsthalle, Hamburg

1992 *"Degenerate Art": The Fate of the Avantgarde in Nazi Germany*, Los Angeles County Museum of Art, 2.17–5.12.1991; The Art Institute of Chicago, 6.22– 9.8.1991; International Gallery, Smithsonian Institution, Washington, DC, 10.8.1991–1.12.1992; Altes Museum, Berlin, 3.4–5.31.1992 (cat.)

1993 *Otto Freundlich et ses amis*, Musée de Pontoise (cat.)
Kurt Weber 1893–1964, Neue Galerie am Landesmuseum Joanneum, Graz, 7.9–8.29 (Otto Freundlich not in the catalogue)

1994 *Otto Freundlich: Ein Wegbereiter der abstrakten Kunst*, Museum Ostdeutsche Galerie, Regensburg, 9.24–10.30; Kulturgeschichtliches Museum – Kunsthalle Dominikanerkirche, Osnabrück, 11.13.1994–1.15.1995 (cat.)

1995 *Okkultismus und Avantgarde: Von Munch bis Mondrian 1900–1915*, Schirn-Kunsthalle, Frankfurt am Main, 6.3–8.20 (cat.)
Von Gabriele Münter bis Georg Baselitz – Linolschnitt im 20. Jahrhundert, Städtische Galerie Delmenhorst, 3.12–4.30

1997 *Deutschlandbilder: Kunst aus einem geteilten Land*, 47. Berliner Festwochen im Martin-Gropius-Bau, Berlin, 9.7.1997–1.11.1998 (cat.)

1998 *Picasso. Klee. Giacometti – Die Sammlung Steegmann*, Staatsgalerie Stuttgart, 10.15.1998–2.21.1999 (cat.)

2000 *L'école de Paris 1904–1929: La part de l'Autre*, Musée d'Art moderne de la Ville de Paris, 12.1.2000–3.11.2001 (cat.)

2001 *Otto Freundlich – Kräfte der Farbe*, Westfälisches Landesmuseum für Kunst und Kulturgeschichte, Münster, 2.18–5.13; Kunstmuseum Liechtenstein, Vaduz, 5.27–8.19 (cat.)
Otto Freundlich: Sculpture, Michael Werner Gallery, New York, 9.26.–11.3 (cat.); Michael Werner Kunsthandel, Cologne, January–February 2002
Farblicht – Kunst und Künstler im Wirkungskreis des Glasmalers Gottfried Heinersdorff (1883–1941), Kunst-Museum Ahlen, 2.18–4.22; Edwin Scharff Museum Neu-Ulm, 5.6–7.15; Clemens-Sels-Museum Neuss, 8.19–10.28 (cat.)
Ornament und Abstraktion: Kunst der Kulturen, Moderne und Gegenwart im Dialog, Fondation Beyeler, Riehen/Basel, 6.10–10.7 (cat.)

2002 *Sammlung Rosenkranz*, Von der Heydt-Museum, Wuppertal, 2.10–3.31 (cat.)
Akrobaten, Harlekine und Amazonen: Graphische Sammlung Delmenhorst. Neuerwerbungen 1999 bis 2001, Städtische Galerie Delmenhorst, Haus Coburg, 1.11–2.10 (cat.)

2004 *Freundlich – Gangolf – Kogan: Drei Künstlerschicksale*, Ernst Barlach Haus, Hamburg, 5.2–9.5 (cat.)

2005 *Martin Noël: Treffen mit Otto Freundlich. Hölzer und Postkarten*, Museum Pfalzgalerie, Kaiserslautern, 10.1–11.27 (cat.)
Von Paul Gauguin bis Imi Knoebel: Werke aus der Hilti Art Foundation, Kunstmuseum Liechtenstein, Vaduz, 2.18–5.22 (cat.)

2006 *Fest der Farbe: Die Sammlung Merzbacher-Meyer*, Kunsthaus Zürich, Zurich, 2.10–5.14 (cat.)
Full House – Gesichter einer Sammlung, Städtische Kunsthalle Mannheim, 4.2–9.4 (cat.)
Von Kandinsky bis Tatlin: Konstruktivismus in Europa, Staatliches Museum Schwerin, 5.13–8.13; Kunstmuseum Bonn, 8.24–10.15 (cat.)
Transformation: Aus eigner Sammlung, Kunstmuseum Liechtenstein, Vaduz, 6.9–10.1
Otto Freundlich und die rheinische Kunstszene, August Macke Haus Bonn, 9.29.2006–1.14.2007 (cat.)

2007 *Otto Freundlich und die Skulpturenstraße des Friedens*, Stadtmuseum St. Wendel, 3.23–5.6. Further venues: Centre Culturel de Rossignol-Tintigny; Centre Mondial de la Paix de Verdun; Le Musée Tavet, Pontoise; Coopération de Wiltz (cat.)
Otto Freundlich – Bilder einer sozialen Utopie, Sammlung Moderne Kunst in der Pinakothek der Moderne, Munich, 5.10–8.19
Großes Ey, wir loben Dich: Johanna Ey und ihr Künstlerkreis, Galerie Remmert und Barth, Düsseldorf, 9.4–11.17 (cat.)
Meisterwerke der 20er Jahre, Berlinische Galerie, Landesmuseum für Moderne Kunst, Fotografie und Architektur, Berlin, 4.6–7.2
1937: Perfektion und Zerstörung, Kunsthalle Bielefeld, 9.30.2007–1.13.2008 (cat.)
De la montaña, de la amistad, de los maestros (semblanza de Otto Freundlich, 1978–1943), Museo Experimental El Eco, Mexico City, September

2008 *Otto Freundlich – 1878–1943: Artyska ze Słupsk, Ein Künstler aus Stolp*, Muzeum Pomorza Środkowego w Słupsku, Słupsk, 6.14–9.14 (exhibition brochure)
Gerd Arntz im Kreise von Freunden und Kollegen: Jankel Adler, Gottfried Brockmann, Otto Freundlich, Marta Hegemann, Heinrich Hoerle, Franz W. Seiwert, Galerie Remmert und Barth, Düsseldorf, 11.25.2008–1.31.2009 (cat.)
Die Verborgene Spur: Jüdische Wege durch die Moderne, Felix-Nussbaum-Haus Osnabrück, 12.7.2008–4.19.2009 (cat.)

2009 *Otto Freundlich: 1878–1943*, Musées de Pontoise, 5.23–9.27 (cat.)
Die Neue Galerie – Auftritt im Schloss! Auf dem Weg zur Wiedereröffnung 2011, Museum Schloss Wilhelmshöhe, Kassel, special exhibitions gallery in the Gemäldegalerie Alte Meister, 11.21.2009–4.11.2010

2010 *Wilde Welten: Aneignung des Fremden in der Moderne*, Georg-Kolbe-Museum, Berlin, 01.24–4.5 (cat.)
Otto Freundlich (1878–1943), Musée Géo-Charles, Echirolles, 2.6–5.30 (exhibition brochure)
The Moderns: Wie sich das 20. Jahrhundert in Kunst und Wissenschaft erfunden hat, mumok – Museum Moderner Kunst Stiftung Ludwig, Vienna, 6.24.2010–1.23.2011 (cat.)
Entartet? Das Schicksal moderner Kunst in Deutschland 1933–45, Edwin Scharff Museum, Neu-Ulm, 9.4–11.21

2011 *Liebermanns Gegner: Die Neue Secession in Berlin und der Expressionismus*, Stiftung Brandenburger Tor, Max Liebermann Haus, Berlin, 2.4–3.7; Stiftung Schleswig-Holsteinische Landesmuseen, Schloss Gottorf, Schleswig, 7.17–10.23 (cat.)
Unsere Moderne – Cézanne, Miró, Matisse, Kirchner, Beckmann, Klee, Staatliche Kunsthalle Karlsruhe, 4.30–10.3
Der Berliner Skulpturenfund: "Entartete Kunst" im Bombenschutt, Staatliche Museen – Museum für Vor- und Frühgeschichte, Berlin (cat.)
Glasmalerei der Moderne: Faszination Farbe im Gegenlicht, Badisches Landesmuseum Karlsruhe, 7.9–10.9 (cat.)

2012 *Der Sturm: Zentrum der Avantgarde*, Von der Heydt-Museum, Wuppertal, 3.13–6.10 (cat.)
1917, Centre Pompidou-Metz, 5.26–9.24 (cat.)
La sculpture des peintres: Arp, Bonnard, Braque, Chabaud, Clavé, Daumier, Degas, Derain, Fautrier, Freundlich, Gauguin, Giacometti, Kirchner, De La Fresnaye, Matisse, Picasso, Renoir, Rouault, Valloton, Venet, Musée de L'Annonciade, Saint-Tropez, 7.7–10.8 (cat.)
1912 – Mission Moderne: Die Jahrhundertschau des Sonderbundes, Wallraf-Richartz-Museum und Fondation Corboud, Cologne, 8.31–12.30 (cat.)
La Collection Michael Werner, Musée d'Art moderne de la Ville de Paris, 10.5.2012–3.3.2013
L'art en guerre, France 1938–1947: De Picasso à Dubuffet, Musée d'Art moderne de la Ville de Paris, 10.12.2012–2.17.2013 (cat.)
L'œil cosmique: Otto Freundlich, Galerie Applicat-Prazan, Paris, February

2013 *Gebaute Bilder: Werke aus der Sammlung Hupertz*, Ernst Barlach Haus, Stiftung Hermann F. Reemtsma, Hamburg, 2.10–5.26
Traum-Bilder: Ernst, Magritte, Dalí, Picasso, Antes, Nay . . . – Die Wormland-Schenkung, Bayerische Staatsgemäldesammlungen – Pinakothek der Moderne, Munich, 9.14.2013–1.26.2014 (cat.)

2014 *Degenerate Art: The Attack on Modern Art in Nazi Germany 1937*, Neue Galerie, New York, 3.13–6.30 (cat.)
Sur les pas de Van Gogh, un chemin vers la couleur, Musée Daubigny, Auvers-sur-Oise, 4.5–8.31

2016 *Wir nennen es Ludwig: Das Museum wird 40!* Museum Ludwig, Cologne, 8.27.2016–1.8.2017
The Power of the Avant-Garde, BOZAR, Brussels, 9.29.2016–1.22.2017
The Shadow of Color: Otto Freundlich, Len Lye, Lygia Clark and Blinky Palermo, The Israel Museum, Jerusalem, 12.22.2016–4.22.2017

1 Information from Jürgen Freundlich, Cologne. Where not otherwise specified, all information has been taken from the biographies *Otto Freundlich: Monographie mit Dokumentation und Werkverzeichnis*, ed. Joachim Heusinger von Waldegg, exh. cat. Rheinisches Landesmuseum Bonn et al. (Cologne, 1978), pp. 281–284; Joachim Heusinger von Waldegg, *Otto Freundlich und die rheinische Kunstszene mit Briefen an Herwarth Walden und Wilhelm Niemeyer*, ed. Verein August Macke Haus, exh. cat. August Macke Haus (Bonn, 2006), pp. 294–322; *Otto Freundlich: Ein Wegbereiter der abstrakten Kunst*, ed. Gerhard Leistner and Thorsten Rodiek, exh. cat. Ostdeutsche Galerie Regensburg et al. (Regensburg, 1994), pp. 190–234.

2 Information from Jürgen Freundlich, Cologne.

3 Cf. the official list of students: "Amtliches Verzeichnis des Personals der Lehrer, Beamten und Studierenden an der königlich bayerischen Ludwig-Maximilians-Universität zu München; Winter-Semester 1904/1905," p. 60. Online: http://epub.ub.uni-muenchen.de/9657/1/pvz_lmu_1904_05_wise.pdf (accessed October 2016).

4 Letter from Freundlich to Walden, early 1907, cited in Heusinger, *Rheinische Kunstszene*, op. cit. (note 1), p. 114.

5 Letter from Freundlich to Walden, March 5 [1908], cited in Heusinger, ibid., p. 116.

6 Cf. Irène Lesparre, "Biografie," in Egbert van Faassen, Sjoerd van Faassen, et al., *Otto van Rees* (Zwolle et al., 2005), pp. 13–65, here p. 23.

7 Letter from Freundlich to Niemeyer, July 9, 1912, see Heusinger, *Rheinische Kunstszene*, op. cit. (note 1), p. 143.

8 Letter from Freundlich to Niemeyer, December 24, 1913, see Heusinger, ibid., p. 164.

9 Letter from Freundlich to Niemeyer, December 26, 1913, see Heusinger, ibid., p. 166.

10 Letter from Freundlich to Heinersdorff, December 22, 1917, Archiv Puhl & Wagner–Gottfried Heinersdorff (APWGH), Berlinische Galerie. Cf. the article by Julia Friedrich in the present volume.

11 Letter from Freundlich to Niemeyer, April 27, 1914, see Heusinger, *Rheinische Kunstszene*, op. cit. (note 1), p. 179.

12 Postcard from Freundlich to de Souza-Cardoso, July 6, 1914, in Coleção Amadeo de Souza-Cardoso, I ASC 13/29; ASC 13/30; ASC 13/31 I FCG-BA, Biblioteca de Arte, Fundação Calouste Gulbenkian, Lisbon. Cf. the article by Lena Schrage in the present volume.

13 Information from Wolfgang Schöddert, Berlinische Galerie.

14 Letter from Freundlich to Niemeyer, February 17, 1915, see Heusinger, *Rheinische Kunstszene*, op. cit. (note 1), pp. 215–216.

15 Letter from Freundlich to Niemeyer, October 11, 1915, cited in Heusinger, ibid., pp. 223–224.

16 "Artists should work in communities as they did in the Middle Ages. In 1915, O. van Rees, C. van Rees [*sic*], Freundlich, S. Taeuber, and myself made an attempt of that sort." Arp, "Concrete Art" (1944) in *Arp on Arp*, cited in Bibiana K. Obler, *Intimate Collaborations: Kandinsky & Münter, Arp & Taeuber* (New Haven and London, 2014), p. 139.

17 Letter from Freundlich to Niemeyer, June 11, 1915, cited in Heusinger, *Rheinische Kunstszene*, op. cit. (note 1), p. 302.

18 Letter from Freundlich to Niemeyer, July 17, 1916, cited in Heusinger, ibid, pp. 228–229.

19 Letter from Freundlich to Niemeyer, March 12, [1917], cited in Heusinger, ibid., p. 238.

20 Letter from Feinhals to Heinersdorff, January 11, 1918, APWGH, Berlinische Galerie.

21 Otto Freundlich, "An die Novembergruppe" [February 11, 1919], in Uli Bohnen, ed., *Otto Freundlich: Schriften. Ein Wegbereiter der gegenstandslosen Kunst* (Cologne, 1982), p. 108.

22 Letters from Heinersdorff to Feinhals, March 11, 1918, and Freundlich to Heinersdorff, April 23, 1918, APWGH, Berlinische Galerie.

23 Letter from Freundlich to Heinersdorff, March 26, 1918, APWGH, Berlinische Galerie.

24 Cf. also field postcard to Heinersdorff, May 16, 1918, APWGH, Berlinische Galerie.

25 Cf. Letter from Heinersdorff to Feinhals, May 24, 1918, APWGH, Berlinische Galerie.

26 Cf. Letter from Freundlich to Heinersdorff, May 28, 1918, APWGH, Berlinische Galerie.

27 Letter from Freundlich to Heinersdorff, May 28, 1918, APWGH, Berlinische Galerie: "I was yesterday in the Secession . . . My picture has been hung a little too high, yet I am happy to see it in this form."

28 Franz Wilhelm Seiwert, "hoerle und ich," *a bis z* 10 (1930), p. 38.

29 Program of the Workers' Council for Art, cited in Uli Bohnen, "Zwischen Utopie und Konfusion: Einige Anmerkungen zum Berliner Arbeitsrat für Kunst," in *Arbeitsrat für Kunst 1918–1921*, ed. Manfred Schlösser, exh. cat Akademie der Künste Berlin (Berlin, 1980), pp. 7–8, here p. 7.

30 Letter from Freundlich to Heinersdorff, September 15, 1919, APWGH, Berlinische Galerie.

31 Cf. *Von Dadamax zum Grüngürtel: Cologne in den 20er Jahren: Bildende Kunst, Fotografie, Rundfunk, Architektur, Musik, Theater, Literatur mit Reprint: "Bulletin D" 1919, Katalog "Brauhaus Winter" 1920, Katalog "Stupid" 1920, "Dokumente der Progressiven" 1920–26 und andere zeitgenössische Texte*, ed. Wulf Herzogenrath, exh. cat. Kölnischer Kunstverein (Cologne, 1975), p. 35.

32 Otto Freundlich, "Absage," in *Arbeitsrat für Kunst 1918–1921*, ed. Manfred Schlösser, exh. cat. Akademie der Künste Berlin (Berlin, 1980), p. 113.

33 Letter from Freundlich to Max Sauerlandt, December 26/28, 1925, Archiv Museum für Kunst und Gewerbe (MKG), Hamburg.

34 Letter from Freundlich to Willi Ganske, February 20, 1921, archive Association Les Amis de Jeanne et Otto Freundlich (AAJOF), IMEC, FRN 19.2.

35 Künstlerarchiv der Berlinischen Galerie, Landesmuseum für Moderne Kunst, Photographie und Architektur, ed., *Hannah Höch: Eine Lebenscollage. Band II 1921– 1945, 2. Abteilung Dokumente* (Ostfildern, 1995), p. 90.

36 Letter from Benjamin to Gershom Scholem, October 27, 1921, in Walter Benjamin, *Gesammelte Schriften, Briefe I* (Frankfurt am Main, 1978), p. 279.

37 Manifesto of the commune, March 1922, cited in Bohnen, *Otto Freundlich: Schriften*, op. cit. (note 21), pp. 122–123, here p. 122.

38 Cf. Peter Mantis, "Versuch einer Rekonstruktion," in *Versuch einer Rekonstruktion: Internationale Ausstellung Revolutionärer Künstler 1922 in Berlin*, ed. Neuer Berliner Kunstverein e.V., exh. cat Artothek Berlin (Berlin, 1975), unpag.

39 Letter from Freundlich to Julius Wissinger, August 4, 1923, cf. Christoph Fischer, Volker Welter, eds., *Frühlicht in Beton: Das Erbbegräbnis Wissinger von Max Taut und Otto Freundlich in Stahnsdorf. Geschichte und Hintergründe der Entstehung. Dokumentation der Restaurierung 1987/88* (Berlin, 1989), p. 45.

40 Cf. Waldemar Grzimek, "Otto Freundlich," in Grzimek, *Deutsche Bildhauer des zwanzigsten Jahrhunderts: Leben – Schulen – Wirkungen* (Munich, 1969), pp. 97–104, here p. 102.

41 Letter from Freundlich to Jeanne Kosnick-Kloss, November 10, 1939, archive AAJOF, IMEC, FRN 4.3.

42 Otto Freundlich, "Brief an den Photographen August Sander, Cologne" [December 1, 1925], in Bohnen, *Otto Freundlich: Schriften*, op. cit. (note 21), pp. 149–150, p. 149.

43 Letter from Freundlich to Wissinger, August 12, 1927, archive of Joachim Heusinger von Waldegg.

44 Letters from Seiwert to Freundlich, August 4 and September 21, 1928, archive AAJOF, IMEC , FRN 14.23.

45 Letter from Sauerlandt to Solmitz, January 28, 1929, Archiv MKG Hamburg

46 Letter from Seiwert to Freundlich, January 16, 1930, archive AAJOF, IMEC, FRN 14.26.

47 Letter from Seiwert to Freundlich, November 26, 1931, archive AAJOF, IMEC, FRN 15.1.

48 Letter from Klee to Freundlich, September 21, 1930, archive AAJOF, IMEC, FRN 11.9.

49 The address given in *Groupe 40: Première Exposition*, exh. cat Galerie de la Renaissance, 11, rue Royale, Paris (June 11–30, 1931), p. 6.

50 Cf. Joël Mettay, *Die verlorene Spur* (Göttingen, 2005), p. 84.

51 Otto Freundlich, "Brief an 'abstraction-création,' Paris," cited in Bohnen, *Otto Freundlich: Schriften*, op. cit. (note 21), p. 195.

52 Otto Freundlich, "Die Wege der abstrakten Kunst" [1934], cited in Bohnen, *Otto Freundlich: Schriften*, op. cit. (note 21), pp. 188–194, here p. 189.

53 Cf. Mettay, *Spur*, op. cit. (note 50), pp. 65–67.

54 Cf. Joël Mettay, Edda Maillet, *Otto Freundlich et la France: Un amour trahi* (Perpignan, 2004), p. 48.

55 Cf. Hélène Roussel, "German Speaking Artists in Parisian Exile: Their Routes to the French Capital, Activities There, and Final Flight—a Short Introduction," in Ines Rotermund-Reynard, ed., *Echoes of Exile: Moscow Archives and the Arts in Paris 1933–1945* (Berlin et al., 2015), pp. 1–26, here p. 19.

56 "Dem Andenken meiner Freunde," cited in Bohnen, *Otto Freundlich: Schriften*, op. cit. (note 21), pp. 205–206, p. 205.

57 Letter from Wagner to Kosnick-Kloss, January 27, 1937, APWGH, Berlinische Galerie. Cf. letter from Wagner to Günter Aust, May 25, 1959, Ausstellungsakte Freundlich, Archive Museum Ludwig.

58 Letter to Robert and Sonia Delaunay, May 26, 1937, archive AAJOF, IMEC, FRN 3.13.

59 Letter to Irmgard Burchard, Zurich, April 29, 1938, archive AAJOF, IMEC, FRN 3.5.

60 Letter from Gropius to Kosnick-Kloss, June 1, 1938, archive AAJOF, IMEC , FRN Correspondance P à Z.

61 Cf. Mettay, Maillet, *Otto Freundlich*, op. cit. (note 54), p. 88.

62 Cf. ibid., p. 95.

63 Cf. ibid., p. 101.

64 Cf. *Otto Freundlich: Leuchtturm der sieben Künste. Ein utopisches Denkmal*, ed. Joachim Heusinger von Waldegg, exh. cat Stadtmuseum St. Wendel (St. Wendel, 2007), p. 74.

65 Cf. Mettay, Maillet, *Otto Freundlich*, op. cit. (note 54), p. 104.

66 Jules Schelvis, *Vernichtungslager Sobibor* (Berlin, 1998), p. 272.

67 Cf. ibid., p. 272.

68 Cf. ibid., p. 272.

69 Cf. Gabi Heleen Bollinger, *Der Plan des Bildhauers: Eine Straße des Friedens für Otto Freundlich*, TV-documentary, Saarländischer Rundfunk, March 9, 2013.

70 Serge Klarsfeld, *Vichy-Auschwitz: Die Zusammenarbeit der deutschen und französischen Behörden bei der "Endlösung" der Judenfrage in Frankreich* (Nördlingen, 1989), p. 499.

71 Schelvis, *Sobibor*, op. cit. (note 66), p. 65.

Writings of Otto Freundlich

"Herwarth Waldens Tonlyrik," *Kampf: Zeitschrift für gesunden Menschenverstand (Neue Folge)* 18 (1905), pp. 529–530.

"Kollektiv-Ausstellungen," *Das Magazin* 4 (1908), pp. 66–67.

"Eine Umrahmung für manche Bilder" [1912], in Joachim Heusinger von Waldegg, *Otto Freundlich und die rheinische Kunstszene mit Briefen an Herwarth Walden und Wilhelm Niemeyer*, edited by Verein August Macke Haus, exh. cat. August Macke Haus Bonn (Bonn, 2006), pp. 249–251.

"Über eine unveröffentlichte Schrift," *Die weissen Blätter* 9 (1916), pp. 297–300. Excerpt in Uli Bohnen, ed., *Otto Freundlich: Schriften. Ein Wegbereiter der gegenstandslosen Kunst* (Cologne, 1982), pp. 100–101.

"Der Bau," *Zeit-Echo* 1–2 (July 1917), pp. 11–12. Reprinted in Ludwig Rubiner, ed., *Die Gemeinschaft: Dokumente einer geistigen Weltwende* (Berlin, 1919), pp. 68–71; and in *Otto Freundlich: Monographie mit Dokumentation und Werkverzeichnis*, edited by Joachim Heusinger von Waldegg, exh. cat. Rheinisches Landesmuseum Bonn et al. (Cologne, 1978), pp. 247–248.

"Das kommende Reich," *Die Aktion* 45/46 (1917), cols. 600–602.

"'. . . durch äonenlange Erfahrung'" [on Ernst Marcus, *Kants Weltgebäude*], *Die Aktion* 15/16 (1918), cols. 183–185. Excerpt in Bohnen, *Otto Freundlich: Schriften*, op. cit., p. 102.

"Der Turm zu Babel," *Die Aktion*, special issue *"Polnische Kunst"* 21/22 (1918), cols. 267–270.

"Hans Bols [sic.], meinem Freunde," *Die Aktion* 31/32 (1918), cols. 393–394.

"Welt—Urwelt," *Die Aktion*, special issue *"Otto Freundlich"* 37/38 (1918), cols. 469–474. Reprinted in Diether Schmidt, ed., *Schriften deutscher Künstler des zwanzigsten Jahrhunderts. Band I: Manifeste, Manifeste. 1905–1933* (Dresden, 1965), pp. 132–138; and in Heusinger, *Freundlich: Werkverzeichnis*, op. cit., pp. 248–250. Excerpt in Bohnen, *Otto Freundlich: Schriften*, op. cit., pp. 103–105.

"Unvergängliche," *Die Aktion* 45/46 (1918), cols. 587–589.

"Das Perpetuum-Mobile," in Otto Freundlich, *Aktive Kunst* (Berlin-Wilmersdorf, 1918) (= *Der rote Hahn* 13), pp. 5–14.

"Aktive Kunst: Vorwort zu meinen Zeichnungen," in Otto Freundlich, *Aktive Kunst* (Berlin-Wilmersdorf, 1918) (= *Der rote Hahn* 13), pp. 17–20. Reprinted in Heusinger, *Freundlich: Werkverzeichnis*, op. cit., pp. 252–254.

"Die namenlose Welt," *Der Strom* 1 (1919), pp. 14–16.

"Der Raum," *Die weissen Blätter* 2 (1919), pp. 82–87. Reprinted in Heusinger, *Freundlich: Werkverzeichnis*, op. cit., pp. 254–256. Excerpt in Bohnen, *Otto Freundlich: Schriften*, op. cit., pp. 106–107.

"An die Novembergruppe" [letter, Berlin-Wilmersdorf, February 11, 1919], *Kunst der Zeit*, special issue *"Zehn Jahre Novembergruppe"* 1–3 (1928), pp. 33–34. Reprinted in Schmidt, *Manifeste*, op. cit., pp. 182–183; in Heusinger, *Freundlich: Werkverzeichnis*, op. cit., p. 251; and in Bohnen, *Otto Freundlich: Schriften*, op. cit., pp. 108–109.

"Bürger und Proletarier!" [probably in collaboration with Franz W. Seiwert; signed: Antischmitz], *Der Ventilator* 5 (1919), pp. 5–7. Reprinted in Walter Vitt, *Auf der Suche nach der Biographie des Kölner Dadaisten Johannes Theodor Baargeld* (Starnberg, 1977).

"Es wird ernst," *Die Erde* 5 (1919), pp. 129–135. Reprinted in Klaus Schuhmann, ed., *sankt ziegenzack springt aus dem ei* (Leipzig and Weimar, 1991), pp. 362–367.

"Die Lach-Rackete," *Bulletin D* (1919), unpag. [p. 2]. Facsimile reprinted in *Dada Zeitschriften*, edited by Lutz Schulenburg (Hamburg, 1979).

"Intellektuelle und Proletarier oder Das System der Entmündigung," *Der Ventilator* 6 (1919), pp. 1–6. Reprinted in Vitt, *Auf der Suche*, op. cit.; excerpt in Heusinger, *Freundlich: Werkverzeichnis*, op. cit., p. 260.

"Zur Synthese Architektur—Plastik—Malerei," *Die Erde* 8 (1919), pp. 233–237. Excerpt in Bohnen, *Otto Freundlich: Schriften*, op. cit., pp. 109–111.

"Zur Politik der Unpolitischen" [on Richard Janthur and Franz W. Seiwert], *Die Erde* 10 (1919), p. 320.

"Die optische Moral," *Der Strom* 3 (1919), pp. 7–10. Reprinted in Heusinger, *Freundlich: Werkverzeichnis*, op. cit., pp. 251–252. Excerpt in Bohnen, *Otto Freundlich: Schriften*, pp. 111–113.

"Wir wollen Heiden sein," *Die Erde* 13 (1919), pp. 390–393.

"Wir gehen . . .," *Das Tribunal* 7 (1919), pp. 83–84.

"Die Welttragik der Lüge," *Die Erde* 18–19 (1919), pp. 555–563.

"Wenn der Künstler untergeht, fängt der Mensch an; Wenn der Mensch untergeht, fängt der Künstler an," *Der Strom* 4 (1919), pp. 8–11; *Westdeutsche Wochenschrift* 30 (1919), pp. 473–475; and in *Katalog zur Ausstellung der Gesellschaft der Künste in Köln im Kölnischen Kunstverein* (Cologne, 1919).

"Wollt ihr impotenten Revolutionäre . . .," *Bulletin D* (1919), unpag. [p. 7]. Reprinted in *Von Dadamax zum Grüngürtel: Köln in den 20er Jahren. Bildende Kunst, Fotografie, Rundfunk, Architektur, Musik, Theater, Literatur mit Reprint: "Bulletin D" 1919, Katalog "Brauhaus Winter" 1920, Katalog "Stupid" 1920, "Dokumente der Progressiven" 1920–26 und andere zeitgenössische Texte*, edited by Wulf Herzogenrath, exh. cat. Kölnischer Kunstverein (Cologne, 1975); and in Heusinger, *Freundlich: Werkverzeichnis*, op. cit., pp. 259–260. Facsimile reprinted in *Dada Zeitschriften*, op. cit.

"Absage. Eine endgültige Auseinandersetzung mit den drei Instituten: Deutscher Werkbund, Arbeitsrat für Kunst in Berlin, Novembergruppe," *Die Erde* 24 (1919), pp. 686–687. Reprinted in *Arbeitsrat für Kunst 1918–1921*, edited by Manfred Schlösser, exh. cat. Akademie der Künste Berlin (Berlin, 1980), pp. 113; and in Bohnen, *Otto Freundlich: Schriften*, op. cit., pp. 116–118.

"Janthur als Graphiker," *Der Cicerone* (1919), pp. 510–518. Excerpt in Bohnen, *Otto Freundlich: Schriften*, op. cit., pp. 113–116.

"In tyrannos intellectuales," *Die Aktion* 3/4 (1920), cols. 52–53.

"Um was es geht! Auf die Worte Max Creutz' vom 'Primitiven in der Kunst,'" *Westdeutsche Wochenschrift* 10 (1920), pp. 136–137.

"Die Verwandlung der sichtbaren Welt" [lecture given on March 2, 1921, at the Graphisches Kabinett J. B. Neumann, Berlin]. Excerpt in Bohnen, *Otto Freundlich: Schriften*, op. cit., pp. 118–119.

"Der Mensch in seiner Form ist ein Bruder des Kosmos," *Veröffentlichungen der Novembergruppe* 1 (1921), p. 18. Reprinted in *Kunst der Zeit: Organ der Künstler-Selbsthilfe*, special issue *"Zehn Jahre Novembergruppe"* 1–3 (Berlin 1928), pp. 64–65; and in Schmidt, *Manifeste*, op. cit., pp. 184–185.

"Dem Bildhauer Max Reinhold Krause," *Veröffentlichungen der Novembergruppe* 1 (1921), p. 23.

"Die schöpferische Macht im Kommunismus," *Die Aktion* 39/40 (1921), cols. 550–552. Excerpt in Bohnen, *Otto Freundlich: Schriften*, op. cit., pp. 119–122.

"Anläßlich Karl Liebknechts Nachlaßwerk," *Die Aktion* 45/46 (1921), cols. 621–623.

"Was wollt ihr von Picasso?" *Die Aktion* 33/34 (1922), cols. 479–481. Reprinted in Bohnen, *Otto Freundlich: Schriften*, op. cit., pp. 128–129.

"Technik und Religion" [1922]. Excerpt in Bohnen, *Otto Freundlich: Schriften*, op. cit., p. 130.

"Moderne Kannibalen," *Die Aktion* 19/20 (1923), cols. 262–263. Excerpt in Bohnen, *Otto Freundlich: Schriften*, op. cit., pp. 130–131.

"Bekenntnis eines Intellektuellen," *Die Aktion* 1/2 (1924), cols. 31–33. Excerpt in Bohnen, *Otto Freundlich: Schriften*, op. cit., pp. 132–134.

"Des yeux nouveaux," *Montparnasse* 36 (1924), p. 9.

"Die gesehene Form," *Die Aktion* 13/14 (1924), cols. 687–688. Reprinted in Heusinger, *Freundlich: Werkverzeichnis*, op. cit., p. 257; and in Bohnen, *Otto Freundlich: Schriften*, op. cit., pp. 146–148.

"Um den Achtstundentag," *8 Stunden: Publikation der Künstlerhilfe (IAH)* (Berlin, 1924), pp. 28–30. Reprinted in Schmidt, *Manifeste*, op. cit., pp. 326–327; and in Bohnen, *Otto Freundlich: Schriften*, op. cit., pp. 145–146.

"Der raumlose Himmel" [1925]. Excerpt in Bohnen, *Otto Freundlich: Schriften*, op. cit., pp. 148–149.

"La matière et l'esprit," *Montparnasse* 47 (1926), p. 5.

"Gedanken des Malers," *Annalen: Eine schweizerische Monatsschrift* 7 (1927), p. 550. Reprinted in Bohnen, *Otto Freundlich: Schriften*, op. cit., p. 152.

"Beethoven in der Notre Dame," *Annalen: Eine schweizerische Monatsschrift* 10 (1927), pp. 791–793.

"Quand un poète meurt: À Paul Husson," *Montparnasse*, special issue in memory of Paul Husson 50 (1928), p. 9. Reprinted in *Deux sculptures monumentales de Otto Freundlich*, exh. cat. Galerie Claude Bernard, Paris, Galerie René Drouin, Paris, Otto Gerson Gallery, New York (Paris, 1962), unpag.; and in *Otto Freundlich, Jeanne Kosnick-Kloss: Exposition commémorative avec le concours de l'Association des amis d'Otto Freundlich*, exh. cat. Centre Culturel Allemand Paris, Goethe-Institut Paris (Paris, 1968), unpag.

"Die Welt, die sich selbst schafft" [1929]. Excerpt in Bohnen, *Otto Freundlich: Schriften*, op. cit., p. 154.

"ein brief über malerei" [to Franz W. Seiwert], *a bis z: Organ der Gruppe progressiver Künstler, Köln* 2 (1929), p. 7. Reprinted in Otto Freundlich, *Aus Briefen und Aufsätzen*, edited by Günter Aust (Cologne, 1963); and in Bohnen, *Otto Freundlich: Schriften*, op. cit., pp. 155–156.

"an wilhelm niemeyer: ein beitrag zur geschichte des sonderbundes," *a bis z: Organ der Gruppe progressiver Künstler, Köln* 4 (1930), pp. 13–14. Reprinted in Freundlich, *Aus Briefen und Aufsätzen*, op. cit.

"Der Künstler ist ein Barometer . . .," *Cercle et Carré* 2 (1930). Reprinted in *Deux sculptures monumentales*, op. cit. [under the title "Destin de l'artiste"]; and in *Hommage à Otto Freundlich à l'occasion du 100ème anniversaire de sa naissance*, exh. cat. Goldman-Schwartz Gallery Jerusalem, The Israel Museum, Jerusalem (Jerusalem, 1978).

"Der Untergang der deutschen Malerei II," *Kunst und Wirtschaft* 12 (1929), pp. 188–189. Reprinted in Bohnen, *Otto Freundlich: Schriften*, op. cit., pp. 156–157.

"Bachs 'Kunst der Fuge,' Aufführung unter Scherchen in Paris nach der Ausgabe von Wolfgang Graeser am 29.12.29." Abridged under the title "bachs 'kunst der fuge,'" *a bis z: Organ der Gruppe progressiver Künstler, Köln* 18 (1931), pp. 70–71. Reprinted in Freundlich, *Aus Briefen und Aufsätzen*, op. cit.

"modigliani," *a bis z: Organ der Gruppe progressiver Künstler, Köln* 6 (1930), pp. 21–22. Reprinted in Freundlich, *Aus Briefen und Aufsätzen*, op. cit.; in Heusinger, *Freundlich: Werkverzeichnis*, op. cit., p. 247; and in Bohnen, *Otto Freundlich: Schriften*, op. cit., pp. 158–159.

"Erdkreis (Orbis Terrarum)" [1930]. Excerpt in Bohnen, *Otto Freundlich: Schriften*, op. cit., p. 160.

"abstrakt – konkret" [1930; title from Uli Bohnen]. Excerpt in Bohnen, *Otto Freundlich: Schriften*, op. cit., pp. 160–162.

"gino severini," *a bis z: Organ der Gruppe progressiver Künstler, Köln* 14 (1931), pp. 53–54. Reprinted in Bohnen, *Otto Freundlich: Schriften*, op. cit., pp. 163–165.

"Die Gräber Vincent und Theo van Goghs," *Kölnische Zeitung* (August 19, 1930), p. 2. Reprinted in *Das Werk: Schweizer Monatsschrift für Architektur, Freie Kunst, Angewandte Kunst* 3 (1931), p. 96.

"Zu van Gogh's 40. Todestag," *Neues Winterthurer Tagblatt* (August 27, 1930), p. 1 [under the title "Van Gogh"]. Excerpt in Bohnen, *Otto Freundlich: Schriften*, op. cit., pp. 165–166.

"Ein deutscher Maler in Paris (Erinnerungen an das Künstlerleben in Paris vor dem Kriege 1914)" [1930]. Excerpt in *Prisme des Arts* 8 (1957), pp. 2–5 [under the title "Le Journal d'Otto Freundlich"; dated there 1931]. Reprinted in *Deux sculptures monumentales de Otto Freundlich*, op. cit. [under the title "Idées d'un peintre revolutionnaire"]; in *Das Kunstwerk* 1 (1959), pp. 24–25; in Otto Freundlich, *Aus Briefen und Aufsätzen*, op. cit.; and in Heusinger, *Freundlich: Werkverzeichnis*, op. cit., pp. 243–247. Excerpt in Bohnen, *Otto Freundlich: Schriften*, op. cit., pp. 166–172.

"zum tode walter opheys," *a bis z: Organ der Gruppe progressiver Künstler, Köln* 11 (1930), p. 44.

"Wir steuern." Amended version in *Der Künstler* 4 (1931), p. 28.

Reader's letter [in response to Karl Scheffler, "Der mißbrauchte Einstein oder Über die Grenzen der Malerei und Mathematik," *Vossische Zeitung*, March 7, 1931], *Vossische Zeitung*, March 15, 1931, supplement, p. 2.

"Die Malerei und ihr Weg" [ca. 1930–31]. Excerpt in Otto Freundlich, *Aus Briefen und Aufsätzen*, op. cit.; excerpt in Bohnen, *Otto Freundlich: Schriften*, op. cit., p. 174.

"Der Künstler und die Wirtschaftskrise," *Das Kunstblatt* 2 (1932), pp. 10–13 [under the title "Der Künstler in der Krise"]. Excerpt in Bohnen, *Otto Freundlich: Schriften*, op. cit., pp. 174–177.

"Picasso, zu seinem 50. Geburtstag" [1931], in Heusinger, *Freundlich: Werkverzeichnis*, op. cit., pp. 257–259; excerpt in Bohnen, *Otto Freundlich: Schriften*, op. cit., pp. 178–180.

"Vortrag" [1931?], *Die Umschau* 1 (1948), pp. 51–58 [under the title "Gedanken über das Werden der neuen Kunst"]. Excerpt in Otto Freundlich, *Aus Briefen und Aufsätzen*, op. cit.; and in Bohnen, *Otto Freundlich: Schriften*, op. cit., pp. 180–185.

"Helligkeiten und Dunkelheiten . . .," *abstraction-création: art non figuratif* 1 (1932), p. 13 [under the title "Le clair et l'obscur . . ."].

"ein vorwort," *a bis z: Organ der Gruppe progressiver Künstler, Köln* 25 (1932), p. 99. Reprinted in *Otto Freundlich, Jeanne Kosnick-Kloss: Exposition commémorative*, op. cit., unpag.

"Für das Bauhaus und gegen die Kulturreaktion" [ca. April 1933], in Bohnen, *Otto Freundlich: Schriften*, op. cit., pp. 187–188.

"Das Nackte . . ." [1933]. Excerpt in *abstraction-création: art non figuratif* 2 (1933), p. 12 [under the title "Le nu et l'homme . . ."].

"Zum Andenken des Freundes Franz W. Seiwert" [1933], in *Franz W. Seiwert—Leben und Werk*, edited by Uli Bohnen, exh. cat. Kölnischer Kunstverein et al. (Cologne, 1978), p. 64.

"Die Wege der abstrakten Kunst" [1934]. Excerpt in Otto Freundlich, *Aus Briefen und Aufsätzen*, op. cit.; in *Hommage à Otto Freundlich*, op. cit.; in Heusinger, *Freundlich: Werkverzeichnis*, op. cit., p. 261; and in Bohnen, *Otto Freundlich: Schriften*, op. cit., pp. 188–194.

"Zur Nationalisierung des Geistes" [1935]. Excerpt in Bohnen, *Otto Freundlich: Schriften*, op. cit., pp. 195–196.

"Bekenntnisse eines revolutionären Malers" [1935]. Excerpt in Otto Freundlich, *Aus Briefen und Aufsätzen*, op. cit.; and in Bohnen, *Otto Freundlich: Schriften*, op. cit., pp. 197–202. English translation published in full in the present volume.

"Richtlinien für den Unterricht in der bildenden Kunst" [1935], in Otto Freundlich, *Le Mur* (Paris, 1936) [under the title "Academie de l'art mural: Introduction"]; in *Anthologie* 1 (1938), pp. 8–9 [under the title "D'un Enseignement"]. Reprinted in *Deux sculptures monumentales de Otto Freundlich*, op. cit.; in *Otto Freundlich, Jeanne Kosnick-Kloss: Exposition commémorative*, op. cit., unpag.; in *Hommage à Otto Freundlich*, op. cit. [dated there 1936]; and in *Otto Freundlich et ses amis*, exh. cat. Musée de Pontoise (Pontoise, 1993), pp. 136–137.

"Die Einheit des Lebens und des Todes" [1936]. Excerpt in *Pour et contre l'art abstrait* 11 (1947), pp. 56–57. Reprinted in Otto Freundlich, *Aus Briefen und Aufsätzen*, op. cit.; excerpt in Bohnen, *Otto Freundlich: Schriften*, op. cit., pp. 204–205.

"Sculptures-Montagnes" [1936], in *Association des Amis d'Otto Freundlich* (Paris, undated [1959]). Reprinted in Heusinger, *Freundlich: Werkverzeichnis*, op. cit., p. 261.

"Dem Andenken meiner Freunde F[ranz] W. Seiwert u. H[einrich] Hoerle" [1936], in Bohnen, *Otto Freundlich: Schriften*, op. cit., pp. 205–206.

"Dialektik" [ca. 1937], in Bohnen, *Otto Freundlich, Schriften*, op. cit., pp. 207–208.

"Der bildhafte Raum" [1938]. Excerpt in Otto Freundlich, *Aus Briefen und Aufsätzen*, op. cit.; excerpt in Bohnen, *Otto Freundlich: Schriften*, op. cit., pp. 211–220.

"Notice biographique du peintre-sculpteur Otto Freundlich, par lui-même" [1941], in *Association des Amis d'Otto Freundlich*, op. cit.; and in Bohnen, *Otto Freundlich: Schriften*, op. cit., pp. 252–253 [under the title "Biographische Notiz des Malers und Bildhauers Otto Freundlich, von ihm selbst verfaßt"].

"Ideen und Bilder" [1940–42], *Maintenant* 7 (1947), pp. 99–102 [under the title "Vie Nouvelle de l'Art"]. Excerpt in *Deux sculptures monumentales de Otto Freundlich*, op. cit. [under the title "Idées et intuitions d'un artiste"]; abridged version in Heusinger, *Freundlich: Werkverzeichnis*, op. cit., pp. 263–266; excerpt in Bohnen, *Otto Freundlich: Schriften*, op. cit., pp. 221–249.

"Aphorismen und Marginalien" [15 quotations from various texts by Freundlich], in Bohnen, *Otto Freundlich: Schriften*, op. cit., pp. 250–251.

"La vie demande tant de sacrifices . . ." [ca. 1938], in *Association des Amis d'Otto Freundlich*, op. cit. [under the title "Pensées d'Otto Freundlich"].

Collective texts with the participation of Otto Freundlich

"Über Cézanne," with Max Ernst and Heinrich Hoerle, *Bulletin D* (1919), unpag. [p. 8]. Reprinted in Schumann, *sankt ziegenzack springt aus dem ei*, op. cit., p. 376.

"Manifest der Kommune (Berlin, im März 1922)," signed by Melchior Hala, Stanislawowa [= Margarete Kubicka], Else Hala, Doris Homann, Felix Gasbarra, Franz Josef Esser, Stanislaw Kubicki, Oskar Fischer, Hermann F. A. Westphal, and Otto Freundlich; presumably distributed as a pamphlet. Published in *Die Aktion* 33/34 (1922), cols. 481–482 [under the title "Ein Manifest kommunistischer Künstler"]. Reprinted in Helga Kliemann, *Die Novembergruppe* (Berlin, 1969), p. 66; and in Bohnen, *Otto Freundlich: Schriften*, op. cit., pp. 122–123.

"Zweites Manifest der Kommune" [undated, but before May 1922], signed by Stanislaw Kubicki, Otto Freundlich, Tristan Rémy, Felix Gasbarra, Hermann F. A. Westphal, Stanislawowa, Ludwig Hilbersheimer, Doris Homann, Franz Josef Esser, Raoul Hausmann, and Hedwig Mankiewitz [= Hedwig Hausmann]; presumably distributed as a pamphlet. Reprinted in Kliemann, *Die Novembergruppe*, op. cit., pp. 66–68; excerpt in Bohnen, *Otto Freundlich: Schriften*, op. cit., pp. 124–126.

Selected Bibliography

Catalogue Raisonné

Otto Freundlich (1878–1943): Monographie mit Dokumentation und Werkverzeichnis. Edited by Joachim Heusinger von Waldegg. Exh. cat. Rheinisches Landesmuseum Bonn et al. Cologne, 1978.
The catalogue raisonné by Joachim Heusinger von Waldegg is abbreviated throughout the present catalogue as "HvW."

Monographs and Other Publications

Aust, Günter. *Otto Freundlich: 1878–1943.* Cologne, 1960.

Association des Amis d'Otto Freundlich. Paris, undated [leaflet, 1959].

Bohnen, Uli, ed. *Otto Freundlich: Schriften. Ein Wegbereiter der gegenstandslosen Kunst.* Cologne, 1982.

Grzimek, Waldemar. "Otto Freundlich." In Grzimek, *Deutsche Bildhauer des zwanzigsten Jahrhunderts: Leben – Schulen – Wirkungen.* Munich, 1969, pp. 97–104.

Heusinger von Waldegg, Joachim. *Otto Freundlich. Ascension: Anweisung zur Utopie.* Frankfurt am Main, 1987.

Heusinger von Waldegg, Joachim. *Otto Freundlich und die rheinische Kunstszene mit Briefen an Herwarth Walden und Wilhelm Niemeyer.* Edited by Verein August Macke Haus. Exh. cat. August Macke Haus. Bonn, 2006.

Kliemann, Helga. *Die Novembergruppe.* Berlin, 1969.

Kornbrust, Leo, ed. *Straße des Friedens: Straße der Skulpturen in Europa. Hommage à Otto Freundlich.* Dillingen, 2001.

Lütge, Karena. *"In der Malerei wird die Materie zum Geist": Otto Freundlich zwischen Jugendstil, Expressionismus und Konstruktivismus.* Berlin and Weimar, 1997.

Mettay, Joël. *Die verlorene Spur: Auf der Suche nach Otto Freundlich.* Göttingen, 2005.

Mettay, Joël, and Edda Maillet. *Otto Freundlich et la France: Un amour trahi.* Perpignan, 2004.

Schmidt, Diether, ed. *Schriften deutscher Künstler des zwanzigsten Jahrhunderts. Band I: Manifeste, Manifeste. 1905–1933.* Dresden, 1965.

Schrage, Lena. *Otto Freundlich (1878–1943). Individualist im Netzwerk der Pariser Avantgarde. Das Frühwerk,* PhD dissertation. Frankfurt am Main, 2017.

Schuhmann, Klaus, ed. *Sankt Ziegenzack springt aus dem Ei. Texte, Bilder und Dokumente zum Dadaismus in Zürich, Berlin, Hannover und Köln.* Leipzig and Weimar, 1991.

Schulz, Maria-Katharina. "Glasmalerei der klassischen Moderne in Deutschland" (= Europäische Hochschulschriften – Reihe XXVIII). Frankfurt am Main, 1987.

Vernerey-Laplace, Denise. "Regards de l'est sur l'abstraction: Otto Freundlich, Étienne Béothy, Jean Leppien." PhD dissertation. Villeneuve d'Ascq, undated.

Wildegans-Krollpfeiffer, Rita. "Otto Freundlichs Werk im Kontext naturwissenschaftlicher und gesellschaftspolitischer Erkenntnisse." PhD dissertation. Hamburg, 1989.

Essays and Articles

Anonymous. "Freundlich, Otto." *Réalités Nouvelles* 1 (1947), unpag.

Anonymous. "Das Mosaik von Freundlich." *Kölner Stadtanzeiger*, November 20, 1954.

Becker, Andreas. "Die Zeitschrift *a bis z.* Erinnerungen an Otto Freundlich." In *Hoerle und Seiwert: Moderne Malerei in Köln zwischen 1917 und 1933. Eine Monografie.* Edited by Hans Schmitt-Rost, exh. cat. Kölnischer Kunstverein. Cologne, 1952, pp. 45–48.

Bovey, Louis. "Compte-rendu de l'exposition 'Cent sculptures de peintres, de Daumier à Picasso à Yverdon.'" *Aujourd'hui, art et architecture* 9 (1956).

Brion, Marcel. "Otto Freundlich." In *Otto Freundlich, Jeanne Kosnick-Kloss: Exposition commémorative avec le concours de l'Association des amis d'Otto Freundlich,* exh. cat. Centre Culturel Allemand Paris, Goethe-Institut Paris. Paris, 1968, unpag.

Bussman, Valérie. "Une vision de l'homme nouveau: Otto Freundlich (1878–1943), un artiste entre l'Allemagne et la France." *Documents. Revue du dialogue franco-allemand* 3 (2001), pp. 112–118.

Creutz, Max. "Ein Mosaik: Eine Ausstellung des Kölner Kunstvereins." *Westdeutsche Wochenschrift* 1 (1919), p. 473.

Da Cunha, Carlos. "Otto Freundlich: Un pioneiro da Arte Abstrata." *Revista da Semana* 7 (February 16, 1952), p. 13.

Da Cunha, Carlos. "Otto Freundlich: Precursor da Arte Abstrata." *Sombra* 135 (1954), pp. 44–45.

Daix, Pierre. "Hypothèses sur Chaissac, Freundlich et Picasso." In *Gaston Chaissac*, exh. cat. Galerie nationale du Jeu de Paume, Paris. Paris, 2000, pp. 17–23.

Deicher, Susanne. "Abstraktion und Begehren: Otto Freundlichs Konstruktion eines Unbewußten der Kunst." In *Die weibliche und die männliche Linie: Das imaginäre Geschlecht der modernen Kunst von Klimt bis Mondrian.* Edited by Susanne Deicher. Berlin, 1993, pp. 141–181.

Diehl, Gaston. "Pour et contre l'Art Abstrait." *Cahiers des Amis de l'Art* 11 (1947), p. 56.

Fenster, Hersh. "Otto Freundlich." In Fenster, *Undzere farpainikte kinstler. Nos artistes martyrs.* Paris, 1951, pp. 190–194.

Franz, Erich. "Otto Freundlich – Dynamischer Raum." In *Freiheit der Linie: Von Obrist und dem Jugendstil zu Marc, Klee und Kirchner.* Edited by Erich Franz, exh. cat. Landesmuseum für Kunst und Kulturgeschichte, Westfälisches Landesmuseum Münster. [Bönen], 2007, pp. 242–247.

Gacon, Jean. "Pour l'anniversaire de mon ami Otto Freundlich." *Le Lunain* 16 (1938).

Giesen, Sebastian. "Der Künstler ist der Mikrokosmos des sozialen Lebens: Otto Freundlich in Hamburg." In *Freundlich – Gangolf – Kogan: Drei Künstlerschicksale.* Edited by Ernst Barlach Haus Hamburg, exh. cat. Ernst Barlach Haus Hamburg. Hamburg, 2004, pp. 11–25.

Géo-Charles. "Le 60e anniversaire d'un précurseur de l'art abstrait." *Anthologie* 5 (1938), pp. 8–9.

Géo-Charles. "Précurseur de l'Art Abstrait." *Revue Sept Arts* 4 (1948).

Goeritz, Mathias. "Highway Sculpture: The Towers of Satellite City." *Leonardo. The International Society for the Arts, Sciences and Technology* 3 (1970), pp. 319–322.

Goeritz, Mathias. "The Route of Friendship: Sculpture." *Leonardo. The International Society for the Arts, Sciences and Technology* 4 (1970), pp. 397–407.

Hagen, Jens. "Die Kölner Progressiven." *Tendenzen. Zeitschrift für engagierte Kunst* 102 (1975), pp. 42–45.

Heusinger von Waldegg, Joachim. "In memoriam Hanns Bolz (1885–1918)." *Aachener Kunstblätter* 47 (1976/1977), pp. 193–298.

Heusinger von Waldegg, Joachim. "Über Otto Freundlichs plastisches Werk." *Bruckmanns Pantheon. Internationale Jahreszeitschrift für Kunst* 4 (1981), pp. 347–351.

Heusinger von Waldegg, Joachim. "Otto Freundlich 'Mon ciel est rouge' (1933). Zum Realitätscharakter ungegenständlicher Malerei." *Bruckmanns Pantheon. Internationale Jahreszeitschrift für Kunst* 46 (1988), pp. 131–141.

Heusinger von Waldegg, Joachim. "Otto Freundlichs Modell eines 'Leuchtturm der sieben Künste': Ein utopisches Denkmal." In *Mythen – Symbole – Metamorphosen in der Kunst seit 1800. Festschrift für Christa Lichtenstern zum 60. Geburtstag*, edited by Helga Schmoll, J. Adolf Schmoll gen. Eisenwerth, and Regina Maria Hillert. Berlin, 2004, pp. 261–273.

Klingbeil, Almut. "Zur Korrespondenz Otto Freundlich – Max Sauerlandt." *Jahrbuch des Museums für Kunst und Gewerbe Hamburg* 9/10 (1990–1991). Hamburg, 1993, pp. 141–152.

Koch, Hans. "Rheinländer in der neuen Kunst." *Bonner Zeitung*, August 5, 1919.

Kracht, Isgard. "Vom Symbol der Freiheit zum Sinnbild 'entarteter' Kunst: Otto Freundlichs Plastik 'Der neue Mensch.'" In *Das verfemte Meisterwerk: Schicksalswege moderner Kunst im 'Dritten Reich,'* edited by Uwe Fleckner. Berlin, 2009, pp. 3–27.

Kracht, Isgard. "Otto Freundlich, Kopf, 1925." In *Der Berliner Skulpturenfund: 'Entartete Kunst' im Bombenschutt*, edited by Matthias Wemhoff, exh. cat. Staatliche Museen Berlin, Museum für Vor- und Frühgeschichte. Regensburg, 2012, pp. 175–181.

Krieger, Peter. "Otto Freundlich: Einzelgänger und Mystiker der Ecole de Paris." *Speculum Artis. Zeitschrift für alte und neue Kunst* 5 (1965), pp. 37–40.

Müller, Ute. "Skulpturale Großprojekte in architektonischen Dimensionen." In Ute Müller, "Zwischen Skulptur und Architektur: Eine Untersuchung zur architektonischen Skulptur im 20. Jahrhundert," PhD dissertation. Aachen, 1998, pp. 119–131.

Müller, Ute. "Die figurativ-architekturale Plastik: Freundlich – Arp." In Ute Müller, "Zwischen Skulptur und Architektur: Eine Untersuchung zur architektonischen Skulptur im 20. Jahrhundert," PhD dissertation. Aachen, 1998, pp. 156–159.

Niemeyer, Wilhelm. "Von Wesen und Wandlung der Plastik." In *Genius. Zeitschrift für werdende und alte Kunst*, edited by Carl Georg Heise, Hans Mardersteig, and Kurt Pinthus. Leipzig, 1919, pp. 77–89.

Otterbeck, Christoph. "Auf der Suche nach einer elementaren Ästhetik: Von der Holzbildhauerei der Brücke-Künstler zum Werk Otto Freundlichs." In *Wilde Welten: Aneignung des Fremden in der Moderne*, edited by Ursel Berger, exh. cat. Georg-Kolbe-Museum Berlin. Leipzig, 2010, pp. 58–72.

Poley, Stefanie. "Skizze zu einem 'Museum des 'neuen Menschen' im 20. Jahrhundert.'" In *Kunst im Kontext: Kunstmuseum und Kulturgeschichte*, edited by Stefanie Poley. Weimar, 1996, pp. 163–198.

Richter-Berlin, Heinrich. "Das Leben des Malers Richter." *Kunstblätter der Galerie Nierendorf* 32 (1974).

Roditi, Edouard. "The Fate of Otto Freundlich: Painter Maudit." *Commentary Magazine*, September 1, 1955 [online https://www.commentarymagazine.com/articles/the-fate-of-otto-freundlichpainter-maudit/ (accessed November 2016)].

Schäfer, Jörgen. "Otto Freundlichs radikale Sozialkritik in 'Die Lach-Rackete.'" In Jörgen Schäfer, *Dada Köln: Max Ernst, Hans Arp, Johannes Theodor Baargeld und ihre literarischen Zeitschriften*. Wiesbaden, 1993, pp. 103–111.

Sonnabend, Martin. "Der neue Mensch: Eine Plastik von Otto Freundlich." In *Verfolgt und Verführt: Kunst unterm Hakenkreuz in Hamburg 1933–1945*, exh. cat. Hamburger Kunsthalle, Hamburg. Marburg, 1983, pp. 86–90.

Springer, Peter. "Blauer Dunst für die Moderne: Der Sammler und Mäzen Josef Feinhals." In *Hülle und Fülle: Festschrift für Tilmann Buddensieg*, edited by Andreas Beyer, Vittorio Lampugnani, and Gunter Schweikhart. Alfter, 1993, pp. 535–546.

Weber, Gerhard Werner. "Die Ideen Otto Freundlichs." *Das Kunstwerk. Zeitschrift für Moderne Kunst* 1 (1959), pp. 18–23.

Wildegans, Rita. "Otto Freundlichs Skulptur im Erbbegräbnis Wissinger." In *Frühlicht in Beton. Das Erbbegräbnis Wissinger von Max Taut und Otto Freundlich in Stahnsdorf: Geschichte und Hintergründe der Entstehung. Dokumentation der Restaurierung 1987/88,* edited by Christoph Fischer, and Volker Welter. Berlin, 1989, pp. 48–56.

Ziesche, Angela. "'Die Verwandlung der sichtbaren Welt': Otto Freundlichs gelbe Frauenbüste von 1910." In *Wallraf-Richartz-Jahrbuch* 53 (1992), pp. 177–188.

Ziesche, Angela. "Otto Freundlich." In Angela Ziesche, *Der neue Mensch: Köpfe und Büsten deutscher Expressionisten.* Frankfurt am Main et al., 1993, pp. 103–113.

Exhibition Catalogues
Solo Exhibitions

Otto Freundlich: 1878–1942. Exh. cat. Galerie Rive Droite. Paris, 1954.

Otto Freundlich 1878–1943: Gemälde – Graphik – Skulpturen. Edited by Günter Aust. Exh. cat. Wallraf-Richartz-Museum, Cologne. Cologne, 1960.

Deux sculptures monumentales de Otto Freundlich. Exh. cat. Galerie Claude Bernard, Paris; Galerie René Drouin, Paris; Otto Gerson Gallery, New York. Paris, 1962.

Otto Freundlich, Jeanne Kosnick-Kloss: Exposition commémorative avec le concours de l'Association des amis d'Otto Freundlich. Exh. cat. Centre Culturel Allemand Paris, Goethe-Institut Paris. Paris, 1968, unpag.

La Donation Freundlich au Musée de Pontoise: Exposition de vingt-deux œuvres de Otto Freundlich et treize œuvres de Jeanne Kosnick-Kloss. Exh. cat. Musée de Pontoise. Pontoise, 1969.

Hommage à Otto Freundlich. Exh. cat. Musée de Pontoise. Pontoise, 1978, unpag.

Hommage à Otto Freundlich à l'occasion du 100e anniversaire de sa naissance. Exh. cat. Goldman-Schwartz Gallery Jerusalem, The Israel Museum, Jerusalem. Jerusalem, 1978.

Otto Freundlich et Jeanne Kosnick-Kloss, les œuvres retrouvées. Exh. cat. Museé de Pontoise. Paris, 1982.

Otto Freundlich (1878–1943): La donation Freundlich au Musée de Pontoise. Edited by Anton Regenberg. Exh. cat. Goethe-Institut Brussels. Brussels, 1985.

Otto Freundlich. Exh. cat. Musée départemental de Rochechouart. Rochechouart, 1988.

Otto Freundlich. Exh. cat. Galerie Franka Berndt Bastille. Paris, 1990.

Otto Freundlich et ses amis. Exh. cat. Musée de Pontoise. Pontoise, 1993.

Otto Freundlich: Ein Wegbereiter der abstrakten Kunst. Edited by Gerhard Leistner and Thorsten Rodiek. Exh. cat. Museum Ostdeutsche Galerie Regensburg et al. Regensburg, 1994.

Otto Freundlich – Kräfte der Farbe. Exh. cat. Westfälisches Landesmuseum für Kunst und Kulturgeschichte Münster; Kunstmuseum Liechtenstein. Cologne, 2001.

Otto Freundlich: Sculpture. Exh. cat. Michael Werner Gallery, New York; Michael Werner Kunsthandel, Cologne. Essen, 2001.

Martin Noël: Treffen mit Otto Freundlich. Hölzer und Postkarten. Edited by Britta E. Buhlmann. Exh. cat. Museum Pfalzgalerie Kaiserslautern. Kaiserslautern, 2005.

Otto Freundlich (1878–1943): Leuchtturm der sieben Künste. Ein utopisches Denkmal. Edited by Joachim Heusinger von Waldegg. Exh. cat. Stadtmuseum St. Wendel et al. Dillingen, 2007.

Otto Freundlich – 1878–1943: Artyska ze Słupsk, Ein Künstler aus Stolp. Exhibition brochure Muzeum Pomorza Środkowego w Słupsku. Słupsk, 2008.

Otto Freundlich: 1878–1943. Edited by Christophe Duvivier. Exh. cat. Musée de Pontoise. Pontoise, 2009.

Otto Freundlich (1878–1943). Exhibition brochure Musée Geo-Charles. Échirolles, 2010.

L'œil cosmique: Otto Freundlich. Exh. cat. Galerie Applicat-Prazan, Paris. Paris, 2012.

Otto Freundlichs Kopf-Plastiken: Stufen der Verwandlung. Edited by Joachim Heusinger von Waldegg. Exh. cat. Museum St. Wendel. St. Wendel, 2014.

Exhibition Catalogues Group Shows

Neue Secession Berlin. I. Graphische Ausstellung 1910. Exh. cat. Berlin, 1910.

Neue Secession Berlin 1911. IV. Ausstellung: Gemälde. Exh. cat. Berlin, 1911.

Internationale Kunstausstellung des Sonderbundes Westdeutscher Kunstfreunde und Künstler. Exh. cat. Cologne, 1912.

Moderne Kunst Kring (Cercle de l'Art Moderne). Catalogue des Ouvrages de Peinture, Sculture, Dessin, Gravure. Exh. cat. Stedelijk Museum Amsterdam. Amsterdam, 1912.

Beiträge zur Kunst des 19. Jahrhunderts und unserer Zeit. Published for the opening of Galerie Alfred Flechtheim Düsseldorf. Edited by Paul Mahlberg. Exh. cat. Galerie Flechtheim, Düsseldorf. Düsseldorf, 1913.

Erster Deutscher Herbstsalon Berlin 1913. Edited by Herwarth Walden. Exh. cat. Galerie "Der Sturm," Berlin. Berlin, 1913.

Offizieller Katalog der Deutschen Werkbund-Ausstellung. Cöln 1914. Edited by the exhibition directors. Exh. cat. Cologne, 1914; reprint Cologne, 1981.

Otto van Rees, Paris, Hans Arp, A.C. van Rees-Dutilh, Paris: Moderne Wandteppiche, Stickereien, Malereien, Zeichnungen. Exh. cat. Galerie Tanner Zürich. Zurich, 1915.

Freie Secession Berlin 1918. Exh. cat. Berlin, 1918.

Kunstausstellung Berlin 1919. Exh. cat. Landesausstellungsgebäude Berlin. Berlin, 1919.

Kollektiv-Ausstellung: Otto Freundlich, Richard Janthur, Erich Heckel, Lene Schneider-Kainer, Willi Jaeckel, Ernst Ludwig Kirchner, César Klein, Heinrich Nauen, Max Pechstein. Exh. cat. Galerie Fritz Gurlitt. Berlin, 1919.

Katalog zur Ausstellung der Gesellschaft der Künste in Köln im Kölnischen Kunstverein. Exh. cat. Kölnischer Kunstverein. Cologne, 1919.

Catalogue de la 39e exposition au Grand Palais de Champs-Elysées. Edited by Société des Artistes Indépendants. Exh. cat. Paris 1928.

Abstrakte und Surrealistische Malerei und Plastik. Exh. cat. Kunsthaus Zürich. Ostfildern, 1929.

Catalogue de la 40e exposition au Grand Palais de Champs-Elysées. Edited by Société des Artistes Indépendants. Exh. cat. Paris, 1929.

Cie de Peintres et Sculpteurs Professionnels. 16. Exposition. Exh. cat. Brasserie Terminus Paris. Paris, 1929.

Expositions sélectes d'art contemporain (ESAC). Exh. cat. Stedelijk Museum Amsterdam. Amsterdam, 1929.

Exh. cat. Galerie Herter Zürich. Zurich, 1929.

98. Große Kunstausstellung. Edited by Künstlerverein Hannover. Exh. cat. Hanover, 1930.

Catalogue de la 41e exposition au Grand Palais des Champs-Elysées. Edited by Société des Artistes Indépendants. Exh. cat. Paris, 1930.

Ausstellung Moderner Bildwirkereien. Edited by Ludwig Grote. Exh. cat. Kunstgewerbe-Museum im Grassi Museum, Leipzig. Leipzig, 1930.

La Compagnie de Peintres & Sculpteurs Professionnels est à Montrouge. 17e Salon. Exh. cat. Brasserie Terminus, Paris. Paris, 1930.

Association Artistique Les Surindépendants: Indépendance, discipline. 2e Exposition. Exh. cat. Paris, 1930.

Association Artistique Les Surindépendants: Indépendance, discipline. 3e Exposition. Exh. cat. Paris, 1930.

"1940": Première Exposition. Exh. cat. Galerie de la Renaissance, Paris. Paris, 1931.

November-Gruppe: Ausstellung im neuen Hause des Vereins Berliner Künstler. Gemälde, Plastik. Exh. cat. Berlin, 1931.

Düsseldorf-Münchener Kunst. Exh. cat. Kunstpalast, Düsseldorf. Düsseldorf, 1932.

Premier Salon des Artistes Musicalistes. Exh. cat. Galerie de la Renaissance, Paris. Paris, 1932.

Catalogue de la 44e exposition au Grand Palais des Champs-Elysées. Edited by Société des Artistes Indépendants. Exh. cat. Paris, 1933.

Exposition du cinquantenaire au Grand Palais des Champs-Elysées. Edited by Société des Artistes Indépendants. Exh. cat. Paris, 1934.

Catalogue de la 46e exposition au Grand Palais des Champs-Elysées. Edited by Société des Artistes Indépendants. Exh. cat. Paris, 1935.

Les Artistes Musicalistes. Troisième salon. Exh. cat. Galerie de la Renaissance, Paris. Paris, 1936.

Art réaliste et abstrait. Edited by Irmgard Burchard. Exh. cat. Z-Haus, Zurich. Zurich, 1937.

Catalogue de la 48e exposition au Pavillon des salons. Edited by Société des Artistes Indépendants. Exh. cat. Paris, 1937.

Catalogue de la Xe Salon des Artistes Indépendants Bordelais 1937 à Bordeaux. Exh. cat. Ville de Bordeaux. Bordeaux, 1937.

Konstruktivisten. Exh. cat. Kunsthalle Basel. Basel, 1937.

1937 Exhibition: Unity of Artists for Peace, Democracy and Cultural Development. Exh. cat. London, 1937.

Tentoonstelling Abstracte Kunst. Exh. cat. Stedelijk Museum Amsterdam. Amsterdam, 1938; reprint Redding, 1974.

Entartete "Kunst." Exhibition guide. Munich and Berlin, 1938. Reprinted in *Nationalsozialismus und "Entartete Kunst": Die "Kunststadt" München 1937.* Edited by Peter-Klaus Schuster. Munich, 1998.

Exhibition of 20th Century German Art. Exh. cat. New Burlington Galleries, London. London, 1938.

Tentoonstelling Abstracte Kunst. Exh. cat. Stedelijk Museum Amsterdam. Amsterdam, 1938.

Abstract and Concrete Art/Art abstrait. Exh. cat. Galerie Guggenheim Jeune, London; Galerie de Beaune, Paris. Published in *London Bulletin* 14 (1939), pp. 2–4, 21–22.

Catalogue de la 16e exposition au Palais de Chaillot. Edited by Salon des Tuileries. Exh. cat. Paris, 1939.

Catalogue de la 51e exposition au Grand Palais de Champs-Elysées. Edited by Société des Artistes Indépendants. Exh. cat. Paris, 1939.

Konkrete Kunst. Edited by Max Bill. Exh. cat. Kunsthalle Basel. Basel, 1944.

Art Concret. Exh. cat. Galerie René Drouin, Paris. Paris, 1945.

Premier Salon des Réalités Nouvelles – art abstrait, concret, constructivisme. Exh. cat. Palais des beaux-arts de la Ville de Paris. Paris, 1946.

Do Figurativismo ao Abstracionismo. Edited by Léon Degand. Exh. cat. Museu de arte Moderna São Paulo. São Paulo, 1949.

L'art abstrait: Ses origines, ses premiers maîtres. Edited by Michel Seuphor. Exh. cat. Galerie Maeght, Paris. Paris, 1949.

Surréalisme + Abstraction: Choix de la collection Peggy Guggenheim/ Surrealisme + abstractie: keuze uit de verzameling Peggy Guggenheim. Exh. cat. Stedelijk Museum Amsterdam; Palais Beaux-Arts Brussels. Amsterdam, 1951.

Collection Graindorge. Exh. cat. Van Abbe Museum, Eindhoven. Eindhoven, 1954.

Ausgewanderte Maler. Exh. cat. Städtisches Museum Morsbroich, Leverkusen. Leverkusen, 1955.

Œuvres d'artistes juifs morts en déportation. Edited by Léon Meiss and Chil Aronson. Exh. cat. Musée d'art juif, Paris; Galerie Zak, Paris. Paris, 1955.

20th Century Painting and Sculpture from the Collection of Mr. and Mrs. Harry L. Winston. Exh. cat. University of Michigan Museum of Art, Ann Arbor. Ann Arbor, 1955.

100 Sculptures: Daumier à Picasso. Exh. cat. Hôtel de Ville d'Yverdon. Yverdon, 1956.

Skulpturen von Malern – von Daumier bis Picasso. Exh. cat. Kunsthaus Zürich. Zurich, 1956.

Cinquante ans de peinture abtraite. Exh. cat. Galerie Creuze, Paris. Paris, 1957.

Collecting Modern Art – Paintings, Sculpture and Drawings from the Collection of Mr. and Mrs. Harry Lewis Winston. Exh. cat. The Detroit Institute of Art et al. Boston, 1957.

Art abstrait: Les premières générations (1910–1939). Exh. cat. Musée d'Art et d'Industrie de Saint-Etienne. Saint-Etienne, 1957.

Cent Sculptures de Daumier à nos jours. Edited by Maurice Allemand. Exh. cat. Musée d'Art et d'Industrie de Saint-Etienne. Saint-Etienne, 1960.

Construction and Geometry in Painting: from Malevitch to "Tomorrow." Exh. cat. Galerie Chalette, New York. New York, 1960.

Expressionismus, Literatur und Kunst, 1910–1923. Edited by Bernhard Zeller. Exh. cat. Deutsches Literaturarchiv im Schiller National Museum, Marbach. Munich, 1960.

Hommage à Jeanne Bucher 1925–1960. Exh. cat. Galerie Jeanne Bucher, Paris. Paris, 1960.

Konkrete Kunst: 50 Jahre Entwicklung. Exh. cat. Helmhaus Zürich. Zurich, 1960.

L'art moderne Pontoise, L'art sacré Auvers-sur-Oise: Peintures, sculptures, vitraux, gemmaux, céramiques, tapisseries. Exh. cat. Musée Tavet de Pontoise; Église et Mairie d'Auvers-sur-Oise. Pontoise, 1960.

Modern Masters in West Coast Collections: An exhibition selected in celebration of the twenty-fifth anniversary of the San Francisco Museum of Art 1935–1960. Edited by George D. Culler. Exh. cat. Museum of Art San Francisco. San Francisco, 1960.

Berliner Bildnisse aus drei Jahrhunderten. Edited by Irmgard Wirth and Dora Lüttgen. Exh. cat. Städtische Galerie München. Munich, 1962.

Europäische Kunst 1912: Zum 50. Jahrestag der Ausstellung des Sonderbundes Westdeutscher Kunstfreunde und Künstler in Köln. Exh. cat. Wallraf-Richartz-Museum, Cologne. Cologne, 1962.

La Sculpture Contemporaine. Text von René de Solier. Exh. cat. Musée Maison de la Culture du Havre. Le Havre, 1962.

Monumental sculpture. Exh. cat. Otto Gerson Gallery, New York. New York, 1962.

Formes Mathématiques: Peintres, sculpteurs contemporains. Exh. cat. Université de Paris; Palais de la Découverte, Paris. Paris, 1963.

Wilhelm Lehmbruck and Other German Sculptors of His Time. Exh. cat. Otto Gerson Gallery, New York. New York, 1963.

Kunstdiktatur Gestern und Heute. Exh. cat. Galerie Ben Wargin, Berlin. Berlin, 1963.

Catalogue du XIVe salon d'art sacré. Exh. cat. Paris, 1964.

Documenta III, Internationale Ausstellung, Malerei/Skulptur. Exh. cat. Alte Galerie Kassel et al. Cologne, 1964.

Meisterwerke der Plastik. Exh. cat. Museum des 20. Jahrhunderts, Vienna. Vienna, 1964.

Traum-Zeichen-Raum: Benennung des Unbekannten. Kunst in den Jahren 1924–1939. Exh. cat. Wallraf-Richartz-Museum, Cologne. Cologne. 1965.

Kunst des 20. Jahrhunderts aus rheinisch-westfälischem Privatbesitz. Edited by Uwe M. Schneede. Exh. cat. Städtische Kunsthalle Düsseldorf, Kunstverein für die Rheinlande und Westfalen. Düsseldorf, 1967.

Sammlung Marguerite Arp-Hagenbach. Exh. cat. Kunstmuseum Basel. Basel, 1967.

Spektrum der Farbe: Eine Züricher Privatsammlung. Text by Max Henri Welti. Exh. cat. Kunsthaus Zürich. Zurich, 1967.

Vom Bauhaus bis zur Gegenwart: Meisterwerke aus deutschem Privatbesitz. Exh. cat. Kunstverein Hamburg. Hamburg, 1967.

Jewish Artists Who Perished in the Holocaust. Edited by Pola Eichenbaum. Exh. cat. Tel Aviv Museum. Tel Aviv, 1968.

Attraction 1924–1969. Exh. cat. Centre Culturel Allemand, Goethe-Institut Paris. Paris, 1969.

Depuis Rodin. Exh. cat. Musée Municipal de Saint-Germain-en-Laye. Saint-Germain-en-Laye, 1969.

Sammlung Wilhelm Hack: Kunst der Römer- und Völkerwanderungszeit, Kunst des Mittelalters, Kunst des 20. Jahrhunderts. Edited by Kunstverein für die Rheinlande und Westfalen Düsseldorf. Exh. cat. Kunsthalle Düsseldorf. Düsseldorf, 1969.

Die Zwanziger Jahre (I): Deutsche Kunst von 1914–1923. Exh. cat. Galerie Nierendorf, Berlin. Berlin, 1970.

Hoerle und sein Kreis. Exh. cat. Kunstverein Frechen. Frechen, 1970.

L'Art en Europe autour de 1925. Exh. cat. L'Ancienne Douane de Strasbourg, Ville de Strasbourg. Strasbourg, 1970.

Verzameling Marguerite Arp-Hagenbach. Text by Rudolf Willem Daan Oxenaar and Franz Meyer. Exh. cat. Rijksmuseum Kröller-Müller, Otterlo. Otterlo, 1970.

Kunst des 20. Jahrhunderts – Freie Berufe sammeln. Edited by Jaroslav Borovička. Exh. cat. Städtische Kunsthalle Düsseldorf. Düsseldorf, 1971.

The Non-Objective World. 1939–1955. Exh. cat. Annely Juda Fine Art, London, et al. London et al., 1972.

Weltkulturen und moderne Kunst: Die Begegnung der europäischen Kunst und Musik im 19. und 20. Jahrhundert mit Asien, Afrika, Ozeanien, Afro- und Indo-Amerika. Exh. cat. Haus der Kunst, Munich. Munich, 1972.

Futurism: A Modern Focus, Selection from the Lydia & Harry L. Winston Collection, Dr. and Mrs. Barnett Malbin. Exh. cat. Solomon R. Guggenheim Museum, New York. New York, 1973.

Kunst in Deutschland 1898–1973. Edited by Werner Hofmann et al. Exh. cat. Hamburger Kunsthalle, Hamburg; Städtische Galerie Lenbachhaus, Munich. Hamburg, 1973.

Sculptures de peintres. Exh. cat. Musée Rodin, Paris. Paris, 1973.

The non-objective world 1914–1955/Die Gegenstandslose Welt 1914–1955. Exh. cat. Annely Juda Fine Art, London; University Art Museum, Austin, TX. Bromley, 1973.

Art abstrait 1910–1940. Dessins. Exh. cat. Musée national d'art moderne, Paris. Paris, 1975.

Die Progressiven. Edited by Wulf Herzogenrath. Exh. cat. Galerie Brockstedt, Hamburg. Cologne, 1975.

Le Bateau-Lavoir: Berceau de l'art moderne. Exh. cat. Musée Jacquemart-André, Paris. Paris, 1975.

Otto en Adya van Rees, levenen werk tot 1934. Exh. cat. Centraal Museum Utrecht; Gemeentemuseum Den Haag, The Hague. Wijchen, 1975.

Politische Konstruktivisten: Die Gruppe "progressiver Künstler" Köln. Edited by Neuen Gesellschaft für bildende Kunst. Exh. cat. Akademie der Künste, Berlin. Berlin, 1975.

Versuch einer Rekonstruktion: Internationale Ausstellung Revolutionärer Künstler 1922 in Berlin. Edited by Neuer Berliner Kunstverein e.V. Exh. cat. Artothek Berlin. Berlin, 1975.

Vom Dadamax bis zum Grüngürtel. Köln in den 20er Jahren. Bildende Kunst, Fotografie, Rundfunk, Architektur, Musik, Theater, Literatur mit reprint: "Bulletin D" 1919, Katalog "Brauhaus Winter" 1920, Katalog "Stupid" 1920, "Dokumente der Progressiven" 1920–26 und andere zeitgenössische Texte. Edited by Wulf Herzogenrath. Exh. cat. Kölnischer Kunstverein. Cologne, 1975.

Die reine Form: Von Malewitsch bis Albers. Edited by Susanne Köngeter and Stephan von Wiese. Exh. cat. Kunstmuseum Düsseldorf. Düsseldorf, 1976.

Hommage à Max Jacob, 1876–1944. Edited by Jeanine Warnod. Exh. cat. Musée de Montmartre, Paris. Paris, 1976.

Aspects historiques du constructivisme et de l'art concret: La McCrory Corporation et sa collection. Exh. cat. Musée d'Art moderne de la Ville de Paris. Paris, 1977.

Aspekte konstruktiver Kunst: Sammlung McCrory Corporation New York, Zürich. Edited by Willy Rotzler. Exh. cat. Kunsthaus Zürich. Zurich, 1977.

Die Dreißiger Jahre. Schauplatz Deutschland. Exh. cat. Haus der Kunst, Munich, et al. Munich, 1977.

Tendenzen der Zwanziger Jahre: 15. Berliner Kunstausstellung Berlin 1977. Edited by Dieter Honisch, Ursula Prinz, et al. Exh. cat. Neue Nationalgalerie Berlin et al. Berlin, 1977.

Wem gehört die Welt? Kunst und Gesellschaft in der Weimarer Republik. Edited by Jürgen Kleindienst. Exh. cat. Staatliche Kunsthalle Berlin. Berlin, 1977.

Abstraction-Création 1931–1936. Edited by Westfälisches Landesmuseum für Kunst und Kulturgeschichte des Landschaftsverbandes Westfalen-Lippe. Exh. cat. Westfälisches Landesmuseum für Kunst und Kulturgeschichte Münster; Musée d'Art moderne de la Ville de Paris. Münster, 1978.

Chemins de la création: Dessins de peintres, dessins de sculptures. Exh. cat. Château d'Ancy-le-France. Ancy-le-France, 1978.

Franz W. Seiwert – Leben und Werk. Edited by Uli Bohnen. Exh. cat. Kölnischer Kunstverein et al. Cologne, 1978.

L'Art moderne dans les musées de province. Edited by Ministère de la Culture et de l'Environnement, Galeries Nationales d'Exposition du Grand Palais. Exh. cat. Grand Palais, Paris. Paris, 1978.

Le Bateau Lavoir. Exh. cat. Museum voor Schone Kunsten, Ghent. Ghent, 1978.

Paris–Berlin 1900–1933: Rapports et contrastes France–Allemagne. Exh. cat. Centre Georges Pompidou, Paris. Paris, 1978.

The Non-Objective World: Twenty-Five Years 1914–1939. Exh. cat. Annely Juda Fine Art, London. London, 1978.

Éloge du petit format: Peintures – sculptures – dessins – collages – pastels – estampes. Collection Pierre Bourut. Exh. cat. Musée de Pontoise. Pontoise, 1979.

L'art dans les années 30 en France. Edited by Jacques Beauffet. Exh. cat. Musée d'Art et d'Industrie de Saint-Etienne. Saint-Etienne, 1979.

Arbeitsrat für Kunst 1918–1921. Edited by Manfred Schlösser. Exh. cat. Akademie der Künste, Berlin. Berlin, 1980.

Exposition Résistance, Déportation: Création dans le bruit des armes. Edited by Michelle Michel. Exh. cat. Chancellerie de l'Ordre de la Libération, Paris. Paris, 1980.

Max Ernst in Köln: Die rheinische Kunstszene bis 1922. Edited by Wulf Herzogenrath. Exh. cat. Kölnischer Kunstverein, Cologne. Cologne, 1980.

Montparnasse. La Revue de Géo Charles: La collection complète de 1914 à 1930, ses poèmes sur le sport, ses portraits, les œuvres de ses amis peintres. Exh. cat. Musée de Pontoise. Pontoise, 1980.

Van Gogh bis Cobra: Holländische Malerei 1880–1950. Edited by Geurt Imanse et al. Exh. cat. Württembergischer Kunstverein, Stuttgart. Stuttgart, 1980.

Westkunst: Zeitgenössische Kunst seit 1939. Edited by Laszlo Glozer. Exh. cat. Museen der Stadt Cologne. Cologne, 1981.

Die Sammlung Theo Wormland. Edited by Hartwig Garnerus. Exh. cat. Haus der Kunst, Munich. Munich, 1983.

German Expressionist Sculpture. Edited by Stephanie Barron. Exh. cat. Los Angeles County Museum of Art et al. Los Angeles, 1983.

Maler bauen Barrikaden: Grafik der 20er Jahre. Edited by Gerd Gruber. Exh. cat. Haus der Kultur und Bildung Neubrandenburg; Kunsthalle Rostock. Neubrandenburg, undated [1983].

Verboten, Verfolgt: Kunstdiktatur im 3. Reich. Edited by Barbara Lepper. Exh. cat. Wilhelm-Lehmbruck-Museum Duisburg et al. Duisburg, 1983.

Verfolgt und Verführt: Kunst unterm Hakenkreuz in Hamburg 1933–1945. Exh. cat. Hamburger Kunsthalle, Hamburg. Marburg, 1983.

Schwebend-Heiter: Gemälde, Aquarelle, Zeichnungen, Drucke, Skulpturen und Objekte. Exh. cat. Galerie Pels-Leusden, Berlin. Berlin, 1984.

Contrasts of Form: Geometric Abstract Art, 1910–1980. From the Collection of the Museum of Modern Art, including the Riklis Collection of McCrory Corporation. Edited by Magdalena Dabrowski. Exh. cat. The Museum of Modern Art, New York. New York, 1985.

De la Bible à nos jours: 3000 ans de l'art. Edited by Société des Artistes Indépendants et le Comité Français Terre d'Israël. Exh. cat. Paris, 1985.

Kandinsky in Paris: 1934–1944. Exh. cat. The Solomon R. Guggenheim Museum, New York. New York, 1985.

Masterpieces of the Avantgarde: Three Decades of Contemporary Art, The Sixties – The Seventies – The Eighties. Exh. cat. Annely Juda Fine Art, London; Juda Rowan Gallery, London. London, 1985.

Vom Klang der Bilder: Die Musik in der Kunst des 20. Jahrhunderts. Edited by Karin von Maur. Exh. cat. Staatsgalerie Stuttgart. Munich, 1985.

Contrastes de forma, Abstracción Geométrica, 1910–1980 de la colecciones del Solomon R. Guggenheim Museum y The Museum of Modern Art de New York. Edited by Magdalena Dabrowski. Exh. cat. Museo de Arte Contemporaneo de Caracas. Caracas, 1986.

Delaunay und Deutschland. Edited by Peter-Klaus Schuster. Exh. cat. Bayrische Staatsgemäldesammlung – Staatsgalerie moderner Kunst, Munich. Cologne, 1986.

Europa-Amerika: Die Geschichte einer künstlerischen Faszination. Edited by Siegfried Gohr. Exh. cat. Museum Ludwig, Cologne. Cologne, 1986.

Formen auf weißem Grund: Konstruktivismus und geometrische Kunst. Exh. cat. Galerie Stolz, Cologne. Cologne, 1986.

1912, Break Up of Tradition. Edited by Louise d'Argencourt. Exh. cat. Winnipeg Art Gallery. Winnipeg, 1987.

"... und nicht die leiseste Spur einer Vorschrift" – Positionen unabhängiger Kunst in Europa um 1937. Edited by Freya Mühlhaupt. Exh. cat. Kunstsammlung Nordrhein-Westfalen, Düsseldorf. Düsseldorf, 1987.

"Entartete Kunst": Dokumentation zum nationalsozialistischen Bildersturm am Bestand der Staatsgalerie Moderner Kunst in München. Edited by Peter-Klaus Schuster. Exh. cat. Staatsgalerie moderner Kunst im Haus der Kunst, Munich. Munich, 1987.

Le eredità sconosciute di Peggy Guggenheim: Da Max Ernst a Jackson Pollock. Exh. cat. Solomon R. Guggenheim Museum, New York; Peggy Guggenheim Collection, Venice. Milan, 1987.

The Cologne Progressives 1919–1933. Exh. cat. Rachel Adler Gallery, New York. New York, 1987.

German Expressionism: The Second Generation 1915–1925. Edited by Stephanie Barron. Exh. cat. County Museum of Los Angeles et al. Los Angeles et al., 1988.

The Non-Objective World Revisited. Text by Stephen Bann. Exh. cat. Annely Juda Fine Art, London. London, 1988.

Bilderstreit, Widerspruch, Einheit und Fragment der Kunst seit 1960. Edited by Siegfried Gohr and Johannes Gachnang. Exh. cat. Museum Ludwig, Cologne. Cologne, 1989.

Corps-Figures: La figuration humaine dans la sculpture du XXe siècle. Text by Dominique Le Buhan. Exh. cat. Artcurial, Centre d'art plastique contemporain, Paris. Paris, 1989.

Der Traum einer neuen Welt, Berlin 1910–1933. Edited by Patricia Rochard. Exh. cat. Museum Altes Rathaus, Ingelheim am Rhein. Mainz, 1989.

Fall 1989. Exh. cat. Graphisches Kabinett Kunsthandel Wolfgang Werner, Bremen; Helen Serger/La Boetie, New York. Bremen, 1989.

Max Jacob et les artistes de son temps, de Picasso à Dubuffet. Exh. cat. Musée des Beaux Arts d'Orléans. Orléans, 1989.

Lambert Rucki et les modernes classiques. Exh. cat. Galerie Franka Berndt Bastille, Paris. Paris, 1990.

"Degenerate Art": The Fate of the Avantgarde in Nazi Germany. Edited by Stephanie Barron. Exh. cat. County Museum of Art Los Angeles et al. Munich and Los Angeles, 1992.

Kurt Weber 1893–1964. Edited by Gottfried Biedermann et al. Exh. cat. Neue Galerie am Landesmuseum Joanneum, Graz. Salzburg, 1993.

Okkultismus und Avantgarde: Von Munch bis Mondrian 1900–1915. Edited by Bernd Apke and Veit Loers. Exh. cat. Schirn-Kunsthalle, Frankfurt. Ostfildern, 1995.

Deutschlandbilder: Kunst aus einem geteilten Land. Edited by Eckhart Gillen. Exh. cat. Martin-Gropius-Bau, Berlin. Cologne, 1997.

Picasso. Klee. Giacometti – Die Sammlung Steegmann. Edited by Ina Conzen. Exh. cat. Staatsgalerie Stuttgart. Ostfildern-Ruit, 1998.

L'école de Paris 1904–1929: La part de l'Autre. Text by Laurence Bertrand Dorléac et al. Exh. cat. Musée d'Art moderne de la Ville de Paris. Paris, 2000.

Ornament und Abstraktion: Kunst der Kulturen, Moderne und Gegenwart im Dialog. Edited by Markus Brüderlin. Exh. cat. Fondation Beyeler, Riehen/Basel. Cologne, 2001.

Die Graphische Sammlung: Klassische Moderne II. Edited by Barbara Alms. Exh. cat. Städtische Galerie Delmenhorst, Haus Coburg. Bremen, 2002.

Sammlung Rosenkranz. Edited by Sabine Fehlemann. Exh. cat. Von der Heydt-Museum, Wuppertal. Wuppertal, 2002.

Freundlich – Gangolf – Kogan: Drei Künstlerschicksale. Edited by Ernst Barlach Haus. Exh. cat. Ernst Barlach Haus, Hamburg. Hamburg, 2004.

Werke aus der Hilti Art Foundation: Von Paul Gauguin bis Imi Knoebel. Edited by Uwe Wieczorek. Exh. cat. Kunstmuseum Lichtenstein, Vaduz. Vaduz, 2005.

Fest der Farbe: Die Sammlung Merzbacher-Meyer. Exh. cat. Kunsthaus Zürich. Cologne, 2006.

Full House – Gesichter einer Sammlung. Edited by Rolf Lauter. Exh. cat. Städtische Kunsthalle Mannheim. Mannheim, 2006.

Von Kandinsky bis Tatlin: Konstruktivismus in Europa. Edited by Kornelia von Berswordt-Wallrabe. Exh. cat. Staatliches Museum Schwerin, Kunstmuseum Bonn. Schwerin, 2006.

Großes Ey wir loben Dich: Johanna Ey und ihr Künstlerkreis. Exh. cat. Galerie Remmert und Barth, Düsseldorf. Düsseldorf, 2007.

1937: Perfektion und Zerstörung. Edited by Thomas Kellein. Exh. cat. Kunsthalle Bielefeld. Tübingen, 2007.

Gerd Arntz im Kreise von Freunden und Kollegen. Exh. cat. Galerie Remmert und Barth, Düsseldorf. Düsseldorf, 2008.

Die Verborgene Spur: Jüdische Wege durch die Moderne. Edited by Martin Roman Deppner. Exh. cat. Felix-Nussbaum-Haus, Osnabrück. Bramsche, 2008.

Wilde Welten: Aneignung des Fremden in der Moderne. Edited by Ursel Berger. Exh. cat. Georg-Kolbe-Museum, Berlin. Berlin, 2010.

Der Berliner Skulpturenfund: "Entartete Kunst" im Bombenschutt. Edited by Matthias Wemhoff. Exh. cat. Staatliche Museen Berlin, Museum für Vor- und Frühgeschichte. Regensburg, 2011.

Liebermanns Gegner: Die Neue Secession in Berlin und der Expressionismus. Edited by Stiftung Brandenburger Tor et al. Exh. cat. Stiftung Brandenburger Tor et al. Cologne, 2011.

1912 – Mission Moderne: Die Jahrhundertschau des Sonderbundes. Edited by Barbara Schaefer. Exh. cat. Wallraf-Richartz-Museum und Fondation Corboud, Cologne. Cologne, 2012.

1917. Edited by Claire Garnier and Laurent Le Bon. Exh. cat. Centre Pompidou-Metz. Metz, 2012.

Der Sturm: Zentrum der Avantgarde. Edited by Antje Birthälmer and Gerhard Finckh. Exh. cat. Von der Heydt-Museum, Wuppertal. Wuppertal, 2012.

L'art en guerre, France 1938–1947: De Picasso à Dubuffet. Edited by Laurence Bertrand Dorléac. Exh. cat. Musée d'Art moderne de la Ville de Paris. Paris, 2012.

La Collection Michael Werner / The Michael Werner Collection. Exh. cat. Musée d'Art moderne de la Ville de Paris. Paris and Cologne, 2012, pp. 504–509.

Meisterwerke der Moderne: Die Sammlung Haubrich im Museum Ludwig. Edited by Julia Friedrich. Exh. cat. Museum Ludwig, Cologne. Cologne, 2012.

La sculpture des peintres: Arp, Bonnard, Braque, Chabaud, Clavé, Daumier, Degas, Derain, Fautrier, Freundlich, Gauguin, Giacometti, Kirchner, de La Fresnaye, Matisse, Picasso, Renoir, Rouault, Valloton, Venet. Edited by Jean-Paul Monery. Exh. cat. Musée de L'Annonciade, Saint-Tropez. Saint-Tropez, 2012.

The Moderns: Wie sich das 20. Jahrhundert in Kunst und Wissenschaft erfunden hat. Edited by Cathrin Pichler. Exh. cat. mumok – Museum Moderner Kunst Stiftung Ludwig, Vienna, et al. Vienna, 2012.

Traum-Bilder – Ernst, Magritte, Dalí, Picasso, Antes, Nay . . . Die Wormland-Schenkung. Edited by Oliver Kase. Exh. cat. Bayerische Staatsgemäldesammlungen – Pinakothek der Moderne, Munich. Ostfildern, 2013.

Degenerate Art: The Attack on Modern Art in Nazi Germany, 1937. Edited by Olaf Peters. Exh. cat. Neue Galerie, New York. Munich et al., 2014.

List of Works

The "HvW" numbers refer to the catalogue raisonné edited by Joachim Heusinger von Waldegg, *Otto Freundlich (1878–1943): Monographie mit Dokumentation und Werkverzeichnis*, exh. cat. Rheinisches Landesmuseum Bonn et al. (Cologne, 1978).

Tapestries, mosaics, stained glass works

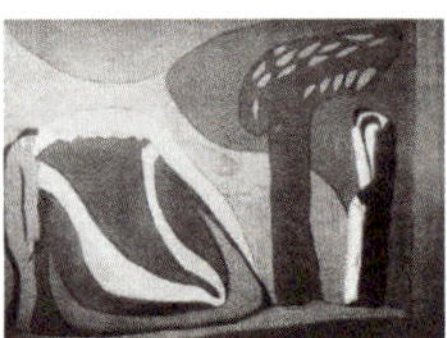
Composition, 1912
HvW 3
Wool tapestry
Large format
Lost
Woven by Adya van Rees after a design by Freundlich in tempera or oils from 1911
p. 32

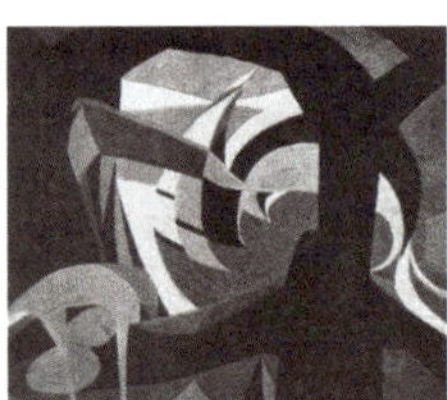
Composition, 1912–13
HvW 5
Wool tapestry
Large format
Lost
Woven by Adya van Rees after a design by Freundlich in tempera or oils
p. 33

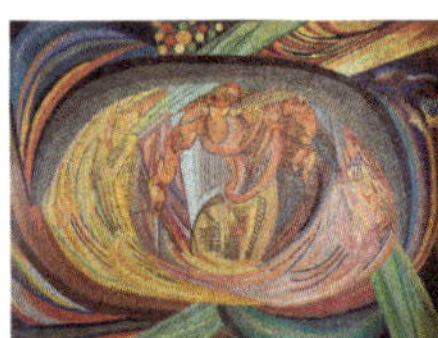
The Birth of Man, 1919
HvW 8
Mosaic
215 × 305 cm
Bühnen Köln–Cologne Theatre
pp. 131–132

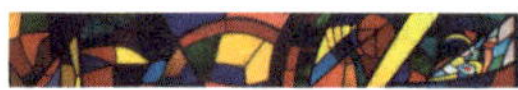
Reclining Woman, 1924
HvW 10
Stained glass painting
24 × 163 cm
Donation Freundlich – Musées de Pontoise
pp. 145–146

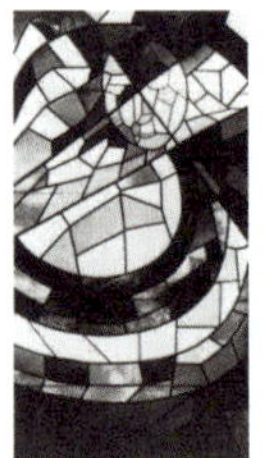
Composition, 1924
HvW 11
Stained glass painting
200 × 100 cm
Lost
p. 140

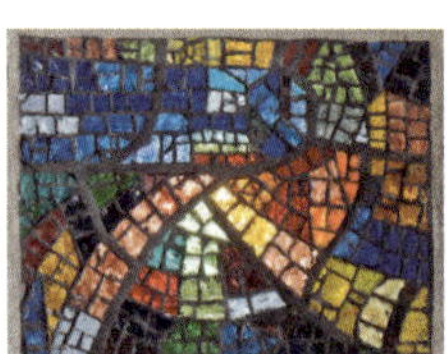
Composition, ca. 1938, or posthumous
HvW 16
Concrete stained glass (dalle de verre)
51 × 67 cm
Donation Freundlich – Musées de Pontoise
p. 153

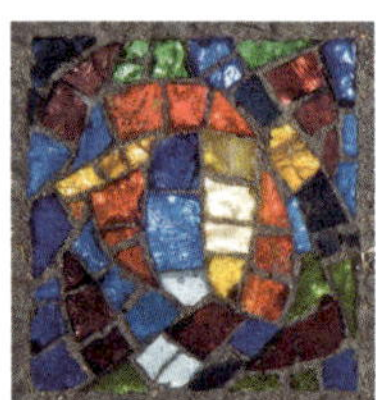
Composition, 1938?
HvW 33
Concrete stained glass (dalle de verre)
22.5 × 22.5 cm
Donation Freundlich – Musées de Pontoise
p. 152

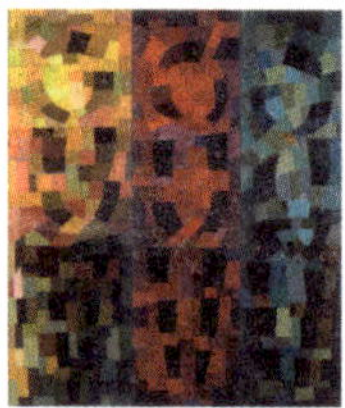
Homage to the Peoples of Color (Hommage aux peuples de couleur), 1938
HvW 36
Three-part mosaic
175 × 58 cm; 175 × 50 cm; 175 × 48.5 cm
Donation Freundlich – Musées de Pontoise
p. 245

Sculptures

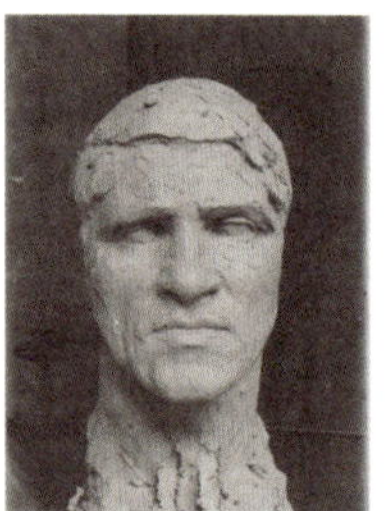
Self-Portrait, ca. 1908
HvW 51
Clay
Lost
p. 48

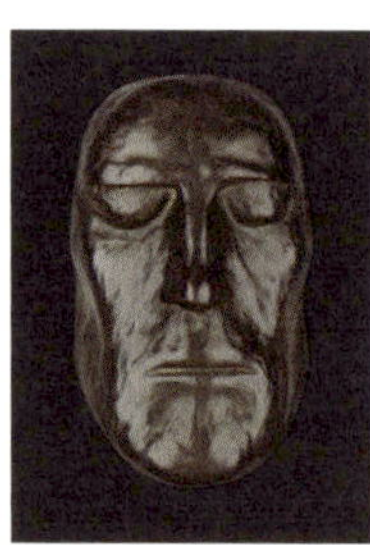
Mask, 1909
HvW 54
Bronze, patinated in antique gray
32.7 × 22 cm
Private collection, Munich
p. 102

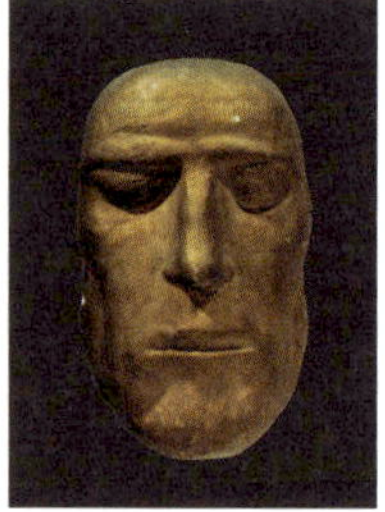
Mask, 1909
HvW 54
Plaster, painted golden-brown
32.7 × 22 cm
Donation Freundlich – Musées de Pontoise
p. 102

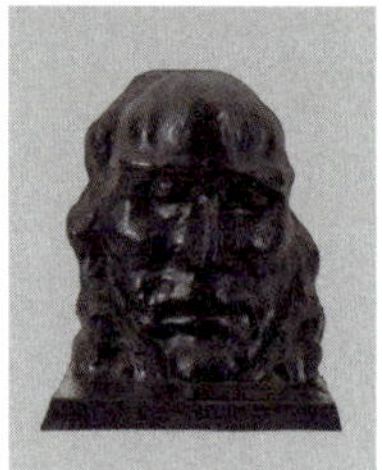
Standing Mask, 1909
HvW 55
Bronze
51.7 × 42.5 × 44.6 cm
Berlinische Galerie – Landesmuseum für moderne Kunst, Fotografie und Architektur
p. 86

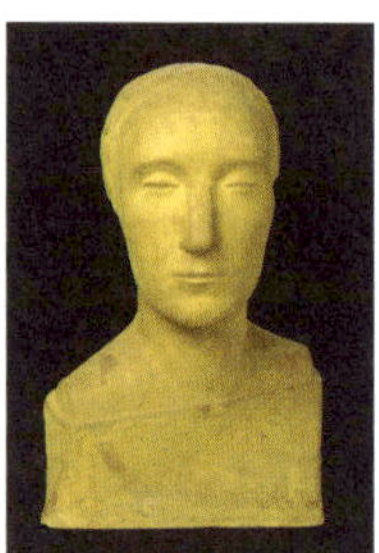
Bust of a Woman, 1910
HvW 56
Plaster, painted yellow
52 × 34 × 29 cm
Museum Ludwig, Cologne
p. 106

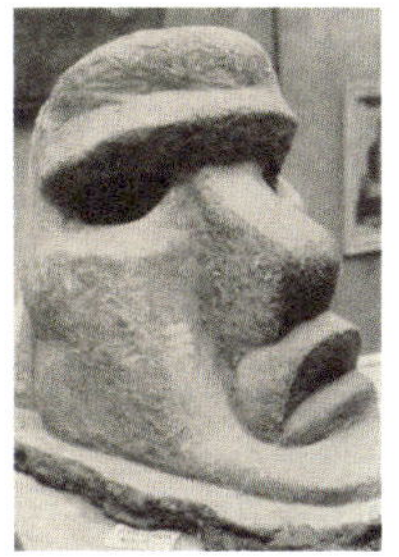

Male Mask, ca. 1910/1920
HvW 58
Plaster
Monumental format
Lost
p. 96

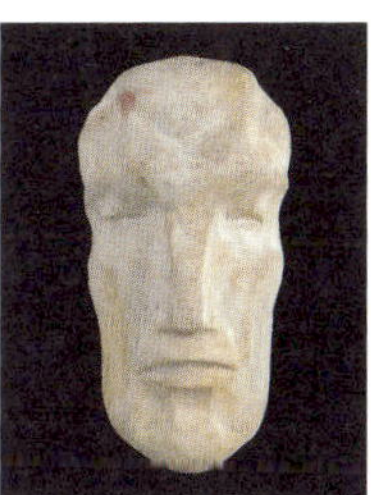

Male Mask, 1911
HvW 61
Plaster
H. 47 cm
Private collection, Cologne
p. 103

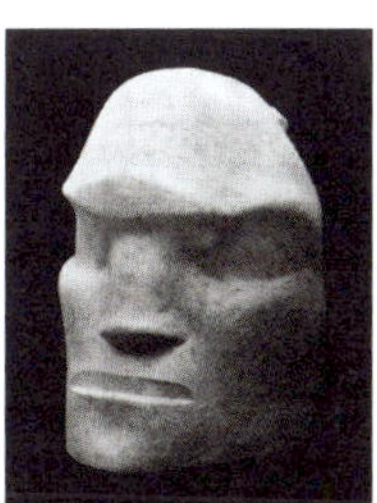

Head, 1912
HvW 62
Plaster
Lost
p. 110

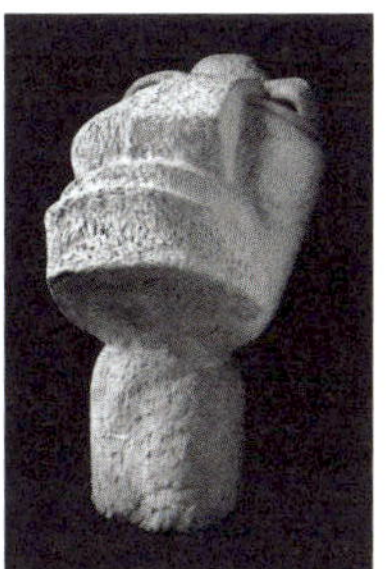

Large Head ("The New Man"), 1912
HvW 63
Plaster
H. 139 cm
Lost
p. 77

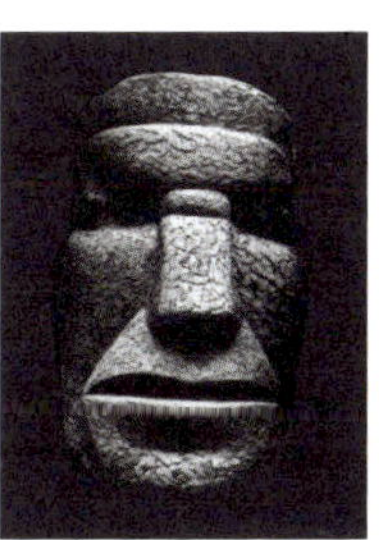

Male Mask, 1915
HvW 64
Colored plasticine on wood
Monumental format
Lost
p. 101

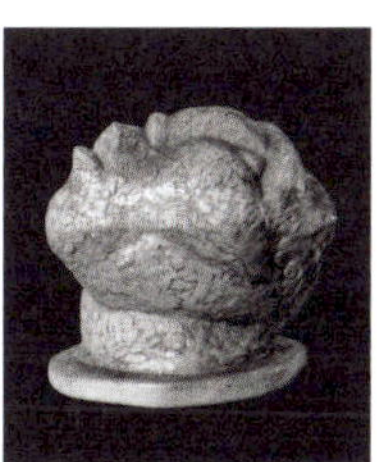

Head, 1916
HvW 65
Lacquered plaster
H. 32 cm
Lost
p. 80

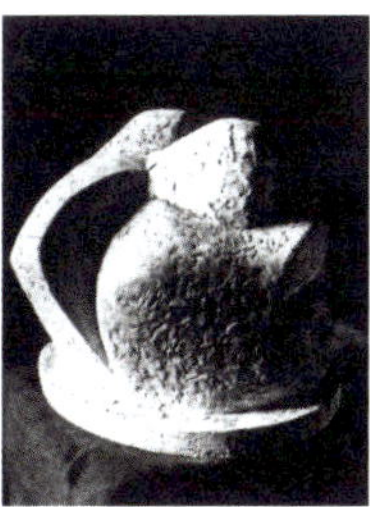

Head, ca. 1915/1922
Not in HvW
Plaster
Lost
p. 79

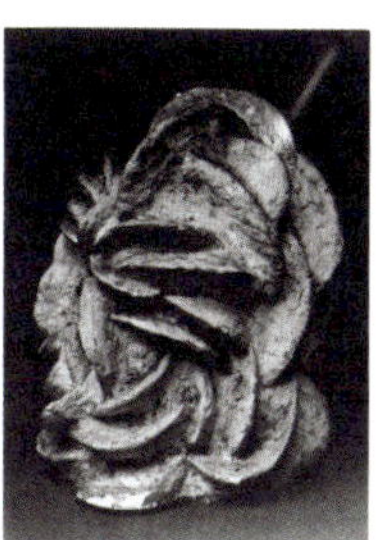

Abstract Sculpture (Head Signs)/Head with its Externalizations, 1916
HvW 66/70
Plaster
Lost
p. 50

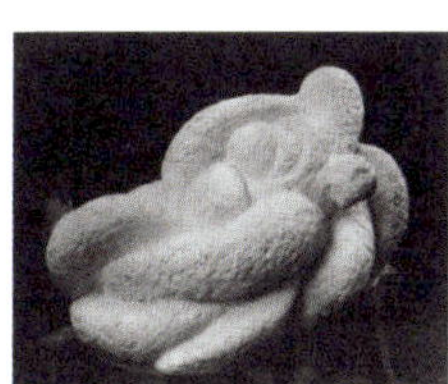

Reclining Figure/Study for a Reclining Woman, ca. 1917
HvW 67/72
Plaster
Lost
p. 100

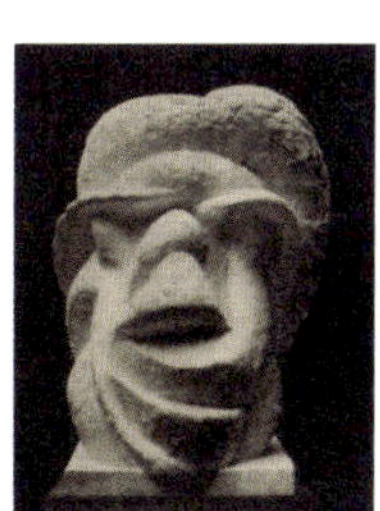

Head, ca. 1919
HvW 68
Plaster
Lost
p. 51

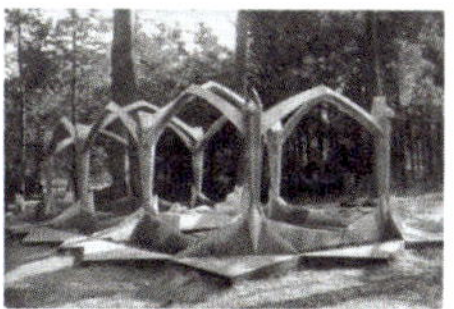

Ground Sculpture for the Wissinger Family Tomb, Berlin-Stahnsdorf, 1922–23
Not in HvW
Concrete
Destroyed in 1923
p. 195

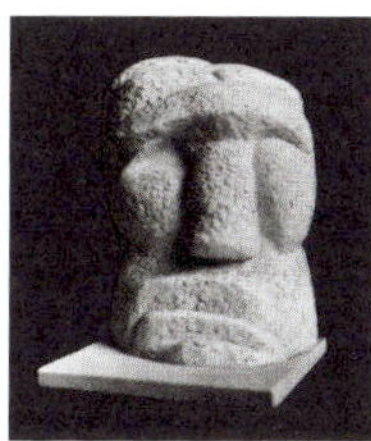

Head, 1925
HvW 75
Plaster
Lost
p. 95

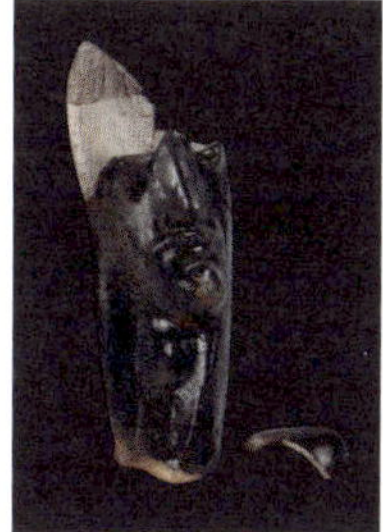

Head, 1925
Not in HvW
Terracotta with black glaze
H. ca. 31 cm, incomplete
Staatliche Museen zu Berlin, on loan from the Bundesrepublik Deutschland
p. 83

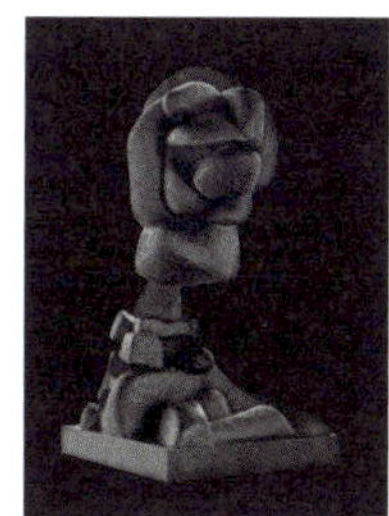

Ascension, 1929/1960*
HvW 76
Bronze, 1/6
200 × 104 × 104 cm
Museum Ludwig, Cologne
pp. 188–189

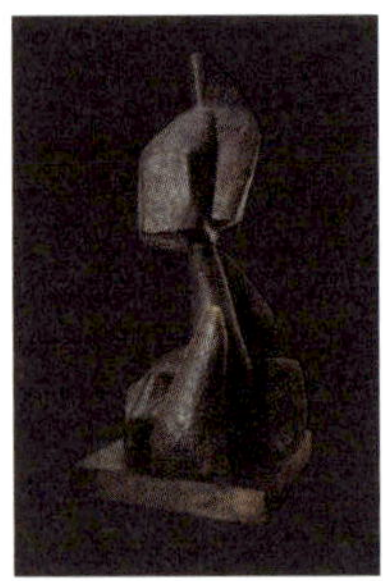

Composition, 1933/2009*
HvW 78
Bronze, HC2
230 × 100 × 100 cm
Galerie Michael Werner, Märkisch Wilmersdorf, Cologne & New York
pp. 190–191

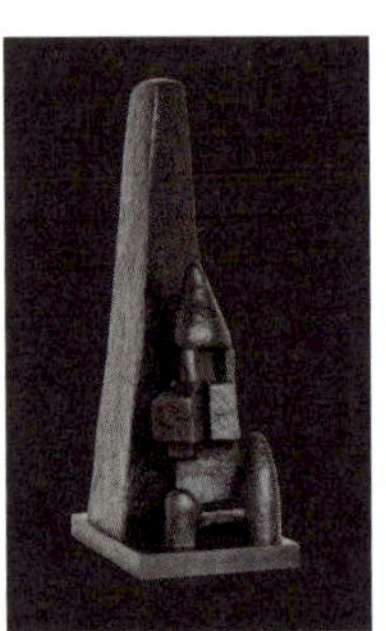

Architectural Sculpture (Sculpture architecturale), 1934–35/1988–89*
HvW 79
Bronze, 5/6
128 × 69 × 43 cm
Museum Ludwig, Cologne
p. 192

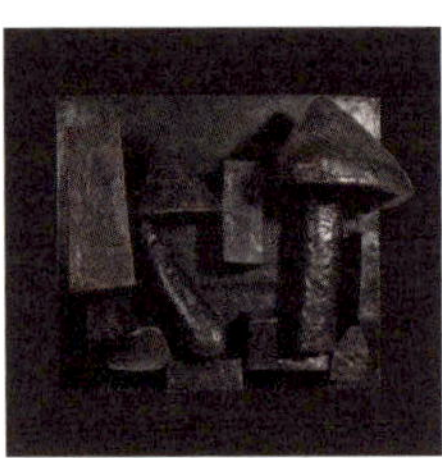

Composition, 1936
HvW 80
Bronze relief, 1/6
67 × 77 × 14 cm
Donation Freundlich – Musées de Pontoise
p. 194

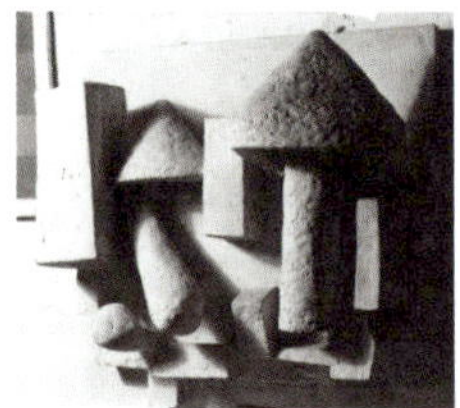

Composition, 1936
HvW 80
Plaster
67 × 77 × 14 cm
Donation Freundlich – Musées de Pontoise
p. 183

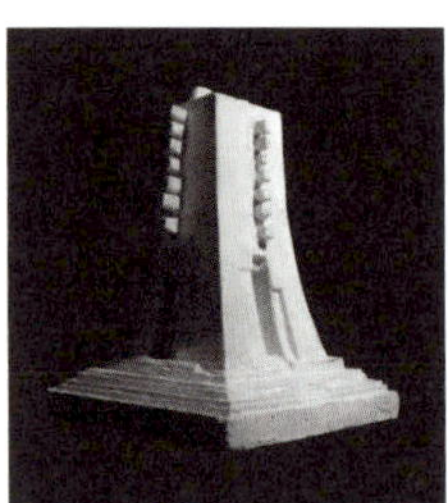

The Lighthouse of the Seven Arts (Le phare des sept arts), after 1945
HvW 81
Plaster model, after a sketch by Freundlich
35.5 × 37 × 46.5 cm
Donation Freundlich – Musées de Pontoise
p. 193

Oil paintings, watercolors, gouaches

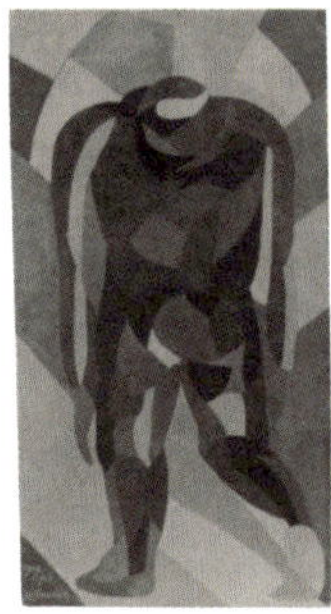

Striding Figure (From Behind), 1909/1941
HvW 101
Gouache
53.5 × 29 cm
Lost
p. 111

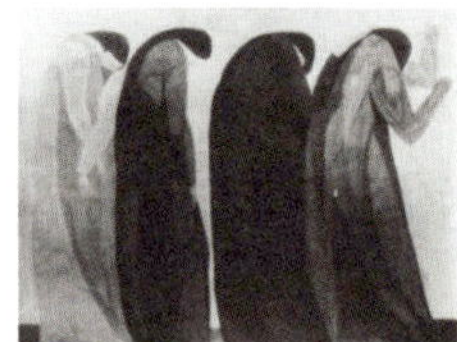

Four Parallel Figures, ca. 1910
HvW 103
Watercolor
Lost
p. 87

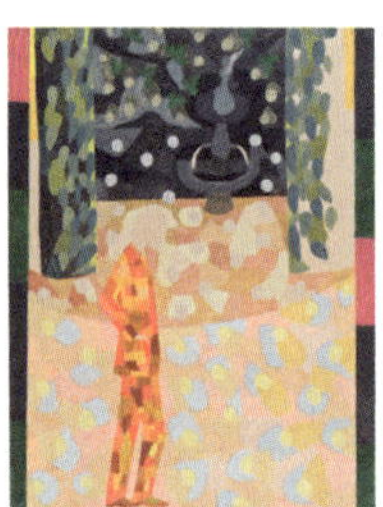

Man in Front of a Fountain, 1911/1942
HvW 105
Gouache on paper
49 × 39 cm
Donation Freundlich – Musées de Pontoise
p. 90

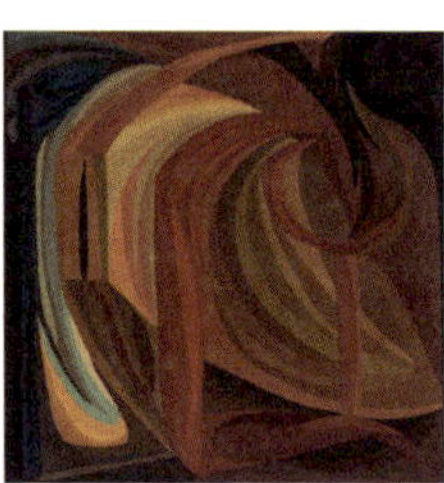

Composition, 1911
HvW 107
Oil on canvas
200 × 200 cm
Musée d'Art moderne de la Ville de Paris
p. 113

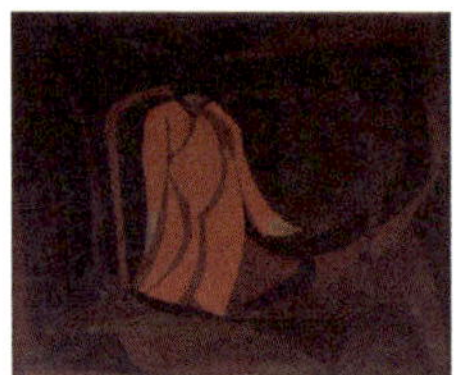

Composition with Figure, 1911
HvW 108
Oil on canvas
54 × 65 cm
Donation Freundlich – Musées de Pontoise
p. 88

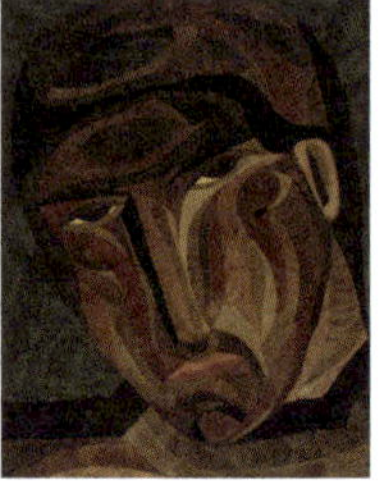

Head, 1911
HvW 109
Watercolor and ink on paper
63 × 48.5 cm
Private collection
p. 84

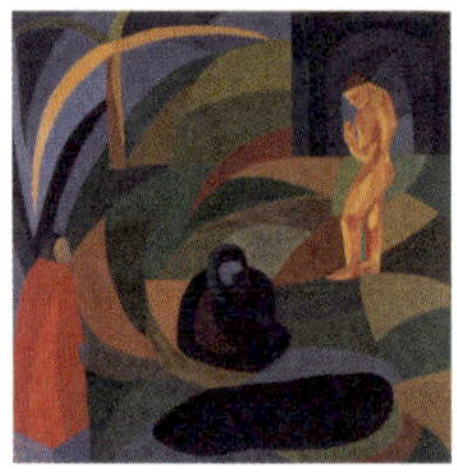

Composition with Three Figures, 1911/1941
HvW 111
Gouache on cardboard
50 × 50 cm
Donation Freundlich – Musées de Pontoise
p. 91

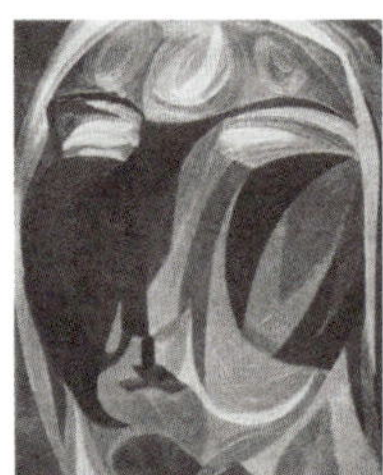

Head, 1912
HvW 115
Oil on canvas
Lost
p. 54

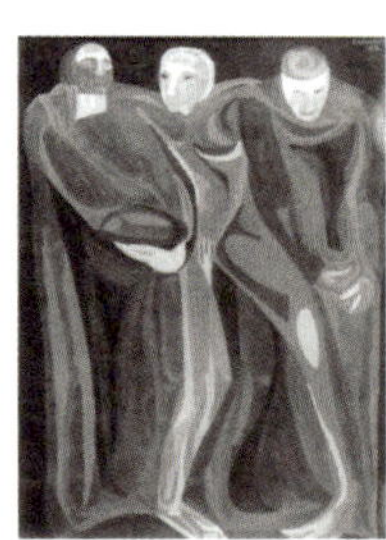

The Sick Man, 1912
HvW 116
Oil on canvas
Lost
p. 85

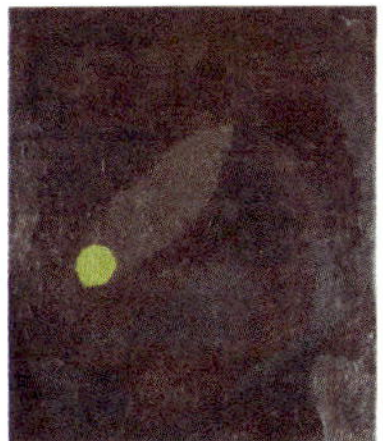

Composition I, 1916
HvW 121
Oil on canvas
70.5 × 61 cm
Private collection
p. 58

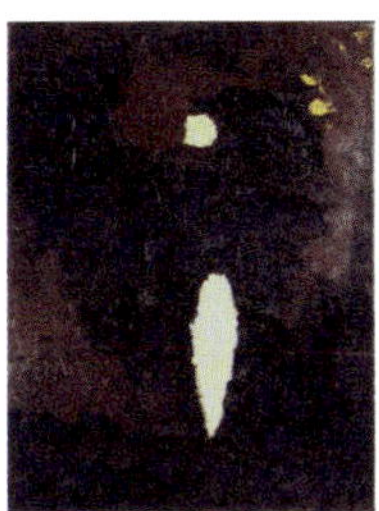

Composition II, 1916
HvW 122
Oil on canvas
65 × 50 cm
Private collection
p. 58

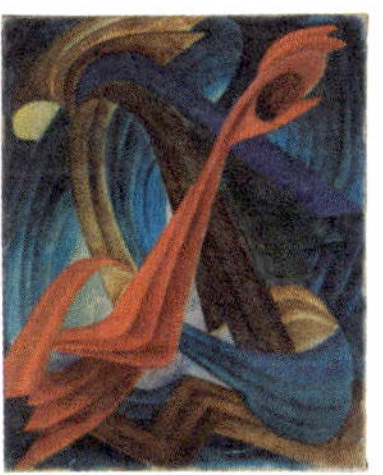

Composition, 1918–19
HvW 126
Oil on canvas
65 × 53 cm
Private collection, Berlin
p. 104

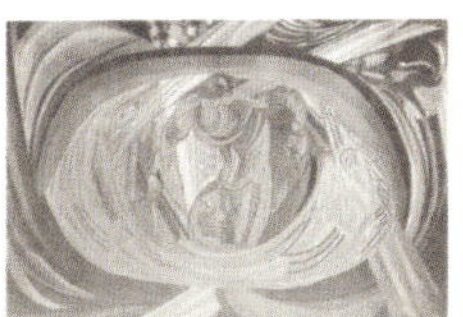

The Birth of Man, ca. 1918–19
HvW 127
Gouache
22 × 32 cm
Lost
p. 130

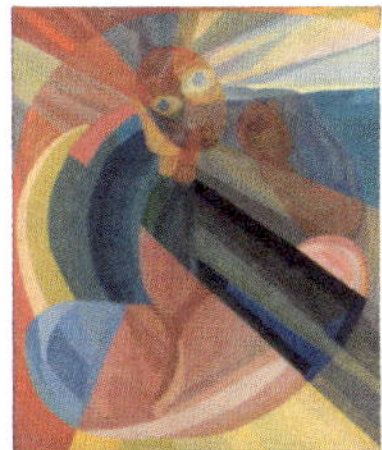

The Mother, 1921
HvW 129
Oil on canvas (muslin)
120 × 100 cm
Berlinische Galerie – Landesmuseum für moderne Kunst, Fotografie und Architektur
p. 142

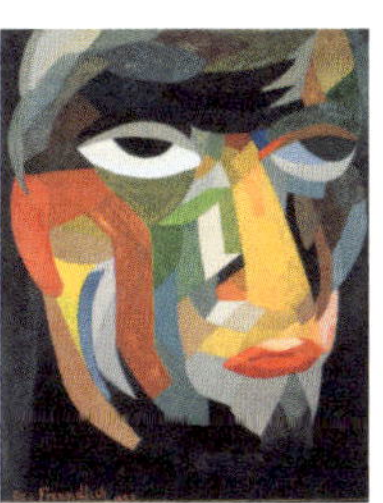

Head (Self-Portrait), 1923
HvW 131
Gouache on paper
73 × 59 cm
Private collection
p. 133

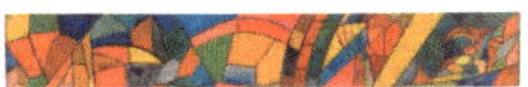

Reclining Woman, 1924
Not in HvW
Watercolor on paper
5.3 × 39.5 cm
Association Les Amis de Jeanne et Otto Freundlich, Musées de Pontoise
p. 144

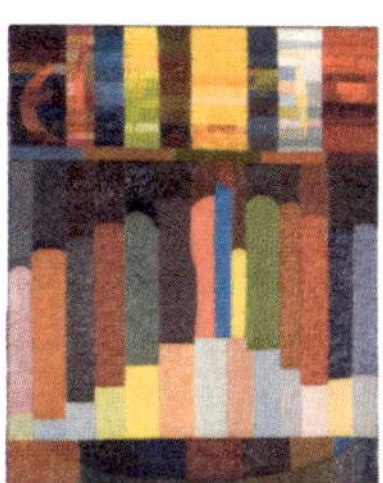

Composition, 1926
HvW 134
Oil on canvas
46 × 39 cm
Berlinische Galerie – Landesmuseum für moderne Kunst, Fotografie und Architektur
p. 157

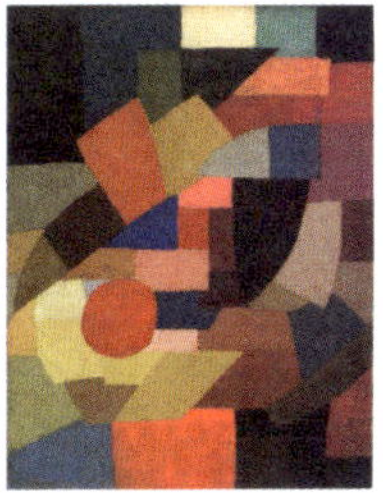

Fragments of Figures in a Context of Planes (Fragments de figure à l'ensemble des plans), 1927
HvW 136
Oil on canvas
55 × 46 cm
Private collection
p. 236

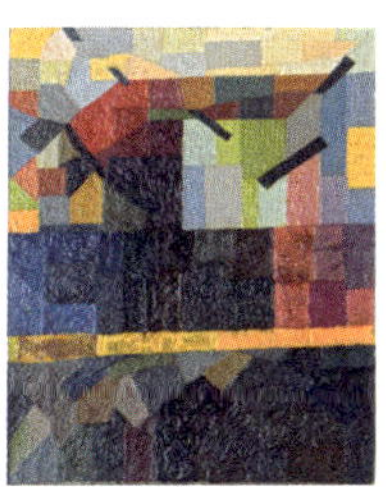

A Tree, 1927
HvW 137
Oil on canvas
54 × 45.5 cm
Gabriele Münter- und Joannes Eichner-Stiftung, Städtische Galerie im Lenbachhaus, Munich
p. 158

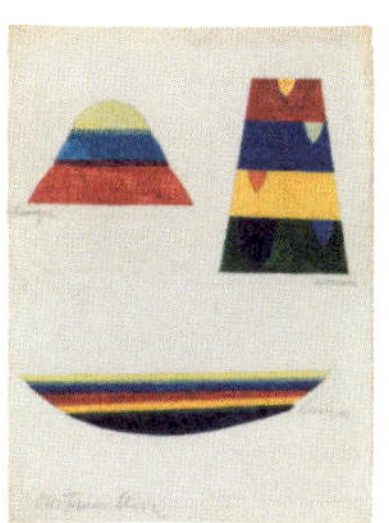

Designs for Lamps, ca. 1927
Not in HvW
Watercolor and pencil on paper
58 × 46 cm
Stiftung Jüdisches Museum, Berlin
p. 147

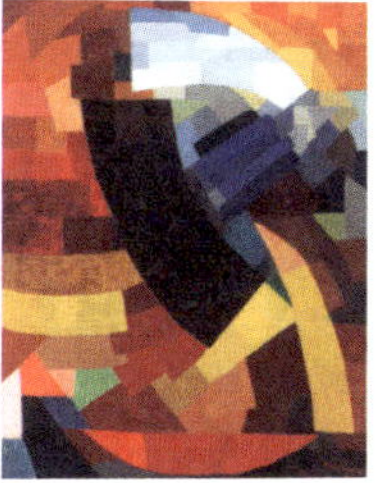

Fragments of Figures in a Context of Planes (Fragments de figure à l'ensemble des plans), 1928
HvW 141
Oil on canvas
91 × 72.5 cm
Private collection
p. 237

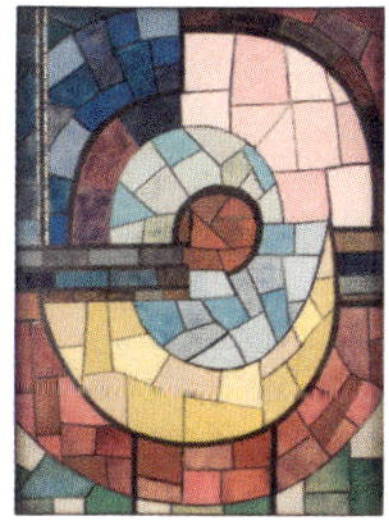

Composition I (Stained Glass Window Design), 1929
HvW 146
Gouache on paper
30.50 × 23 cm
Private collection
p. 148

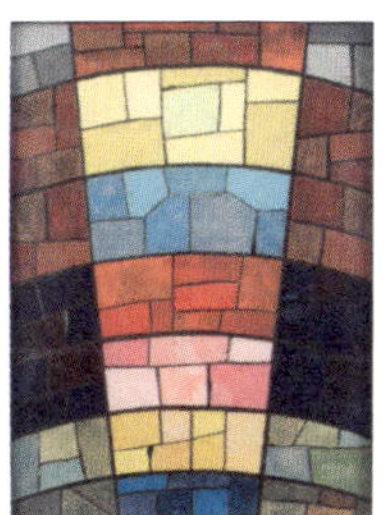

Composition II (Stained Glass Window Design), 1929
HvW 147
Gouache on paper
30.50 × 23 cm
Private collection
p. 149

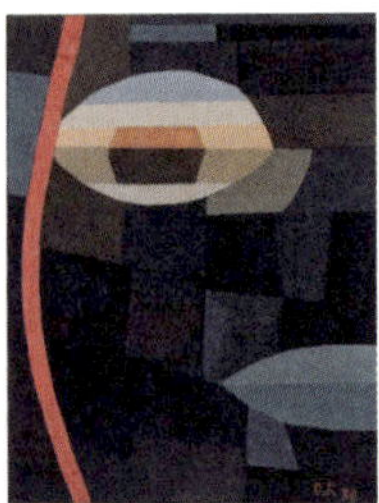

Composition, 1930
HvW 148
Gouache on paper
73.5 × 58.5 cm
Staatliche Museen zu Berlin, Kupferstichkabinett
p. 235

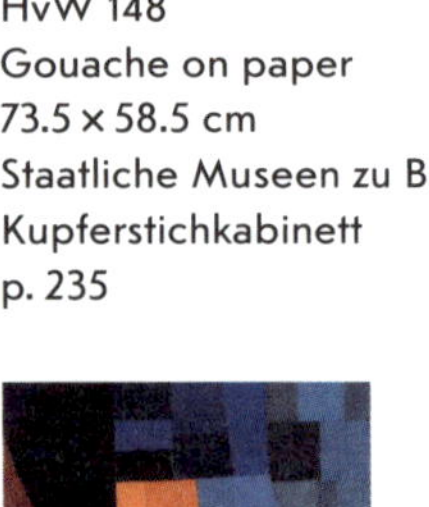

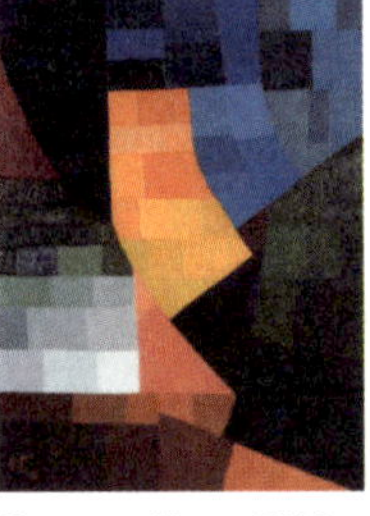

Composition, 1930
HvW 149
Oil on canvas
116 × 89 cm
Musée d'art moderne et contemporain Saint-Étienne Métropole
p. 261

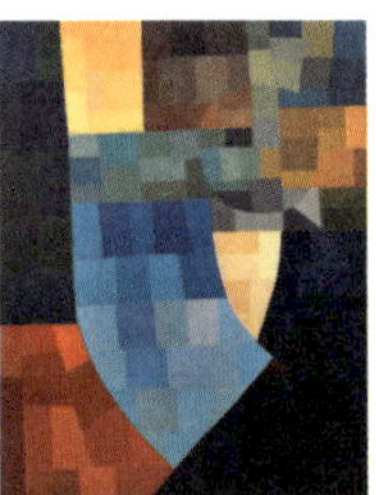

Composition, 1930
HvW 151
Oil on canvas, mounted on plywood
147 × 113 cm
Donation Freundlich – Musées de Pontoise
p. 259

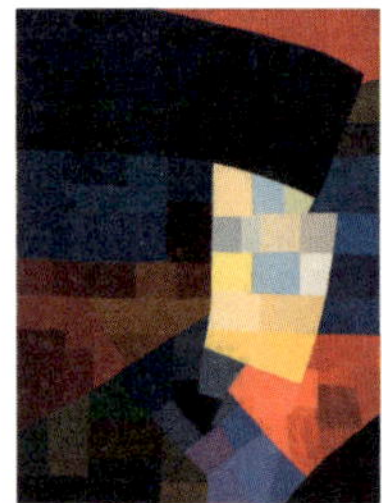

Composition, 1930
HvW 152
Oil on canvas
117 × 89 cm
Private collection
p. 260

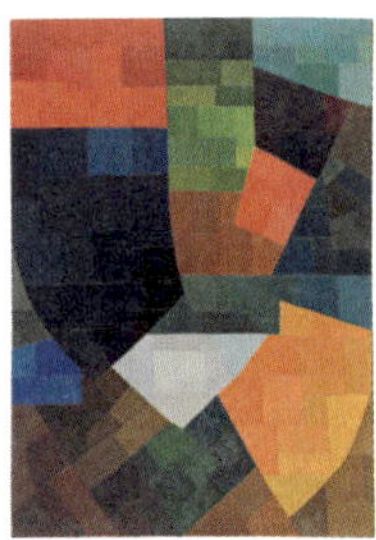

Composition, 1930
HvW 154
Oil on canvas
130 × 97.1 cm
Museum of Modern Art, New York. The Riklis Collection of McCrory Corporation, 1983
p. 258

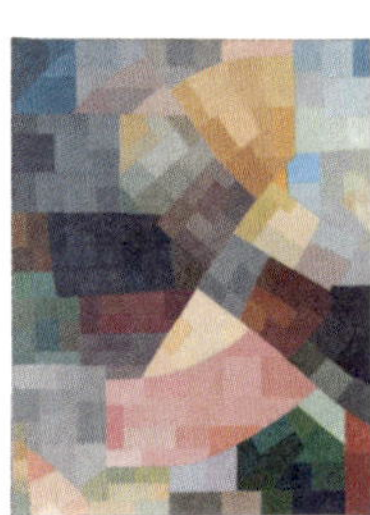

Composition, 1931
HvW 156
Oil on canvas
146 × 114 cm
Donation Freundlich – Musées de Pontoise
p. 276

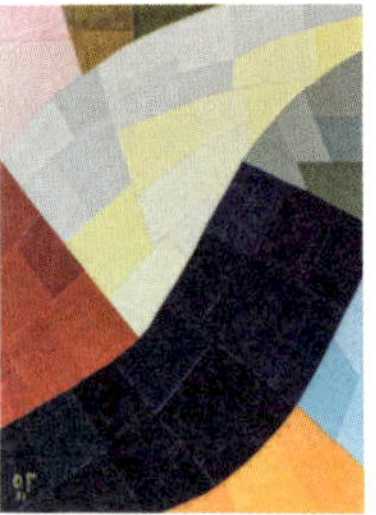

Composition, 1931
HvW 159
Oil on canvas
81 × 60 cm
Von der Heydt-Museum, Wuppertal
p. 253

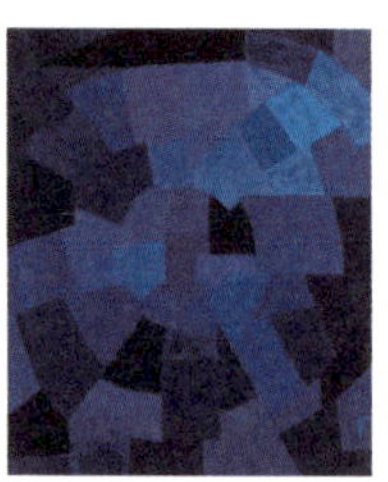

Composition in Blue, 1931
HvW 161
Oil on canvas
54.5 × 45.5 cm
Private collection
p. 271

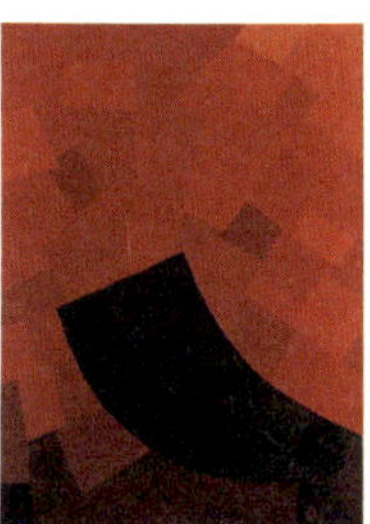

Composition in Red, 1931
HvW 162
Oil on canvas
80 × 59 cm
Museumslandschaft Hessen, Kassel
p. 270

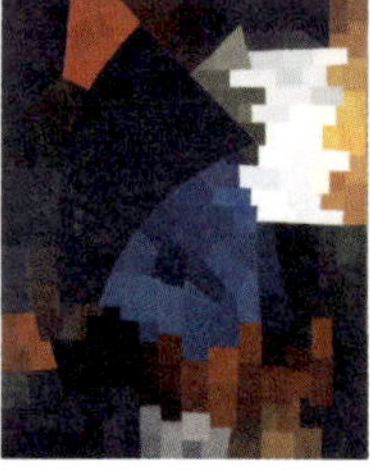

Composition, 1932
HvW 165
Oil on canvas
161.5 × 130 cm
Kunstmuseum Basel. Gift of Dr. h.c. Richard Doetsch-Benziger 1947
p. 233

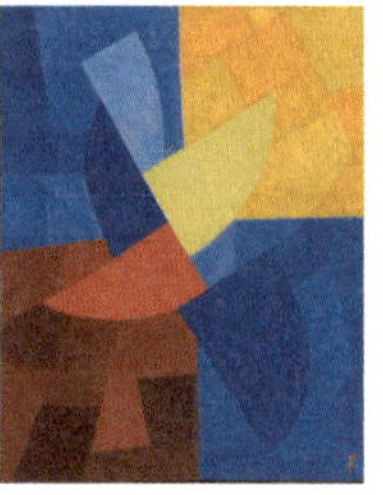

Composition, ca. 1932
HvW 166
Tempera on wood
21.5 × 17 cm
Kunstmuseum Basel. Gift of Marguerite Arp-Hagenbach 1968
p. 265

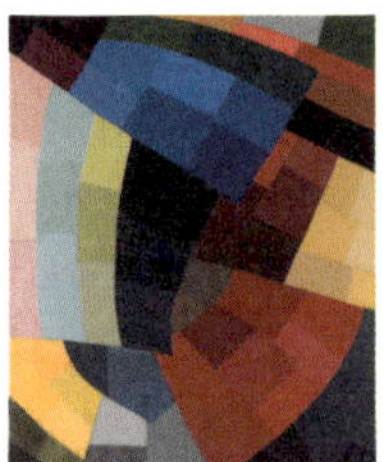

Composition, 1932
HvW 167
Oil on canvas
65 × 54 cm
Institut Valencia d'Art Modern, IVAM, Generalitat, Spain
p. 262

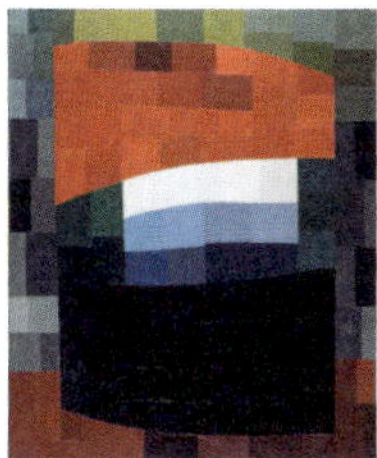

My Sky is Red (Mon ciel est rouge), 1933
HvW 168
Oil on canvas
155.5 × 128 cm
Centre Pompidou, Paris; Musée national d'art moderne/Centre de création industrielle
p. 272

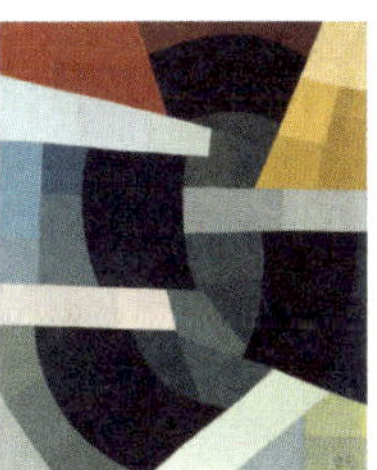

Forces, 1934
HvW 172
Oil on canvas
64 × 53 cm
Museum moderner Kunst Stiftung Ludwig, Vienna, acquired in 1965
p. 252

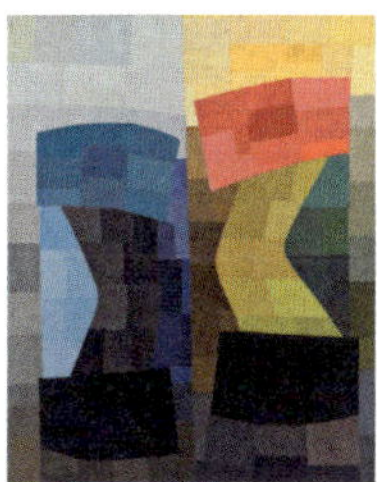

Two Motifs, 1934
HvW 173
Oil on canvas
98 × 80 cm
Museu Coleção Berardo
p. 268

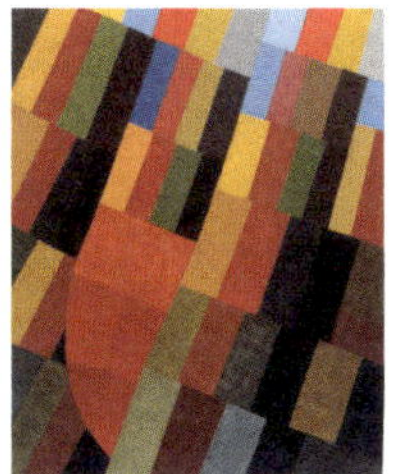

Autumnal Vision, 1935
HvW 174
Oil on canvas
92.9 × 74.2 cm
Hamburger Kunsthalle; permanent loan of the Stiftung für die Hamburger Kunstsammlungen
p. 238

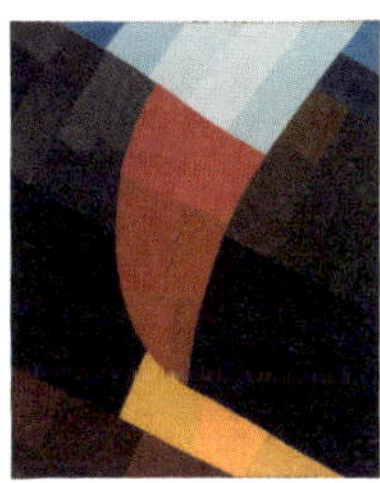

Composition, 1935
HvW 176
Oil on canvas
63 × 52 cm
The Israel Museum, Jerusalem. Gift of Charlotte and Rodolphe Gutmann, Paris
p. 257

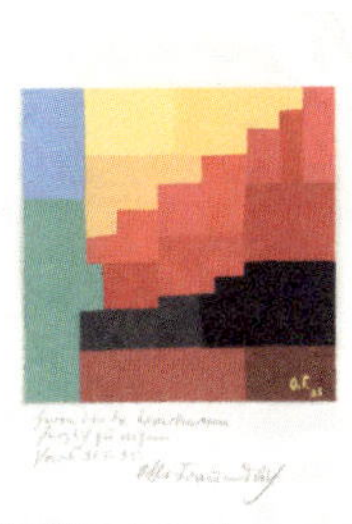

Composition, 1935
Not in HvW
Gouache on paper, mounted on backing
18 × 18.5 cm (picture)
30 × 21 cm (mount)
Private collection
Written on the mount: "Warmly dedicated to Herr Director Dr. Wartmann, Paris 31.5.35. Otto Freundlich."
p. 239

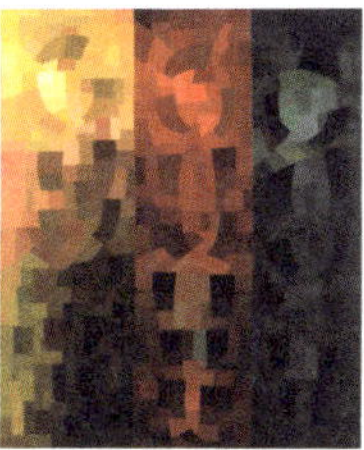

Homage to the Peoples of Color (Hommage aux peuples de couleur), 1935
HvW 178
Gouache on paper on canvas
165 × 138 cm
Centre Pompidou, Paris, Musée national d'art moderne/Centre de creation industrielle
p. 244

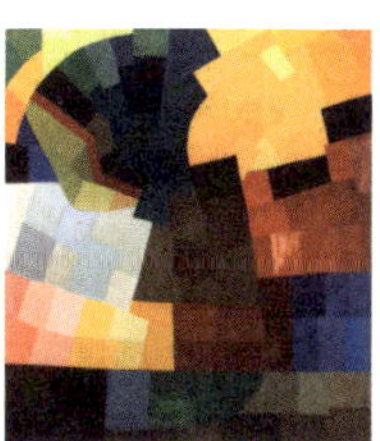

Composition, 1935
HvW 179
Gouache on paper on plywood
108 × 99 cm
Donation Freundlich – Musées de Pontoise
p. 266

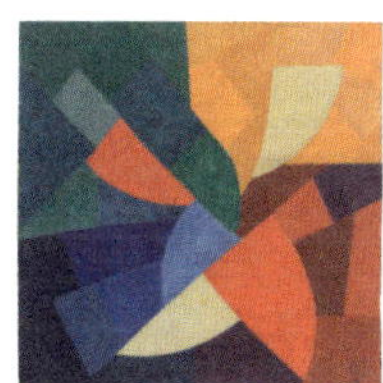

Composition, 1936
HvW 181
Tempera on wood
20.6 × 21.4 cm
Private collection
p. 264

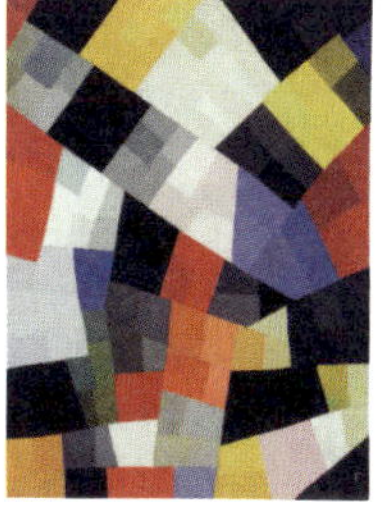

The Unity of Life and Death (L'unité de la vie et de la mort), 1936–38
HvW 185
Oil on canvas
115 × 86.5 cm
The Museum of Modern Art, New York. Lydia Winston Malbin Bequest in memory of Alfred H. Barr, Jr., 1990
p. 240

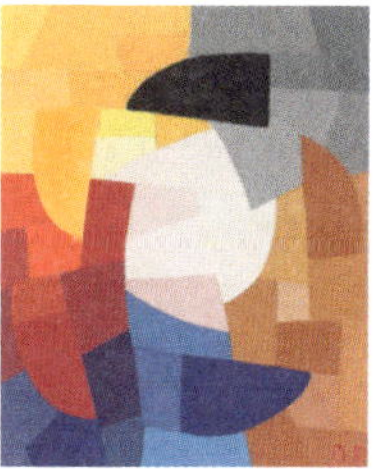

Composition, 1937
Not in HvW
Tempera on wood
17.6 × 15 cm
Private collection
p. 265

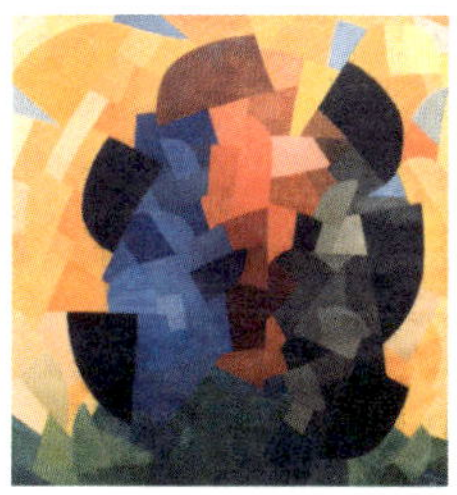

Rosette I (La Rosace I), 1938
HvW 192
Gouache on paper, mounted on canvas
208 × 202 cm
Donation Freundlich – Musées de Pontoise
p. 279

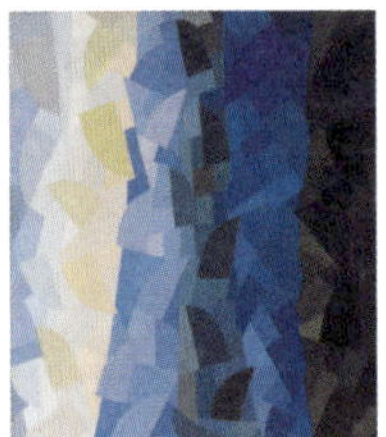

Composition, 1938
HvW 195
Tempera on cardboard
54.5 × 45 cm
Stiftung Jüdisches Museum Berlin
p. 248

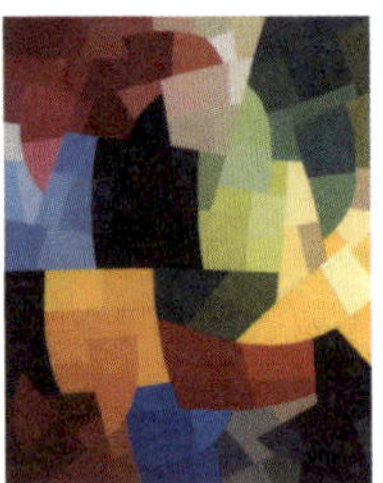

Composition, 1939
HvW 196
Gouache on paper
54 × 43 cm
Donation Freundlich – Musées de Pontoise
p. 267

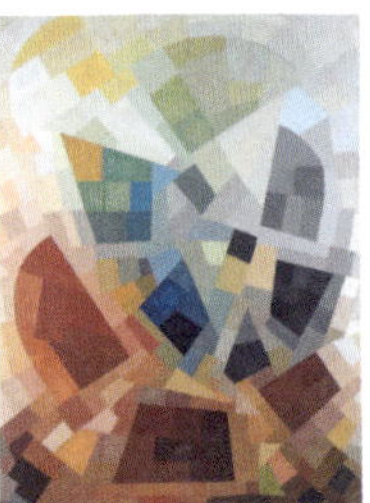

Composition, 1939
HvW 197
Tempera on paper mounted on canvas
193 × 146 cm
Donation Freundlich – Musées de Pontoise
p. 277

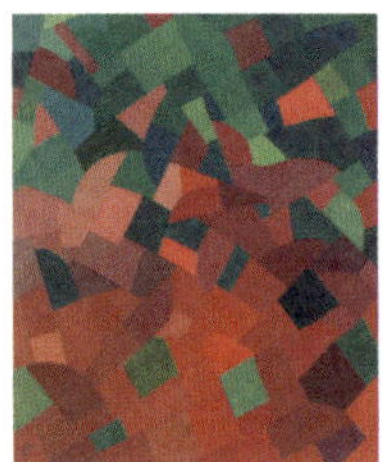

Composition Red-Green, 1939
HvW 199
Oil on canvas
65 × 54.5 cm
Museum Ludwig, Cologne
p. 249

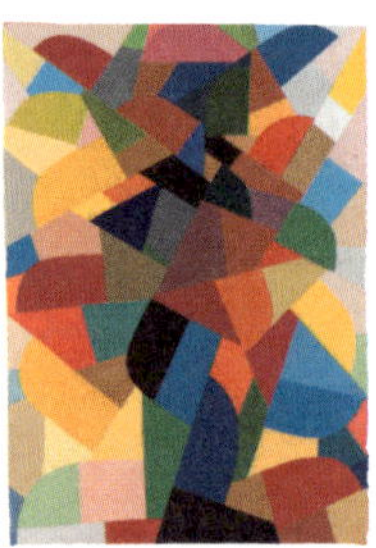

Composition, 1940
HvW 200
Gouache on paper
84 × 60 cm
Wilhelm-Hack-Museum, Ludwigshafen
p. 246

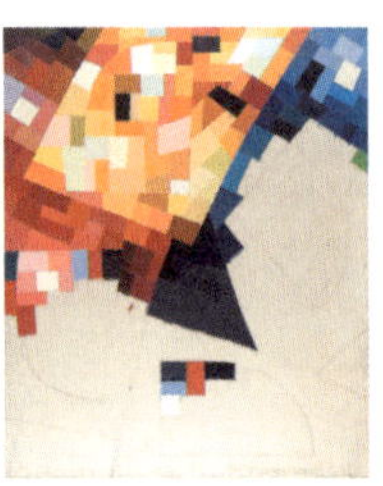

Composition, 1940, unfinished
HvW 203
Oil on canvas
183 × 154 cm
Donation Freundlich – Musées de Pontoise
p. 221

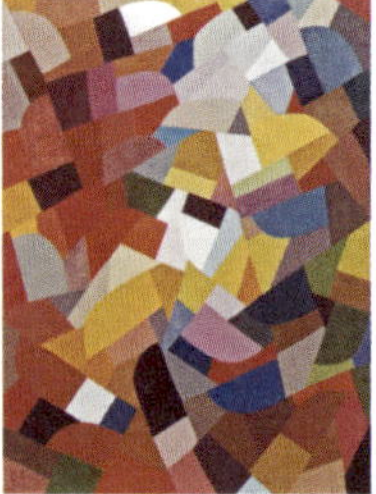

Composition, 1941
HvW 207
Tempera on cardboard
67 × 51.5 cm
Kunstmuseum Bonn
p. 242

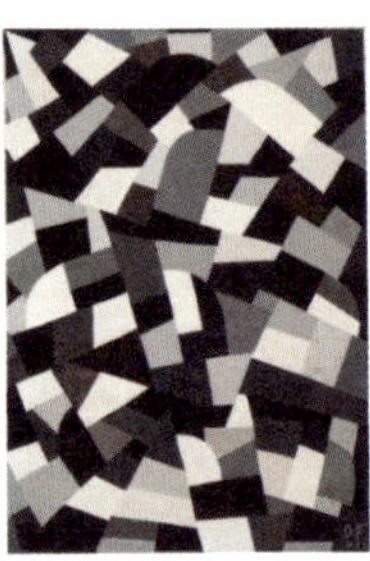

Composition, 1941
HvW 208
Gouache on paper
83 × 59 cm
Merrill C. Berman Collection
p. 243

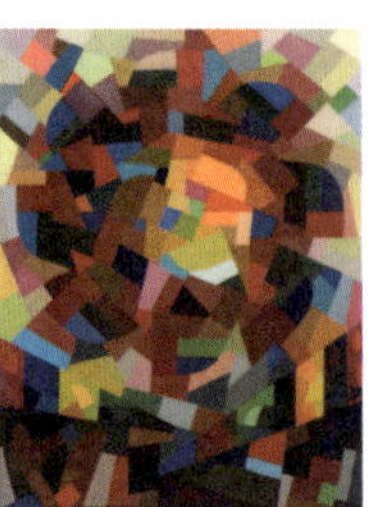

Rosette II (La Rosace II), 1941
HvW 210
Gouache on cardboard
65 × 50 cm
Donation Freundlich – Musées de Pontoise
p. 280

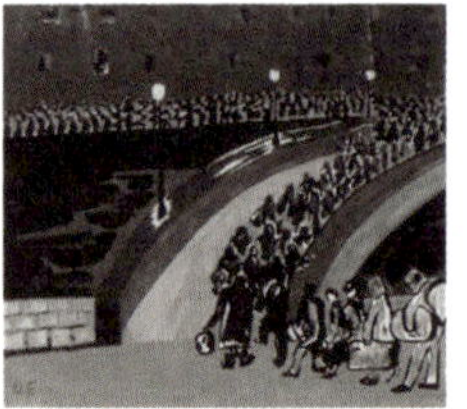

The Inmates from Colombes Crossing a Bridge While Being Transferred (Les internés de Colombes transférés traversent un pont), 1942
HvW 214
Gouache
20.5 × 20.5 cm
Lost
p. 315

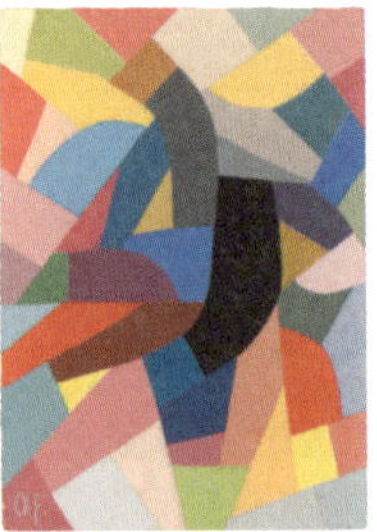

Composition around Two Planes in Black and Gray (Composition autour de deux plans noir et gris), 1942
Not in HvW
Opaque paint on cardboard
16.9 × 12.2 cm
Staatliche Graphische Sammlung, Munich
p. 255

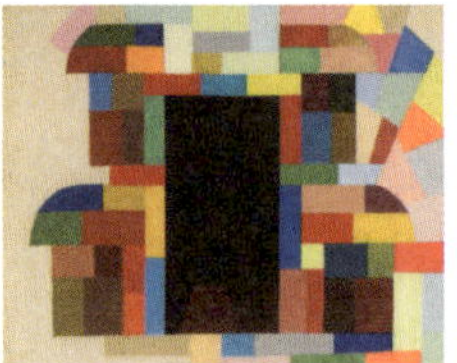

Composition, 1940–43, unfinished
HvW 218
Gouache on cardboard
22.5 × 29 cm
Donation Freundlich – Musées de Pontoise
p. 218

Pastels

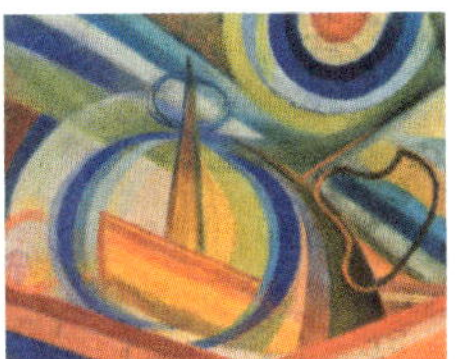

Composition with Ship,
ca. 1918–19
HvW 219
Chalk pastel on wove paper
34.5 × 45.7 cm
Private collection
p. 151

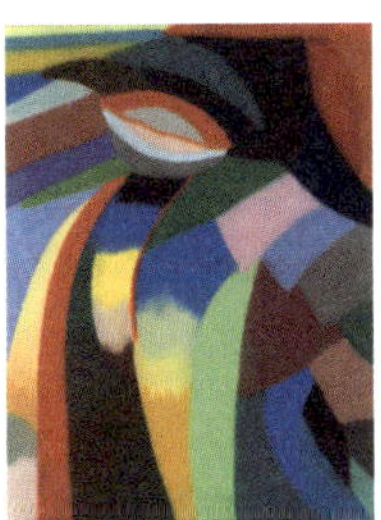

Composition, 1919
HvW 223
Pastel on paper
68 × 52 cm
Donation Freundlich –
Musées de Pontoise
p. 164

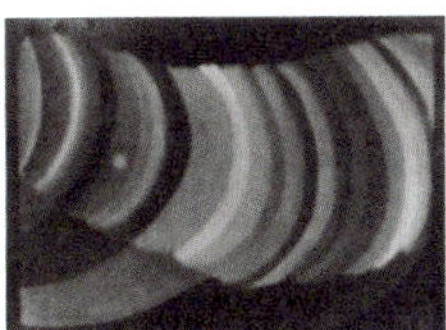

Composition, 1921
HvW 226
Pastel on paper
Lost
p. 172

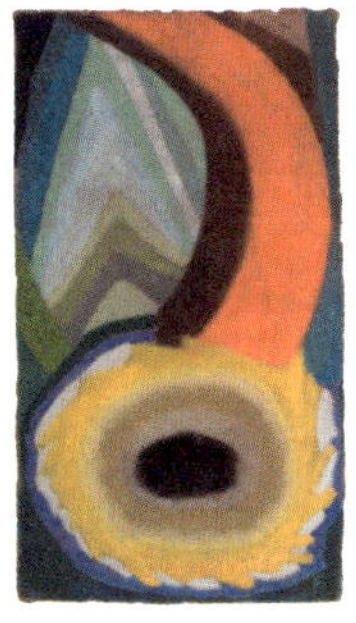

Composition, 1921
HvW 227
Chalk pastel on paper
77.5 × 44.2 cm
Berlinische Galerie –
Landesmuseum für
moderne Kunst, Fotografie
und Architektur
p. 169

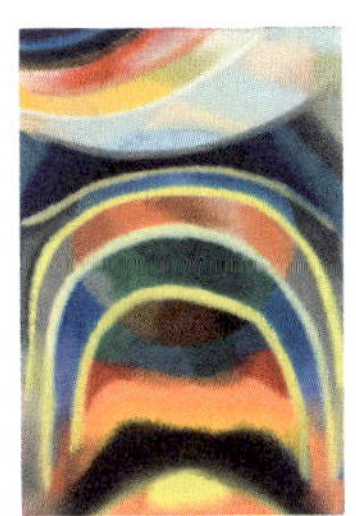

Circles of Light
(Cosmic Rainbow), 1922
HvW 228
Pastel on paper
32.5 × 23 cm
Collection David Ghezelbash
p. 173

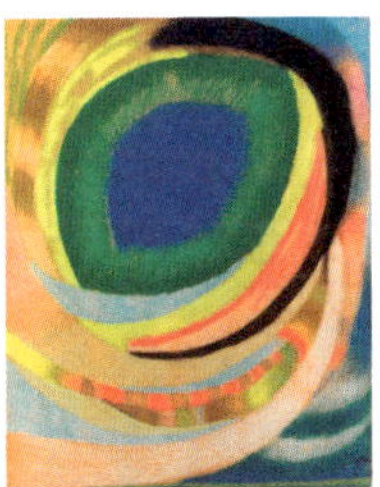

Cosmic Eye, 1921–22
HvW 229
Pastel on paper
81 × 65 cm
Private collection. Courtesy
Applicat-Prazan, Paris
p. 167

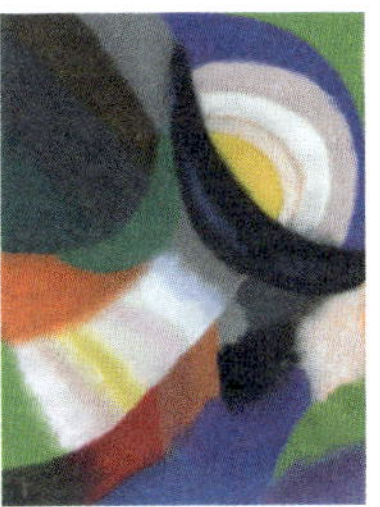

Cosmic Composition,
ca. 1922
Not in HvW
Pastel on paper
34.15 × 26 cm
Brigitte G. Alexander,
Kennett Square, PA, USA
p. 166

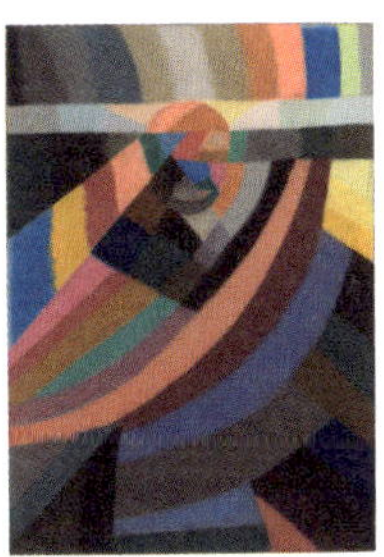

Composition, 1924
HvW 230
Pastel on paperboard
74.7 × 53.8 cm
The Cleveland Museum
of Art. Bequest of
Lockwood Thompson
p. 141

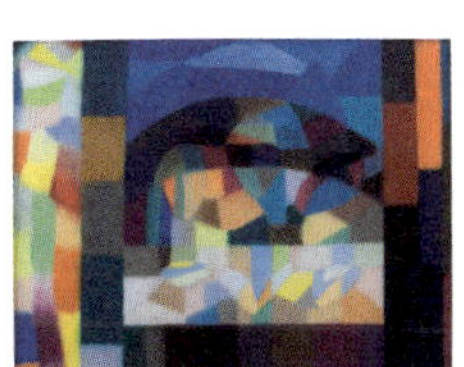

View from the Window, ca.
1924–25
HvW 231
Pastel on paper
50 × 65 cm
Private collection
p. 160

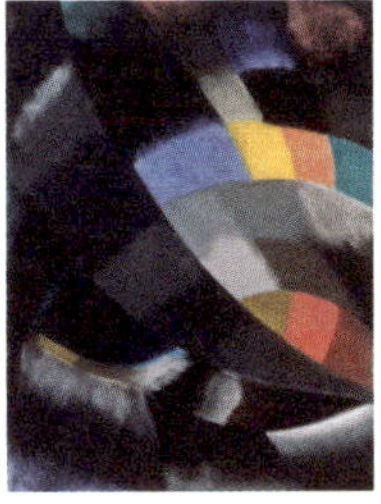

Ship in a Storm, 1924
HvW 232
Pastel on wove paper
63.5 × 48.5 cm
Hilti Art Foundation,
Schaan, Liechtenstein
p. 170

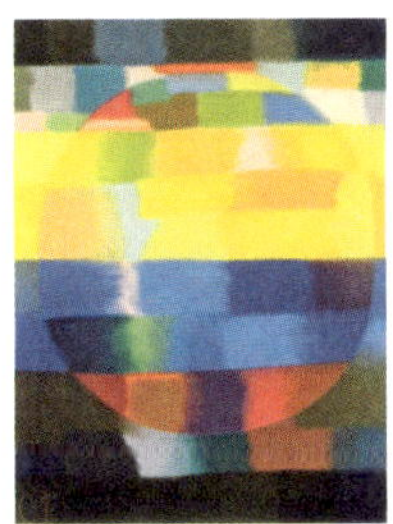

Spherical Bodies, 1925
HvW 234
Pastel on paper
65 × 50 cm
Private collection, Bonn
p. 162

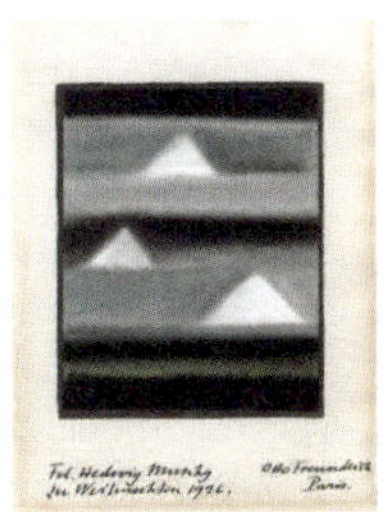

Composition, 1926
HvW 235
Pastel on paper
9.7 × 11.8 cm
Private collection
Below:
"For Miss Hedwig Muschg,
Christmas 1926.
Otto Freundlich, Paris."
p. 231

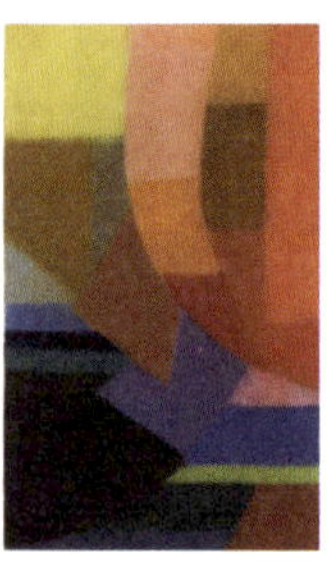

Composition, 1927
HvW 236
Pastel on paper
17 × 10.5 cm
Private collection, Berlin
p. 254

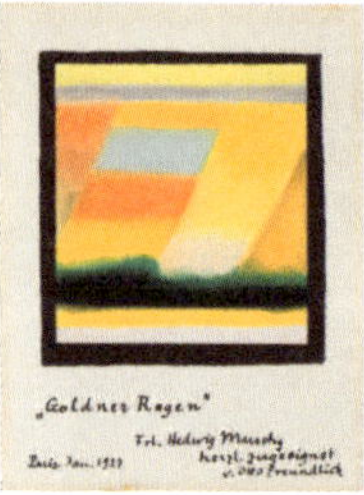

Golden Rain, 1927
HvW 240
Pastel on paper
11.5 × 10.5 cm (picture)
21.5 × 17 cm (paper)
Private collection, Munich
Below: "'Golden Rain' warmly dedicated to Miss Hedwig Muschg, Otto Freundlich, Paris, Jan. 1927"
p. 231

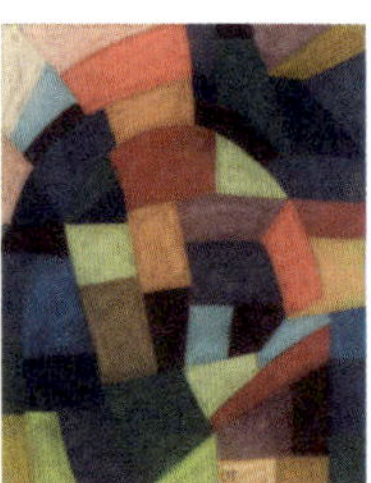

Composition, 1928
HvW 246
Pastel on canvas
40.5 × 33 cm
Private collection. Courtesy Applicat-Prazan, Paris
p. 175

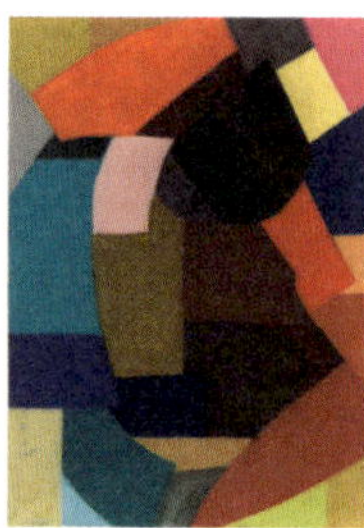

Composition, 1928
HvW 247
Pastel on paper
65 × 48.3 cm
The Israel Museum, Jerusalem. Gift of Jacob Schulman, Gloversville
p. 176

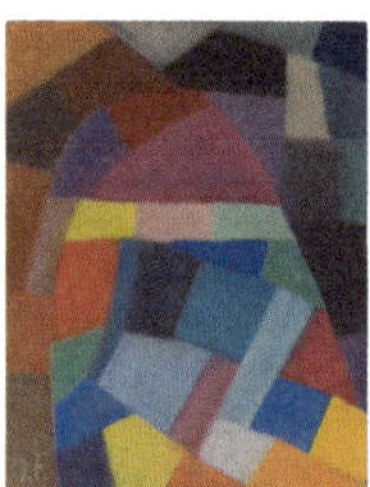

Composition, ca. 1929
HvW 252
Pastel on mottled paper
30.2 × 24 cm
Kunstmuseum Basel, Kupferstichkabinett
p. 174

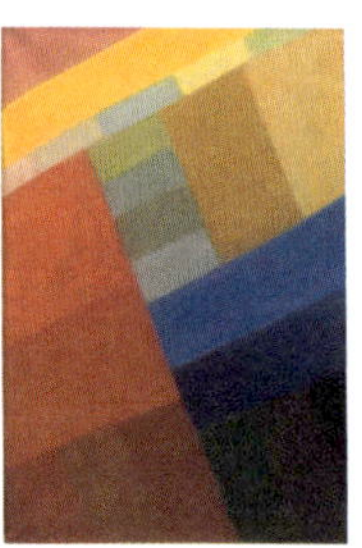

Composition, ca. 1931
HvW 256
Pastel on velvet paper
44 × 31 cm
August Sander Stiftung, Cologne. Courtesy Galerie Julian Sander, Cologne
p. 159

Drawings

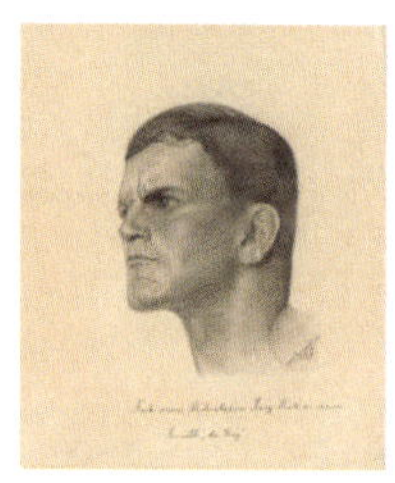

Copy after Franz von Stuck, 1901
HvW 259
Charcoal on paper
42 × 36 cm
Private collection
Right: "Otto Freundlich Bützow 1901"; below: "After a study of a head by Franz Stuck for his painting 'der Krieg'"
p. 40

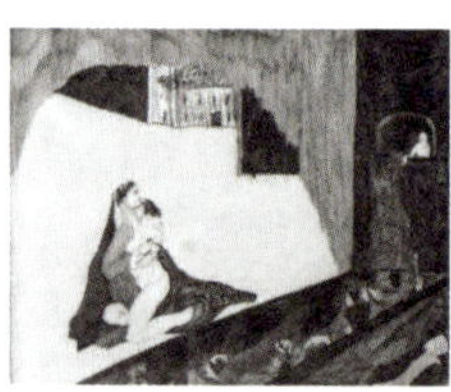

Opera Scene, 1905
HvW 260
Pencil on paper
26 × 33 cm
Michael Taylor, New York
p. 99

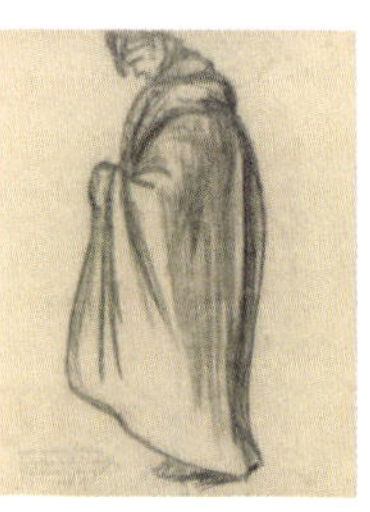

Robed Figure with Bowed Head, 1910
HvW 263
Charcoal on paper
62 × 50 cm
Private collection, Cologne
Right: "Otto Freundlich 1910"; below: "Warmest wishes to my father on 24.9.19"
p. 87

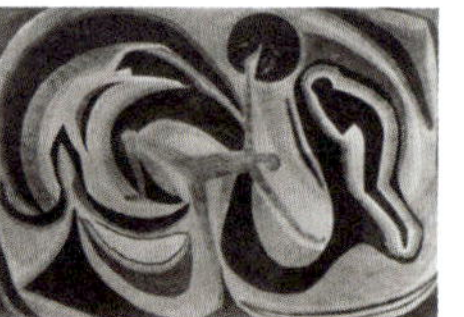

Cosmic Composition, 1910
HvW 264
Pencil on paper
Lost
p. 89

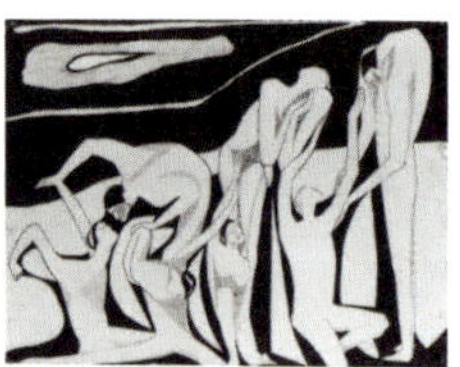

Group, 1911
HvW 265
Pencil on paper
48 × 62.5 cm
Musée d'Art moderne de la Ville de Paris
p. 107

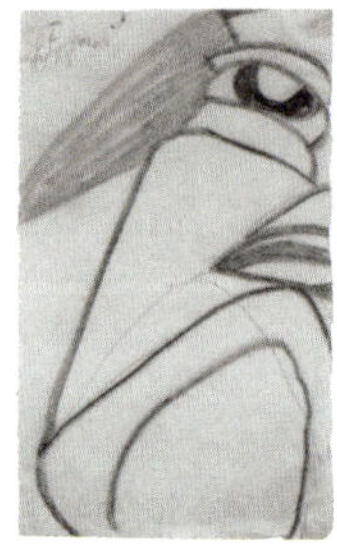

Protruding Figure II (Study of Head), 1913
HvW 267
Pencil on paper
20 × 12.5 cm
Lost
On the mount: "Study of Head"
p. 78

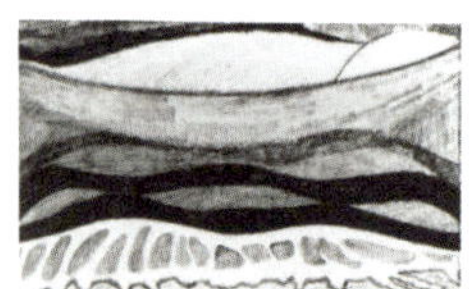

Marne Landscape, 1913
HvW 268
Pencil on paper
12.7 × 21 cm
Lost
p. 92

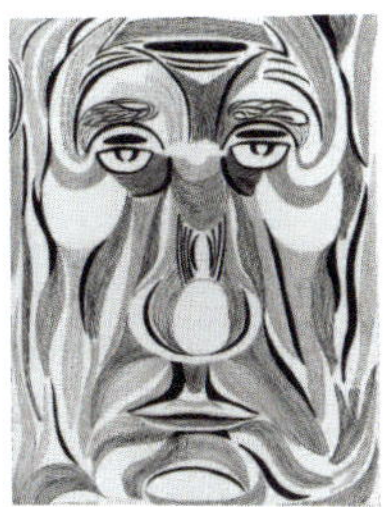

Head, 1914
HvW 269
Ink on cardboard
63 × 48 cm
Private collection
p. 94

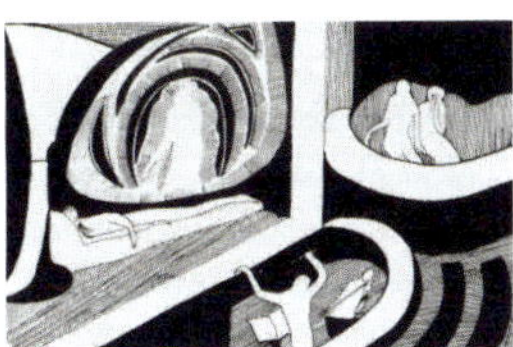

Egmont's Dream, 1915
HvW 270
Ink on paper on cardboard
20.8 × 32.7 cm
Donation Freundlich –
Musées de Pontoise
p. 98

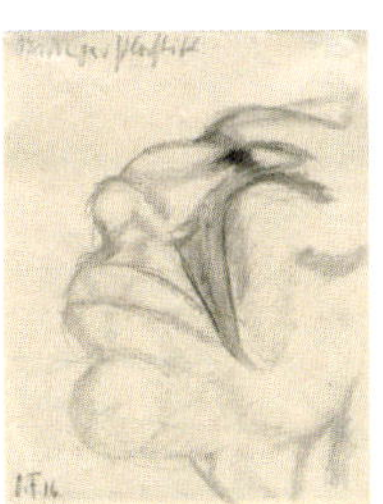

Sketch for Sculpture, 1916
Not in HvW
Pencil on paper
21 × 16.7 cm
Anthony Plaut, Mount Vernon,
Iowa, USA
Above: "Sketch for sculpture"
p. 81

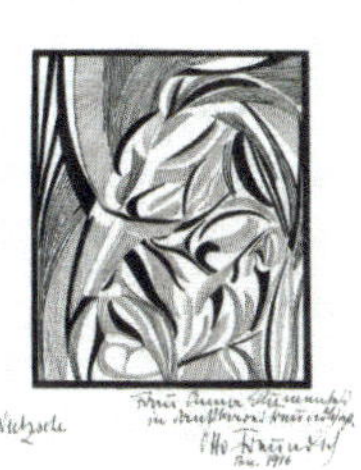

Nietzsche, 1916
Not in HvW
Ink on paper
27 × 20.8 cm
Anthony Plaut, Mount Vernon,
Iowa, USA
Below: "Nietzsche. For
Frau Anna Blumenfeld in
friendship and appreciation.
Otto Freundlich Aug. 1916"
p. 112

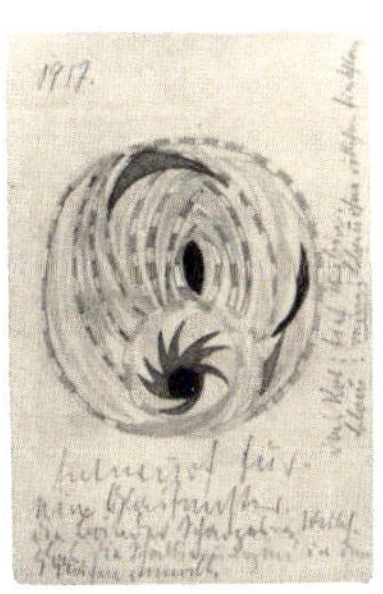

Design for a Stained Glass Window, 1917
HvW 276
Pencil and watercolor on
paper
15.2 × 10.2 cm
Private collection
Below: "Design for a stained
glass window. The strips
bl[ack]&. opaque glass.
The shading painted on the
surfaces." Right: "The red:
deep ruby. Blue: pure blue
with no hint of red."
p. 154

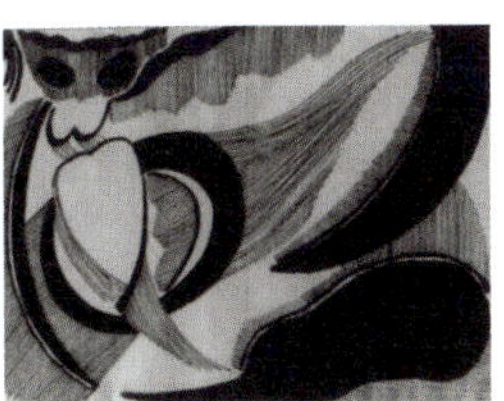

Composition, 1917
HvW 277
Ink on paper
14.4 × 19 cm
Private collection
p. 92

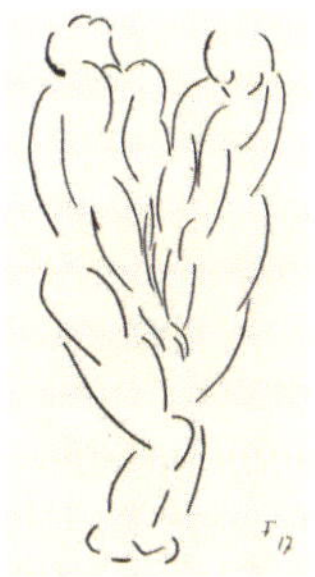

Naked Couple, 1917
HvW 278
Pen and ink drawing
Lost
In *Die Aktion* 37/38 (1918)
p. 63

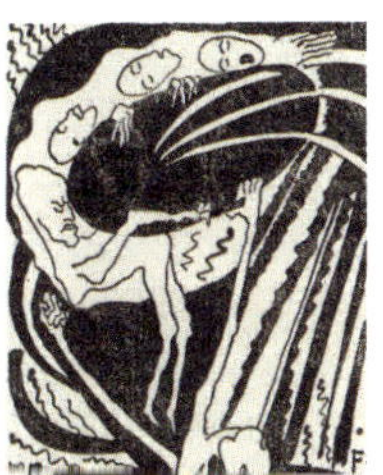

Composition, 1917
HvW 290
Pen and ink drawing
Lost
In *Die Aktion* 37/38 (1918)
p. 72

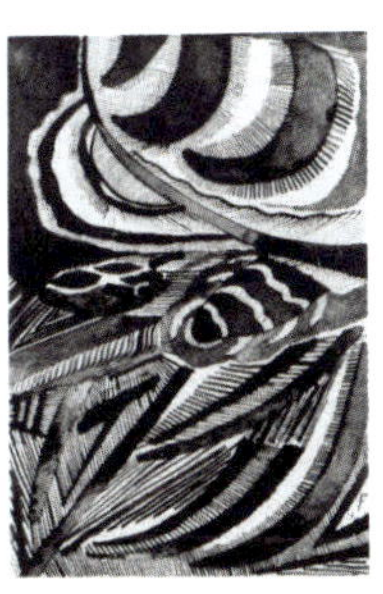

Landscape, 1918
HvW 292
Ink on cardboard
26.2 × 18 cm
Private collection
p. 93

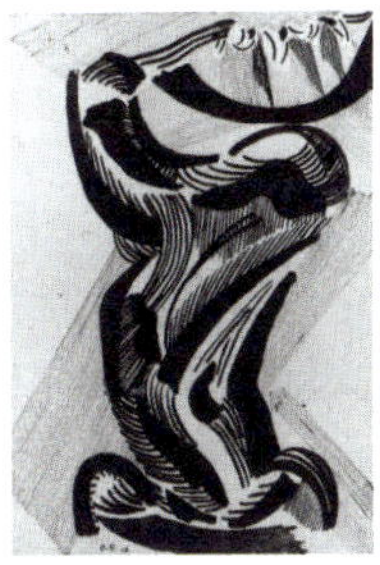

A Tree, 1918
HvW 293
Ink on Bristol paper
26.5 × 18 cm
Private collection
p. 108

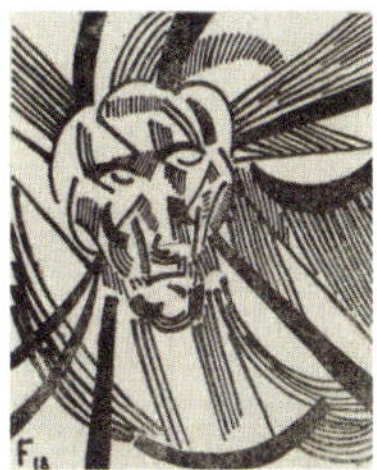

Head, 1918
HvW 295
Ink on paper
Lost
In *Die Aktion* 33/34 (1918)
p. 60

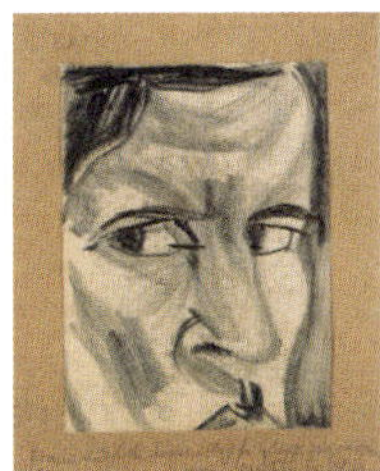

Self-Portrait, 1918
HvW 296
Chalk on paper on mount
20 × 15 cm
Le Claire Kunst, Hamburg
On the mount: "Warmly
dedicated to Erwin and
Käte from Otto Freundlich,
12.1.18"
p. 114

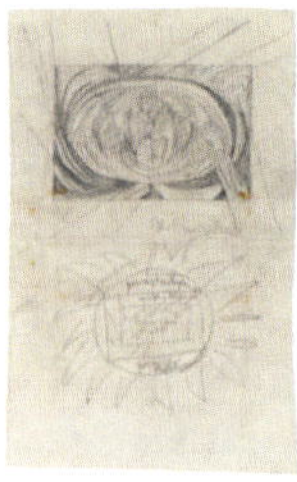

Sketch for the mosaic The Birth of Man, 1919
HvW 297
Pencil on tracing paper
40.5 × 26.5 cm
Museum Ludwig, Cologne
In the sketch from top to bottom: "Second frame; first frame; formative [?] image; second frame"
p. 130

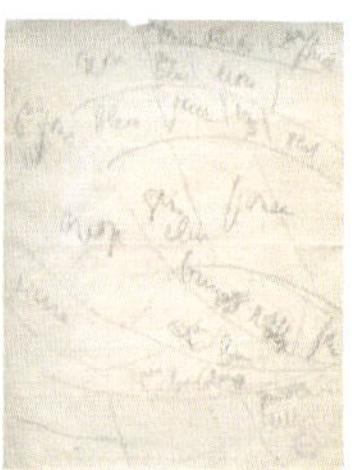

Ship in a Storm, 1924
HvW 307
Pencil on graph paper
27 × 21 cm
Association Les Amis de Jeanne et Otto Freundlich, Musées de Pontoise
p. 171

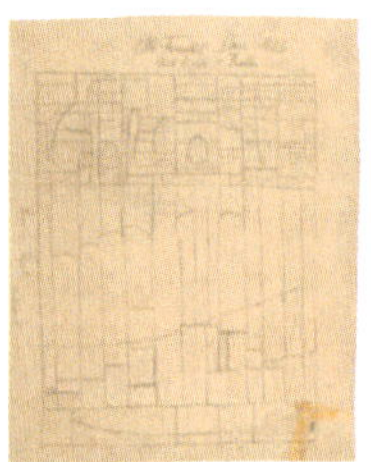

Design sketch for the painting Composition, 1926
Not in HvW
Pencil on vellum
54.5 × 44.5 cm
Berlinische Galerie – Landesmuseum für moderne Kunst, Fotografie und Architektur
Above (in the hand of Jeanne Kosnick-Kloss): "Otto Freundlich Paris 1926 à H. Hoech à Berlin"
Left: "Berlin Tegel H. Hoech"
p. 156

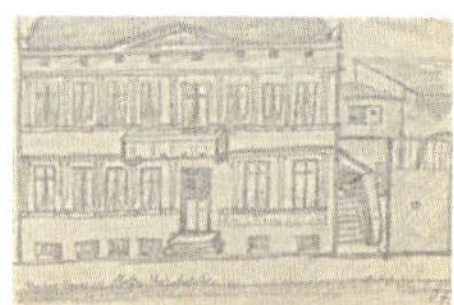

Our House in Stolp, ca. 1919
Not in HvW
Pencil on copying paper
14 × 21 cm
Private collection, Cologne
Below: "Our house in Stolp. Hospitalstr. O.F." Beneath the window: "Emil Freundlich"
p. 302

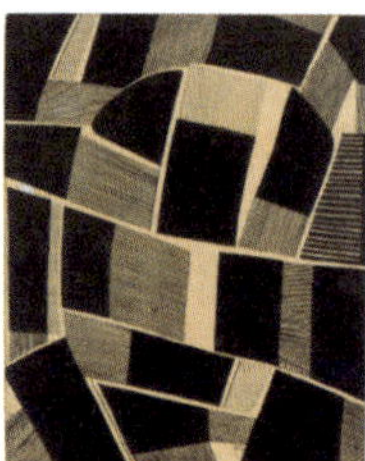

Composition in Black and White, 1931
HvW 322
Ink on cardboard
72 × 58 cm
Museum Ludwig, Cologne
p. 263

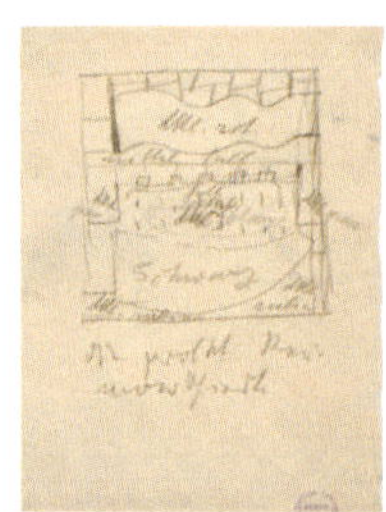

My Sky is Red (Mon ciel est rouge), 1933
HvW 336
Pencil on Ingres paper
21 × 13.5 cm
Association Les Amis de Jeanne et Otto Freundlich, Musées de Pontoise
Below: "the prolet[arian] Rev[olution] marches on"
p. 273

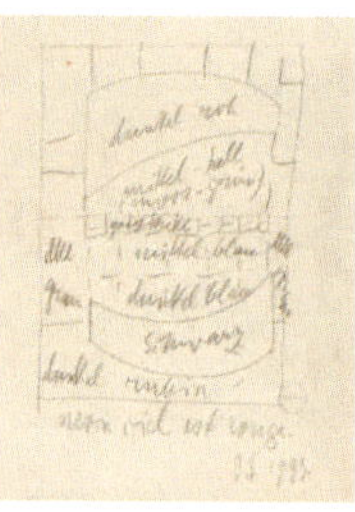

My Sky is Red (Mon ciel est rouge), 1933
HvW 337
Pencil on Ingres paper
27 × 21 cm
Association Les Amis de Jeanne et Otto Freundlich, Musées de Pontoise
Below: "mon ciel est rouge. O.F. 1933"
p. 273

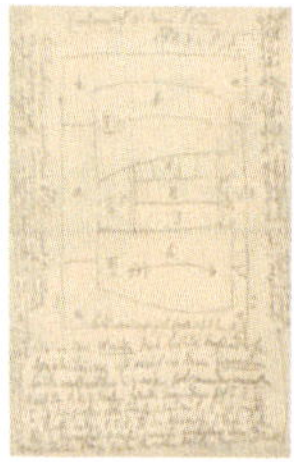

My Sky is Red (Mon ciel est rouge), 1933
HvW 338
Pencil on Ingres paper
27 × 21 cm
Association Les Amis de Jeanne et Otto Freundlich, Musées de Pontoise
Above: "Design for the painting. 1933 O.F." Left: "The picture contains the most impersonal element there is: the number. And yet it is realistic, which is to say neither occult nor mystic. Through the number, mass enters art, and through it, art comes to be mass." Below: "The threefold division in the middle of the painting likewise extends throughout the entire work, as follows: I,II,III refer to the 1,2,3 at the middle. I is the large red surface above the 1. II is beside 1,2,3 on the right and left. III the black surface beneath the 3. The entire complex is framed by the angular surface 1 above the red surface, right and left." Right: "under that 2 (as central piece of the perimeter) and beneath that as underlying sequence 3 in dark ruby red. Additionally the relationship between the surfaces denoted by a to the b-surfaces and c-surfaces." In the drawing: "Painting done. End of 1933. O.F."
p. 273

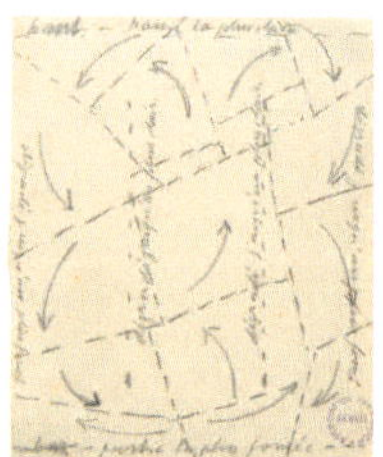

Composition, ca. 1934
HvW 340
Pencil on paper
14 × 11.5 cm
Association Les Amis de Jeanne et Otto Freundlich, Musées de Pontoise
Above: "top. Brightest section" Right: "Graduated to the darkest shade" Below: "beneath. Darkest section" Left: "Graduated to the darkest shade" Center, twice: "Graduated to the brightest tone."
p. 250

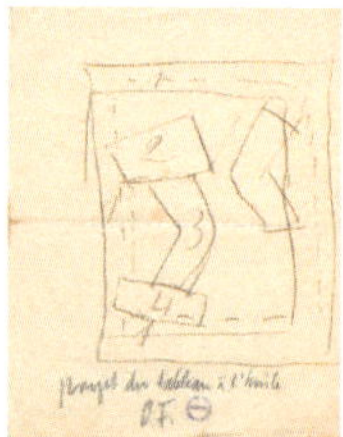

Composition, 1934
HvW 343
Pen on paper
27 × 21 cm
Association Les Amis de Jeanne et Otto Freundlich, Musées de Pontoise
Below: "Project for an oil painting O.F."
p. 269

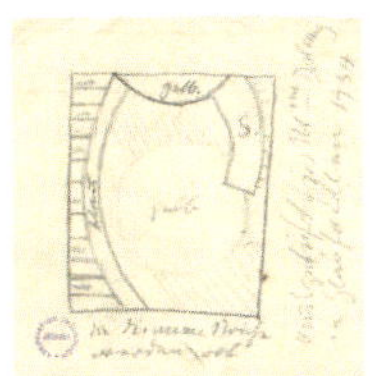

Composition, ca. 1934
HvW 346
Pencil on paper
13.5 × 13.3 cm
Association Les Amis de Jeanne et Otto Freundlich, Musées de Pontoise
Below: "The thin lines will be in red." Right: "Done for Madame [Dolang/Dodang?] in glass stains 1934"
p. 155

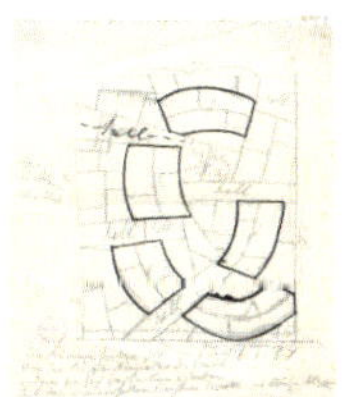

Composition, 1934
HvW 347
Pencil and ink on sketching paper
20.5 × 18 cm
Association Les Amis de Jeanne et Otto Freundlich, Musées de Pontoise
Below: "O. F. 34. The curves have liberated themselves from physical slavery by dividing themselves up and every section gazes the universal powers straight in the eye."
p. 251

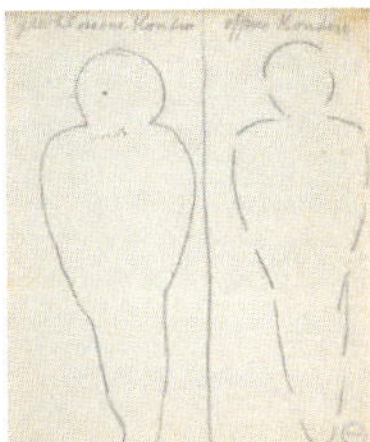

Contour Scheme, ca. 1935–36
HvW 359
Pencil on watercolor paper
29 × 22.5 cm
Association Les Amis de Jeanne et Otto Freundlich, Musées de Pontoise
Recto of HvW 360
Above: "closed contour/ open contour"
p. 37

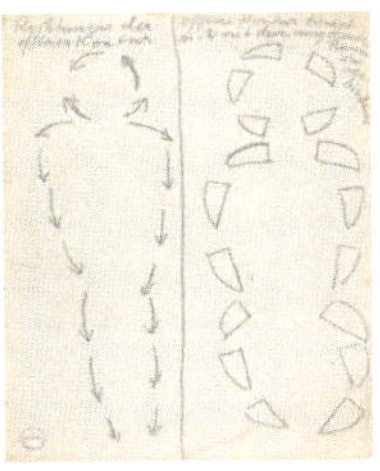

Contour Scheme, ca. 1935–36
HvW 360
Pencil on watercolor paper
29 × 22.5 cm
Association Les Amis de Jeanne et Otto Freundlich, Musées de Pontoise
Verso of HvW 359
Above: "Directions of the open contour/open contour ready to join up with the surrounding space."
p. 37

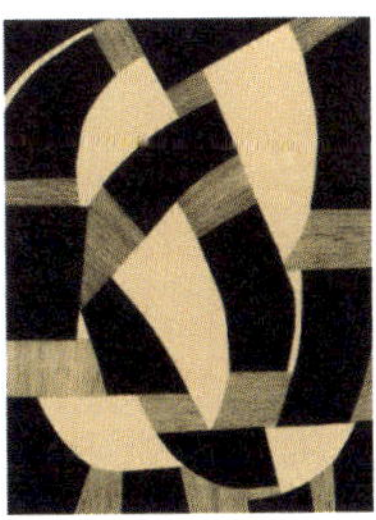

Composition, 1936
HvW 363
Ink on paper
63 × 48 cm
Donation Freundlich – Musées de Pontoise
p. 256

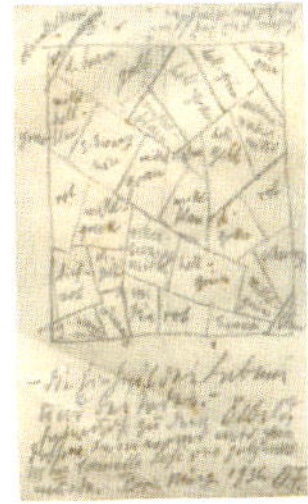

Sketch for the painting The Unity of Life and Death, 1936
Not in HvW
Pencil on paper
20.5 × 13.4 cm
Association Les Amis de Jeanne et Otto Freundlich, Musées de Pontoise
Above: "Life and death are the same forces." Below: "The unity of life and death. Design for the oil painting whose canvas was given to me as a gift by M. Camille. Paris. March. 1936. O.F."
p. 241

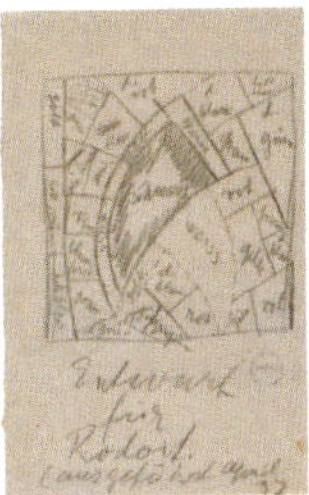

Composition, 1937
HvW 371
Pencil on paper
21 × 13.5 cm
Association Les Amis de Jeanne et Otto Freundlich, Musées de Pontoise
Below: "Design for Rodoit. (done April 37.)"
p. 155

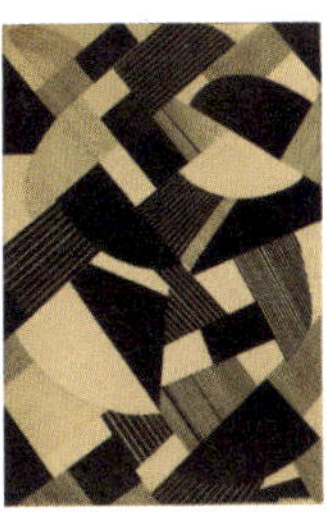

Composition/Geometric Abstraction, 1938
HvW 376/191
Ink on paper
104.1 × 71.1 cm
Seattle Art Museum
p. 247

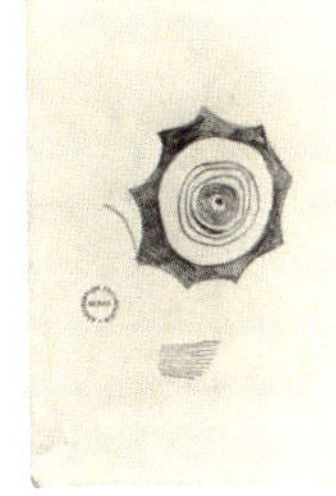

Composition, 1941
HvW 408
Pencil on sketching paper
21 × 13.5 cm
Association Les Amis de Jeanne et Otto Freundlich, Musées de Pontoise
p. 278

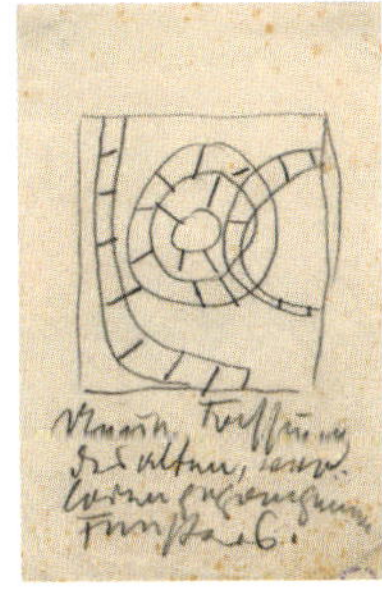

Design for a Stained Glass Window, ca. 1941
HvW 415
Pencil on Ingres paper
21 × 13.5 cm
Association Les Amis de Jeanne et Otto Freundlich, Musées de Pontoise
Below: "New version of the old window that was lost."
p. 154

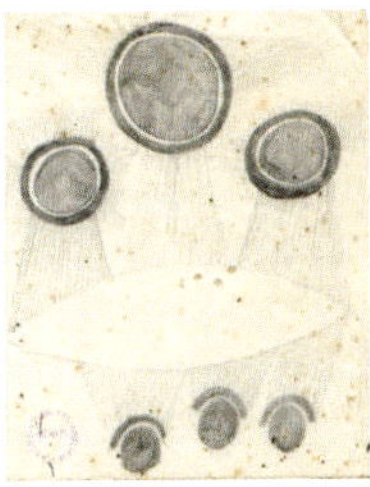

Composition, 1943
HvW 435
Pencil on sketching paper
20 × 15.5 cm
Association Les Amis de Jeanne et Otto Freundlich, Musées de Pontoise
p. 278

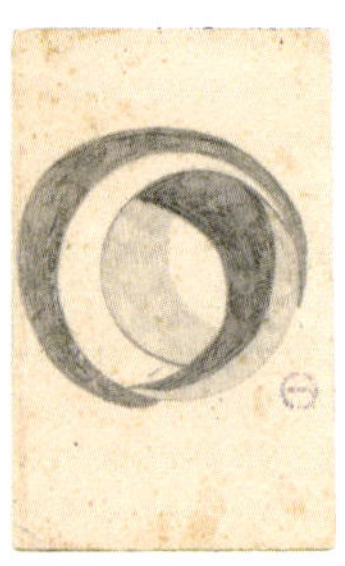

Composition, 1943
HvW 437
Pencil on cardboard
21 x 13.3 cm
Association Les Amis de Jeanne et Otto Freundlich, Musées de Pontoise
p. 278

Prints

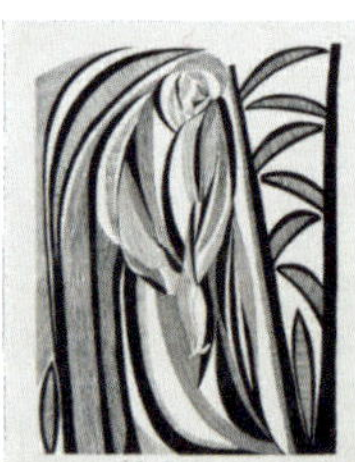

Man and Vegetation, 1916
HvW 440
Zinc engraving on paper
64 x 49.5 cm (picture)
72 x 59 cm (sheet)
Donation Freundlich – Musées de Pontoise
Below: "for Georg Fuchs. Otto Freundlich 1917."
p. 105

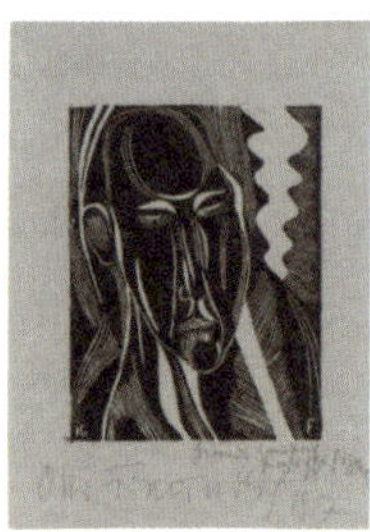

Head, 1916
HvW 441
Woodcut on gray paper
29.5 x 23 (picture)
45 x 33 (sheet)
Museum Ludwig, Cologne
Below: "For Dr. Haubrich, warm regards Freundlich 1917."
p. 82

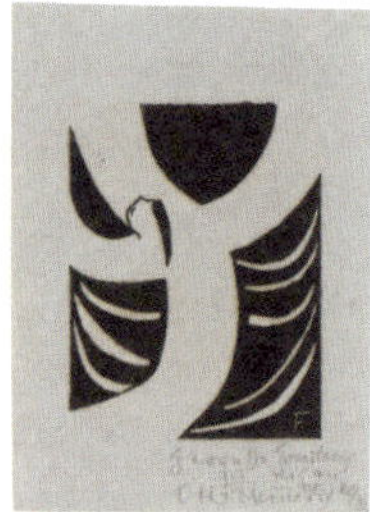

Upsurge, 1917
HvW 442
Woodcut on gray paper
29.2 x 23 (picture)
44.7 x 33 (sheet)
Museum Ludwig, Cologne
Below: "For Dr. Haubrich, best regards Freundlich 20/II. 17."
p. 109

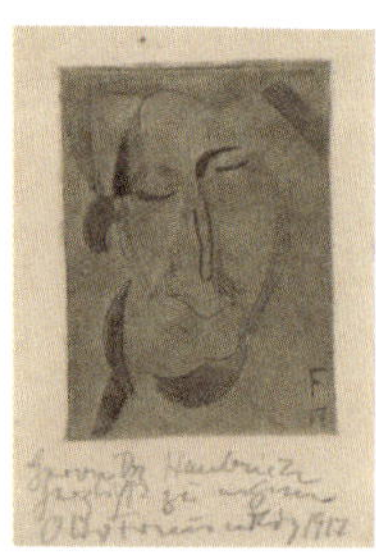

Head, 1917
Not in HvW
Etching on paper
11.5 x 8.7 cm (picture)
16.6 x 12 cm (sheet)
Museum Ludwig, Cologne
Below: "For Dr. Haubrich, warm regards Freundlich 1917."
p. 82

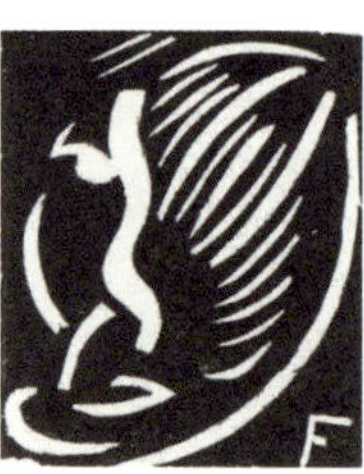

Ecstasy, 1917–18
HvW 443
Woodcut
13 x 11.4 cm
Cover picture *Die Aktion* 1/2 (1918)
p. 56

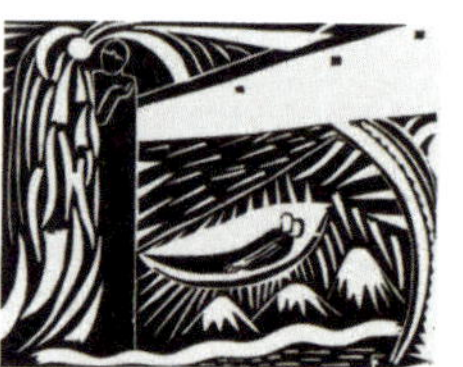

Figural Composition, ca. 1918
HvW 444
Woodcut on paper
30.5 x 39.7 cm
Donation Freundlich – Musées de Pontoise
p. 150

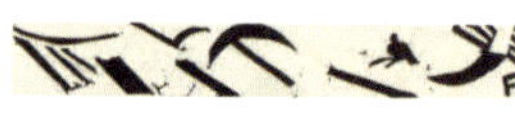

Landscape, 1918
HvW 445
Linocut
3 x 19.6 cm
In *Die Aktion* 13/14 (1918)
p. 56

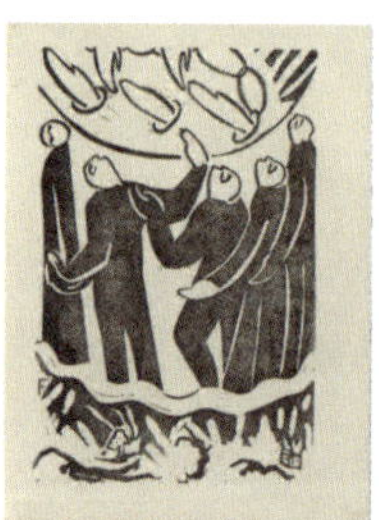

Leaflet on the Communist Manifesto, 1918
HvW 446
Linocut
28 x 18.5 cm
In *Die Aktion* 17/18 (1918)
p. 108

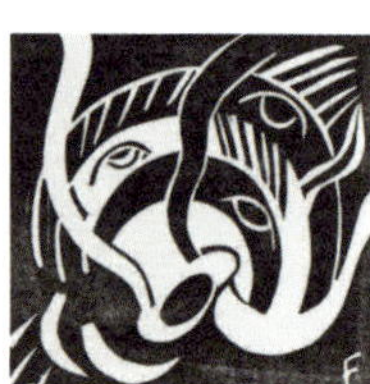

Vision, 1918
HvW 447
Woodcut
14.7 x 15.5 cm
In *Die Aktion* 25/26 (1918)
p. 56

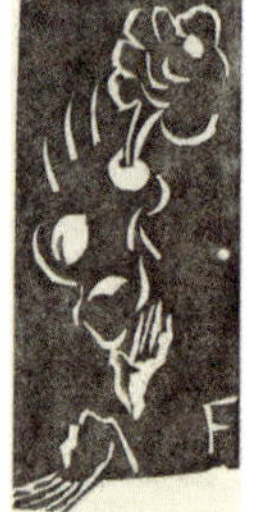

The Dagger, 1918
HvW 448
Woodcut
20.5 x 9 cm
In *Die Aktion* 27/28 (1918)
p. 57

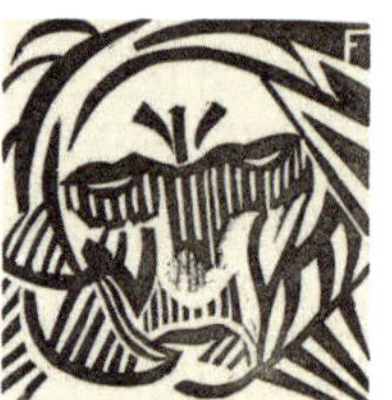

Self-Portrait, 1918
HvW 449
Woodcut
13 x 12.5 cm
In *Die Aktion* 37/38 (1918)
p. 61

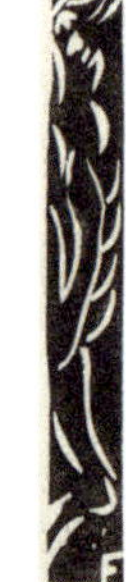

Nude, 1918
HvW 450
Woodcut
15.6 x 2 cm
In *Die Aktion* 37/38 (1918)
p. 64

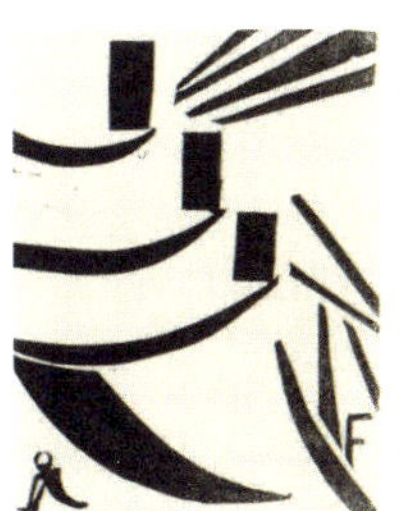

Man in the Landscape, 1918
HvW 451
Woodcut
14.5 × 11 cm
In *Die Aktion* 37/38 (1918)
p. 65

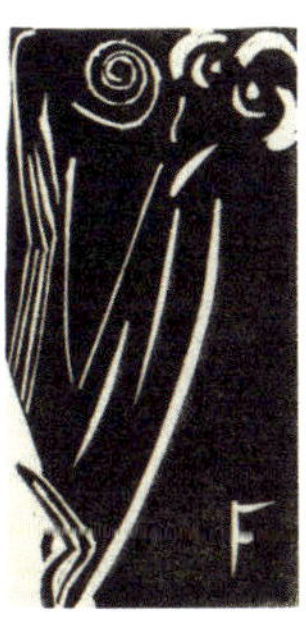

Cello Player, 1918
HvW 453
Woodcut
15.7 × 8 cm
In *Die Aktion* 37/38 (1918)
p. 69

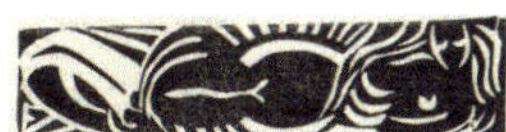

Nude, 1918
HvW 454
Woodcut
3.7 × 17 cm
In *Die Aktion* 37/38 (1918)
p. 144

Reclining Nude, 1918
HvW 455
Woodcut
3.9 × 17.8 cm
In *Die Aktion* 37/38 (1918)
p. 144

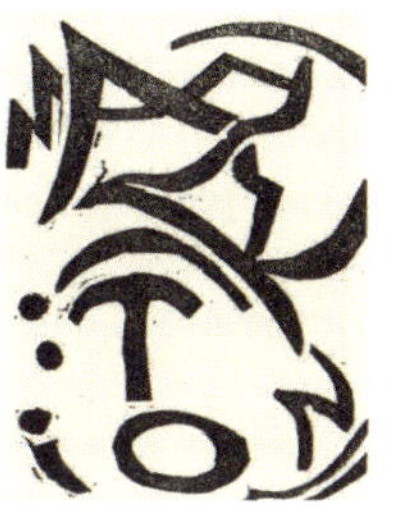

Dedication to "Die Aktion,"
1918
HvW 456
Woodcut
11.5 × 8.3 cm
In *Die Aktion* 37/38 (1918)
p. 75

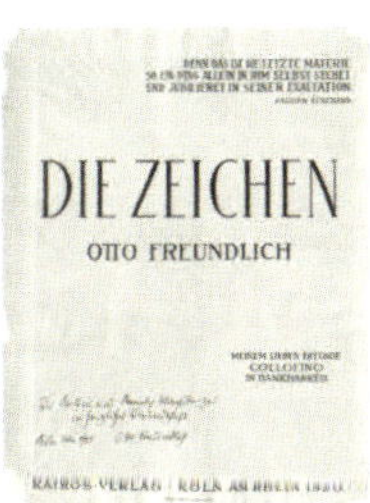

DIE ZEICHEN
OTTO FREUNDLICH

The Signs (Die Zeichen),
1919–20
HvW 461–466
Zinc engraving on paper
Each 78 × 62 cm,
or 62 × 78 cm (sheet)
Museum Ludwig, Cologne
Portfolio with 6 zinc engravings done from ink drawings, a text by Bekja Gusyk, and printed dedication to Josef Feinhals ("Collofino"), Kairos-Verlag, Cologne 1920.
On the title page:
"For Arthur and Annely Wachsberger in warmest friendship. Cologne Feb. 1920 Otto Freundlich"
pp. 134–139

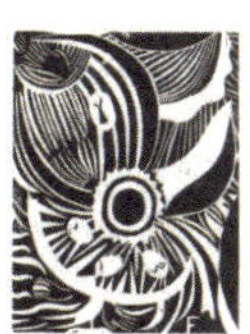

Composition, ca. 1920–21
HvW 469
Woodcut on handmade laid paper
39.9 × 30.7 cm (picture)
62.5 × 49.2 cm (sheet)
Kunstmuseum Basel, Kupferstichkabinett
p. 165

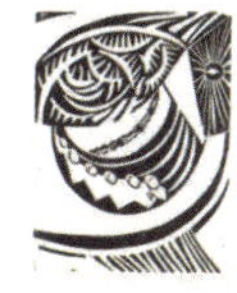

Composition, 1921
HvW 470
Woodcut on paper
39.8 × 30.7 cm (picture)
70.2 × 55.8 cm (sheet)
Kunstmuseum Basel, Kupferstichkabinett
p. 161

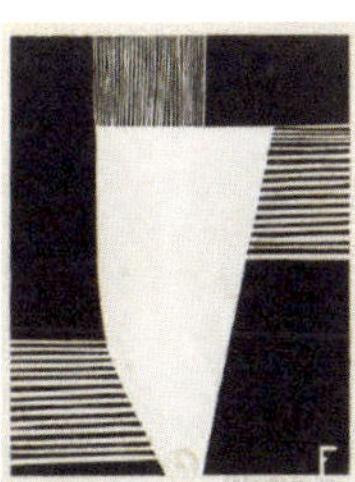

Composition, 1936
HvW 471
Woodcut on laid paper
38.2 × 30.7 cm (picture)
40.4 × 32.8 cm (sheet)
Kunstmuseum Basel, Kupferstichkabinett
Below: "Otto Freundlich. Paris 1936"
p. 274

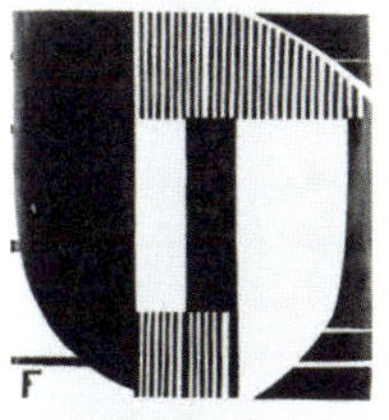

Composition, 1937
HvW 473
Linocut on Japanese paper
36.5 × 37.5 cm (picture)
48 × 38 cm (sheet)
Centre Pompidou, Paris Musée national d'art moderne/Centre de creation industrielle
Below: "for my friend and comrade Hans Arp.
Otto Freundlich Paris 1937"
p. 275

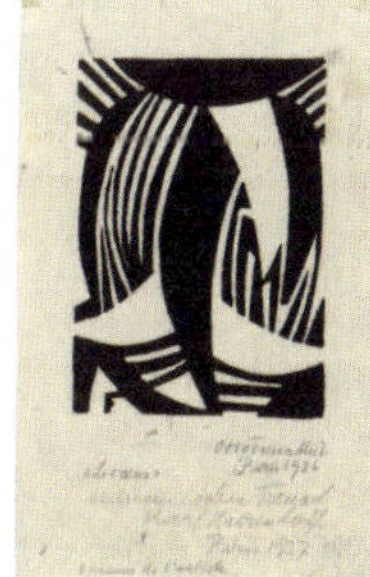

The Heart (Le Cœur), 1936
HvW 477
Linocut on Japanese paper
16.6 × 12 cm (picture)
27.1 × 17.4 cm (sheet)
The Museum of Modern Art, New York. Gift of Samuel A. Berger
Below: "'Le cœur' Otto Freundlich Paris 1936. To my dear friend Karl Nierendorf 1937. Artist's proof."
p. 274

* All bronze castings are posthumous.

This catalogue is published in conjunction with the exhibition

Otto Freundlich
Cosmic Communism

Curated by Julia Friedrich

Museum Ludwig, Cologne
February 18 – May 14, 2017

Kunstmuseum Basel
June 10 – September 10, 2017

Museum Ludwig

Director
Yilmaz Dziewior

Secretary
Ursula Hübner

Curatorial Assistant
Mandy Wignanek

Interns
Corinna Fix, Lara Höfchen, Neele Ziesing

Registrar
Christin Wähner

Conservation
Kathrin Keßler, Isabel Gebhard, Petra Mandt, Yvonne Garborini, Sophia Elze

Exhibition Coordination
Iris Maczollek

Carpentery
Leif Lenzner with Michael Bangert, Rodrigo Alexandre Ferreira Melo, Johannes Gabler, Milan Scharf, Marie-Charlott Stenzel

Facility Manager
Lukas Hofmann, Dirk Otter

Technical Staff
Guido Fassbender with Thomas Loerzer, Mario Morawitz, Peter Pier, Thomas Sydlik, Isa Uzun, Ingo Weber, Andreas Wischum, Michael Zorn

Press and Public Relations
Kirsten te Brake, Sonja Hempel, Anne Niermann, Donata aus der Wieschen

Fundraising
Lisa Schade with Dagmar von der Burg

Education
Angelika von Tomaszewski

Administration
Angela Coenen, Marion Funken, Pia Christoph, Ursula Meyer-Krömer, Susanne Brentano

Museum Ludwig
Heinrich-Böll-Platz
D-50667 Köln
Tel.: +49 221 26165
Fax: +49 221 24114
www.museum-ludwig.de

Museum Ludwig thanks

ART MENTOR FOUNDATION LUCERNE

KULTUR
STIFTUNG · DER
LÄNDER

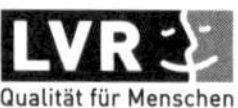

Freunde des Wallraf-Richartz-Museum und des Museum Ludwig e.V.

Kunstmuseum Basel

Director
Josef Helfenstein

Chief Executive
Annette Schönholzer

Coordination
Salome Schnetz

Registrar
Charlotte Gutzwiller

Conservation
Werner Müller, Sophie Eichner, Simone Flubacher, Annette Fritsch, Amelie Jensen, Viola Möckel, Chantal Schwendener, Annegret Seger, Caroline Wyss

Education
Simone Moser, Andrea Saladin, Christine Müller Stalder

Communication/Marketing
Gerrit Terstiege, Michael Mathis, Christian Selz, Malik Becker

Exhibition Set Up
Claude Bosch, Stefano Schaller, Andreas Schweizer, Muriel Utinger

Kunstmuseum Basel
St. Alban-Graben 16
CH-4010 Basel
Tel. +41 61 206 62 62
Fax +41 61 206 62 52
www.kunstmuseumbasel.ch

Kunstmuseum Basel thanks

stiftung für das kunstmuseum basel

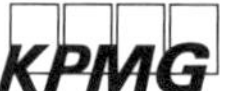

Catalogue

Editor
Julia Friedrich

Graphic Design
Petra Hollenbach

Translation
Malcolm Green, Jim Gussen

Copy Editing
Anne O'Connor

Publication Management
Iris Maczollek

Copyrights
Siri Effelsberg

Reproduction
farbanalyse, Cologne

Editorial Direction, Prestel
Constanze Holler

Production Management
Cilly Klotz

Typeface
Journal Sans New

Paper
Multi Art Silk, Munken Lynx

Printing and Binding
Passavia, Druckservice GmbH & Co. KG, Passau

Verlagsgruppe Random House
FSC® N001967

Printed in Germany
ISBN 978-3-7913-5639-6
(German edition)
ISBN 978-3-7913-5640-2
(English edition)

Prestel Publishing Ltd.
14-17 Wells Street
London W1T 3PD

Prestel Publishing
900 Broadway, Suite 603
New York, NY 10003

A CIP catalogue record for this book is available from the British Library.

www.prestel.com

Front cover
Otto Freundlich, *Composition*, 1931,
Von der Heydt-Museum, Wuppertal

Photo Credits

Applicat-Prazan, Paris: pp. 167, 175; Association Les Amis de Jeanne et Otto Freundlich: pp. 154 (r.), 155 (l.), 241, 251, 269, 278 (upp. r. & bot.); Association Willy Maywald: pp. 124, 193, 197, 312 (bot.); Karen Bartsch, Berlin: p. 114; Kai-Annet Becker, Berlin: pp. 86, 142, 156, 157, 169; Berlinische Galerie: p. 79 (r.); Bibliothek der Friedrich-Ebert-Stiftung, Bonn: p. 57 (ctr.); bpk/CNAC-MNAM/ Constantin Brancusi: p. 185; bpk/CNAC-MNAM/ Philippe Migeat: p. 272; bpk/ Hamburger Kunsthalle/Elke Walford: p. 238; bpk/Kupferstichkabinett, SMB/ Jörg P. Anders: p. 235; bpk/Museum für Vor- und Frühgeschichte, SMB/ Achim Kleuker: p. 83; bpk/Museumslandschaft Hessen Kassel: p. 270; bpk/ Paris, Centre Pompidou-CNAC-MNAM Centre de création industrielle: p. 275; bpk/RMN-Grand Palais/Béatrice Hatala: p. 220 (bot.); bpk/RMN-Grand Palais/ Adam Rzepka: p. 184; bpk/RMN-Grand Palais, Centre de création industrielle/ Philippe Migeat: p. 244; bpk/Staatsbibliothek zu Berlin: p. 207 (top); Constantin Brancusi, by SIAE 2008: p. 181; Yves Bresson/ Musée d'art moderne et contemporain de Saint-Etienne Métropole: p. 261; Bridgeman Images: p. 183 (l.); Brücke Museum Berlin/Roman März: p. 125 (top); Martin P. Bühler: pp. 161, 165, 174, 233, 265 (r.), 274 (l.); The Cleveland Museum of Art: p. 141; Collection Gemeentemuseum Den Haag: p. 55; Collection Kröller-Müller Museum, Otterlo, the Netherlands, Van Moorsel donation to the Dutch State, 1981: p. 217 (bot.); Colourworks, Wilmington: p. 166; farbanalyse, Cologne: pp. 32 (top), 33 (top), 47 (l.), 48, 50 (top), 54 (r.), 56 (top), 78, 79 (l.), 87 (top), 89, 92 (bot.), 93, 95, 96, 100 (upp. l. & r.), 101, 108 (r.), 140, 154 (l.), 172, 182, 195, 208 (upp. r.), 209 (upp. l.), 213, 278 (upp. l.), 302 (ctr.), 306, 312 (ctr.), 315 (top); Hannes Flach-Archiv, Cologne, Sig. 27/31: p. 310 (bot.); Fonds Otto Freundlich/IMEC: pp. 92 (top), 97, 111, 186-187, 198, 200, 202, 220 (top), 227, 228, 282-301, 307, 309 (bot.), 312 (top), 313 (r.), 314 (r.); Galerie David Ghezelbash: p. 173; Galerie Hasenclever, Munich: pp. 160, 231 (r.); Alberto Giacometti Estate (Fondation Alberto e Annette Giacometti + ADAGP), Paris, 2016: p. 183 (r.); Grisebach, Berlin: p. 151; Reni Hansen, Bonn: p. 242; Harvard Art Museums/Busch-Reisinger Museum: p. 308; Benjamin Hasenclever, Munich: p. 243; Hilti Art Foundation, Schaan, Liechtenstein: p. 170; Institut für Zeitungsforschung, Dortmund: pp. 51, 100 (bot.); Institut Valencia d'Art Modern, IVAM, Generalitat, Spain: p. 262; The Israel Museum, Jerusalem by Elie Posner: pp. 176, 257; Kunstmuseum Winterthur: p. 217 (top); Philipp Mansmann, Munich: p. 102 (l.); Medienzentrum, Antje Zeis-Loi / Von der Heydt-Museum Wuppertal: Cover, p. 253; Wolfgang Morell: p. 183 (ctr.); Gabriele Münter- und Johannes Eichner-Stiftung, Munich: p. 158; Musée d'Art Moderne/Roger-Viollet: pp. 33 (bot.), 107, 113; Musées de Pontoise: pp. 32 (bot.), 36, 54 (ctr. r.), 84, 88, 90, 91, 98, 102 (r.), 105, 125 (bot.), 144 (top), 145-146, 150, 152, 153, 164, 171, 194, 218, 221, 226 (top), 236, 245, 250, 256, 259, 260, 266, 267, 276, 277, 279, 280, 313 (low. l. & r.); Museu Coleção Berardo/ David Rato: p. 268; Museum für Kunst und Gewerbe Hamburg: pp. 47 (r.), 77, 80, 207 (ctr.); Museum moderner Kunst Stiftung Ludwig Wien: p. 252; Museum moderner Kunst Stiftung Ludwig Wien, formerly Hahn Collection, Cologne: p. 315 (bot.); 2016. Digital image. The Museum of Modern Art, New York/Scala, Florence: pp. 57 (r.), 240, 258, 274 (r.); Photographic Archives Museo Nacional de Arte Reina Sofía: p. 50 (bot.); Die Photographische Sammlung/SK Stiftung Kultur - August Sander Archiv, Cologne: p. 309 (top); Tony Plaut: pp. 81, 112, 310 (top); Rheinisches Bildarchiv Köln: pp. 18-19, 40, 54 (ctr. l.), 58, 82, 87 (bot.), 103, 106, 109, 110, 118 (bot.), 130, 131-132, 134-139, 180, 188, 189, 192, 224 (top), 225 (low. l. & r.), 239, 249, 263, 264, 265 (l.), 302 (top), 311, 314 (l.); Jean-Michel Rousvoal Photographe: pp. 155 (r.), 231 (l.), 273; August Sander Stiftung, courtesy Galerie Julian Sander, Cologne: pp. 159, 310 (ctr.); Scherl/ Süddeutsche Zeitung Photo: p. 207 (bot.); Seattle Art Museum: p. 247; Luca Spano, www.lucaspano.com: p. 99; Staatliche Graphische Sammlung München, Inv. 1955: 516 D: p. 54 (l.); Inv. 1994:17 Z: pp. 225 (upp. l.), 226 (bot.), 255; Stadtarchiv Halle (Saale): p. 208 (upp. l.); Stadtarchiv Salzburg, Fotoarchiv Franz Krieger: p. 208 (bot.); Nic Tenwiggenhorn, Berlin: p. 190, 191; Universitäts- und Landesbibliothek Düsseldorf. "Die Aktion," 1918. Signatur: 19 zb 8575: pp. 56 (ctr. & bot.), 57 (l.), 60, 61-75, 108 (l.), 144 (ctr. & bot.); Jean Vong Photography Inc., New York: pp. 148, 149; Günter Weber, Bonn: p. 162; Joachim Werkmeister, Ludwigshafen: p. 246; Wirtschaftsarchiv der Wirtschafts- und Sozialwissenschaftlichen Fakultät der Universität zu Köln/Schmalenbach-Bibliothek: p. 209 (bot.); 2016. The Yale University Art Gallery: p. 118 (top); Jens Ziehe, Berlin: pp. 147, 248

The editor wishes to thank all the many people who have contributed to the success of the exhibition and the catalogue:

Christine Adolphs, Volker Adolphs, Beatrix Alexander, René Allonge, Tobias Bäumer, Anita Beloubek-Hammer, Marion Bertram, Inka Berz, Rodrigo Bettencourt da Camara, Diana Blumenroth, Antje Birthälmer, Uli Bohnen, Birgit Brauner, Sabrina Buchhorn, Ralf Burmeister, Keith Cheng, Yves Chevrefils Desbiolles, Geneviève Debien, Anne Delfieu, André Derval, Cornelia Desaga, Georg Dietz, Stephanie Dietz, Jürgen Döring, Christophe Duvivier, Björn Eggert, Alexander Eiling, Franz Esser, Marion Euskirchen, Gerhard Finckh, Barbara von Flüe, Verena Franken, Erich Franz, Jürgen Freundlich, Stefan Frey, Dominique Gagneux, Anne Ganteführer-Trier, Kristina Gell, Bettina Gembruch, Sebastian Giesen, Thomas Gilbhard, Dorothee Grafahrend-Gohmert, Wolfram Hagspiel, Oliver Hahn, Benjamin Hasenclever, Michael Hasenclever, Ute Haug, Stefanie Heckmann, Michael Hering, Céline Hersant, Georg Heusch, Joachim Heusinger von Waldegg, Gunnar Heydenreich, Joachim Hiltmann, Annegret Hoberg, Marie-Thérèse Hochwartner, Katrin Holzherr, Tobias Iglhaut, Isabel Jansen, Antje Janssen, Alexandra Käss, Oliver Kase, Hannelore Kersting, David Klemm, Eva-Maria Klother, Carlo Knöll, Robert Knöll, Isgard Kracht, Michael Krajewski, Mario Kramp, Sylvie Kyeck, Laurent Le Bon, Gerhard Leistner, Katharina Liebetrau, Stephan Lohrengel, Caroline Louvet, Annelie Lütgens, Edda Maillet, Paul Mattick, Birgit Meyer, Camille Morando, Pia Müller-Tamm, Karsten Müller, Katharina Müller, Adolf Muschg, Brigitte Muschg, Christina Nägler, Janina Nentwig, Andrei Nakov, Friederike Naumann-Steckner, Susanne Neuburger, Jutta Niemann, Doris Oltrogge, Jaques Paparo, Virginie Pertrissot, Gallus Pesendorfer, Andreas Piel, Tanja Pirsig-Marschall, Tony Plaut, Hans Portsteffen, Franck Prazan, Ina Reiche, Astrid Reuter, Franziska Rübsteck, Esther Ruelfs, Gerd Sander, Julian Sander, Iris Schaefer, Andreas Schalhorn, Nina Schallenberg, Karin Schick, Wolfgang Schöddert, Dirk Schönbohm, Lena Schrage, Christiane Schuessler, Bernhard Schwenk, Michael Semff, Jérôme Serri, Katy Siegel, Alfons Söllner, Rainer Stamm, Maike Steinkamp, Jonas Storsve, Bernd Streitberger, Sonja Tesche, Hans Robert Thomas, Agnes Tietze, Susanne Titz, Markus Trier, Marcus Vaillant, Denise Vernerey-Laplace, Gerson Waechter, Rita Wagner, Christiane Wanken, Patrick Wasserbauer, Nina Watrin, Eva Weissweiler, Michael Werner, Uwe Wieczorek, Erika Wieprecht, Rita Wildegans, Dagmar Willecke, Eric Wychlacz, Kyllikki Zacharias.